A Note From The Authors

Special Edition Using Microsoft Commercial Internet Sy...
a powerful information network for your company and ...
systems and companion servers. We show you how to ...
gether so you can set up your Internet system or Intr...
commercial-grade services. This book focuses on the rea...
giving hints, suggestions, and information about lessons we learned, so you can ...
time on providing the best possible service for your users and clients.

By providing information ranging from the basic understanding and installation details for
these technologies, then addressing administration and troubleshooting all along the way,
we save you time and effort in bringing the products online.

Microsoft has stepped into the Internet arena with a vengeance. This is easily seen in their
providing the tools necessary to control content, the server engine, and additional functionality that ranges from gateway and proxy services to site-wide search engines. This
book brings these different tools into perspective and shows how you can implement them,
allowing either you or your users to develop content, while you continue to control access
to your system.

People reading this book learn how to install, configure, use, and understand the different
servers and understand the manner in which these servers interact with your site. This
book provides excellent advice for administrators who have the task of implementing the
Web site and other integrated components. Managers learn to use and understand the
technologies to improve their business footing and leverage their automated information
systems to maximize return on investment: not only what to do with their site, but how to
do it, and most important of all, why they should.

With the variety of material presented in *Special Edition Using Microsoft Commercial Internet System*, coupled with its up-to-date material, level of detail, and easy to follow "how-to"
format guides, this will be the all-encompassing book you can depend upon for answers to
your installation and administration questions.

Pete Butler

Roy Cales

Judith Petersen

Special Edition

USING
MICROSOFT
COMMERCIAL
INTERNET
SYSTEM

QUE®

Special Edition

Using
Microsoft
Commercial
Internet
System

*Written by Pete Butler, Roy Cales,
and Judy Petersen with*

*Steve Banick • Chris Denschikoff •
Scott McPherson • David Melnick*

que®

Special Edition Using Microsoft Commercial Internet System

Credits

PRESIDENT
Roland Elgey

PUBLISHER
Stacy Hiquet

PUBLISHING DIRECTOR
David W. Solomon

DIRECTOR OF MARKETING
Lynn E. Zingraf

PUBLISHING MANAGER
Fred Slone

SENIOR TITLE MANAGER
Bryan Gambrel

EDITORIAL SERVICES DIRECTOR
Elizabeth Keaffaber

MANAGING EDITOR
Sandy Doell

ACQUISITIONS EDITOR
Kelly Marshall

SENIOR EDITOR
Susan Ross Moore

EDITORS
Matthew B. Cox
Sean Dixon
Sherri Fugit
Patricia Kinyon
Mike LaBonne
Juliet MacLean
Jade Williams

PRODUCT MARKETING MANAGER
Kristine Ankney

ASSISTANT PRODUCT MARKETING MANAGERS
Karen Hagen
Christy M. Miller

STRATEGIC MARKETING MANAGER
Barry Pruett

TECHNICAL EDITOR
Matthew Brown

TECHNICAL REVIEWER
Steve Hegenderfer

TECHNICAL SUPPORT SPECIALIST
Nadeem Muhammed

SOFTWARE SPECIALIST
Brandon K. Penticuff

ACQUISITIONS COORDINATOR
Carmen Krikorian

SOFTWARE RELATIONS COORDINATOR
Susan D. Gallagher

EDITORIAL ASSISTANTS
Andrea Duvall

BOOK DESIGNER
Ruth Harvey

COVER DESIGNER
Dan Armstrong

PRODUCTION TEAM
DiMonique Ford
Julie Geeting
Laura A. Knox
Kaylene Riemen
Julie Searls

INDEXER
Craig Alan Small

Composed in *Century Old Style*, *MCPDigital*, and *ITC Franklin Gothic* by Que Corporation.

To Karen and Anna Grace for their prayers, love, and support and to my mother, father, and sister, Maureen, for their patience and guidance. Blessings upon you, dear.

Pete Butler

For Dawn Cales, my lovely, patient, and incredibly understanding wife; Gareth Cales, my 11-year-old who helped me figure out how this stuff worked; and Courtney Cales for the hugs that kept me going. Last, but far from least, my mom, Gladdy Cales, who always said I should go into that "computer stuff."

Roy Cales

For my mom, Nina Jane Petersen, who always walks in while I am playing computer games, and therefore wonders if actually I have a real job.

Judy Petersen

About the Authors

Pete Butler is a graduate of Florida A&M University School of Journalism, Media, and Graphics Arts and is presently involved in the development of the highly regarded Florida Communities Network (visit us at **fcn.state.fl.us**). When he's not handling project management of the Florida Communities Network implementation of the Microsoft Commercial Internet Servers, Pete spends his time playing the drums, reading *Wired* Magazine, and hanging out with his wife, Karen, and one year old daughter Anna Grace. Pete can be reached at **pete@supernet.net**.

Roy Cales   The overpowering urge for bigger and better toys, combined with many years of managing strange and unusual projects, led **Roy Cales** to found Integrity Data, Inc., a north Florida based Network Integrator, specializing in business and government technology. His desire to be the ruler of his own domain also drove him to co-found one of the oldest ISPs in the three-state region. The trials and tribulations experienced there have now culminated in the Genesis Communications Network, an ISP focused on providing high bandwidth, secure Internet access to businesses and government. He has been responsible for most of the site design and implementation featured in this book. He can be reached at **rcales@integritydata.com**.

Judy Petersen has been writing for Que since 1991. She has contributed to Que's *Using WordPerfect 6, Using WordPerfect 6 for Windows, Using WordPerfect 5.1 for Windows, Using Corel WordPerfect 7, Using PC Tools 8, Using Microsoft Works for Windows 95, Killer Windows Utilities*, and *Upgrading to Windows 3.1*, and been revision author for the *Que's Computer User's Dictionary, 5th Edition*, and lead author for *Using PC Tools for Windows, Special Edition*.

She provides software training and support in all the popular desktop applications and operating systems at Integrity Data, Inc. Before she discovered what she wanted to do with her life, she practiced law (and still does when sufficiently tempted), managed a restaurant, and drafted soil profile illustrations for an engineering firm that still hires her from time to time to perform environmental history title searches. She is also designing classes to train attorneys in using the Internet as a legal research tool. However, she would rather spend her time cheering on her beloved FSU Seminoles and puttering in the garden. Judy can be reached at **judy@integritydata.com**.

Steven Banick   Having thrown off the shackles of a detour career as a tech and network administrator, Steve's returned to his roots as a graphic designer and writer. Principal of the appropriately named "Steven Banick and Associates" studio in Edmonton (Canada), Steve works primarily in electronic mediums like the World Wide Web and interface design, as well as traditional print work. His sideline employment writing is a throw back to a rebellious youth belief: If you can't be a rock 'n' roll star, you can always be a writer. He can be reached at **Steve@Banick.com**, or **http://www.Banick.com**.

Chris Denschikoff writes a lot. He writes for arts and entertainment magazines, he writes for online publications. Despite all this, he still has time to write for Que, and sometimes, for himself. He finds that his Hunter S. Thompson on geriatric drugs is ideally suited to the kill or be killed world of computer technical reference publishing. After a long day slaving over hot computer components, he kicks back and relaxes casually in whatever socially approved fashion you don't object to personally. He also likes cats.

David Melnick, who is currently consulting on Electronic Commerce for the Deloitte and Touche LLP Solutions Group, has over six years of experience in applying technology to support process re-engineering, with a special focus on implementing database-driven Internet/intranet-based applications for business.

He holds both an MBA from the Anderson School at UCLA and the Microsoft Certified Professional status, providing him with both the technical and business skills to address the opportunities that businesses face in leveraging advanced technologies.

David has implemented Microsoft's premiere Internet BackOffice technologies, including Active Server and Merchant Server, into production applications for Fortune 500 clients, providing integrated inventory management, order fullfilment, and online authorization capabilities over the Internet.

Scott McPherson   When people talk of reinventing themselves, they should use Scott McPherson as the poster boy. Entering the record industry in 1973 at age 17, Scott was soon traveling to England and Europe on business. Dissatisfied with what he perceived as a lack of quality elected leadership, Scott ran for—and won—a seat in Florida's House of Representatives in 1980, at age 25. This led Scott to serve in the 1980s as a consultant for local, state, and Federal political candidates, as well as a major Presidential candidate. In the late 1980s, Scott entered the relatively new field of personal computer consulting—and has served nearly a decade in that capacity. His weekly column for Knight-Ridder newspapers, The Help Screen, is read by nearly a million newspaper subscribers weekly, and he enjoys a profitable career as a consultant and information technology director. Scott is married to Marta McPherson, and is stepfather to Marta's two children, Danny, age 11, and Mailin, age 14. The McPhersons reside in Tallahassee, Florida. His hobbies include politics, sports, music, and trying to sleep in Saturday mornings.

Acknowledgments

Building the servers and sites that are described in this book, starting with nothing but a bare box and some software (most of it in beta version), takes a variety of skills and untold hours of installing, testing then retesting, and starting over, with plenty of aspirin and antacid tablets always on hand. Without the technical skills and efforts of Douglas Singletary, Ken Sain, and Bryan Blank, the graphics-design capabilities of Colleen McCants, and the ability of Brooke Bassage to effortlessly pick up scripting language, this project would not have come to fruition.

We believed it is important that the Integrity Checks included throughout this book should describe the efforts that were actually required to create sites that will be serving the needs of real enterprises. We are therefore grateful to George Varn with the Tallahassee-Leon County Civic Center, Mimi Jones of The Public Agenda, and Scott McPherson of The Help Screen for their willingness to allow their sites to be the first and their commitment to providing the best services to their users.

Thanks to Bill Lindner and the rest of the talent at Florida Communities Network for their energy and vision. The FCN site and the universal acclaim it has received has set an example for us all. Our hats are off to Pete Butler's contacts at Microsoft for keeping him in the loop on this product, especially Steve Pruett, Laura Metzer, Paul Kavanaugh, and Mike Flanigan.

Particular thanks are due to Kelly Marshall of Que, our Acquisitions Editor, for believing that we really could write this book. She was a source of unfailing support and encouragement in those moments when we were suddenly not so sure after all. Matt Brown served us well in his role of Technical Editor. Many of his suggestions were invaluable; his ability to pick up our oversights was uncanny. Senior Editor Susan Moore nitpicked us to death and scrubbed this book thoroughly, all with unending cheerfulness; any errors that remain are ours.

The authors and publisher give many thanks to Steve Hegenderfer for his invaluable comments, expertise, and patience in reviewing page after page of manuscript while traveling the world.

We'd Like to Hear from You!

As part of our continuing effort to produce books of the highest possible quality, Que would like to hear your comments. To stay competitive, we *really* want you to let us know what you like or dislike most about this book or other Que products.

Please send your comments, ideas, and suggestions for improvement to:

The Expert User Team
Email: euteam@que.mcp.com
CompuServe: 105527,745
Fax: (317) 581-4663

Our mailing address is:

Expert User Team
Que Corporation
201 West 103rd Street
Indianapolis, IN 46290-1097

You can also visit our Team's home page on the World Wide Web at:

http://www.mcp.com/que/developer_expert

Thank you in advance. Your comments will help us to continue publishing the best books available in today's market.

Thank You,

The Expert User Team

Contents at a Glance

VIII | Appendixes

Table of Contents

II | Microsoft Commercial Internet System Conference Systems

7 Advanced Internet Mail Server Administration   165

8 Adding a Chat Server   191

III | Commercial Internet System Membership Services

9 Understanding Commercial Internet Personalization System   223

10   The Internet Locator Service   251

IV | Commercial Internet System Content Management Servers

14 Building a Merchant System 381

18   Server Administration Via the Web   485

Introduction

Until recently the home of only academics and computer scientists, the Internet has become *the* place to visit for millions of computer users around the world.

Yet in spite of hearing every day how the Internet is going to change the way we do business, few of us in fact have Internet access, fewer still know how to use the access we have for anything other than e-mail, and only an infinitesimal number of us actually conduct any business on the Web. To our dismay, our children might be more accomplished and regular users than we are. A 10-year-old friend of mine knows his HTML 6-digit color numbers better than he knows his multiplication tables!

This should not be surprising to people reading this book. We are all looking for ways to better access and distribute information, yet network administrators, business owners, and Internet Service Providers spend hours figuring out how to make a mail server program interface reliably with the authentication system only to have a hacker invade the system and wipe out everyone's password. Meanwhile, individual users buy a fast modem and a browser, and then sign up with an online service only to learn it is not always easy to find information, or that servers are "down" whenever they try to dial in, and are reluctant to buy anything online because they have no idea if it's wise to give out credit card numbers or don't see why they should pay to read a few more sports stories on a sports magazine site.

Recognizing a need and an opportunity when they see one, Microsoft has designed the Microsoft Commercial Internet System (MCIS) as the complete answer to online commerce. The set of Internet servers that make up MCIS is designed to enable users to conduct business, access information, and communicate with others on the Internet, and to provide more comprehensive management of Internet sites and activities. MCIS is built on a foundation of Windows NT Server 4.0 and the Internet Information Server. Tightly integrated, with a common user interface, Microsoft Commercial Internet System and its foundation offer scalability, stability, and security that cannot be found by cobbling together pieces of whatever else is out there.

This book is designed to guide you through the complex administration and implementation issues associated with the Microsoft Commercial Internet System. To better accomplish that task, a group of individuals employed full-time in developing and delivering Internet services to users has written *Special Edition Using Microsoft Commercial Internet System*. Each author brings to this book a level of expertise and perspective that assures the reader the fullest discussion of design, installation, management, and training issues.

There is, however, very little discussion of the membership, content replication, and address book components of CIS. Because of the late public availability of these components, we were unable to adequately verify the final features and test operability problems before going to press. ∎

Who Should Read This Book?

This book addresses itself to information system managers and administrators who are responsible for Internet site management or for moving elements of their business onto the Web, to software developers who develop applications and interfaces for use with the Internet, to commercial Internet Service Providers interested in providing the highest level of services for its business customers, and to readers interested in implementing a full-fledged commercial Internet system. The reader is assumed to be thoroughly familiar with installing and administering a Windows NT 4.0 server and have a working knowledge of SQL Server 6.5, the Internet, and the World Wide Web.

This book's readers will learn how to install, configure, and use the individual servers that make up the Microsoft Commercial Internet System as well as the Proxy Server, Index Server, and the Merchant System. Special attention is paid throughout the book to real-world applications for each server, providing administrators with the information necessary to decide how and to what extent to implement a commercial presence on the Web.

With each of the servers that make up the Microsoft Commercial Internet System given separate attention, this book will serve as a complete reference with clear step-by-step instructions for how to install, configure, and administer all components of Microsoft Commercial Internet System, as well as integration issues and techniques, background material designed to enhance your understanding, and discussion of advanced topics to improve the effectiveness of Internet and intranet ventures.

In addition, the book is based in part on the actual implementation of Microsoft Commercial Internet System on a site that presently consists of four enterprises: a retail store, a syndicated columnist, a nonprofit community-building entity, and the statewide management structure for local charitable agencies. Each chapter includes a discussion of the implementation of its server software in one or more of the site enterprises and provides screen-shots and URL links to actual online pages.

How This Book Is Organized

This book begins with a description of the Microsoft Commercial Internet Service and its foundation, Windows NT 4.0 and Internet Information Services, and addresses issues of site planning and hardware requirements. Subsequent sections describe each of the MCIS servers in turn, using a step-by-step approach to planning, installation, configuration, administering, and troubleshooting the application.

NOTE Throughout the book, all descriptions and installation notes were written based on one of the early Beta versions of the software, which were available for public download from the Microsoft Web site. Unfortunately, there were no Release Copies available for any of the products at the time of the writing. According to Microsoft, the public release of the software will happen during the fourth quarter of 1997. ■

Part I

Part I, "Preparing for the Microsoft Commercial Internet System," covers what Microsoft Commercial Internet System is and how you prepare for it in your enterprise.

Chapter 1, "Meet the Microsoft Commercial Internet System," describes the Microsoft Commercial Internet System, the reasons why Microsoft has developed this suite of servers, and reviews the reasons why commercial Internet applications are the right choice in today's marketplace. The site that the authors have built to illustrate the applicability of MCIS is described.

Chapter 2, "Getting Started with Microsoft Commercial Internet System," provides an overview of each of the servers that makes up the Microsoft Commercial Internet System and the foundation. The chapter describes the ways an Internet connection can be established and concludes by identifying the issues you need to consider when planning an MCIS site.

Chapter 3, "Building the Foundation," describes the features and installation procedures of Windows NT 4.0 and the Internet Information Server. Information about maintaining the Windows NT 4.0 system, setting up virtual domains, and scaling the foundation is also provided.

Part II

Part II, "Microsoft Commercial Internet System Conference Systems," covers the servers that support Internet communities by providing users access to a variety of information and more powerful ways to communicate with each other.

Chapter 4, "Delivering Discussion Forums with MCIS," examines the ways a news server supports and simplifies the gathering and dissemination of information, reviews the history of Network News Transfer Protocol (NNTP), and describes UseNet. Step-by-step procedures for setting up and administering the Internet News Server, including items such as building a news hierarchy, and adding feeds and newsgroups, are provided.

Chapter 5, "Advanced Administration of the Internet News Server," discusses the advantages and implementation of master/slave relationships, then describes how to index the news feeds set up in the previous chapter as well as how to create local and global news groups. The chapter discusses why it might be wise to create moderated groups and how to tune the performance of News Server.

Chapter 6, "Instant Communication—Microsoft Commercial Internet Mail," begins with an overview of Internet Mail, details the procedure for installing and configuring each of the components of Commercial Internet Mail Server, and concludes with information about managing mailboxes and monitoring the mail server.

Chapter 7, "Advanced Internet Mail Server Administration," addresses planning and scaling Internet Mail Server for both Internet Mail and Groupware clients, backing up and restoring IMS, hosting mail and using listserver applications, and looks at ways to fine-tune the mail server performance.

Chapter 8, "Adding a Chat Server," provides a basic understanding of how the Chat Server can serve the needs of your organization. The procedures for installing and configuring the Chat Server, including step-by-step instructions for setting up a three-server and an eight-server network, are provided. Administering, monitoring, and troubleshooting the Chat Server are addressed, as well as suggestions for testing Chat with several popular IRC clients.

Part III

Part III, "Commercial Internet System Membership Services," explores some of the ways Microsoft Commercial Internet System enables providers to manage and enhance the relationship with their customers and other users.

Chapter 9, "Understanding the Commercial Internet Personalization System," describes how the Personalization System can help attract and satisfy new customers, analyze site traffic, and increase the effectiveness of your Web site. The chapter continues with detailed information designed to help you plan for and install the Personalization System for your enterprise, as well as maintain and monitor the system.

Chapter 10, "The Internet Locator Service," provides an overview of the Locator Server and the procedures for installing and configuring ILS. Using Locator Server for activities such as obtaining real-time user information, NetMeeting, and tracking Web site visitors is described, along with several examples of ILS in action.

Part IV

Part IV, "Commercial Internet System Content Management Servers," can be used to acquire, classify, and effectively distribute information within and outside the enterprise.

Chapter 11, "Using Microsoft Index Server," explores the importance and advantages of indexing to assist users in finding information accurately, quickly, and easily. The chapter describes installing Index Server, the considerations involved in efficiently and effectively indexing documents in all formats and many languages, how to create and use query forms, and the ongoing administration that makes an Index Server a truly useful tool.

Chapter 12, "Replicating Internet Content with the Content Replication System," provides an overview of Content Replication Server and instructions for preparing the system for CRS, running setup, and testing the installation. Examples are given for replicating a Web site structure and propagating content with CRS.

Part V

Part V, "The Merchant System," provides information to aid in understanding, installing, configuring, and tuning the Merchant System for use with your enterprise.

Chapter 13, "Microsoft Merchant Server—Enabling Commerce on the Web," considers why to use the Merchant System and looks at the types of merchant servers, such as single stores, online malls, and multiple merchants, that will provide the most benefit to your business. The chapter provides detailed information on installing and testing the server, building a store, and effectively merchandising goods. Interfacing with the SQL server is also described.

Chapter 14, "Building a Merchant System," describes processing orders and payment methods and looks at how shopping is conducted by the store patrons. Administration issues such as synchronizing and changing configurations and adding stores are described, as well as the administrative tools that can assist this process.

Part VI

Part VI, "The Active Server," aids you in getting a Microsoft Internet Information Server off the ground, and tells you why you should be using it. This part includes coverage from base functionality to helpful installation hints.

Chapter 15, "Introduction to Internet Information Server 3.0," is a concise overview of the new Microsoft Web server technology. This chapter goes into detail on how the new facets of IIS 3.0 will affect administration and content delivery models, and allow you to decide if it's the server software for you.

Chapter 16, "Serving Active Content on the Internet," details the power and implementation of Internet Information Server 3.0's Active Server Pages (ASP). This includes brief code examples and a look into the significance of active versus static content on a Web site.

Part VII

Part VII, "Administration, Data Access, and Extended Capabilities," addresses how Microsoft Commercial Internet System can assist in analyzing, administering, and securing the enterprise site.

Chapter 17, "Using the Microsoft Proxy Server," describes the necessary preparation of disk drives, network adapters, the LAT, and service ports, and provides instructions for installing, configuring, and administering the Proxy. Procedures for authenticating clients, granting permissions, controlling Web Proxy user access, monitoring activity, and securing the server are presented. The chapter also provides information on configuring the cache to obtain maximum system performance.

Chapter 18, "Server Administration Via the Web," provides an overview of the Internet Service Manager, describes administration by using a Web page, the standard Internet Service Manager, and the Windows NT 4.0 Internet Service Manager. The reader will become familiar with site administration and troubleshooting, establishing site security, how to monitor multiple servers, and to conduct remote administration.

Chapter 19, "Interpreting Logfiles and Monitoring Server Performance," describes the information that logfiles can provide your business, how to interpret logfiles by using a SQL server, and reviews third-party software that can provide similar data.

Chapter 20, "Developing an Intranet with MCIS Servers," presents information about the ways an intranet can enhance in-house communications, then addresses site planning and the implementation of the MCIS servers that the site plan requires.

Part VIII

Appendix A, "Hardware Requirements," covers in detail the minimum, average, and optimum hardware requirements for each server. Requirements are presented in the context of an actual site where the consequences of various designs are displayed.

Appendix B, "Performance Monitor Counters," details more than 80 performance counters available in Performance Monitor and the operating information each provides about a server.

Appendix C, "Glossary," provides a reference for readers who want more information about many of the terms you must know when working with Microsoft Commercial Internet System.

Conventions Used in This Book

This book assumes that you are already familiar with the graphical user interface used in Windows-based applications. Consequently, no attempt is made to describe how to select or choose various options in the dialog boxes discussed throughout this book. Instead, the terms click, select, choose, highlight, activate, disable, and turn on/off have been used to describe the process of positioning the cursor over a menu command or a dialog box element (option button, check box, command button, drop-down list arrow, and so on) and clicking a mouse button. Those familiar with using the keyboard to select various menu and dialog box options may relate this selection process to keystrokes instead of mouse clicks. Either method is equally acceptable.

Mnemonics in the name of menu commands and dialog box options are indicated by underscoring the letter. However, in the Windows NT 4.0 environment, keyboard access is limited. For example, mnemonics do not appear in the Start menu cascading submenus, and dialog boxes do not have menus but instead use tabs to organize the many options available in each box. In addition, it is possible to administer MCIS using a Web browser and Web pages are not keyboard-friendly. However, wherever keyboard shortcuts are available (such as pressing Ctrl+P to print), the shortcut will be given.

References to paragraph headings that have appeared previously in the book or that will follow later in the book are generally annotated as cross-references and appear near the text to which they pertain. Look for these special features throughout the book to enhance your learning experience.

The following type and font conventions are used in this book to help make reading it easier:

- *Italic type* is used to introduce new terms.
- On-screen messages, code listings, and command samples appear in `monospace type`.
- Code that you are instructed to type appears in **`monospace bold type`**.
- Shortcut keys are denoted with underscored letters or multiple-key combinations. For example, "choose File, Edit" means that also you can press Alt+F, and then press E to perform the same steps as clicking the File menu and then clicking Edit.

Tips, Notes, and Cautions appear in these specially formatted boxes to make this important information easier to locate.

TIP Tips present short advice on a quick or often overlooked procedure. These include shortcuts.

NOTE Notes present interesting or useful information that isn't necessarily essential to the discussion. A note provides additional information that may help you avoid problems or offers advice that relates to the topic.

CAUTION

Cautions look like this and warn you about potential problems that a procedure may cause unexpected results, or mistakes to avoid.

References to section headings that have appeared previously in the book or that will follow later in the book are annotated as cross-references and appear near the text to which they pertain.

▶ **See** "Testing the Installation," **p. 234**.

ON THE WEB

http://www.quecorp.com   These special sections point you to useful Web pages. This, for example, is Que's home page.

Preparing for the Microsoft Commercial Internet System

Meet the Microsoft Commercial Internet System

The Internet is probably the most over-hyped and, at the same time, under-hyped technology in the history of computing. We hear every day how it is going to change the way we work, play, and even think. Our mailboxes are bombarded with claims of fantastic new ways to bring the power of the Internet to our businesses and our homes. No one's business card or stationery seems complete without an e-mail address and an URL. Break room conversations revolve around the latest e-zine or Webcast of last night's game.

No matter where we turn the Internet intrudes, yet has it changed your life? Has it affected the way your company functions? Have you made even one purchase online or really used the Internet for work and not play? In many ways, the Internet is way over-hyped. Millions of people still read the newspaper to get their news or turn on the television to catch the game. Office memos are still more frequently distributed by hand or fax than via e-mail. Few consumers are willing to actually purchase items without speaking to a "real" human being. So does this mean the Internet is just the latest media sweetheart and doomed to fade away? Most definitely not!

Let's look at the facts. According to the Business Research Group, in 1993 there were 1.2 million Internet hosts; by 1996 that number had increased to 9.6 million. On top of that, it is estimated that there are four times as many "hidden" networks within the com domain as there are visible ones. That means the Internet could easily have over 20 million hosts.

Every day more companies announce their Internet strategy. Many schools now have direct access to the Internet and teach our children how to use it. The Vice President of the United States has made the "Information Superhighway" a priority in his platform. If you are an IT director, corporate executive, network administrator, business owner, or Internet Service Provider, you must realize the effect the Internet is having and will have on your life and your business.

We also need to face today's reality. The Internet is just coming out of its infancy. It is still bewildering to the average user. Most of the people in the world have never used a computer, much less the Internet. Yet, the staggering growth in Internet usage shows the sheer power it represents. Choose almost any business in America, give them Internet access, and train them to use it. Then try to take it away. They will fight you tooth and nail.

Corporate executives have been looking for ways to better access and distribute information since the dawn of the computer age. Many ideas have had their day in the spotlight; most, if not all, have failed. Now the Internet and the applications developed to support it offer the most promising options ever. In the corporate world, information is power. Having the right information when you need it can make or break a business. With the incredible amounts of information scattered across the Internet, it is possible to access almost any information imaginable. Not only is it out there, it's available almost instantaneously.

Yet the Internet is not just about information. Perhaps even more important is the power to communicate. The single most popular use of the Internet is still e-mail. If a business or individual has an Internet e-mail account, you can bet they use it every day. E-mail enables us to communicate, to share ideas and information in a personal manner. It can also take the place of phone calls and voice mail. How many of us have had to wait on hold or suffer through numerous transfers just to leave a voice mail message?

In addition to enabling us to communicate or access information, the Internet is changing the way we all do business. Once an individual has access to the Internet, they use it to keep up with the world, to research business projects, and to make purchase decisions. So even though online commerce has not yet lived up to its hype, it will.

People today think nothing of calling a mail order company and giving their credit card number to a complete stranger. So as soon as they find something online they want to buy, they will order it. Many estimates placed online purchases around 200 million dollars in 1996. They also predict that by the year 2000 that number will exceed two billion dollars. This means that no business can afford to ignore the Internet. It will change the way all businesses think of themselves and their market.

So why hasn't the Internet already taken over the world? No single leader has shown the way. Until recently, the Internet has been the home of academics and computer scientists. Only in the last few years has Internet access even been available to individual users and commercial entities. Even then, if you could get access there was no real benefit to the average person. The advent of HTTP and the World Wide Web led the way to the Internet of the future. Now there is a way to present information in a user-friendly manner and make it easily attainable.

But this is only half the problem. Sure, users can access information, but how is that information gathered, distributed, and controlled? Until now, MIS departments had to either buy numerous software packages from disparate vendors or build their own applications. Now Microsoft is introducing the Commercial Internet System. This is a group of eight different server products, each designed to integrate seamlessly with Windows NT Server and the Internet Information Server. No longer will administrators need to spend hours figuring out how to make a mail server program interface reliably with their News server or Authentication systems. The Microsoft Commercial Internet System consists of:

- The Internet News Server
- The Internet Mail Server
- The Membership System
- The Information Retrieval Server
- The Personalization Server
- The Conference System
- The Internet Address Book Server

In this book, you look at each of these systems. You also look at the underlying foundation required to run the MCIS. Also, you look at these additional servers:

- The Microsoft Proxy Server
- The Microsoft Index Server
- The Microsoft Merchant System

These applications, combined with the Commercial Internet System, will enable any corporation or business group to offer a complete Internet or intranet solution. ■

How This Book Can Help You

Building an Internet or intranet site is significantly different from developing any other software implementation. It is not simply a software application, nor is it a marketing device or a sales tool. An effective Internet site must be all of this and even more. There will be many different departments involved in planning an Internet site. Corporate management will of course set the tone and direction of the site. Marketing and Public Relations will most likely develop the actual page copy. Graphics designers will produce the logos and designs which will uniquely identify the site. Accountants will most assuredly watch every expense and require justification of every decision. All of these factors will be a vital part of developing an Internet site. However, when it is all said and done, there will be an IT Director and a staff of network administrators who will make it all happen.

These are the people who can benefit from this book: the IT executives who are responsible for implementing Internet plans, the network administrators who actually make things happen, the software developers who develop the ActiveX controls, and the consultants who advise management on what actually works. These individuals, as well as Internet Service Providers, businesses with an Internet site, and anyone who wants a better understanding of how to build a full commercially scaled Internet site, will want to read this book.

History of MCIS

Internet Service Providers (ISPs) have been in constant need of stronger, more scalable applications to support their services. Most of the larger sites have developed their own extremely customized, extremely proprietary solutions. These solutions are, by their nature, expensive to maintain and notoriously nonscalable. Microsoft faced these same problems with its own Microsoft Network (MSN). To overcome these problems and develop an open architecture solution, Microsoft developed the Commercial Internet System (code-named Normandy).

"Internet providers now have an extensible, scalable, and open solution that combines the power and reliability they require with the simplicity and ease they demand," says Brad Silverberg, senior vice president of the Internet platform and tools division at Microsoft. "Our platform allows commercial services to easily customize their information to fit the personal interests of their subscribers." In addition to extensive testing under lab conditions, components of the MCIS platform have been field-tested for more than a year as an underlying technology for the Internet services on MSN.

The Needs of CompuServe

CompuServe claims to have millions of users around the world, and yet they too were caught up in the explosive growth of the Internet. To handle this growth and expand into new Internet-related markets, CompuServe needed to replace their aging proprietary network. In June of 1996, CompuServe announced that they would migrate their network over to the Microsoft Commercial Internet System.

"Microsoft's Commercial Internet System is the solution that gives us the salability and reliability we need to support five million CompuServe users in 185 countries around the world," says Bob Massey, CompuServe president and CEO. "Microsoft is a crucial component of our new strategy to bring CompuServe services to the Internet."

Lack of Common Internet Server Suite

CompuServe and the Microsoft Network were just two of the thousands of Commercial ISPs looking for a better Internet solution. The only real solution was to run a combination of UNIX-based servers and software from numerous sources. Much of this software had been developed by universities or other research organizations. Support and updates were difficult to find. The commercial solutions that were available were either very costly and difficult to use or were unproved in a high-pressure, commercial environment. Netscape Communications was on the verge of introducing its Internet Suite, yet it was still based upon high-end UNIX servers. This was not an acceptable alternative to thousands of corporations and ISPs who did not have personnel who were knowledgeable in UNIX.

These needs, combined with their own, are what led Microsoft to develop the Microsoft Commercial Internet System. Of course, there may be an additional reason.

Why Normandy?

The Allied invasion of occupied France was a turning point in the war against Hitler's Germany. The battle plan, code-named Overlord, called for the largest amphibious assault ever. It began in the early morning hours of June 6, 1944, now known as D-Day. Thousands of American, British, Canadian, and French soldiers, backed by warships, bombers, and paratroopers, stormed a 50-mile stretch of French beach in the province of Normandy. Following huge initial losses, the allied forces gained a foothold and surged inland. This invasion marked the beginning of the end for Nazi Germany, as only eleven months later, the war in Europe came to an end.

It is interesting to note that just after the 50-year anniversary of D-Day, Microsoft chose the code name Normandy for its suite of Commercial Internet Services. In the past two years we have been inundated with reports of the "Browser Wars" between Microsoft and several competitors. Then, in a surprising move, Microsoft began to give away its browser, the Internet Explorer. This strategy placed Microsoft very much on the attack against Netscape and its Netscape Navigator. Then Microsoft launched another attack against the Java programming language with its ActiveX technology.

As all of this was happening, Microsoft was forming alliances with major hardware and software vendors to bundle Internet Explorer with its offerings. Now Microsoft is designing its suite of Internet servers, the Commercial Internet System. By choosing Normandy as the codename, it is possible that Microsoft considers the release of the Commercial Internet System as a sort of "D-Day" for control of the Internet.

The Genesis Communications Network Commercial Internet Site

Genesis Communications Network, Inc., is an Internet Service Provider to businesses and government in North Florida. We were looking for better ways to meet our customers' growing needs. Many of the customers are looking into conducting some kind of online commerce within the next year. All of them are trying to find a way to better learn who is using their Internet site. Each also wants to find ways to keep site visitors returning. We were already anticipating the introduction of the Microsoft Commercial Internet System when the opportunity arose to contribute to this book. We decided that the most practical and useful discussion of how to use the Commercial Internet System would be to build our site as we wrote the book. This enables you to come along with us on this roller coaster ride. You will be able to see exactly what mistakes we made and how we overcame them. We will share with you the way we came to decisions and how they worked out. You will be able to see how the various components work together and what it takes to support a full-blown commercial Internet site.

In Chapter 2, "Getting Started with Microsoft Commercial Internet System," you see how we developed the site plan and learn what information you need to gather to develop your Internet strategy.

To demonstrate all of the Commercial Internet System servers, we chose four of our client sites:

- Integrity Data
- The Public Agenda
- The Tallahassee-Leon County Civic Center
- The Help Screen

These clients, along with the Genesis Communications site, allow us to demonstrate the entire line of Commercial Internet Servers in a development and production environment. All of the examples we use and the forms and applications we demonstrate will be in actual use on the Web site, **www.gencom.net**. All of the sample forms, pages, and applications may also be found on Que's Web site—**http://www.quecorp.com/mcis**.

In the following sections, you learn a little more about the four clients and what they expect from the Commercial Internet System.

Integrity Data, Inc.

Integrity Data, Inc., is a North Florida-based Network Integrator. It specializes in designing and implementing network systems for businesses and government. These services include Internet and intranet sites. Integrity Data has full-service Training and Programming departments in addition to the standard Sales and Service offerings. They also differ from many integrators in that they are also an Internet Service Provider (Genesis Communications). In this book, we will be looking at the Integrity Data site from two different perspectives, first as the commercial site provider and second as a computer reseller.

As a computer reseller, Integrity Data will use several components on its Internet site.

- Merchant System

  Using the Merchant Server, Integrity Data hopes to market and sell laptop computers and training classes via the Internet.
- Chat and Internet Location Servers

  Utilizing the Chat Server, Integrity Data will host a virtual help desk manned by trained technicians. This will enable customers to get real-time answers to questions.
- The Internet Mail Server

  E-mail is already an important part of Integrity Data's external and internal communications strategy.

- Internet News Server

  The staff uses UseNet groups to help keep up with technical issues. It also plans to host several technical and strategic discussion groups on its Internet news server.

- Membership System

  Integrity Data plans to utilize the Membership system to control access to specific areas of content. This will enable them to provide a premium service to selected customers without having to build an independent site.

The Public Agenda

In Tallahassee, Florida, there is a public community service effort called The Public Agenda. Operating under a grant from The Pew Charitable Trusts and other funding sources, The Public Agenda project's goal is to promote the return to participatory democracy, where people are involved with their social environment in an informed and active way.

To this end, The Public Agenda has conducted research and surveys in the community, staged public meetings with follow-up discussion groups, and has conducted training sessions to instruct citizens on the deliberative method of discussion aimed at reaching a common voice. It is their hope that purposeful discussions wherever people meet, in their living rooms, churches, workplaces, or online, for example, will become the norm. While the product of these discussions is certainly of interest and potential benefit to the community, it is the process that is essential to the realization of the goal: that people come together, not apart, to solve community problems.

The Public Agenda has conducted Community Dialogues, intended to bring different segments of the community together to learn that they have many things in common: concerns and conclusions. The Community Dialogues have resulted in a number of committees that continue to meet to explore problems and possibilities related to special concerns, such as crime, race relations, children, and education.

The Public Agenda, by helping to raise awareness and form connections, is the catalyst. It is up to the people to "public agenda" items of concern and then to carry them forward to their agreed-upon conclusions.

The Public Agenda has put a lot of effort into making contact with the public. Some of that effort has been directed to developing an Internet site that has already shown results. In the continuing effort to enhance dialog in the community, The Public Agenda Project will use several of the Microsoft Commercial Internet Servers:

- Internet Mail Server

  Public Agenda intends to use Mail as an important means of communication with the public.

- Internet News Server

  The Public Agenda will have discussion groups for each of its committee areas. This will add another area of input for the public as well as an ongoing dialog.

■ Chat Server

Communication and discussion are the two methods The Public Agenda utilizes to reach its goals. The Chat Server will give them the capability to take these discussions into cyberspace. This will give them access to a different constituency in real time. By doing so, they hope to broaden the discussion and further enrich the community understanding.

■ Internet Locator Server

The Locator Server will be used to enhance the online chats. Before you can talk with someone, you have to know they are around. The locator server will be utilized to provide a dynamic list of the Internet site's visitors.

By utilizing these systems, the Public Agenda will be able to enhance the dialog process by expanding the capabilities of their Internet site. This will enable them to reach parts of the community in a dynamic manner not fully implemented until now.

Tallahassee-Leon County Civic Center

The Tallahassee-Leon County Civic Center is the sports and entertainment mecca for the surrounding communities. It is the "home court" for Florida State University's basketball team and the East Coast Hockey League's Tiger Sharks. It also hosts numerous concerts and Broadway plays throughout the year and schedules public ice skating during hockey season. Numerous seminars, meetings, conventions, and trade shows are held in various meeting rooms and exhibition halls.

The Civic Center wants to use the Internet to improve its communication with the community and as a value-added service to its clients. In order to facilitate this, they plan to use these components of the MCIS:

■ Internet Mail Server

TLCCC plans to utilize the e-mail as an internal and external medium. Many of the groups utilizing the civic center prefer to communicate via e-mail. The difficult schedules followed by touring groups make it difficult to coordinate telephone calls. E-mail also gives local community members an easy way to communicate with civic center staff.

■ Chat and Internet Location Servers

The civic center plans to offer public forums with guest artists and sports figures. This will allow fans to communicate directly with public figures they normally could not reach.

■ The Proxy Server

Since the Civic Center will be used for multiple events, bandwidth usage is a concern. The Proxy Server will allow them to build a large cache of frequently accessed sites thus reducing bandwidth usage.

The Help Screen

The Help Screen is a weekly column that is carried via the Knight-Ridder/Tribune News Wire. It answers questions from computer users across the country. Currently the Help Screen is seen in over 300 local papers across the United States. As more papers are added on a weekly basis, the readership continues to expand. This produces several difficult challenges. Each time an additional new paper picks up the column, many of the same questions are asked by the local readers. How does the column remain fresh while still responding to those readers? Another problem is delivering the current or archived columns to the individual papers. The author plans to utilize the Commercial Internet System to address these issues as well as others. In order to accomplish this, the Help Screen will use:

■ Chat Server

One of the new plans for the Help Screen is to host occasional online chats with the readers. This will enable the author to not only meet his public, but also to get a feel for what they would like to get from The Help Screen.

■ Membership Server

The Membership server system will provide the means to track who accesses the Help Screen site. Thus the author will be able to look for new markets that might be interested in carrying his column.

■ Merchant Server

The Merchant system, in conjunction with the Membership system, provides the vehicle to distribute columns to the various papers without spending massive numbers of man-hours. It will also generate billing events. This will simplify knowing which subscribing papers owe what amount.

■ Content Replication System

Since the Help Screen site will be constantly changing content and the way it is presented, version tracking will be an area of concern. The Content Replication System will allow the Webmaster and the author complete control over the content of the site. Updates can be made without fear of broken links or overwriting newer data.

Common Concerns

There are several items that all of the preceding sites will have in common. They will all be running on Windows NT Server 4.0. They will each also run the Internet Information Server. A SQL Server version 6.5 will also be available to support the Commercial Internet System. In addition, all of the sites will utilize:

■ Active Server Pages

Active Server pages will allow the sites to take full advantage of the Internet Information Server 3.0 and the ActiveX control technology.

■ Personalization Server

The Personalization Server is an important tool for gathering information about site visitors. This kind of information will enable the site developers to change the site to meet the needs and desires of the users. It will also allow the users to customize the site to their own preferences, thus encouraging users to return more frequently.

■ Proxy Server

The Proxy Server will be one line of security covering the entire commercial site. Since there is an intranet operating behind firewalls, the Proxy server will be an integral part of the Internet strategy.

From Here...

This chapter introduced the Microsoft Commercial Internet System. It showed you why it was developed and the needs it addressed. It also introduced the WWW site that was built to accompany this book and the client groups it supports.

■ Chapter 2, "Getting Started with Microsoft Commercial Internet System," takes a closer look at each of the Commercial Internet servers. It also discusses how to plan your Internet site. The types of Internet connections will be examined and you learn what is required to establish an Internet site.

■ Chapter 3, "Building the Foundation," describes the hardware and software required to run Microsoft Commercial Internet System. Information on setting up your domain and scaling the system when activity warrants is also provided.

Getting Started with Microsoft Commercial Internet System

The Microsoft Commercial Internet System is a set of Internet servers designed to enable Internet Service Providers, their customers, and corporations with their own Internet site to conduct their business on the Internet, to more easily access the information available on the Web, and to provide more comprehensive management of Internet and intranet sites and activities.

This chapter introduces you to each of the servers that make up the Commercial Internet System package. We will discuss some of the key features as well as give some examples of how they can be used. You will learn about a variety of considerations that will aid in planning an MCIS-based site. Finally, we will look at the many ways to establish an Internet connection and set up your domain. ■

See what is underneath a successful Internet site

Learn about the different elements required to build an Internet Server. Look under the hood at Windows NT Server and the Internet Information Server.

Meet the Microsoft Commercial Internet servers

Find out what is included in the MCIS. See which servers are right for your site, and learn how the different components all work together to build the complete Internet site.

Learn how to plan an Internet site

Learn the difference between a T1 and a T3. Figure out how much bandwidth you need. Determine which MCIS components are required at your site.

Experience an Integrity Check

Look in and learn from our decisions and mistakes as we build the Genesis Communications Network and Integrity Data Internet site.

Understanding the Microsoft Commercial Internet System Foundation

Windows NT Server 4.0 and Internet Information Server provide the foundation on which Microsoft Commercial Internet System is built. Like any organization, the final product can be no better than the underlying platform. MS Windows NT Server 4.0 is Microsoft's latest entry in the enterprise server arena. It provides a stable, robust, and scalable foundation for the entire BackOffice suite as well as for Microsoft Commercial Internet System. Windows NT Server 4.0 provides the tools and power necessary to manage and develop Internet as well as intranet sites.

The Internet Information system provides a versatile base on which to build an Internet site. Its ease of use and administration allow it to integrate easily with the Microsoft Commercial Internet System Suite. The virtual server capabilities in Internet Information Server allow the hosting of multiple virtual domains. These virtual sites can then be managed through the Internet Service Manager and the HTML extensions for the Internet Service Manager. This ease of administration allows the network administrator the luxury of leaving the office from time to time.

The Internet Information Server supports many industry standards including Common Gateway Interface scripting and Perl. It is also built with an open API, the Internet Server API (ISAPI). This allows custom extensions to be added to Internet Information Server for logging, indexing, database access, and third-party applications.

Perhaps the greatest benefit of building the Microsoft Commercial Internet System upon NT and Internet Information Server is the scalability inherent in NT. This ability to easily grow a site allows for the massive and sudden growth so often associated with an Internet site. Since Microsoft Commercial Internet System is primarily designed for sites serving millions of customers, it is imperative that the site be stable and manageable.

All of these features combine to give Microsoft Commercial Internet System a solid foundation upon which to build. As mentioned in Chapter 1, "Meet the Microsoft Commercial Internet System," five of the servers plug into Internet Information Server as additional services. This tight integration and common user interface greatly reduces the time spent learning how to use a new piece of software. In today's frantic pace, this alone could warrant using Microsoft Commercial Internet System.

Obtaining the Software

Currently, the Microsoft Commercial Internet System is still in development. However, 10 beta versions of the components are available from the Microsoft Web site at:

http://backoffice.microsoft.com

When you arrive at the site, select the option for "Microsoft Commercial Internet System," and then click the "Download" button. You are then launched to the MCIS download site.

From here, simply select the components you are interested in and follow the download procedure for each. Version 1.0 of the following components are currently available for download:

- Chat
- Content Replication
- Internet Locator
- News
- Personalization
- Merchant
- Proxy

Part
I
Ch
2

Throughout the book, all descriptions and installation notes were written based on one of the early beta versions of the software; all were available for public download from the Microsoft Web site. Unfortunately, there were no Release Copies available for any of the products at the time of this writing. According to Microsoft, the public release of version 2.0 of the software will happen during the fourth quarter of 1997.

Introducing the Microsoft Commercial Internet System Servers

There are several individual components of the Microsoft Commercial Internet System, each utilizing a common System Administration Architecture. They are the newest server applications to be added to Microsoft's BackOffice servers.

Each piece of the Commercial Internet System is covered in detail in one or more chapters later in the book. However, each is truly designed to be only one part in the cast of characters that make up a complete package. So, take some time now to learn about all the individual components, the part each plays, and how they all work together to provide Internet solutions for your business.

The Commercial Internet Mail Server

The most popular use of the Internet today is still e-mail. In spite of all the hype about the World Wide Web and Commerce, the Internet runs on e-mail. Any successful site must have a solid and dependable e-mail server. Savvy network administrators realize that they will get no peace if the staff's Mail does not get through.

ISPs and network administrators require a heavy-duty, reliable mail system. Most ISPs host mail for multiple domains. Web pages and sites are filled with mail-to's and forms, which require a stable mail platform. Intranets require that inter- and intra-office mail not only be reliable and user-friendly, but integrate seamlessly with group scheduling and workflow applications.

Microsoft's Commercial Internet Mail Server is an Internet Standards-based electronic mail service. Built as an add-on service to Internet Information Server, the mail server can theoretically be scaled to millions of users. It is fully SMTP and POP3 compliant and supports any SMTP/POP mail clients, including the Microsoft mail client, Eudora, Netscape, and others. Since the Internet Mail Server is standards-based, it eliminates the need for many gateways or format conversions. In future versions of the software, Microsoft plans to support the Internet Message Access Protocol (IMAP), version 4, for remote mailbox access.

FIG. 2.1

The Commercial Internet System mail server.

The Internet Mail Server is administered either through the Internet Service Manager or through Web-based administration. The Internet Information Server on which the Internet Mail Server is built allows for advanced monitoring and performance tuning of the Internet Mail Server. The Internet Mail Server also allows for remote monitoring and administration of mailboxes. The ability to create, delete, expire, and view mailboxes remotely is integral in the scaling of the Internet Mail Server. Internet Mail Server allows for increasing capacity by allowing mailboxes to be distributed across multiple servers in multiple locations. The message storing processing is separate from the client connection processing. This allows the number of concurrent connections to be scaled separately from the number of mailboxes.

Like all of the Microsoft Commercial Internet Servers, the Internet Mail Servers support three different security options:

- Standard, clear-text AUTH user/pass commands to the NT server 4.0 account database
- Distributed Password Authorization, which is a more secure method
- SSL, which authenticates the users and encrypts the data stream between the client and the server

The Microsoft Commercial Mail Server is designed to be able to not only support systems such as CompuServe with millions of mailboxes spread over multiple servers in multiple locations, but also a corporate intranet with hundreds of users in one location. Since it is based on established Internet Standards for Mail transport and delivery, it can be integrated into almost any situation.

The Commercial Internet News Server

Information sharing is the cornerstone of today's corporate environment. No longer are clients content waiting for answers. In order to succeed, companies as well as individuals need access to information when *they* need it, not when it is convenient. Customers today want to build relationships with their suppliers. They want quick answers to their problems and 24-hour access to information. A full-featured Internet News System can help deliver all of this. Millions of users turn everyday to Internet News groups such as UseNet for information and discussion (see Figure 2.2). No successful ISP or corporate intranet can hope to succeed without a stable, robust News System.

FIG. 2.2
A wide range of newsgroups can be accessed easily in the point-and-click interface the News Server offers to users.

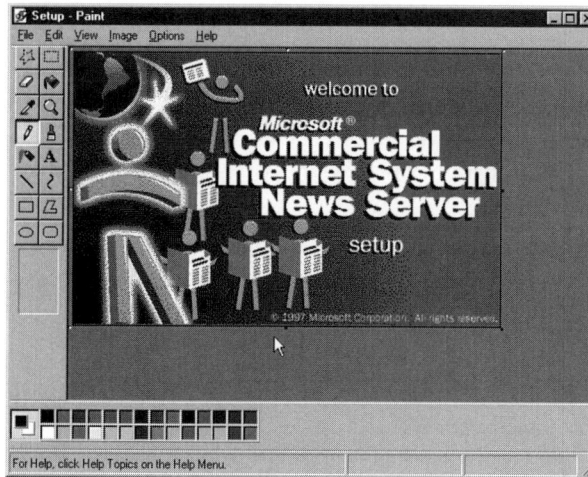

The Microsoft Commercial Internet News Server is a full-featured, NNTP-compatible News Server. It supports public, moderated, and authenticated groups. Since it is based upon Microsoft Windows NT Server 4.0 and the Internet Information Server, it is inherently scalable. The INS features:

- True NNTP server and client compatibility
- NNTP security extensions, which allow encrypted password transmission
- Full native support for control-group messages, allowing automated newsgroup administration
- Full-featured transaction and usage logging

The INS is highly compatible with INN, the public domain NNTP software, which is used to host the UseNet newsgroups. It uses a standard Master/Slave relationship to replicate data across multiple servers. This allows sites to deploy multiple servers to distribute the client load. In sites using slave servers, clients only connect with the slaves, thus freeing the masters to process news. According to Microsoft, a dual processor P160 with 256M of RAM can support up to 3,000 concurrent users.

Hand-in-hand with scalability goes usability. Quite simply, managing a news server has never been easier. This implementation of NNTP is outstanding and most all of the functions are managed from the intuitive Microsoft Internet Service Manager. This drastically reduces the development and implementation time for a News Server. Lest the purists in the group despair, Microsoft has included a full set of command line utilities, such as nntpbuild and list.

The Chat Server

The most frustrating part of Internet News is waiting for a response. This can take from several minutes to several days. This is not helpful during a crisis. If the Internet is supposed to be this wonderful interactive medium, why do we have to wait? Masters of the command line have another opportunity that most do not—Internet Relay Chat (IRC). Many people first joined the online community via organizations such as The Portal or The Well. These were online bulletin boards with chat rooms. The chat room was where several users could meet online and "talk" about issues. The popularity of these chat rooms helped spur the development of IRC, which many users from different systems use to chat online. The problem with this method is the command line knowledge required. Today's typical computer users cannot survive without their GUI.

Large commercial online services such as America Online and CompuServe developed nice graphical chat rooms. They quickly became two of the most popular services. As long as users had access to these types of services they could utilize the chat rooms there.

Then the Internet and World Wide Web exploded onto the scene. Suddenly people had access to a much wider range of services and content. Millions of users "surfed the Web" without access to the commercial online services. The need developed to create a standards-based system that not only supported the IRC protocols but also incorporated a GUI interface. Then the system had to be highly scalable and extensible.

The Chat server is based on Internet Chat standards and also allows for additional features by including its own Chat protocol. This allows it to support most IRC clients as well as additional Microsoft chat clients. The Chat server incorporates many features, some of which are:

- Compatibility with standards-based IRC Servers and Clients
- The ability to allow "whispers" and private chats for confidential business-to-business communication
- Built-in support for queries to locate other chats
- The ability to include document shortcuts and URLs through Chat
- Built-in support for data-based messages
- An SDK which includes ActiveX controls for incorporating Chat into Web pages (see Figure 2.3)

The Microsoft Chat Server uses data packets, which are roughly half the size of normal IRC packets. This, coupled with the native NT Server scalability, allows a Microsoft Chat Network to grow to approximately 48,000 concurrent users. An individual Chat server can support in excess of 2,500 users. Combine this with the ability to support multiple channels and you have a full-featured server.

FIG. 2.3

The Chat Server can simplify communication both in-house and with the outside world.

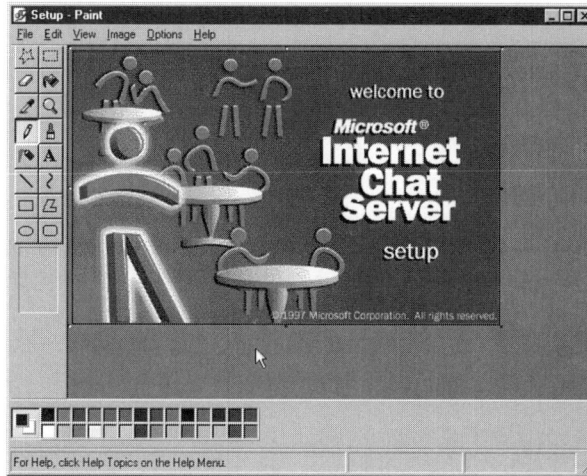

Administration of the Chat server is once again accomplished via the Internet Services Manager. This gives the Chat administrator access to the same transaction logs and usage information as the other services. This greatly reduces the effort and time spent in Performance tuning and maintenance required of a high-volume Chat server.

The Internet Locator Server

FIG. 2.4

The Commercial Internet System Internet Locator Server.

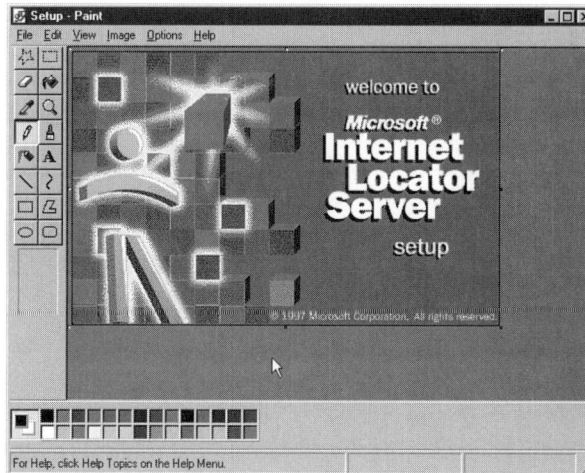

Now you have the ability to chat in real time on a Web page. Who are you going to talk to? What if you need to reach a client and you do not know what channel the client is on? Sure, you can manually search all of the channels, if you don't have anything better to do with your time, but there is a better way.

The Microsoft Internet Locator Server allows the real-time lookup of who is logged on. This is accomplished by a dynamic database of current users and their IP addresses. This database is based upon the Lightweight Directory Access Protocol RT (Real Time) person object. The Locator Server stores the database in RAM and constantly updates it with user information.

This Real Time capability allows businesses to conduct online meetings and conferences within a chat environment. It also allows users to identify clients or colleagues online and then initiate an "IP Phone" session or link them to a chat.

The Internet Locator Server uses a GUI administration system that is compatible with the IIS. This allows the administrator access to all logs and usage statistics. The ILS is presently compatible with clients supporting the Lightweight Directory Access Protocol. NetMeeting and Intel Phone both support LDAP.

Using the Chat and Locator servers together allows companies to host multiple online meetings and conferences. They also give administrators a vastly improved method for integrating a productive chat server with a Web site, a function that eludes most administrators by its complexity.

The Content Replication System

Internet usage is growing at a phenomenal rate. That fact is well known by anyone who reads a paper or watches the news. What the uninitiated do not think about is how all that information gets on the Web. If questioned, most would realize that someone has to create the pages and write the material. However, how many know how to make that material available to the public? If you have ever administered an Internet site, you know the problem. Sites with thousands of pages and hundreds of graphics look great on the development systems. Then they tell you to move them out to the production environment. Then, by the way, 500 of those pages may change daily. Either you have an excessive personnel budget and can hire someone to manually move the data from the development systems out to the production systems or you automate the process.

The Microsoft Content Replication System (CRS) allows the secure movement and mirroring of information across both intranet and internet servers. Most present systems use some type of File Transfer Protocol-dependent distribution process. This has several inherent shortcomings, such as:

- Most systems of this type are not reliable. If a file transfer is interrupted they cannot recover.
- Most replication is accomplished via some type of batch process, which must be manually developed and maintained.
- Most systems are unavailable or out of sync while the transfer is taking place.
- Most of the current systems are unable to easily add additional sources or destinations of the data.

The MCRS addresses all of these problems and adds several key features:

- *ACL Replications*   The replication of NT and Membership Access Control Lists allows security to be transferred with data.

- *Automatic File Replication*   Allows the administrator to link updates with Directory Change Notifications. This provides for extremely quick updates with minimal user input.

- *Chained Replications*   Servers not directly connected to the source systems can be updated based on project name and route definition. This is extremely useful when data developed within a fire wall must be distributed to multiple points outside the wall.

- *Incremental Replication*   Allows the automatic replication of incremental changes without checking file synchronization, thus allowing much quicker transfer for "real-time" information.

- *Transaction-Based Replication*   This creates a temporary directory on the production system. All of the data to be replicated is copied into this directory. Then the previous production directory is renamed and the temporary directory is named to replace it. This allows for a nearly instantaneous update of information, reducing the window of "Broken Link Time" common with current replication. It also provides a way to fall back to previous versions by keeping the renamed directories.

- *"Get" support for FTP and HTTP built into the CRS*   Allows information to be pulled from Web and FTP sites and then replicated (see Figure 2.5).

FIG. 2.5

The Commercial Internet System Content Replication Server.

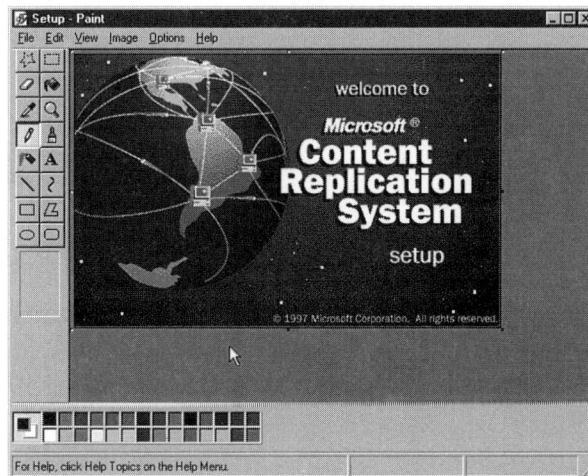

The Content Replication system can secure the transfer of this information by utilizing both NTLM Authentication and MD5 Transmit Stream Hashing "Signing." This not only protects the information on the server but also allows the system to sign each session stream to prevent data hijacking.

The MCRS utilizes the NT Event Logs to track all performance-based information and utilization records. It also produces text-based diagnostic logs and Performance Monitor counters.

Part

I

Ch

2

The MCRS improves a company's ability to provide time-critical information. It allows for publishing of current, near real-time information across multiple platforms. The Microsoft Network utilized the MCRS during the 1996 Super Bowl and the Oscar Awards. Game and Award recipient information was kept constantly updated during the events.

The Microsoft Personalization System

Most Web sites have multiple products, services, and information they want to aim at specific users. The difficulty for Web designers is to get users to return again and again by creating a site that is compelling and useful. To be effective, the site must be customizable to the individual user.

The designer must create the appropriate combination of customization to the user's preferences while also targeting content to provide the proper information to the selected types of users. Internet service providers and commercial Web sites normally personalize a site by developing scripts that run on the Web server, and that create content via the Common Gateway Interface (CGI), or by a Service Access Point Identifier (SAPI) interface such as IIS Internet Services Application Programming Interface (ISAPI) or the Netscape Application Programming Interface (NSAPI). Information about each user is typically stored on the user's client in the form of a "cookie." The "cookie" solution is easy to implement because it pushes the burden of storing user information onto the user.

This method does have some shortcomings, which include:

- Designers must be proficient in C or PERL programming.
- To store pertinent information the "cookies" must be quite large.
- The information stored in a cookie is not available for analysis.
- Cookies are an insecure mechanism and can be counterfeited.

The MPS utilizes the Microsoft Active Server Pages (ASP). This provides a way to gather the information necessary to construct a server-based user profile database. The tools and components to take full advantage of this database are included in the ASP.

The store of user information in the database makes it easier for companies to use this information to build individual and group user profiles. User properties can include data recorded and gathered from a user's Web activity, and not just information provided directly by the user. Properties can be changed and new properties added offline via server-based APIs.

Two key features of MPS are the support of Active Server Pages and the User Properties Database. The support of Active Server Pages allows a site to more fully utilize ActiveX components in gathering and analyzing user information (see Figure 2.6).

The User Properties Database object offers the following benefits:

- Make it easy to gather and maintain information about each user.
- Are centralized on the Web site server, and can be secured.
- Can be partitioned across multiple servers to scale with user load.

■ Can be replicated onto multiple servers to provide a hot "backup."

■ Can hold a large amount of information about a single user.

FIG 2.6

The Commercial Internet System Personalization Server.

Part
I

Ch
2

Perhaps the biggest benefit is the ability to create a unique user ID. This ID can be stored in a cookie on the user's system, thus allowing the user information to be shared across multiple participating Web sites.

These features allow sites to offer users dynamic and personal content, which should increase return traffic and customer loyalty. It also should enable advertisers to get more complete user information from the site, based both on a user's stated preferences and the user's actions on the Web.

The MPS also incorporates several control objects:

■ User Property Database

■ SendMail

■ Voter

These controls allow the developer to further personalize and enhance the user experience. The user controls include browser detection. *Browser detection* allows the server to see which browser is accessing the system and serve pages which best suit the browser.

By mixing the features of IIS and MPS, the following Content Controls can be used:

■ *An Ad Rotator*   Allows advertisements to be placed on the site.

■ *User Voting*   Allows surveys to be conducted.

■ *Content Navigation*   Allows users to create individual home pages.

■ *An Information Pump*   Allows the developer to provide customized content to each user.

The Service Controls include a Direct Mailer for automated response and a Database Connector for automated access to the user database.

The Microsoft Membership Server

Now you have all of these wonderful ways of providing information and enjoyment to millions of users. Do you want to provide all of them with the same information? Do you want to give it all away for free? If you provide services for multiple clients, do they have restrictions they want to place on their sites? What happens if employees need to access your information through different servers? Most administers would have a different answer for each question. All of them requiring long hours and custom programming.

The Microsoft Membership System attempts to address these issues and more. Basically, the Membership System is a distributed authentication and access control system. It integrates with the other MCIS servers to allow users to build an extremely robust and scalable Commercial Internet Service. Unfortunately, due to beta testing cycles we were unable to fully review the Membership system before we went to print. We can therefore only give you a brief overview of the Membership system's potential.

The Membership System includes the ability to authenticate users, control access to specific areas of an Internet site, and create accounting events to be processed by an external-billing engine (see Figure 2.7).

FIG. 2.7
The Commercial Internet System Membership Server.

Some of the key features of the Membership System include:

- Integrated support for a wide range of Microsoft clients and servers, such as Web, Chat, Mail, and News.
- A security database provides a central storage facility for user rights and product offerings.

- Distributed Password Authentication (DPA) includes a customizable user logon to authenticate users against the Security Database. DPA allows this authentication to take place on any server deployed by the site administrators anywhere across the Internet. It also allows a user to have a single ID and password for all services offered by a site, even if the content is from multiple content providers.

- Integration with external billing systems allows third-party software to gather billing events directly from the Membership system.

- A "token" feature allows the grouping of users and products into Product and Service Class Definitions. Coupled with an expiration feature, this allows content to be offered by type, group of users, or expiration date.

The Microsoft Address Book

The Microsoft Internet Address Book provides White Pages-type service to handle user information. This allows for easily accessed Web directories of members and customized information about them, such as e-mail addresses, chats and newsgroups subscribed to, and other personal information.

The Address Book utilizes the Microsoft SQL to store user information. This access is available to clients via an HTTP interface or through an LDAP interface. The LDAP allows custom clients to query the Address Book Server.

The Address Book is a low resource server. Microsoft estimates that a single server can handle up to two million entries and millions of hits per day.

Templates for creating custom HTML pages are included with the Address Book Server. It also integrates with the Internet Services Manager to provide easy administration and event logging.

The Address Book Server includes its own built-in security technology. This protects not only the individuals having information in the database, but also the entire database. Individual users can determine the amount of personal information they wish to display. The Server also includes "anti-data mining" technology to prevent unauthorized use of information by online marketeers.

The Microsoft Merchant System

The World Wide Web has enjoyed unprecedented growth and exposure. Millions of people "surf" the Web daily and millions more utilize e-mail or News. Yet more and more people are asking if this is all there is? Isn't this supposed to make life easier or better? What reasons do I have to keep using this? Well, how about making money? That's the quickest answer. However, how do you do this and is anybody doing it already? Until recently no one really had the answers to those questions. The only way to sell online was to either accept a nonsecure transfer of payment information or to spend thousands of dollars creating custom applications to display the merchandise and take the payment information. You then had to integrate the information with some type of authorization method and then figure out how to process and deliver the merchandise.

The Microsoft Merchant Server is an Internet-retailing software product that companies can use to sell goods and services over the Internet. The Merchant Server is designed so merchants can present an enjoyable shopping experience with limited custom development. It allows for all of the above difficulties in a near turnkey package. However you still have to get your own products and deliver them. While the Merchant Server is not technically a part of MCIS, it is designed to work hand in hand with MCIS to provide a complete Internet solution.

The Merchant System allows businesses to:

- Provide an enjoyable customer experience. When consumers connect to sites running Merchant Server, they use a process that is consistent and easy to use across shopping sessions and client platforms.

- Create personalized shopping experiences based on registered profiles. In addition, merchants can build stores using tools such as ActiveX and Java. The Merchant Server supports industry-standard protocols such as the Secure Sockets Layer and the Secure Electronic Transaction protocol, which secures the transfer of data.

- Minimize custom development of Internet stores. Merchant Server supports flexible configurations that can be easily changed as a store grows. The system components can run on a single computer or on multiple computers across a network to support heavy traffic loads. In addition, Merchant Server can be integrated with existing inventory or order-processing systems by means of its open application programming interfaces (APIs).

- Enable real-time merchandising capabilities. Merchants can track consumers and orders, analyze store activity, and respond quickly to user preferences or market pressures.

Built-in features of the Merchant Server are:

- HTML templates to dynamically generate pages from a database.

- Administrative Web pages enable merchants to manage the products and organization of the store from their browser. Changes are automatically reflected on the store pages without requiring changes to the HTML markup.

- The ability to create and update promotions based on purchase or shopper characteristics.

- A Shopping Basket, which holds items that the shopper has selected for purchase.

- Forms which collect the shopper's name, shipping address, shipping method, and credit card information; and online receipts confirm the purchase.

- Shipping and tax charges on purchases can be calculated using third-party services.

- APIs to integrate incoming Internet orders with existing inventory management, tax, shipping, and fulfillment systems.

- Forms which collect information about orders, shoppers, and store traffic, either for all data or for data sorted according to various criteria such as product or shopper for easy viewing.

These features allow companies to build sites that go beyond the norm and actually conduct commerce over the Web.

Planning the Site

Now that you have a better idea of the services that are available with the Commercial Internet System, it's time to start thinking about a site. The first part of developing an Internet site is determining exactly what type of site you need. There are several considerations:

- Are you serving a single entity or multiple clients?
- What type of business are you?
- What type of content are you going to provide?
- Where do you fit into the plan?
- What type of services are you going to offer?
- How much traffic do you project?
- What kind of budget do you have?

In this section we will address each of these issues and explain how we developed the base plan for our site.

What Type of Site You Will Build

In broad terms there are only two main types of Internet Sites:

- The stand-alone company
- The commercial Internet Services Provider

A stand-alone company is a business or organization that chooses to develop its own Internet site. They provide information and services from their own location and equipment. These sites may be as large as Hewlett-Packard or as small as an individual home-based business.

The commercial provider encompasses many types of businesses. They may be a large commercial online service such as MSN or CompuServe. They could be a typical ISP or a local Web site host. Government agencies can also fall into this category as they often carry information from many different divisions or agencies. In any case, they have to take multiple client concerns into consideration when planning and administering their site.

What Type of Business You Conduct

Along with the question of what type of site you are going to create goes the question of what kind of business you are. Different types of organizations have different needs. Large online services such as MSN or CompuServe require extremely large and scalable platforms with as many types of services as possible. They provide access and services to millions of users and distribute content from thousands of clients. The slightest unreliability or performance lag can result in the loss of millions of dollars. Regional and local ISPs face most of the same concerns on a much smaller scale. However, they depend on the ease of use of a platform. Government agencies and nonprofit organizations can be restricted by policy makers and security concerns. They need to offer specific services, but have a lot of control over who accesses it and what is available.

Every organization has different needs. It is vital to have a solid understanding of what your organization envisions for the Internet site. What type of information do you wish to distribute and how are clients going to access it?

What Type of Content You Are Going to Provide

Okay, you know who you are and what you want to say. Now, how do you say it? What type of content is it? The MCIS provides multiple ways of distributing information and products. You need to look at the content or need you have and determine how best to deliver it. If you need basic communication and accessibility, all you may need is e-mail. If you need to have ongoing discussions or provide support to your users, News may be the answer. Do you need to control access to clients or content? If so, then you need the Membership System. Look back at the features of the individual components previously listed. Decide which ones fit your particular needs. Be careful to not just look at the distribution, but also at the development. The Information Retrieval and Content Replication Servers may not seem very appealing, but they can save hundreds of manhours.

Where Your Organization Fits into the Plan

If you are a stand-alone organization, it is obvious where you fit in the site plan—smack dab in the center. However, if you are a commercial provider, then you need to evaluate what role your organization will play.

Online service providers are concerned with meeting the needs of their clients. All of their staffing and security planning revolve around those needs. Other providers often find themselves providing content and services to other groups as well as their own. This practice raises numerous security concerns. How do you protect your sensitive information from others? How do you separate the public site from the private network?

What Type of Services You Are Going to Offer

Earlier you determined what type of content you were going to provide. Now it's time to decide what services to provide. Almost every site will want to provide e-mail. Many will also want to utilize Membership and News. Evaluate all of the content you provide and clients you serve, and then decide how best to accomplish this. We had our four clients to address. All of our clients needed Mail services. They also needed access to Membership services and the Personalization server. After that they all had different needs. Integrity Data is a Merchant and Service provider. Therefore it needs the Merchant Server to sell goods. It also utilizes the

News server to provide support to its clients. Integrity Data also makes use of the Information Retrieval Server to gather current product information and updates. The other clients all have their individual needs. In order to develop an overview of the services needed, we utilized a simple spreadsheet to lay out the site, as shown in Table 4.1.

Table 4.1   Genesis Communications Network Internet Plan

MCIS Server	Integrity Data	Public Agenda	TLCCCC Help Screen	Scott McPherson
NNTP (News)	X (inter)	X (intra) X (inter)	X (intra)	
Chat		X (forums) (lectures)	X (Meet performers)	X (meet the author)
Merchant	X (hardware) (training)			X (syndication)
Personalization	X	X	X	X
Membership:	X	X	X	X
Location		X		X
White				
Pages	X		X	
Index	X		X	X
Info Retrieval	X	X		X
Replication				X
ActiveX	X	X	X	X
Proxy	X	X		X
Mail	X	X	X	X

A word processor or spreadsheet table makes it easy to begin organizing a site on paper. However you accomplish it, you need to know what services you will offer in order to plan your site effectively.

How Much Traffic You Project

Now for some reality. How many people are *really* going to access your site? How quickly do you expect it to grow? How much data do you have to distribute? How vital is the speed at which it can be accessed? All of these questions figure into traffic projections.

Accurately predicting and measuring Internet traffic is an elusive art. It is also an area of visionary fuzziness. Many organizations develop an Internet site believing that if they build it, users will come. It's not the movies, folks. If you do not have a compelling reason for people to come to your site, they are not going to visit. You must not only have a reason for them to come once, but also to keep returning.

Corporations such as Microsoft and HP have compelling reasons for users to return. They provide product information and support to their users. Sites such as Yahoo! and *Wired* Magazine provide useful services or information. Sites such as these have millions of users a day and require the platform to support it. Other sites may be for company use only, or have a limited appeal. They still require all of the planning and implementation, but on a smaller scale. In fact, if your organization has a local appeal it will receive much less traffic than one with international appeal.

What Kind of Budget You Have

It always comes down to money. Whatever you originally thought it would cost to build an Internet site, triple it. It still will cost more. There are no real rules of thumb here.

You are attempting to build something that will serve you in multiple ways. The site will add marketing and communications; it can provide new opportunities to sell your product. It can provide new insight and information about your customers and it can allow you to interact with them in new and exciting ways.

Developing a budget for an Internet site can be extremely difficult. If you do not have experienced developers and administrators in-house you face even more questions. We believe that unless you have done this before you would benefit from bringing in a qualified consultant to help plan and budget your site. If you then choose to implement it yourself you have a plan to rely on.

Now you know what content you are going to provide and how you want to deliver it. Where do we go from here? Before we start installing software and building pages we need to look at one more item. What is the Internet and how do I get there? In the next section we will take a look at how to establish your Internet connection.

Establishing the Internet Connection

We now have a plan for building an Internet site. Yet we are still missing one crucial piece. How do we connect our network to the Internet? The first thing we need to do is define what we mean by the Internet.

The Internet can be described as a worldwide network of computers linked together and configured to share information. Originally, the Internet started as a research project of the Advanced Research Projects Agency (ARPA). The original intent of the ARPA network was to create a means of connecting computers across the country. To achieve this, ARPA funded research that included specifying standards for communications between networked computers, as well as establishing conventions for handling and routing network traffic. This work evolved into the development of the TCP/IP protocol suite, a set of standards for networking computers.

As the ARPA network grew, its membership and purpose grew as well. The first ARPA network, created in 1969, was a small number of leased telephone lines used to interconnect four ARPA sites. Later designs included the addition of other research sites for use by academic and military organizations, as well as by schools and universities throughout the world. By the 1980s, the original ARPA network term, "ARPANet," was no longer valid. As network membership expanded considerably beyond the original ARPA sites, the network became increasingly called "the Internet," to indicate an internetwork connecting government agencies, and later private industries.

Today, the Internet is continuing to grow rapidly. Due to public funding and the global participation of over 61 countries worldwide, no single business or organization controls the Internet. Instead, it can be seen as the internetwork formed by all the businesses and organizations that choose to link their computers to a global public network. The Internet is now a universal carrier of electronic mail, text files, multimedia objects, and real-time audio. In the future, even more information will be available in these and other formats.

The original ARPA network team saw the difficulty in implementing reliable communications between computers that used different hardware and software. Because of differences in vendor designs, a common set of openly published standards was seen as the best solution to resolving this problem. All vendors could then have access to the standard specifications and new products could be designed to operate for networked use in predictable ways. These standards have come to be known collectively as TCP/IP.

ON THE WEB

www.ietf.cnri.reston.va.us   TCP/IP refers to all of the established protocols approved and published by the Internet Engineering Task Force (IETF) that support two basic protocols:

- *Transmission Control Protocol (TCP)*   The main protocol that is used to handle connection-based service between networked computers. It specifies methods for reliable delivery of data between networked computers.
- *Internet Protocol (IP)*   The protocol that is used to move data through the network. It uses a standard addressing scheme of unique addresses to determine how data is routed through the network.

For example, if an e-mail is composed and sent to your computer as text-based data, this data is sent in pieces called *packets*, which are fixed-length parts of the data contained within the message. These packets are then forwarded to your computer by using its Internet Protocol (IP) address. An IP address consists of four numbers, each between 0 and 255, separated by periods, such as 198.199.199.199. These numerical addresses are then translated into names, such as gencom.net, by Domain Name Service (DNS).

The use of TCP and IP in this way, combined with other TCP/IP protocol sets, allows your computer to communicate with other computers on the Internet or on your local intranet. In the preceding example, the other member protocols might include either the Simple Mail Transfer Protocol (SMTP) or the Post Office Protocol (POP), which are specific standards within TCP/IP for e-mail messaging services.

Another method of TCP/IP addressing beyond IP addressing is the Domain Name System (DNS), which uses conventional names to identify computers and services available on the network. Domain names, which are easier to remember than IP addresses, are then mapped to specific IP addresses.

Domain names consist of the following elements, separated by periods:

- *A host name*   The host name is the name of the specific computer, such as WWW.
- *A subdomain name*   The subdomain name is usually the name of the private organization that manages the site, such as integritydata. These domain names are registered and administered through the Internet Network Information Center (InterNIC).
- *A top-level domain name, such as .com*   The top-level domain, which indicates the type of organization that hosts the Web site, is assigned by the InterNIC.

For example, **www.integritydata.com** is the domain name for the Integrity Data World Wide Web site. The host name, **www**, indicates that it is a World Wide Web site. The subdomain, **integritydata**, is the name registered with InterNIC by the owner of the site. In this case, the owner is Integrity Data. The top-level domain, **.com**, indicates that the Web site is operated by a commercial organization.

Internet top-level domain names include:

Abbreviation	Designation	Description
.com	Commercial	Used by all businesses and other organizations involved in commercial uses of the Internet
.edu	Educational	Used by all public schools, colleges, and universities
.org	Nonprofit organization	Used by nonprofit organizations only
.mil	Military	Used by member agencies of the U.S. Department of Defense only
.net	Network	A more recent addition to the list of top-level domains. This domain is reserved for ISPs providing large-scale access to the Internet backbone or other organizations providing Internet access

ON THE WEB

rs.internic.net   In order to connect your network to the Internet, you need to be running some form of TCP/IP protocol on the systems connecting to the Internet. You also need to have registered your domain with the InterNIC. You can do this by filling out the template at the InterNIC Web site.

An *intranet* is another name for a private network. A TCP/IP intranet is an organization's internal network of computers based on the Internet model. This internal network can be as small as a local area network (LAN) that connects two PCs over a serial link, or as large as a wide area network (WAN) that connects hundreds of computers worldwide. An intranet can be thought of as any network whose computers and network hardware are under the responsibility of a single organization. Many organizations use intranets to publish information for their network users. An intranet can be connected to the Internet via a gateway. A *gateway* is special software, or a computer running special software, that enables two different networks to communicate. The gateway acts as a barrier that allows you to make requests to the Internet and receive information, but does not necessarily allow access to your network by outsiders.

Part

I

Ch

2

An intranet can utilize conventional TCP/IP addresses or it can opt to use its own scheme. However, if a computer will be interacting with others via the Internet, it must either have a valid Internet address or utilize some sort of Proxy system.

Okay, we are almost ready. We have a site plan. We have a registered Domain Name and TCP/IP addresses. Wait, where did we get the addresses from? Each block of addresses can be broken down into four segments: 199.199.199.199. They correspond to the type of address block, as shown here:

IP address	199.199.199.199
block	A B C D

Each segment of the address has the potential for 255 addresses, such as 199.199.199.1– 199.199.199.255. When you plan your network you will need some idea as to the number of computers or other networks connecting at any given moment. This will help give you an idea of what size block you require. If you have less than 200 systems connecting, then a Class C block (199.199.199.0) would be sufficient. If, however, you also expect to have several other large networks connecting, then you may need part of, or maybe all of, a Class B block (199.199.0.0).

The size of the block requested determines where you get the addresses. If all you need is a Class C or less, then your ISP can provide them. If, however, you need a much larger block, then you will wind up working with your ISP and the InterNIC to acquire them.

Now you have everything you need except the connection itself. Here there are numerous choices presently available, all of them again dependent upon your traffic projections. Each of these connections is based upon the amount of "bandwidth" you need, that is, how much data you need to move and how fast you need to move it. A site with only very few users and little data needs much less bandwidth than a site with millions of users and gigabytes of data.

The "connections" break into several types:

- *The Dial-Up Connection* This is a connection through an ISP via a standard modem. As of now the fastest standard connection via modem is a 33,600 bps connection. This is the type of connection the home user uses to connect to the Internet. It is fine for one user or in rare cases a small group. Data moves very slowly at this speed and bandwidth intensive applications such as live video are impractical.

- *The ISDN Connection* ISDN stands for "Integrated Services Digital Networks." ISDN is basically the telephone network turned digital from end to end, utilizing the existing infrastructure. This allows the basic "call" to be a 64kbps end-to-end channel. This technology coupled with ISDN modems allows for bandwidth of 64kbps to 128kbps. This is a much faster Internet connection, yet is still better suited for getting information rather than distributing it.

- *The T1 Connection*   This is where ISPs begin. A T1 connection has a throughput of 1.45 Mbps. This is a sizable increase in available bandwidth. Most local and many regional ISPs utilize a single T1 line for all of their needs. Many support over 1,500 users and multiple content providers. This level of connection should be readily available in your area. Most telephone carriers have them available and many of the National ISPs will also provide them upon request. The T1 will allow you to have bandwidth readily available to your users and leave plenty to distribute your information out over the net. If you need a little more, then you might want to look at getting multiple T1s. This can allow you to separate internal use from external use. You can also use this method to separate incoming News and Data feeds from your client traffic.

- *The DS3 Connection*   Until recently this was the promised land. A DS3 connection can pump 45 Mbps to your network. Much of the Internet "backbone" is run over DS3 connections. If you are planning to be a large online service or you have massive amounts of data to distribute, this is for you. The difficulties with DS3 are twofold. First, you can have trouble finding a local connection, and secondly, it is significantly more expensive. Many times a group of companies or providers will share a DS3 connection, thus distributing the cost.

- *ATM, Fiber Optic, and Beyond*   The Internet's growth has been explosive. Millions of new users are accessing the Internet every year. This, of course, requires that access and content providers find ways to provide greater and greater amounts of bandwidth. These new technologies are already in use on many large sites. If you are building a site requiring this much bandwidth then you already have the knowledgeable staff to select the method that is right for you.

Integrity Check

We decided, as shown in Table 4.1, to utilize all of the different servers in various capacities. Obviously, this puts us in the ISP category of business. Yet we also had to concern ourselves with building our corporate intranet and serving our employees needs. In order to keep expenses down we decided to use a two-step bandwidth approach. During the testing and early development stages we opted for a Fractional T1, 128kbps connection. This was sufficient for testing the various servers and developing the applications we would use. Then, as we approached the production rollout, we upgraded our connection to a full T1. We have also begun arrangements to access either a DS3 or ATM connection when the need arises.

In any case, no matter which connection speed you choose the MCIS provides the platform on which to build your site.

From Here...

You are now finally ready to move into actually building the site. In this chapter, you examined the different Microsoft Commercial Internet System servers and decided which ones you need to use. You also learned how to get a registered Domain Name and Addresses. You have chosen which type of Internet Connection you will use and are ready to begin.

■ In Chapter 3, "Building the Foundation," you look at the Foundation. First you look at Microsoft Windows NT Server 4.0 and second at the Internet Information Server. These are the two pieces the entire Commercial Internet Service will be built upon.

Building the Foundation

It's no secret that the Internet is exploding in popularity. Among the aftershocks of this explosion we're seeing an incredible growth in the number of computers required for dispensing information. In the past, these machines (servers) were primarily UNIX or UNIX-derivative systems. With the advent of low-cost PC servers—as opposed to pricey high-end systems—and the evolution of the Microsoft Windows NT Network Operating System, there is now a powerful alternative to existent server options. More than ever, Windows NT Server 4.0 creates a powerful framework for Internet applications. This chapter describes what Windows NT offers individuals and organizations as a content-delivering platform. ■

What NT Server 4.0 offers

Two of the most appealing aspects of NT Server 4.0 are its scalability and ease of administration. NT provides a robust and elegant server for both administrators and users.

What Internet Information Server is

Microsoft's Internet Information Server platform offers a powerful and attractive set of services for delivering content onto the Internet or intranets.

How to maintain your system

Server up and delivering information? Well, you can't stop there. Administering your server is an often-overlooked and crucial step in providing content from Windows NT.

When to use virtual domains

More than one server is not required to provide information for more than one site thanks to virtual servers.

Where to go next

Expanding a server's potential audience through upgrades.

Using Windows NT Server 4.0

Microsoft Windows NT provides an appealing platform for Internet services. This section explores why NT is growing in popularity and why it may be ideal for you.

The NT Server 4.0 Advantages

Microsoft Windows NT has grown from its humble LAN-based heritage to a capable WAN-based server platform. NT Server 3.51 saw the maturation of NT as an Internet-capable platform, which could then be expanded to service any variety of roles on the Internet. With NT Server 4.0, Microsoft has created a platform which, out-of-the-box, provides almost everything people will need in a network server.

Aware of several shortcomings in previous versions of Windows NT, Microsoft has released a product with many benefits. The new NT is easier to install, use, and manage than any previous version. By adopting the standard "Windows 95" Explorer interface, a pleasant and easier to use new face has been added to the operating system.

Integration   NT 4.0 provides a significant change in the underlying structure of the Windows NT architecture. By re-writing the root levels of the operating system, Microsoft was able to bring considerable enhancements in speed and stability to the OS. Continuing beyond a re-working of the NT internals, Microsoft united software titles which were add-ons in the past.

Previously, content-serving software for the Internet, such as Web servers, were delivered as third-party packages to build upon existing transport layers of NT. In NT 4.0 this changes with the combination of basic Internet services (WWW, FTP, Gopher, and DNS) into the operating system. By designing the architecture of NT 4.0 around these services, Microsoft was able to coax tremendous performance over traditional services of the previous model.

Integration within NT 4.0 is not limited to Internet services. Network interoperability also received considerable enhancements at the root of NT. By improving not only the NT Server content-provision, but also the lowest level transport layers of the operating system, NT now provides some of the fastest and most stable network services available in modern network operating systems.

Not content with merely upgrading the core of NT, Microsoft continued the improved integration of the administrative tools present in the operating system. Unlike most UNIX systems, NT offers a set of centralized tools for monitoring and managing the server. By providing a standardized interface and common tools, the previously daunting task of maintaining a network server is now simplified. Because there is only ever one program to use, an administrator's learning curve and workload lessen considerably. The NT administration tools enable an administrator to control almost any aspect of the server including, but not limited to:

- Performance Monitoring
- System Diagnostics
- Disk and Device Management
- Security and User Management

- Internet Services
- Task and Process Control
- DNS/WINS Name Services
- System and Application Events
- Security Events
- Connection Status

Scalability   Better performance in Windows NT 4.0 also sees improvements in the expandability of the OS to suit growth requirements. NT 4.0 delivers scalability through support for multi-processor systems and symmetric multi-processing (SMP) for over four processors. In addition to processor expansion, NT 4.0 provides improved throughput and scalability for applications that demand considerable overhead.

NT 4.0's framework has allowed for system clustering using several industry vendors and the forthcoming Microsoft WolfPack. By using multi-processing systems in a clustered environment, sizeable network installations can grow or shrink as needed. As the cost of systems decreases, expansion of an installation can be achieved in short order.

Fault Tolerance   As reliability is a key requirement in any installation, NT uniformly handles all hardware and software faults. By having fault tolerant technologies for reliability built into the core of NT, there is greater insurance that data has better protection. While maintaining the safety of the data and the system, NT also maintains the availability of system services and resources over the network. The elements that comprise NT's fault tolerance strategy are:

- *Protected Sub-Systems and Error Handling*   Windows NT Server employs protected subsystems in its design. In case of a fault (program error or crash), properly designed software reports an error to the system reporting service (Event Viewer) and gracefully exits. This ensures the operating system is not brought to its knees by an application exception. With this capability, new server-based applications can be run with less risk of crashing the server.

- *Recoverable File System*   The Windows NT File System (NTFS) excels at recovering from disk and system faults. By using unique transaction records for each I/O operation, NT stores both redo and undo information in the Log File Service. If a transaction is completed properly, the update is completed. In the event of a fault such as a disk failure, NTFS rolls back the transaction using the undo information. Additionally, NTFS supports "hot fixing" if a physical error is encountered due to a bad sector on the device. Hot fixing forces NT to relocate the data to a different sector on the device and marks the original as bad, never to be used again.

- *Automatic Restarts*   Through the use of protected sub-systems and error handling, system failures are extremely rare. In case a system-wide failure does occur, NT can be configured to automatically restart itself to reduce downtime. Like UNIX systems,

Part

I

Ch

3

administrators have the option of having NT transfer the complete memory contents to disk, similar to a "core dump." This provides a wealth of debugging information for skilled administrators and programmers in the event of a problem.

■ *Backup Support*   Integral to any fault-tolerant system are regular backups. NT's backup has tape support built into it. NT backup allows you to create multiple-set backups with standard, incremental, and even differential archival methods. The basic NT Server backup service is extensible through third-party products to provide additional functionality.

■ *Uninterruptible Power Supply Support*   Using UPS guarantees less downtime for any server during a power failure. The NT UPS service is able to detect a loss of power and warn all connected users. After notifying currently connected users, predefined commands may be executed before a graceful shutdown of the system. This ensures all data is safely stored and applications end normally.

RAID Support   Another key element of the scalability of NT Server 4.0 is its robust support for high capacity, expandable storage devices using RAID (Redundant Array of Inexpensive Disks). RAID enables you to create a large information store which spans multiple physical drives. When you use RAID, you are employing a series of relatively inexpensive hard disk drives using in-groups to store your data. In a RAID system, not all data is necessarily stored consecutively on the first hard drive. Instead, RAID may scatter your data across several devices to increase efficiency and access time.

One of the main appeals of NT's support for RAID, aside from its storage expandability, is the nature of fault-tolerant disk systems. RAID systems are categorized into six levels, RAID 0 through 5. By using a different algorithm to implement its fault tolerance, each level provides differing performance and reliability. Briefly, the six RAID levels are:

■ *Level 0*   RAID 0 is also known as "Disk Striping." By using a file system known as a *stripe set*, data is split across all disks in the array in blocks. This is primarily used for speed reasons so that access can be done independently of each device.

■ *Level 1*   Mirroring, or "Disk Mirroring." Identical copies of selected disks are created. When the primary disk is modified, the change is duplicated on the mirror. As there are duplicate copies of the data, read access is improved but write access is typically slower.

■ *Level 2*   Disk striping with error correcting is the basic idea. Error correction in RAID 2 uses multiple drives. Due to the marginal improvements and increased costs, this level is rarely used.

■ *Level 3*   Unlike RAID Level 2, this disk-striping alternative only requires one disk for error correction using parity data.

■ *Level 4*   Using larger segments than Levels 2 and 3, RAID 4 uses disk-striping and keeps user data away from error-correcting data. As it is not efficient in comparison to other levels, it is rarely used.

■ *Level 5*   RAID 5 is one of the newest and most popular RAID designs. Also known as "striping with parity," it stripes data in large blocks across all disks in the array. As in Level 4, data and parity information are always arranged in the array so they are on separate disks.

RAID technology provides considerable flexibility for systems to grow. By spanning multiple devices while yielding performance improvements, you have few effective limits on your system. One thing to keep in mind is that system-based RAID performs slower than hardware-based RAID systems. As the server must use CPU cycles to handle the RAID array, expect slow-downs on software-based RAID setups.

Installing and Configuring Windows NT Server 4.0

Before beginning installation of Windows NT Server 4.0, several pieces of important information are required. Although Microsoft documentation details the process to follow when installing and configuring Windows NT Server, you should still have this information for convenience's sake.

When planning to set up an NT Server to provide content to the Internet or an intranet, you should be dealing with a set of static network addresses. It is crucial that you provide proper addressing information for the server, otherwise NT won't even know where to "look" for a network. Before starting, set aside a pad of paper to record your information. It is best to have these numbers lying around for future reference.

Your Internet Service Provider will give you most of the information you need. If you work with an intranet only, you can use your own network numbering scheme. Contact the Network Administrator—if that isn't you—for information on your corporate network configuration. When obtaining network addresses, be sure to get the following before beginning NT Server installation:

■ Your IP Address, or if you are supporting virtual servers, IP Addresses

■ Your Gateway or Router address

■ Your Network Subnet Mask

■ Your Domain Name Servers (DNS)

You also will want to confirm your server's domain name. If you are setting up your server as a part of your Internet Service Provider or corporation's domain, ensure that the proper DNS changes have been made and propagated. If you are using your own domain, ensure that it has been registered with the appropriate agency and the proper DNS set-up has been done.

If you are working within a corporate network, you may also require network addresses for:

■ DHCP Server(s) for dynamic IP

CAUTION

Use DHCP with extreme caution on a server; never use it for your primary IP addresses. Only use static DNS-mapped IP addresses for your primary addresses; otherwise, visitors will not be able to see your site.

Part

I

Ch

3

- WINS Server(s) for Windows Naming Service over TCP/IP networks
- WINS Address Scope
- Whether or not you are setting up your server as a Primary or Backup Domain Controller
- Whether you are using a standalone server, such as a PDC or BDC.

By carefully recording the network information and keeping it on hand, you can ensure that you have the right information. It is the quirky nature of networking that last-minute changes are often required, and it is much easier to work from a list of settings than memory. If this server is the first server in your network, you will likely need to configure your new server as the Primary Domain Controller to contain all of the security and user information for the network. If you have an existing NT Primary Domain Controller in place, you may wish to add this server as a Backup Domain Controller rather than creating a new NT domain.

Now that you have all of your network addresses, you can proceed with NT Server installation according to the documentation included with the software. Once complete, you move on to setting up the server software.

Using Internet Information Server

It was Microsoft's goal to introduce a powerful Internet content server that fit the overall Windows NT structure, saving you from relying on a third-party product that may not perform. The Internet Information Server (IIS) has been accepted as one of the standards of the field since its initial introduction.

IIS offers a number of significant advantages over other content servers on the market. Most importantly, IIS provides blinding speed and reliability while providing incredibly simple maintenance tools. It is safe to say that anyone can learn how to extend and administer his or her own IIS server.

N O T E Windows NT Server 4.0 includes IIS 2.0. Later in the book, we will be exploring the newest version of IIS, version 3.0. You must be running Windows NT 4.0 and IIS 2.0 to install the newer version. ■

ON THE WEB

http://www.microsoft.com/iis You can obtain IIS 3.0 and its components from the Microsoft Web site.

Built-In Services

Internet Information Server is actually a set of three content services built into one server application. IIS's unique integration with the NT Server architecture provides these three services an efficient and robust utility. These services are covered in more detail in the following sections.

WWW　IIS's World Wide Web service offers not only a complete open-standards based HTTP server, but also an extensible architecture for the next generation of Web sites. One of the most notable advancements with IIS is the Internet Service API, or ISAPI.

With previous Web servers, server-side or back engine-driven interactivity was achieved by using the Common Gateway Interface (CGI) standard. CGI allowed programmers and Webmasters to take information from the client through the Web browser. This information, usually in the form of a URL or data submitted through a form, could then be processed and a response returned. The response could be a new page, a direction to a different site, or a series of instructions executed to store the information retrieved.

CGI is intentionally simple by nature. This allows the CGI "programs" to be created in almost any compiled language, such as C++, or scripted language, such as Perl. At its heart, CGI is just a standard on how information comes into the program and how it is sent out to the Web server. No more, no less. And although this provides a great deal of simplicity in design, it does create a number of significant issues.

First, CGI takes overhead. Each time a bit of information, such as a URL is passed to the Web server to then again be passed off to a CGI program, the system must start the CGI program so that it may process the information and return its result. Once the result is returned, the CGI program closes and waits to be called again. This happens every time a bit of information or a request for information from a CGI program is needed. This translates into a great deal of server overhead in starting and stopping the CGI program each time.

Second, CGI is platform independent. Although compiled binaries are platform specific, the general idea is that CGI programs from a UNIX server will work on an NT server without much work. This is especially true for CGI scripted programs. Though this may sound appealing, and in many cases it is, it does mean that CGI may not take full advantage of the platform it is running on. Think of CGI as "the lowest common denominator."

To address some of the shortcomings of CGI, several newer standards have appeared. The WinCGI standard for many Windows-based WWW servers, such as O'Reilly's Website and Website Pro, allow interactivity that is tied much closer to the Windows architecture. Another newer standard is Netscape's Netscape Server API (NSAPI) standard. NSAPI is a standardized set of programming instructions for developers to create more optimized server side Web applications. The power of NSAPI is that it is available on any platform the Netscape Web server is available on.

In cooperation with Process Software, the developers of a Web server called Purveyor, Microsoft developed its own standardized API for IIS, called ISAPI. ISAPI allows optimized server applications for Windows system developers. The key advantage to ISAPI over CGI is that unlike CGI, which opens the program as it needs and then closes it, ISAPI programs are "in process" applications. By enabling server applications to run inside the memory space and sub-system of IIS, tremendous speed gains are achieved over conventional methods.

Part

I

Ch

3

IIS not only gives extensibility, but also comprehensive security. This occurs in all IIS services and allows administrators to guarantee data is only accessible by people who should be seeing it. Web security is handled through the standard Windows NT security settings on directories and files. By allowing certain users and groups access to selected files, you can effectively limit what a visitor can view.

In addition to directory and file security, IIS supports data security through encryption. Used for transferring confidential information such as credit card numbers, the Secure Sockets Layer (SSL) standard provides the required level of security to let people transfer information without concern. SSL is implemented by using unique digital keys that isolate where the data is from, and its destination. If a person intercepts the data, they have almost no chance of understanding it, as its encryption is a unique digital key and a number of random variables.

Aside from the ability to deliver information from a single Web site, IIS WWW supports "virtual servers." This allows you to provide the content for more than one Web server from one machine in a transparent fashion. For example, if your main Web server was accessible from the address http://www.BigCo.com—but you wanted to have a second Web server which delivered separate content, you could create a virtual server using a different address (say, http://www.OtherCo.com) that physically resides on the same server as the main Web site. This saves you the cost of maintaining multiple servers and connections. However, to create virtual servers you require multiple IP Addresses. You will have to contact your Internet Service Provider or corporate administrator to arrange for more IP Addresses.

The IIS implementation of WWW is a powerful and attractive package for content providers due to the speed and reliability of the service. In addition, its extensibility and security is an added bonus.

FTP   The *File Transfer Protocol* has existed on the Internet for a considerable time. Before the advent of the Web, it was the most widely used method for transferring volumes of data and programs across the Internet. FTP works like all Internet services, by using the raw transport layers of the Internet protocol TCP/IP. By establishing a session through a standard TCP connection, the FTP client "hooks up" to an FTP server. This TCP connection maintains a constant link between client and server to transfer data about the session. Once the client requests a file from the FTP server, a second connection, this time using a "stateless" UDP connection, is opened and transfers the requested file in a stream to the client.

FTP is still in widespread use as a method for transferring software, data files, and resources over the Internet. Although it is not required as much as it was before the Web appeared, FTP provides a quick and convenient method for clients to request information from a content provider and receive it at their own convenience.

The IIS implementation of FTP enjoys the same flexible security that the WWW service has. By setting directory and file-based permissions, certain clients can have access to material that other clients may not. IIS's FTP supports both guest or "anonymous" FTP users and named accounts. This is ideal for setting up personal transfer points so that "graced" users may access files that the general public may not.

IIS FTP also supports virtual directories. This allows you to create a centralized FTP server to deliver content spanning many computers. You can allow a user to request information that may be stored on a different machine than the server. The information would be transferred over a network through the FTP server, transparent to the client.

Gopher   Long before the World Wide Web appeared, Gopher was a simple interface for navigating the Internet. Using a menuing structure, Gopher linked several sites across the Internet in an easily digestible form. Far simpler than the Web in nature, Gopher allowed content providers to categorize data types and arrange menu structures.

Although Gopher has almost disappeared from general use, it is a predominant legacy system. Many secondary education centers and "freenets" still use Gopher to allow their users to interact on the Internet. Gopher will most likely fade as the Web continues to grow, but in the meantime many content providers must still support Gopher as a method for access.

The IIS implementation of the Gopher service provides the full capabilities of UNIX-based Gopher services, in addition to comprehensive security options. This is achieved through setting NT access permissions on directories and files.

The Benefits of a Single Interface

Internet Information Server provides you with one interface to control all services.

True to NT Server's policy of smooth integration and convenient administration, IIS provides a single utility for administration. The Internet Service Manager provides a seamless central tool for you to maintain and configure your content server. Not only are the built-in services such as WWW, FTP, and Gopher managed through this interface, but so are add-on products like the Microsoft Commercial Internet platform.

Ease of Use   One of the main reasons most people move to Windows NT from other operating systems is for the ease of use. IIS recognizes this, as shown in Figure 3.1.

FIG. 3.1

Internet Service Manager provides you with convenient menu access for management.

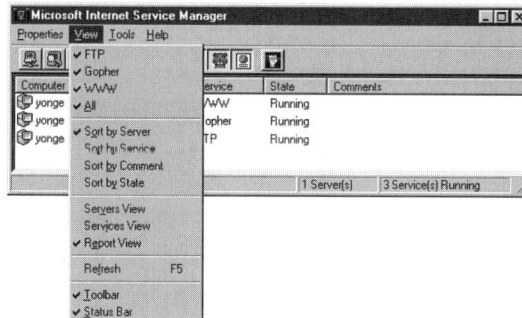

In the past, if you were so lucky to have administration programs for content services such as WWW, it was extremely unlikely that the same utility would be used to administer another service. With IIS, you now have one tool where you can conveniently control your content provision and configure it to your preference. The Internet Service Manager allows you to start and stop your services, not to mention pause them, configure the properties for your services, and even control the services on an entirely separate server.

Centralized Control   Unlike other similar products, IIS provides you with one place to go for controlling your services. This is shown in Figure 3.2.

FIG. 3.2

Whenever you need to stop or restart your services, Internet Service Manager locates it all in one spot.

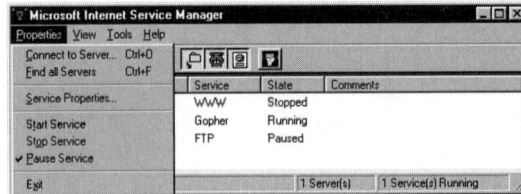

By providing one standard control program, Microsoft has ensured that you will be able to control your server without confusion. In addition, it has provided a framework for future content delivering services to grow into the existing architecture. Rather than relying on separate applications or control panels to configure services, you now can manage all of them from one interface.

The Internet Service Manager provides a convenient at-a-glance view of a service's status. By selecting a service, on either your server or a separate network server, you can restart it, stop it, and make it unavailable. If you want to temporarily make your site unavailable, you can pause the service, which prevents visitors from accessing it while you make changes.

Configuration is also a simple process. By selecting Properties, you set up the service as required. More comprehensive information on configuring services is provided below and within the documentation included with Windows NT Server 4.0.

Integration with Windows NT 4.0

As you learned earlier, Windows NT 4.0 integrates network services and administration tools into the operating system. IIS is no exception to this trend. Unlike some third-party content servers, IIS does not run as an application in your operating system. Instead, the IIS services operate as system-level services integral to the operating system. System-level services perform below the user interface, in the background of the system.

By not requiring a user interface, the IIS services operate considerably faster. All interaction with the user is carried out through the Internet Service Manager, and events are reported to the Event Viewer application, like all NT services. As with other NT services, you can control the IIS services' start-up behavior from the Services Control Panel. This allows you to decide whether or not you want the services to begin when you restart your server.

By using the integration of NT, IIS provides convenient and manageable administration and event tracking while also retaining considerable speed. Count on saving a lot of time by taking advantage of this architecture.

Installing and Configuring IIS

IIS is added to an NT server much like any NT network service. Once you have configured the network, you can add the service. By following the instructions from Microsoft, you will be provided with the required software and documentation for IIS on disk.

Once IIS is installed on your server, the Program Menu from "Microsoft Internet Server (Common)" from the Start Menu provides a link to documentation on IIS. Complete configuration and maintenance information is detailed therein, as shown in Figure 3.3.

FIG. 3.3
All documentation on the Internet Information Server is provided online, accessible through your Web browser.

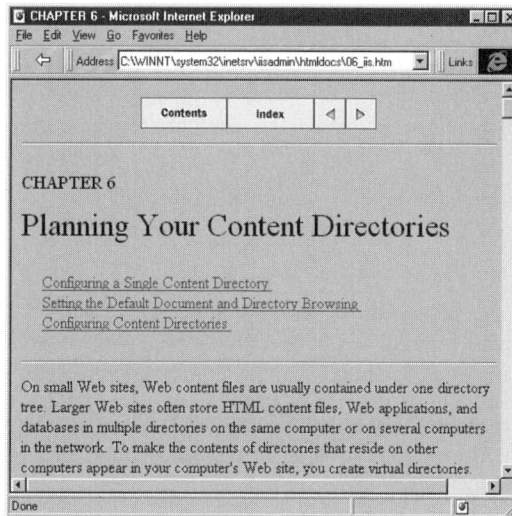

Performing System Maintenance

Although your server is set up and operational, your job is not done yet. The ongoing administration and support for a server can be a rigorous task. By using the Windows NT administration tools, you have simple utilities for server management.

Aside from the Internet Service Manager, the core tools you use are the following:

■ *Event Viewer* The Windows NT Event Viewer allows you to examine detailed logs of what happens in the server. These logs are split into three categories: System, Security, and Application. Sorting events by these categories reduces those dauntingly long logfiles.

Part
I

Ch
3

- *Performance Monitor*   Curious as to how the server is holding up? The Performance Monitor provides a graphical chart of almost every aspect of the server and the services running on it. You can also create stored charts which can be modified as you see fit.

- *User Manager*   If you want secured areas on the server, you will need the User Manager to create and modify user accounts and groups. By grouping users into logical arrangements, you can assign security permissions and accessibility in a large bundle as opposed to one user at a time.

- *Explorer*   File and directory maintenance, including security permissions, uses the GUI file management utility named Explorer. If you are familiar with the File Manager from Windows 3.1 and NT 3.51, the Explorer is not much different. A direct duplication of the Windows 95 Explorer, the interface allows improved control over the system.

In addition to these basic utilities, there are several other tools which will prove useful to you, depending on your installation; they are:

- *Microsoft DNS*   If you are maintaining your own DNS service, you may choose to use Microsoft's implementation of the standard naming service. MS DNS benefits from a simplified GUI interface, as opposed to configuration files and command line utilities.

- *WINS Administrator*   If you are using a Windows NT Wide Area Network over a TCP/IP network, you need the WINS naming service.

- *DHCP Administrator*   If you require dynamic IP allocation on your network, the DHCP service is an industry standard method for handling IP address management for clients.

- *Server Manager*   When dealing with multiple servers, the NT Server Manager allows you to control and monitor all of the computers on your network. The Server Manager lets you control directory shares, connected users, services, and event alerts.

If you need help with any of these utilities, they each have online documentation accessible from the Help menu. More information on system maintenance and administration is provided in the appendixes of this book.

Setting Up Virtual Domains

The appeal of hosting several independent Web sites on one server is a strong one. Rather than have the cost and overhead of maintaining multiple servers, virtual servers let you provide differing content on the same machine without users ever noticing. Virtual servers work by using differing IP Addresses, which in turn can have unique fully-qualified domain names, to identify to the server which site a visitor wishes to view. If the server does not support more than one IP address, you can only have a single main Web site.

Adding the IP Address to Your NT Server

The process of adding new IP addresses to your NT Server is simple. Just follow these steps:

1. Open the Network Control Panel and select the Protocols tab from along the top, as shown in Figure 3.4.

FIG. 3.4

The Protocols Tab from the Network Control Panel lists the network protocols installed on your machine. From here you can add or remove protocols, or edit their properties.

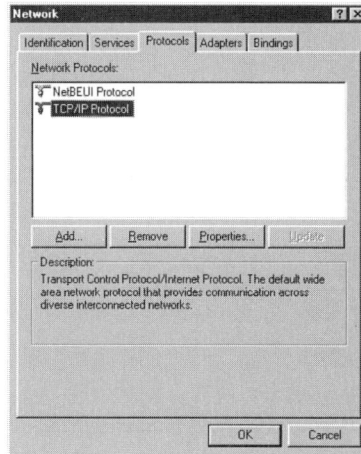

2. From the protocol list, select TCP/IP Protocol and click the Properties button.

The Microsoft TCP/IP Properties sheet appears, as shown in Figure 3.5.

FIG. 3.5

From the TCP/IP Protocol Properties sheet, you can configure your TCP/IP network settings. TCP/IP is the underlying protocol for the Internet, which makes it one of the most important aspects for your Internet-based server.

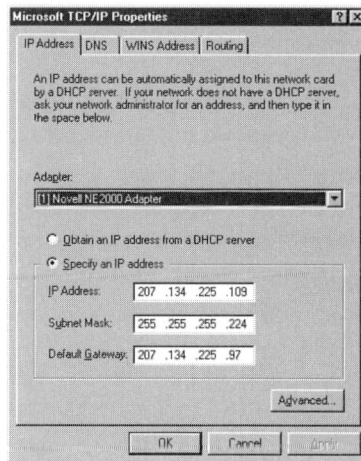

3. At the bottom of the TCP/IP properties dialog box, click the Advanced Button.

4. The top box of the Advanced IP Addressing window lists the IP addresses bound to the current network adapter. You may select a different network adapter if you have more

Part

I

Ch

3

than one installed in your server to view a different list of IP addresses, as shown in Figure 3.6.

To add a new address, click the Add button.

FIG. 3.6

The Advanced IP Addressing Dialog Box is the place to be if you want to add or remove more than one IP address for your server. This dialog box is a drastic improvement over the one in previous versions of Windows NT.

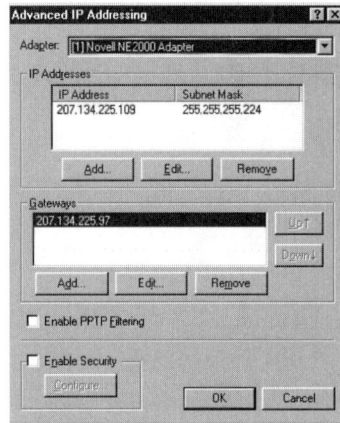

5. Enter the new IP Address in the pop-up dialog box, and then the subnet mask, as shown in Figure 3.7. Click OK.

FIG. 3.7

After clicking the Add Button, you enter the new IP Address and Subnet Mask.

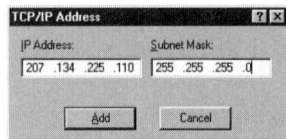

6. This completes the process, as shown in Figure 3.8. Continue the process for any additional IP Addresses you want to add. When finished, click OK. You may be required to restart your system for these changes to take effect.

FIG. 3.8

After you've added the new IP Address, it appears in the IP Addresses list for your server.

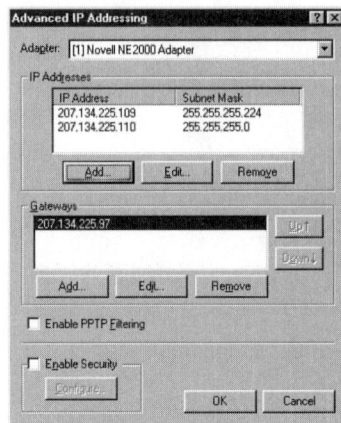

Configuring the New Site for IIS

When NT server knows the IP Address is available for a virtual server, it is a simple matter to set up a new virtual Web server. Follow these steps to do so:

1. Open the Internet Service Manager and double-click the WWW service. The WWW Properties sheet appears, as shown in Figure 3.9.

FIG. 3.9

After double-clicking the WWW Service, you see the WWW Service Tab.

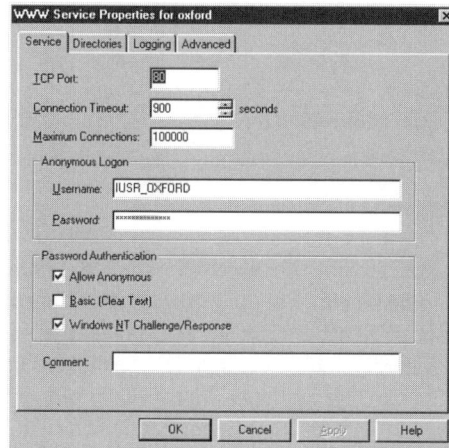

2. Click the Directories tab along the top, as shown in Figure 3.10.

FIG. 3.10

The Directories Tab lists the virtual directories and virtual servers you currently have configured.

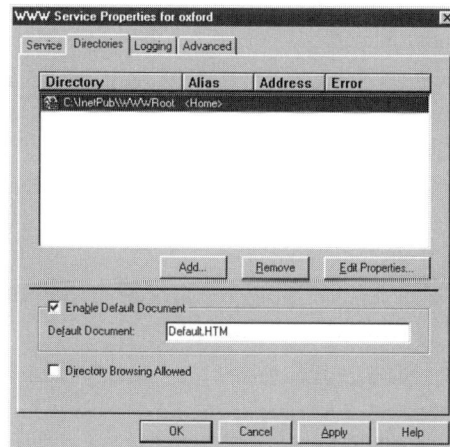

3. Click the Add button. The Directory Properties window opens (see Figure 3.11), in which you set up your new virtual Web server.

FIG. 3.11

The Directory Properties dialog box enables you to set up virtual directories and virtual servers for your server.

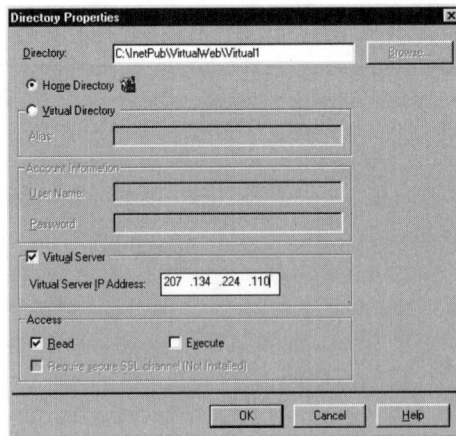

4. In the first text entry box, provide the directory path to the home directory for this virtual server. This should be either in the form of a local directory path (C:\Path\Directory), or a UNC (Uniform Naming Convention) network directory path for a shared resource (\\Server\Share\Directory). UNC paths are used by Windows Networking to point to shared resources on network servers or workstations. Similar to a directory path, they point to a machine instead of a physical drive.

5. Click the Home Directory radio button to set this to be the home directory for this virtual server. If you were adding a virtual directory for this virtual server, you would click the Virtual Directory radio button and provide the virtual directory name.

6. If you provided a UNC directory path for this directory, you must enter a username and password under Account Information, which is used to connect to the network resource.

7. Click the Virtual Server check box to tell IIS that this directory is used by a virtual server IP address.

8. Enter the new virtual server's IP address into the text box.

9. Under Access, click the Read check box to allow people to read this directory. If you need this directory's contents to be executable for scripts or ISAPI programs for example, click the Execute check box.

10. Click the OK button. Your new virtual server directory is now listed in the directory list, as shown in Figure 3.12.

Once your virtual server is configured, make sure that you or your network administrator have carried out the required changes to your DNS entries. Visitors will then be able to access your new virtual server by the proper fully qualified domain name.

FIG. 3.12

Your new virtual server appears in the Directories list. You can differentiate what directory belongs to what server by referring to the IP Address listed under the Address column.

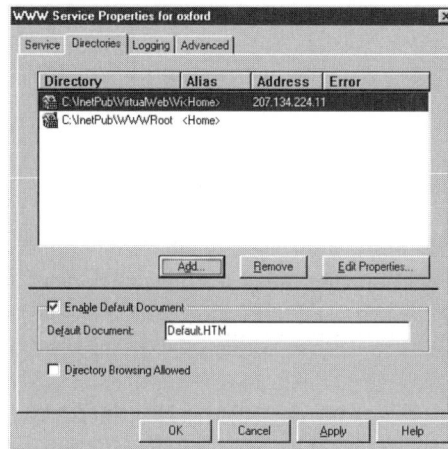

Scaling the Foundation

As previously discovered, NT Server 4.0 provides a lot of growth options. As your server grows you will need to address a list of priorities dependant on your situation. The key considerations are:

- *Storage*   Everyone knows that you can never have too much disk space. This holds especially true when you are delivering content on to the Internet or an intranet. As you need to grow your storage, you can begin by adding hard disk space to your server. This process and the limitations depend on your hardware platform. Beyond simply adding hard disk space or removing files, you can look to larger storage solutions such as RAID arrays.

- *Memory*   The only commodity more valuable than disk space is RAM. As your server's load increases, expanding your system's memory will add relief in many ways. By increasing RAM, your server will be able to not only deliver content to more people, but also be able to deliver more faster.

- *Processing power*   If you've looked to more memory and that simply hasn't helped the growing pains, you may want to look to a faster processor, or even multi-processor options. NT's support for multiple processors and symmetric multi-processing makes it a great platform for delivering content in high volume sites.

- *Distributing the load*   Growing your one server may be a losing battle when you may be better off moving some services to separate servers. Windows NT's network operating system (NOS) heritage enables you to distribute your services to other NT Servers running within the same NT "Domain" (no relation to Internet domains). By selecting one server in your pool to become the Primary Domain Controller (PDC) and each subsequent server a Backup Domain Controller (BDC), your servers can take advantage of shared user accounts and permissions. If you are running several systems with different user bases, you may want to look at setting up multiple PDCs.

■ *Clustering*   So, you've tried more storage, more memory, more processors, and more servers. It still didn't do the trick? Maybe it's time to look at clustering. *Clustering* is the powerful ability to group similar—or even dissimilar—servers to share the load. Clustering allows an entirely new level of fault-tolerance for servers, as well as performance increases. Clustering is available through third-party products, such as Digital Clustering from Digital Equipment, and from the forthcoming Microsoft WolfPack Clustering API.

Adding New Servers

How do you know when to add a new server? How do you do it? Thankfully, Windows NT includes facilities for monitoring your network to know just when you should start shopping for that extra machine. The Windows NT Performance Monitor is one of the most indispensable tools for managing your NT network. The Performance Monitor (covered in detail in Chapter 19, "Interpreting Logfiles and Monitoring Server Performance") allows you to examine nearly every aspect of your server's behavior. Key areas to watch for are processor and memory usage. If you find that on an ongoing basis your server is suffering from loads that upgrading simply won't handle, it's time to add a new server.

When you begin the installation of your new server, the install process asks you to set up your network. By specifying the new server as part of an existing NT domain, you have the option of specifying the new server as a Back Up Domain Controller (BDC). In doing so, the new server shares the same security and access settings as the existing server. You are asked to specify the existing domain, which should be that of your existing server.

Because your new server is part of the existing domain, the chores of maintaining information about the domain are split between the Primary Domain Controller (the PDC, likely your original server) and your new BDC. The new server has a unique name and address, but can easily share some of the loads by distributing access.

Regardless of which route you pursue for expansion, NT can expand with it. Scaling requires careful planning. Make sure to properly explore your options, and what will work best for your particular installation. Make sure you are finding a solution that works for your needs and that you are making the changes when you need to. Carefully monitor your server's performance and total load before even considering implementing a change. It is best to plan ahead when considering scaling and to remember not to overcomplicate things too quickly.

Keeping Your NT Server Current

Software has bugs. Everyone knows it. To address the issue of problems in Windows NT, Microsoft periodically releases "Service Packs." Service Packs are updates to existing Windows NT installations to fix problems in releases. You should generally ensure that you are running the most recent Service Pack, as many software releases require these updates.

Service Packs contain all the changes present in previous Service Packs. This simplifies things so that you do not need to always retrieve and hold on to older Service Packs before updating with the newest one. This means, for example, Windows NT 4.0 Service Pack 2 contains all of the updates that were present in Windows NT 4.0 Service Pack 1. Always make sure you are obtaining the Service Pack appropriate for your release and hardware platform.

ON THE WEB

http://www.microsoft.com/ntserver   To obtain the latest Service Pack, visit the Microsoft Web site.

From Here...

Windows NT has been long regarded as a platform that was best suited for LAN and niche-markets. With recent developments, Microsoft has taken an aggressive stance to create a powerful network operating system which is capable of handling many diverse roles. The Internet popularity explosion in the last few years has fueled an entirely new passion for interoperability and performance. NT has not been unaffected by this. Windows NT is now, finally, proving itself as a robust and cutting-edge solution for network services.

By choosing NT and IIS as your platform of choice, you can feel safe in knowing you are among millions of others, but also that you can enjoy the experience of some of the most advanced content delivering software in the industry. The development time has drastically been reduced for sizeable enhancements to the operating system. You won't likely see a change in the pace that has begun, which ultimately provides you with a stable and fast-growing platform.

Now that you have learned more about the foundation of Windows NT Server 4.0, you will begin your exploration of the Microsoft Commercial Internet System.

Part
I

Ch
3

- Chapter 15, "Introduction to Internet Information Server 3.0," will let you explore the revolutionary Active Server Pages and how it radically changes how you work with Web sites.

- Chapter 19, "Interpreting Logfiles and Monitoring Server Performance," clearly explains the process of digesting the logs and monitoring your system performance.

Microsoft Commercial Internet System Conference Systems

CHAPTER 4

Delivering Discussion Forums with MCIS

How to benefit from the news server

Learn a variety of uses for the news server and acquire a basic understanding of the history of UseNet and the NNTP protocol.

How to set up the news server

Gain an understanding of how to install and set up the news server. Then get an overview on how to check to make sure that it is functioning properly.

How to administer the news server

Learn how to gather your server's news feed, handle the maintenance of the new hierarchy, and then deliver it to your customer base.

Imagine walking into a massive Superdome-like stadium, containing hundreds of thousands of people, many of them employed by your company. There are clusters of people scattered around the room discussing topics like computer software, workplace child-care centers, alternative marketing strategies, fantasy baseball, and employee training options. Every voice and idea can be heard, and anyone who wants to contribute an idea may do so. People pass from one group to the next freely. There are few rules, but that doesn't stop the effectiveness of the experience. Is this Nirvana? Absolutely not!

In reality this could never work. There simply would be too much chaos in the room. In fact, it would be hard to hear anybody.

So step outside of reality for a moment and face the facade of the digital world, a world that provides an opportunity for the above mentioned example with a sense of order. Call it controlled chaos. On second thought, call it UseNet News. That's what Internet users have been calling this discussion tool for the past 15 or so years.

Sure, it's text based, but users can submit messages on any topic of their choice, and read information from people all over the world. It's freeform and it's funky. And, it's a powerfully useful tool.

On UseNet, there's something for everyone, even folks who have interests that are slightly off the beaten path. Take my friend Bert. He likes to study and talk about foxes, the kind of foxes that you find in the wilderness. He's hooked on their habitat. He has more information about foxes than anyone I know. Where could a guy learn so much? Is there a fox school? Not at all...he's finding his information on the Internet in UseNet newsgroups.

UseNet is a big pool of ideas and discussion groups. Like my pal Merlin says, "If you think you have a weird quirk, or think you've just discovered something new, forget about it. There's already someone who has created a UseNet group on the topic and there are 50 people discussing the issue right now." That's what led to alt.animals.foxes. Here are over 100 messages covering topics from Japanese foxes to red foxes. This is the hot zone for fox aficionados. Indeed, there are thousands of discussion groups on the Internet.

UseNet is an incredible network of information. It's a fast way to transfer information and the conversations are freeform.

This chapter is designed to help you take this wealth of information, and put it to use in your organization with Microsoft's Commercial Internet News Server. Specifically, you'll learn how to install and maintain the Internet News Server. This is about information distribution kicked into high gear. ■

Reasons for Setting Up a News Server

The Microsoft Internet News Server is a conferencing tool that provides an easy way to launch an effective information resource. Let's face it, getting answers is tough business. There's always a busy signal when you try to call the company's answer man...and the answer man is tired of having to give the same answer to three dozen people. Since we all have the same questions, why not use a bulletin board strategy so the information can be posted once, and then it's available to the whole workforce. If a unique question comes up, it benefits the entire office. Business offices need this sort of resource.

UseNet probably has the largest collection of experts on every subject you can imagine, and they're all right at your fingertips. Simply go to the newsgroup and learn from your peers, both those within the business and those around the world. If you can't figure out how to use a Word macro, there's probably someone on the staff who can help.

N O T E In reality you won't always get an immediate response to the questions you post on newsgroups. Sometimes you'll have to be patient, or rephrase your question and report it to the newsgroup. ■

Company and Product Information

The word intranet remains one of the hottest buzz words in the corporate office. People in the front offices are asking for intranet strategies before they even know what can be wrapped into an intranet. Many limit the scope to a World Wide Web page, with a business card approach. There is so much more, but the conversations you hear in the front offices are all too familiar.

"We have to have an intranet," says the boss. "Yes sir, and I think we should have a news server for sharing ideas," says the subordinate technologist. "What in the heck has news got to do with anything? Let the employees buy their own newspapers," retorts the boss.

There are just too many opportunities, with internal NNTP groups, to let ignorance stop progress. Imagine how informed this boss would be if he were reading an internal newsgroup entitled **intranet.offerings.unlimited**. He would become a person who was not only familiar with Web pages, but he might also know a little about file transfer, e-mail, and UseNet.

In the office place, if this technology is presented properly, both management and employees will understand the concept. Not only can an office set up public discussion forums featuring discussions on everything from parking to holiday leave, it can also create private or moderated newsgroups.

This means an office could launch an NNTP strategy and implement some of the following:

- Closed discussion groups
- Open discussion groups
- External discussion groups for customers
- Internal/External private newsgroups for work teams
- Moderated discussion groups

With the Internet News Server, all these opportunities are available, through a simple administrative interface. With private groups the messages are not visible to users without the proper permissions, and access to those newsgroups and the information contained in them is prevented. The Microsoft Internet News Server supports the Internet standard Secure Sockets Layer (SSL) protocol, which creates a secure channel between client and server or between server and server and prevents people outside the group from intercepting information. Suffice it to say that if you transmit a message to a private newsgroup, it will remain secure.

Low-Cost Technical Support

Though UseNet is a hot technology, it has had its shortcomings. For instance, the typical news server is built on a UNIX system and requires an experienced employee who can handle the complexity of the operating system platform and the interface with the Network News Transport Protocol (NNTP). These administrators can be hard to find and hard to replace. However, you won't need to be a genius to manage the Microsoft Commercial Internet News Server. Unlike UNIX, this news server is configured primarily through a graphical user interface. We're talking Windows here—that familiar point and click interface you will recognize.

To manage the Internet News Server, the administrator of the system needs a basic understanding of:

- *Windows NT*   The operating system
- *Internet Information Server*   Provides the server platform for the Internet News Server and handles the connections of news clients.
- *Internet Service Manager*   The administration tool of the Internet Information Server, which is used to manage the Internet News Server.

Understanding NNTP

The Network News Transfer Protocol, or NNTP, is the standardized protocol for the transmission of news messages across the Internet. NNTP is driven by a collection of computers sharing what might be best described as a universal bulletin board.

The movement of messages through the NNTP protocol is an interesting process. When a user submits a message to a news group, the message is first sent to the news machine which was accessed by the user and remains on that machine. Using the NNTP protocol, the message is sent onward to many other machines on the Internet. With this method, the original message sent by the user will make its journey across the Internet to every news machine that subscribes to the group where the message was posted.

For users, it's not terribly important to understand how NNTP works. If you want to read news, you simply open a news reader and access the server that provides you with a feed to UseNet news. With the news reader, the user can also post a message. It shouldn't be too difficult to get this concept.

Of course, maintaining a news server requires a bit more effort. But it's worth it, and we owe the creation of the concept to a handful of adventurous Internet users.

History of NNTP

The birth of UseNet was a spin off of a UNIX feature that was created almost 20 years ago. The feature, which came to be known as UNIX-to-UNIX copy, or UUCP, allowed developers to have one UNIX computer connect with another over phone or data lines and exchange information. Communication was the key, and this was important stuff for anyone with a UNIX box.

The advancement from UUCP to NNTP was natural. Legend has it that two graduate students from Duke University, James Ellis and Tom Truscott, envisioned a way of taking the plain vanilla interface of UUCP, and expanding it into a categorized presentation of information to be distributed to people in the UNIX community. Actually, the first examples of NNTP were demonstrated on a much smaller scale. A huge leap came when the duo from Duke tag teamed with two folks at the University of North Carolina and connected the computers with their custom made conferencing software. At this point, Network News Transfer Protocol caught on and, like all things Internet, more people got involved and helped NNTP take shape.

The original version of the program was designed to send a few articles per newsgroup, per day. Still, this ability created quite a buzz.

NOTE Why call the network UseNet? The early releases of this conferencing program were intended for the USENIX Association, an organization made up of UNIX users. As a result, the network was named UseNet. ▪

UNIX users around the country were incorporating NNTP. Enhancements were natural and the big next step was taken on the west coast, at the University of California, Berkely. In 1982, Matt Glickman and Mark Horton released a new version of the technology which improved the feature set and also allowed for better organization through categories and topics.

Since UseNet was growing so quickly, the developers implemented better ways to accommodate the growing number of sites. NNTP had matured and the framework for UseNet as we know it today was in place.

UseNet continues to grow at a phenomenal rate, connecting hundreds of thousands of sites. There are over 20,000 available UseNet topics (or UseNet groups) that users can subscribe to. And the growth is massive because every day millions of UseNet users continue to add information to this network of networks.

Uses of NNTP

The Network News Transport Protocol (NNTP) provides newsgroup property control settings which allow local, remote, and moderator-approved article posting, processing, sending, and storage of news data. The process flows within the Internet News Server can be seen in the way NNTP servers exchange news feeds (see Figure 4.1). The master server gathers, or pulls, news feeds from the Internet, replicates this content to slave servers, collects new content from slaves, and transmits, or pushes, it to downstream Internet NNTP servers. Slave servers in turn host newsgroup discussion threads and replicate new news articles to the master. The NNTP service manages the exchange of files that carry the news between servers.

FIG. 4.1

The master server is linked to the slave servers, which in turn are linked to the news clients.

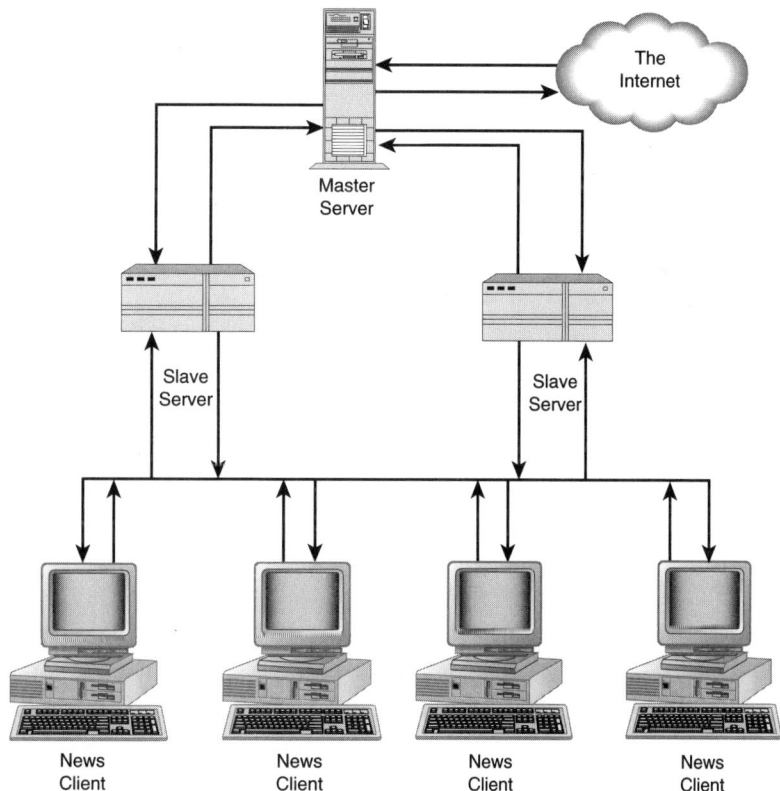

Part
II

Ch
4

■ *NNTP client*   Includes any client that supports NNTP for reading news. For example, this might be a high school student accessing his Internet Service Provider's news feed through Netscape News.

■ *Slave servers*   In this scheme, the Internet Service Provider is a slave server. It pulls a thread from the master server, and can replicate responses to the master.

■ *Master server*   In my neck of the woods, this is the local phone company's UseNet server, which services incoming and outgoing peer and slave news feeds.

To get an understanding of the basic master/slave process, review the following process:

1. The master server retrieves news feeds from the Internet.

2. Replication occurs between the master and slave servers.

3. Clients place news requests to the slave server.

4. Clients post responses to news to a slave server.

5. News feed is distributed by the master server to other Internet servers.

Of course, every news server isn't participating in a master/slave scheme. You could simply set up a master server to manage all of the above. The strategy may not be as robust, but it works.

Group Headings on UseNet

The library of data that can be found on UseNet is categorized by top directories and subdirectories. Each UseNet group begins with a header that describes the general category and then gets more specific. For instance, if you were looking for information on animals, you might start at **alt.animals**. From there, you may drill down to **alt.animals.foxes**. But you could also peruse **alt.animals.kangaroos**, or even deeper still to **alt.animals.kangaroos.boxing**.

Here is a sampling of some of the major headers you can find on UseNet:

■ alt: alternative groups, discussion on a variety of topics

■ bionet: biological groups

■ comp: discussion about computers

■ gnu: the Free Software Federation GNU project

■ misc: miscellaneous discussion

■ news: UseNet related news

■ rec: recreational matters

■ sci: scientific discussion

■ soc: social chat, psychology, sociology

■ talk: various discussions

UseNet groups are also broken down into geographical areas:

- na: North America
- fl: Florida
- ga: Georgia

For intranet, or site-specific newsfeeds, the UseNet groups are divided by organization:

- freenet: Freenet
- microsoft: Microsoft
- sprint: Sprint

In geographic and organizational examples, the concept of additional elements being added on to the prefix still carries. For instance, Microsoft's main discussions on the initial release of the Microsoft Commercial Internet Server are carried on at **microsoft.public.normandy.beta.newserver**. That has since changed to **microsoft.public.mcis.newserver**. You can access this group and groups dedicated to discussion on the other MCIS components at **msnews.microsoft.com**.

With the Internet News Server, articles are stored on a *newstree*. There is a virtual root, which is the top directory, with newsgroups stored as subdirectories under the virtual root. The name of the newsgroup will correspond to the subdirectory. Anytime newsgroups are nested within other groups they are referred to as trees. In the case of **alt.animals.foxes**, the subgroup of "foxes" falls within the group of "animals."

N O T E All articles stored in the Internet News Server's newstree will have a .nws extension. Files with an .xix extension are files holding the subject headers for article threads. There will be one .xix file for every 128 articles.

Part

II

Ch

4

Setting Up the Internet News Server to Serve News

Setting up a UseNet News Server has never been a picnic. Even with an unhealthy mix of patience, determination, obsession, and coffee, getting through your first configuration of a UNIX-based news server successfully is an extremely iffy project.

With Microsoft Internet News Server, providing a news feed to the user base is amazingly easy. Follow the basic steps, and you will be on your way to grabbing a feed and providing UseNet to your customers in no time. This is no joke. Administration and setup can be conducted in the typical Microsoft graphical user interface. In less than an hour, the news server should be installed, and your first news feed should be available for access.

The Features of the Internet News Server

Managing a news server has never been easier. This implementation of the Network News Transport Protocol is outstanding and most all of the functions are managed from the intuitive Microsoft Internet Service Manager. In a very short time you will benefit from the point and click approach to reaping the following benefits:

■ *Performance and scalability*   This is a tight-knit, integrated package, sharing services such as Chat and Mail quite well. From the client perspective, this is quite efficient.

■ *An open platform, with NNTP based client support*   The Internet News Server is a native NNTP server that supports open news reader clients and operates effectively with other NNTP servers.

■ *User authentication, using the standard NNTP security protocols and extensions*   The Internet News Server can be configured to provide the Windows NT Challenge/Response protocol that doesn't require sending passwords in clear text over the Internet, or the server can be configured in the standard NNTP protocol. The Internet News Server also supports Secure Socket Layer (SSL) encryption.

■ *Built-in support to control news server property settings*   Local, remote, and moderator-approved article posting.

■ *Analysis logs containing usage statistics*   Provide usage statistics and the ability for administrators to track messages and transactions, and analyze usage.

Requirements Regarding the Server, Connectivity, and the Client

To launch the Internet News Service, it's very important that you have enough resources to do it right. Depending on the number of feeds you intend to have your server pull, you need to allocate an appropriate amount of space. Thousands of megabytes are posted in UseNet feeds daily. If you only have a two gig hard drive, there won't be much room for storing your news feed. You may want to limit your feed to one group, like **alt.animals.foxes**, as opposed to a hundred sites that look interesting to you.

A minimalist setup for News would entail the following system requirements:

■ Windows NT, version 4.0

■ Internet Information Server 3.0

■ Microsoft Internet News Server

■ Pentium 100 MHz

■ 32M of RAM

■ 2G of storage space

■ A high speed TCP/IP connection with a domain name

If you want to pack more punch from the start, you should consider the following. Obviously, you can build your server in an even more robust environment. However, this isn't a bad start.

■ Windows NT, version 4.0

■ Internet Information Server 3.0

■ Microsoft Internet News Server

- Index Server
- Pentium 200 MHz (dual processors)
- 128M of RAM
- 25G of storage space
- A high speed TCP/IP connection with a domain name
- TCP/IP connectivity
- A properly configured Domain Name Service

▶ **See** "Establishing the Internet Connection," **p. 38**, for more information.

Getting There from Here—Installation

Before beginning the setup process, you must log on as an administrator to the computer where the Internet News Server Machine is to be installed. To avoid pesky error messages, be sure to exit all running Windows programs and shut down any Windows NT IIS server programs that are running.

1. Open the folder which contains the Internet News Server setup program, which is **SETUP.EXE**, to begin the setup process.
2. At the Internet News Service Installation Welcome Screen shown in Figure 4.2, click the Next button. Read and acknowledge the License Agreement and click the Yes or No button, depending on your preference.

FIG. 4.2
The Internet News
Server Welcome screen.

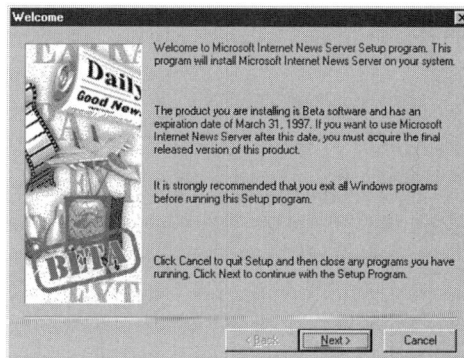

3. At the Registration screen (see Figure 4.3), enter your name and company name, or accept the default.

N O T E The information submitted at the Registration screen is simply for reference and will not affect the operation of the program. ▪

FIG. 4.3

Enter personal information at the Registration screen.

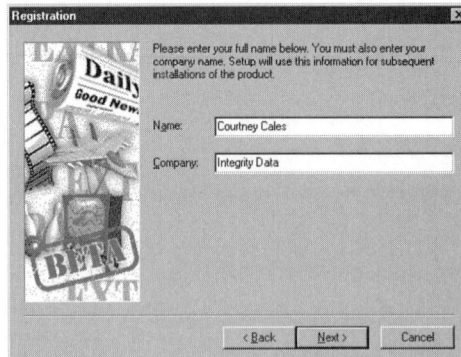

4. Prepare to select the components of the Internet News Server. Select both the Internet News Server NNTP Service and the Internet Service Manager extensions, as shown in Figure 4.4. Click the Next button.

FIG. 4.4

Select the components for the Internet News Server.

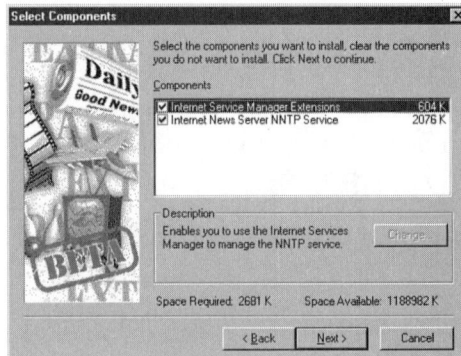

5. If the Internet News Server setup program says that there are Internet Information Server services running (see Figure 4.5), choose Yes to have the system shut down the IIS services.

FIG. 4.5

The Internet News Server can be instructed to shut down services that are running and thereby interfering with installation.

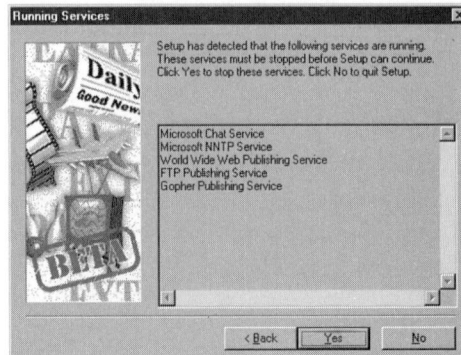

6. Setup will request users to select the NNTP Root Folder. Confirm the default of c:\InetPub\nntproot or submit another directory. Click the Next button.

N O T E After Setup is completed you can configure additional space by accessing the Internet Service Manager, entering the properties for the Internet News Server, and adding your selections under the Directories tab. ▪

7. Setup will ask users to select the NNTP Database Files Folder. Confirm the default of c:\InetPub\nntpfile or submit another directory. Click the Next button.

8. When selecting a desktop folder, choose Microsoft Internet Server (Common) from the existing list of folders (see Figure 4.6). Click the Next button.

FIG. 4.6

Place the News Server in the Microsoft Internet Server folder.

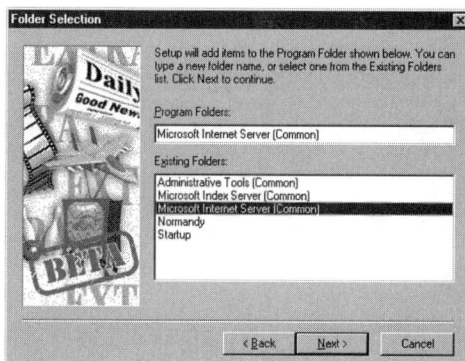

9. Review the setup information, as shown in Figure 4.7.

FIG. 4.7

Review selections and setup information carefully before proceeding.

10. Click the Next button. Installation kicks into gear.

N O T E Here's what's happening during installation. An NNTP Root folder is created if it doesn't exist, the Registry Keys are set, the performance monitor counters are loaded, as well as a Simple Mail Transport Protocol agent, and the application files. ▪

11. At the Setup Completion dialog box, choose I would like to start the NNTP service, and select Finish.

N O T E Remember, before doing the setup you stopped the other IIS services, so don't forget to restart those services after completing the setup. Services will need to be started again by Setup. To verify which services are running, launch the Internet Services Manager and review the list of services. Press F5 to refresh this screen. ▧

Now is the time to ensure that the Internet News Service was installed correctly and is up and running. Check the Internet Service Manager to see if the Services are running. You get to the Internet Services Manager by clicking the Start button, selecting Programs, choosing Microsoft Internet Server, and then Internet Service Manager (see Figure 4.8).

FIG. 4.8

Launching Internet Service Manager from the Start menu.

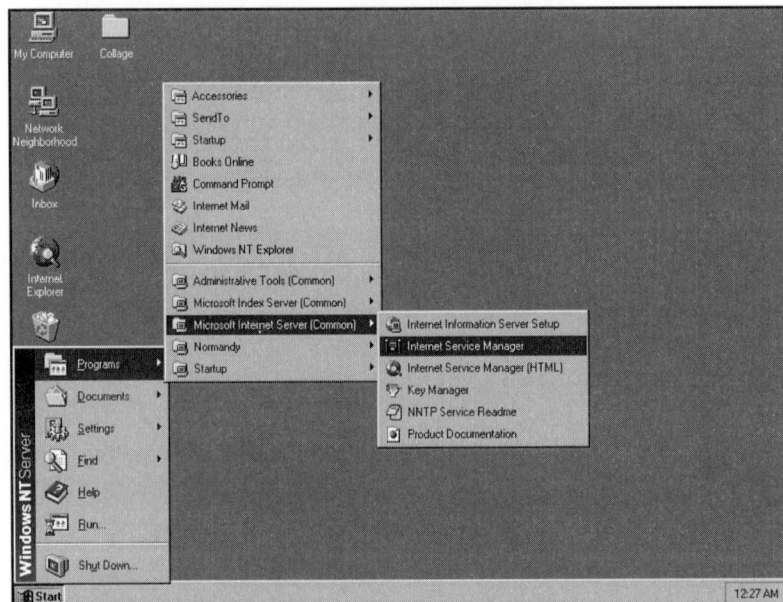

The dialog box for the Microsoft Internet Service Manager appears and displays the name of the computer, all the services that are presently running, and what state they are in (see Figure 4.9). After a restart, all services, including the Internet News Server, should be running.

FIG. 4.9

The Internet Service Manager dialog box provides information about the services that are currently active.

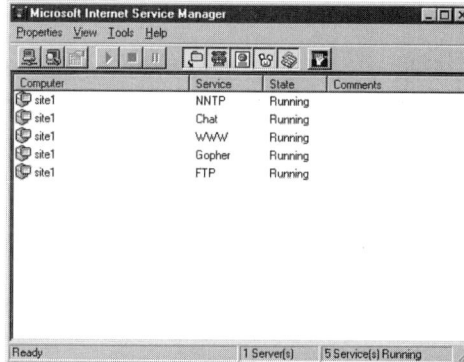

Configuring the INS to Pull a News Feed

After you have completed the Internet News Server installation procedure, it's time to get this Ferrari of a program out of park and see how effective it is on the proverbial highway. Since you should already be located at the dialog box for the Microsoft Internet Service Manager, you're ready to begin.

From the Internet Services Manager open the configuration options for the NNTP service.

The Feeds Tab

At the NNTP Service Properties page, there is a series of tabs across the top of the dialog box and service properties displays by default. For now, start by selecting the option tab for Feeds as shown in Figure 4.10.

FIG. 4.10

Select the Feeds tab and submit information on feeds.

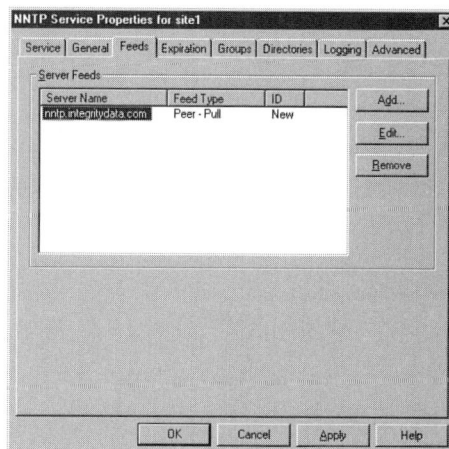

Part
II
Ch
4

The following list shows you how to configure your NNTP feeds:

1. This is the area to select the particulars on the Feed. Begin by choosing the Add button.

2. Enter the name of the server to pull the news feed from (see Figure 4.11). Remember, you must have access to the news server from which you intend to pull your feed. Microsoft has a public news feed at msnews.microsoft.com. If you do not have any other options, you may want to enter this into the Feed Server Name text box. It's worth noting that some major providers have multiple news machines. Users will need to make an entry for every news server (such as news1.integritydata.com, news2.integritydata.com, and so on). Currently, INS does not handle wildcard addresses, so there's no quick way around this.

FIG. 4.11

Provide details on Feed properties in the Feeds tab.

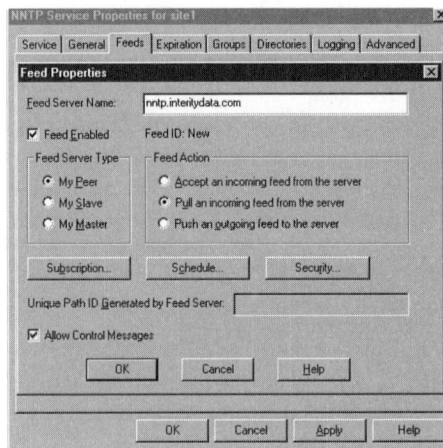

3. Under the option for Feed Server Type, Select the My Peer radio button, which designates the remote server type as a peer.

4. For Feed Action, choose the Pull an incoming feed from the server option, which pulls incoming newsgroup articles from the feed server by using the "newnews" NNTP command. This option is disabled if My Slave or My Master are selected for Feed Server Type.

5. Be sure that Allow Control Messages box is checked.

TIP Control Messages are not the typical News Articles that UseNet fans read. Instead, Control Messages allow for a degree of remote administration by notifying the program of things like newly established groups, or that a group has been deleted. Basically, this keeps the active news list up to date.

6. Now it's time to determine what groups to select, as seen in Figure 4.12. From the Feeds tab, select the Subscription button.

FIG. 4.12

Enter feed information, such as **comp.***, in the Subscription List box.

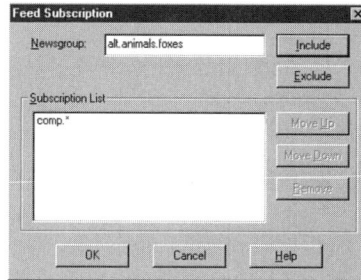

7. By default, the Subscription list is scheduled to pull every group off the server. It is recommended that you highlight the wildcard and select Remove so you won't download thousands of unwanted newsgroups. Now, add a specific group or category to limit your first pull in the text box for Newsgroup. Perhaps you may want to enter a wildcard for comp.*—which will pull all the feeds under the comp header, which is specific to computers. If you want a much smaller feed for your first test, you may want to choose something a little more specific, like **alt.animals.foxes**.

N O T E The term wildcard refers to the use of the character "*". When used to pull a newsgroup feed, such as comp.*, the wild card allows you to retrieve a list of every newsgroup under the comp header. █

T I P It's important to remember that you can only select newsgroups that exist on the server from which you are pulling your feed. If you want to see the present newsgroup list that is available, you can do so by clicking the Start button, choosing Run, and typing **telnet newsserver.name 119** to telnet to the news server. The newsserver.name command is the name of the news server where you will be pulling your feed, and the 119 signifies the port to which you are telnetting. Once you are connected to the server, type list active at the command prompt. A list of all the newgroups on the server will be displayed. Be prepared; this can be a long list. My news feed comes from a server with over 20,000 groups.

8. At this point you should have an item in your Subscription list; click the OK button. Select the OK button, which returns you to the Feed Properties options.

9. From the Feed Properties dialog box, select the Schedule button.

10. In the Feed Schedule dialog box, shown in Figure 4.13, you configure a schedule for incoming and outgoing feeds. Beginning with the Run option, for testing purposes, select the Every option button and set the time factor for the pull feed to 15 minutes. Here, we are specifying the frequency of connections.

11. If you choose, there is a checkbox option to Automatically Disable Feed of a site. Depending on the number that is entered, that is how many times the Internet News Server will attempt to connect before the feed is disabled. Since you are only connecting to one server right now, don't check the Automatically Disable Feed feature.

FIG. 4.13

In the Feed Schedule dialog box, specify the frequency of connections.

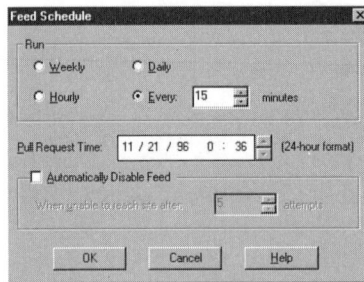

12. Select the OK button.

13. From the Feeds tab, select the Security button. This is where you specify the security to be used with the selected feed.

    By default, the option button for No Authentication Necessary is selected. This uses no security features.

    If you select the Basic (No Encryption) option, the servers exchange user names and passwords over the Internet via clear text (see Figure 4.14). This method provides no security.

FIG. 4.14

Choose from NNPT Server security options available in the Feed Security dialog box.

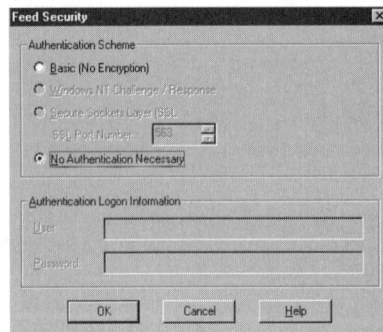

You also have the ability to use the Windows NT Challenge/Response option, which allows the servers to exchange authentication via Windows NT Challenge/Response.

You may also choose the Secure Sockets Layer (SSL) option; however, you must enter the SSL Port Number box.

You may also submit a User Name and Password in the Authentication Logon Information. However, this option will only function in the Clear Text or Windows NT Challenge/Response authentication scheme. For testing purposes, keep the default of No Authentication Necessary.

N O T E   Secure Sockets Layer (SSL) protocol creates a secure channel between client and server or between server and server. If you elect to use the SSL option with the Internet News Server, encryption is used to transmit private secure newsgroups. During server to server communications, a separate secure session is initiated if private newsgroup articles need to be replicated. ▪

14. Select the OK button.

The Service Tab

Next, you will choose the Service tab and enter TCP/IP connection information, which is connection-specific information (see Figure 4.15).

FIG. 4.15

Submit TCP/IP service options for the news server.

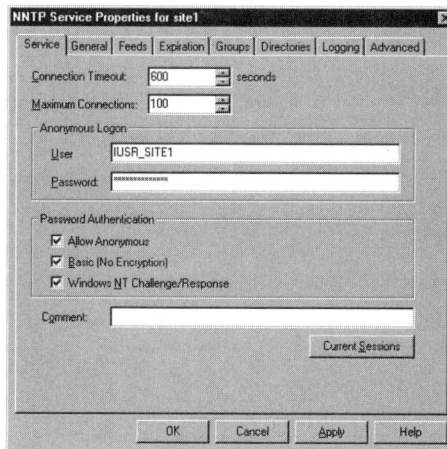

Part

II

Ch

4

1. Set a Connection Timeout, which determines the amount of time before an inactive connection is closed. The default is 600.

2. Enter a number for the Maximum Connections, which determines the amount of simultaneous connections. The default is 100.

3. The Anonymous Logon option provides a space to type a User name to use for anonymous connections. The default is IUSR_<machine name>. The Password field provides a space to type a password to use for anonymous connections. The default is the valid password for the default user's name.

N O T E   Don't be concerned with changing the default User name. The IUSR translates into the current user's name, and <machine name> is replaced with the name of the Internet News Server. ▪

4. The Password Authentication options allow for Anonymous, Basic (No Encryption), and Windows NT Challenge/Response, which uses Windows NT log on accounts to authenticate users.

5. Here, you can also add a Comment, which will be displayed on the initial Internet Service Manager (ISM) window for the NNTP service.

6. If you click the button for Current Sessions, the NNTP User Sessions dialog box is displayed. This is where you can view current connections and disconnect some or all of them.

The General Tab

On the General tab, shown in Figure 4.16, you provide more connection-specific information. Here you can create specifics for the Allow Client Posting area. Maximum Post Size relates to the maximum size (in kilobytes) of articles that clients can post. NNTP will not post articles larger than this size. Maximum Connection Size relates to the maximum size (in megabytes) of articles that users can post before NNTP disconnects them.

FIG. 4.16

Select connection-specific information in the General properties sheet.

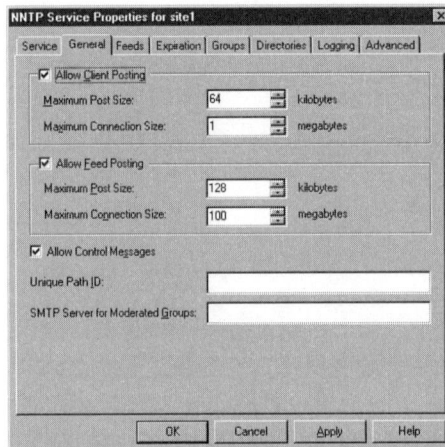

N O T E The Allow Client Posting concerns an individual client's machine posting to your news server. The Allow Feed Posting concerns the posting of the entire feed from another news server. ▓

1. Under Allow Feed Posting, the Maximum Post Size and Maximum Connection Size are controlled. Under Maximum Post Size, the number submitted dictates the maximum size (in kilobytes) of articles that feeds can post. With Maximum Connection Size, this entry controls the maximum size (in megabytes) of articles that feeds can post before NNTP disconnects them. You may want to start with 1,000K maximum to begin with; that way, there is enough room to move segments of binary files.

2. The Internet News Server also has the option to turn on or off the ability to Allow Control Messages. If the box is checked, Control Messages are automatically processed; if the box is unchecked, a Unique Path ID is needed. Also, if your news server offers a moderated group, you must specify the SMTP Server for Moderated Groups.

The Expiration Tab

Select the Expiration tab and view the property page, (see Figure 4.17), which displays the criteria for deleting newsgroups. The Expiration Policies dialog box displays the newsgroups that are set up for expiration and outlines the expiration information. The default size displayed is the maximum size that the newsgroup may attain before included articles are expired. The time option controls the maximum age that the newsgroup may attain before it is expired. If you need to edit Expiration Policies, click the Edit button. To add a new Expiration Policy, choose the Add button. You also have the option to Remove a policy.

FIG. 4.17

Establish the expiration policies for newsgroups.

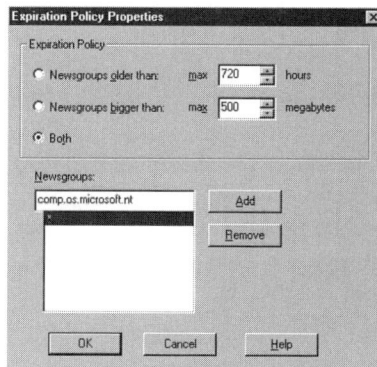

NOTE Careful on the expiration dates. If you choose a long stretch on the expiration, you'll need a lot of disk space to store the news articles. ■

The Groups Tab

Use the options available in the Groups tab shown in Figure 4.18 to add, edit, and delete newsgroups.

FIG. 4.18

Find newsgroups from the NNTP properties dialog box.

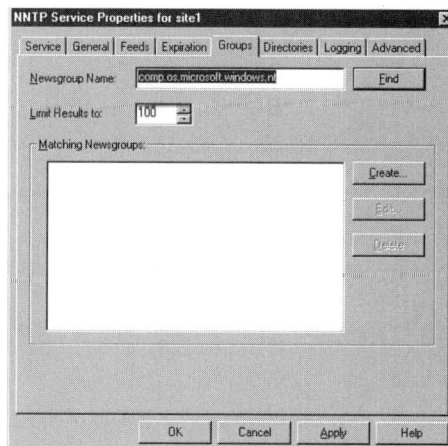

Part

II

Ch

4

1. Select the Groups tab. Under the Newsgroup Name option, there is a space provided to type the newsgroup name that you want to look up. When you finish typing the name, click the Find button. Newsgroups that match the criteria you specify are displayed in the Matching Newsgroups box.

2. Limiting results shows the maximum number of groups that will be displayed. With this feature, a wildcard for the comp.* group would only list the first 100 groups in the comp category.

3. In the Matching Newsgroups window, a list of the newsgroups that matched your search will be displayed.

4. You can Create, Edit, or Delete a group from the Matching Newsgroups box by clicking the appropriate button.

The Directories Tab

Under the Directories tab shown in Figure 4.19, you will find the property page which contains the directory configuration information. The default entry in the Directory list box is the home directory for news; in this case it is c:\InetPub\nntproot. If no other directories are listed, it is assumed that all newsgroups are contained under this directory. The user can change the properties associated with the home directory but cannot remove the home directory. For the NNTP service, the Alias is a list of newsgroup specifications similar to the newsgroup specification in the Feed Subscriptions dialog box.

FIG. 4.19

In the Directories properties sheet, submit and review directory configuration information.

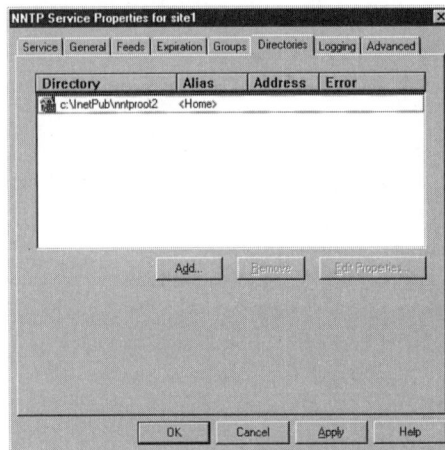

> **T I P** For optimum performance, if you are running anonymous access to your Web server, uncheck the Restricting Newsgroup Visibility option located in the Directories tab. If you fail to do this, the server will unnecessarily check every user's permission when they list newsgroups.

The Logging Tab

The logging feature with the Internet News Server provides valuable information about the accesses to the server. If you Enable Logging (see Figure 4.20), the server will build a plain text log file based on the criteria you select. For instance, you can choose to create a new log Daily, Weekly, Monthly, or create a new log file after the file reaches a certain size. There is also the capability to select the directory containing all log files.

FIG. 4.20

Enable logging and capture information on accesses to the server.

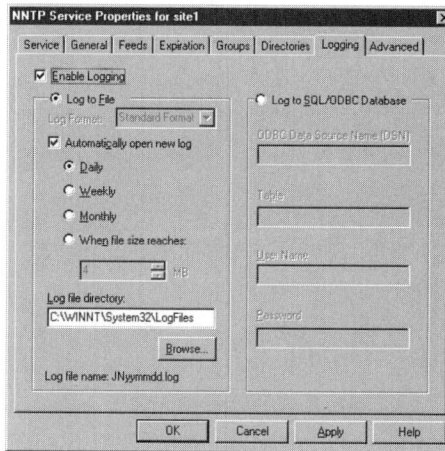

You also have the choice to send the log files to an Open Data Base Connectivity (ODBC)–supported database. This may come in handy when you have multiple servers or services on a network. With this feature you can log all of their activities to a single file or database on any network computer. If you log to an ODBC data source, you must specify the ODBC Data Source Name (DSN), the table name, and the valid user name and password for the database.

The Advanced Tab

Select the Advanced Tab, shown in Figure 4.21, to control access configuration. Here, you have the option to set access by specific IP address and block individuals or groups from gaining access to your server. To control the maximum amount of traffic on your server, you can also set the maximum network bandwidth for outbound traffic.

Follow these steps to get an overview on how to set up access permissions, and in effect restrict some users:

1. Select the Granted Access option button to grant access to all computers. If you need to deny access to some computers, click the Add button.

2. Select the Denied Access option to deny all computers. To then grant access to some computers, click the Add button.

FIG. 4.21

Use the options available in the Advanced tab to set additional access controls.

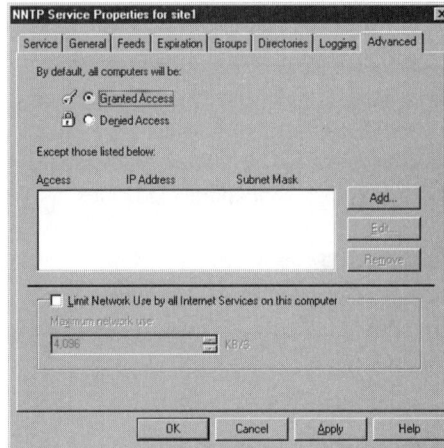

3. Specific access list allows you to set up approvals or denials based on submitting the specific IP address of the computer.

4. You may also <u>L</u>imit Network Use By All Internet Services On This Computer by clicking in the check box and entering a number for Ma<u>x</u>imum Network Use by limiting the network bandwidth allowed for all of the Internet services on the server. Set the maximum kilobytes per second of outbound traffic permitted on this computer.

▶ **See** "Bandwidth Allocation," **p. 123**

CAUTION

If you choose to limit the bandwidth, you are cautioned that this value applies to *all* Microsoft Information Services on this computer, and not just the news server.

Applying the Selections

If you are ready to test the Internet News Server, choose the Apply button. Now click the OK button, which will close the properties sheet. A pull feed begins.

N O T E   If you're grabbing a feed with any substance, you'll definitely have time for a long coffee break—expect this to take a couple of hours. ■

Are We There Yet? Testing INS

To find out whether your Internet News Server is installed successfully, set up a news reader application, called a *news client*, on a separate machine and try accessing a newsgroup.

T I P

If your news client fails to connect to the News Server, double-check the Domain Name Server settings described in Chapter 2, and the authorizations in the NNTP Service Properties dialog box.

If you prefer to work in the UNIX environment, you can use the UNIX-based news reader **tin**. In Windows, you can use Netscape News or try a shareware program such as Free Agent. Any client will do, but for our purposes we'll use the Microsoft Mail and News client.

ON THE WEB

www.microsoft.com/ie/download/   If you don't have a news client, the latest version of Microsoft Mail and News can be downloaded from Microsoft.

Configuring Mail and News

To get your news client running, follow these steps:

1. Click the start button on the tool bar, and select Programs/Internet News. The configuration wizard will start. Click Next.

2. In the dialog box enter your name as you want it to appear in news postings, and your e-mail address so people can reply to your postings. Click the Next button.

3. In the news server field, enter the name of the Internet News Server you are trying to access. Leave the field My news server requires me to logon blank. Click the Next button.

4. Select the I use a LAN connection option. Click the Next button.

5. In the next dialog box you are told installation is complete. Click the Finish button.

6. When setup is complete, you are given the option to download a list of the present newsgroups available and review the list. Choose to receive the list.

7. From the list, select groups of interest and select the subscribe button. Click the OK button and close the options page.

8. From the news reader, use the drop-down list and select a group. Notice the hierarchy presented in the drop-down list shown in Figure 4.22.

9. Post items to the group and be sure to confirm that the expiration policy is working.

Part

II

Ch

4

FIG. 4.22

Acces UseNet feed with a news client.

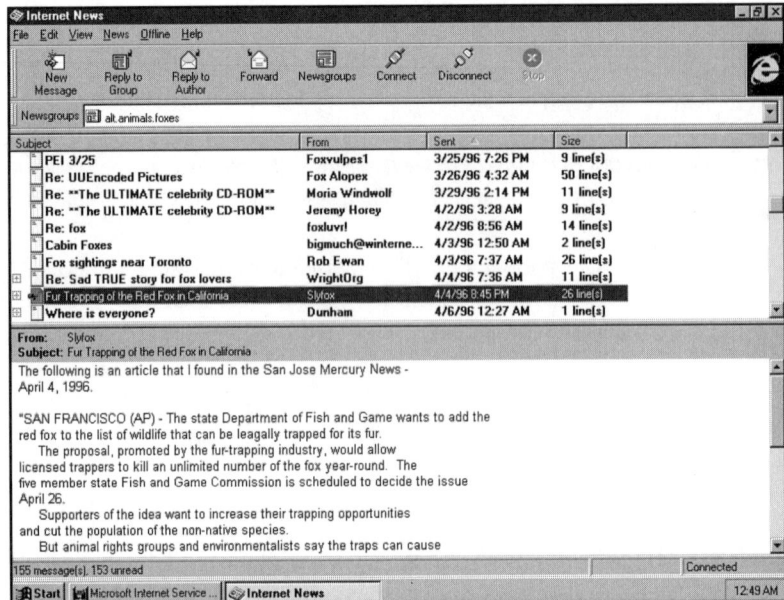

Administering the Internet News Server

Before you can come up with an offering of newsgroups for your client base, you have to know what's on the master list. This section will clarify how to complete this process.

Compiling the Active File

When we went through the step-by-step configuration of the Internet Server, we used wild cards to subscribe to the news groups of interest. For instance, instead of choosing to pull the feed for **alt.animals.foxes**, we could have chosen to pull the feed for **alt.animals.***. Not only would we receive the group specific to foxes, but we'd also get the rest of the groups that were listed in the *alt* category, with a subheading of *animals*. Though, it's obviously possible to use wildcards to build your subscription list, you may want to try creating an active list from a plain text file. In order to do this, you will need to build a new newstree. To do so, you need to capture the active newsgroup from the server. To accomplish this task, the Internet News Server looks at a text file of each newsgroup on the server's active file to create a directory structure. Where directories exist and articles are contained, the INS server will open these and build its data structures.

Getting an active list is not incredibly difficult to pull off. But you do need to get into a different frame of mind. This time you'll be working from a prompt, instead of a nice graphical user interface.

N O T E   You may want to buckle up for a moment, because we're departing from the graphical user interface; this will require us to conduct some command-line activity. ▨

Follow these steps to retrieve the active list:

1. Begin by clicking the Start button, and selecting Run. In the Open text entry area, type **telnet nntp.domain.com 119** (substitute your specific server information where it says nntp.domain.com).

2. When you are connected to the site, turn on logging in telnet. You can accomplish this by selecting the file selection for Terminal. Specify the file name and the file location and a text file of your activity during the connection will be generated (see Figure 4.23).

FIG. 4.23

Acquiring the active list through a telnet session.

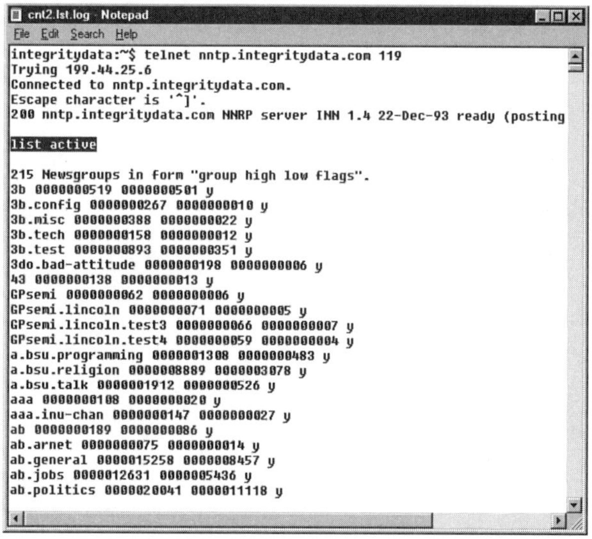

```
cnt2.lst.log - Notepad                                          _ □ ×
File  Edit  Search  Help
integritydata:~$ telnet nntp.integritydata.com 119
Trying 199.44.25.6
Connected to nntp.integritydata.com.
Escape character is '^]'.
200 nntp.integritydata.com NNRP server INN 1.4 22-Dec-93 ready (posting

list active

215 Newsgroups in form "group high low flags".
3b 0000000519 0000000501 y
3b.config 0000000267 0000000010 y
3b.misc 0000000388 0000000022 y
3b.tech 0000000158 0000000012 y
3b.test 0000000893 0000000351 y
3do.bad-attitude 0000000198 0000000006 y
43 0000000138 0000000013 y
GPsemi 0000000062 0000000006 y
GPsemi.lincoln 0000000071 0000000005 y
GPsemi.lincoln.test3 0000000066 0000000007 y
GPsemi.lincoln.test4 0000000059 0000000004 y
a.bsu.programming 0000001308 0000000483 y
a.bsu.religion 0000008889 0000003078 y
a.bsu.talk 0000001912 0000000526 y
aaa 0000000108 0000000020 y
aaa.inu-chan 0000000147 0000000027 y
ab 0000000189 0000000086 y
ab.arnet 0000000075 0000000014 y
ab.general 0000015258 0000008457 y
ab.jobs 0000012631 0000005436 y
ab.politics 0000020041 0000011118 y
```

3. Now type **list active** and a list of the newsgroups will start zipping across your screen. In the meantime, your logfile is capturing all of the groups to the text file that's being written.

N O T E   Telnet is a text-based Internet service that allows Internet users to log on to another computer on the Internet through a command-line interface. Telnet establishes a terminal interface, and the user interfaces with the computer it has logged onto from a command prompt. Windows NT Resource Kit 4.0 provides a Telnet application. There's also a variety of shareware Telnet applications available for download. ▨

FTPing the Active File

If you are transitioning from a UNIX news server to a MCIS server, you might want to FTP directly into the news server and grab the active file. Typically, the active file is located in /usr/

local/lib/news. The file itself is called "active." Send the file via FTP and proceed with building your news hierarchy, which is discussed in the following section.

Building Your News Hierarchy

With a text file containing the active list for the news server you will be pulling your feed from, you are now ready to build your news hierarchy. First you need to edit the active list so that it only contains the groups in which you want to subscribe. Launch your text file in Microsoft's Wordpad program, or a similar text editor, and cut all the groups you don't want to subscribe to (see Figure 4.24).

FIG. 4.24

Use a text editor to develop an active list.

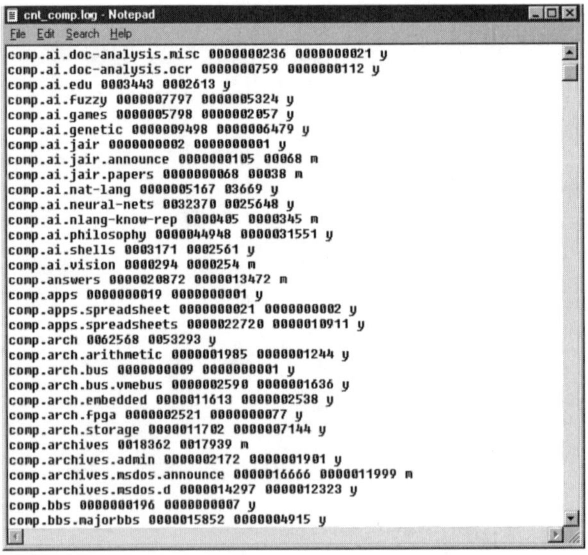

```
cnt_comp.log - Notepad
File  Edit  Search  Help
comp.ai.doc-analysis.misc 0000000236 0000000021 y
comp.ai.doc-analysis.ocr 0000000759 0000000112 y
comp.ai.edu 0003443 0002613 y
comp.ai.fuzzy 0000007797 0000005324 y
comp.ai.games 0000005798 0000002057 y
comp.ai.genetic 0000009498 0000006479 y
comp.ai.jair 0000000002 0000000001 y
comp.ai.jair.announce 0000000105 00068 m
comp.ai.jair.papers 0000000068 00038 m
comp.ai.nat-lang 0000005167 03669 y
comp.ai.neural-nets 0032370 0025648 y
comp.ai.nlang-know-rep 0000405 0000345 m
comp.ai.philosophy 0000044948 0000031551 y
comp.ai.shells 0003171 0002561 y
comp.ai.vision 0000294 0000254 m
comp.answers 0000020872 0000013472 m
comp.apps 0000000019 0000000001 y
comp.apps.spreadsheet 0000000021 0000000002 y
comp.apps.spreadsheets 0000022720 0000010911 y
comp.arch 0062568 0053293 y
comp.arch.arithmetic 0000001985 0000001244 y
comp.arch.bus 0000000009 0000000001 y
comp.arch.bus.vmebus 0000002590 0000001636 y
comp.arch.embedded 0000011613 0000002538 y
comp.arch.fpga 0000002521 0000000077 y
comp.arch.storage 0000011702 0000007144 y
comp.archives 0018362 0017939 m
comp.archives.admin 0000002172 0000001901 y
comp.archives.msdos.announce 0000016666 0000011999 m
comp.archives.msdos.d 0000014297 0000012323 y
comp.bbs 0000000196 0000000007 y
comp.bbs.majorbbs 0000015852 0000004915 y
```

TIP This may be terribly obvious, but we found that the newsgroup's active list was so large, editing it would take forever. Heck, there were 19,850 groups that we weren't interested in. We simply highlighted the groups we wanted in my hierarchy and then we cut and pasted the list into a new text document. We gave it a new name, saved it as text, and we were ready to go.

Building the newstree requires you to run a command-line program, plugging in the appropriate parameters. Be forewarned; this process can take a long time if you have a large list.

To build a server newstree from an active file with Nntpbld.exe, follow these steps:

1. Click the Start button, select Programs, and then choose Command Prompt.
2. At the prompt, enter the following: **cd c:\WINNT\system32\inetsrv**.
3. Now enter the following: **nntpbld -c -a NameOfFile.log**.
4. Restart the NNTP service in the Internet Service Manager.

N O T E   If the NNTP server fails to start running, review the Event Log and search for details on errors. To get the Event Viewer, select the Start button, choose Administrative Tools, and then select the Event Viewer. You are looking for any NNTPSVC problems that are listed. Any events causing errors are colored in red. Simply double-click the event to review the details. If the NNTP event mentions corrupt or missing files, you will need to rebuild the corrupt or missing files. ■

Rebuilding the News Hierarchy

If the Internet News Server failed to start after being set up, it may be because of corrupt or missing files. If so, you will need to rebuild the News Hierarchy. Here are the steps:

1. Click the Start button, select <u>P</u>rograms, and then choose Command Prompt.
2. At the prompt, type the following: **cd c:\WINNT\system32\inetsrv**.
3. Now enter the following: **nntpbld -c -G -e**. (This may take a while to rebuild. A long while...)
4. When the rebuild is complete, restart the computer and check the Internet Service Manager to see if the NNTP service is running.

CAUTION

In order to rebuild the news tree, nntpbld has to review every data file in the tree, and the present process only uses a single thread. Microsoft developers have said they realize this is an inefficient way to conduct a rebuild and are working on a multi-thread solution, but don't expect the new feature to be available until after the first release of the product. For the sake of perspective, expect the rebuild to take at least two and one-half hours for every gigabyte of data in the tree.

You can control the nntpbld configuration process with some additional parameters. Use any of the following parameters when running "nntpbld":

Switch	Name	Description
-v	Verbose mode	Increases the amount of information that is generated into the output file, which is specified through the -o option.
-o \<filename\>		This will be the name of the file where the rebuilt report is saved.
-t \<filename\>		This scans the news tree and creates a file called \<filename\> which can be used to rebuild the group file.
-g \<filename\>		Rebuilds a server based on the newsgroups contained in the file.

continues

Part

II

Ch

4

continued

Switch	Name	Description
-G		Combines option -t and -g, automatically scanning the virtual roots and producing a file containing the list of newsgroups.
-a <filename>		Rebuilds a server news tree based on an active file. Remember, the active file is generated through a telnet session, where you log on to Port 119 and then issue the "list active" command. The nntpbld.exe file expects this list to contain only the newsgroup names.
-c		Deletes all files before starting rebuild.
-I		Indicates that the existing news list stores files with sequential, increasing decimal numbers. The server will handle the conversion to the present numbering system.
-h		This stops a deletion of the history file. This option overrides all others.

Adding and Removing Feeds

Once you've had the Internet News Service operating for a while, you'll be ready to make some changes to your original configuration. If you are pulling feeds from multiple servers, changing your selection of UseNet feeds may be one of the top items that you need to change. Working with the feeds is a pretty straightforward process.

Simply follow these steps to add or remove feeds:

1. Click the Start Button, choose Programs, and then select the Microsoft Internet Server option. In the dialog window, double-click the NNTP server listing to access the properties page.

2. Select the Feeds Property tab.

3. Add, edit, or remove feeds as necessary.

Changing expiration settings, which might be necessary to cut down on the amount of space your news feed is occupying on your hard drive, is equally as simple:

1. From the NNTP properties sheet select the Expiration Property tab.

2. Add, edit, or remove expirations as necessary.

To activate your new settings, you will need to click the Apply button before you exit the Internet News Server properties page. The changes will take effect without a restart of the NT server.

N O T E As a rule of thumb, many administrators limit all of the binary groups to a two-day expiration. All other articles expire after two weeks. Start with a large expiration for the binary groups—a week perhaps. Monitor it, using the Performance Monitor (which is covered in Chapter 5) and then scale it down after you have gotten a good feel for the load. As far as the other groups go, the traffic is minor. It is possible for a news administrator to keep custom groups indefinitely because the file sizes are relatively small. ▦

Creating, Editing, or Deleting a Newsgroup

With over 20,000 newsgroups available on the Internet, making changes to the choices in your group list will probably be a pretty common occurrence. Changing newsgroup configuration is as easy as changing the feeds:

1. From the Internet News Server, select the Groups property sheet.
2. Type the name of the newsgroup to create, edit, or delete.
3. Select Create, Edit, or Delete.

It's simple and straightforward and again, to activate the changes, you'll need to click the Apply button. Changes will go into effect immediately.

Moving Hierarchies to a Different Directory

There may be a time when you need to move a hierarchy to another directory. Perhaps the feed has gotten so big, it's time to move the files to a larger drive. If you need to make a change to the directory, simply follow these instructions:

1. Open the Internet Services Manager and access the NNTP services information. Turn off the Allow Client Posting and Allow Feed Posting options by selecting each to remove the checkmark. Click Apply.
2. When the changes take effect, use the Windows Explorer to move the desired groups to their new directories.
3. Go to the Directories page in the NNTP service property pages. If the directory is new, select add and enter the hierarchy for the root of the subtree, such as **alt.animals**. Click Apply and wait for the process to be completed.
4. On the General page, recheck the appropriate posting parameters and click Apply.

The Directory structure change is now complete.

Types of News Feeds

There are two types of news feeds, both of which are based on the UNIX standard of IHAVE/YOUHAVE, INEED/YOUNEED.

The Pull Method   It's helpful to put the major processes of the news server into perspective. Since the pull method is the key component to receiving your news feed, let's break it down.

Part

II

Ch

4

With the pull method, the news server accesses another server (the feed server) to access its newsfeed. Think of it as a place that houses a library of discussions in over 20,000 different categories. Obviously, few client bases will ever need access to that many groups. But there's plenty there for the taking. Clearly, it's the server administrator's job to help weed through the list and select an appropriate newsfeed.

N O T E   Making a determination on the appropriate newsgroups for your organization will require some time and effort. Obviously, the title of the UseNet newsgroup gives you a preview of the subject matter contained in the topic. For instance, when we accessed alt.animals.foxes, we were 99 percent sure that the information we were retrieving would relate to the type of animal found in the wild, as opposed to the animal found on a swimsuit calendar. Still, we wondered. With that said, it's important to make a habit of screening the content to establish validity. Clearly, if you're in a technology shop, you'll want to access most of the computer groups (comp). However, if your organization doesn't use IBM's OS2, there's no need to pull a feed from the group. There are truckloads of data out there, and there's no need to store unnecessary newsgroups on your server. Conserving hard drive space is a must, so take the time and weed out the garbage. You'll be glad you did if you ever have to rebuild your news tree. ▪

Selecting the appropriate discussion groups (you're making your selections from the Feeds dialog box in the NNTP properties under the Subscription option) to include using the Microsoft Internet News Server is a snap and the scheduling of your next pull is a simple point-and-click solution.

The Internet News Server can handle the following tasks smoothly:

- Receiving and sorting of news
- Updating the news tree
- Allowing the ability for users to read, reply to, and generate news

These three issues are the most important items in managing a news server. The bottom line: Is the end user getting a quality product that is timely and reliable? It's imperative that you can answer yes to this question. With the Internet News Server, you can count on a yes answer when you are asked that question.

The Push Method   When using the push method, the Microsoft Internet News Server not only retrieves newsgroups, but the messages your user base has submitted to the news server are pushed to the news feed server. From there, the message gets distributed to additional servers and eventually to an Internet backbone site. This is when the message is on its way to mass distribution, and eventually arrives at more and more news servers on the Web. This all begins with the push method.

Here's how it works: The message is pushed (think of a package being wrapped and sent) from your server to the machine providing your feed. The push from your server is complete. The job of mass distribution is truly the job of the backbone sites. Each backbone handles the hard work of moving the news. Of course, all of the UseNet groups on your news server may not be designed for mass distribution. Local groups will not be pushed to the rest of the Web because distribution is restricted to the local area.

N O T E The process of sending and distributing messages across the Internet via NNTP is often called the "flooding algorithm" because of the way the messages move in a similar fashion to water flooding from rivers, to tributaries, to streams, and creeks.

Integrity Check: What We Experienced

After installing Windows NT 4.0 and the Internet Information Server, we checked to make sure our IP address and domain were valid. No problems; we were ready to go. Our hardware arrangement was a P166 MHz, with 64 megabytes of RAM and a 2 gigabyte hard drive. Not a commercial grade box, but certainly enough to handle the installation of the Microsoft Commercial Internet News Server. Rolling through the install was pretty easy—very intuitive interface and no confusion over how to get to the properties and make changes.

We selected the server to pull our feed from and decided to limit it to the comp.* groups. We also created a group of our own. After applying the selections, the server began chugging along and in the meantime we decided to use another computer on the LAN to access the new news server. The results were very impressive; the test group we created was listed, as well as the comp groups. For fun we submitted a test message to our test group and, impressively, the server was updating the group rather quickly. Then we checked the comp groups…

All the groups from the server we pulled from were listed. But each group had fewer than half a dozen messages. Hmmmmm… It was doubtful that these groups were getting that little traffic, so we went directly to the main news server and checked the groups. Sure enough, we were only getting a portion of the feed.

Checking the manual, a solution appears. We'll try to create an active news file from the server that we intend to pull the feed from. We found out that you have to build a news tree, but don't close that manual. This is not a point-and-click solution. It required us to go to a command prompt, run the Nntpbld.exe program, and create an active news file with a command like "nntpbld -c -a groups.log".

That seemed to run fine, but after a reboot, we were informed by the Internet Information Server that the NNTP server failed to run. According to the Event Viewer, we were missing files, or there was a corrupt file.

From here we had to conduct a rebuild using nntpbld -c -G -e . It seemed to work. After a reboot, the server confirmed we were back in service. Since then, there has been little to no trouble. However, some folks report that they have to build and rebuild the active file every time they bring up a new news server. Admittedly, we're grabbing a limited feed and not really testing the limits of the "Commercial" aspects of the Microsoft Internet News Server.

However, our small-scale intranet/Internet approach has helped us to understand that UseNet enhances communication abilities dramatically and can be used in office environments to

Part

II

Ch

4

supplement information resources. Here are a few of the side effects we experienced from our news distribution strategy:

- Motivates employees to share their expertise on a wider scale.
- Provides for a way to distribute massive amounts of information to its workforce, who can review the information at their own pace. And, employees can reference the information at a later date.
- Allows workgroups to conduct discussion over a private newsgroup.
- Opens up new opportunities for the organization to communicate with its external customers.

From Here...

At the conclusion of this chapter, you should understand how to install, configure, and run the Internet News Server at your site. You have explored the methods for acquiring and editing an active file, creating news trees, pulling a server feed, and setting specifics on connection information. You have also been provided with different diagnostic tools offered by NT to monitor your News Server's performance.

- For an overview on expanding your news server strategy, indexing news feeds, and working with discussion groups, see Chapter 5, "Advanced Administration of the Internet News Server."
- For information on setting up electronic mail, see Chapter 6, "Instant Communication—Microsoft Commercial Internet Mail Server."
- To set up chat services to implement real-time communication, see Chapter 8, "Adding a Chat Server."

Advanced Administration of the Internet News Server

In the last chapter, you learned the basic administrative techniques needed to maintain the News Server. In this chapter, advanced administrative features including Scaling Servers, Indexing the News Feed, and other advanced topics are explored. Although this chapter is not required reading for every server administrator, the information will expand on the basic skills you learned about in Chapter 4, "Delivering Discussion Forums with MCIS." ■

How to improve performance through server scaling

Learn how to establish a multi-server news strategy through the scaling of servers using a master/slave relationship. Find out how to establish this relationship between multiple servers on the network.

How to create and manage newsgroups

Learn how newsgroups are created and then delivered to the user community. Discover how to create moderated newsgroups, and handle advanced administrative features, such as access control and relocating directories.

How to manage performance

Explore the tools which allow you to monitor the performance of the News Server and view the results.

Scaling Servers Through a Master/Slave Relationship

Administering a news server presents many challenges. If your business has a large user base with a wide variety of interests, you may plan on pulling over 20,000 newsgroups to offer to your clientele. To serve up that much information, you will need more than one server to manage this mass of data effectively. When you start adding multiple servers to your network architecture, you'll need tools to string them together. Thankfully, the Internet News Server is prepared for this sort of growth and is rather easy to configure.

If your organization will only be offering a small fraction of the 20,000 newsgroups, scalability will still be of interest to you. The Internet News Server retains an excessive amount of information in the newsgroup directories. This is a situation where it's imperative to build a platform that is bigger, better, and faster.

This chapter outlines the steps involved in expanding the server to handle the newsgroup load better. You're introduced to details on developing a strategy for adding multiple and replicated servers, expanding capacity, and reconfiguring the system.

N O T E In the Master/Slave relationship, there are two roles. The Master server, which generally has no end-user clients, is the primary server and receives a newsgroup feed from other servers on the Internet and replicates the feed to the Slave servers. The Slave receives the content from the Master and makes it available to clients. ▨

Advantages of Master/Slave

Let's consider the three areas that were listed in the previous section. If you need to increase the number of clients that can be served, developing a commercial-sized news server strategy will require the addition of more systems to the architecture.

N O T E When adding additional servers to participate in this Master/Slave relationship, each will need to be Windows NT servers, because the same NT-based software that was used to configure the Master server will be used to configure the Slave. ▨

In the present configuration, all clients and feeds connect to the same server. Consequently, when traffic is high the server takes a beating and your users see a decrease in service. By adding additional NT servers, the load can be distributed among other systems and, as a result, improve service for your user base.

In the area of improving client performance, this boils down mostly to hardware upgrades. The bottom line for getting the server to perform faster is to make improvements by increasing physical memory or increasing processor speed.

N O T E If you intend to launch a multiple-server scheme for your news delivery strategy, you must have a license for each server on which the Commercial Internet System News Server is installed. ■

If you are running out of storage space on the server, you can either increase the physical disk space or eliminate some groups from your feed. Also, you can spread newsgroups over multiple machines by putting newsgroups on different virtual roots.

Purchasing an additional hard drive or a faster processor will help you deliver the news, and will do a lot for client performance. You may even want to consider mirroring your hard disk. But if you want to make significant improvements in the number of clients that can be served simultaneously, and overcome storage space problems, you'll have to come up with a change in the architecture. If that's the case, you'll find answers in the next section on implementing a Master/Server approach to delivering news.

Adding Master/Slave Servers

With this procedure, you need at least one more Windows NT server. It is recommended that you add at least two machines to transition from one machine to a Master/Slave relationship. That said, you are ready to proceed in configuring the Master/Slave strategy when the additional machines are configured and successfully operating with the following components:

- ■ *Windows NT 4.0* The operating system
- ■ *Internet Information Server* Provides the server platform for the Internet News Server and handles the connections of news clients
- ■ *Internet Service Manager* The administration tool of the Internet Information Server used to manage the Internet News Server
- ■ *Microsoft Internet News Server* The commercial grade UseNet news server

Assuming that you have the additional servers prepared, with software installed and functioning properly, this is the process for scaling servers through a Master/Slave relationship. On one of the new servers, follow these steps:

1. Click the Start button, choose Programs, Microsoft Internet Server, and then select the Internet Service Manager.
2. Select the NNTP service from the list of services and access the configuration files by choosing Properties, Service Properties.
3. From the NNTP Service Properties sheet, select the Feeds tab.
4. Select Add Server, and in the Feed Properties text box, under Feed Server Name, type in the name of the primary server that has been handling the news server function, as shown in Figure 5.1.

Part

II

Ch

5

FIG. 5.1

The Feed Properties sheet provides configuration options for Master/Slave configuration.

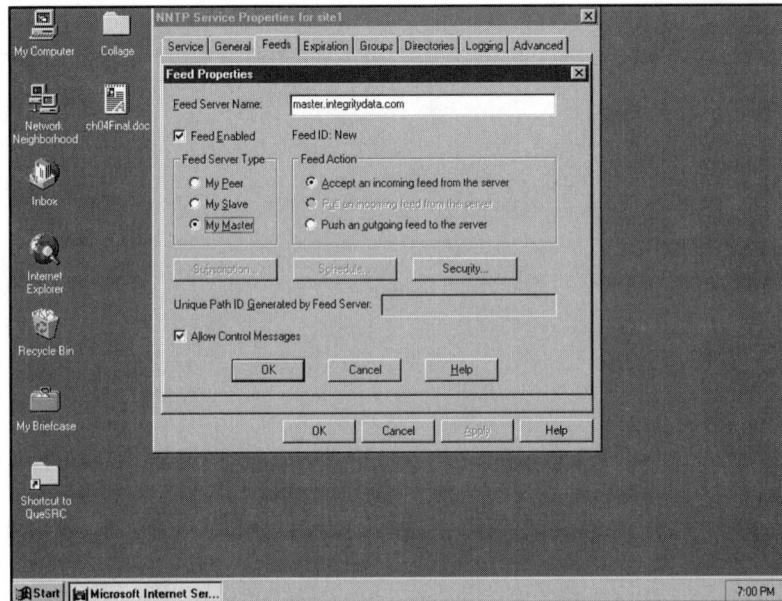

5. Select Feed Enabled so that a check appears in its box.

6. In the Feed Server Type category, select the My Master option. This designates the remote server type as a slave. The slave services clients and forwards all posted articles to the master server.

7. In the Feed Action category, select the option to Accept an Incoming Feed from the Server, then click the OK button.

8. Select the Add server option again, and in the Feed Server Name text box, type the name of the primary server that has been handling the news server function.

9. Select Feed Enabled so that a check appears in its box.

10. In the Feed Server Type category, select both the My Master option and the Push an Outgoing Feed to the server, as shown in Figure 5.2.

11. Click the Apply button to set the configuration.

12. Repeat the process for each additional slave server.

CAUTION

When INS servers are configured in a master/slave topology, administrative changes must be made on each server individually. This includes the creation and deletion of newsgroups and cancellation of messages.

FIG. 5.2

The Feeds tab allows the user to configure options to push a feed from the server.

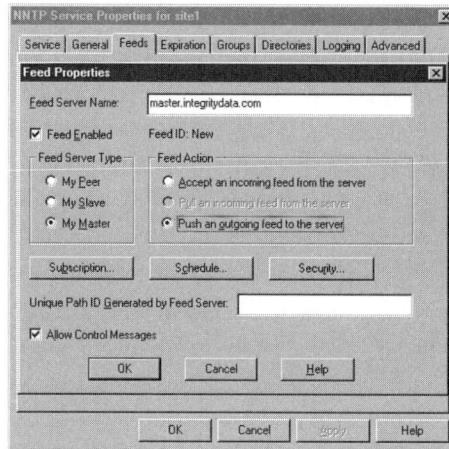

Creating Newsgroups

The ability to create newsgroups for specific discussion topics should be especially useful in an office environment. Over an intranet, communications can be improved dramatically through the offering of newsgroups. As an example, here's how a local group within the company intranet might work. A group will be created to discuss training opportunities. Let's call the group **ourcompany.training.opportunities**. Employees can check in the group to see what training offerings are available in the upcoming months and possibly even be notified of additional class availability because of cancellations from a class. It's simple and easy, and allows this information to disseminate in a speedy fashion.

This section outlines the specifics on Local Groups, Global Groups, and Moderated Groups.

Local Groups

To set up a local group, complete the following steps:

1. Click the Start button, choosing Programs, then Microsoft Internet Server, and then the Internet Service Manager.

2. Select the NNTP service from the list of services and access the configuration files by choosing Properties, Service Properties.

3. From the NNTP Service Properties sheet, select the Groups tab, and choose Create.

4. Complete the dialog box requesting the name of the Newsgroup. In this case, you may type **integritydata.training.opportunities** (see Figure 5.3).

5. Submit a Description for the group; for example, title it Information on Department Training Opportunities.

Part
II

Ch
5

FIG. 5.3

Enter the newsgroup name and a description in the Newsgroup Properties dialog box.

6. You can set the newsgroup up to be Read Only. When this box is checked, users and feeds will not be able to post articles to this newsgroup.

7. You can also make the group moderated (please see the later section, "Moderating Newsgroups").

8. Choose OK. A dialog box reporting that the newsgroup was added successfully will appear, as shown in Figure 5.4. Click OK.

FIG. 5.4

The Internet Service Manager will inform you if the newsgroup was added properly.

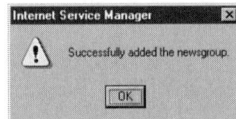

To view the Newsgroup list, choose the Groups tab and type an * in the Newsgroup Name text box, and then click the Find button. All of the newsgroups on the server will be displayed, as shown in Figure 5.5, including the local group you just created.

FIG. 5.5

Review a list of the groups in the site by using the options in the Groups tab.

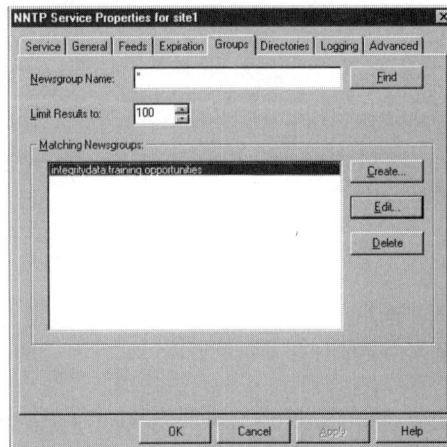

Global Groups

Creating a UseNet group for global distribution is a fascinating process. The true democratic nature of approval for a global newsgroup is amazing. Before you begin to think about requesting a new group, it's very important that you acquire an understanding of the process. The best place to learn the process is in the UseNet groups **news.announce.newgroups** and **news.groups**.

T I P If creating a new UseNet group is a new experience for you, it is recommended that you seek assistance in the process. Send e-mail to **group-mentors@acpub.duke.edu**, explain what you are proposing, and ask for help. This body of volunteers really understands the newsgroup creation process and can help you avoid reinventing the wheel. If you intend to propose a new group and you want to know the ins and outs of submitting a good proposal, it is in your best interest to seek assistance from this group before submitting a formal proposal.

To go global with a new UseNet group, the process would work like this:

1. Submit a Request for Discussion (RFD), outlining the intention of the group, to **news.announce.newgroups**.

2. There will be a month of discussion on the request in **news.groups**.

3. After a month of discussion, a Call for Votes (CFV) will be issued, explaining the specifics of the group and the length of the voting period.

4. The UseNet Volunteer Votetakers, a group of neutral, third-party vote-takers who currently handle vote gathering on new proposals will begin the voting process. To win the proposal there must be 100 more yes votes than no votes and two thirds of the votes must be yes.

5. After the vote result is posted, there is a five-day waiting period, allowing an opportunity to correct any errors in the voter list or the voting procedure.

6. If there are 100 more yes votes than no votes and two thirds of the votes are yes, the group is approved and a message will be sent to the **news.announce.newgroups** with the outcome.

7. Any requests for discussion that failed through a vote cannot be brought up for discussion again until six months have passed since the vote.

The result is that your local newsgroup becomes a globally distributed UseNet group. There is no guarantee that every server will pick up your feed. However, for each server that does, there will be opportunities for their user base to join and participate in the group. When that happens, expect a more populist approach to discussion and a greater input base from a potentially international user base. Also, in UseNet fashion, there is a great opportunity for the group's flow of discussion to be disjointed and outside your local interest. That's all part of going global.

Part

II

Ch

5

If the possibility of disjointed and irrelevant discussion makes you consider managing the flow of discussion, perhaps a moderated newsgroup is the solution, which leads us to the next section on moderating newsgroups.

Moderating Newsgroups

Although there is a beauty to the freeform atmosphere of UseNet groups, there are times when conducting discussions in the traditional UseNet fashion is simply unsatisfactory. In this atmosphere, there's simply too much noise (miscellaneous messages) to weed through and there's a lack of ability to stay on the topic.

For instance, take an organization like state government. Perhaps the governor of the state is interested in soliciting feedback and sharing ideas on workers' compensation. If a basic, public UseNet newsgroup called **gov.forum.workers_comp** were created, the discussion may start with an introduction by the governor, requesting feedback on a proposed piece of workers' compensation legislation which has been drafted. The second message to the group might include the actual language of the bill. Initially, the messages from the public may focus on workers' compensation, and the merits of the proposed legislation. But it won't be long before the subject matter takes a detour. A whole new line of topics will be created.

Here's an example of what might happen:

Message 1

from: Governor

subject: Workers' Compensation

Message 2

from: Governor

subject: Soliciting comments on language of bill

Resulting Messages

subject: Excellent language

subject: I don't understand the accompanying bill

subject: What happened to last year's draft

subject: Hey idiots, let's focus on Education

subject: What's the point, bureaucrats have never listened to the public

subject: Make money fast

subject: Can we tie this legislation onto SB0001a

subject: Let's have casino legislation

subject: Can't you people stay on the subject

subject: My brush with the Governor

It doesn't take long for the discussion to veer into other directions and get emotional. The effort that goes into reading and sorting through the controversial messages detracts from the purpose of the group.

Certainly, if you weed through the garbage, there are some valid comments and helpful information. The governor can cull specific information to assist in the legislative effort. Also, the focused participants are experiencing a new type of relationship with their state government. However, a portion of the people who really want to discuss workers' compensation will grow tired of the nonsense and choose to leave because it's simply too hard to focus on the issue.

When this happens, the solution may be the moderated newsgroup, where every message that is sent to the group is immediately forwarded to a moderator. The moderator reviews the message for content, and if it meets the criteria for the group, the moderator posts the message to the UseNet group. All messages, whether on recurring topics or a new concept, will pass through the moderator before they are submitted to the newsgroup for public access.

Creating a Moderated Group

In Chapter 4, "Delivering Discussion Forums with MCIS," you learned how to maintain a news server through the Internet Services Manager. This is the same place you will go to set up a moderated newsgroup. To set up a moderated group, simply follow these steps:

1. Click the Start button, choose Programs, Microsoft Internet Server, and then the Internet Service Manager.

2. Select the NNTP service from the list of services and access the configuration files by choosing Properties, and the Service Properties.

3. From the NNTP Service Properties sheet, choose the Groups tab, and then select Create.

4. Complete the dialog box requesting the name of the Newsgroup.

5. Enter a Description for the group.

6. Place a check in the box for Moderated, as shown in Figure 5.6. When articles are posted to the newsgroup, e-mail will be sent to the moderator. The moderator will review the content of the articles and then post with an "approved by" header.

Part

II

Ch

5

FIG. 5.6

In Newsgroup Properties, a check in the Moderated check box signifies that a group is moderated.

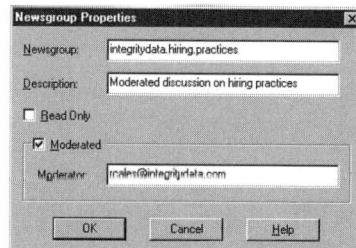

7. Enter the e-mail address of the Moderator.

8. Click the OK button. The Internet Service Manager will report that it has successfully added the newsgroup. Click OK to acknowledge the message.

9. To view the Newsgroup list, in the Groups tab simply type an * in the Newsgroup Name text box and click the Find button. All of the newsgroups you are accessing will be displayed, as seen in Figure 5.7, including the moderated list you created.

FIG. 5.7

Review the list of matching newsgroups in NNTP Service Properties for the site.

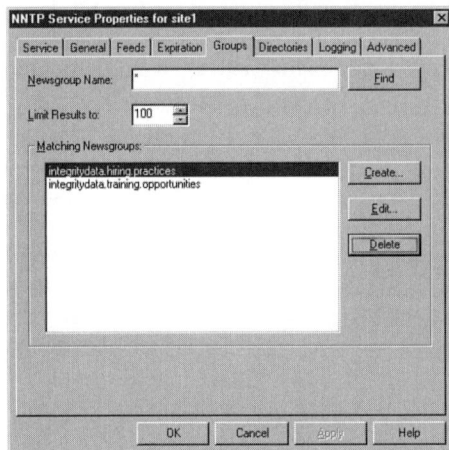

N O T E If you do not have a Mail Server configured, all message postings to moderated groups will fail. In Chapter 6, "Instant Communication–Microsoft Commercial Internet Mail Server," you learn how to install, configure, and administer the Microsoft Commercial Internet Mail Server. ∎

Moderating the Group

A newsgroup moderator's job is demanding. Managing, maintaining, and reviewing messages sent from a large group of people is tough. It is essential that the administrator have the time and patience to carefully review the content of each message and then distribute it to the rest of the group.

From the user's erspective, a moderated group should provide a more consistent flow of discussion. However, there are a few shortcomings. For instance, in the traditional UseNet group, messages posted by users are submitted and available to the rest of the group to read in a timely manner. With a moderated group, all messages submitted to the group are sent to another person, who controls when the message will be made public to the group. Of course, the moderator is checking the content of the messages to ensure that the subject matter is relevant to the group. This leads some folks to have concerns about all of their ideas going through a gatekeeper (whatever happened to freedom of speech, cry the users).

Frankly, the biggest problem is when the moderator fails to process the messages in a prompt fashion. You can forget about activity in the group if the moderator goes on vacation, gets sick, or has something else occupying their time. The newsgroup is only active when the moderator is on top of things.

Maintaining the moderated newsgroup is all handled through a mail client. Here's how it works:

1. The moderator launches the mail program of their choice, perhaps Eudora, Microsoft Mail, or Netscape Mail.

2. When mail is sent to the newsgroup, it is retrieved by your mail client.

3. Any newsgroup mail will be reviewed for content by the moderator and if the content passes the review process, the message will be forwarded to the newsgroup by sending the message to the newsgroup.

If the configuration of a moderated newsgroup needs to be edited, the server administrator can make changes by doing the following:

1. Click the Start button, choose Programs, Microsoft Internet Server, and then the Internet Service Manager.

2. Select the NNTP service from the list of services and access the configuration files by choosing Properties, Service Properties.

3. From the NNTP Service Properties sheet, choose the Groups tab.

4. View the Newsgroup list by submitting a wildcard, *, in the Newsgroup Name text entry field and click the Find button.

5. Select the group that needs to be edited and click the Edit button.

6. Make any necessary changes, such as the Description or the Moderator, as shown in Figure 5.8.

FIG. 5.8

Update the newsgroup description or other settings in Newsgroup Properties.

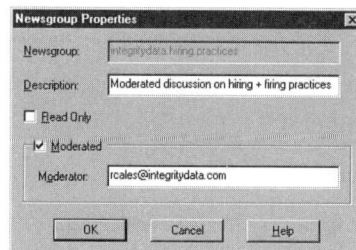

Part

II

Ch

5

7. Click the OK button and the Internet Service Manager will report that it has successfully set newsgroup properties. Click the OK button to acknowledge the message.

The changes you make will go into effect immediately.

Handling Advanced Administration

The Microsoft Internet News Server has made great strides in interface design for news servers. If you've had some experience in managing a UNIX news server, you would probably agree that there was no end to the confusion. It required a great deal of patience. Managing the news server is still time-consuming, but it's good to know that the interface of the news server makes sense. Also, it isn't too difficult to figure out, even when you get into the tough administrative features.

The objective of this section is to describe the particulars for Relocating Newsgroup Directories, Updating News Subjects, and Controlling Access to News.

Relocating Newsgroup Directories

With a UseNet news server, making adjustments to get optimum performance is natural. If you ever add a new hard drive to help share the wealth, you might consider moving a newsgroup hierarchy to another directory. If that is the case, simply follow these instructions:

1. Click the Start button, choose Programs, Microsoft Internet Server, and then the Internet Service Manager.

2. Select the NNTP service from the list of services and access the configuration files by choosing Properties, Service Properties.

3. From the NNTP Service Properties sheet, select the General tab.

4. Uncheck the Allow Client Posting and Allow Feed Posting options by selecting each, as seen in Figure 5.9. Each check box should be empty. Click Apply.

FIG. 5.9
Deactivate Client
Posting and Feed
Posting when changing
your directory structure.

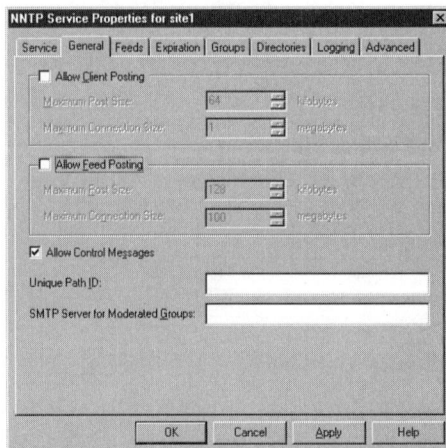

5. Right-click the Windows NT Start button and choose Explore to launch the NT Windows Explorer, the file management system for Windows NT.

6. If you followed the installation instructions in Chapter 4, you can access the group hierarchies by accessing the **c:\InetPub\nntproot** directory. This directory contains folders for all the newsgroups offered by the server. Select the desired group, then drag and drop it on the directory/drive of your choice, as seen in Figure 5.10.

FIG. 5.10

Windows Explorer supports drag-and-drop when moving directories.

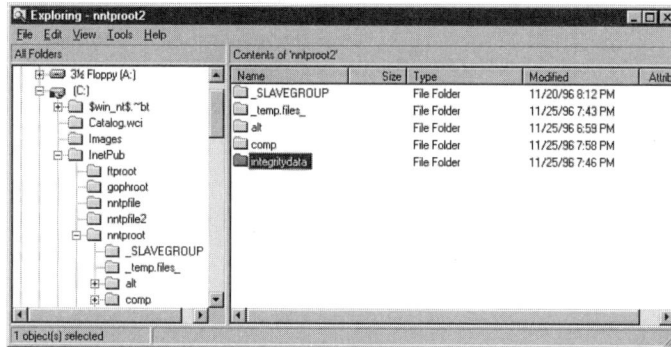

7. When the file transfer is complete, return to the NNTP service property pages located in the Internet Service Manager. Select the Directories tab and click the Add button.

8. In the Directory properties dialog box, enter the name of the directory either by typing it or by clicking the Browse button and selecting it. This is a required field and cannot be the same as any of the presently submitted directories listed in the Directory list on the NNTP Directories property page. It will end up looking something like this: **c:\InetPub\ nntproot\alt\animals\foxes**, as seen in Figure 5.11.

FIG. 5.11

In the Directory Properties dialog window you can enter the directory where the files have been moved.

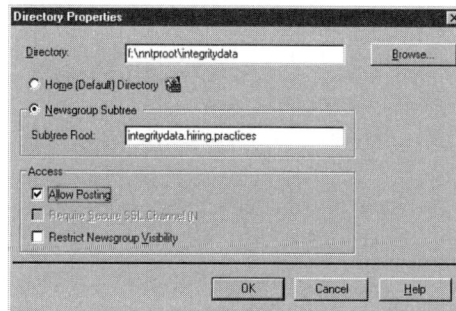

9. Select the Newsgroup Subtree option, to indicate that the named directory should be used for a specified subtree only, as shown in the Subtree Root box.

10. Enter a Subtree Root that corresponds with the hierarchy which you just added. For instance, **alt.animals.foxes** would be the subtree root for the directory example in Step 10.

11. Select the Allow Posting option if you want clients to be able to post to newsgroups.

12. Select the Require Secure SSL Channel option if you want clients to connect using secure sockets layer SSL.

13. Select the Restrict Newsgroup Visibility option if you want only clients with read or post permission to be able to see the newsgroups under the specified directory.

CAUTION

According to Microsoft, because of the overhead in processing permissions on a per-group basis, using the Restrict Newsgroup Visibility feature may cause a loss in performance.

14. Click the OK button, and then choose the Apply button on the General tab, recheck the appropriate posting parameters, and click Apply Option.

The directory structure addition is now complete and operational.

Updating News Subjects

As the server administrator, you can count on having to update UseNet groups on a regular basis. There's just so much information out there, and your user base will be discovering topics that they need to access. You can count on your users calling upon you to ask why you are accessing one group over another. More often than not, you'll need to go into the Internet Services Manager to add the requested group. When you get those calls, here's the easiest way to handle it:

1. Click the Start button, choose Programs, Microsoft Internet Server, and then the Internet Service Manager.

2. Select the NNTP service from the list of services and access the configuration files by choosing Properties, Service Properties.

3. From the NNTP Service Properties sheet, select the Feeds tab and highlight the name of the server name you are accessing for your feed. This is located in the Server Feeds box.

4. Click the Edit button.

5. Select the Subscription button and the Feed Subscription dialog box opens. In the Subscription List are the present groups to which you have subscribed.

6. Type the specific newsgroup that you want to access, such as **comp.sources.unix**, into the Newsgroup text field, as seen in Figure 5.12.

7. If you want to retrieve an entire category, take the wildcard approach again (for example, **comp.sources.***). For a single category, enter the name of the specific newsgroup that you want to access, such as **comp.sources.unix**.

8. If there are any groups that you are receiving that you want to remove from the list, highlight the group name in your subscription list and click the Remove button.

9. When your additions are complete, choose the OK button, which returns you to the Feed Properties dialog box.

FIG. 5.12

Subcribe to groups from
the Feed Subscription
dialog box.

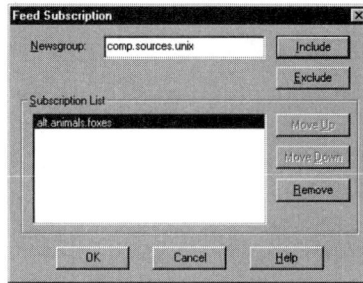

10. The Feed properties should require no changes, so click the OK button.

11. Click the Apply button to update the Internet News Server and complete the updating
    process.

The Internet News Server will pull the group on the next scheduled feed.

Controlling Access to News

There will come a time when you will need to specify access controls to the news server. One
example is to limit IP access to specific IP addresses. This will limit activity on the Internet
News Server to a specific group of users. For instance, you can close off anyone outside your
complex.

To limit access by IP address, follow these steps:

1. Click the Start button, choose Programs, Microsoft Internet Server, and then the
   Internet Service Manager.

2. Select the NNTP service from the list of services and access the configuration files by
   choosing Properties, Service Properties.

3. From the NNTP Service Properties sheet, select the Advanced tab, as seen in
   Figure 5.13.

FIG. 5.13

The Advanced Tab
provides opportunities
to set accessibility
options.

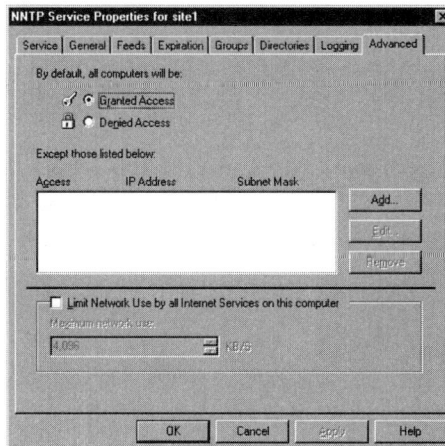

4. Here you can set access by specific IP address and block individuals or groups from gaining access to your server. By default, all computers are Granted Access to the News Server. If you choose to grant access to all users by default, you can specify the computers to be denied access.

5. Click the Add button, which launches the Deny Access On dialog box, as seen in Figure 5.14.

FIG. 5.14

Enter specific IP addresses and subnet masks to deny access to a group of computers.

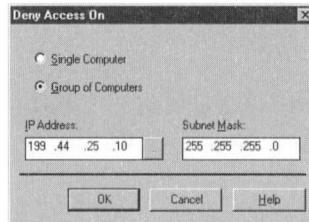

6. Choose to limit access on a single computer by identifying its IP address, or choose to deny access to a Group of Computers by identifying their IP addresses and subnet mask.

7. If you are denying access to a single computer, enter the IP address for the single computer in the IP Address entry field. If you don't know the IP address, click the button to the right of the IP Address box to look up the IP address for a specific computer name by entering the domain name.

8. If you are denying access to a group, you will need to select the Group of Computers option and then enter the IP Address and the Subnet Mask.

N O T E   Another way to set up the access privileges is to deny access to all users by default, and then specify those computers that are allowed access. For an intranet situation, this may be the best option. When you click Add, you will add the Group of Computers in your office place. ■

9. Click the OK button, and then click Apply to update the Internet News Server and activate the Access submissions.

Performance Tuning the News Server

Windows NT offers a number of tools to assist with managing the Internet News Server. Specifically, you'll want to learn the basics on operating the Windows NT Performance Monitor, which provides two important functions to help you maintain the News Server:

■ *Charting*   A graph of the item you are monitoring displayed in real-time.

■ *Alerts*   Provide the ability to set a value and if the performance falls below the level specified, an alert is triggered.

N O T E The Windows NT Performance Manager is a well documented tool and the Windows NT Resource Kit features a great user guide, written by Russ Blake, the designer of the Performance Manager. This section is only designed to provide you with an example of how it can assist you in analyzing the performance of the News Server. ▨

Monitoring

The Windows NT Performance Monitor will enable you to get a thorough handle on the performance status of the Internet News Server. It will allow you to access information on everything from current anonymous users to article posted. In order to access this resource, you have to activate the LogicalDisk object, which is inactive by default.

Follow these steps to activate the LogicalDisk object:

1. Click the Start button, choosing Programs, Command Prompt.

2. At the C:\ prompt type **diskperf -y** and press Enter. A message is posted that the change will take effect after the system is restarted. An example of this message is shown in Figure 5.15.

3. Reboot the computer.

FIG. 5.15
Working from a DOS prompt, the logical disk is activated.

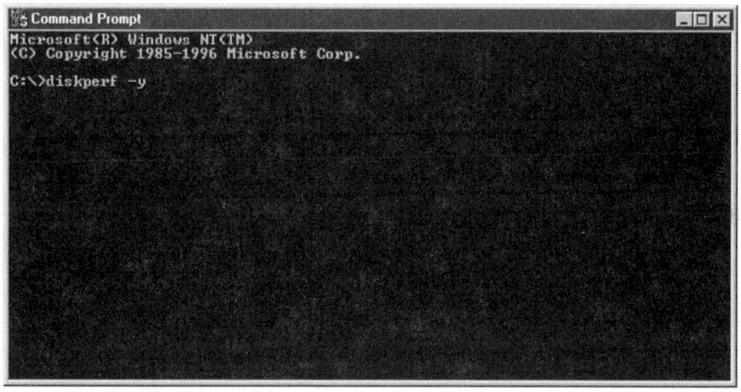

Part
II

Ch
5

To access the Performance Monitor and evaluate the status of the Internet News Server, follow these steps:

1. Click the Start button, choosing Programs, then Administrative Tools, and then choose the Performance Monitor.

   The Performance Monitor is launched.

2. Select View, and verify that you will be viewing by Chart, as seen in Figure 5.16.

3. Choose to add to the chart by choosing Edit, Add to Chart, as seen in Figure 5.17. You can also activate this feature by clicking the + button on the toolbar.

FIG. 5.16

Configure Performance
Monitor to display
results in a chart.

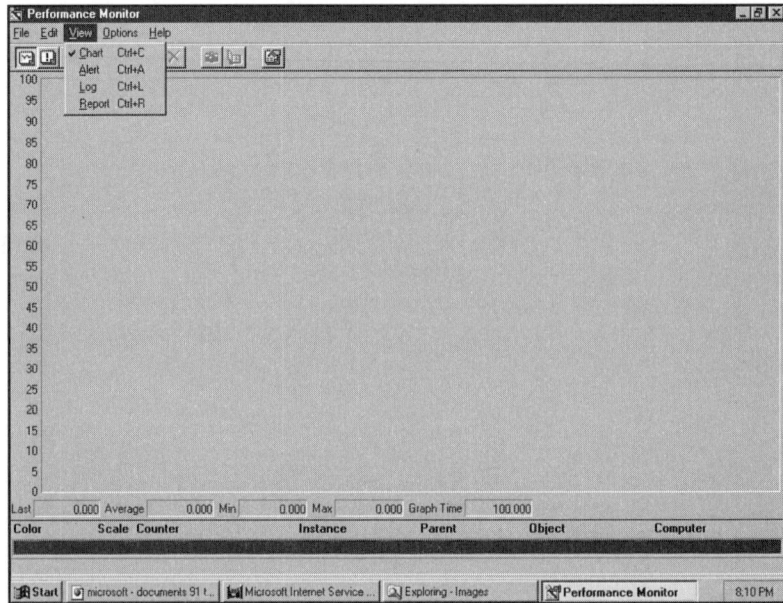

FIG. 5.17

Preparing to add groups
to the chart.

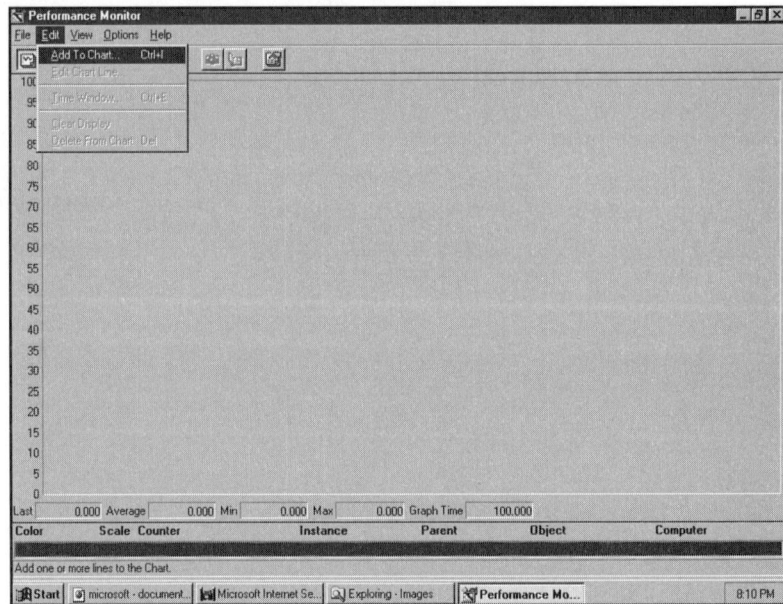

4. The Performance Monitor launches the Add to Chart dialog box, as seen in Figure 5.18. Some of the main options in the Performance Monitor are:

Computer   Select the computer you want to monitor. Your server appears as the default. If the Internet News Server resides on another server, click the ellipses button (...) and a Select Computer dialog box is launched.

Object   Select an object to monitor from those residing on the computer you have chosen to monitor.

Counters   Select the counter you want to monitor.

FIG. 5.18

Specifically select the items to monitor.

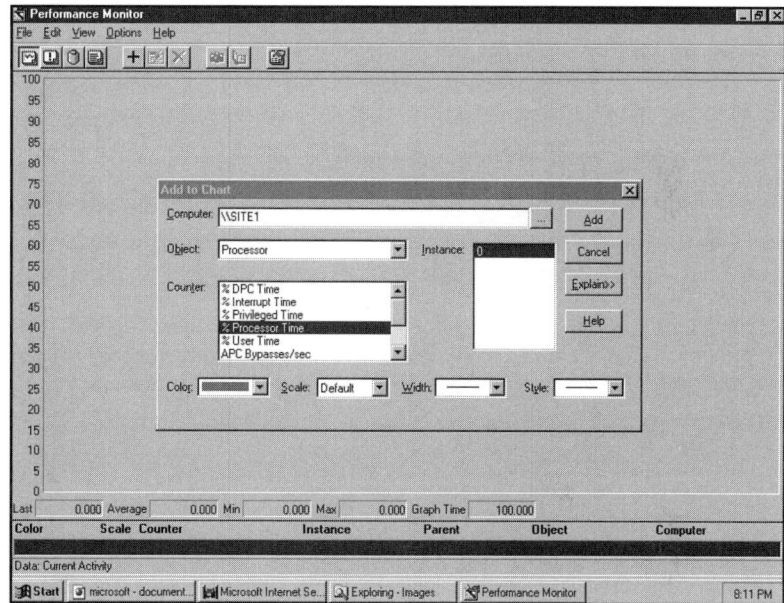

5. Leave the Computer as the default.

6. Change the Object feature to Processor.

7. Select the counter of interest. To review what the counters are designed to do, select the option and click the Explain button. For this test, select %Processor Time, which will chart the elapsed time that a processor is busy executing a non-Idle thread. It can be viewed as the fraction of the time spent doing useful work, as seen in Figure 5.19.

8. Now, click the Add button and the counters will be launched.

9. Click Done and the Performance Monitor begins charting the graph as shown in Figure 5.20.

Part

II

Ch

5

FIG. 5.19

You can view an explanation of the counter by clicking the Explain button.

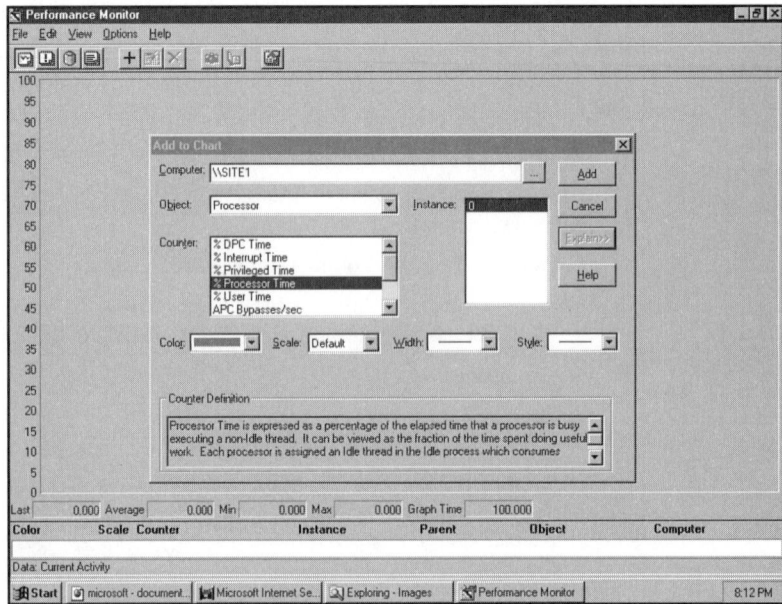

FIG. 5.20

The Performance Monitor at work.

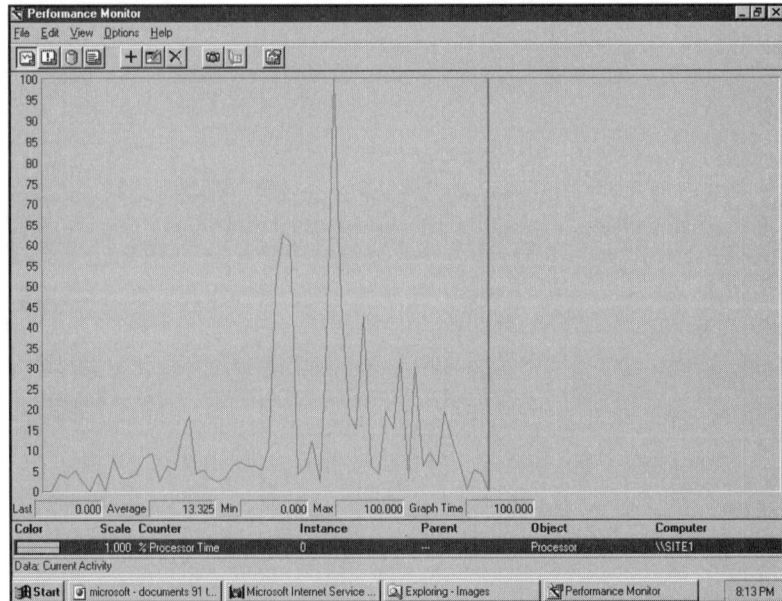

10. To customize the chart, choose Options, Chart.

11. Select the option to add a Horizontal grid, as seen in Figure 5.21.

12. Click OK and review the outcome.

FIG. 5.21

Use a grid for the background to make chart interpretation easier.

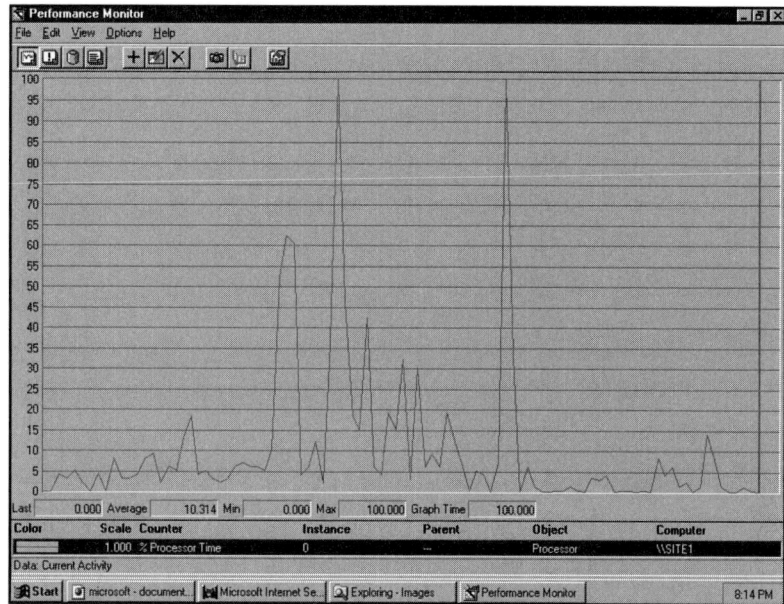

N O T E According to Microsoft, the normal reading of the counter should be less than 75 percent. If the reading is greater, it means the processor is limiting the data and the user should consider adding another processor. ■

Obviously, a system monitor is good only if it can notify the administrator when the server is not performing up to standards. Windows NT has the solution for this: the Performance Monitor's alert feature. The key is to be judicious in setting the sensitivity of the levels, especially since you will be notified whenever the monitor records the server crossing the threshold of each level.

Here's how you set up the alert feature for Performance monitor:

1. Click the Start button, choose Programs, Administrative Tools, and then select the Performance Monitor. The Performance Monitor is launched.

2. Select the View the Alerts button on the button bar, or choose View, Alert, as shown in Figure 5.22.

3. Click the Add Counter button (+), or choose Edit, Add to Alert.

4. Select Processor for the Object and %Processor Time as the Counter.

5. In the Alert If section, select Over and type **50** in the text entry field, as seen in Figure 5.23. This will cause the server to notify you when the time a processor is busy executing a non-idle thread exceeds 50 percent.

6. Click the Add button.

Part

II

Ch

5

FIG. 5.22

Preparing to set alert modes.

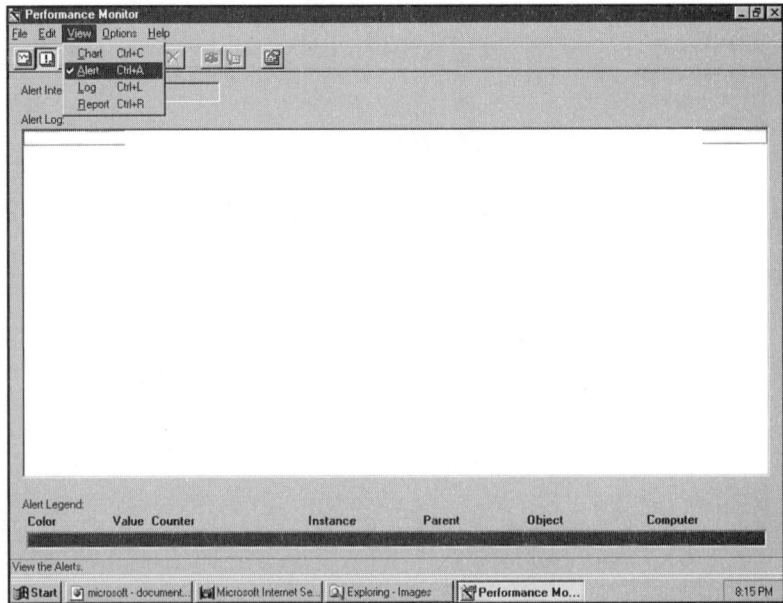

FIG. 5.23

Enter a number in Alert If to indicate the level at which you want to be notified.

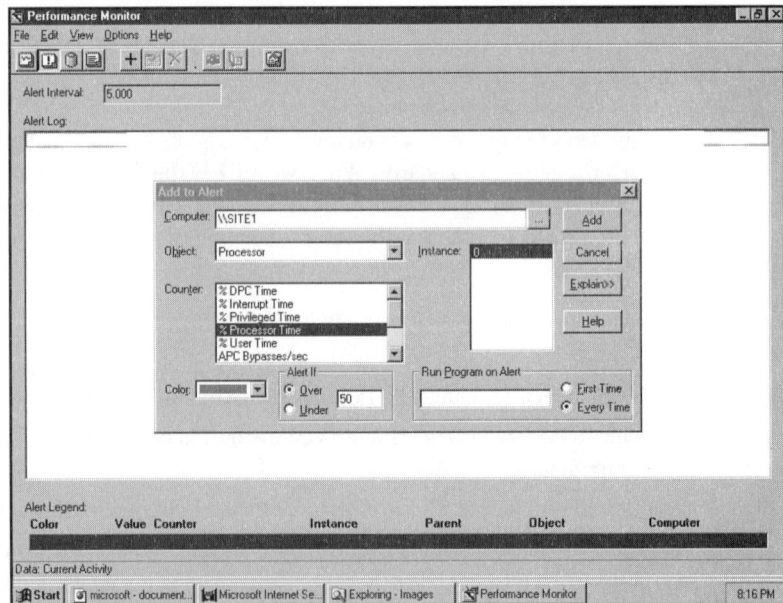

7. Choose Options, Alert to launch the Alert Options dialog box, as seen in Figure 5.24. The Alert Options dialog box opens.

FIG. 5.24

Launch Performance
Monitor into alert mode
from the menu bar.

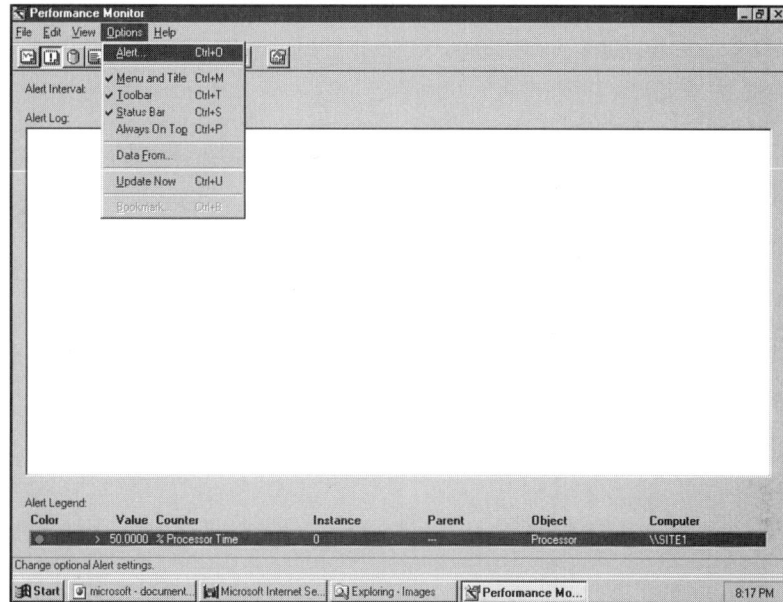

8. If an alert is necessary, Performance Monitor can be configured to Switch to an Alert
View, or Send Network Message to the administrator. For now, select Switch to an Alert
View, as seen in Figure 5.25.

FIG. 5.25

Choose Switching to
Alert View in the Alert
Options dialog box.

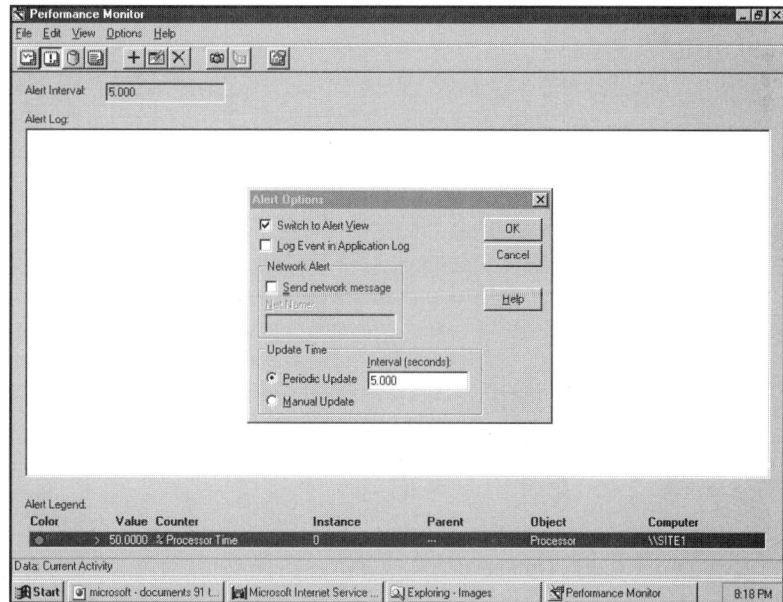

The Performance Monitor will track anything that crosses the alert threshold and will log the activity on the Performance Monitor page, as seen in Figure 5.26. You can now monitor the server resources and adjust as needed.

FIG. 5.26

The Performance Monitor Alert View displays detailed information for every instance an object does not perform as specified.

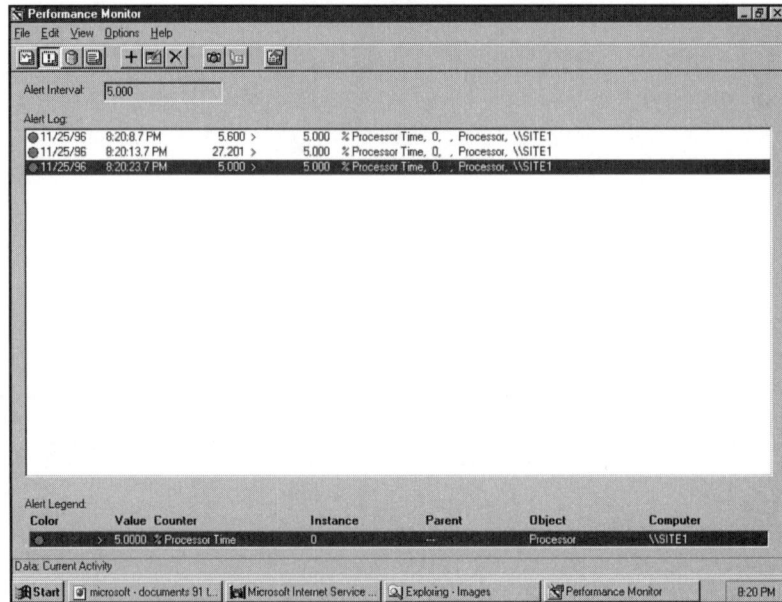

Multiple Drives

Additional hard drive space is a must if you are in the business of administering a newsgroup. You simply can't have enough hard drive space. Plenty of drive space is essential, and since there are gigabytes of data available via news feeds, the more you want to access, the more space is required. That's where multiple drives come into play.

To provide additional headroom, the best approach may be to consider a more powerful disk subsystem, such as a Redundant Array of Inexpensive Disks, also known as a RAID. In a RAID atmosphere, you can distribute data over several disks. The result is an ability to realize more potential, through faster read/write speeds across multiple disk drives. The bottom line is to enable users to get to the news in a prompt fashion. A single disk drive can deliver news, but it won't provide optimum performance. Improved speed is not the only benefit. In a RAID configuration, the chance of failure is decreased, because RAID stores redundant information, which allows the automatic re-creation of your data should a single drive fail. In a news server situation this is extremely useful.

Your user base will be potentially accessing hundreds of megabytes of data each day; it's important to protect your deliverables with a high-end strategy, such as a RAID.

Bandwidth Allocation

The Internet News Server will also enable you to control your Internet services by limiting the network bandwidth allowed for all of the Internet services on the server. *Bandwidth* is the amount of information and the rate of speed it travels through the network. As more features are added to your server, the more the network bandwidth is spread thin. Additional bandwidth is a must if you want to get optimum performance from the server.

The next option in Internet News Server options is to limit the bandwidth allowed, providing for a little extra headroom. However, please be advised; this option will change the bandwidth for *all* Internet Services on the Windows NT server.

To limit network use by all Internet Services on the network, follow these steps:

1. Click the Start button, choose Programs, Microsoft Internet Server, and then the Internet Service Manager.
2. Select the NNTP service from the list of services and access the configuration files by choosing Properties, Service Properties.
3. From the NNTP Service Properties sheet, select the Advanced tab.
4. At the bottom of the Advanced dialog box, choose the option to Limit Network Use by All Internet Services on This Computer. When you check this box, the Internet Services Manager brings up a warning that the value applies to all Microsoft Information Services on the server and asks for confirmation that you want to change the present bandwidth allocation, as shown in Figure 5.27. Choose Yes.

FIG. 5.27
Confirm that you want to change the bandwidth allocation for all services.

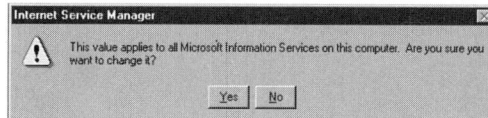

Internet Service Manager

This value applies to all Microsoft Information Services on this computer. Are you sure you want to change it?

Yes   No

If you choose No in the confirmation dialog box, the default is restored. If you choose Yes, you have the ability to adjust the Maximum Network Use, which is the maximum kilobytes of outbound traffic permitted on this computer. If you limit the amount of data that can move per second, it will lighten the load on the server. If you raise the number, the load will increase, as shown in Figure 5.28.

5. Once you've settled on the maximum kilobytes of traffic that will be allowed per second, choose Apply to update the Internet News Server and activate the new bandwidth configuration.

FIG. 5.28

Changing the default
bandwidth configura-
tion.

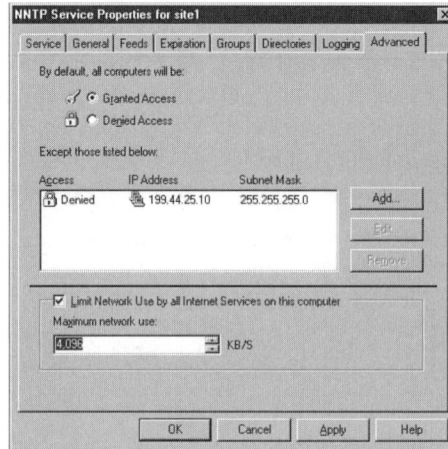

From Here...

At the conclusion of this chapter, you should have a general understanding of how to scale
servers, create newsgroups and moderated groups, apply advanced administration techniques,
and conduct performance tuning.

■ For further performance-tuning information, please refer to Que's *Special Edition Using
Microsoft BackOffice*.

Instant Communication— Microsoft Commercial Internet Mail

The most popular use of the Internet today is still e-mail. In spite of all the hype about the World Wide Web and Commerce, the Internet runs on e-mail. Any successful site must have a solid and dependable e-mail server. Savvy network administrators realize that they will get no peace if the staff's mail does not get through. To meet this need, ISPs and Network administrators require a heavy-duty reliable mail system.

For most ISPs this need is even greater because they host mail for multiple domains. Web pages and sites are filled with mail-to's and forms that require a stable mail platform. Intranets require that inner- and intra-office mail is not only reliable and user friendly, but integrate seamlessly with group scheduling and workflow applications.

Microsoft's Commercial Internet Mail Server is an Internet Standards-based electronic mail service. Built as an add-on service to Internet Information Server, the mail server can theoretically be scaled to millions of users. It is fully SMTP and POP3 compliant and supports any SMTP/POP mail clients, including the Microsoft mail client, Eudora, Netscape, and others. Since the Internet Mail Server is standards-based it eliminates the need for many gateways or format conversions.

The Microsoft Commercial Mail Server is designed to not only support systems such as CompuServe with millions of mailboxes spread over multiple servers in multiple locations, but also a corporate intranet with thousands of users in one location. However, the Mail Server's ease of use allows it to also fill the needs of smaller companies and organizations. Since it is based on established Internet Standards for Mail transport and delivery, it can be integrated into almost any situation. ■

Introducing the Mail Server Features

The Mail Server provides the following key advantages for an ISP or commercial Web site:

- *Standards support*   Mail Server provides full support for the Internet standard Simple Mail Transfer Protocol (SMTP) and Post Office Protocol, version 3 (POP3) and is fully compatible with SMTP mail clients.
- *Scalability*   It is designed for high scalability, reliability, and performance. The Mail Server can scale to support millions of users at a single data center and supports thousands of concurrent users in a single-server configuration.
- *Easy administration*   It supports management by using Microsoft Windows NT Server and Microsoft Internet Information Server administration tools.
- *Multiple security options*   It supports Internet-standard security options, Windows NT domain security, and Microsoft Distributed Password Authentication to provide secure logon and user authentication.
- *Distribution lists*   It supports creation and management of distribution mailing lists.
- *Directed mail drop and pickup*   It supports specifying drop and pickup locations for incoming and outgoing mail, respectively.

Uncovering the Mail Server Architecture

The Mail Server has four basic components:

- *Simple Mail Transport Protocol (SMTP) server*   Send and receive mail
- *SQL routing table database server*   Look up addresses and route mail messages to the correct mailbox
- *Post Office Protocol (POP3) server*   Manage the mailbox files
- *Mailbox file server*   Store mail messages in user mailboxes

Figure 6.1 shows the physical components of Mail Server.

FIG. 6.1
Here's now the various components of Mail Server are organized. Note that the numbers correspond to the Components listed in the following table.

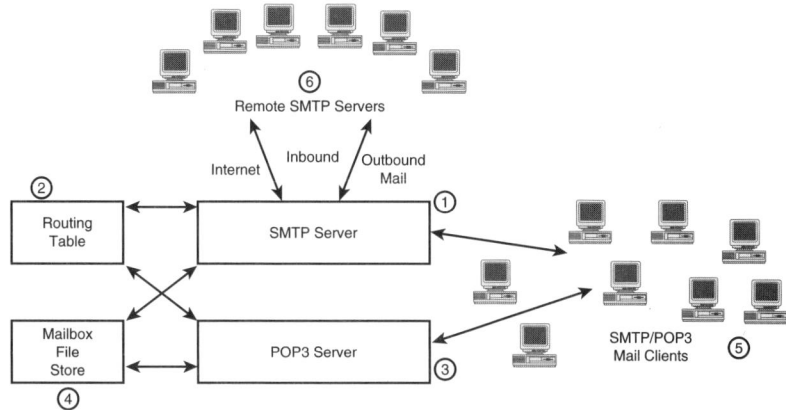

Component	Name	Description
1	SMTP server	Delivers mail for remote servers and mail clients
2	Routing table	Database that contains mailbox addresses and mailbox details such as location, size, and forwarding records
3	POP3 server	Manages the mailboxes for mail clients
4	Mailbox file store	Server where mailboxes and messages are stored
5	Mail clients	Various Internet and local SMTP/POP3-compatible clients
6	Remote SMTP servers	Servers that send and receive mail to the SMTP server

Installing Commercial Internet Mail Server

This section will walk you through setting up the Mail Server at your site. The process is divided into four steps:

- Preparing the Platform
- Running Setup
- Testing the Installation
- Cutting Over

If you have a small site, it is possible to run all of the Mail Server components on a single NT server. However, this is not recommended for sites of any size at all because the performance of the entire Mail system may suffer if individual services have to compete for system resources. In this chapter, you install the Mail Server in a two-computer scenario.

Part
II

Ch
6

Preparing the Platform

This section examines the steps required before installing the Mail Server. The Mail Server consists of several components. Review these preparation instructions carefully to assure than the minimum requirements for each component are met before proceeding.

Before You Begin

Table 6.1 gives you the minimum requirements, according to Microsoft, for each of the Mail Server components:

Table 6.1   Client Requirements

Client Type	OS Requirements	Software Requirements
User	Windows 95, Windows NT Workstation, or Windows NT Server version 3.51 or later, or any operating system that supports an SMTP/POP3 mail client	Microsoft Internet Mail and News client or any third-party SMTP/POP3 mail client
Mail Server Administrative	Windows NT Server or Windows NT Workstation version 4.0	Internet Service Manager (ISM) Microsoft Internet Information Server (IIS) version 2.0 or later Internet Service Manager Extension for Mail

You can use either the SMTP or POP3 server as the administrative client. Alternatively, you can set up the administrative client on a separate computer.

Server Requirements

The Routing Table Database Server has the following minimum requirements:

- *Processor*   Intel 486+, Digital Equipment Corporation (DEC) Alpha, or PowerPC
- *Operating system*   Windows NT Server version 4.0
- *Other software*   SQL Server version 6.5
- *Random access memory (RAM)*   16M
- *Hard drive storage*   50M of free disk space for SQL Server and basic database setup, plus 0.5G per million users

The minimum requirements for the Mailbox File Server are:

- *Processor*   Intel 486+, DEC Alpha, or PowerPC
- *Operating System*   Windows NT Server version 4.0
- *Other software*   Windows NT 4.0 Service Pack 2
- *Random access memory (RAM)*   16M
- *Hard drive storage*   Space equivalent to the number of anticipated mailbox accounts multiplied by the maximum size allowed for mailboxes, plus 30 percent for system overhead NTFS file format on the drive partition that will be used for the mail root directory (SMTP only).

The SMTP and POP3 Servers require the following minimum configuration:

- *Processor*   Intel 486+, DEC Alpha, or PowerPC
- *Operating system*   Windows NT Server version 4.0
- *Other software*   Windows NT 4.0 Service Pack 1

  Microsoft IIS version 2.0 or later with at least one service (WWW, Gopher, or FTP) installed
- *Random access memory (RAM)*   16M
- *Hard drive storage*   1G

  10M of free disk space for SMTP and POP3 program files. SMTP requires additional space for the mailroot directory; the size depends on the amount of mail that will be queued for delivery by SMTP.

N O T E   According to Microsoft, in a small Mail Server installation, all four services can operate on a computer with 16M of RAM and a 1G hard disk drive. However, realistically you would need at least 64M of RAM and 2–4G of hard drive space to achieve accepatable performance on one system.

Connectivity requirements:

- TCP/IP connectivity among all components.
- LAN connectivity between the Mail Server machines for performance and reliability.
- LAN or Windows NT Server connectivity is required between the administration client and the servers because of the use of remote procedure calls (RPC) for administration.
- Remote servers must be able to locate the local Mail Server SMTP and POP3 servers by name, and local SMTP servers must be able to locate remote servers by name. DNS must be configured with the computer name and DNS domain used by these servers
- SQL Server version 6.5 must be configured to use named pipes for network access.

Part

II

Ch

6

The Windows NT Server and IIS

Each server must have the Windows NT Server version 4.0 operating system installed. In addition, the following software requirements must be met:

- Each computer must have a unique computer name that reflects the primary function of the server. For example, you can name your servers Mail _Router, Mail _SMTP, Mail _POP3, Mail _Mailboxes. Write down the names that you use because you will need them during Mail Server setup.

- IIS must be installed on the SMTP and POP3 servers. This allows the Mail Server to communicate with the Internet.

- At least one service from IIS must be installed (WWW, FTP, or Gopher) so that files required by the Mail Server SMTP and POP3 services are properly installed.

- Internet Service Manager (ISM) must be running on at least one NT server. When you install IIS and select one of the three services required, Internet Service Manager is automatically selected for you. You can also install the ISM extension independently on a computer running Windows NT Server, Windows NT Workstation, or Windows 95. This computer can be used to administer Mail Server remotely on any server running IIS.

- The SMTP server uses the advanced file security features of the NT File System (NTFS) and will not work with the FAT file system. When installing SMTP, you must specify the hard disk drive partition that you plan to use for the mail root directory. It must be a local drive and must be formatted as NTFS. The POP3 service does not require NTFS, and works equally well on either the FAT or NTFS file formats.

- The Mail Server is designed to use the standard Internet protocol, Transport Control Protocol/Internet Protocol (TCP/IP). Install the Windows NT TCP/IP network protocol on every NT server, giving each a valid TCP/IP address. Then register each of the addresses in the Domain Name Tables for your domain.

Once all of the systems have the proper software installed and configured you are ready to begin setting up the Mail System.

▶ **See** "Installing and Configuring Windows NT 4.0," **p. 49** and "Installing and Configuring IIS," **p. 55**, for more information.

Running Setup

This section details the process of installing the Mail Server. We will look at an overview of the setup, then detail the steps to actually install and configure the Mail Server and finally present some troubleshooting steps.

Overview of the Setup Process

Mail Server Setup installs many of the Mail Server services and configures the routing table. For a single-server setup, Mail Server components can be set up in any order as long as the SMTP and POP3 services are not started until the routing table component is set up. However, for a multiple-server installation, it is recommended that you set up the routing table database server and mailbox file server before setting up SMTP and POP3 because the SMTP and POP3 setup requires information about these servers before they can be started.

The following list outlines the setup process that is detailed in the sections that follow:

1. Install SQL Server, then create the Mail Server routing table database.
2. Install the SMTP service. When asked for the SMTP mailroot directory, specify a directory located on an NTFS partition.
3. Install the POP3 service.
4. Install the Internet Service Manager Extension on a separate computer if you want to use an administrative client computer or it can be installed on either the SMTP or POP3 system.
5. Populate the routing table database with account information using the POP3 Internet Service Manager interface.

You must have the following information on hand before installing the Mail Server:

■ SMTP and POP3 mailroot directory path (where SMTP will queue mail)
■ Default domain name
■ Computer name of SQL Server computer
■ SQL Server administrator account name and password
■ Number of SMTP and POP3 servers to be installed
■ Approximate number of individual mail user and distribution list routing table entries
■ Drive and directory path for the routing table device on the computer running SQL Server
■ File name you will use for the routing table device

Setting Up SQL Server

The Mail Server routing table is stored in a SQL database. In order for it to function properly, there are several specific setup requirements for the SQL system.

1. Install Microsoft SQL Server version 6.5 on the routing table server. If you need information on how to setup SQL refer to Que's *Special Edition Using SQL Server 6.5, Second Edition*.
2. Choose the following options during the SQL installation:
   • Mail Server routing table requires a case-insensitive sort in SQL Server. The sort order you pick for SQL Server will affect the order that mail aliases are displayed on the SMTP Aliases tab in Internet Service Manager.
   • Set the MSSQLServer service and the SQLExecutive service to start automatically. In a standard Mail Server installation, all Mail Server services will start automatically when the host servers are started. The SQL Server installation does not set the database to start automatically so you should choose this option during setup.

Part
II

Ch
6

3. Install Service Pack 1 for SQL 6.5. This is available from the Microsoft Web site at **www.microsoft.com**.

4. Restart the system.

When you reboot SQL Server, check to be sure that the automatic settings are correct, and that no errors are encountered when automatically starting the services.

To check the automatic settings for MSSQLServer and SQLExecutive services, use the following procedure:

1. Log on as an administrator to the routing table server.

2. Open Control Panel and double-click the Services icon.

3. Locate the MSSQLServer and SQLExecutive services and confirm that each has a status of Started and a Startup condition of Automatic.

If the services status is Stopped, you need to set the MSSQLServer and SQLExecutive services for Automatic startup by following these steps:

1. Locate the MSSQLServer service.

2. Click Startup.

3. Click Automatic.

4. Repeat the process for the SQLExecutive service.

Once you have SQL Server installed, change the system administrator (sa) account password because by default, sa does not require a password.

To change the sa account password:

1. In SQL Server Enterprise Manager accessed from the Server menu, click Register Server to display the Register Server dialog box.

2. In the Login ID box, type **sa**.

3. Leave the Password box empty.

4. Click Close.

5. In the Server Manager window, click the plus icon (+) next to the server name, and then click the plus icon next to Logins.

6. Double-click the sa account.

7. In the Password box, type a non-null password for the sa account and then click Modify.

8. Confirm this password.

You will need this account and password later in the installation process.

SQL Server stores databases in objects called devices. The Mail Server installs a single SQL Server device, called the data device. The data device stores all the actual user data, and in the case of the routing tables, must be sized in proportion to the number of users and distribution lists it will hold. The default settings created during SQL Server setup might have to be changed to accommodate your mail site size and memory requirements.

The routing table database can be adjusted to allow for the volumes you anticipate for your mail service.

To configure SQL Server locks, open objects, and memory, use this procedure:

1. Open the SQL Server Enterprise Manager (see Figure 6.2).

FIG. 6.2
Use the SQL Enterprise Manager to configure SQL.

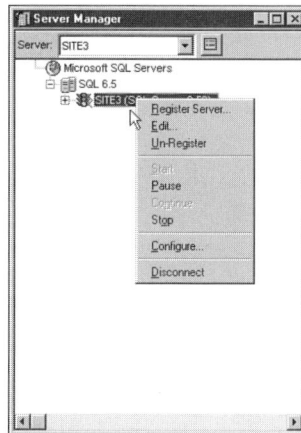

2. Right-click the newly installed server in the Server Manager window.
3. Click Configure.
4. If the newly configured server is dimmed, expand the server branch by clicking the + icon next to it. This expands and activates the server tree so you can access the server.
5. Click the Configuration tab (see Figure 6.3).

FIG. 6.3
Change the SQL configuration options to the correct Mail Server settings.

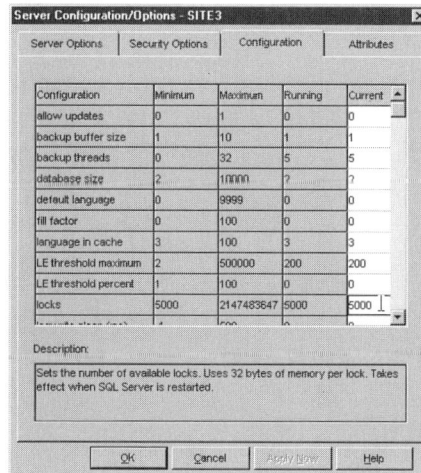

In the Configuration column change the settings in the Current column as follows:

6. Set Locks using the following formula:

 (SMTP servers + POP3 servers * 10) * 5000

 For example, using 1 SMTP server and 1 POP3 server:

 (1 +1 * 10) * 5000 = 20 * 5000 = 100,000 locks

7. Set Memory using the following formula:

Total System Memory Allocation to SQL Server	Approximate Memory
24	8
32	16
48	28
64	40
128	100
256	216
512	464

8. Set Open Objects as follows:

 (SMTP servers + POP3 servers * 10) * 400

 For example, using 1 SMTP server and 1 POP3 server:

 (1 + 1 * 10) * 400 = 20 * 400 = 8000 open objects

9. Click Apply Now and then click OK.

Review the amount of space allocated to the SQL Server temp database. Since the temp database is used for intermediate query results, it is recommended that the temp database size be proportional to the data device. Use SQL Server Enterprise Manager to reconfigure the temp database if needed.

First use the following formula to estimate the amount of disk space to allot to the temp database.

 SMTP servers * Distribution Lists (DLs) * (average number recipients per DL * average length recipient name) * 50

For example, a site has 3 SMTP servers, 75 DLs, an average DL (distribution list) size of 200 recipients with an average recipient name length of 30 bytes.

 3*75*(200*30)*50 = 11,250*(200*30) =11,250*(6000) = 67,500,000 bytes temp database = 67.5M

CAUTION

Be sure you do not attempt to create SQL devices that take up more space than you have available on your hard disk drives. SQL will attempt to create the devices and fail.

To expand the tempdb database:

1. Open the SQL Enterprise Manager.
2. Click the plus (+) icon next to the SQL Server name.
3. Click the plus (+) icon next to Databases and then double-click tempdb.
4. In the Database tab, click Expand.
5. In the Data Device box select <new> to create a new device, as shown in Figure 6.4.

FIG. 6.4

Create a new database device.

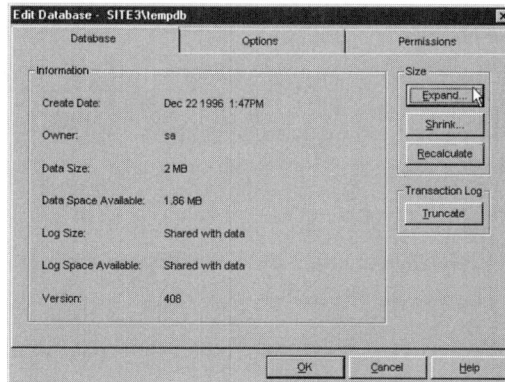

6. In the Name box, type a device name (for example, RTtempdb).
7. In the Location box, type or select the letter of the disk drive for the device, as shown in Figure 6.5.

FIG. 6.5

Configure the new database device as described previously.

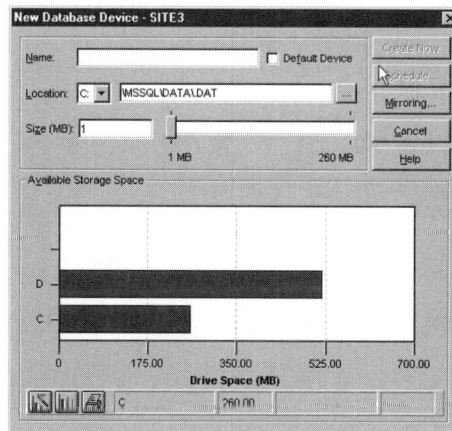

8. In the Path box, type the full path name to the device.
9. In the Size box, type the size of the device in M, or use the slider.

10. Click Create Now to create the device. When the device has been created, click OK.

11. Click Expand Now and then click OK.

Installing the Routing Table Server

Now that SQL Server has been configured, you can run the Mail Server setup program and configure the routing table database. If you are setting up Mail Server on a single server, you can run setup once to install all Mail Server components. For multiple-server setups, run Setup on each server.

The setup instructions that follow are for setting up Mail Server on two computers. The routing table will be set up on one computer and the SMTP and POP3 components will share a second computer. As mentioned earlier, the Mail Server can be set up on a single computer, in which case the Mail Server services can be installed simultaneously (that is, you need only run setup once to install all of the components on a single server).

To install the Routing Table Server complete the following steps:

1. Open the folder containing the Mail Server and launch setup.exe.

2. Complete the Licensing Agreement and Register the software in your name.

3. Choose the destination directory and then click Next (see Figure 6.6).

FIG. 6.6
Choose the location where you want to store the Mail Server files.

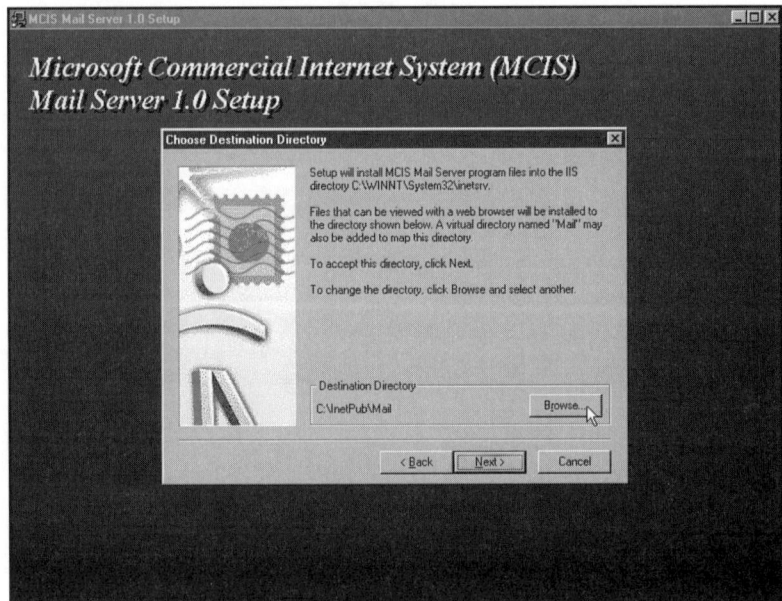

4. Select the Routing Table option, as shown in Figure 6.7, and then click Next.

FIG. 6.7
Select the components to install in the Select Components dialog box.

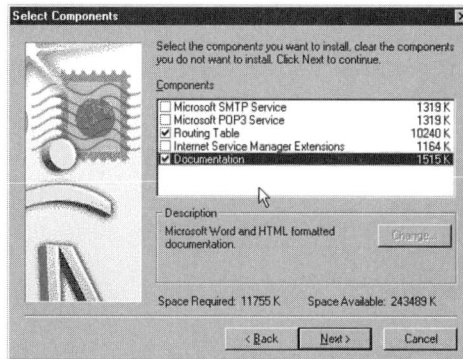

5. Fill in the appropriate Domain Name in the Default Domain Name dialog box. Click Next.

6. Complete the Specify the Database Login box (see Figure 6.8). Use the password you set up earlier in this section. Click Next.

FIG. 6.8
Specify the properly authorized database login to be used.

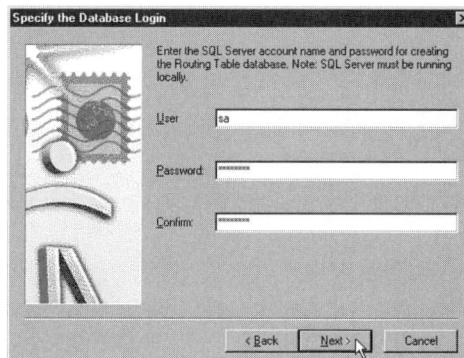

7. When the Routing Table Database Location box appears (see Figure 6.9), fill in the name of the Routing Table database, for example, Routing_Table.

FIG. 6.9
Provide the location of the Routing Table Database.

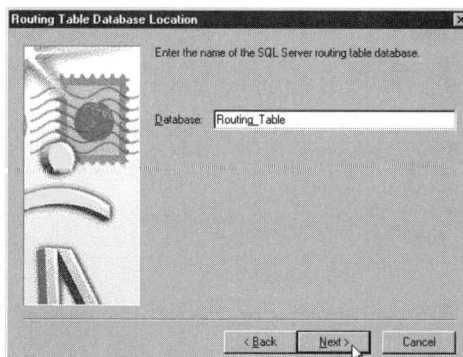

Part II Ch 6

8. Click Next, and then choose Yes when it asks if you want to create the database.

9. Enter the number of SMTP and POP3 servers in the Server Sizing Information box, as shown in Figure 6.10.

FIG. 6.10

Indicate how many servers there will be.

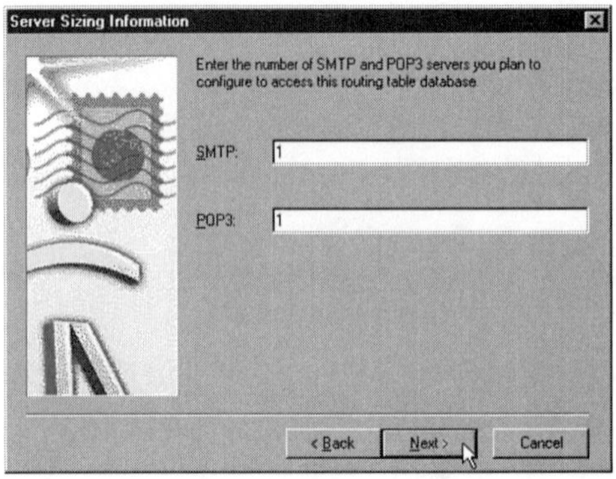

10. Click Next.

11. Enter the number of Users and Distribution Lists (Dist. Lists) you plan to service in the Routing Table Sizing Information dialog box (see Figure 6.11), and then click Next.

FIG. 6.11

Indicate how many users will be in the routing table.

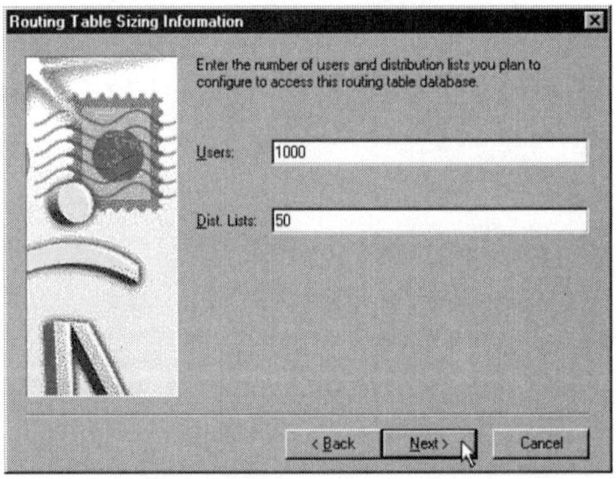

12. Enter the location of the routing table data device file in the Data Device File Configuration box and then click Next (see Figure 6.12).

13. Enter the name and size of the Routing Table file. Click Next.

14. Review the information in the Confirm Setup Information box. If there are any errors, use Back to return to the appropriate dialog box and correct them. When all information is correct, click Next.

15. Setup will copy files to your computer. When the files are copied, click Finish and Setup is complete.

FIG. 6.12

Name the Routing Table file for the current mail system.

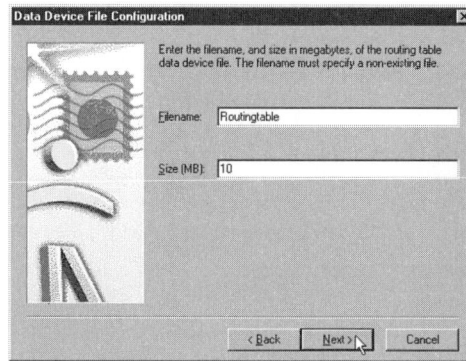

Before restarting the computer you should make two configuration changes:

- Separate your log device from the database device by using the SQL Enterprise Manager to create a new log device.
- Enable the Guest Account in the Windows NT User Manager.

To create a separate routing table log device, follow these steps:

1. Open the SQL Enterprise Manager.
2. Click the plus (+) icon by the SQL Server name.
3. Click the plus (+) icon by Databases and then double-click the Routing Table you created.
4. Click Expand.
5. In the Data Device box, select the routing table device.
6. In the Log Device box, select <new>.
7. In the Name box, type a device name (for example, RTlog).
8. In the Location box, type or select the letter of the disk drive for the device.
9. In the Path box, type the full path name to the device.
10. In the Size box, type the size of the device in M, or use the slider bar.
11. Click Create Now to create the device, as shown in Figure 6.13. When the device has been created, click OK.
12. Click Expand Now and then click OK.
13. Close the Enterprise Manager.

Next, the Guest Account must be enabled in the Windows NT User Manager. The default setup for SQL Server version 6.5 disables the Guest account. This account is needed to access a remote mail file store, and should be enabled in Windows NT Server.

Part

II

Ch

6

FIG. 6.13

Create a new Database Device.

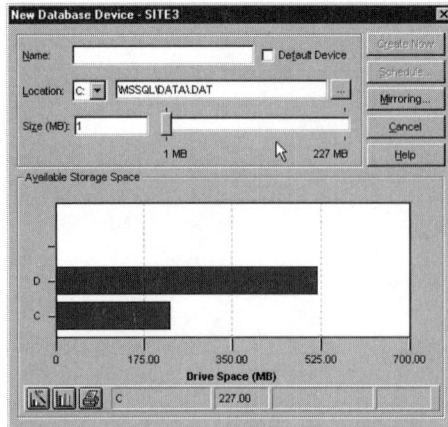

To enable the Guest account in Windows NT Server User Manager, use these steps:

1. Log on to the routing table server as local administrator.

2. Open the User Manager for Domains and double-click the Guest account, as shown in Figure 6.14.

FIG. 6.14

Enable the Guest Account in the User Properties dialog box.

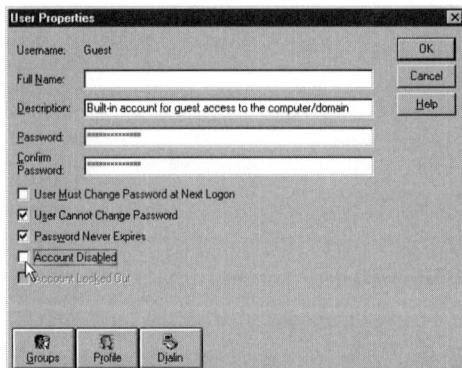

3. Clear the Account Disabled check box, and then click OK.

You have now completed the Routing Table Server installation. Restart the system and prepare to install the remaining Mail Server components.

N O T E   All of the components can be installed on one system. You should still restart the system after installing the Routing Table Server. This will make it easier for the other components to properly link to the table. ▪

Installing the SMTP and POP3 Servers

Now that the Routing Table Server has been installed, you are ready to install the SMTP and POP3 servers. In this example, they will be installed on the same computer. To install the SMTP/POP3 servers complete the following steps:

1. Insert the Mail Server CD and choose Setup.
2. Complete the Licensing Agreement and register the software in your name.
3. Choose the destination directory, and then click Next.
4. Select the all options except Routing Table, as shown in Figure 6.15. Click Next.

FIG. 6.15

Select all of the desired components in the Select Components dialog box.

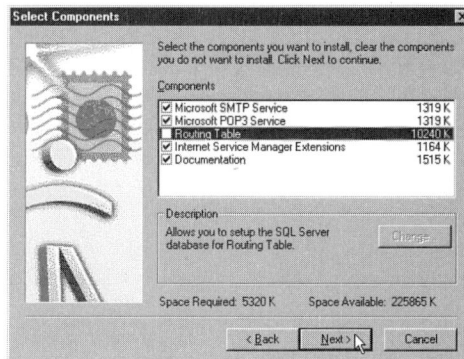

5. In the Running Services dialog box that appears, select Yes to allow the services to be shut down.
6. Select the Mail Root Directory path in the Mail Root Directory box shown in Figure 6.16, and then click Next.

FIG. 6.16

Specify the mailroot directory. This is where the Mail Server will store the actual messages.

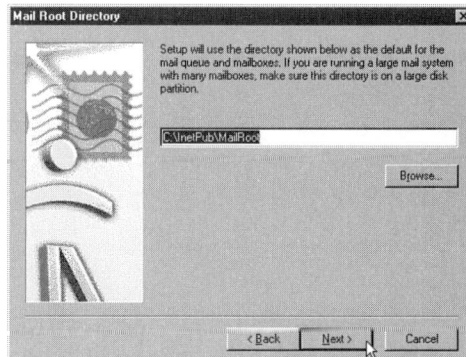

Part
II

Ch
6

7. Fill in the appropriate Domain Name in the Default Domain Name dialog box and then click Next.

8. Complete the Routing Table Database Settings dialog box (see Figure 6.17). Use the name of the system where the Routing Table is installed and the database name you selected.

FIG. 6.17

Fill in the database and system names.

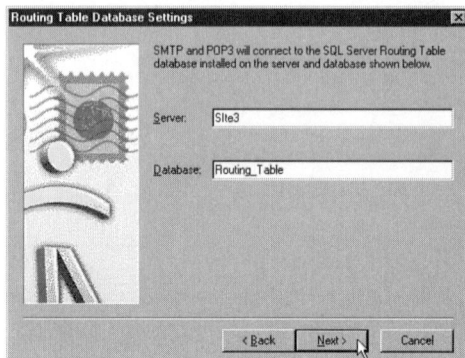

9. Enter the sa user and password from the SQL server in the Routing Table User Account Settings dialog box (see Figure 6.18). Click Next.

FIG. 6.18

Configure user account settings.

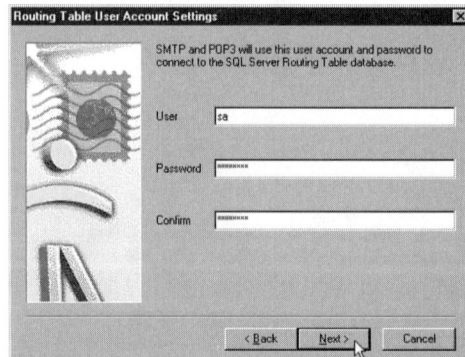

10. Select the Folder in which you want the Mail Server components to appear, and then click Next.

11. Review the information in the Confirm Setup Information box. If there are any errors Click Back to return to the appropriate dialog box and correct them. If there are no errors, click Next.

12. Setup will copy files to your computer. When this is done, click Finish and Setup is complete.

13. Restart the system.

14. After the system restarts, check the Windows NT Event Viewer to see if there were any errors during startup, then verify that SMTP and POP3 are running. To verify the services started, open the Internet Service Manager. If the SMTP and POP3 services are running then Running will be in the State column next to the services.

15. If you need to manually start a service, simply select the service you need to start by clicking the computer name next to the service. Now the service can be started by clicking the Start button.

The SMTP and POP3 components are now installed on the second system.

Setting Up an Administrative Client

If you have not already done so, you can install the administrative client on a separate computer or on either the SMTP or POP3 servers.

Setting up the administrative client involves using the Mail Server Setup program to install the Mail Server Internet Service Manager Extension.

To set up an administrative client, run Mail Server Setup on the administrative client computer. This computer must have IIS version 2.0 or later installed. Clear all of the services except Internet Service Manager Extension, then continue as you did for the SMTP and POP3 setup in the previous section.

Populating the Routing Table Database

Without data in the routing table, SMTP and POP3 will start but SMTP will not deliver any mail to the mailbox file servers. POP3 will also not allow any client connections. For configurations in which Mail Server SMTP is used as a mail router, you may have little or nothing in the routing table database. However, to properly process local mail, two sets of data must be added to the routing table database: user account names and domain names.

New user accounts can be added to the routing table by means of the SMTP Aliases tab in the Internet Service Manager administration tool.

To add user information using the Internet Service Manager administration tool, use this procedure:

1. Open the Internet Service Manager (ISM).

2. If the computer name of the server that hosts the SMTP service is not listed, click Connect to Server to connect to the desired server, as shown in Figure 6.19.

3. Double-click the SMTP server, and then click the Aliases tab.

4. Click New User, as shown in Figure 6.20.

Part

II

Ch

6

FIG. 6.19

Connect to a remote server.

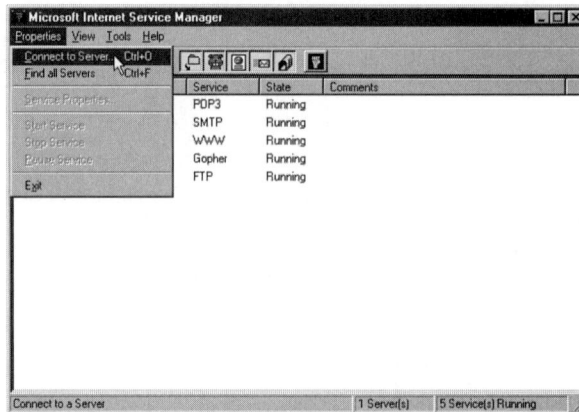

FIG. 6.20

Add new users under the Aliases tab.

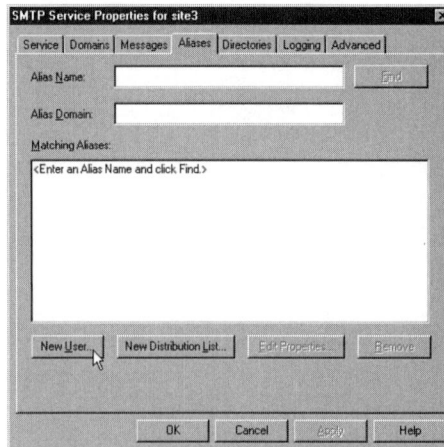

5. If the user is to have a local mailbox, click Local Address, as shown in Figure 6.21.

FIG. 6.21

Configure users and mail settings for each account.

6. In the User Name box, type the user name.

7. In the Address Domain box choose the user's domain.

8. Specify the virtual directory name in the Mailbox Virtual Root box.

9. Set the Maximum Mail Box Size to either Unlimited or the number of megabytes.

N O T E You should strongly consider limiting the size of most mailboxes. Otherwise, an errant user could eat up significant space. ■

10. If the user has a mailbox on some other mail system, click Remote Address and then enter the Address Domain.

11. Click the Auto Forward button if mail is to be forwarded for the user.

12. If Auto Forward is chosen, fill in the Forward Name and the Forward Domain.

13. Click OK and the user is created.

By using the Internet Service Manager, you can add new local domains to the routing table. Local Domains are the domains for which the SMTP service processes mail.

To add a local domain using the Internet Service Manager; follow these steps:

1. Open the Internet Service Manager.

2. If the computer name of the server that hosts the SMTP service is not listed, click Connect to Server to connect to the desired server.

3. Double-click your SMTP server.

4. On the SMTP properties page, click the Domains tab shown in Figure 6.22, and then click Add (as shown in Figure 6.23).

FIG. 6.22

Configure Mail domains under the Domains tab.

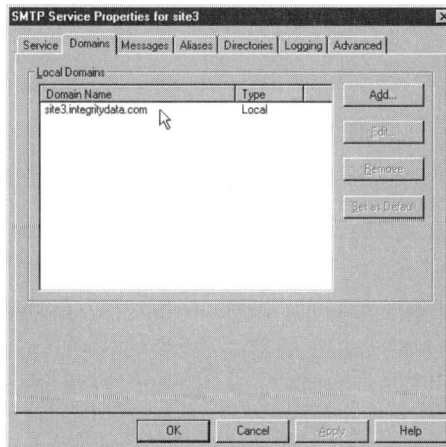

Part

II

Ch

6

5. In the Domain Properties dialog box, type the name of the domain. Click OK.

FIG. 6.23

Add new domain names
in the Domain
properties box.

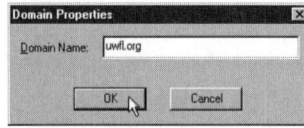

6. If you want the new domain to be the default domain, select the newly added domain in the list and then click Set As Default.

7. Click OK.

N O T E   In order for a POP mail user to read mail, the user must have a Windows NT account on the POP mail server. This account should not have local logon privileges. ▪

You have now finished installing and configuring the Mail Server. Now let's move on to testing the installation.

Testing the Mail Server Installation

The first step in testing the installation is to open the Internet Services Manager and verify that the SMTP and POP3 services are running. If the server on which the Mail Server SMTP and POP3 services are installed does not appear on the list of servers and services, click Connect to Server to connect to the server hosting the SMTP or POP3 services.

Now, view the services installed on the server. Find the Mail Server SMTP or POP3 service and double-click it. If the service is functioning properly, a Properties dialog box appears with the Service tab on the far left.

If Mail Server SMTP or POP3 are not displayed, then Setup was not completed successfully.

Testing the Servers

Now that the services are set up, they should be used to try sending and receiving mail. To test that a client can send and receive mail use a POP3 mail client such as the Microsoft Internet Mail and News client shown in Figure 6.24, install the client on a system that has TCP/IP connectivity to the Mail Servers. Send a message to your own account, wait a few seconds, and then download the mail.

If no mail arrives, check the event logs on the computers that are running the SMTP and POP3 services. Look specifically for a message such as SMTP failed to start. Also, check the \badmail directory on the computer that is running the SMTP service and read the *.ltr and *.rtr files for troubleshooting information.

FIG. 6.24
Send and receive mail
with POP3 clients.

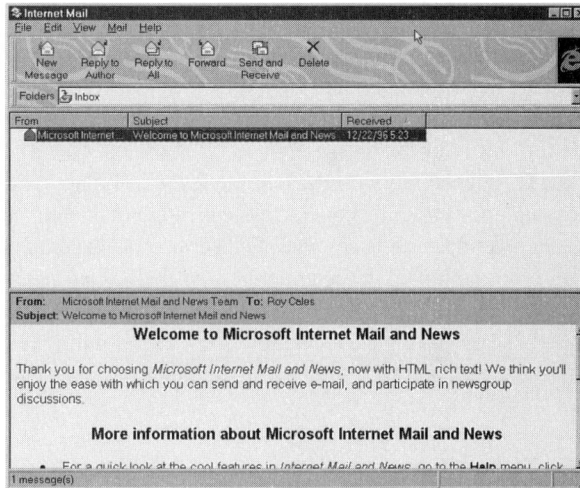

Troubleshooting Your Mail Server Installation

There are some common installation errors that can cause your system to malfunction:

■ *One of the two services is not installed properly*

Because Mail Server has two services, SMTP and POP3, both must be functioning properly in order for mail to flow through the system. Mail clients use the SMTP service only when sending mail. If the POP3 service is functioning properly while the SMTP service is not functioning properly, no mail is delivered to the user's mailbox. Therefore, a proper test includes both sending and receiving a mail message from a mail client. For a newly installed system, the mail message should appear in a few seconds. If this is not the case, then it is likely that there is an installation problem.

■ *The default domain for POP3 is incorrect*

A common installation problem is specifying the wrong default domain for the POP3 service. If SMTP is configured with test1.com as the default domain but the POP3 service uses test2.com as the default domain, then mail sent to the user Courtney@test1.com will not be retrievable with the POP3 server because the POP3 protocol does not allow the specification of the domain for the user connecting to the service. The Mail Server POP3 service receives the Courtney user identifier but incorrectly assumes that the domain is test2.com. If there is no such user as Courtney@test2.com, then POP3 will return an error stating that the user inbox could not be found. In this scenario, for Courtney to receive mail, either the POP3 service default domain would have to be test1.com, or the alias Courtney@test1.com would have to be changed on the test2.com POP3 server to Courtney@test2.com.

Part

II

Ch

6

■ *Mailbox locations are incorrectly defined for multiple local domains*

Sites that have configured multiple local domains often have installation problems. A local domain is a domain serviced by SMTP for local users. If a user can't be found at a local domain, then SMTP will not attempt further delivery and will return a nondelivery report to the author of the message stating that the user does not exist. A feature of Mail Server SMTP is the ability to service multiple local domains with a single SMTP server. However, you must carefully configure the location of mailboxes for different local domains. For example, consider an SMTP server that is configured with the two local domains a.com and b.com. If the administrator defines a Gareth@a.com and a Gareth@b.com, the administrator must specify a different virtual root for the mailbox location if these two users are indeed different users. If the same virtual root is used for both Gareth@a.com and Gareth@b.com, then mail to either user will end up in the same mailbox.

Servicing Users

The final step in the installation process is "going live." What good would a Mail Server be if it did not allow real-world users to send and receive mail?

This section provides procedures for switching the Mail Server from a testing environment to full production. It details the setup, configuration, and testing issues that must be addressed in order to "go live." When this is completed, the Mail Server should be fully available to users.

In order to make the Mail Server available it may be necessary to reconfigure routers, set up a firewall, or reconfigure the access rights on your Mail Server installation.

Before you continue, identify the group of users that will be using the Mail Server, and identify the critical nodes (firewalls, DNS servers, routers, and so on) in the network path between your Internet users and Mail Server. All of these nodes will have to be configured to allow client access to the Mail Server.

Reconfiguring for Live Service

Several changes must be made to the configuration before going live:

1. Add an entry that maps the Mail Server computer names to their IP addresses in your DNS tables.

2. Confirm that the DNS recognizes the Mail Servers by pinging the named systems.

   Ensure that Mail Server packets can pass through the firewall. The Mail Server accepts SMTP packets on server port 25 and POP3 packets on port 110. If you want to expose the Mail Servers to users outside the firewall, your firewall needs to be configured to pass packets on these ports through to the Mail Servers.

   ▶ For information on configuring DNS and firewalls see the documentation provided with the services. For information on configuring Microsoft Proxy Server see Chapter 17, "Using the Microsoft Proxy Server."

3. Reconfigure the Mail Server security settings:

   Open the Internet Service Manager (ISM).

   Select the POP3 server.

   Click Service Properties.

   Click the Service tab.

   In the Password Authentication dialog box (see Figure 6.25), set the authentication mechanisms that POP3 will allow: Basic and/or Challenge/Response.

FIG. 6.25
Select the user authentication method under the Password Authentication option.

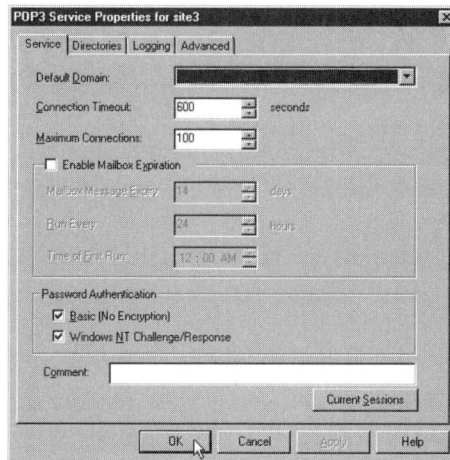

Now, restart the Mail Server Systems, and the Mail Servers will be in production mode.

You can confirm that the cutover process was successful by having the same access that your user base has to a server. For example, if your Mail Server users all sit outside the company firewall, you will need to test the setup using the same access, then run through some of the same tests that used for the Mail Server installation.

▶ **See** "Testing the Mail Server Installation," **p. 146**

Troubleshooting the Cutover Process

If you find that your intended users are not able to access the Mail Server, check for the following conditions:

■ Confirm that the client system is set up properly and that the mail client has been properly configured.

■ Client computers are not able to see the Mail Server computer on the network. You can test this by pinging the server by computer name (not by IP address) from the client machine. If pinging the server name is unsuccessful, DNS is probably not configured correctly.

Part
II

Ch
6

- If client computers can successfully ping the server but still cannot use Mail Server, be sure the firewall, if any, is allowing SMTP and POP3 packets through.

- If the firewall is properly configured but users still cannot access Mail Server, be sure the users have security rights that satisfy the security requirements you set.

- Be certain that the user has an NT account on the POP server.

When you have completed all of these steps you will have a full production Mail system. Next, we will look at some of the day-to-day administration requirements of the Mail Server.

Administering the Internet Mail Server

A reliable mail system is the backbone of Internet and intranet sites. Nothing bothers users more than not having access to their e-mail when they want it. The Mail Server provides a stable environment but no matter how reliable the engine, daily maintenance is required. In this section, we will look at some of the basic fundamentals of administering the Mail Server.

Starting, Pausing, and Stopping Mail Server Services

Although the default configuration for Mail Server is to start automatically when the server starts, the services can be manually stopped and restarted. The default can also be changed to require that the service be started manually. However, once Mail Server is in operation, stopping, pausing, and restarting services must be done carefully so that users are not affected.

You use the Internet Service Manager (ISM) to stop, pause, and start the SMTP or POP3 services. You use the Services icon in Control Panel to change the default setting for how services are started when the system is turned on. The options are Automatic, Manual, or Disabled.

All IIS computers on an organization's network can be stopped, paused, and restarted remotely from any computer on which Internet Service Manager (ISM) is installed. In order to administer Mail Server remotely, the user running ISM must be defined in the Windows NT accounts database as an administrator of the remote computer.

Changing the functional status of Mail Server services while they are in service involves the following tasks:

- Manually starting Mail Server
- Manually pausing Mail Server
- Manually stopping Mail Server
- Starting and stopping multiple servers
- Smart bleeding of user connections

The following procedures provide information for starting, pausing, and stopping the Mail Server services using ISM or the command line.

Manually Starting Mail Server Services   To manually start or stop the SMTP or POP3 services, you can use either ISM or the net start command. Before starting either the SMTP or POP3 services, check that SQL Server is running on the computer hosting the routing table database. Use SQL Enterprise Manager to connect to the computer running SQL Server, and check to be sure that the status light is green.

The SMTP and POP3 services can be stopped in any order.

To manually start the SMTP or POP3 service using ISM, follow these steps:

1. Open the Internet Service Manager (ISM).
2. If the computer on which you want to run the SMTP or POP3 service is not the local computer, click Connect to Server to connect to the remote server.
3. Click the SMTP or POP3 service and then click the Start button on the ISM toolbar. Alternatively, click the service, and then click Start on the popup menu.

To manually start the SMTP service using the command line, at the command prompt on the SMTP server, type

> net start smtpsvc

To manually start the POP3 service using the command line, at the command prompt on the POP3 server, type

> net start pop3svc

Manually Pausing Mail Server Services   Use the following procedures to pause the Mail Server services for updates or maintenance on either the local or a remote computer. Pausing prevents new client connections, but continues to service existing client connections, as well as allowing SMTP to deliver queued mail.

To manually pause the SMTP or POP3 service using ISM, use this procedure:

1. Open the Internet Service Manager (ISM).
2. If the computer on which you want to pause the SMTP service is not the local computer, on the ISM Properties menu, click Connect to Server to connect to the remote server.
3. Click the SMTP or POP3 service.
4. Click the Pause button on the ISM toolbar. You can also pause the service by right-clicking the service and clicking Pause in the popup menu.

To manually pause the SMTP or POP3 service using the command line, at the command prompt on the SMTP or POP3 server, type **net pause smtpsvc** or **net pause pop3svc**, whichever applies.

Part
II

Ch
6

Manually Stopping Mail Server Services   Use the following procedures to stop the Mail Server services for updates or maintenance on either the local or a remote computer.

To manually stop the SMTP or POP3 service using ISM, follow these steps:

1. Open the Internet Service Manager (ISM).
2. If the computer on which you want to stop the SMTP service is not the local computer, on the ISM Properties menu, click Connect to Server to connect to the remote server.
3. Click the SMTP or POP3 service
4. Click the Stop button in the ISM toolbar. You can stop the service by right-clicking the service and clicking Stop in the popup menu.

To manually stop the SMTP or POP3 service using the command line, at the command prompt on the SMTP or POP3 server, type **net stop smtpsvc** or **net stop pop3svc**, whichever applies.

Clearing the Mail Server Before Shutting Down   All servers must be periodically taken out of service for maintenance, during which time clients are unable to connect. For large sites with multiple SMTP and POP3 servers, client service does not have to be interrupted if you have proper Domain Name Service (DNS) configuration. That is, by having the DNS name for both the SMTP and POP3 services resolve to multiple servers, or by defining proper MX records, one server can be taken out of service while the other servers continue to accept client connections. This process involves removing the server from new client connections while allowing existing clients to clear.

The process for clearing users from either the SMTP or POP3 service is the same. If both services are running on the same server, it is necessary to perform the steps for both SMTP and POP3 individually before moving to the next step.

To clear user connections from the Mail Server SMTP and POP3 services:

1. Open the Internet Service Manager (ISM).
2. Pause the SMTP or POP3 service as previously described. Pausing prevents new client connections, but continues to service existing client connections.
3. Double-click the SMTP or POP3 service.
4. On the SMTP or POP3 Service tab (see Figure 6.26), click Current Sessions to monitor the number of client connections to the service.

When the number of client connections is zero, it is safe to shut down the server.

FIG. 6.26

Current users can be viewed under the Service tab.

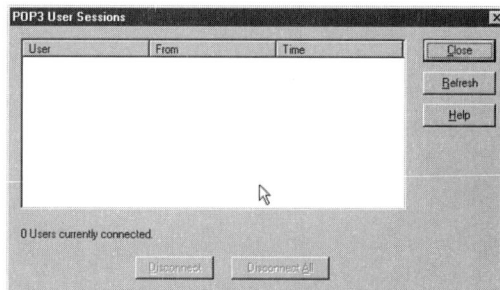

Configuring Mail Server Options

Configuring the Mail Server involves setting and updating the configuration options. You can configure Mail Server using a variety of administration tools, including Windows-based and command-line tools.

The Mail Server provides two sets of commands to administer and configure services. Each Mail Server service has a Windows-based graphical user interface (GUI) tool and a command-line administration tool to carry out the administration commands.

The Mail Server administration tools can be used to remotely configure Mail Server components from any computer running Windows NT Server version 4.0 and IIS version 2 or later. The remote administration is done via the Remote Procedure Call (RPC) protocol.

Configuring the Mail Server involves the following administrative tasks:

- Configuring SMTP/POP3 services
- Configuring SMTP local domains
- Configuring SMTP message parameters
- Configuring SMTP aliases

Configuring SMTP Services

Both SMTP and POP3 have a Service property page in ISM where you can review or update service settings. This section looks at configuring SMTP to the needs of your site.

To configure SMTP services using ISM, follow these steps:

1. Open the Internet Service Manager (ISM).
2. Locate the SMTP or POP3 server to be configured. If the server is not listed, on the Properties menu, click Connect to Server to add the server to the list.
3. Double-click the SMTP or POP3 service that you want to configure.

   The SMTP Service Properties box will open.

Part

II

Ch

6

The Service Tab   Under the Service tab (see Figure 6.27), you configure the basic SMTP service:

- *Connection Time-out*   Allows you to set the number of seconds the server will keep an idle connection before killing the connection
- *Maximum Incoming Connections box*   Allows you to limit the number of simultaneous incoming connections
- *The Maximum Outgoing Connections box*   Allows you to do the same for outgoing connections
- *The Badmail Directory*   The directory where SMTP will place any mail that fails to deliver

N O T E   This is a good directory to keep an eye on, especially at first. If you see a lot of material being dumped here, it's a good sign you have a problem somewhere. ■

FIG. 6.27

SMTP service configuration tab.

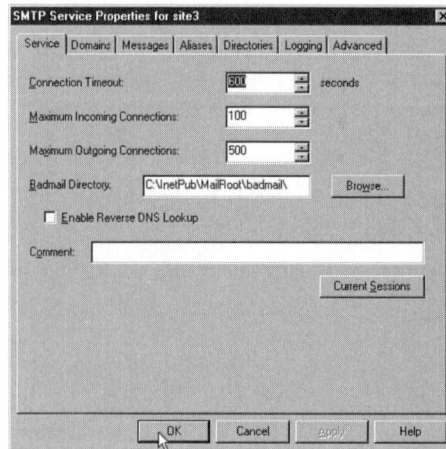

- *The Enable Reverse DNS Lookup box*   Allows you to force the Mail Server to use reverse ARP before accepting mail
- *The Current Sessions button* Opens the SMTP User Sessions box (see Figure 6.28), where you can monitor current connections

FIG. 6.28

Current SMTP user sessions can be monitored in the SMTP User Sessions dialog box.

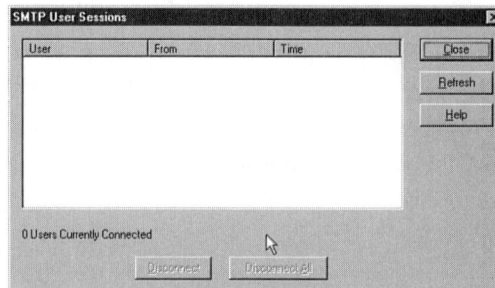

The Domains Tab   Under the Domains Tab (see Figure 6.29), you configure the Domains serviced by SMTP.

FIG. 6.29

The Domain tab is where you can configure the SMTP domains.

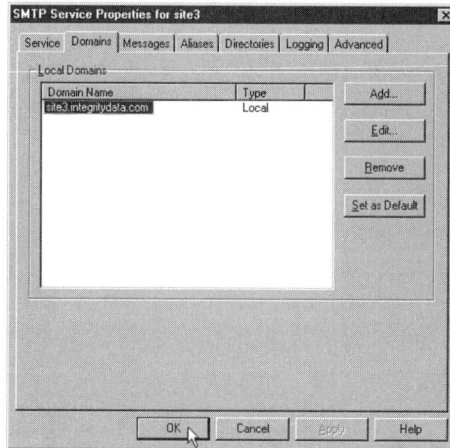

- Use the A**dd** button to add Domains in the Domain Properties box.
- Use the E**dit** button to change the name of a Domain, as shown in Figure 6.30.

FIG. 6.30

Edit SMTP Domain names.

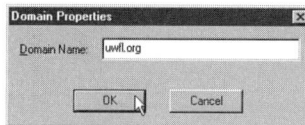

- Use the **Remove** button to delete Domains.
- Use the **Set** as the Default.

The Messages Tab   The Messages Tab is where allowed message parameters are set (see Figure 6.31).

- *The Postmaster Display Name*   Sets the preferred name to be displayed as the Postmaster
- *The Postmaster Mail Alias*   Sets the account which will receive all mail for the Postmaster
- *The Limit Message Size checkbox*   Allows you to limit the size of messages accepted by the mail server
- *Maximum Message Size box*   Allows you to limit the size of each mail message and the Maximum Session Size limits the total size of all messages transacted in a single session
- *Maximum Message Recipients*   Limits the number of addresses to which a single e-mail can be sent

Part

II

Ch

6

FIG. 6.31

The Messages tab.

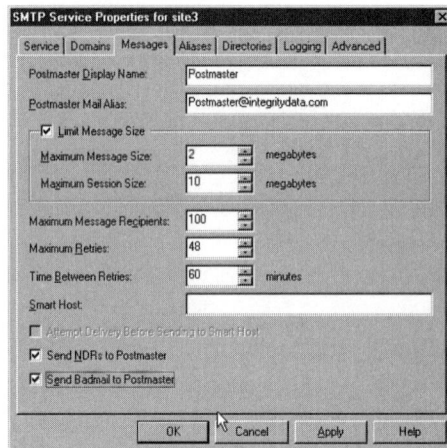

T I P Be sure to set some limit on the number of addresses. This can help knock out spam.

■ *Time Between Retries* Determines how long the SMTP service waits, after an unsuccessful delivery attempt, before trying again

■ *Send NDRs to Postmaster* Allows you to receive a report of any failed deliveries

■ *Send Badmail to Postmaster* Automatically sends all non-deliverable mail to the Postmaster

---

T I P Sending bad mail to the Postmaster can result in an admin getting overwhelmed by e-mail. It is much better to get an NDR report and check the badmail directory.

The Aliases Tab The Aliases Tab is used for adding and editing users and creating distribution lists. Adding users was covered previously in "Populating the Routing Table Databases."

If you want to edit a user's properties, follow these steps:

1. Enter the name in the Alias Name box.
2. Locate the user by clicking the Find button. This will highlight the appropriate user.
3. Click the Edit Properties button. The User Properties box appears, as shown in Figure 6.32. You can only edit two properties here.

The Maximum Mailbox Size can be set to Unlimited or a specific number of megabytes.

You can also set mail to Auto Forward. If you select to forward mail then you need to fill in the Forward Name and the Forward Domain boxes.

FIG. 6.32

Edit user properties.

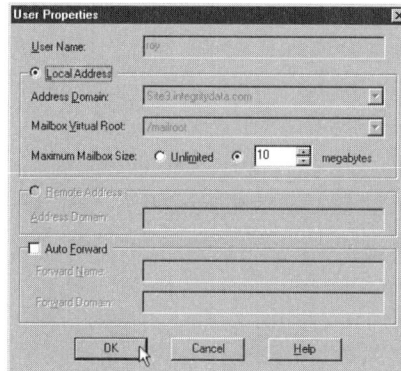

To create a Distribution List click the New Distribution List button under the Alias Tab. The Distribution List Properties dialog box will open in which you set up and administer mailing lists.

FIG. 6.33

Create mailing lists.

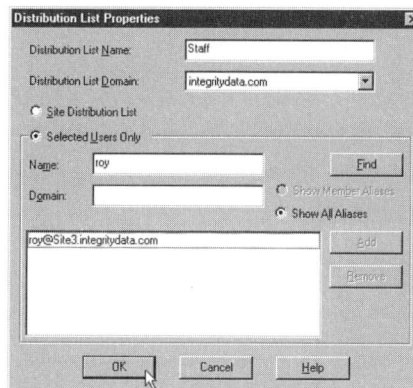

1. Fill in the name of the mailing list in Distribution List Name (refer to Figure 6.33).
2. Enter the domain in which the list is stored in Distribution List Domain.
3. Activate Site Distribution List if you want the list to include all users with an account on this server.
4. Activate Selected Users Only if you want to designate members of the list. If you choose to select members, enter the user name in the Name box and click the Find button to display user aliases with that name.
5. Use the Domain box to specify a domain for the user.
6. Activate the Show All Aliases box if you want aliases from all Domains to be displayed.

Part

II

Ch

6

7. To list members of the distribution list only, check the Show Members Only box, and then highlight the users you want to add to the DL and click the Add button.

8. To remove a user from a DL, highlight the user and click the Remove button.

9. Click OK and the Distribution List will be created or modified.

The Directories Tab The Directories Tab is where the SMTP directories are managed and where you can add a Routing Table to the SMTP service.

Figure 6.34 shows a listing of all SMTP directories where mail is stored is in the Directory list. If only the mailroot directory is listed, then all mail is stored under that directory.

FIG. 6.34

View a list of current mail directories under the Directories tab.

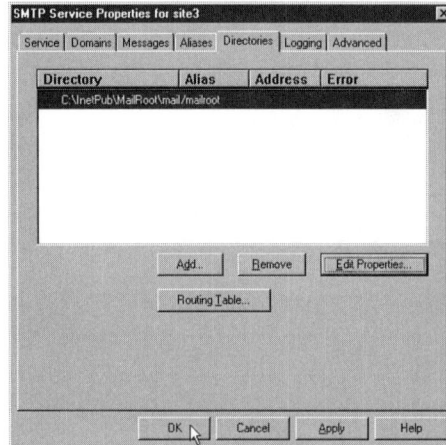

To add a new mail directory, click the Add button. The Directory Properties dialog box will open. This is where you can configure a new mail directory; follow these steps:

1. The Directory box, as shown in Figure 6.35, is where you designate the path for the new mail directory. Check the Home Directory box if this is the actual directory.

FIG. 6.35

The Directory Properties dialog box.

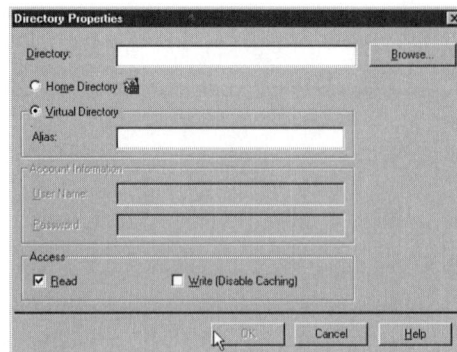

CAUTION

Other IIS services use the Home directory function. SMTP should not be configured to use the Home Directory.

2. Activate Virtual Directory if you are creating a virtual mail directory. In the Alias box, provide the alias name or the virtual directory.

3. In the Access section, configure the directory for either Read or Write access.

4. Click OK and the directory will be created.

The Directories Tab also allows you to either Edit a directory or Remove a directory by clicking the appropriate button. Editing a directory utilizes the same Directory Properties box as adding a directory.

If you need to configure the Routing Tables that the SMTP service utilizes, click the Routing Table button under the Directories tab. The Routing Table List box will open and display a list of all current routing tables (see Figure 6.36).

FIG. 6.36

Add or edit routing tables.

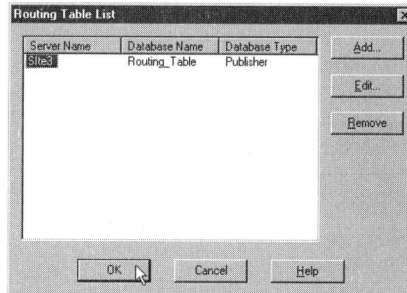

To add a Routing Table, follow these steps:

1. Click the Add button. The Routing Table Properties dialog box will open (see Figure 6.37).

FIG. 6.37

Configure routing tables for SMTP.

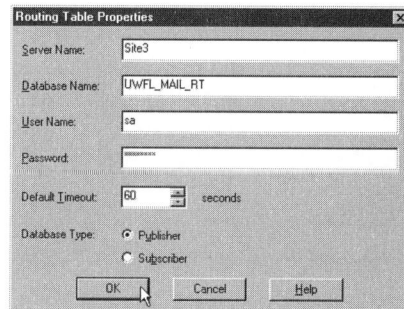

Part
II

Ch
6

2. Type the name of the routing table server in the Server Name box.

3. Fill in the Database Name box.

4. Specify the user who will administer the routing table in the User Name box. Remember, this user needs administrative rights.

5. Put the user password in the Password box.

6. Limit the database time-out in the Default Timeout box.

7. Set the type of database to either Publisher or Subscriber in the Database Type boxes.

8. Click OK and the routing table will be configured.

To edit a Routing Table, highlight the chosen table, choose the Edit button to display the Routing Table Properties box, then edit the settings as described previously.

To delete a Routing Table highlight the table and click the Remove button.

CAUTION

Be very careful deleting Routing Tables. Other SMTP or POP3 servers may be linked to the same Routing Table.

When you are finished, close the Routing Table Properties dialog box.

The Logging Tab   The logging feature with the Internet Mail Server provides valuable information about the server usage. Figure 6.38 shows the Logging tab, where you can configure logging for your site.

FIG. 6.38

Logging can be configured under the Logging tab.

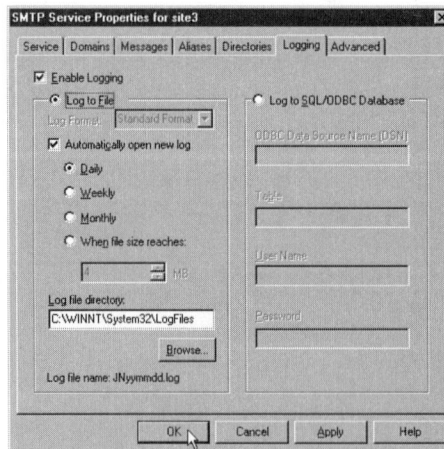

- If you check the Enable Logging box the server will build a plain text log file based on the criteria you select.

- Choose the interval for logging: Daily, Weekly, Monthly or When File Size Reaches a certain size.

- In the Log File Directory box, specify the directory containing all log files.

- The log files can be sent to an Open Data Base Connectivity (ODBC)–supported database. Select this option by checking the Log to SQL/ODBC Database box. This may come in handy when running multiple servers or services on a network. The activities of all servers can be logged to a single file or database on any network computer. To successfully log to an ODBC data source, specify the ODBC Data Source Name (DSN), the Table name, and the valid User name and Password for the database.

When the logging is configured, click the OK button to move on to the Advanced options.

The Advanced Tab Select the Advanced Tab, as shown in Figure 6.39, to control access configuration. Here, you have the option to set access by specific IP address and block individuals or groups from gaining access to your server. To control the maximum amount of traffic on your server, you can also set the maximum network bandwidth for outbound traffic.

FIG. 6.39

Set server access rights under the Advanced tab.

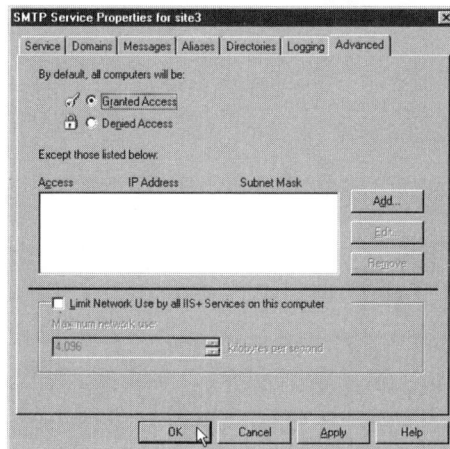

- Select the Granted Access radio button to grant access to all computers. If you need to deny access to some computers, click the Add button.

- Select the Denied Access option to deny all computers. To then grant access to some computers, click the Add button.

- You may also Limit Network Use by All Internet Services on This Computer by clicking in the check box and enter a number for Maximum network use by limiting the network bandwidth allowed for all of the Internet services on the server. Set the maximum kilobytes per second of outbound traffic permitted on this computer.

Part

II

Ch

6

CAUTION

If you choose to limit the bandwidth, you are cautioned that this value applies to *all* Microsoft Information Services on this computer, and not just the Mail Server.

Click OK and configuring the SMTP server is complete. Restart the system so that all changes can take effect.

Configuring POP3 Services

To configure POP3 services using ISM, use this procedure:

1. Open the Internet Service Manager (ISM).

2. Locate the POP3 server to be configured. If the server is not listed, choose Properties, Connect to Server to add the server to the list.

3. Double-click the POP3 service that you want to configure and the POP3 Service Properties dialog box, as shown in Figure 6.40, will appear.

FIG. 6.40

The POP3 Service Properties sheet is where you configure the POP3 server.

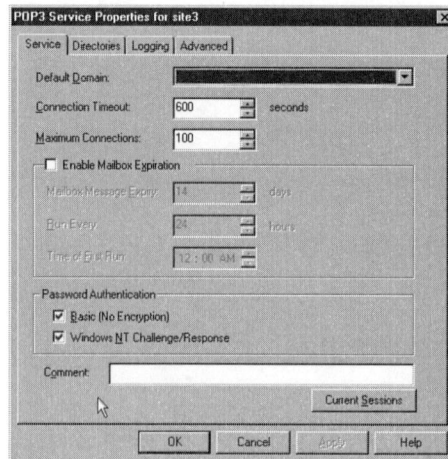

The Service Tab   The Service tab allows you to configure the basic POP3 parameters:

- Use Default Domain to specify the default for users of this POP3 service. If no domain is specified, the POP3 service will attempt to deliver the mail to the default domain.

- Specify a time-out value for POP3 clients by using the Connection Timeout box. Any connection that is idle for longer than this value will be dropped.

- The Maximum Connections box limits the number of simultaneous connection allowed for the POP3 service.

- Activate the Enable Mailbox Expiration to schedule mail expiration. Set the maximum mail age in the Mailbox Message Expiry box.

- Schedule how often to expire mailboxes in the Run Every box.

- Set the original start time in the Time of First Run box.

N O T E Expiring mailboxes can reduce the amount of mailbox file storage space required. However, be careful to allow your users plenty of time to access and respond to their e-mail. Many sites choose to expire mail every 30–45 days. ▨

■ Choose the type of authentication in the Password Authentication box: Basic or Windows NT Challenge/Response. Remember that not all POP3 clients support Challenge/Response authentication.

When you have finished with Services, click OK to apply your changes.

The Directories Tab The Directories Tab is where the POP3 directories are managed and where you can add a Routing Table to the POP3 service. To configure the Directories tab under POP3, use the same technique discussed previously in "Configuring SMTP Directories Tab." Follow these steps:

1. In the Directory box, designate the path for the new mail directory. Check the Home Directory box if this is the actual directory.

2. Activate Virtual Directory if you are creating a virtual mail directory. In the Alias box, provide the alias name or the virtual directory.

3. In the Access section, configure the directory for either Read or Write access.

4. Click OK and the directory will be created.

The Directories Tab also allows you to Edit or Remove a directory.

The Logging Tab To configure the Logging tab under POP3 use the following technique:

1. Check the Enable Logging box and the server will build a plain text log file based on the criteria you select.

2. Choose the interval for logging: Daily, Weekly, Monthly, or When File Size Reaches a certain size.

3. In the Log File Directory box, specify the directory containing all log files.

4. To send log files to an Open Data Base Connectivity (ODBC)–supported database the Log to SQL/ODBC Database box. To successfully log to an ODBC data source, specify the ODBC Data Source Name (DSN), the Table name, and the valid User name and Password for the database.

When the logging is configured, click the OK button to move on to the Advanced options.

The Advanced Tab To configure the Directories tab under POP3 use the same technique discussed previously in the Configuring SMTP Logging Tab section.

When you are finished configuring the POP3 services click OK and then restart the POP3 server.

Part
II

Ch
6

From Here...

This chapter covered a basic overview of the Internet Mail Server and how to install and configure it. It then covered some of the basic configuration and administration of the Mail Server.

■ Chapter 7, "Advanced Internet Mail Server Administration," covers logging, monitoring, and backing up the Mail Server along with other more advanced Mail Topics.

■ If you need more information on Using or Configuring Windows NT or IIS, see Chapter 3, "Building the Foundation," or for even more in-depth coverage see Que's *Special Edition Using Windows NT 4.0* or *Special Edition Using Internet Information Server*.

Advanced Internet Mail Server Administration

Monitor Mail Server performance

Learn how to gauge the health of your mail system. Test system performance with Performance monitor and other tools.

Maintain Mail Server logs

See how to set up Mail Server logs using text files or third-party products.

Protect your mail with proper backups

Learn how to perform a proper backup and restoration of your e-mail and mailboxes. See how to prevent the nightmare of restoring lost files.

One of the most important parts of any Internet or intranet site is e-mail. If an administrator cannot provide a stable and dependable mail system he will probably quickly find himself job hunting. Most e-mail systems are extremely difficult to manage. Ask any UNIX administrator what his least favorite thing to do is and you will very likely hear about the sendmail.cf file. Many administrators throw up their hands at the thought of having to edit that file. Many newer programs have simpler interfaces but lack all the tools necessary to run a busy site.

Microsoft has taken a huge step in reducing the pain and suffering required of mail administrators. The Microsoft Internet Mail Server is one of the easiest and most robust systems available. In this section we will look at some the more advanced areas of administering the Mail Server such as:

- Monitoring the Mail Server
- Maintaining the Mail Server logs
- Backing up and restoring mailboxes and routing tables

When you are finished with this chapter and Chapter 6, "Instant Communication—Microsoft Commercial Internet Mail Server," you will be ready to implement the Mail Server at your location. ■

Monitoring Mail Server

Administration of any server begins with monitoring. If you are not aware that something is wrong, you can't fix it. In this section you look at monitoring:

- Stability
- Configuration
- Performance
- Capacity
- Security

Monitoring Service Stability

Monitoring the stability of the Mail Server services is critical to maintaining performance. Monitoring informs you which services are running at a given time and if the service has frozen or failed.

The Mail Server SMTP and POP3 services are both TCP/IP services. Windows NT comes with several utilities that are useful for monitoring services based on TCP/IP, such as ping and Telnet. Also, the Windows NT Performance Monitor and Windows NT Event Viewer are tools for monitoring services.

Monitoring service stability involves the following tasks:

- Running the ping command
- Running the telnet command
- Consulting event logs using Windows NT Event Viewer
- Consulting Windows NT Performance Monitor

Running Ping   Ping is a command-line tool used to determine if there are network problems between different components of the system. Ping can be used between Mail Server components, such as the SMTP/POP3 services and the SQL Server routing table or mailbox file servers.

A failure to connect to the server causes ping to return an error result. Always ping by IP address first to determine whether you have network connectivity.

To use ping:

- Go to a Windows NT command prompt.
- Type **ping ###.###.###.###** (the Internet protocol address of the remote system).
- Or you can type **ping computer_name** (the name of the remote system).
- Then press Enter. If successful, the reply shown in Figure 7.1 appears.

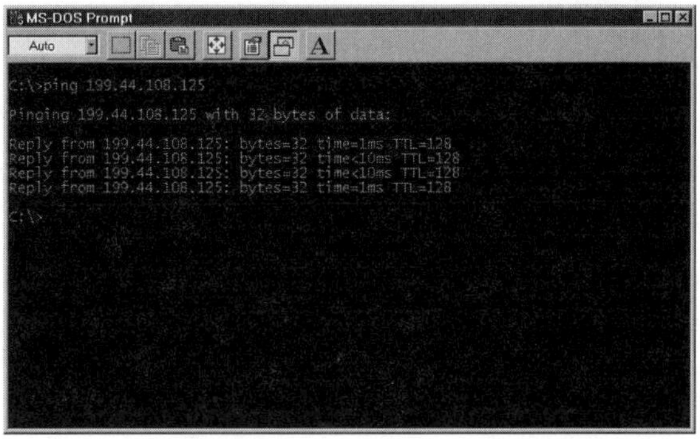

FIG. 7.1
Use ping to test
network connectivity.

If using ping with an IP address fails, it indicates a network problem between the computer running ping and the remote computer. Check the network cabling and the protocol settings on each system.

Failure of ping by computer name usually indicates a problem with the DNS service.

In this case check to be sure your DNS services are running and that they are configured properly.

▶ **See** "Setting Up Virtual Domains," **p. 56**, for more information on TCP/IP protocol settings and DNS.

Running Telnet to Monitor Service Stability   Telnet is a command-line tool that can be used to determine whether a TCP/IP service is responding to connections. The Mail Server SMTP port number default is 25 and the POP3 port default is 110.

Using the telnet command, you can check to see if the SMTP and POP3 services are responding. If the service is functioning properly, a welcome banner is returned after successful network connection. The following is an example of an SMTP banner (see Figure 7.2):

```
220-integritydata.com Microsoft SMTP MAIL
ready at Sun, 29 Dec 1996 14:17:31 -05
00
220 ESMTP spoken here.
```

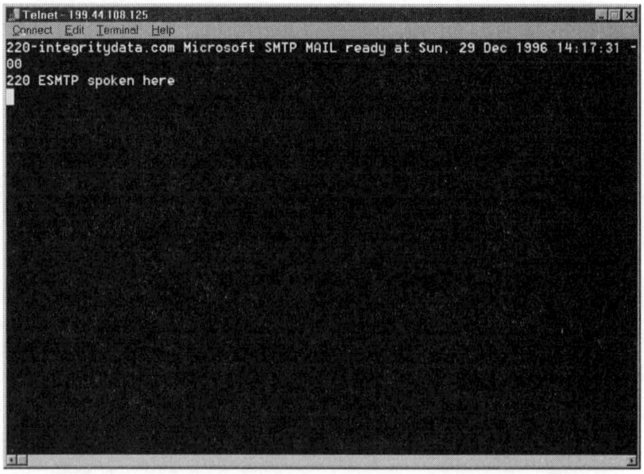

FIG. 7.2

If SMTP is running a banner, Welcome will appear.

The following is an example of a POP3 banner:

```
+OK SITE3.integritydata.com POP3 Server
```

To use telnet:

- Go to a command prompt (see Figure 7.3).

- type **telnet computer_name 25** to test the SMTP connection (for example, **telnet SITE3.integritydata.com 25**).

- Or, type **telnet computer_name 110** to test the POP3 connection (such as **telnet SITE3.integritydata.com 110**).

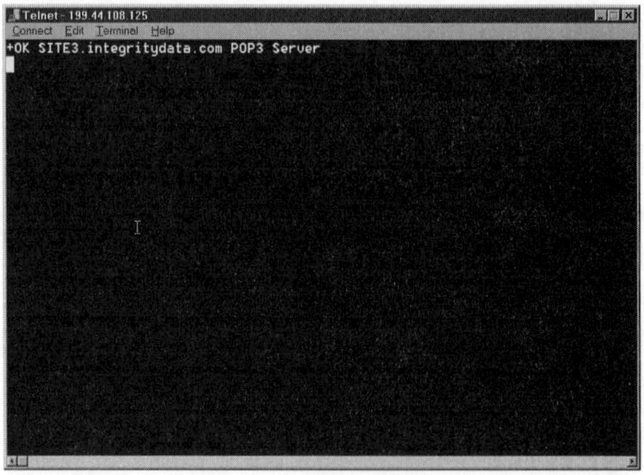

FIG. 7.3

Telnet to Port 110 to check the POP 3 service status.

If you fail to get a response from either port, do the following:

1. Open the Internet Service Manager.
2. Check to see if the SMTP or POP3 service is running. If not, start the service.
3. Open the appropriate service and verify that the service ports have not been changed. If they have re-run, telnet with the appropriate port number.
4. If the service is still not running, go back and check the original configuration steps.

▶ **See** "Configuring Mail Server Options," **p. 153**, for more information on Mail Server configuration.

Consulting the Event Viewer   The Windows NT Event Viewer can be used to view system, application, and security log events on each computer hosting either the SMTP or POP3 service.

In particular, you should look for warning or error events generated by either Smtpsvc or Pop3svc.

To use the Windows NT Event Viewer, follow these steps:

1. Click the Start Menu button.
2. Click Programs
3. Click Administrative Tools (Common).
4. Click Event Viewer.

   The system events for the host system will appear as shown in Figure 7.4.

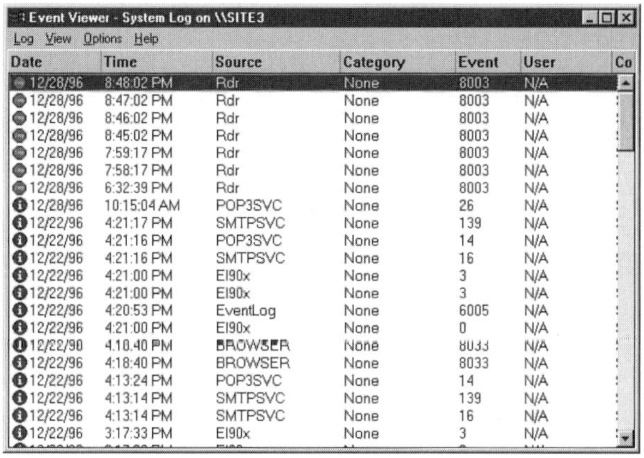

FIG. 7.4

System error messages are flagged in the Event Viewer.

Date	Time	Source	Category	Event	User	Co
12/28/96	8:48:02 PM	Rdr	None	8003	N/A	
12/28/96	8:47:02 PM	Rdr	None	8003	N/A	
12/28/96	8:46:02 PM	Rdr	None	8003	N/A	
12/28/96	8:45:02 PM	Rdr	None	8003	N/A	
12/28/96	7:59:17 PM	Rdr	None	8003	N/A	
12/28/96	7:58:17 PM	Rdr	None	8003	N/A	
12/28/96	6:32:39 PM	Rdr	None	8003	N/A	
12/28/96	10:15:04 AM	POP3SVC	None	26	N/A	
12/22/96	4:21:17 PM	SMTPSVC	None	139	N/A	
12/22/96	4:21:16 PM	POP3SVC	None	14	N/A	
12/22/96	4:21:16 PM	SMTPSVC	None	16	N/A	
12/22/96	4:21:00 PM	EI90x	None	3	N/A	
12/22/96	4:21:00 PM	EI90x	None	3	N/A	
12/22/96	4:20:53 PM	EventLog	None	6005	N/A	
12/22/96	4:21:00 PM	EI90x	None	0	N/A	
12/22/90	4:18:40 PM	BROWSER	None	8033	N/A	
12/22/96	4:18:40 PM	BROWSER	None	8033	N/A	
12/22/96	4:13:24 PM	POP3SVC	None	14	N/A	
12/22/96	4:13:14 PM	SMTPSVC	None	139	N/A	
12/22/96	4:13:14 PM	SMTPSVC	None	16	N/A	
12/22/96	3:17:33 PM	EI90x	None	3	N/A	

Part

II

Ch

7

If you need to monitor a system other than the local computer in the event viewer, follow these steps:

1. Open the Log menu.
2. Click Select Computer.
3. Highlight the computer you want to monitor.
4. Click OK.

When you have the proper event list open, double-click an event to view specific details about that event.

Consulting the Performance Monitor   The Windows NT Performance Monitor is used to monitor system activity. The Mail Server SMTP and POP3 services have bytes-per-second counters. These counters give a good indication of whether the services are processing data. When these counters approach zero, the indication is that either the services have no data to process or that the services are not functioning properly. Most installations have periods of time where there is little or no activity, so this tool must be used carefully to determine service stability.

To use the Performance Monitor, follow these steps:

1. Click the Start Menu button.
2. Click Programs.
3. Click Administrative Tools (Common).
4. Click Performance Monitor.
5. Choose Edit, Add to Chart.
6. Select either SMTP or POP3 server in the Object box.
7. Select the counters related to bytes sent and received per second in the Counter list.
8. Click Add to add the counters.
9. Click one to add the counters and monitor performance as shown in Figure 7.5.

FIG. 7.5
You can choose which counters to use to chart the Mail Server activity with the Performance Monitor.

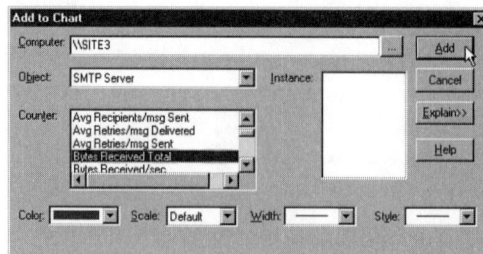

For a list of available Performance Monitor counters see Appendix B, "Performance Monitor Counters."

For more information on using the Performance Monitor see Que's *Special Edition Using Windows NT 4.0.*

Monitoring Security

Security monitoring involves knowing if the service is secure from attack or compromise. Proper monitoring can warn you if the service is at risk or is being compromised.

The main function of the SMTP and POP3 services is to service client connections. Unfortunately, these services are typically where attackers try to breach service security. The Mail Server utilizes two tools to monitor for such attacks:

- The Internet Information Server transaction log for viewing transaction history
- The Windows NT Event Viewer for viewing security events

Using the IIS Transaction Log to Monitor Security   The Internet Information Server (IIS) logs transactions carried out by particular service actions. For example, transaction logs can be used to track the commands issued by a particular user. They can also be used to monitor attacks on a service.

The transaction log is written either to a flat file or to a SQL/ODBC database. If written to a flat file, a simple text editor can be used to view the file. If written to a SQL/ODBC database, database query tools can be used to view the transaction log records.

To set up transaction logging for a service:

1. Open the Internet Service Manager (ISM).
2. Click the service you want to log.
3. Click the Logging tab (see Figure 7.6).
4. Click Enable Logging.
5. Click Log to File or Log to SQL/ODBC Database.
6. Choose the appropriate settings.
7. Click OK.

After you have configured the Mail Server event logging you should review the logs on a regular basis. You need to look for:

- Consecutive failed login attempts
- Telnet or ping attempts to the Mail Server service ports
- Attempts to log in as an administrator
- Any other unusual activity

If you do not check the logs, you might as well not create them.

Part

II

Ch

7

FIG. 7.6

Proper logging can help
secure a site.

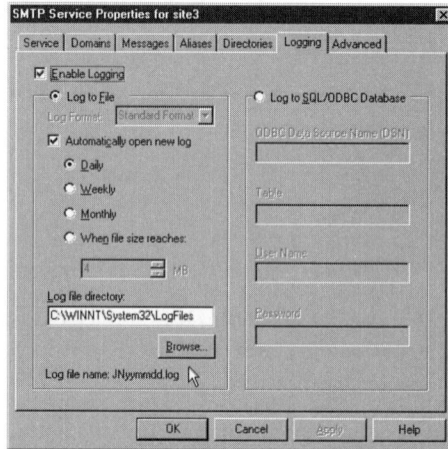

> **N O T E** Do not make the logging period too long. Daily logging is a good place to start. As you
> become familiar with the site you may be able to increase the logging period. The Mail
> Server logs can quickly grow to an unmanageable size. They can also take up valuable space on your
> hard drive. ■

Using Windows NT Event Viewer to Monitor Security   The Windows NT Event Viewer is used
to monitor service events, including informational, warning, and error events. It can be used to
view the security log events on each computer hosting either the SMTP or POP3 service.

To use the Event Viewer to view the security log:

1. Click the Start Menu button.
2. Click Programs.
3. Click Administrative Tools (Common).
4. Click Event Viewer.

    The system events for the host system will appear.

If you need to monitor a system other than the local computer in the event viewer, follow these
steps:

1. Choose Log, Select Computer.
2. Highlight the computer you want to monitor.
3. Click OK.

    When you have the proper system open:

4. Choose, Log, Security.
5. Double-click an event to view details about the logged event.

Review the events for unauthorized activity. In particular, watch for connection failures. They can indicate a possible attack by someone who is either making excessive connection requests or is maintaining a connection for an extended period of time. The event should include the IP address or computer name of the computer used by the possible attacker.

Monitoring Configuration

An improperly configured system will not run properly. Therefore, it is important to keep an eye on the Mail Server configuration. Changes to the system that are made intentionally or otherwise can affect performance and stability. Monitoring the configuration requires identifying the critical settings and registry keys and monitoring their use. This will tell you if there are new service settings or if any of the settings have been changed.

There are two main things to monitor with respect to system configuration:

- Service configuration changes
- Incorrect system configurations

To monitor for service configuration changes, you can use the Windows NT Event Viewer.

Monitoring Service Configuration Changes   To monitor incorrect system configuration, you can use Windows NT Performance Monitor, telnet, and the SQL Server ISQL tools.

To use the Windows NT Event Viewer to monitor service configuration changes, follow these steps:

1. Click the Start Menu button.
2. Click Programs.
3. Click Administrative Tools (Common).
4. Click Event Viewer.

    The system events for the host system will appear.

If you need to monitor a system other than the local computer in the event viewer:

1. Choose Log, Select Computer.
2. Highlight the computer you want to monitor.
3. Click OK.

Examine all error events and review all warning and informational events. For example:

- Error events will show any services that failed to start.
- Warning events will show incorrect configuration settings and other less critical errors.
- Informational events will show when configuration changes have been made.

Reviewing these events allows you to keep on top of unexpected changes to the system.

Part

II

Ch

7

Using Telnet to Monitor Incorrect Service Configuration   You can issue telnet commands to the Mail Server SMTP and POP3 services. These services do not echo commands, so to see results you must use the Telnet program in Windows NT Accessories and turn on local echo. A good test of service configuration is to use telnet to submit a message to the SMTP service and retrieve the same message via POP3.

To turn on local echo for telnet:

1. Open the Start menu.
2. Point to Accessories.
3. Click Telnet. The Telnet window appears.
4. Choose Terminal, Preferences.
5. Check the Local Echo box.
6. Click OK.

To use telnet to submit a message via SMTP (see Figure 7.7), open a command prompt and then type the following (press Enter at the end of each line):

```
telnet [hostname] 25
ehlo postmaster
mail from: postmaster
rcpt to: postmaster
data
Test Message

Quit
```

Hostname is the name of the SMTP server.

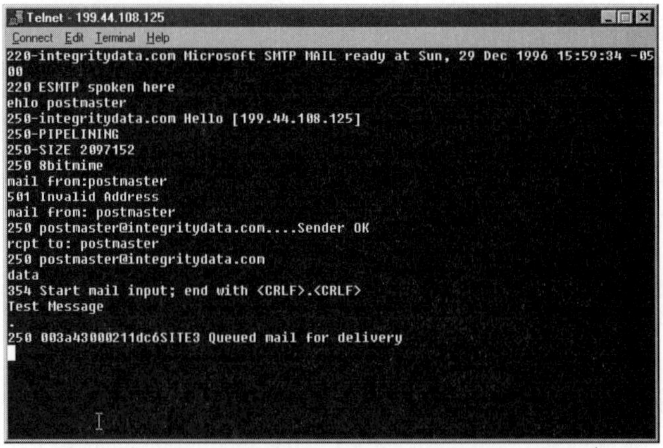

FIG. 7.7
You can test SMTP from the telnet command.

To use telnet to retrieve the message via POP3, open a command prompt and then type the following (press Enter at the end of each line):

```
telnet [hostname] 110
user postmaster
pass password
retr 1
quit
```

If the test message is returned after the POP3 command, you have verified that SMTP has properly performed local delivery and that POP3 has the message in the mailbox.

Using Performance Monitor to Monitor Incorrect Configuration   The performance counter can be used to monitor system activity as described earlier in the section titled "Consulting the Performance Monitor." If the system begins to fail to process data it may indicate that the system is not properly configured. You should then use the service stability tests described earlier in "Testing System Stability" to make sure that the network is configured properly.

Monitoring SQL Server Configuration   SQL Server ISQL_w is used to submit queries to a SQL Server database. If installed, this tool is usually found in the SQL Server 6.5 program group. SQL Enterprise Administrator also has a query window you can use. You can use these tools on any computer running SQL Server to query the SQL Server routing table used by the Mail Server SMTP and POP3 services.

To open a query window in SQL Enterprise Administrator, follow these steps:

1. Open SQL Enterprise Administrator from the SQL Server program group.

2. Choose Tools, SQL Query Tool.

   The Query Tool window opens.

3. In the Query box type the following commands (see Figure 7.8):
   ```
   USE database name
   GO
   SELECT * FROM ABINFO
   ```

4. Click the Execute Query button on the toolbar.

FIG. 7.8

A properly configured Routing Table will return results.

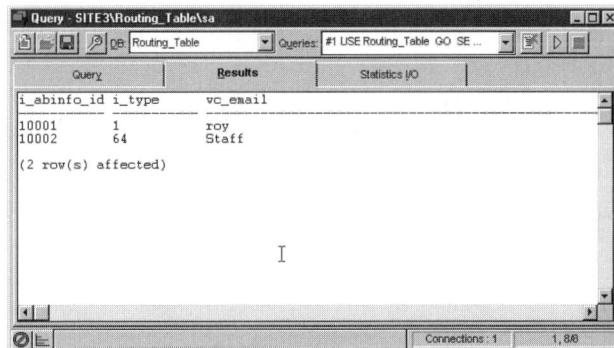

Part

II

Ch

7

If results are returned, the system is configured properly. If no results are returned, the SMTP and POP3 services may not be configured to use the correct SQL Server database.

If an error is returned, the routing table database is probably not set up correctly on this SQL Server database.

To open a query window in ISQL_w:

1. Open the Start Menu.
2. Click Programs.
3. Click SQL Server 6.5.
4. Click ISQL_w. The Connect Server dialog box appears, as shown in Figure 7.9.

FIG. 7.9
ISQL_W can be used to query the routing table.

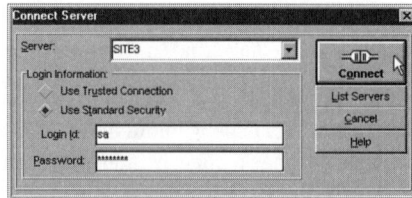

5. Type or select the routing table server name in the Server box.
6. Type the Login ID, if needed, and your Password.
7. Click Connect. The Query Tool window opens.
8. In the Query box type the following commands:

```
USE database name
GO
SELECT * FROM ABINFO
```

9. Click the Execute Query button on the toolbar.

If results are returned, the system is configured properly. If no results are returned, the SMTP and POP3 services may not be configured to use the correct SQL Server database.

If an error is returned, the routing table database is probably not set up correctly on this SQL Server database.

For more information on configuring SQL see "Setting up SQL Server" in Chapter 6, "Instant Communication—Microsoft Commercial Internet Mail," or Que's *Special Edition Using Microsoft SQL Server 6.5*.

Monitoring Performance

Monitoring the performance of the Mail Server involves measuring its responsiveness. This type of monitoring tells you if the service is performing as expected, and warns you about processing slowdowns and latencies that need attention.

Each Mail Server component stresses different types of resources. Of the four Mail Server components, SMTP, POP3, and the mail routing database tend to stress the CPU, while the mailbox file store stresses disk performance.

In general, the three key hardware resources you need to monitor are:

- CPU utilization
- Disk utilization
- Memory utilization

In addition, you need to monitor network connections and key counters in Mail Server to help you identify the performance of the various components of the Mail Server.

The Performance Monitor uses a series of counters that track data, such as the number of processes waiting for disk time, the number of network packets transmitted per second, and the percentage of process utilization. You can set up Performance Monitor to store data in logs for later use, and also to view performance in real time without creating a log.

The following tasks are involved in monitoring performance:

- Setting up the Performance Monitor logging
- Monitoring performance in real time
- Viewing performance logs

Setting Up Performance Monitor Logging   When you set up event logging you will capture the following objects:

- Memory and System objects on all mail servers
- The SQL object on the routing table server
- The SMTP object on their servers
- POP3 objects on the POP servers
- Logical Disk objects on the file store and SMTP servers

You must activate the diskperf tool if you want to monitor the logical disk object. On the server you want to monitor, run diskperf -y from the command prompt and then reboot.

For more information on running the Performance Monitor, see "Launching Performance Monitor" in Appendix B, "Performance Monitor Counters," or Que's *Special Edition Using Windows NT 4.0.*

The following table provides a list of counters for monitoring performance. The table also includes the range of readings to expect for each counter, and what it means if the readings are outside the expected range.

Part
II

Ch

7

Counters	Normal Readings	Deviations and Probable Causes
Local queue length (SMTP)	0	>0 indicates that the server is receiving more messages than it can handle; that the local mail store is not accepting messages.
Remote queue length (SMTP)	0	>0 indicates that the server is receiving more messages than it can process, or that the remote mail store is not accepting messages.
Available memory (memory object)	>10% of total memory is available	<10% of available memory free indicates excessive processing.
Current connections (SMTP/POP3)	> 0	A value of zero may indicate that there are network problems.
Failed authentications per second (POP3)	< 1	>1 may indicate that POP3 is having trouble connecting to the routing table SQL Server database.

To set up Performance Monitor logging, follow these steps:

1. Open the Start menu.
2. Click Programs.
3. Click Administrative Tools.
4. Click Performance Monitor.
5. Choose View, Log. The Log window opens.
6. Choose Options, Log. The Log Options window opens.
7. In the File name box, type the name of your new log file.
8. In the Update Time box, select Periodic Update or Manual Update.
9. If you select Periodic Update, enter an interval in seconds in the Interval box (see Figure 7.10).
10. Click Save.

FIG. 7.10

Set up Performance
Monitor logs.

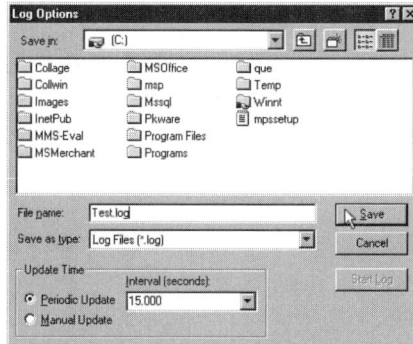

N O T E When choosing an update interval, consider the size of the log, the overhead introduced by logging performance data, and your viewing needs. Generally, use a 10- to 15-minute interval when creating a log file for analysis (use a 10- to 15-second interval for troubleshooting performance problems in real time). ▊

11. Choose Edit, Add to Log.

12. Select the computer from which you want data.

13. Click the objects you want to capture (see Figure 7.11).

14. Click Add after selecting each object.

15. Click Done when you are finished selecting objects.

FIG. 7.11

Select Performance
Monitor counters.

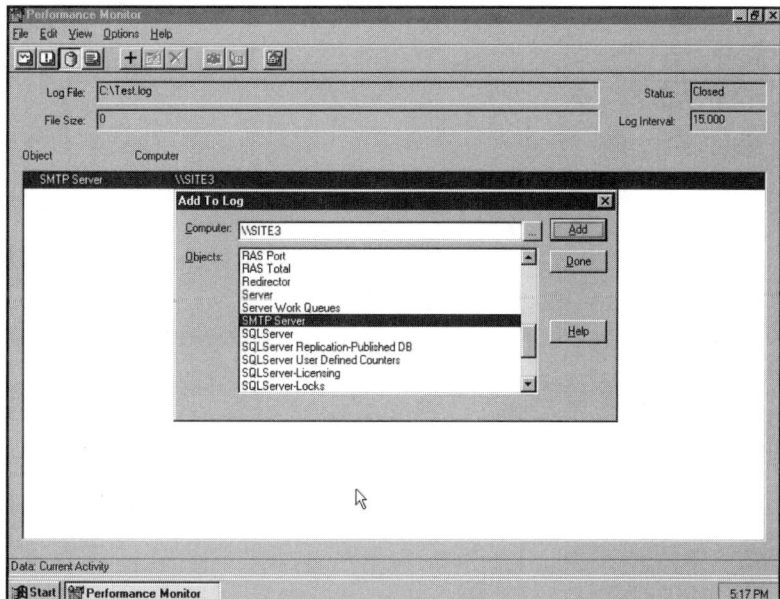

16. Choose Options, Log.

17. Click Start Log. The logging process starts and you should see the file size increase in the File Size box.

   Your computer is now logging the data.

To stop logging, follow these steps:

1. Choose Options, Log.

2. Click Stop Log.

Monitoring Performance in Real Time   When you monitor performance in real time, you use the Chart window in the Performance Monitor. You select an object to monitor and then add counters for the object. You can add multiple counters for an object, and as you add the counters, they appear as graph lines.

To monitor performance in real time:

1. Open the Start menu.

2. Click Programs.

3. Click Administrative Tools.

4. Click Performance Monitor. The Performance Monitor opens.

5. Choose Edit, Add to Chart.

6. Select the computer you want to monitor from the Computer box.

7. Select the object you want to monitor from the Object box.

8. Click a counter in the Counter list, as shown in Figure 7.12.

9. Click Add.

10. Click Done when you have finished selecting counters.

FIG. 7.12
Select Performance
Monitor counters.

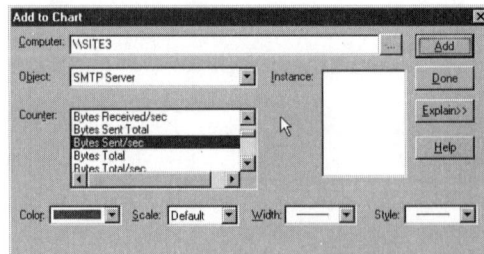

You now see the Performance Monitor charting the performance counters you selected. If you have only limited activity you may need to adjust the scale of a specific counter.

To adjust a scale on a counter:

1. Double-click the counter name at the bottom of the screen. The Edit Chart Line window opens.
2. Click the Scale box.
3. Select the new scale, as shown in Figure 7.13.

FIG. 7.13
You can change the scale of chart lines.

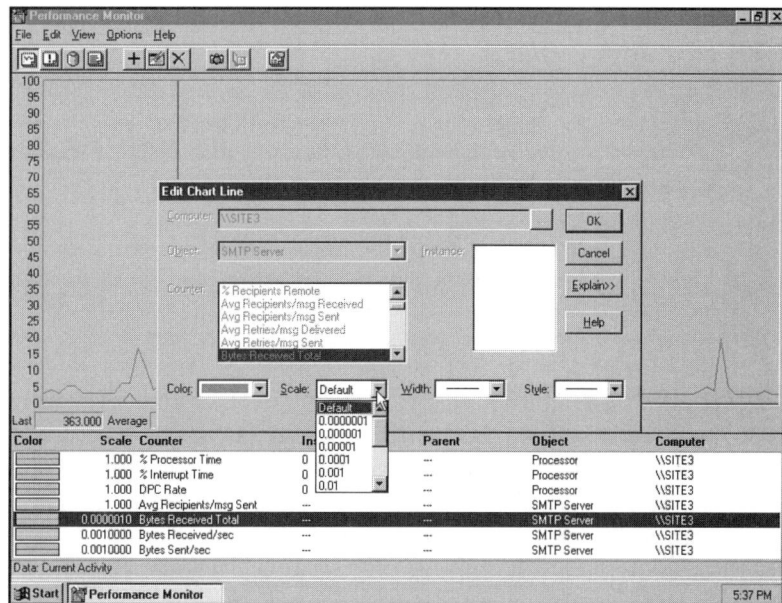

Viewing Performance Logs   The logs you configured in the Performance Monitor give you data to analyze. When you want to view the data you use the Log window in Performance Monitor. In the Log window, the same objects and counters are available as in the Chart window you use to monitor objects in real time.

To view data from a Performance Monitor log:

1. Open the Start menu.
2. Click Programs.
3. Click Administrative Tools.
4. Click Performance Monitor.
5. Choose View, Log. The Log window opens.
6. Choose Options, Data From. The Data From dialog box opens, as shown in Figure 7.14.

Part
II

Ch
7

FIG. 7.14

Specify the log file you
want to view.

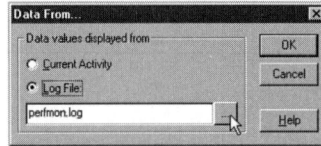

7. Click Log File.

8. Click Perfmon.log.

9. Click OK.

10. Select the drive and directory where you have stored the Performance Monitor logs.

11. Select the log you want to view.

12. Click Open.

The log will be displayed in the Log window. Review the log and look for performance levels that are under or over your normal site activity.

N O T E When you first set up the mail server you will have no data to compare your performance against. Therefore you should run logs frequently so you can build up a realistic measure of your Mail Server's performance. ■

Monitoring Capacity

An unexpected shortage of Mail Server capacity can have dire consequences for an unsuspecting administrator. Monitoring server capacity involves comparing the actual usage to the available resources. Monitoring tells you the level of resource utilization relative to the system capacity. This type of monitoring provides advanced warning of resource shortages.

To monitor Mail Server capacity you need to look at physical resource capacity as well as Mail Server service capacity. A physical resource reaches capacity when it is busy 100 percent of the time. A service reaches capacity when requests for service start experiencing delays.

The following table provides a list of counters for monitoring capacity. The table also includes the range of readings to expect, and what it means if readings are outside the normal range.

Counters	Normal Readings	Deviations and Probable Causes
%disk (logical disk object)	<70%	>70% indicates that either SMTP is not keeping up with the mail queue or that a mailbox directory is running out of space.
%CPU utilization (system)	<70%	>89% indicates nearing capacity.
Available memory (memory)	>10% of total memory	<10% of available memory free may indicate excessive processing.

Capacity monitoring should be set up at the time as Performance monitoring. This allows both sets of data to be analyzed simultaneously.

The steps for setting up capacity monitoring are described earlier in the Performance Monitoring section. Only the counters are different.

Use the Performance Monitor to monitor physical resource capacity by observing critical resource utilization such as:

- % disk time
- % CPU time
- Available memory

To monitor physical capacity, diskperf must be turned on. To run diskperf:

1. Open a command prompt on the server you want to monitor.
2. Type **diskperf -y**.
3. Press Enter.
4. Reboot the system.

T I P Diskperf utilizes a lot of system resources. It should only be turned on for specific testing periods. When you are finished, turn diskperf off by issuing the diskperf -n command and then reboot the system.

Maintaining Mail Server Logs

Server logs can be used to improve system performance, increase site security, and predict the need for system upgrades. In order to produce this information they must be properly configured.

The Mail Server uses two different logging mechanisms to track service activity:

- The Windows NT Event logs
- Internet Information System (IIS) transaction logs

The Event logs can be used for tracking server related issues such as errors, warnings, and configuration changes. The IIS logs are used for following individual mail transactions through the mail process.

Each of these requires periodic maintenance.

Maintaining Windows NT Event Logs

Event log maintenance involves clearing the log before it becomes full and saving the cleared events in archive format. Use Windows NT Event Viewer to monitor the log regularly so you know when it is getting full. When you clear the log, you save the log at the same time.

Part
II

Ch
7

To clear and archive an event log:

1. Open the Start menu.
2. Click Programs.
3. Click Administrative Tools.
4. Click Event Viewer. The Event Viewer opens.
5. Choose Log, System. The system events are displayed.
6. Choose Log, Clear All Events. The Clear Event Log dialog box opens, as shown in Figure 7.15.

FIG. 7.15

Save the log to a file.

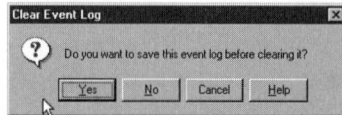

7. Click Yes to save the log to a file.
8. Name the file and supply a location to save the log file.
9. Click Save.
10. Click Yes to confirm clearing the log.
11. Choose Log, Application.
12. Repeat Steps 7–12 for the application log.

The SQL Server logs events to the application log, whereas the Mail Server SMTP and POP3 log events to the system log.

You can now analyze the saved log files using either a custom SQL database or a third party log analysis product. If you use flat file logs be sure to move them off the Mail Servers before they take up too much space on the log drive.

Maintaining IIS Transaction Logs

The Internet Information Server logs transactions to either SQL database files or flat table files. When you need to analyze the transaction log files use the Internet Service Manager to locate the file, copy the transactions to a backup file, and then delete the transactions to clear the log.

To determine the location of the transaction log file:

1. On either an SMTP or POP3 server, open the Start Menu.
2. Click Programs.
3. Click Microsoft Internet Server (Common).
4. Click Internet Service Manager (ISM). The ISM opens.
5. Double-click the SMTP or POP3 service.

6. Click the Logging tab.

7. Read the location of the transaction log file in the Log to File directory box (see Figure 7.16).

FIG. 7.16

Determine the location of the log files.

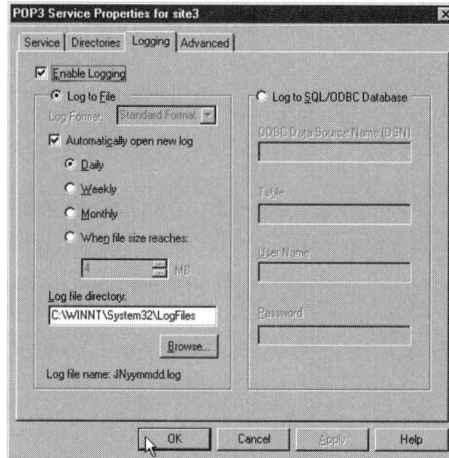

You can use any backup system to copy the old files from the location shown in the ISM Logging tab. They can be saved to removable media or archived on a network system. When you have backed up the files you should always verify the integrity of the backups and conduct periodic restores for confirmation.

When you have verified that you have a good backup up the transaction logs you can delete the files from the mail server. The files can be deleted from either the command prompt or Windows NT Explorer. The files can be pulled into any third-party log product or a custom SQL database for study.

Backing Up and Restoring Mail Server Files

System failures can ruin an administrator's day or month. Not only do you have to determine why the system crashed, but then you have to restore the system, correct the problem, and restore the data. If you properly documented your setup, then restoring the system may be tedious, but not difficult. However, the only way to restore the data is with a good backup.

E-mail can be especially vulnerable due to its dynamic state. The contents of user mailboxes change continuously and it is difficult to require individuals to back up their own mail.

Properly backing up the Mail Server can be more difficult than it appears. The interrelationships between the various components are not always clear. In this section we will discuss some of the issues you need to consider in preparing your system backup policy.

Part

II

Ch

7

Backing up and restoring Mail Server data files involves working with the SQL Server routing table and the mailbox virtual directories. Mailbox virtual directories point to an NTFS file partition. The Mail Server does not include NTFS backup software, but you can use either the backup software that is included with Windows NT Server or third-party backup software. Depending on the backup software used, backup and restoration can be performed while the SMTP and POP3 services are running. The same software that is used to back up Mail Server data must be used to restore it.

The Mail Server is designed so that mailboxes can be stored on different computers from the SMTP and POP3 services. Therefore, mailbox storage size is not limited to the disk capacity of a single computer. For large installations with many file servers, backing up all the mailbox virtual directories can present a challenge. To reduce the backup time in large organizations, the backup process should be performed on the file server hosting the actual virtual directory drive. This makes the file backup a local operation rather than a network operation. Each mailbox file server can also be backed up separately.

Backing up and restoring involves:

- Creating backup media for mailbox data and the SQL Server routing table database
- Restoring mailbox data and routing table database

Backing Up Mail Server Files

To back up Mail Server mailboxes:

1. Make a list of all virtual directories that host user mailboxes.
2. On each POP3 computer start Internet Service Manager (ISM).
3. Click the Directories tab, and note the full directory path of all the virtual directories that contain mailboxes.

> **CAUTION**
>
> The list of virtual directories must be complete. A missing virtual directory will result in mailboxes that are not backed up.

4. Back up the virtual directory paths, including the root directory and all subdirectories.

Backing up only the root directory does not back up user mailboxes. The actual mailboxes are subdirectories of the root. The backup software must be configured to back up all subdirectories of the virtual directory path.

To back up the SQL database:

1. On the SQL system, open the Start menu.
2. Click Program.
3. Click SQL Server 6.5.

4. Click SQL Enterprise Manager.

5. Choose Tools, Database Backup/Restore. The Database Backup/Restore window opens.

6. Click the Backup tab.

7. Select the proper database in the Database Backup drop-down list box.

8. Choose Entire Database.

9. If you want the SQL server to initialize the backup device choose Initialize Device.

10. Highlight the Backup device in the Backup Devices list box, as shown in Figure 7.17.

11. Click Backup Now.

12. Specify the Volume Label.

13. Click OK.

14. When the backup is completed, click Close.

FIG. 7.17
You can back up the
SQL database by using
the SQL Enterprise
Manager.

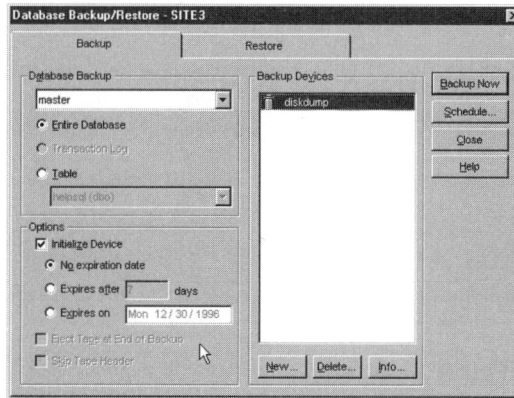

Restoring Mail Server Files

The SMTP service continuously delivers messages to mailbox directories, and it is very likely that the status of a mailbox will change during the time the directory is being backed up.

The Mail Server uses an index file in each mailbox directory for performance purposes. The index file is a quick summary of the messages contained in the mailbox directory. POP3 marks entries as deleted in this file but does not actually remove the entries. Since the index file in a mailbox directory can be out of synchronization with what is on the backup media, the inetcfg POP3 build_index command-line tool can be used to make sure that the index file is synchronous with the actual contents of the mailbox directory.

Restoring Mailbox Files   When you need to restore mailbox files, use the same software that you used to back up the files. Be certain to verify that you are restoring to the same system and directory as the original. When you have finished the restore you will need to use the inetcfg POP3 build_index to ensure index file-mailbox directory synchronization.

Part

II

Ch

7

To run the build index command:

1. Open a command prompt.
2. Type **inetcfg.exe POP3 BUILD_INDEX {arguments}**.
3. Press Enter.
4. The index file will be rebuilt and the results written to the specified log.

Following is the proper syntax for using the build_index command and a description of the arguments.

```
BUILD_INDEX [-rv] [-e <days_to_expire>] [-l [log_file_name]]
            [MailFolderName]
```

Parameter	Description
-r	Run this command recursively over subdirectories.
-v	Verify. Do not make any updates, but just verify that the mailbox directory is not corrupt.
-e	Number of days to expire mail messages. Messages that are older than the specified number of days will be deleted and removed from the index file.
-l	Write a log to Standard out. Creates a log file named [*log_file_name*].
MailFolderName	The full path to the mail folder to repair.

This command will rebuild the index files in the specified directories. The POP users will then have a current listing of the messages in their mailboxes.

By closely tracking the location where data corruption occurred and using the command-line tool to synchronize the index file with the contents of the mailbox directory after restoration, you can minimize the time that a mailbox is unavailable to users due to data corruption.

Restoring the SQL Database   When you need to restore the SQL database:

1. On the SQL system, open the Start menu.
2. Click Program.
3. Click SQL Server 6.5.
4. Click SQL Enterprise Manager.
5. Choose Tools, Database Backup/Restore. The Database Backup/Restore window opens.
6. Click the Restore tab.
7. Select the database to be restored in the Database box, as shown in Figure 7.18.
8. Choose Database or Transaction Logs.

FIG. 7.18

Restore the SQL
database file.

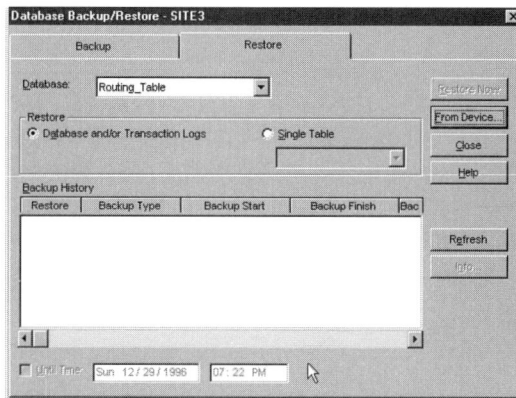

9. Click From Device. The Restore From Device On Server window opens (see
   Figure 7.19).

FIG. 7.19

Choose the proper
device to restore the
database.

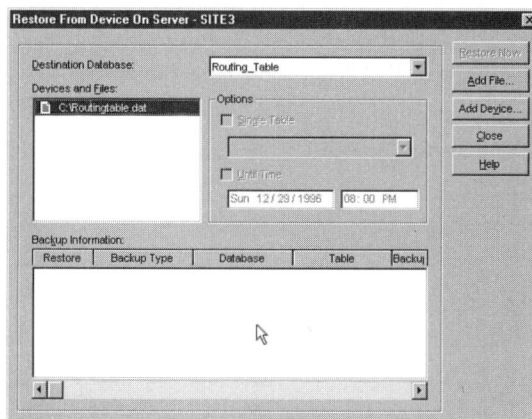

10. Choose the Destination Database.

11. Highlight the device in the Devices and Files list box.

12. Click Restore Now.

13. When the restoration is complete, click Close.

14. Reboot the system to ensure a clean database.

For more information on backing up and restoring SQL databases see Que's *Special Edition
Using Microsoft SQL Server 6.5*.

Part

II

Ch

7

Integrity Check

When we were setting up the Integrity Data Web site, we started with UNIX Sendmail. In typical admin fashion we spent many long nights hacking and customizing the sendmail.cf file to get just what we wanted. Even then we had to keep making continuous updates and fixes to keep up with the current standards and security holes. Imagine our delight when we discovered the ease of setting up the MCIS Mail Server. While it took us several tries to get the SQL Database and routing tables set up to our satisfaction, it was much, much easier than setting up SendMail. It still leaves a little to be desired in configuring multiple virtual e-mail domains, but its overall ease of use has made it a much better choice for us than sendmail.

From Here...

This chapter covered some of the advanced parts of administering the Mail Server: monitoring the server, using the server logs, and backing up and restoring the Mail Server files. This gives you an excellent foundation on which to construct your Mail Server installation.

- For more information on configuring the Mail Server see Chapter 6, "Instant Communication—Microsoft Commercial Internet Mail."

- Chapter 8, "Adding a Chat Server," shows you how to install and configure the Microsoft Chat server.

- Chapter 9, "Understanding Commercial Internet Personalization Server," looks at how you can customize your site for every user.

- For more information on SQL Server 6.5 see Que's *Special Edition Using Microsoft SQL Server 6.5*.

Adding a Chat Server

Successful deployment of any communications platform requires support for instant communication. The Microsoft Internet Chat Server is an instant communication tool that facilitates the exchange of information in a real time environment, meaning when a message is sent in the chat room, the other participants will see the message almost instantly. It's a live conversation tool and it's not difficult to get running.

In this chapter you explore the capabilities of the Chat Server. You also learn about its functionality and pick up a few techniques for resolving problems that may occur. ■

How to implement the Chat Server

Learn a variety of uses for the chat server to determine if you have a need for this method of interaction. Gain a basic understanding on how the chat server functions and the differences between the Microsoft chat server and the traditional Internet Relay Chat protocol.

How to install and configure the Chat Server

Understand the ins and outs of installing the chat server and verify that the server is functioning properly. Then, learn how to implement the features available in the chat server.

How to expand your Chat Server network

Learn how to scale a network of servers to deliver a commercial scale chat server strategy.

How to manage Chat Server performance

Acquire an overview of the monitoring tools available through Windows NT; these allow you to keep track of the performance of the Chat Server.

Introducing Microsoft Commercial Internet Chat Server

What is communication without real-time discussions? No office runs well without a live conversation. Sure, you can accomplish a lot with a bulletin board, post-it notes, and memorandums, but when it's time to make a decision or get some answers, you need a real person who's ready to respond immediately.

This has been one of the tricky areas of digitizing the office place. There's e-mail, which is a convenient way to communicate but with no guarantee for a reply, not to mention whether any reply will be timely. The News Server is another avenue for discussions, but it's not real time. Ahhhh, but chatting, that's real time. Here, as you can see in Figure 8.1, you are actually interacting with other people, on-the-fly. Certainly, you'll be working hard to type your thoughts quickly without a whole bunch of grammatical errors, but it's real time and answers come at you with a quickness that is unmatched!

FIG. 8.1
Online chats can be quite helpful in the office place.

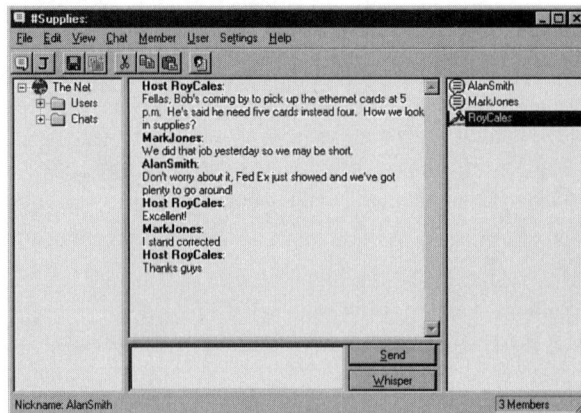

However, you have to forget the term "chat" to make the most of this technology. Chats are things people have on their coffee break. A chat is informal, and it's far too passive a term for most office places. Let's think of this tool a little differently. Instead of chat, think conferencing. Now that's something a lot of executives and managers do!

Why Have a Chat Server?

The Microsoft Chat Server provides the Internet conferencing tool that offices need. Employees no longer need to get up from their desks to ask another staff member a question. Telecommuters can be called upon by their supervisors. Even discussions with customers can be handled through the chat server. Talk about prompt, courteous, and efficient service.

The bottom line is that location is no longer important for the average discussion. What used to require advanced scheduling and warm bodies can now be handled on-the-fly in a chat room. This tool can also manage private discussions, open forums, and closed forums. The server can run exclusively on the office intranet, or it can be a public server.

N O T E The Microsoft Internet Chat Server was designed as a multiuser chat system based on the same standards as the Internet Relay Chat (IRC) protocol. IRC was originally created in 1988 in Finland by Jarkko Oikarinen. It was designed, and presently functions, as a multiuser chat system where people talk in groups, or in private. ■

Public Forums The Chat Server provides an excellent environment for public forums. This provides a place where users can meet to discuss a particular subject of interest. If necessary, the group can be closed to members only and the substance of the discussion can be logged to a text file for future reference.

This can be a valuable tool, because companies need input from their user base. The Chat Server can be accessible to external users, as well as internal users.

Online Support The concept of an online customer support strategy is quite enticing. Not only can you provide an online support desk, but you can also take advantage of customer input sessions. Imagine a weekly input session, where customers can log on and gain product assistance (see Figure 8.2). How about an environment where users can arrive at a scheduled time and have their questions answered?

FIG. 8.2
The Chat network can provide access to discussion in a wide variety of topics. Simply select a topic of interest and enter the channel.

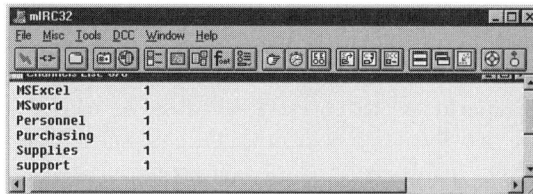

The uses for online support are not limited to external customers. On an intranet, the computer support desk can begin handling the majority of its phone calls through the Chat Server.

The Microsoft Internet Chat Server opens up these opportunities.

Interviews Imagine a forum where key personnel on your staff can be available for interviews by the user public, or better yet, the internal users. Every organization has key people who drive it. Here's an opportunity to let these folks share their techniques with the rest of the staff. Perhaps the company president wants to go live for a session as well. You can set up the chat session in a moderated format and let the users submit questions to be answered by the interviewee, or you can open it up as a freeform discussion.

Public interviews can also be quite effective. The public loves an organization that's responsive to its needs. Let them have an opportunity to share input and get up close and personal with the policy makers. If you're a government organization, this is the sort of stuff you ought to be doing.

Chat Server Features

The Chat Server extends the range of options for live conferencing with the Microsoft Internet Chat protocol while supporting the Internet Relay Chat protocol. Chat clients that are developed using all the capabilities of the Microsoft Internet Chat protocol can send and receive messages from clients using the native Internet Relay Chat protocol and vice versa.

Here are some of the additional features:

- The server can operate as a stand-alone or can be linked with other chat servers to form a large chat network.
- Offers excellent conferencing capabilities, where users can whisper and participate in private chats.
- Users can initiate queries easily to find other chats.
- Allows for authentication and can easily be configured to perform security confirmation on each user.
- The server administrators can grant or deny access to specific anonymous clients based on their Domain Name Server host name.

How Does Chat Work?

Discussions take place in a typical client/server environment, where users enter their comments and transfer them to the chat server. The chat server receives the comment and instantaneously distributes it to the other members in the chat room. Servers may also be connected to a network of servers. In this interconnected format the messages are passed from user to user. One server can be connected to several other servers, and the servers can contain hundreds of thousands of users.

Installing Chat Server

Like the rest of the Microsoft Commercial Internet Servers, the Internet Chat Server is also a pretty easy product to implement. With the familiar Windows NT graphical user interface you can easily install the Internet Chat Server.

Before you start, you really need to determine what your anticipated number of users will be. Microsoft describes three configurations: Minimal, Recommended, and Optimal. Here's a breakdown of the components of each configuration:

Installation	Hardware	Platforms	Software
Minimal— handling up to 1,000 concurrent users	1 machine i486 Compaq Proliant 64M RAM 1G hard drive	I486 Alpha (RTM) MIPS (RTM) PowerPC (RTM)	Windows NT 4.0 IIS Chat
Recommended— 5,000–10,000 concurrent users	3 machines dual P133 Compaq Proliant 128M RAM 2G hard drive	P133+ Alpha (MIPS) PowerPC (RTM)	1–2 Windows NT 4.0 MIPS (RTM) IIS Chat
Optimal— 30,000–50,000 concurrent users	20 machines (load balance) Quad P133 Compaq Proliant 256–512M RAM 2–4G hard drive	P133+ Alpha (RTM) MIPS (RTM) PowerPC (RTM)	1–3 Windows NT 4.0 IIS Chat

Once you've determined how big your user base is, you'll be ready to begin your install. In this section, you learn about the setup procedure for configuring one Windows NT server to act as your chat server. Then, you test the installation.

Running Setup

Before beginning the setup process, log on as an administrator to the computer where the Internet Chat Server will be installed. You should exit all running programs before you begin.

The following steps show you how to install the Chat Server:

1. Open the folder containing the Internet Chat Server setup program, which is setup.exe, and launch the executable program to begin the setup process.

2. At the Internet News Service Installation Welcome Screen, shown in Figure 8.3, click the Next button. Read and acknowledge the License Agreement, and click the Yes button.

FIG. 8.3
Select the Next button to proceed with Setup.

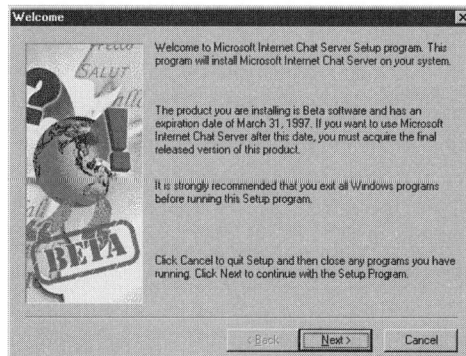

Welcome

Welcome to Microsoft Internet Chat Server Setup program. This program will install Microsoft Internet Chat Server on your system.

The product you are installing is Beta software and has an expiration date of March 31, 1997. If you want to use Microsoft Internet Chat Server after this date, you must acquire the final released version of this product.

It is strongly recommended that you exit all Windows programs before running this Setup program.

Click Cancel to quit Setup and then close any programs you have running. Click Next to continue with the Setup Program.

< Back   Next >   Cancel

3. At the Registration screen (see Figure 8.4), enter your name and company name, or accept the default and click the Next button.

FIG. 8.4

Enter your name and your company's name at the Registration screen.

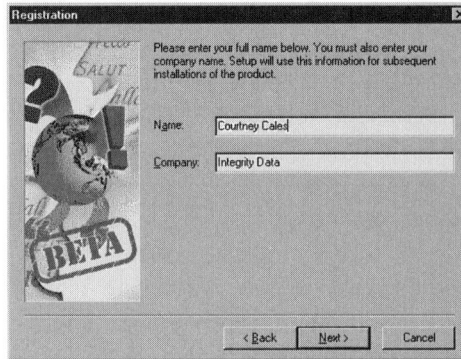

4. In the Select Components dialog box, shown in Figure 8.5, select all of the individual components listed in the Components list box and then click the Next button.

FIG. 8.5

Select all of the components listed to install the Chat service and additional components.

N O T E If the Internet Chat Server setup program says that there are Internet Information Server services running, choose Yes to have the system shut down the IIS services. ▦

5. When selecting a desktop folder, choose the Microsoft Internet Server from the existing list of folders. Click the Next button.

6. Review the setup information in the Confirm Setup Information dialog box, shown in Figure 8.6.

7. Click the Next button, and Setup begins.

8. At the Setup Completion dialog box, place a check mark in the box to the left of `I would like to start the Chat service`, and select Finish.

FIG. 8.6

Verify the setup information by ensuring that the proper components have been selected.

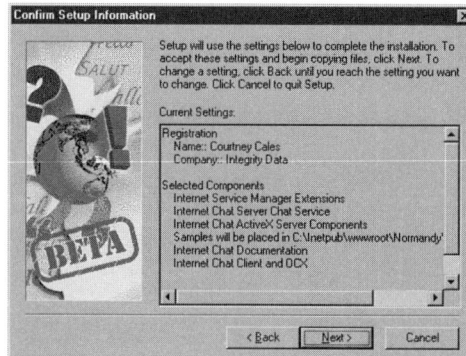

Testing the Installation

To test the Chat Server, you will need to launch a chat client and connect to the site. If you do not have an IRC chat program already installed on your server, you can use the chat client that was placed on your server during the program installation. The Chat Client can be found in the ics/client folder. Again, if you would prefer, you can use the IRC Client of your choice.

For those who want to use the Microsoft Chat Client, follow these steps:

1. From the ics/client folder, launch the program michat.exe.

2. In the Connection Settings dialog box, enter your server name (see Figure 8.7).

FIG. 8.7

Type your Server name to identify the server to which you want to connect.

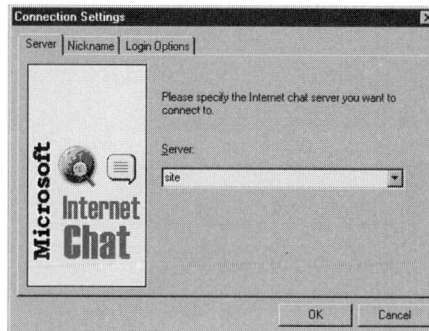

T I P If you are unsure of the server name, launch the Microsoft Internet Service Manager to see a list of the services running. The name of your server is listed under Computer. That's the name to enter in the server name field.

3. Select the Nickname tab and enter a <u>N</u>ickname to be used for the chat. For this text, type **User1** and in the <u>B</u>ackup nickname field enter **User2** (see Figure 8.8).

FIG. 8.8

Enter your Nickname and a Backup Nickname in case someone else is using your primary nickname.

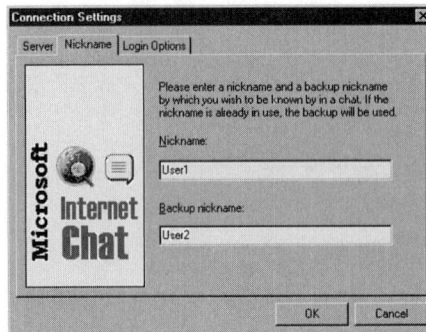

N O T E   What's a nickname? This is how users are identified while they are engaged in a chat. When using the Microsoft Internet Chat client, the nickname can be up to 23 characters in length. On Internet Relay Chat, nicknames must be 9 characters or less. Since MIC clients will be interacting with IRC clients, it's probably a good idea to keep nicknames under 9 characters. ■

4. Under the Login Options tab, you have the option to enter a Username to identify yourself. For now, leave this blank and select OK.

5. The Current Settings dialog box is displayed. Click the <u>C</u>onnect button.

6. In the Create Personal Chat dialog box enter a <u>N</u>ame and <u>T</u>opic for the chat. For now, enter the <u>N</u>ame as **#testchat** and the <u>T</u>opic as **ChatServer test #1**, as seen in Figure 8.9. Also, place a check in the box to the left of the <u>E</u>xpose chat to IRC users if you will be running the test with the Microsoft Internet Chat program or any other shareware Internet Relay Chat program.

FIG. 8.9

Enter the Name and topic of the discussion you want to join.

N O T E   When you select the Expose chat to IRC users option, notice that a # sign is placed before the Name of the group. If you want the group to be accessible only to users of Microsoft Internet Chat clients, an & should be placed before the group name. ■

7. Under the Chat Type tab, choose to make the chat Public. Later, you may want to test the Private and Secret features.

N O T E   The difference between Public, Private, and Secret groups is pretty straightforward. If you create a public group, anyone on the server can join the group. However, if you create a private group, only invited parties may join the channel. A secret group is the same as a public group, but users would have to know the group exists to enter the chat. Secret groups will not be visible when users view the list of groups available. ■

8. Under the Advanced tab, you have the option to configure further permissions for your group. For now, leave these fields at their default.

9. Click the OK button and the Microsoft Internet Chat program is launched. In the lower left-hand corner of the chat window, as seen in Figure 8.10, you will notice the nickname you selected is displayed. In the right-hand corner is a list of how many members are presently involved in the discussion.

FIG. 8.10

The Microsoft Internet Chat interface places the user's name in the lower left-hand corner of the chat window.

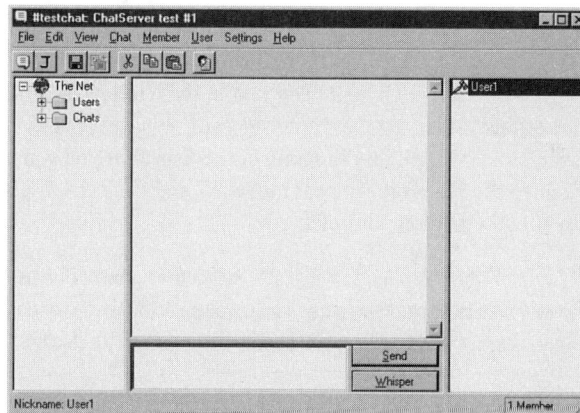

10. Minimize this copy of the Microsoft Internet Chat client, and launch another copy of the michat.exe program from the ics/client folder. We'll use this to simulate a conversation.

11. There is no need to change your settings, because the Microsoft Internet Chat client will automatically use the Backup Nickname if your Nickname is taken. Since you already have one chat launched using the nickname *User1,* the backup nickname will be used. Click the Connect button.

12. In the Create Personal Chat dialog box enter **testchat** in the <u>N</u>ame field and leave the <u>T</u>opic area blank. Place a check in the box to the left of the <u>E</u>xpose chat to IRC users. Click OK.

13. Microsoft Internet Chat launches a chat session in the *testchat* chat room.

14. In the lower left-hand corner of the chat window, the nickname for User2 is displayed. The right-hand corner now shows there are two members presently involved in the discussion, as seen in Figure 8.11.

FIG. 8.11

The number of users involved in a chat is displayed in the lower right-hand corner of the chat window.

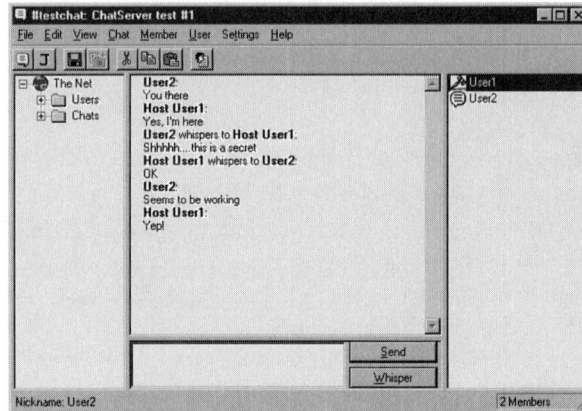

15. Have a chat with yourself by entering text in the window to the left of the <u>S</u>end and <u>W</u>hisper buttons. After you have entered your message, press Enter to send. If you want to <u>W</u>hisper, simply highlight the name of the user that you want to whisper to in the right column, enter the message you want to send, and click the Whisper button. The message is sent to only the person you selected.

N O T E If you want to Whisper to multiple users, highlight the name of one user then press the Ctrl key while you click each of the other names (all selected names should be highlighted at this point). Type your message and it will only be sent to the names you selected. ■

16. At this point, you should be properly connected and chatting.

The additional functions and features of the Microsoft Internet Chat client are pretty straight-forward. In the left column is a globe labeled The Net, and underneath it are folders entitled Users and Chats. Each folder has a plus (+) sign next to it.

If you click the + next to Users, the List Users dialog box opens. You can enter the name of a user you are searching for in the List Users dialog box and click OK to conduct a search for that user, or you can leave the field blank and click OK to get a list of all the users presently logged on to the server, as seen in Figure 8.12.

FIG. 8.12

To view a list of users, click the + next to the Users folder.

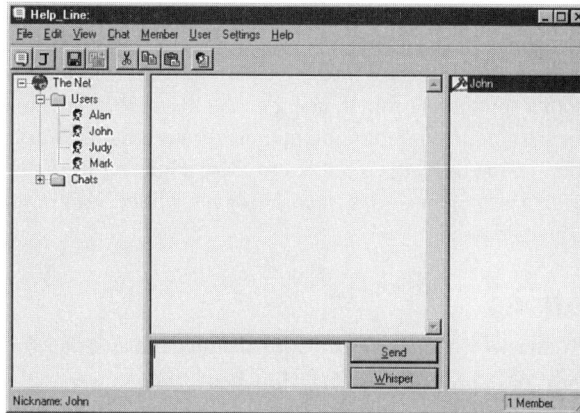

Part
II

Ch
8

If you click the + next to Chats, the List Chats dialog box opens. You can enter the name of a chat you are searching for in List Chats dialog box and click OK to search for that chat, or you can leave the field blank and click OK to get a list of all the chat channels that presently have users in them, as seen in Figure 8.13.

FIG. 8.13

To view a list of available chat groups, click the + next to the Users folder. The number in parentheses to the right of the group name determines how many users are currently logged in to the channel.

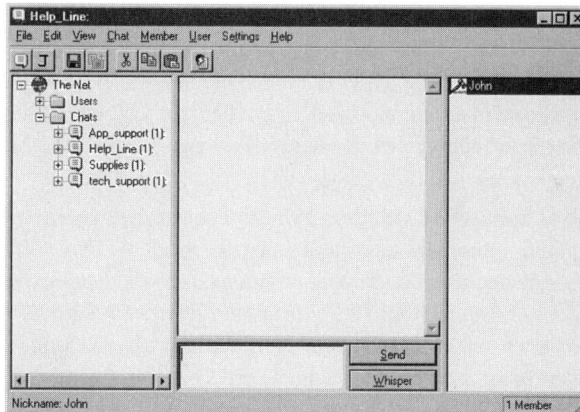

There is also a feature which allows you to list groups according to user count. This may come in handy when there are several groups listed on your server and you only are interested in finding lively chatrooms that have more than 10 users.

Configuring the Chat Server

You can configure the Chat Server through the Internet Service Manager's graphical user interface or from a command prompt, using chatcmd.exe to make changes. In this section you get an overview of the configuration options through the Internet Service Manager. The Microsoft Internet Chat Server is intended to allow administrators the ability to manage the Chat Server from a graphic user interface. However, whenever it is appropriate, the command line utility will be discussed.

Chat Server Options

The Microsoft Internet Chat Server provides a simple interface for the administrator to configure options for Services, Channels, Portals, Classes, Banned Users, Channel Services, Server Information, Security, and Logging. To configure the Chat Server, follow these steps:

1. Click the Start button, select Programs, Microsoft Internet Server, and then the Internet Service Manager.

2. Select the Chat service from the list of services and access the configuration files by selecting Properties, and then Service Properties.

3. From the Chat Service Properties, select the Service tab. The name that is presently displayed in the Name field was retrieved from the Domain Name Server Host Name setting, which was set up during the Internet Information Server installation.

4. In the field for ANSI title, enter the name of your site to be displayed to ANSI clients. The title must be 63 characters or less. In the field for Unicode title, enter the name of your site to be displayed to Unicode clients. Typically, you'll enter the same text in each of these fields. This title must also be 63 characters or less.

5. Proceed to Connection Limits and you can adjust the maximum number of Total chat clients and the Anonymous connections allowed. The Total setting is a combination of the authenticated users and the anonymous users. The anonymous connections refers to users who connect without authentication. The default for both is set at 1,000. The value must be between 0 and 4,096. Change the settings by clicking the up/down arrows or directly entering the numeric value. There's no need to change these defaults until you have a user base that requires a higher number.

6. The Chat Server administrator can control the maximum number of channel members allowed into a channel.

N O T E   A *channel* is the discussion group or topic header where conversations take place. Depending on the size of the server, several channels can be active simultaneously. Chat provides a dynamic environment, where anyone can create a new channel. Each channel remains active until the last person leaves. ▪

7. The Chat Server Administrator can also make changes to the mode of operation by placing a check in the desired Server Mode box, which is on the left side of each Server Mode option. The options are as follows:

- *Client Game Mode*   Allows clients to enable game mode.

- *Server to Server Game Mode*   Enables server-to-server game mode.

- *Server is MIC Only*   Blocks IRC clients from connecting to the server.

- *Disable New Connections*   Blocks new client connections.

- *No Host Mode on Channel Creation*   Prevents members from becoming channel hosts when they create a new channel.

- *No Dynamic Channels*   Stops clients from creating channels.

- *Sysop is Host*   Allows the system operator to be a host in any channel they are permitted to join.

- *Intranet*   Configures the service to work with internal network usage.

8. The Ports and Addresses dialog box, as seen in Figure 8.14, allows you to configure network server options.

FIG. 8.14

The Ports and Addresses dialog box lets you configure ports for your Chat server.

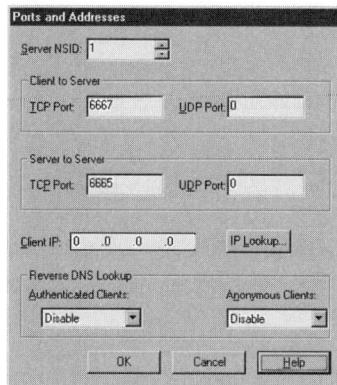

The options are:

- The Server NSID specifies the Network Service Identifier (NSID) on a chat network. The maximum number of servers that can be handled on the network is 255, so the NSID should be between 1 and 255.

N O T E   Each server on a chat network must contain a unique NSID or links between different servers won't work. If a duplicate NSID is detected, an event will be generated and the server-to-server connection dropped. ▨

- The Client to Server TCP Port and UDP Port Addresses should be left at the default, because it will most likely affect your user base which will connect to the mostly universal IRC port of 6667.
- The Server to Server TCP Port and UDP Port Addresses should also remain at the default settings, because it will most likely affect your server's ability to communicate with a chat server network.

NOTE If you make any changes to the Client to Server or Server to Server settings, the Chat Server will need to be stopped and restarted before the changes will take effect. ■

- The Client IP text entry field allows the administrator to set the IP address of the next known available Internet Chat Server in a Chat network. This method is called *dynamic load balancing*, which means that when one server is full, the IP address of the next available server is returned to the client. If the value is zero, there are no additional MIC servers available.
- There is also an option for Reverse Domain Name Server (DNS) Lookup, where the administrator can enter settings for Authenticated Clients and Anonymous Clients. Here you can either disable, attempt, or require the reverse domain lookup. If you choose require, whenever a user attempts to log on to your chat server, the server checks to see if the user's IP address returns a valid Domain Name Server. If there is not a valid DNS returned, a connection is not permitted. If you choose attempt, even if a valid Domain Name Server is not returned, the user is permitted to access.

NOTE Reverse DNS comes in handy when someone who is using your chat server is being disruptive, usually by running bots or clone processes over IRC, which use forged IDs. The only way to counteract that type of behavior is to disallow the entire domain. To do so, run the Reverse DNS and add the domain to the Banned Users list. The UNIX version of IRC calls this feature identd. ■

9. The last field offered under the Service properties is the Comment field, where there is a space to type a comment and will appear next to the service in the Microsoft Internet Service Manager window.

Configuring Portal Properties Portals are the connections that link Microsoft Internet Chat servers together. In this section, you learn to add, copy, remove, and edit properties for portals.

Following are the necessary steps to configure portal properties:

1. From the Chat Service Properties dialog box, select the Portals tab, and then click the Add button.
2. Type the Name, as seen in Figure 8.15, of the server you want to connect to.
3. Enter the IP address for the computer.
4. Type the Port Number for the new server.
5. Enter the Network Server Identifier for the computer.

FIG. 8.15

Portal properties include options such as portal names, server ports, and network server identifiers.

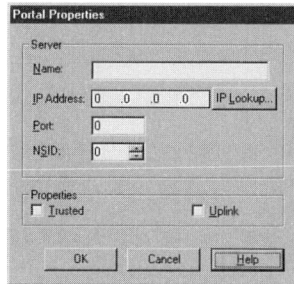

6. In Properties, select Uplink.

7. Click OK, and then choose Apply.

8. When the reminder to stop and restart the service displays, choose OK.

9. Click Properties, and then click Stop. After the Service has stopped, click Properties and then Start.

10. Now connect to the server named in the Portal Name and create a portal connection to the first server.

11. If the first server had a Portal Property of Uplink, the server must either be Trusted or have neither of the properties checked. If the first server had a selection of Trusted, this server should be checked as Uplink.

12. Stop and restart the Chat Service on the second system.

If both Chat Services have been restarted, a two-server Chat Network now exists.

Using ChatCmd to Add a Connection (Portal) to the Network If you want to try to configure Portals from the command line using the chatcmd.exe feature, follow these steps:

1. Begin at a command prompt. Run the ChatCmd /addportal switch with the following parameters: Enter the name of the server this will run on (* for current server), Name of New Server, NSID, IP Address, IP Port, and Modes of the new server. For instance:

    ChatCmd Server02 /addportal:New24=123, 199.44.108.2, 6665, uplink

2. To stop the service, type **net stop chatsvc**.

3. To start the service, type **net start chatsv**.

The administrator uses the /AddPortal switch to add a connection between other servers and to form a network of Chat servers. To create a Portal connection between two Chat servers, it is necessary to build corresponding Portals on each of the servers. The following rules apply when updating ChatCmd:

■ You'll want to use a pound sign (#) to accept the current value.

■ Submit an asterisk (*) when the value should return to the default for that switch.

You can also use the additional commands:

- /DeletePortal
- /GetPortal
- /ListPortals
- /SetPortal

Configuring Chat Classes Properties   This feature will allow you to restrict access rights and privileges to the server. Administrators will first identify users who fall into a class, and then determine rights and privileges given to the current class.

Here are the necessary steps to configure chat classes properties:

1. From the Chat Service Properties dialog box, select the Classes tab, and then click the Add button.
2. Enter a Class Name (for example, internal users). The Class Name can be no more than 63 characters in length.
3. In the Class Properties dialog box, displayed in Figure 8.16, select the modes you want to filter.

FIG. 8.16
Use the Class Selection tab on the Class Properties Sheet to identify which users fall into a selected class.

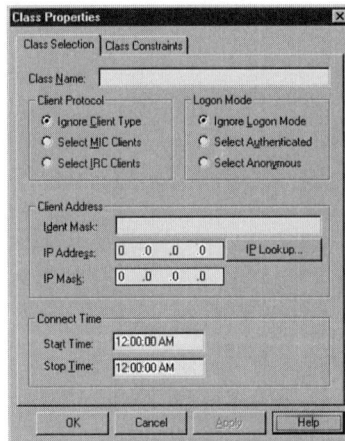

The following list provides an explanation of the modes available for the chat classes properties:

- *Client Protocol*   Here you can either choose to Ignore Client Type, or add the MIC client or the IRC client to this user class.
- *Logon Mode*   You may disable class selections based on logon mode by selecting Ignore Logon Mode. To add authenticate users to this class, select Authenticated. To add anonymous users to this class, select Anonymous.

- *Client Address*   The administrator can add an Ident Mask string for adding users to a class. For instance, if @integritydata.com is added to the Ident Mask text entry field, any users with @integritydata.com in their ident mask string will automatically be added to this user class. Classes can also be configured by the client's IP Address or IP Mask.

- *Connect Time*   Classes can also be set by Start Time and by Stop Time. The administrator simply defines a start time and a stop time that the server can use to add users to a user class. For instance, when a user logs on during the defined start and stop times, then they are automatically added to this user class.

T I P   Keep in mind that when you set Class Properties based on Connect Time, all times are based on Greenwich Mean Time (GMT), also known as Zulu time. Since Eastern Standard Time is five hours behind GMT, you'll need to add five hours to your start time.

4. Once you have completed your class selections, choose the tab for Class Constraints to define privileges and restrictions for a selected class. Begin by selecting Restrictions.

   The following list provides an explanation of the class constraints available in the class properties:

   - *Cannot Log On*   Stops users in this class from logging in.
   - *Cannot Create Dynamic Channels*   Stops any users in this class from creating a dynamic channel.
   - *Cannot Host Channel*   Stops users in this class from hosting a channel.

   Additional Class Constraint settings:

   - *Enable Sysop*   When checked, this feature lets users in this class have system operator privileges if other security requirements are met.
   - *Maximum Channels*   The administrator can set the maximum channels to a value between 0 and 10.
   - *Input Flood Limit*   Configures the amount of unprocessed input data (in bytes) before a user is disconnected. The value must be between 256 and 4096.
   - *Output Saturation Limit*   Sets the maximum number of kilobytes in the output queue before disconnection occurs.
   - *Ping Delay*   Defines an idle ping delay. The value should be between 15 and 3600.

5. After completing your selections, click Apply and your properties in the Classes category will go into effect and also be displayed in the Class Names category.

6. Click OK to close the Class Properties dialog box.

Using *Chatcmd* to Add a Class to the Network   The /AddClass switch is used with chatcmd to add a class from the command line. These classes allow the administrator the ability to filter user connections, along with assigning certain properties to any users who fall into a particular class.

The following steps provide details on how to add a class from the command prompt:

1. First, determine the properties desired for the new class.

2. Run Chatcmd: chatcmd * /addclass:<class_name>=<class properties>.

You can also use these additional commands:

- /DeleteClass
- /GetClass
- /ListClasses
- /SetClass

Configuring Banned User Properties   Use the Banned Users property page to ban users from the chat service. You can ban users with a specific nickname, username, or domain name.

The following steps provide details on how to set up your configuration to ban particular users:

1. From the Chat Service Properties dialog box, select the Banned Users tab, and then click the Add button to create the Names of Banned Users list.

2. In the Banned Properties dialog box, enter the Nickname of the user you intend to ban.

3. Submit the User Name of the person whom you are banning from the chat service, as seen in Figure 8.17. Submit an asterisk if banning by Nickname or Domain Name.

FIG. 8.17

Enter the name of the user you want to ban.

4. Submit the Domain Name of the user you are banning. Submit an asterisk if banning by Nickname or User Name.

5. A ban can also be set by Start Time and by Stop Time. The administrator simply defines a start time and a stop time that the server can use to add users to a user class. For example, if a banned user logs on to the service between the defined start and stop times, then the user will be denied access.

6. If you desire, enter the Reason for Ban.

7. Click OK, then click Apply.

N O T E After you enter information into these fields and click OK, the information is committed to the server and it cannot be edited. Should you need to edit properties for an existing user ban, the Nickname box, the Username box, and the Domain box are not available. But you can, however, edit the connect time options. When you are ready to remove a ban, simply highlight the Name of the banned user, and click the Remove button. ▦

8. To immediately Kill a user off the server, highlight the name of the banned user, and click the Kill a User button.

9. A dialog box is launched that verifies this is the user you want to kill. Enter a message in the Reason text entry field, and then click the Kill button.

10. The Internet Service Manager asks you to verify that you are sure you want to kill that user from the site. When you click Yes, the Kill feature is executed. The result is that the user is disconnected from the server and the information you typed in the Reason For Kill box is displayed to them.

Using *Chatcmd* to Add a Ban to the Network   To add a Ban to the network from the command line using the chatcmd.exe feature, follow these steps:

1. Decide on the properties of the new class.

2. Run Chatcmd: chatcmd * /addclass:<class_name>=<class properties>.

You can also terminate the user by using the /KillUser Command. These additional commands are available:

- ▦ /AddBan
- ▦ /DeleteBan
- ▦ /GetBan
- ▦ /ListBans
- ▦ /SetBan

Configuring Channel Services Properties   Channel Services provide the administrator some flexibility in configuration by allowing extensions that customize individual chats and can provide a variety of automated capabilities. These customized features can be interactive (bots and games) or data feeds (stock ticker, voting results in real time, and so on), are implemented as DLLs on the server, and can be loaded as needed.

N O T E The term *bot* comes up frequently in discussions about IRC. A bot is a simple program that is designed to respond to things that are done to it. For instance, many bots are programmed to grant channel operator status to any qualified user who messages the bot with the proper command character. A real life example would involve a user sending the following message to the bot "!op" to request channel operator status. If the user is authorized for operator status, the request is granted. Bots can be programmed to do a number of things, such as the automated transferring of files. ▦

This section does not provide an explanation on how to create the automated features. It is only designed to explain where channel service DLL files are stored and define the channel service data field.

The following list explains configuring Channel Service Properties:

1. From the Chat Service Properties dialog box, select the Channel Services tab, and then click the Add button to open the Channel Services property page.

2. Type the Name of the Channel service.

3. Type the Path.

4. Type the Data.

5. Click OK and the Channel Service is added.

To remove a channel service, simply highlight the service and click the Remove button. If you need to edit the properties of a channel service, simply highlight the service and click the Edit Properties button.

Configuring Channel Services Properties   The Server Information property page is used to edit server messages that are displayed to clients. The configuration page is separated into two sections, ANSI and Unicode, allowing you to send different messages to each type of client.

The following steps explain how to modify the server message:

1. In the text entry field for ANSI Admin Information, enter the contact information for the Server Administrator. This field is limited to 119 characters.

2. In the text entry field for the ANSI Message of the Day, type in a message for the day. This field is limited to 1,007 characters.

3. In the Unicode text fields, the text entered for Admin Information and Message of the Day is displayed. If you desire to make any changes, place your cursor in the text box and edit as necessary. The field limitations for both are the same as above.

4. Click the Apply button, and then click OK.

Configuring Security Properties   Security functions for the Admin Tool are not supported in this version, but will be implemented in later versions. A class will be like a chat group that can be accessed by or denied to users with the correct privileges.

Configuring Logging Properties   In this section, you'll want to uncheck the box to enable logging. According to Microsoft, you can open a log for chat from the Logging tab in the Chat Service Properties dialog box; however, the chat server adds no information to the logs generated by IIS. Therefore, you can log what goes on in the Internet Information Server, but there's no specific chat information in it.

Adding Channels

The Channels tab allows the administrator to add, delete, or modify persistent channels on the server. Persistent channels may be created with a wide range of values and options.

N O T E Remember, channels are either dynamic or persistent. Any Chat user can create a dynamic channel that focuses on their topic of interest on the network. The channel will remain active until the last person leaves the room. However, only the server administrator can create a persistent channel. The persistent channel remains active, whether it is occupied by a user or not. ■

To add a persistent channel, follow these steps:

1. From the Chat Service Properties dialog box, select the Channels tab, and then click the Add button to create a channel, as seen in Figure 8.18.

FIG. 8.18

Creating a persistent channel using channel properties.

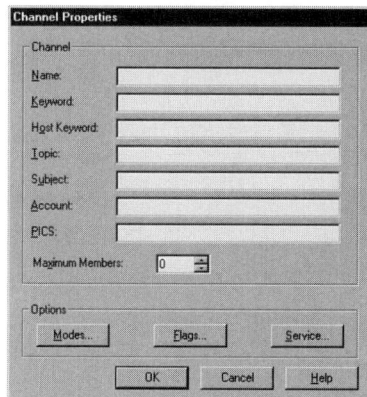

2. Enter a Name for the new channel.
3. Enter values for any of the optional parameters: Keyword, Host Keyword, Topic, Subject, Account, PICS, and Maximum Members.
4. If modes other than Public will be used, click Modes and choose the appropriate settings.
5. If special flags will be used, click Flags and choose the appropriate settings.
6. If this is a service, click Service and enter the client GUID and the Service GUID.
7. Click OK, and Apply.

N O T E A persistent channel that is empty will not be seen when a client searches for available channels. Only after someone joins the channel will it become visible. ■

Filtering Channels

Microsoft's Internet Chat Server allows administrators to control features in each channel. To set configuration and restriction options, follow these steps:

1. Access the Chat Service Properties dialog box, and select the Channels tab.
2. Highlight the group that you want to edit and then click the Edit Properties Button to access the properties.

3. Click the <u>M</u>odes button and you will be presented with a dialog window with the access and restriction options, which are:

Channel Visibility:

- Public
- Private
- Secret

Access options:

- *<u>I</u>nvitation Only*   Only invited users are allowed to enter the channel.
- *Moderated*   Turns off the default speaker setting for new members.
- *<u>K</u>nock Notification*   Messages the channel hosts if an uninvited user tries to join an invite-only channel.
- *<u>S</u>ysop is Host*   Causes users with system operator privileges to host status when they enter a channel.
- *<u>A</u>uditorium*   Only allows messages from non-host members to be sent to host members. With this option, only the hosts are notified when non-host members enter and leave the channel.

Restriction options:

- *<u>N</u>o Alias*   Causes the client's real identity to be broadcast to all channel members. For instance, upon entering a channel, the user's e-mail address, such as **doe@integritydata.com**, is displayed. This option is only supported in MIC-only channels.
- *No <u>D</u>ata*   Stops the capability to send data to members of a channel.
- *No <u>R</u>eal Names*   Stops the ability for users to query the identity or name of other members.
- *No <u>W</u>hispering*   Stops the ability for users to whisper to one another in a channel.
- *No Remote <u>U</u>sers*   Only local users will be allowed to join the channel.
- *No <u>E</u>xternal Messages*   Stops messages from non-members to the channel.
- *Only Host <u>C</u>hanges Topic*   Allows only the channel host to change the topic of the channel.

The following steps explain how to set restriction options:

1. Click the checkboxes to the left of the features you would like to use and then click OK.
   This returns you to the Channel Properties Page.
   Click OK again.
2. Click <u>A</u>pply when you return to the Chat Service Properties.

Setting Up Additional Chat Servers

To create an infrastructure that can grow and handle the load of thousands of users, it's imperative to plan for adding additional servers. Better yet, start with a multi-server approach in the beginning. This section outlines how to launch a three-server network.

Before you begin, you will need to have the additional servers configured, and successfully operating with the following components:

- *Windows NT 4.0*   The operating system.
- *Internet Information Server*   Provides the server platform for the Internet News Server and handles the connections of news clients.
- *Internet Service Manager*   This is the administration tool of the Internet Information Server and it is used to manage the Internet News Server.
- *Microsoft Internet Chat Server*   This is the commercial grade Internet Chat Server.

A Three-Server Network

With a three-server network, Microsoft reports that you should be able to handle a user base of 5,000 to 10,000 concurrent users. Follow these steps to set up the network:

1. Click the Start button, select Programs, Microsoft Internet Server, and then the Internet Service Manager.
2. Select the Chat service from the list of services and access the configuration files by selecting Properties, and then access the Service tab.
3. Click the button for Ports and Addresses.
4. Assign a unique Server Network Server Identifier (NSID) value for each chat server within the range of 1 to 255. For this example:

   Server1 - NSID = 10

   Server2 - NSID = 11

   Server3 - NSID = 12

5. After adding the NSID values, choose Apply.

Setting up Server 1:

1. Set up Server1 to connect to Server2 by choosing the Portals tab and clicking the Add button.
2. In the Name entry field in Portal Properties, enter **Server2**.
3. Enter the IP address you assigned to Server2, as seen in Figure 8.19.
4. The Port should be left at the default of 0.

FIG. 8.19

Portal properties include options such as portal names, server ports, and network server identifiers.

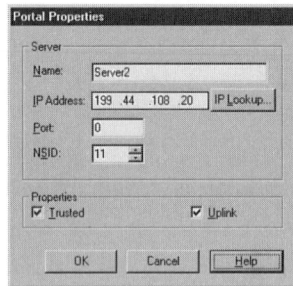

5. Set the NSID to 11.

6. Select the Trusted option and the Uplink option by placing a check in the box to the left of each option.

7. Choose OK.

Setting up Server2:

1. Set up the second chat server (Server2) to permit connections from the other two servers (Server1 and Server3). Access the Portals tab and click the Add button.

2. In the Name entry field, type **Server1**.

3. Submit the IP address you assigned to Server1.

   The Port should be left at the default of 0.

4. Set the NSID to 10.

5. Select the Trusted option and leave the Uplink option unselected. Choose OK.

6. Click the Add button to set up the link to Server3.

7. In the Name entry field, type **Server3**.

8. Submit the IP address you assigned to Server3.

   The Port should be left at the default of 0.

9. Set the NSID to 12.

10. Select the Trusted option and leave the Uplink option unselected. Choose OK.

Setting up Server3:

1. Set up the third server to connect to Server2. Access the Portals tab and click the Add button.

2. In the Name entry field, type **Server2**.

3. Submit the IP address you assigned to Server2.

4. The Port should be left at the default of 0.

5. Set the NSID to 11.

6. Select the <u>T</u>rusted option and the <u>U</u>plink option by placing a check in the box to the left of each option. Click OK.

7. The last step is to stop and restart the chat servers for the portal settings to take effect.

You now have a three-server network.

Comparing MIC with the IRC Protocol

There really isn't a contest here, and Microsoft wasn't looking for one. The Microsoft Internet Chat Server wasn't designed to replace the Internet's traditional Internet Relay Chat (IRC) protocol; it was designed to enhance it and provide a solution for the office that wants to supplement its services with an easy-to-manage online conferencing system.

When you review the features of the Microsoft Internet Chat client, you'll appreciate that fact that it uses a smaller packet size and has an ability to transfer data without converting to text; however, there are a few obvious omissions from the traditional IRC client. The most obvious omission is the user's ability to trade files. But that doesn't mean Microsoft designed a lesser server.

In fact, Microsoft didn't leave any IRC features out of this server package. To the IRC user, a connection to the Microsoft Internet Chat Server looks no different than a connection to your average UNIX server. When you connect to the Chat Server with your favorite IRC client, you can send files, and exploit all the features of IRC.

That said, you have to wonder why Microsoft left out many of the typical IRC features. It appears that the reasoning is fairly obvious. The IRC format is confusing and to the first-time user it can be quite frustrating. There are a number of basic commands that you need to learn just to get connected...and, it's even hard to figure out how to disconnect.

With the Microsoft Internet Chat client, Microsoft created a simple way to participate in an Internet chat without having to get down in the dirt trying to learn the basics. Indeed it's a clever approach, because when the user tires of the average chat, and wants to learn more features, they can graduate to a more robust client and enjoy all the features of IRC.

Going Live

Once you have completed the installation and connected your Chat Server to the Internet or the company intranet, you should consider yourself live, because now clients are hitting a live network. Therefore it's of the utmost importance to be able to keep the Server operating without disrupting the conversations.

Maintaining connections and ensuring that communications between the servers are up to par is the object of staying live. This section provides you with an overview on how to perform routine maintenance.

Administering Chat Server

The chat server seems to be a very solid server component. We experienced no down time or server crashes. The only time we had difficulty was when we were having network errors. If you have users contacting you with complaints that they cannot connect, you'll want to handle the problem like any other—simply figure out the scope of the problem, then narrow the possibilities.

The following list provides a few examples of troubleshooting problems you may encounter.

- If users cannot connect to any of the servers on the Chat Server Network, there is probably some other type of network problem. Resolve those problems first and connectivity to the Chat Network should be functional.

- If there are problems connecting to a particular chat server with all types of clients, there may be a network problem with the server. Also, the service may not be functioning properly on that machine.

- If problems occur with IRC clients connecting to a particular server, check the settings in Internet Service Manager service page for Server Modes. Specifically, this should not be set to MIC only if you also want to allow IRC clients. You may also want to check to make sure that the number of anonymous clients allowed on the Internet Service Manager service page in the Connection Limit settings for Anonymous users is set high enough. You can adjust this setting dynamically, which means you don't need to stop and restart the service; however, you need to be aware of how many clients the server can support before you change it. You should also be aware that if this number is set to zero, all users are forced to be authenticated. Raising this number above zero means that unauthenticated users will be allowed on the server.

- If clients connecting from a specific domain cannot connect, check the Internet Service Manager page for classes. Simply ensure that a class has not been set up to ban a group of users.

Checking the Health of the Channel   If users cannot join a channel, it's most likely because the channel is full. The host of the channel can raise the channel limit to the maximum number of clients allowed as defined in the Internet Service Manager's page for Service. This is configured under Member Limits. If the host sets the number higher, no error is given and the channel limit is set to the maximum as defined in the ISM. It is also possible to set persistent and dynamic channels so that only MIC users can join, or only authenticated users can join, so it is important for the creator of the channel to review the settings that were defined when the channel was created.

To raise the maximum number of members allowed in a channel:

1. Open the Internet Service Manager's page for Service.
2. Set Maximum member limit as desired, and click OK.

    The setting will take effect on all new channels created.

N O T E When users can no longer see channels on the server that exist on the net, the culprit is more than likely a net split. Net splits are a very common occurrence on the Internet. In short, it means another server on the network split off from the network you were on. It's one of the side effects you'll experience when you connect to the global IRC community. Net splits occur for any number of reasons, such as another server crashing.

Sometimes a split happens when another server is too overloaded to handle additional connections. A split may also be the result of another IRC administrator closing their connection for maintenance reasons. To the user who is chatting on the network, when a net split occurs it appears that suddenly a number of people quit simultaneously. Users who are new to IRC may wonder if they said something offensive and chased people away. In reality, there was a net split. Eventually, the servers will rejoin. And the mass of users who quit will rejoin simultaneously. ▪

Monitoring the Chat Server

The Windows NT Performance Monitor enables you to look at the performance status of the Internet Chat Server. With Performance Monitor you can review the status and health of your server by viewing over 80 different performance counters, each of which is designed to give you the most informed information about your Chat Server.

To access the Performance Monitor and evaluate the status of the Internet Chat Server, follow these steps:

1. Click the Start button, select Programs, then Administrative Tools, and then choose the Performance Monitor. The Performance Monitor is launched.

2. Choose View, Chart.

3. Choose to add to the chart by choosing Edit, Add to Chart. You can also activate this feature by clicking the + button on the toolbar.

4. The Performance Monitor launches the Add to Chart dialog box. Some of the main features needed in the Performance Monitor are:

    - *Computer*   Selects the computer you want to monitor. The server you are on appears as the default. If the Internet Chat Server resides on another server, click the ellipsis button (...) and a Select Computer dialog box is launched.

    - *Object*   Select an object to monitor from the computer you selected.

    - *Counters*   Selects the counter you want to monitor.

5. Leave the Computer at the default.

6. Change the Object feature to Chat Server.

7. Select the counter of interest. To review what the counters are designed to do, highlight the option and click the Explain button. For this test, select Current Clients, which is a count of all the clients on the Chat Server.

8. Now click the Add button and the counters will be launched.

9. Click the Done button and the Performance Monitor begins charting a graph. If you presently have no clients, the chart will be flatlined at zero. To initiate a response, launch michat.exe from the ics/client/ directory and log in to the chat server. Perform will immediately record the entrance of the new client.

10. To customize the chart, choose Options, Chart.

11. Select the option to add a Horizontal grid.

12. Click OK and review the outcome.

N O T E   If you have an active Chat Server and the Performance Monitor for "current clients" drops to zero, you have lost your clients and are probably disconnected from the chat network. This may have happened because of a network error, but if the network seems to be working, try stopping and restarting the service. The server should reconnect to the chat network and the performance monitor should begin recording the "current client" load again.

You can also exploit the alert mode feature of the Performance Monitor to automatically notify you when levels do not reach your expectations. Here's how you set up the alert feature for Performance Monitor:

1. Click the Start button, select Programs, Administrative Tools, and then choose the Performance Monitor.

   The Performance Monitor is launched.

2. Select the View the Alerts button on the button bar, or choose View, Alert.

3. Choose the Add Counter button (+), or choose Edit, Add to Alert.

4. Select the Object as Chat Server, and this time set the Counter as Client Bytes Sent/sec.

5. In the Alert if field, select the Under and type the number 1 in the text entry field. This will cause the server to notify you whenever the server has no activity whatsoever.

6. Click the Add button.

7. Choose Options, Alert to launch the Alert Options dialog box.

8. If an alert is necessary, the Performance Monitor can be configured to Switch to an Alert View, or Send a network message to the administrator. For now, select Switch to an Alert View.

9. The Performance Monitor tracks anything that crosses the alert threshold and logs the activity on the Performance Monitor page.

10. Monitor the server resources and adjust as needed.

N O T E   Microsoft's minimum recommended configuration is currently a Proliant Quad Processor machine, 128 MHz or better, with a minimum 128M RAM. Problems are most likely to be experienced on machines that do not meet the suggested configuration.

Reviewing a Variety of IRC Clients

There are several fine IRC clients available for download on the Internet. For the most part, the features are all trying to do the same thing, which is to deliver an automated interface to the confusing Internet Relay Chat architecture. Since you will probably have users accessing your pages with similar clients, it would be a good idea to take a look at a variety of IRC clients to get a look at the interface your users will experience. Here are three examples of IRC clients you may want to review:

- *PIRCH (Shareware)* PIRCH is an IRC client for the Microsoft Windows 3.x, Windows 95, and Windows NT platforms and can be downloaded by visiting **http://www.bcpl.lib.md.us/~frappa/pirch.html**. This is an easy-to-use, customizable client that has lots of extras that improve on the typical IRC client interface, which is barely a step beyond the command line interface. PIRCH makes the most of the graphic user interface. The current registration fee for PIRCH is $10.00.

- *mIRC (Shareware)* For experienced IRC users, this is the best client available. Visit the mIRC homepage at http://www.mirc.co.uk/ to download a copy, which is available in 16- and 32-bit versions. mIRC offers full DCC File Send and Get capabilities, aliases, remote commands, and plenty more. But if you're not an experienced IRC user, you may want to start with a different client. The program is free of charge for 30 days to evaluate. The current registration charge is $15.00.

- *VIRC (Freeware)* Visual IRC is a scriptable IRC client; currently there are 16- and 32-bit versions that can be downloaded at **http://www.megalith.co.uk/virc**. VIRC is quite functional with a number of extra features.

From Here...

At the conclusion of this chapter, you should have a general understanding of the Microsoft Commercial Internet Chat Server, including installation and configuration procedures, setting up additional chat servers and going live.

- For information on how to use ActiveX Chat Control, see the Introduction to Internet Information Server 3.0 in Chapter 16, "Serving Active Content on the Internet."

- For further Performance Tuning information, please refer to Que's *Special Edition Using Microsoft BackOffice*.

Commercial Internet System Membership Services

Understanding Commercial Internet Personalization System

Implement the Personalization Server

Gain an understanding of what the Personalization Server can do for you and take a look at how others are getting the most out of this server.

Install and configure the Personalization Server

Learn how to get the most out of the Personalization Server, along with specific information on how to configure and maintain the product.

Use templates and ActiveX to create personalization

Learn how to adapt Personalization into your site quickly with some easy to use templates and controls.

The key to a successful Internet site boils down to how well you can portray your company's self-concept on a computer screen. Contemporary culture has created a public that loves fast food and makes decisions quickly. If your Web site doesn't have something to offer immediately, you shouldn't expect the public to search through your haystack to find some special nugget of information. Society's attention span is short, and the average Web surfer, unless they are absolutely committed to finding out something specific about your organization, are going to be out of there as quickly as you can say "it's only two clicks off the home page."

What you think you are as an organization is oftentimes not in sync with the public's interpretation. At this level of communication, the public's definition really counts. The Microsoft Internet Personalization System is designed to allow your clients to determine what's important to them, and avoid the things they have no interest in. Interestingly, with the Personalization System, the company can sit back and get a realistic view of what its real deliverables are. There are two tiers in this transaction. First, what does the user want? Second, how can the organization collect that information to target the user's interest later?

In this chapter, you get an overview of the advantages of a Personalized Site, the installation process of the Microsoft Internet Personalization System, and a look at a few sites that are using the system. There will also be information on some of the features of the system, such as identifying users, along with some information on using the ActiveX control pack. When you complete this chapter, you will have found that authoring pages is not too difficult, as there are plenty of templates, wizards, and GUI authoring tools. ■

Taking Advantage of a Personalized Site

It's a whole new Web out there. In a very short time, the way we deliver information over the Web has changed considerably. When the first Web browsers were released, the Web world consisted of static pages. Some Web sites showed the appearance of life, but when look and feel changed, it was because the Web page designers took the initiative to make manual updates to the pages.

At first, that was enough to captivate us. But not for long. We had to liven things up.

In comes the dynamic Web page, as seen in Figure 9.1. Here the user is served up information from databases. The Web pages are written on-the-fly and once again, Web surfers are captivated.

FIG. 9.1

With dynamic pages, the page shows more signs of life because the users see a new look every day.

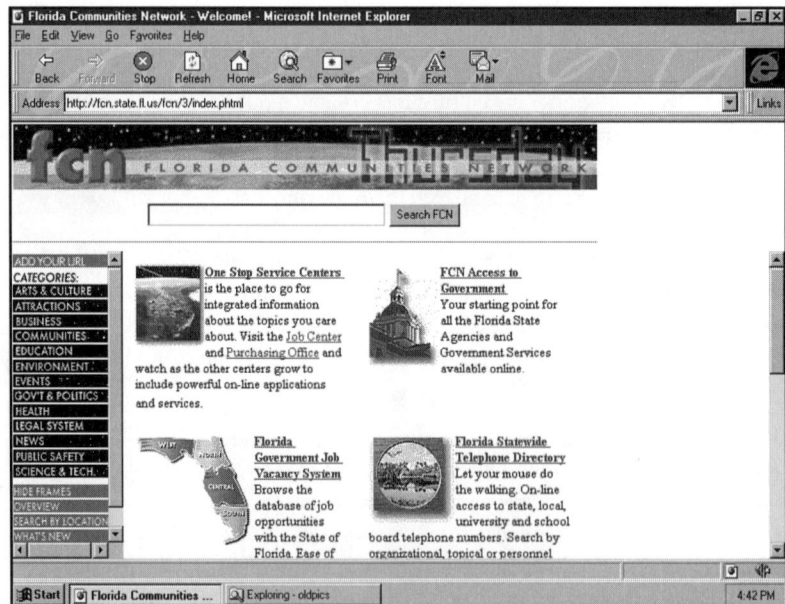

The older sites that required a manual conversion of documents to HTML are now being converted on-the-fly and placed in Web pages. But who could be satisfied with that? The Web surfer wants to be the focal point and wants to be catered to. So let the catering begin.

Today, winning Web pages must also be personalized, specifically delivering information that is based on the current user's interests. Imagine a radio station that could identify who was listening at a certain moment and then deliver customized information based on their interest. Confused? OK, try this. Farmer Ted turns on his radio; at the very moment he flips the dial to 94.9, the disc jockey at the radio station is informed that Farmer Ted has tuned in. Because the DJ knows Farmer Ted likes fishing, football, and computers, he only sends him advertising and marketing information on sports and high tech stuff. Interestingly, Mrs. Jones is listening to the same radio station at the same moment. Instead of hearing about sports and computers, the DJ serves her up shopping information, beauty tips, and food. After all, that's what she cares about. It's an interesting scenario, albeit impossible, but imagine the power behind a marketing approach that adjusts for every listener. That's why the latest developments on the Web are so captivating.

The Microsoft Internet Personalization System is designed to deliver that very thing, as seen in Figure 9.2. With this application, users have a say about what you'll deliver. For them it's an individualized view of the Web, determined by their individual tastes. For you it just might be marketing heaven.

Indeed, the Web will never be the same again. Bravo for that!

FIG. 9.2
Personalization comes in the form of direct marketing to the user, delivering topics based on what they selected through an online questionnaire.

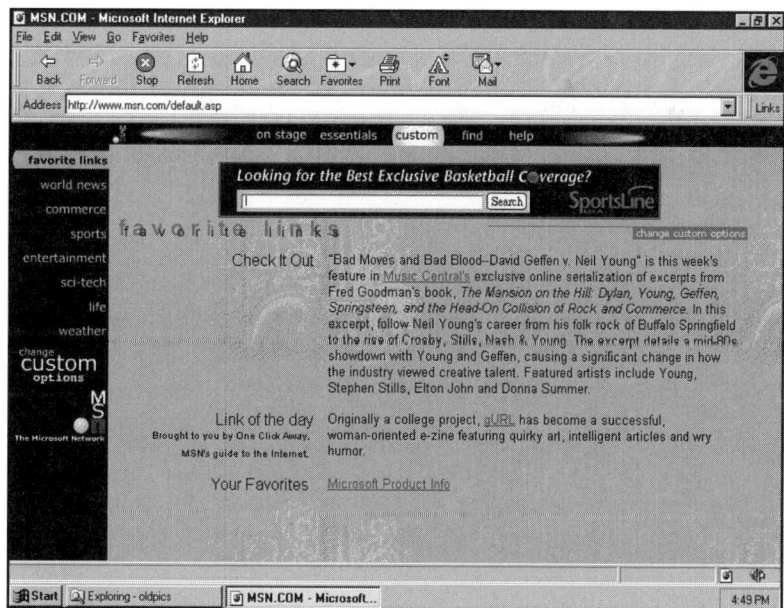

Attracting New Customers

With today's technology, the notion of sending the same message to everybody is absurd.

At the Florida Communities Network there is a steady flow of people visiting the site. Some are accessing purchasing information, others are interested in searching the state phone book, and most are looking for a job. There's a lot to sift through, and it can easily become a tangled mess unless you find a way to let the user determine what is important. That can be done a couple of different ways:

- Let the user fill out a questionnaire asking them to list their top interests, and then deliver them a custom home page based on their interests.
- Over a short amount of time, track what the user is accessing. Then have the custom pages develop without a user request.

The first option is quite direct and the user feels like the organization is giving them the option to take control of the site, which isn't bad from their perspective. The second option is a little more clever because changes occur without asking the user directly what they want. A side effect may be that the users just think that by some weird twist the world is starting to cater to their interest. From their perspective, that's also a good thing.

The bottom line is that the more specific the audience definition is, the more interesting and useful the site becomes to its visitors. When a new visitor stops by to visit your Web page, and the user has the feeling that you are there to cater to their every need, they more than likely will be back. People love good service from an organization that understands their needs. Of course, if the product stinks they may lose interest quickly, but they'll remember the quality service. And that's a step in the right direction.

Increasing Web Site Effectiveness

There's no way around it, each customer is unique. Your ability to create positive one-on-one relationships with your customers dictates your success. Here are a few ways to improve your Web site:

- Enhance the attractiveness of the site by tailoring the information to the visitor's interest.
- Track user information internally to get a better idea of what people like on the site and what they don't like.
- Add functionality and simplicity for the Web visitor. In other words, give up the steering wheel and let the customer drive, as seen in Figure 9.3.

It's all about raising the bar. Gone are the old days, where customers had to wade through a lot of peripheral information to get to what they want. Today, forward thinking organizations can deliver unique information based on the user's personal interests.

Customer Response

Though the new personalized approach to building a Web site sounds like a terrific idea, and many customers applaud the technology, the topic has stirred up some folks. Presently, there is an ongoing debate about the appropriateness of personalization. The debate centers around potential privacy implications. Specifically, the experts are talking about *cookies*, and there are no chocolate chips in these cookies.

FIG. 9.3

At the Microsoft Network, users complete an online form and express what interests them, such as sports or world news, and thereby dictate what topics will be delivered to them when they access the Web page.

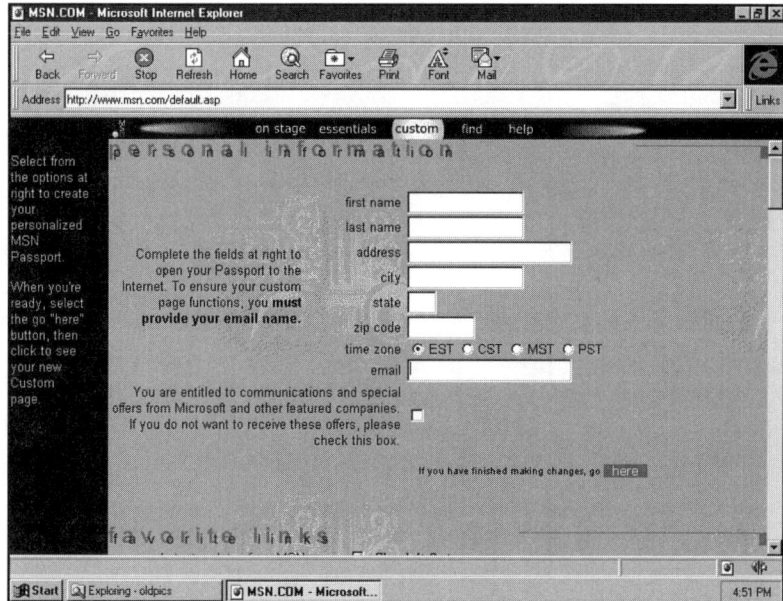

What's a cookie? Basically, it's the placing of information on a user's hard drive, providing details about a user's previous visit to the site.

N O T E The cookie is best described as a "persistent client-side data storage." With MCIS, all the user gets is a GUID (Global User Identification), which is unique to the user. In Personalization, the information (likes and dislikes) is actually stored on the server in a non-SQL database and is read in when the GUID is read from the client. Shawn Trexler, who is handling much of the MCIS development at the Florida Communities Network, considers this a much safer method of persistent data storage since no opinions can be read in without access to the server itself. At the current time, only MCIS Personalization can do that.

The cookie is a file that can, and will, be used by Internet sites to access a user's behavior profile from a database. In effect, through time a site can monitor everything you do, then morph itself into something that better meets your interests. That's why some folks are concerned about privacy invasions.

You'll be hearing a lot more about cookies over the next year. For now, be aware that some people would prefer it if you didn't serve them a cookie. They see it as an invasion of privacy. Heck, you can gather a detailed profile of their online experience without their knowledge or consent, as seen in Figure 9.4. It's important to be sensitive to these issues.

ON THE WEB

http://www.anonymizer.com/   Already, there are free services on the Internet that are designed to protect the identity of users. Check out this site for more information.

FIG. 9.4

Web sites can gather a lot of information about you without your consent, as demonstrated by the Center for Democracy and Technology's Web page.

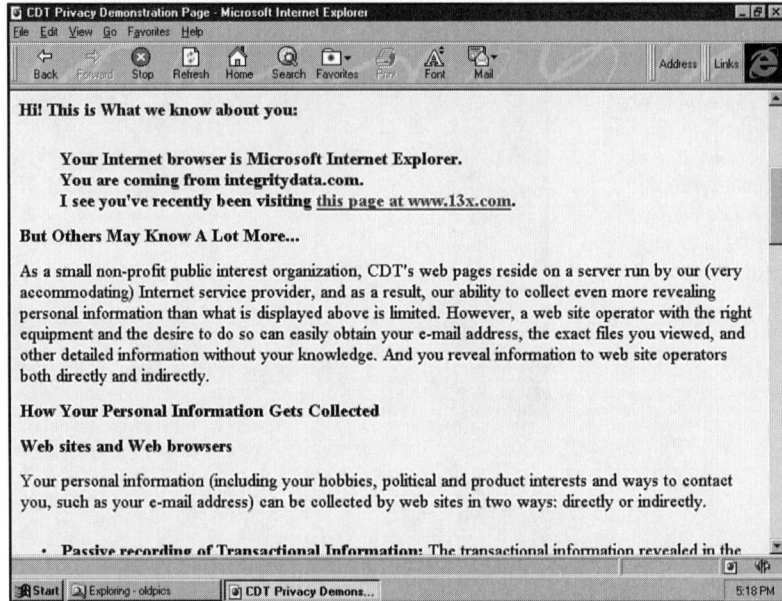

NOTE   Perhaps the best solution for organizations to handle the technology during the privacy battle is to be open and honest about the techniques you use to personalize the site for them. It might be a good idea to let the user decide whether they want to have a personalized site. ▓

Certainly, Web administrators see the benefit to a customized site. It's time you found out from the customer what they want.

Customer Satisfaction

We're a whiz bang world and the next cool feature we unleash on the Internet is designed to be impressive. Our developer friends are turned on by our latest tricks. It's a constant competition to outdo your peers in the development world. Of course, to the average user, a lot of these developments are useless. Does the customer really care if his favorite color combination comes up every time he visits your site? The customer craves information, and if you have little to offer in that department you can forget about return visits.

Now's the time to get in touch with the customer. Perhaps you could offer users the ability to vote on their top interests and then use that information to shape the future of the site. Later in this chapter you learn about the voting feature, which is located in "User Surveys," built into the Internet Personalization System. It's simple, and allows users to have input on the direction of the site. If your success depends on customer satisfaction, then it's imperative to let the customer shape your direction.

Personalization is indeed the wave of the future, but personalization alone will not keep customers coming back. If you have a lack of useful content to offer, you may be wasting your time. Content is king. If you want to please your customers, the job of providing information they are interested in will always be the Number One priority.

Analyzing Site Traffic

Typically, the way to determine how your site is being accessed by the users is to analyze the system log files. With the log files, you can determine which pages are the most popular on your server and how hard your server is working. You can also determine where your accesses are coming from, such as city, state, and country. Unfortunately, it's not easy to figure out what all the numbers in the log files mean.

What the organization needs is specific user information, not an overview of hits. The focus here is user analysis, not exhaustive content usage analysis. The goal is to build a platform for predictive modeling. When you can deliver pages based on what the user wants, before the user even knows what he wants, that's when you're on top of personalization.

Checking Trends   The Internet Personalization System provides the ability to capture user information. There are also tools available to make the most out of the information you collect in the database. That information reveals specific facts about each user and makes it easier for your development teams to create user profiles. User properties include everything from information based on the user's Web activity, to other information provided by the user. This knowledge allows organizations to make buying and surfing recommendations to repeat visitors.

Using Retrieval Information   Personal information can be used in many ways, such as providing information that is specific to the user's taste, as seen in Figure 9.5.

Information can be content-based, or it might be focused on targeted advertising. When it comes to making money, the two most important ingredients are obvious:

- *Website tracking*   In short, what motivates the user. Organizations pay hundreds of thousands of dollars to attain information on the specific makeup of their clientele. The more you know about the client, the easier it is to target sales. And that's where the next ingredient comes in.

- *Online marketing*   Once you have a clue on the user's taste, you can place advertisements that will be of interest to them. Manipulative, perhaps, but this is about service. If your customer has no interest in hardware, there's no need to try to sell them a hammer.

ON THE WEB

An example of hyper-focused online marketing is available at **http://www.doubleclick.net**. At this site they use a tracking method to determine what ads you click, and continue to direct-market to you based on your previous selections.

FIG. 9.5
Hotwired allows users the ability to customize their viewing experience.

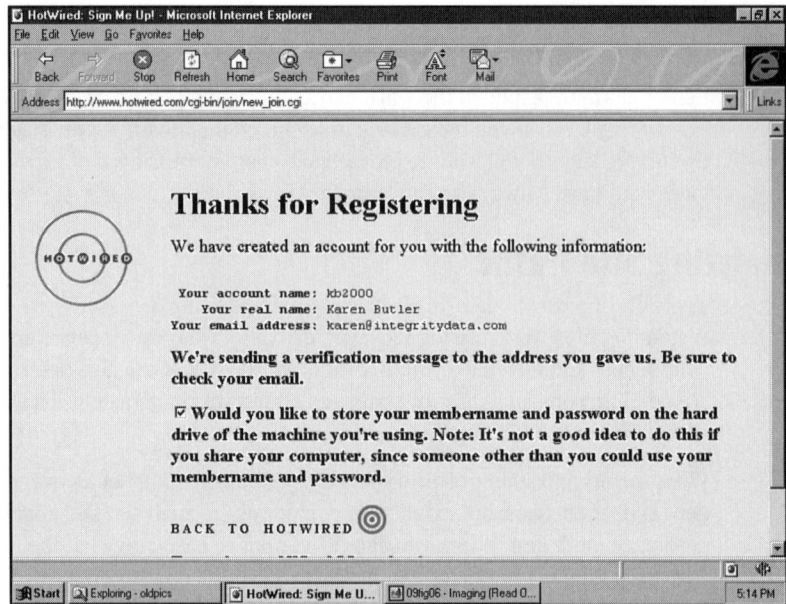

Features of the Personalization System

The best news about the Internet Personalization System is that it doesn't require a hard core programmer to develop the features. There are templates and active scripts available once you install the program, and they're not too hard to understand. Here are several of the intriguing features in the personalization system:

- *User Property Database* Have the user complete a form and then you can display the user's name on the page every time they return to the site. This is the first step to personalization and a good example of the use of cookies.

- *Voting* Allow users to vote on topics, or hot issues. The information is stored in a database which is updated and presented with every vote that is registered.

- *Forms processing* Processing forms is old news on the Web. However, this is a nice integrated feature that allows you to receive comments or information, have it placed in a database, display the results on a Web page, and send an e-mail message to the user to confirm the receipt of the form.

Developers can mix and match these features to accomplish a number of results, including targeted mailings and personalized content.

Sampling Custom Sites

Personalization, and the use of the Microsoft Internet Personalization feature, is alive and well on the Internet. In this section you'll have an opportunity to look at a few sites which are using the Personalization System.

www.gencom.net

Genesis Communications Network, Inc., an Internet Service Provider to businesses and government in north Florida, has recently begun experimenting with personalization on its Web site. If you visit their pages you'll encounter the following:

- *User personalization*   Users fill out a questionnaire and outline their preference for the look and feel of their viewing experience. There is a set of background textures available for the user to choose from, and options. In fact, if the user chooses, they can set a byte threshold for sizes. If you don't want to wait for images that are larger than 50K in size, simply set the filter to exclude images that are above that threshold.

- *Polling*   Genesis Communications Network hosts the Web pages for The Public Agenda Project, which promotes the return to participatory democracy, where people are involved with their social environment in an informed and active way. The Internet Personalization System offers an opportunity to vote on community issues and check the real time status of the poll.

- *Personalization based on preference*   Genesis Communications Network also hosts the pages of Scott McPherson's Help Screen, a syndicated computer column published by Knight Ridder. By using cookies, the Web pages deliver PC or Macintosh related tips. Whichever preference trends the user shows affect the page display.

www.msn.com

The Microsoft Network offers a page that users can configure to provide specific information from news to comics by filling out online forms. The Microsoft Network Web page, seen in Figure 9.6, offers a questionnaire where the users identify their interests. Once complete, a personalized page is developed for each user.

In the process, the user is informed that they are entitled to special offers from Microsoft and other featured companies. If you do not want to receive those offers via e-mail, you choose to turn off that option.

Whenever the user visits the MSN site, they are presented with their custom page and have the option to update their personalization configuration at any time.

FIG. 9.6
The Microsoft Network
features plenty of
customization options.

FIG. 9.6
The Microsoft Network features plenty of customization options.

Identifying Users

It all boils down to cookies and the User Property Database. When the user arrives at your site, the Web server accesses a record of their interest. Based on that information, the server delivers a personalized Web page.

Cookies

Cookies have been around since the introduction of Netscape Navigator 1.1 in March of 1995, but it wasn't until recently that their capability has unfolded. If you access the /cookies directory in your Windows NT folder, you can take a look at the cookies you have received so far.

Here's a cookie I picked up from ESPN SportsZone:

```
SWID 32282422-653C6279-50223DD7-689B4D1F.0000 sportszone.com/
0 2704337024 29165831 1999385824 29092406 *
```

Contained in the cryptic numbers is probably information about my trip through the SportZone. If we could decipher this, it would probably tell us that the user visited the site using the Internet Explorer browser on December 14. The user accessed the results on the winner of the Heisman trophy, and then departed. Nothing too personal, but ESPN has learned something about my interest. So long as they don't confuse me with being a Florida Gator football fan, what do I care?

CAUTION

Deciding how to interpret the user data is of great importance since the interests of the user may not match the interpretations of the designer. Additionally, decisions about what information to track must take into consideration the disk space available and the usefulness of the information. MPS has a limit of 2K per cookie, so you'll want to use it wisely.

Netscape Navigator uses a similar procedure, only the cookies are saved in a single file named cookies.txt found in /Program Files/Netscape/Navigator. A current Netscape Navigator cookie file is shown in Figure 9.7.

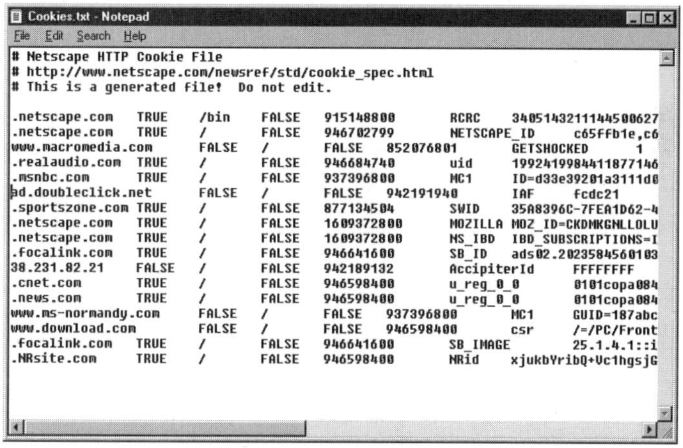


```
# Netscape HTTP Cookie File
# http://www.netscape.com/newsref/std/cookie_spec.html
# This is a generated file!  Do not edit.

.netscape.com   TRUE    /bin    FALSE   915148800       RCRC    340514321144500627
.netscape.com   TRUE    /       FALSE   946702799       NETSCAPE_ID     c65ffb1e,c6
www.macromedia.com      FALSE   /       FALSE   852076801       GETSHOCKED      1
.realaudio.com  TRUE    /       FALSE   946684740       uid     1992419984411877146
.msnbc.com      TRUE    /       FALSE   937396800       MC1     ID=d33e39201a3111d0
ad.doubleclick.net      FALSE   /       FALSE   942191940       IAF     fcdc21
.sportszone.com TRUE    /       FALSE   877134504       SWID    35A8396C-7FEA1D62-4
.netscape.com   TRUE    /       FALSE   1609372800      MOZILLA MOZ_ID=CKDMKGNLLOLU
.netscape.com   TRUE    /       FALSE   1609372800      NS_IBD  IBD_SUBSCRIPTIONS=I
.focalink.com   TRUE    /       FALSE   946641600       SB_ID   ads02.202358456010З
38.231.82.21    FALSE   /       FALSE   942189132       AccipiterId     FFFFFFFF
.cnet.com       TRUE    /       FALSE   946598400       u_reg_0_0       0101copa084
.news.com       TRUE    /       FALSE   946598400       u_reg_0_0       0101copa084
www.ms-normandy.com     FALSE   /       FALSE   937396800       MC1     GUID=187abc
www.download.com        FALSE   /       FALSE   946598400       csr     /=/PC/Front
.focalink.com   TRUE    /       FALSE   946641600       SB_IMAGE        25.1.4.1::i
.NRsite.com     TRUE    /       FALSE   946598400       NRid    xjukbYribQ+Vc1hgsjG
```

FIG. 9.7
A typical Netscape Navigator cookies.txt file includes cookies from several sites.

Cookies identify the user by a name or identification tag and any other information you choose to track. It's client-side information that remains persistent.

NOTE Netscape Navigator writes its cookie files a little differently than Internet Explorer. As mentioned previously, Navigator writes them to a single file, while Explorer writes individual files. However, Navigator only writes to the cookies.txt file upon a proper exit and shutdown of Navigator. This means that if Navigator crashes before the user can exit the program properly, all persistent client-side data is lost. Explorer doesn't have that problem. Another plus with Explorer is that the user can delete cookies from certain sites from within their directory. Navigator warns against editing the cookies.txt file because it is machine generated.

In the Personalization System, the cookie mechanism is built in. When a cookie is placed on the user's hard drive, there is no login or password required when the user next visits the site. Instead, the cookie places a unique ID in the cookie the first time the user visits the site, which enables per-user tracking and becomes a sort of caller ID system for the server.

What can be placed in a cookie? It can be virtually anything. Naturally, it will contain the basics, such as the unique user ID generated by the server, the current date and time, and the IP Address where the browser is logged on to the net. There's plenty of opportunities to place additional chunks of data as long as you keep it under 2K.

N O T E   When a user visits a site, the browser will only send the cookie to the server that originally created and placed it. There's no need to worry about administrators from other servers reviewing what cookies other sites have placed on a particular user's hard drive. ■

For the privacy advocates, a cookie is a text token associated with a domain and a path. This is what we have referred to as the unique user ID and is the information that the browser and server pass back and forth to generate the personalized page. Cookies can be used to record all input from a user, which can then be placed into a database for later use.

HTTP Basic

The Personalization System is based on the HTTP Basic cookie standards. Here is an example on how a sample cookie might be delivered:

The cookie might resemble the following:

```
Visit=1 expires=Wednesday, 09-Nov-1999 23:12:40 GMT;
path=/; domain=.integritydata.com; secure
```

- **Visit=1**   This is the `name` field and 1 is the content of your data.
- **expires=Wednesday, 09-Nov-1999 23:12:40 GMT**   This is the date the cookie will expire. Notice, it's based on Greenwich Mean Time. If a date is not configured, the cookie will go away when the user completed their session.
- **path=/**   This tells the browser to send the cookie when the user requests an URL of at least that path (the root directory). If you set the field to `path=/test` the cookie will only be returned if the browser requests an URL in the path `/test` or a subdirectory in the `/test` directory. If you set the cookie to the root directory, a cookie is sent with every page that is accessed.
- **domain=.integritydata.com**   This is the domain where the cookie will be returned. You must have at least two periods in it, such as .integritydata.com. If your site was www.integritydata.com, it would be fine because there are two periods listed in the domain name.

N O T E   Internet Explorer needs the domain name to be in lowercase while Netscape Navigator is not case-sensitive. ■

User Property Database   The User Property Database component is used to identify visitors to a Web site by creating a unique ID for each visit. This database is made up of a group of files containing user information about each Web site visitor. Basically, here's how it works: When a new user visits your site, an HTML script creates a globally unique ID (GUID) for the new user. With this GUID, the User Property Database is updated and the server can store information regarding the user's preferences. Interestingly, all Microsoft sites share the same common GUID database, and also, the same User Property Database. With this design if you make changes on MSNBC to your news profile, it is conceivable that MSN or **www.microsoft.com** could pick up on the changes and provide you with customized content there.

Installing the Personalization System

This section is a brief overview of the hardware considerations that are needed for the Personalization System and a step-by-step installation guide. You will also get an opportunity to test the installation prior to going live with your user public.

Preplanning

Like any of the Microsoft Commercial Internet Servers, you need to make decisions on the architecture of your site based on present Web traffic and user sessions. Specifically, with the Personalization system you need to decide how much content you intend to personalize and the information you expect to store for each user.

The required storage capacity for the User Property Database is a combination of the anticipated number of users of your Web site, the amount of information you plan to store for each user, and how much your site will use the Voting component. The following table charts required storage space for a typical site; your storage needs may vary.

The following assumptions were made: 100 properties stored for each user, 20 bytes per property, two votes stored at any given time.

Number of Users	User Property Database Storage	Vote Database Storage
1 thousand	2M	32K
10 thousand	20M	320K
100 thousand	200M	3.2M
1 million	2G	30M
10 million	20G	300M

How Many Servers?   The number of Web servers your site needs is largely determined by the:

- Number of HTTP requests received per second by your site at peak load
- Percentage of those requests that are for personalized Web content
- Complexity of those personalized pages

Estimating the exact number of servers needed also depends on a number of variables that affect a Web server's exact performance, such as:

- RAM
- CPU speed and power
- CPU type
- Server architecture
- Network bandwidth
- Script complexity

The delivery of a personalized Web page requires a lot more processing power than a static page containing two images and some text. The more complex the site, the more processing power you will need. According to Microsoft, a 120 MHz quad processor with 128M of RAM can efficiently handle the following:

Page Requests/sec	Requests/day	Web Servers Needed	File Servers Needed
1	86,400	1	0 (same server)
10	860,000	2	1
50	4,300,000	10	1
100	8,600,000	20	2

SendMail Traffic   With Personalization, you also need the ability to send e-mail. This enables you to exploit the SendMail feature when you are communicating with your users through automated programs. Specifically, you want to be able to send automatic mail messages to users based on their needs. In order to use this feature, you need to review your present mail infrastructure.

The number of SMTP servers needed by the SendMail Component is directly related to the estimated maximum number of e-mail messages sent per second. SendMail is typically used to thank users for submitting information or to deliver the submitted information to an e-mail box. In those cases, the number of messages needed per second is usually low. The following table suggests the number of SMTP servers that you will need based on the estimated use of SendMail.

The numbers were calculated for an SMTP server running on a single-processor Pentium 133 with 32M of RAM.

E-Mail Messages/sec	E-Mail Messages/day	Number of SMTP Servers Needed
1	86,400	1
5	432,000	2

For software, you will need Windows NT 3.51 (or higher) with Service Pack 4, Microsoft Internet Information Server (IIS) version 3.0 for basic installation. Personalization System can use an SMTP mail server and an SQL database server to deliver a greatly enhanced level of capability.

Running Setup

To install Microsoft Personalization System, follow these steps:

1. Make sure you are logged on to the server as an administrator and exit all running Windows programs.

2. Launch the Microsoft Personalization System executable program setup.exe to begin the setup process.

3. At the Installation Welcome screen choose Next and at the License Agreement screen select the Yes button to accept the terms of the agreement and proceed with installation.

4. In the Registration dialog box, enter your Name and Company affiliation and click the Next button.

5. Choose the destination directory where the Personalization System should be installed. The default directory is c:\MCIS; to accept the folder, click Next; to choose another, click Browse.

6. Select the components you want to install, as seen in Figure 9.8. The options include:

   - *Microsoft Personalization System*   This installs the User Property Database and the Voting Mechanism.
   - *User Property Database Admin Tool*   A tool that allows administrators to add or reconfigure file servers.
   - *Sample Script Templates*   Installs a few templates that will be used for demonstration purposes.
   - *Documentation*   Installs the Operations, Reference guide, and Web Authors guide for the Personalization System.
   - *SendMail Component*   The feature that allows users to send e-mail from your Web site. In order for this to work you need an SMTP mail server. If you do not have a mail server available for use by the Personalization, unselect this option.
   - *User Logging Filter*   Installs a filter that will allow the administrator to add the identification of the user that is viewing the site to the server's log files.

7. If any services are running, the setup program will notify you. Click Yes to have the setup program automatically shut down the services.

FIG. 9.8

Install all of the components, unless there are features you will be avoiding, such as the SendMail Component.

Part
III
Ch
9

8. Enter the host name or IP address of the mail server that will be used for the SendMail Component of the System and click Next.

N O T E   If you do not enter a valid mail server, Setup will display an error dialog box. The setup program is attempting to Ping the server during this point of the installation. If you get an error it may also be because your network connection is down. ▪

9. In the Transaction log configuration, choose to disable or enable logging. For this installation, leave the properties at their default, with Logging being conducted daily or when the file length reaches 100,000 lines. The destination directory of c:\WINNT\System32\LogFiles is the standard location for the log files. Click Next.

10. At the User ID dialog box, choose to Enable User ID Sharing and enter the host name for the main Web site, for example **site.integritydata.com**. Click Next.

N O T E   Since user identifications are typically stored in cookies, and the information in the cookie can't be shared, you need an alternate means for tracking the user. You'll want to enable User ID Sharing to build a more complete user profile. With this feature, new users are redirected to a single cookie generation URL. This ensures that the same user, across multiple domains, is identified by the same ID. However, if you are configuring a standalone server, there would be no need to include ID sharing. ▪

11. Enter the domain name for the master domain, for instance **.integritydata.com**. It's important to make sure the domain name begins with a leading period. This information will be user by the User Property Database to redirect a user to the master site. Click Next.

12. In the Folder Selection dialog box, either accept the Program Folder default option of MCIS, enter a new Program Folder name, or select from Existing Folders. Click Next.

13. Confirm your selections and click the Next button or click the Back button to access any fields that need to be edited and then return to the Confirm Setup dialog box and proceed. The file installation process begins.

14. At the Property Database Administrator dialog box, Setup will walk you through the configuration process for the User Property Database Administrator. Click Next.

15. Determine if this is the first machine to be configured using the User Property Database. Click Next.

16. Configure the server and directory for the User Property Database and click Next.

17. After the Administration tool displays a dialog box reporting that the configuration is complete, click Next.

18. After finishing the initial setup, select the I Want to Run the Setup Verification Pages checkbox and click the Finish button. If you want to review the release notes for the Personaliztion System, select the checkbox for I Want to View the Release Notes.

Installation is complete! Now it's time to test the Installation to make sure the Personalization System is functioning properly.

Testing Internet Personalization System

Once the Setup program is complete, your Web browser will be launched to the Internet Personalization Verification Page, as seen in Figure 9.9.

FIG. 9.9

The Internet Personalization Verification page helps you determine quickly whether Setup was successful.

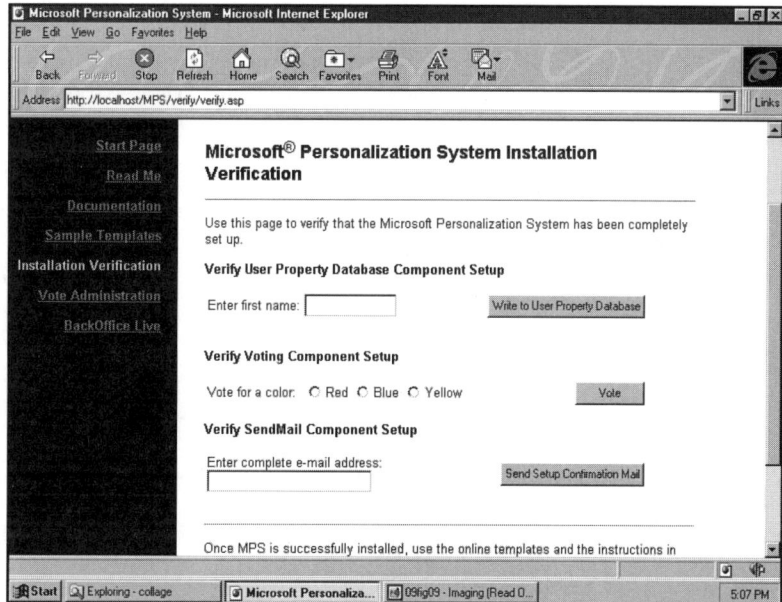

CAUTION

It is necessary to type the complete URL "http://localhost/mcisverify/mps/verify.asp," as seen in Figure 9.9, and not just the file name because it has to be read by the server. For people who just drag files from Windows Explorer into Internet Explorer, you'll be left wondering why the verification page isn't displaying properly.

Here, you will conduct a three-step test to ensure that the User Property Database, the Voting Component, and the SendMail Component were set up properly. Begin with the first field:

1. *Verify User Property Database Component Setup* Enter your first name, then click the Write to User Property Database button. The submission will be processed and a new Web page will be created. If the User Property Database is set up properly, you will receive confirmation with a response using your first name.

If the User Property Database is not working, check the following:

- Did you restart the computer after installing the Personalization System? If not, do so.

N O T E Users may want to bookmark the Verification page before rebooting. This will make it easier for you to verify once you've rebooted. ▬

- Your file server may not be configured properly. Reconfigure the User Property Database by using the administration tool.

- Your Web server may not have security access to the User Property Database file server. Use Windows NT Explorer to check the properties and to change the permissions so that everyone has full access.

2. *Verify Voting Component Setup*   Select the color you want to vote on, then click the Vote button. The submission will be processed and a new Web page will be created, as seen in Figure 9.10. If the Voting component is set up properly, you will receive confirmation through a table that shows the present vote count with the color, the Number of Votes, and the Percentage.

FIG. 9.10

Testing the voting Component through the verification page.

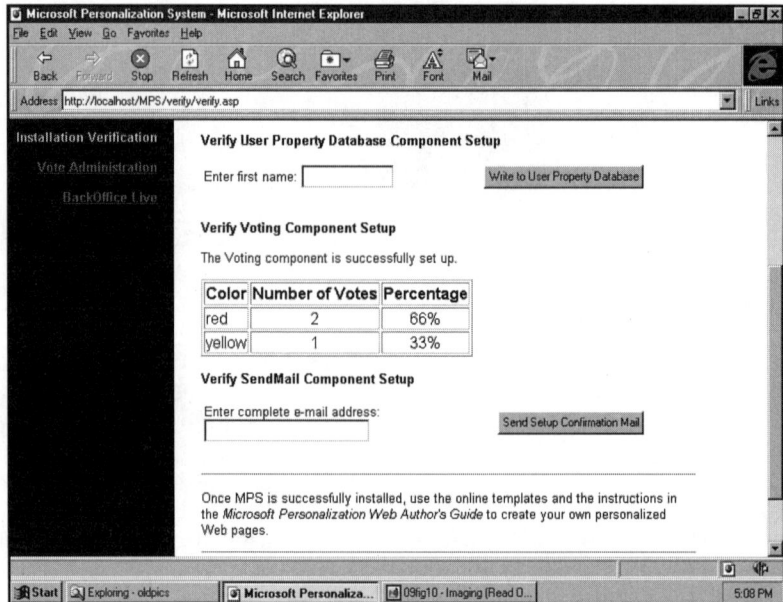

3. *Verify SendMail Component Setup*   Enter your complete e-mail address and click the Send Setup Confirmation Mail button. The submission will be processed and a new Web page will be created. If the SendMail Component is set up properly, you will receive a confirmation to the e-mail address from the Personalization Server.

The following message (appropriately dated, of course) should be received:

```
Date: Sat, 14 Dec 1996 09:12:20 -0500
From: MPS.Setup.Verification@microsoft.com
Subject: Congratulations
The Send Mail component of MPS is set up properly.
See the MPS Web Author's Guide and the online templates
for ideas and sample code.
```

If the SendMail Component is not working, check the following:

- The SMTP server may not be working. Telnet to the SMTP server to test SendMail.

- SMTP is working, but SendMail is not. Review Chapters 6, "Instant Communication— Microsoft Commercial Internet Mail," and 7, "Advanced Internet Mail Server Administration," and correct the mail server setup.

Part

III

Ch

9

Going Public

Personalization should be functional and ready for prime time. However, at this point, you haven't designed any personalization features, so you'll want to hold off your launch until you have something to offer. Once you are ready to go live, it's a simple process. Moving from development to production requires no changes to the Internet Personalization Server. If you are moving directories to a different server, simply make sure your privileges are set correctly.

Using the Internet Personalization System

With the Internet Personalization System, it's important to have a basic understanding of how to monitor and maintain the performance of the system and how to work around potential problems. In this section you'll get an overview of how the Personalization System interacts with the Windows NT Event Viewer and Performance Monitor when monitoring the progress during live personalization.

Maintaining the System

The Windows NT Event Log Viewer is an excellent tool for monitoring any of the service events that are conducted by the server. With the Event Log, administrators can monitor performance and gather useful information on errors and configuration problems that may be occurring with the Personalization System, or more specifically, the User Property Database. Follow these steps to access the Event Log:

1. Click the Start button, choose Programs, select Administrative Tools (Common), and then choose Event Viewer.

2. The main window for the Event Viewer provides detailed information on system events. Displayed from left to right are the date, time, source (the process that logged the event), category (relates mostly to Security issues), event (a numeric identifier), user (the user account where the event occurred), and the computer.

3. To obtain more information about an event, double-click the event. The Event Detail dialog box is launched and provides a description of the event.

4. Review the event description and correct the problem accordingly.

Monitoring Performance

The Windows NT Performance Monitor allows you to take a look at the performance status of the User Property Databases. The Performance Monitor is designed to enable you to review real-time information on the status and health of your server by letting you view a variety of performance counters.

To access the Performance Monitor and evaluate the status of MPS, follow these steps:

1. Click the Start button, select Programs, Administrative Tools, and then choose the Performance Monitor. The Performance Monitor is launched.

2. Choose View, Chart.

3. Choose to add to the chart by choosing Edit, Add to Chart. You can also activate this feature by clicking the + button on the toolbar.

4. The Performance Monitor launches the Add to Chart dialog box. Some of the main features needed in the Performance Monitor are:

   - *Computer* Select the computer you want to monitor. Your server appears as the default. If the Content Replication Service resides on another server, click the ellipses button (...) and a Select Computer dialog box is launched.

   - *Object* Selects an object to monitor from those residing on the computer you selected.

   - *Counters* Selects the counter you want to monitor.

5. Leave the Computer as the default.

6. Change the Object feature to User Property Database.

7. Select the counter of interest. To review what the counters are designed to do, highlight the option and click the Explain button. For this test, Select Reads/Sec, which will record the total number of user property database reads per second.

8. Now click the Add button and the counters will be launched.

9. Click the Done button and the Performance Monitor begins charting the graph. If there is no one accessing the User Property Database, the chart will be flatlined at zero. To initiate a response launch a Web page that utilizes the User Property Database. The Performance Monitor will immediately record the status of the project.

10. Review the outcome.

You can also use the Performance Monitors alert mode feature to automatically notify you when levels do not reach your expectations.

Here's how to set up the alert feature for Performance Monitor:

1. Click the Start button, select Programs, Administrative Tools, and then choose the Performance Monitor.

2. The Performance Monitor is launched. Select the View the Alerts button on the button bar, or choose View, Alert.

3. Choose the Add Counter button (+), or choose Edit, Add to Alert.

4. Select the Object as Processor, and the Counter as %Processor Time.

5. In the Alert If field, as an example, select the Over option and type the number 50 in the text entry field. This will cause the server to notify you whenever the server's processors reach more than 50 percent usage.

6. Click the Add button.

7. Choose Options, Alert to launch the Alert Options dialog box.

8. If an alert is necessary, Performance Monitor can be configured to Switch to an Alert View, or Send Network E-mail message to the administrator. For now, select Switch to an Alert View.

9. The Performance Monitor will track anything that crosses the alert threshold and will log the activity on the Performance Monitor page.

10. Monitor the server resources and adjust as needed.

With this test, you can analyze the performance of the Personalization System against the other offerings on the server and determine whether the server is being taxed excessively.

For a more detailed explanation on how to interpret Performance Monitor results, see Appendix B, "Performance Monitor Counters."

Performance Tuning

Recommended additional tools for Analyzing performance include the Ping Utility and Telnet. When you're uncertain if connectivity is good, use the following tests to test general functionality.

When you have more than one server involved, the Ping utility always comes in handy. Simply open a command prompt on one of the Web servers, and then follow these steps:

1. Determine the name of the machine you need to analyze, and type **ping site1.integritydata.com**, or the server.name of your choice. Press Enter.

2. The server will send a series of bytes to the other machine, which should reply.

3. If the hostname test fails, try to Ping by IP address.

4. The Telnet Utility is the tool that you'll use to determine whether the SMTP server is responding to client connections. In this test, you will attempt to connect to the SMTP server manually to help determine whether the SendMail Component of your mail server is working or not. Simply open a command prompt on one of the Web servers and use this procedure:

5. Determine where the SMTP server is located that you are testing, then type **Telnet site2.integritydata.com 25**, or the server.name of your choice.

Part
III

Ch
9

6. Once connected, you should get a Welcome, which mentions that you are connected via the Microsoft Internet Mail Connector, or something to that effect.

7. Now you'll want to attempt to send mail manually. Type the following code, as shown in Listing 9.1, replacing italicized text with your information and pressing Enter when you see <crlf>.

Listing 9.1 Sending Mail Manually

```
mail from: <sender><crlf>
rcpt to: <recipient><crlf>
data<crlf>
subject: <subject><crlf> (this line isn't required)
<mailmessage><crlf>     (You can enter several lines of information here)
.<crlf>       (be sure the data section ends with a period as the first
& last character on a line)
quit<crlf>                        (this will disconnect you from the server)
```

8. If you do not get a positive response, then the SendMail Component is down and you'll need to review your mail server configuration. Refer to Chapters 6, "Instant Communication—Microsoft Commercial Internet Mail Server," and 7, "Advance Internet Mail Server Administration."

Using Templates to Create Personalization

One of the beauties of the Personalization System is the ease of customization through the simple modification to existing templates. In the MCIS\Templates\IPS folder you'll find the following:

- *upd.asp*   This contains an overview on how to write to the User Property Database and how to read from it. This is a nice template since there is no setup required to use it. It's pretty straightforward the first time the file is accessed. With little effort the user can customize the page. After selecting preferences, the greeting changes accordingly. In future visits, the info on the page changes to match your preferences.

- *vote.asp*   This template will gather polling and voting options. The user will make selections and then a custom table with the results is displayed. One great feature in this template is that if a user tries to vote a second time, the user will get a message that says No Voting twice.

- *sendmail.asp*   This template will gather input from users and then mail the comments to a specific site based on the users' preferences.

Using the ActiveX Control Pack

Organizations are looking for quicker and easier ways to create Internet applications that leverage already existing investments. Also, they want implementation strategies that are easy to deploy. Specifically, they want to avoid the old school techno-development environment—such as CGI—and ensure that the solutions and components can be built quickly. ActiveX and Active Server Pages are the quickest way to create dynamic Web sites. In this section you find information on how to develop personalized pages through the use of Active Server Pages.

User Controls

Users control their personalized pages through their User Properties. Here's an example of how user properties work:

1. A user completes a form that explains what he or she is interested in.
2. That information is submitted to a database.
3. When the user returns to the page, the page accessed will be customized to his or her preferences.

▶ **See** "Included Active Server Components," **p. 429**, for more information about User Controls.

Properties Database   The User Property Database is a file-based system marketed as a low maintenance, high performance solution. It creates property transaction logs, and it's easy to port to other databases, such as SQL, for offline analysis. Here's the crux of what the User Property Database is doing for your organization:

- Collecting information from the user, either through a Web page or by collecting information over time based on the user's choices while visiting the site.
- Storing the data in the User Property Database so that it can be accessed whenever the user returns to the site.
- Retrieving information from the database to develop a custom page for the user.

The User Property Database is the key to customization. Once you gather information about the user, what is displayed is dependent on the user's interest, and perhaps what your marketing offices are offering to the public.

Current Controls

After analyzing the templates, and acquiring some understanding of ActiveX, you should be ready to enhance your pages with the following personalization features:

- User Surveys
- Information Feed
- Direct Mail

This section outlines specific enhancements through the use of Active scripting. If you are unfamiliar with Active scripting, please review Chapter 16, "Serving Active Content on the Internet," for more information.

User Surveys   The template for user surveys is very nice and pretty easy to customize. In this case you modify the template to feature an example of an Integrity Data Intranet application where employees can vote on the Employee of the Year. The template already includes the abilty to stop duplicate votes. Since voting requires a database to hold the information, you will need to create a Microsoft Access database or use the vote.mdb file contained in the /MCIS/ Mps/Bin directory. Now, you must identify the database in the Windows NT Open Database Connectivity Control Panel. To do this, follow these steps:

1. Open the control panel in Windows NT.
2. Choose the ODBC icon and select the tab for System DSN.
3. Click Add and choose the Microsoft Access Driver. Click Finish.
4. In the Data Source Name field, type **Vote**, and then click Select. Go to the c:\MCIS\Mps\Bin\Vote.mdb file.
5. Select OK, apply the changes, then close the ODBC control panel.

To set up the Active server pages for voting, you will modify the showvote.asp file included with the Personalization server, or refer to the vote.asp file included on the CD-ROM. Simply follow these steps:

1. Access the vote.asp file in a text editor. At the top of the file add the following to create an instance of the user voting component:

   ```
   <% set vt = Server.CreateObject ("mps.Vote") %>
   ```

2. Now add the following lines to vote.asp to specify Voting databases and Ballot Name information (see Listing 9.2).

Listing 9.2   Specify Voting Databases and Ballot Name Information

```
<% REM Open vote database. %>
<% openresult = vt.Open("vote", "guest", "guest") %>

<% ballotresult = vt.SetBallotName ("Employee"( %>
```

The REM statement is for informational purposes. The next line, the first parameter, `vt.open` is the datasource name that was specified to set up ODBC for this database. The second item is the userID, followed by the password. Both of these items (the repeated SSOVote) were set up during the creation of the database.

3. Add the following lines to identify each user (see Listing 9.3):

Listing 9.3   Identifying the User

```
<% REM Identify user %>
<% set prop = Server.CreateObject("mps.PropertyDatabase") %>
<% prop.LoadProperties ("", "read") %>
<% userID = prop.ID %>
```

This uses a built-in parameter of the User Properties Component, ID, and sets the groundwork to stop users from submitting multiple votes.

4. Add the code from Listing 9.4 to make sure that users only vote once:

Listing 9.4   Allowing Only One Vote Per User

```
<% REM Notify user if vote was counted or ignored. %>
      <% if (empVote = True) then %>
            Thanks for voting!
      <% else %>
            You cannot vote twice, so this vote was not counted.
      <% end if %> <% REM End of check for whether user voted twice. %>
```

The three parameters to vt.Submit are two column headers to put the results into the table, and the third is the unique user ID that was created.

5. The last step is to display the total number of ballots submitted. Enter the code from Listing 9.5 next:

Listing 9.5   Display the Total Number of Ballots

```
<% REM Display raw results in custom formatted table. %>
      Here are the results of the Employee of the Year vote:
      <blockquote>
      <table border=1 bordercolor=cccc99 cellpadding=5 cellspacing=0 %>
        <tr>        <td>Brooke Bassage-Glock</td>
           <td align=right>
           <% = vt.GetVoteCount("Employee of the Year", "brooke") %></td>
        </tr>
        <tr>   <td>Adam Robinson</td>
           <td align=right>
           <% = vt.GetVoteCount("Employee of the Year", "adam") %></td>
        </tr>
        <tr>   <td>Bo Flynn</td>
           <td align=right>
           <% = vt.GetVoteCount("Employee of the Year", "bo") %></td>
        </tr>
        <tr>   <td>Marshall Howland</td>
           <td align=right>
           <% = vt.GetVoteCount("Employee of the Year", "marshall") %></td>
        </tr>
      </table>
      </blockquote>
```

6. Save the file as plain text and visit the vote.htm page to test the code. Try voting a second time to see if you are limited to only one vote.

Information Pump   This is an Active Server Pages feature that provides real-time feeds of continuous incoming data and demonstrates the use of active pages with Personalization.

To begin, you need to set up a file with the data that will be fed. Follow these steps to get the file in order:

1. The file update.htm contains the strings to add for each person in the Employee of the Year competition. Each contestant needs to be surrounded by an #ipmpstart and an #ipumpend tag, which specify what will be pulled. Enter the following information:

```
<!--#ipumpstart tag = "brooke" -->
Brooke, the current Employee of the Year, is up for re-election
based on his outstanding car wash ticket sales.
<!--#ipumpend tag = "brooke" -->
```

2. Repeat this process for the following additional tag values for the other employees in the update.htm file (see Listing 9.6). Save the file as plain text.

Listing 9.6   Tag Values for Other Employees

```
<!--#ipumpstart tag = "adam" -->
Over the past year, Adam has been our leading sales representative
logging over 400 laptops to all types of customers.
<!--#ipumpend tag = "adam" -->

<!--#ipumpstart tag = "bo" -->
Bryan Oliver, as head of web page development, has repeatedly
proven his programming skill by designing pages for our top customers.
<!--#ipumpend tag = "bo" -->

<!--#ipumpstart tag = "marshall" -->
Marshall's innovative and imaginative hardware designs make him a
contender.  His ideas have pulled our sales into the lead.
<!--#ipumpend tag = "marshall" -->
```

Now set up the feed by editing the following in the default.asp file:

1. First, specify that you want to use the information pump component by adding the following two lines:

```
<% set pump = Server.CreateObject ("mps.infopump") %>
<% pump.UsesDataFile ("update.htm") %>
```

2. Delete any Product update headlines from the original default.asp text, so you can just provide the information each user is interested in.

3. Add the code from Listing 9.7 to display updated information on the four available products:

Listing 9.7   Displaying Live Data After Votes Are Submitted

```
<% REM Display employee update info if user has selected favorite products. %>
  <% if (prop("employee") <> "") then %>
  <p><b>Employees up for Election.  To vote, click the link below</b><p>
  <table>
  <tr>
      <td align=top>
    <% if (prop.product="brooke") then %>
        <b>Why to elect Brooke:</b><p>
        <% = pump.brooke %>
    <% elseif (prop.product="adam" then %>
        <b>Why to elect Adam:</b><p>
        <% = pump.adam %>
    <% elseif (prop.product = "bo") then %>
```

```
        <b>Why to elect Bo:</b><p>
        <% = pump.bo %>
<% elseif (prop.product = "marshall") then %>
        <b>Why to elect Bo:</b><p>
        <% = pump.marshall %>
   <% end if %>
```

4. Save the file as plain text. Look at the default.asp file and review the product updates.

Direct Mail   E-mail still remains the best way to communicate with other users over the Internet. This section takes you through the steps to send mail to users from Active Server script. The mail can be customized to users' properties and you can use any SMTP mail server. Follow these steps to send a receipt via e-mail confirming that you have received feedback from a user:

1. Create a custom Active Server Page using the SendMail Component by entering the following:

```
<% set mail = Server.CreateObject ("mps.smail") %>
```

2. Now enter the following code to send a receipt right after the comment is submitted (see Listing 9.8):

Listing 9.8   Sending the Comment

```
<% if (request ("receipt") = "yes") then %>
    <% result = mail.SendMail ("Integrity Data, Inc.",
    Request ("email") , "Thanks for your  vote." ,
    ("Thanks a bunch for your vote.  Your coworkers appreciate it
     and the management does too. .
     " & chr (13) & Request ("comment") ) ) %>
```

3. To enter the confirmation that mail was sent appropriately, enter the following (see Listing 9.9):

Listing 9.9   Mail Confirmation

```
<p>
<% if (result = 0) then %>
    A receipt has been mailed to your e-mail address ,
    <% iEmail %>
<% else %>
    Uh oh, we tried to send a mail receipt to you but an error
occurred.   <p>
<% result %>
<% end if %>
```

4. Save the file as submit.asp in plain text and test the code to see if you get a return receipt.

From Here...

In this section, you gained an overview of the Microsoft Internet Personalization System. The chapter provided an overview on how to set up and use the service. There were also examples of practical ways to use the application.

- For more information about ActiveX, see Chapter 16, "Serving Active Content on the Internet."
- For additional information on hardware, see Appendix A, "Hardware Requirements."
- For a more detailed explanation on how to interpret Performance Monitor results, see Appendix B, "Performance Monitor Counters."
- For more information on the Windows NT User Manager and Event Log, please review Que's *Special Edition Using Windows NT 4.0.*
- For more information on the use of databases, please refer to Que's *Special Edition Using SQL Server 6.5* and Que's *Special Edition Using Microsoft Access 7.*

The Internet Locator Service

Face the facts; in the past couple of years, finding information on the Internet has gotten easier and easier. But there has been little ground gained in finding the people that are actively surfing the Web. The Microsoft Internet Locator Server may change that. This is a creative new tool which allows Web site administrators the ability to open up communication opportunities on the Internet. With this tool, the Internet Locator Service, not only can you see who is logged on at that very moment, but it also provides the necessary first link in starting a real-time conversation.

The Locator Service is designed to publish on a Web page, as seen in Figure 10.1, the names of users who are presently logged on to the site. On this Web page, users are able to review basic information about other users and, if they choose, they can engage in a live audio chat through the use of another application—Microsoft's NetMeeting, which is an application that allows users to converse through a number of conferencing features.

- **How to implement the Internet Locator Service**

  Understand how the Internet Locator Service functions and see some of the advantages to using the application.

- **How to install and configure the Internet Locator Service**

  Learn how to install the Internet Locator Service, confirm that it is functioning properly, and then test the installation.

- **How to get the most out of the Internet Locator Service**

  Learn how to implement the Internet Locator Service and exploit its features, such as real-time user information and conferencing opportunities.

- **How to integrate the product in the work place**

  Review a couple of real life examples on how this product can be used to improve office communications, as well as open up new interaction with your customers.

FIG. 10.1

Microsoft uses Active Server pages to display users that are presently logged on to its Internet Locator Service.

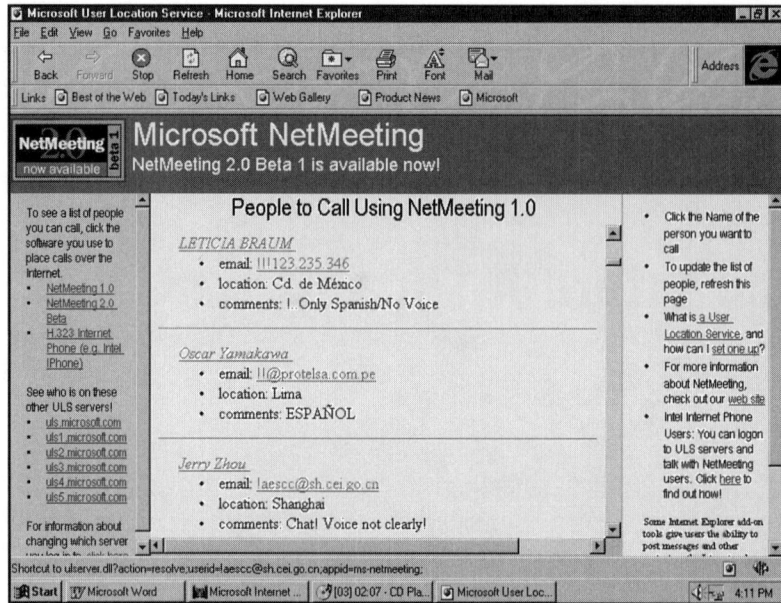

This chapter is designed to provide an overview on the Internet Locator Service and explain how to install and configure the software. The chapter also reviews how to obtain real-time user information, outline some examples of uses of the Internet Locator Service, and provide installation and usage information on the NetMeeting program. ■

An Overview of the Internet Locator Service

With the rapid growth of the Internet, developers have been pushing the limits on communication capabilities by trying to add effective conferencing centers. In the past couple of years, voice communications became a reality through applications such as the Internet Phone. In the early going, these products didn't offer other conferencing tools, such as a whiteboard and file and application sharing. Today, through the use of Microsoft's NetMeeting, all of these tools are available in one package and are tightly integrated for live, real-time virtual conferencing. NetMeeting can be seen in Figure 10.2.

Undoubtedly, NetMeeting is a hot application and stands out as one of the most significant new tools for Internet users. However, it's important to remember that a conferencing tool is of little use if you can't find the people you need to conference with. With the Microsoft Internet Locator Service, that problem is solved. The locator services are pretty new to the Internet and standards are still in development, but the concept is quite clear: You can now access an Internet directory and find dynamic information about users that are connected to the Internet. The dynamic angle is complete with this server, because users are only listed in the directory while they are logged on to the server through a program such as NetMeeting.

FIG. 10.2
NetMeeting provides an intuitive interface for conducting Internet conferencing.

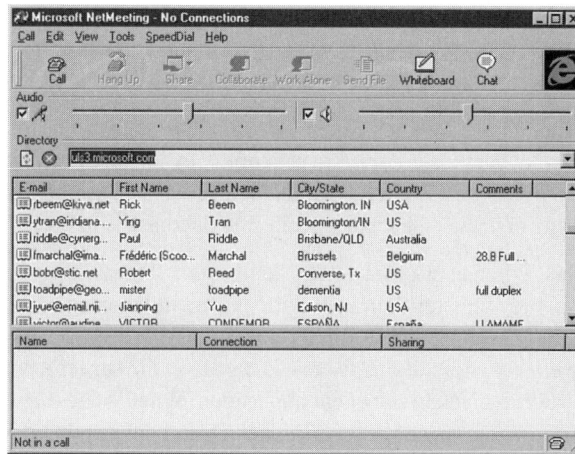

With a directory such as this, programs like NetMeeting become quite significant. Here's why: Knowing who's online is only valuable if you can take it the next step and converse with that person and work together to edit documents and share an online whiteboard to illustrate points.

Microsoft has accomplished a lot with this product and it's quite easy to launch on your Web site. Also, Microsoft says this product is built to take the heat of commercial use and high traffic. For example, the ILS server is designed to accommodate scalability of tens of thousands of users per server handling millions of queries per day on each server.

Following are the hardware and software configuration requirements for launching the Internet Locator Service:

Category	Requirement
Server hardware	32-bit x86-compatible microprocessor (such as Intel 80486/25 or higher), Intel Pentium, or supported RISC-based micro-processor, such as the Digital Alpha or PowerPC.
Software	Windows NT Server version 4.0 (with Service Pack 1) and Internet Information Server version 3.0.
Memory	Minimum 16 megabytes (M) of RAM for x86 systems (32M recommended). Minimum 32M RAM for RISC-based systems

Also, Microsoft recommends one of the following:

- A computer with one Alpha processor and 32M memory
- A computer with one x86 processor and 32M memory

Why Use Internet Locator Service?

The short answer: This is a well thought out, tightly integrated service that will open up a number of options for server administrators.

There's more to it, though. The components of Internet Locator Service provide for a flexible system, which offers a dynamic directory service that can be used for a variety of different client applications.

Internet Location Service handles all the dynamic information. For instance, it makes no difference if a user's IP address is different every time they log on to the Internet. The Internet Locator Service works with live information, and doesn't call on information from past logins to accomplish any of these tasks. Specifically, the database is in RAM.

It works like this: When users connect to the Internet, if they visit a site using the Internet Locator Service, they register their name and pertinent information. As long as they are online, the user's Internet Locator Service entry remains valid and can be displayed to other users. The key to the effectiveness of this feature is based on the server's periodic refresh routine, which updates any changes to the client application. When a client application crashes, the Internet Locator Service recognizes the departure and deletes the user entry when the refresh period has elapsed, keeping the dynamic directory information fresh and up-to-date.

In order to manage the high number of active refreshes, the Internet Locator Service uses the RAM database to store its information, providing for a more effective system than a disk-based database. Your user population will be using the Internet Locator Service Lightweight Directory Access Protocol interface to access this directory information in a Web page. This is new ground and will bring life and interaction to Web sites.

What Is Lightweight Directory Access Protocol?

The Lightweight Directory Access Protocol interface is an Internet standards-based protocol which allows any third-party Internet client to access dynamic directory information, such as a user's current IP address, facilitating point-to-point Internet communication sessions.

Advantages of ILS

The Internet Locator Server puts a new spin on desktop conferencing. With this tool, a live conference can be conducted on the Internet, or an intranet. Here are some excellent opportunities provided by the Internet Locator Service:

- *Business conferencing* Through the company's intranet, employees will benefit greatly from Microsoft Internet Locator Server. With this feature, they can determine what other staff members are online, and if necessary, they can initiate a conference with NetMeeting, Microsoft's conferencing software.

- *Easy administration* Microsoft Internet Locator Server has the same administrative graphical user interface as all of the Microsoft Commercial Internet Servers. There are also the usual tools available to create transaction logs and the ability to conduct performance monitoring.

- *Security features* Microsoft Internet Locator Server can use the Authentication mechanism available in the Microsoft Membership System.

■ *Scalability*   Microsoft Internet Locator Server was designed to handle up to thousands of user connections per server. If that's not big enough, additional servers can be added to the scheme to balance loads and improve response time.

Installing ILS

Before you begin, make sure that each server and the administrative client have Windows NT 4.0, along with Windows NT Service Pack 1a, installed. Also, the Active Server Pages (ASP) script processor will need to be installed with the Internet Locator Service to allow for HTML access. If you install Microsoft Internet Information Server 3.0, the Active Server Page processor is included. Make sure all of these items are installed before you proceed with the Installation of the Internet Locator Service.

To install Microsoft Internet Locator Service, make sure you are logged on to the server as an administrator and exit all running Windows programs, then follow these steps:

1. Open the folder that contains Microsoft Internet Locator Server and launch the setup.exe to begin the setup process.

2. At the Installation Welcome Screen, choose Next to set up the program. Select the Yes button to accept the terms of the License Agreement and proceed with installation.

3. Enter your Name and Company information, and then click the Next button.

4. Accept the default directory name or enter a different location to place the program. To change the directory, click Browse and select another directory from the list or type the directory name you want to use. Click the Next button.

5. Select the components you want to install. The default options are to install the Internet Locator Service, which includes the Lightweight Directory Access Protocol, the sample .htm and .asp files (Web page components and scripts), and ILS documentation as Microsoft Word Files. For a standard Internet Locator Service setup, make sure all check boxes are selected.

6. If you are prompted that all Internet Information Services need to be stopped, click Yes to stop the running services. An informational message informs you as each service is stopped.

7. Setup now verifies if you have the Active Server Pages (ASP) script processor installed. If the program was not installed, a warning appears. If you get this warning, exit from the installation and install the Active Server Pages before attempting to reinstall the Internet Locator Service. If the ASP files were installed, Setup will continue.

8. Verify that the root for the Lightweight Directory Access Protocol is correct and click the Next button. To change the directory, click Browse and select another directory from the list or type the directory name you want to use. Click the Next button.

9. Select the Program Folder on the Start Menu where you want the Internet Locator Service program to reside. The default option is the Microsoft Internet Locator Server. Click Next to accept the default or choose an alternate folder.

10. Confirm Setup Information by reviewing the screen that contains a summary of your settings. If there were any errors, use the Back button to make changes before proceeding. If the information meets your approval, click the Next button.

11. Setup begins copying the files. A progress indicator tracks the status of the installation. When the Setup Complete dialog box is displayed, choose I would like to view the Start Page, which will open a start page in your Web browser that contains an online guide for using the program. Also, choose I would like to start the Administration Tool, which will start the Internet Service Manager to use the Administration Tool for the Internet Locator Service.

12. Select Finish.

Uninstalling the Internet Locator Service

In the event you need to uninstall the service for any reason, follow these steps:

1. Log on to Windows NT as an administrator, and quit all Internet services because they have a tendency to interfere with this process.

2. Launch the Windows NT Control Panel and choose Add/Remove Programs.

3. Review the list of programs in the Add/Remove Properties dialog box, and click Microsoft Internet Locator Server, then click Add/Remove, as seen in Figure 10.3.

FIG. 10.3

Uninstalling a program in Windows NT is conducted through the Windows NT Add/ Remove Programs Properties.

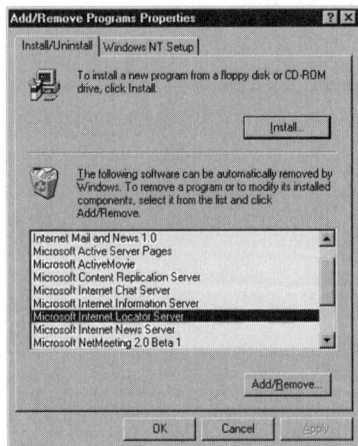

4. When prompted Are you sure you want to completely remove the selected application and all of its components? seen in Figure 10.4, click Yes.

5. When the uninstall process is finished, click OK to close the dialog box.

FIG. 10.4

Choosing Yes will remove all the files that were installed during the Internet Locator Server installation.

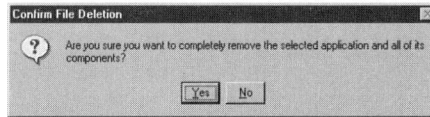

N O T E If there are other Internet services running when you are uninstalling the Internet Locator Service, all of the appropriate files are not immediately deleted. Many files are just marked for deletion and will be cleared when the computer is restarted. To help the uninstall process go a little smoother, stop all other Internet services, such as WWW, FTP, and any others, before you begin the process. ■

Confirming that Setup Was Successful

If you didn't run the verify page at the end of the Internet Locator Service Setup, you should do that now. Launch your browser and go to **http://computer_name/ILS/Verify/Verify.htm**.

Make sure you substitute where it says computer_name with the name of your Internet Locator Server. Once you arrive at the page, choose the Installation Verification option in the left column of the page.

A verification page is launched, as seen in Figure 10.5, displaying a series of steps for testing the Internet Locator Service with the Internet Information Service World Wide Web service. Begin by selecting the Step 1, Create Online Listing button.

FIG. 10.5

The verification page allows you to verify that Internet Locator Server has been correctly set up.

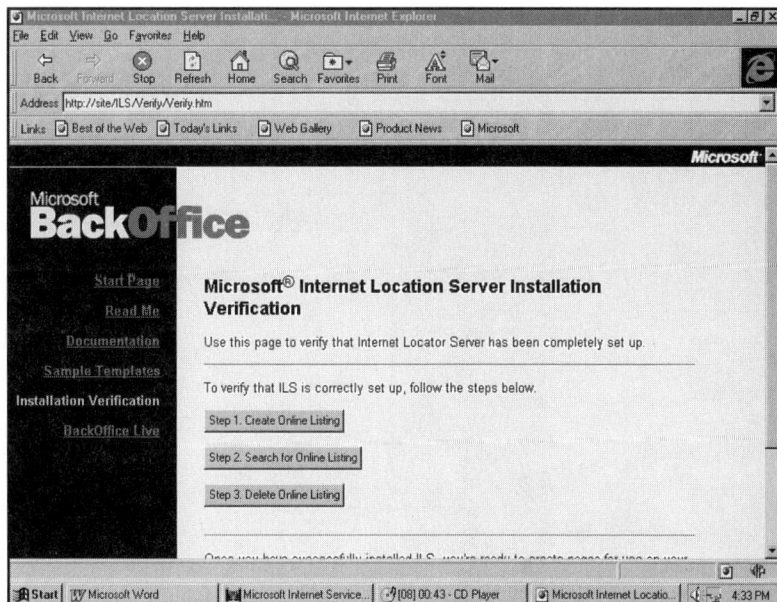

The database reports that your online listing was successfully created, as seen in Figure 10.6. Choose the link to `Return to the Installation Verification Page`.

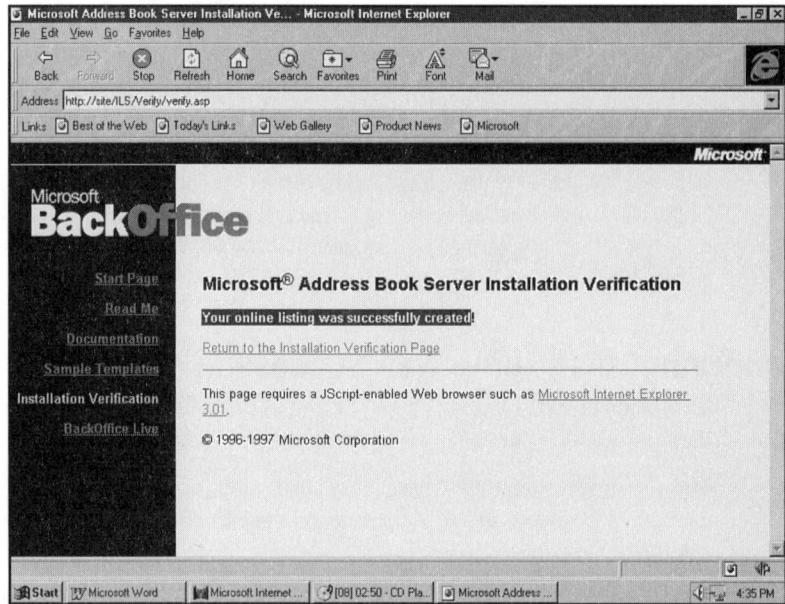

Select the `Step 2, Search for Online Listing` button. The database report indicates that a user is now online, as seen in Figure 10.7. Choose the link to `Return to the Installation Verification Page`.

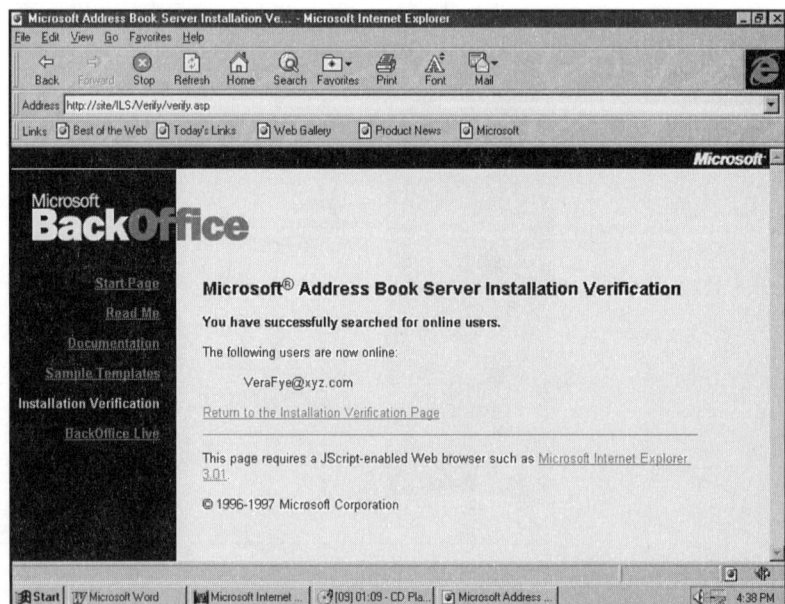

Select the Step 3, Delete an Online Listing button. The database returns a message that the online listing has been successfully deleted (see Figure 10.8). The Internet Locator Server has been correctly installed!

FIG. 10.8
The verification program reports that the online listing was successfully deleted.

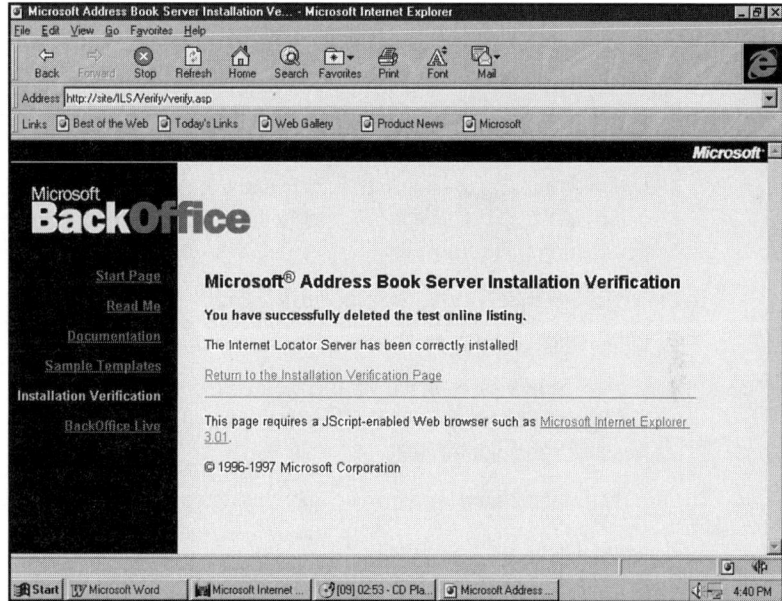

Testing the Installation

The key at this point is to ensure that you have properly installed the services. This section focuses on testing the installation for proper configuration. Before you run these tests, you need the following software components installed on the client side:

- Microsoft Internet Explorer version 3.01 or later or Netscape Navigator 3.0 or later, to access the Internet Locator Service's HTML form
- Microsoft NetMeeting version 1.0, used to test the User Locator Protocol interface of Internet Locator Service

ON THE WEB

http://www.microsoft.com/netmeeting/   Microsoft NetMeeting can be found here.

http://www.microsoft.com/ie/download/   Microsoft Internet Explorer and the Microsoft Mail and News Client Software are at this site.

Use the following sets of instructions to test the installation.

To test the Internet Locator Service—Test 1:

1. Use NetMeeting to log on to the newly installed Internet Locator Service. When NetMeeting is launched, the Internet Locator Service server will create an entry for you based on the preferences you entered during the configuration of the NetMeeting program. Enter **uls.yourserver.com** to test the installation or the appropriate domain.

2. Launch your Web browser and visit your server to see if your entry is now listed on the Internet Locator Service.

3. Quit NetMeeting to ensure that your entry is deleted from the Internet Locator Service database. Once the program has exited, click the Refresh button in your browser to see if your listing was removed.

To create an Internet Locator Service entry using NetMeeting—Test 2:

1. Launch NetMeeting.

2. Choose Select Directory from the menu. Review the list to verify that you are listed on the Internet Locator Service. This test is specifically checking the Lightweight Directory Access Protocol interface.

To view the Internet Locator Service entry through a Web browser—Test 3:

1. Launch your Web browser.

2. In the Address box, type **computer_name/ILS/Verify/Verify.htm**.

   Again, make sure you substitute **computer_name** with the name of your Internet Locator Server.

3. To check the Web interface, follow the directions for entering and viewing an Internet Locator Service entry.

   Also, on the Call menu, click Web Directory and verify that you are listed on the Internet Locator Service server.

If the previous three tests were successful, the Internet Locator Service should be in fine shape. Through these tests, you have checked the following:

- The Web browser's ability to create and manipulate Internet Locator Service entries
- The capability to access the dynamic database through the use of the Lightweight Directory Access Protocol
- The capability to use Microsoft NetMeeting to test the User Location Protocol interface, which is the key to the dynamic directory information accessible in the Internet Locator Service
- The ability to use a Web browser to access Internet Locator Service information

Configuring Internet Locator Service

Like the other services packaged with the Microsoft Commercial Internet System, the Internet Locator Service can be configured easily through the Internet Service Managers graphic user interface. Follow these steps to configure the Internet Locator Service:

On the Start menu, choose Programs, Microsoft Internet Server (Common), and then select Internet Service Manager. Choose the computer name to the left of the Lightweight Directory Access Protocol (LDAP) service to access the configuration options.

Service Properties

The LDAP Service Properties page opens by default on the Service properties, as seen in Figure 10.9. This is the area that controls how users can connect to the service.

The following steps explain how to configure the LDAP Service Properties:

1. Start with the Connection Timeout option, which identifies the amount of time before an inactive connection is closed. The default is set at 600 seconds, which is 10 minutes. This should be adequate, so don't bother changing this option.

2. The next option is for Maximum Connections. This sets the maximum number of simultaneous connections that are allowed. The default number is 1000 and should be fine to begin with.

FIG. 10.9
Service Properties configuration page for the Internet Locator Service offers an intuitive interface.

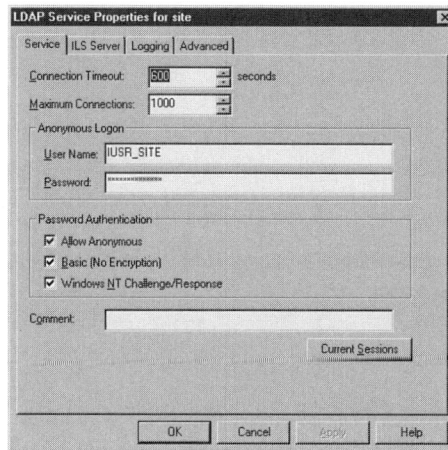

3. In the Anonymous Logon Section, the User Name and Password are set up and configured for anonymous logon. Don't bother changing these options unless you want to close your Internet Locator Service to anonymous users.

Part
III

Ch
10

4. In the Password Authentication section, administrators have the ability to determine how users will be authenticated. The LDAP service can be configured to allow three authentication methods, which are:

   - *Allow Anonymous*   This allows for anonymous connections and uses the default username and password indicated under Anonymous Connections.

   - *Basic (No Encryption)*   Passwords are sent as clear text without encryption.

   - *Windows NT Challenge/Response*   Configures the service to use Windows NT logon accounts for authentication.

5. If the administrator wants to place a comment next to the Service listing in the Microsoft Internet Service Manager, they can enter the text in the Comment text box. The text will be displayed next to the LDAP service in the Internet Service Manager window.

6. To determine how many users are presently logged on to the Internet Locator Service, click the Current Sessions button. An LDAP User Session dialog box appears. With this feature you can determine who is connected to the directory server, each user's IP address, and how long each user has been connected. If necessary, administrators can use the controls in this dialog box to disconnect users from the LDAP service.

   From the LDAP user session dialog box, you may also Refresh the listing. If any new users have logged on since you opened the dialog box, their names are displayed in the refreshed list.

   You may also disconnect a single user by highlighting the user's name and clicking the Disconnect button.

   If you want to disconnect all users from the Internet Locator Service, click the Disconnect All button.

   Choose Close to return to the Service Properties page. To activate your changes, click the Apply button.

ILS Server Properties

The Internet Locator Service is designed to provide dynamic directory information to other users. All Internet Locator Service entries are created when the user logs on to the Internet. This user information, which specifically ties back to the users IP address, can be accessed and the success occurs when one user initiates point-to-point communication with another user.

The following steps detail setting up the server properties:

1. Select the ILS Server tab, which contains settings specific to the Internet Locator Service. It's important to make sure you have checked the box to Enable ILS Server. When this box is selected, all of the controls under it are enabled. When this box is not selected, all of the controls under it are disabled.

2. The Client Time to Live selection, as seen in Figure 10.10, specifies the time frame for which clients will send refresh messages to the server. The server assigns this time

frame to the client when the client connects to the Internet Locator Service. By default, the default is set at 20 minutes, which means every 20 minutes users connected to your server will send a refresh message to the server.

FIG. 10.10

The dynamic angle to the Internet Locator Service is managed through the ILS server Properties Sheet.

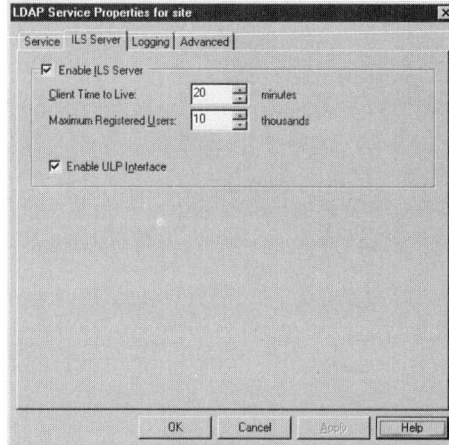

3. You also have the ability to set the Maximum Registered Users that are allowed simultaneously on the ILS server. The default is set at 10,000. There's no need to adjust this number at this point. Later, if your server is struggling, you may want to consider lowering this number.

4. You should also Enable ULP Interface, which allows the Internet Locator Server to offer User Location Protocol Interface. This means that any clients, such as any NetMeeting releases version 2.0 beta 2, that use the User Location Protocol will be able to connect to and use your server.

5. Select the Apply button and proceed to the Logging tab.

Logging Properties

The logging feature with the Internet Locator Service provides valuable information on the total number of accesses to the server. If you Enable Logging, the server will build a plain text log file based on the criteria you select. For instance, you can choose to create a new log Daily, Weekly, Monthly, or Create a new log file when the file reaches a certain size, as seen in Figure 10.11. There is also the capability to select the Log file directory containing all log files.

You also have the choice to send the log files to an Open Data Base Connectivity (ODBC)–supported database. This may come in handy when you have multiple servers or services on a network. With this feature you can log all of their activities to a single file or database on any network computer. If you Log to SQL/ODBC Database, you must specify the ODBC Data Source Name (DSN), the Table name, and the valid User name and Password for the database.

FIG. 10.11

Like any of the Microsoft Commercial Internet Servers, logging options are available.

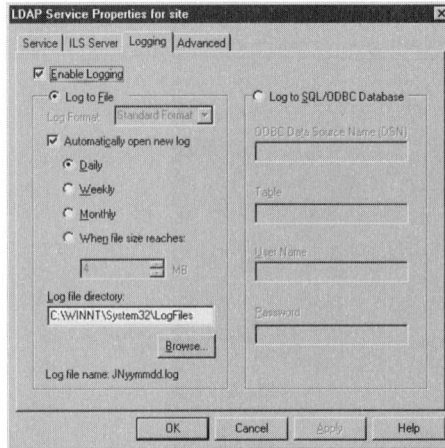

Advanced Properties

Select the Advanced tab to control access configuration. Here, you have the option to set access restrictions by specific IP address and disallow certain users or groups of users from accessing your server. Here, you can also set the maximum traffic on your server. You can also configure the maximum network bandwidth for outgoing traffic.

The following steps describe how to configure advanced LDAP properties:

1. Select the Granted Access radio button to grant access to all computers, as seen in Figure 10.12. If you need to deny access to some computers, click the Add button and add to the list the IP addresses you intend to deny access.

FIG. 10.12

Configuring the access options through the Internet Locator Service.

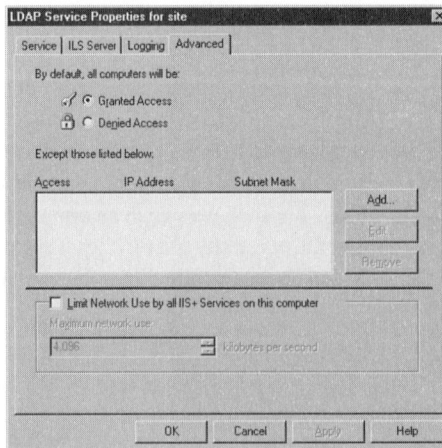

2. Select the De_nied Access option to deny all computers. To then grant access to some computers, click the A_dd button.

3. Specific access list allows you to set up approvals or denials based on submitting the specific IP address of the computer.

> **TIP**
>
> If you choose to grant access to all users by default, you can specify the computers to be denied access. You can also choose to deny access to all users by default, and then specify which computers are allowed access.

4. You may also L_imit Network Use By All Internet Services On This Computer by clicking the check box and entering a number for Maximum network use. This will limit the network bandwidth allowed for all Internet services on the server. You can also change the maximum kilobytes per second for outgoing traffic permitted on the server.

> **CAUTION**
>
> If you choose to limit the bandwidth, you are cautioned that this value applies to *all* Microsoft Information Services on this computer, and not just the Internet Locator Service.

Part

III

Ch

10

Obtaining Real-Time User Information

From an administrator's perspective, the best place to access real-time user information is through the Microsoft Internet Services Manager. From the user's perspective, they can get real-time user information from the Active Server Pages or from the directory listing in the NetMeeting application. This section explains how to accomplish the retrieval of this information.

Administrative Tracking

From the Internet Service Manager, choose the computer name of the computer that you want to check. Choose the Current Sessions button from the Services page to see a display of current users.

Real-Time Information from the Web Page

Since users will not have access to the administrative functionality of the Internet Services Manager, they have to resort to another search method. The first is to search for Real-Time Information from a Web page.

> **ON THE WEB**
>
> **http://uls.microsoft.com**   If the users want to determine if their coworker is connected to the Microsoft server, they can use their browser to access a list of who is connected to the Internet Locator Service by visiting this site.

Users can scroll the page and obtain the name, e-mail address, and location of the users who are connected.

> **N O T E** This is not a flawless approach for user searches. If a user chooses during the setup of the NetMeeting program to not publish their name on the Internet Locator Service, real-time information about that user will not be accessible. ∎

Real-Time Information from the NetMeeting Program

In this scenario, users can access Real Time Information by using the NetMeeting program. Once the user is connected, they can determine if their coworker is also online by scrolling through the directory list. Here, users can acquire the name, e-mail address, and location of the users that are connected.

Applications for Internet Locator Service

Any office with employees who collaborate on projects needs this application. This simple process makes it easy for employees to meet for real-time discussions.

To enhance the communication, you need another application. The tool of choice is NetMeeting, which is covered in the next section. However, Intel's Internet Phone may also be used. This chapter outlines the uses of NetMeeting, and also provides an overview of the Web Page interface.

NetMeeting

Microsoft NetMeeting is a groundbreaking product that includes voice communication and conferencing tools. Keep in mind that NetMeeting is a client application. The Internet Locator Service allows users of NetMeeting to determine who is presently logged on to the server. When users find a person they are interested in communicating with, NetMeeting is the platform that allows users to strike up a conversation or participate in conferencing or collaboration.

NetMeeting is often compared to the present offering of Web Phones that are on the market, but there's really no comparison. Sure, there's real-time audio, but the product also allows users to share applications, draw on a shared whiteboard, use text-based chat, or transfer files. That's groundbreaking stuff!

Interestingly, the most recent beta releases of the NetMeeting product integrate video into the application, a natural addition for a conferencing software package.

> **N O T E** According to Microsoft, NetMeeting follows international standards developed by the International Telecommunications Union and the Internet Engineering Task Force, to ensure the application has support for standard protocols and will work across platforms. ∎

In this section, you learn how to install and operate Microsoft NetMeeting. First, you need to install a copy of the program, which is available for download from Microsoft at **http://www.microsoft.com/netmeeting/**.

Installing Microsoft NetMeeting   Before you start with installation, let's cover the minimum hardware requirements your clients will need to use NetMeeting. According to Microsoft, one of the following configurations is recommended:

Option 1	Option 2
Microsoft Windows 95	Microsoft Windows NT 4.0
486/66 with 8M of RAM	486/66 with 16M of RAM
Sound card, with microphone and speakers	Sound card, with mic and speakers
(Pentium with 12M of RAM recommended)	

N O T E   NetMeeting does not run on Windows 3.1. Also, NetMeeting works best with a fast Internet connection (28.8-baud modem or local area network) and if you plan to use the audio features of NetMeeting, you need a sound card, speakers, and a microphone.

Running Setup   To install Microsoft NetMeeting, follow these steps:

1. After downloading the program, launch the executable program to begin the setup process.

2. At the Installation Welcome Screen, choose Yes to set up the program and select the Yes button to accept the terms of the License Agreement and proceed with installation.

3. Enter the directory name where you want to install NetMeeting. The default is C:\Program Files\NetMeeting. Click the OK button.

4. Program installation begins and, upon completion, a dialog box reporting the successful completion will be displayed. Click the OK button.

5. A dialog box reports that you must restart the computer before the new settings will take effect. Select the Yes button to restart the computer.

Launching NetMeeting for the First Time   After restarting your computer, choose Programs from the Start menu, then select Microsoft NetMeeting.

The following steps explain how to configure NetMeeting:

1. When the program launches, the first dialog box provides a brief outline of what NetMeeting is designed to do. Select Next.

2. Provide User Information about yourself, as seen in Figure 10.13. This information will be displayed to other users connected to the Internet Locator Service. Begin by adding your First name. Tab down to the next text box.

Part
III

Ch
10

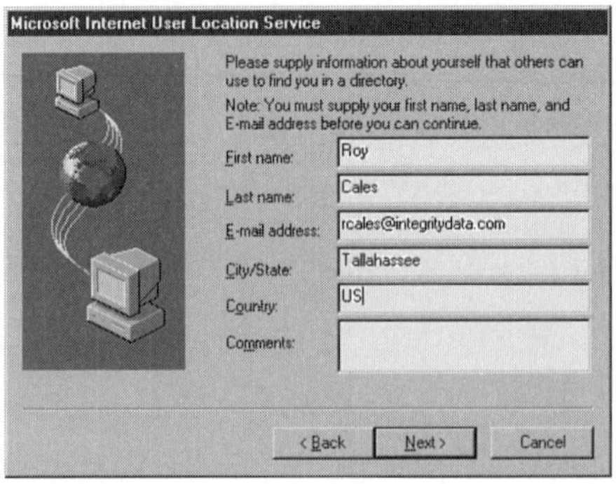

FIG. 10.13

Before you connect you'll need to submit in the text entry boxes some personal information about yourself, such as your name, e-mail address, location, and any comments you want to display.

T I P   Keep in mind that everything you enter into the User Information field will be accessible to anyone connected to the Internet Locator Service. If you want to remain anonymous, you may want to plug in aliases in the User Information fields.

---

3. In the next dialog box, you can choose not to have your name published in the Internet Locator Service. By default, Yes is selected. Leave the default and tab down to the next text entry field.

N O T E   If you choose not to have your information published in the Internet Locator Service, none of the other users will be able to find you. You'll basically be an invisible user. You can see all of the other users; they just can't see you. However, you can still place calls to other users of NetMeeting, but they won't be able to call you unless they know your e-mail address, machine name, or IP address. This is similar to having an unlisted telephone number. The other party needs to know your phone number to place a call to you. ▪

4. Enter the name of the Internet Location Server you want to use. Here you can leave the default of **uls.microsoft.com**, which is Microsoft's public server, or enter the name of the Internet Locator Service you have added to your server. Click the Next button.

5. The Audio Tuning Wizard is launched with an information dialog box explaining that the program will automatically detect the sound card if one is installed on your computer. Click Next.

T I P   Make sure you close any other programs that are open which play or record sounds to avoid interfering with the Audio Tuning Wizard. If you have any faxing software or phone recorder software, close the applications because experts warn that sometimes they will interfere with this process.

---

6. If you have a sound card installed, the Audio Tuning Wizard determines your present audio settings and displays the devices that have been installed for Recording and Playback. Determine if these are the appropriate settings. Also, in the dialog box, the Audio Tuning Wizard reports whether your sound card is capable of Full Duplex audio or Half Duplex Audio. Click Next.

N O T E NetMeeting's Audio Tuning Wizard will detect whether your computer can operate with Full Duplex Audio or Half Duplex Audio. Full Duplex is supposed to allow both users to talk and hear the other user at the same time, like a traditional telephone conversation. When you are operating at Half Duplex, users must take turns speaking, reminiscent of a ham radio conversation. The ability to run a computer in Full Duplex mode depends on the sound card. ▨

7. Determine the speed of your connection in order to set the compression rates when sending audio. The options are 14,400 bps modem, 28,800 bps modem, and Faster than a 28,800 bps (LAN or ISDN). Make the appropriate selection and click the Next button.

8. In order to set the audio settings, you need to speak aloud while the Audio Tuning Wizard sets the appropriate volumes. Click the Start Recording button and read aloud the two paragraphs below the Start Recording button. Your voice will be recorded for a few seconds. Once the status bar shows that the recording has ended, click the Next button.

9. NetMeeting reports audio tuning results form the test. Choose Finish to complete the audio tuning section. The NetMeeting program is then launched for the first time.

Operating Microsoft NetMeeting—The Basics Once NetMeeting is launched the conferencing browser is displayed. To learn about the features included in NetMeeting, follow these steps:

1. Start NetMeeting. The program will try to connect you to the Internet Location Server you selected during the setup process. This is also the same service that will maintain information about the Internet addresses of all the people connected to the server using NetMeeting. If you left the default ILS as uls.microsoft.com the server will have several users listed on the directory list. If you selected a Custom Internet Location Service, the activity will probably be significantly less.

2. In the NetMeeting Directory window you will see a list of the users presently logged on to NetMeeting, as seen in Figure 10.14. Included in the directory window is information on the user's e-mail address, First Name, Last Name, City/State, Country, and Comments. Review the list to determine who you would like to conference with.

T I P You can change the way the directory is sorted by clicking the column headers, making it easier to find a person you want to call. Also, you can reposition the columns in the directory view by clicking the column header and dragging to the left or right as desired, making it easier to find the people you want to.

3. Find the person you want to call, click the user name of the person you want to conference with and your browser will launch you into your NetMeeting session. At the same time, the user you selected will be notified of your call and has the option to accept or reject your call.

Part

III

Ch

10

FIG. 10.14

NetMeeting always keeps the dynamic user list visible. When idle, Not in a call displays in the lower-left corner of the window.

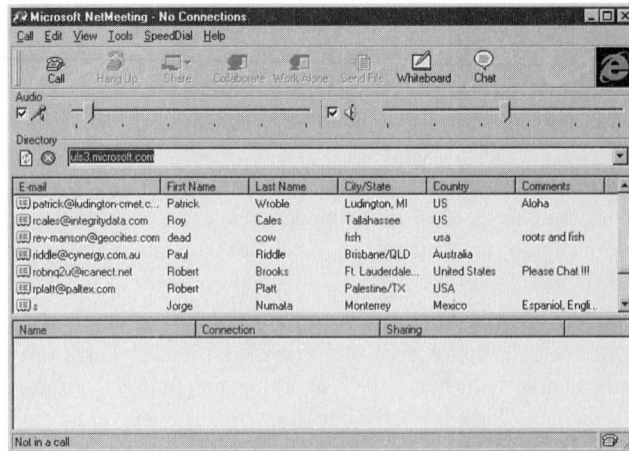

4. When you are succesfully connected, NetMeeting reports by displaying that you are "In a call" in the lower-left corner of the NetMeeting window. Also, the users in the call are listed in the bottom section of the application window.

5. Introduce yourself through the microphone.

N O T E   NetMeeting supports "multipoint" connections, which allow more than two people to join in conversations at a time. However, voice conferencing is currently limited to connections between two points, but you can expand to five points for data conferencing, and even more when using network-based conferencing services. ■

6. If you do not have a microphone, launch a text chat by clicking the Chat button, or choose Tools, Chat. A Chat window opens. Enter your text where the blinking cursor is located. After entering your comment, press Enter. Your user name will be displayed with your comment listed to the right.

7. When the user you are conferencing with responds to your comment, it will be displayed below your previous message.

T I P   If you want to change the way messages are displayed in a chat window, choose Options, Chat Format. Click the header information, such as Person's Name, Date, and Time, then select the message format you want. The options include having the entire message remain on one line, and variations on word wraps.

8. If you have difficulty hearing the other user or if they are having trouble hearing you, adjust the speaker and microphone volume sliders in the NetMeeting window. If the problem doesn't improve, choose Tools, Audio Tuning Wizard, and run the Audio Tuning Wizard process again.

TIP Though it's a hot topic of discussion, don't expect NetMeeting to replace your long distance service. Even when the audio transmission is at its best, it's still awkward using this for the traditional phone call. The voices lag a bit, and the quality of the signal is inconsistent. With the impending improvements in bandwidth, this product might one day be able to compete with the traditional phone service. But it's not there yet.

9. The session proceeds until either user chooses to end the call by selecting the Hang Up button. After a conference, you can save the transcript from Chat by choosing File, Save or File, Save As.

TIP If you display the directory window for a while without selecting a person to connect to, you might want to refresh the directory to update the listing. You can do this by clicking the Refresh button, or pressing F5. This will allow you to see the contents of the directory with the names of new users who have started NetMeeting, and without the names of users who have exited NetMeeting.

What else can users do? Some of the additional features are listed in the next sections.

The Whiteboard Feature If you need to use visual aids during a conversation, you can use the Whiteboard feature to draw a picture, which will be displayed to the other users in the conference. Interestingly, both users can draw on the Whiteboard at the same time. To launch the Whiteboard, follow these steps:

1. Either click the button for Whiteboard or choose Tools, Whiteboard. The Whiteboard will appear on both user's screens.

2. To enter text from the Whiteboard, choose Tools, Text.

3. Click the Whiteboard at the point where you want the text to start, and start typing, as seen in Figure 10.15.

FIG. 10.15

The NetMeeting Whiteboard works a lot like the Windows paint program.

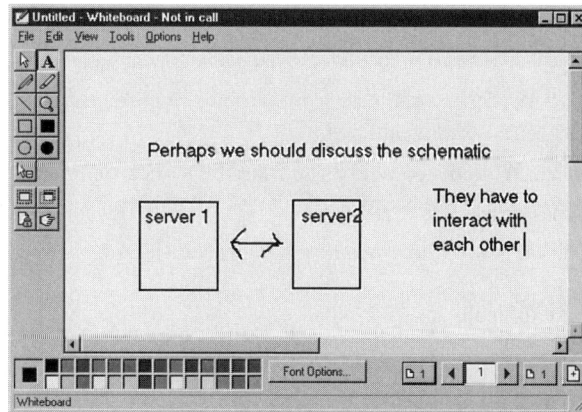

Part III
Ch 10

N O T E To change the color or font of the text, choose Options, Font and make your selections. ▮

To draw on the Whiteboard, follow these steps:

1. In Whiteboard, choose Tools, Pen.

2. From the Tools menu, choose the type of line or shape you want to use, such as an Unfilled Rectangle, Filled Rectangle, Unfilled Circle, or a Filled Circle. If you want simply to draw a line, choose Line. To choose the width or color of the line or shape, choose Options, Line Width or Colors of choice.

3. Click on the Whiteboard where you want to begin your drawing.

It is possible to highlight text and graphics on the Whiteboard. Choose Tools, Highlighter. To highlight an item, drag the mouse pointer over it. The result is similar to using a yellow highlighter on a piece of paper.

N O T E If your monitor is configured to display only 16 colors, the highlighting will appear behind the text or selected graphics. ▮

T I P If you want to use a pointer during a conference, choose Tools, Remote Pointer. This puts a pointer on the page. Just drag it to any spot where you need to direct attention.

If you've worked with many graphics tools, you are aware that zooming in and out is especially useful, particularly if you need to edit anything or correct mistakes. Choose View, Zoom to double the size of the Whiteboard contents. To return to the original screen size, choose View, Zoom.

Copying an area of the screen to the Whiteboard involves a number of steps to be successful:

1. Choose Tools, Select Area.

2. When the Whiteboard Select Area dialog box appears, click OK.

3. Beginning in a corner of the area you want to capture, drag the mouse pointer diagonally until the desired area is outlined.

4. Click on the Whiteboard where you want the screen capture pasted and the capture will be placed on the Whiteboard.

To copy a specific window, the procedure is slightly different:

1. Choose Tools, Select Window.

2. When the Whiteboard Select Area dialog box appears, click OK.

3. Choose the window you want to copy.

4. Return to the Whiteboard and click where you want the window item pasted. The window capture will be placed on the Whiteboard.

Sharing an Application with Another User During a Conference   This feature will come in handy when users need to collaborate on a project, such as editing a Microsoft Word document or a spreadsheet in tandem. Follow these steps to share a document with another user during a NetMeeting Conference:

1. On your computer, start the application you want to share.

2. In NetMeeting, choose Tools, Share Application, and then click the name of the application.

   You are now in sharing mode with the other user.

3. If you want to see the name of the person who is sharing an application, look in the upper right-hand corner above the application window for his or her name.

   If you don't want others in the conference to take control of the application you have shared, choose Tools, Work Alone. If the user has control of the application while you are changing to Work Alone mode, you might also have to click the mouse button or press a key to regain control of your computer.

N O T E   You can only share applications on computers running NetMeeting on Windows 95. Other users can access a shared application on your computer if their computers are running NetMeeting on Windows 95 or Windows NT 4.0. ■

> **CAUTION**
>
> If you should share a Windows Explorer window, such as My Computer or a folder on your computer, you will be sharing every Windows Explorer window you have open. Also, once you have shared a Windows Explorer window, every application you start during this conference will also automatically be shared with participants in the conference.

To work with an application shared by someone else, choose Tools, Collaborate. Take control of the application by double-clicking in the application window. Once you have control of the application you have access to every feature of the application, just as if it were on your computer.

N O T E   Many applications are difficult to share because of bandwidth considerations. Therefore, before attempting to share a graphics-intensive application during a conference, you should consider removing any unnecessary graphics. If you are participating over a dial-up connection, you may want to avoid application sharing altogether. It can be an uncomfortably slow experience. ■

Part
III

Ch
10

If you find that shared programs are responding in an odd fashion, it's most likely because other users engaged in the conference have a different screen resolution. You can solve this by having all of the users agree to use the same screen resolution. To change the screen scroll option, choose Tools, Options, and then choose the appropriate option on the General tab under the When a shared window is too big to fit on my screen section. You'll want to get resolutions set before the conference because usually when you change your resolution, you will need to restart your computer.

Sending Files to Other People in a Conference   It's probably not possible to participate in a conference without finding it necessary to exchange more detailed information with others. Sending files while conferencing may be the solution. Use this procedure to send files:

1. Choose Tools, Send File.
2. Select the file on your hard drive you would like to send, and then click Send File.

If you are in a conference with multiple users, the file will be sent to all users in the conference.

TIP If you only want to send the file to one person in a multiple chat, right-click the icon for that person, and then click Send File. You can also drag and drop the file on the person's name.

It may be important for you to specify where to save files that are received from other users. Follow these steps to set up your incoming file directory:

1. Choose Tools, Options.
2. Select the General tab and select the option to Receive Files Sent To Me In a conference.
3. Type the path of the folder where you want the files to be saved.

TIP You can avoid receiving a file transfer by choosing Cancel in the File Transfer Status dialog box.

Web Site Visitors

The ability for users to query and search for other users via a Web page is one of the hottest features of the Internet Locator Service. This section will outline a basic overview of the use of the Active Server Pages script processor to deliver Web pages displaying directory information from the Internet Locator Service. Please refer to Chapters 15, "Introduction to Internet Information Server 3.0," and 16, "Serving Active Content on the Internet," for a more in-depth overview of the ActiveX scripting language, with some sample scripts to enhance your Internet Locator Server.

The objective of this interface is to provide a way to search for people who have already connected to the server using a real-time communication application, or to automatically register people who are visiting your site as being online.

Here are some of the features that can be provided through a Web page using Active Server Pages.

Searching for Online Users   Users can define queries, execute queries, and display the results of queries. Searches will not only display users who are added by connecting to the server using a real-time communications application, but also users whose listings are added by a Web page.

Enable Conferencing by Clicking a User Name   Web page developers can provide a link in their results page to allow users to click to connect directly to another user using Microsoft NetMeeting or Intel Internet Phone. The conferences are launched through an installed Active Server Pages file called Ulserver.dll, which is installed in the /Scripts virtual root on your server.

> **N O T E**   For these links to work, the person receiving the call must have the appropriate real-time communication application (NetMeeting or the Intel Internet Phone) running on their computer. The link will start the application on the initiator's computer. ■

Part

III

Ch

10

Automatic Refresh of the Web Page so that the Displayed User Information Remains Current   Administrators of the Internet Locator Service can create an automatic refresh feature to keep the user information current. To be able to have a page open for a long period of time and automatically see when people come online or leave, you can use the HTML <meta> tag to set the frequency of refresh.

Registration of Users Online   To register a user online, the Web page adds a listing for the user, and then for each application the user has available, the listing is modified to add the application information.

Authenticating the User   In order to protect online listings from being modified or deleted by anyone other than their owner, administrators can use ActiveX to authenticate the user before allowing modification or deletion of the record. This authentication is done at the script level, because there are several types of authentication environments Internet Locator Service can be used in.

All of these examples require developers to program in the ActiveX scripting language, which uses the .asp file name extension, and must be in a virtual root on your Web server that has both read and execute permission. In order to get a better understanding of ActiveX, and examples of its uses with the Internet Locator Service, please refer to Chapters 15, "Introduction to Internet Information Server 3.0," and 16, "Serving Active Content on the Internet."

Examples of ILS

The Internet Locator Service will become an important part of many offices in the near future. The communications and conferencing software will be deployed for internal uses on company intranets, and will also become a key device for communicating with customers who access the companies intranet site.

The Public Agenda Project

In Tallahassee, there is an effort called The Public Agenda Project. According to its charter, the goal of The Public Agenda Project is to promote the return to participatory democracy, where people are involved with their social environment in an informed and active way.

The Public Agenda has put a lot of effort into making contact with the public. It has conducted research and surveys in the community, and has conducted training sessions to instruct citizens on ways to work together to solve community problems.

In an effort to enhance dialog in the community, The Public Agenda Project will use several features of the Microsoft Commercial Internet Servers, specifically the News Server, the Chat Server, and the Internet Locator Server. The Public Agenda will enjoy the value of the Internet Locator Services ability to allow staff members to be in contact with each other, and with public officials and the citizens in the community.

With improved communications as the goal, the NetMeeting/Internet Locator Service opens up worlds of opportunities. In this day and age, it's important to have a digital business model. This is a communicator's dream and it will be an excellent addition to access points at public libraries and public schools.

Members of the public can meet for real-time conversations, conduct searches of other users who are online, as well as look for users grouped by areas of interest. In an environment where the public has a say and has access to the communities decision-makers, the public will be encouraged and the result will be an improved relationship with their government.

Microsoft Chat Room

Microsoft, in an effort to demonstrate its innovative software, has created an Internet Locator Server. In fact, Microsoft has several servers set up for public access. On any given day there will be thousands of connections to the Service. Microsoft has set up an example of its Active Server Pages strategy and provides information about each user that is presently logged in.

Users can participate in conference calls with other users and exploit the many features that are available, such as Whiteboard, application sharing, text chats, and audio chats. Microsoft's server, though crowded, has proven to be remarkably stable and capable of handling the large user population that is accessing the server.

The Internet Locator Service is hot and necessary for most Internet Service Providers and certainly would be a perfect solution for the majority of Intranets.

From Here...

You should now have a general understanding of the Microsoft Internet Locator Service, including installation and configuration procedures, and setting up additional applications for enhanced communications.

■ For a more detailed explanation on how to use ActiveX, see Chapters 15, "Introduction to Internet Information Server 3.0," and 16, "Serving Active Content on the Internet."

Commercial Internet System Content Management Servers

Using Microsoft Index Server

With Microsoft's Index Server, one of the greatest challenges for the Internet or intranet user—finding information accurately, quickly, and easily—is solved with an easy to install, easy to administer package. As part of Microsoft's Windows NT Server and Internet Information Server, the Index Server indexes and finds documents by using simple Web-based querying tools.

Just as Web browsers brought the power and beauty of the Internet to the average user, Microsoft's Index Server allows users to access the information housed inside an organization's intranet or Internet site in a way never truly possible before.

In this chapter, you learn how to install Index Server, index virtual roots on the Web and elsewhere, perform simple as well as complex queries, administer Index Server, and troubleshoot routine problems. ■

Document indexing

Learn the differences between a file-based LAN and a document-based intranet, and why Index Server plays such a major role in establishing a useful site.

Index Server operation

Indexing documents in several languages, Index Server's tools allow for English-to-foreign language indexing options—and back again.

Index Server and Windows NT

The interaction between Windows NT Server and Index Server allow for much more flexible searches than traditional document indexing technologies.

Mapping documents to virtual roots

To make an indexed directory available to your audience, you want to map that directory to a virtual root. Mapping strategies and security options are discussed here.

Making queries

There are many ways to make queries under Index Server. A list of the more common (and some very unique) query statements are included in this chapter.

Understanding the Role of Index Server

Microsoft Index Server brings the power and ease of use of Web-based indexing and querying to corporate and organizational intranet sites, Internet servers, and other networks, without requiring that documents be reformatted into HTML. Index Server allows Internet or intranet administrators to index documents residing on a Windows NT server, NetWare, or UNIX server on a network within an enterprise. Once documents and their properties are indexed, users can search for and access the indexed documents by using query forms. These query forms allow users to request information based on subject matter, content, file size, or the date, time, and author of a document.

Index Server performs this task by mapping words to documents, indexing the documents behind the scene, and making the whole process transparent to the user. Best of all, the documents can retain their original format.

Importance of Document Indexing

One of the benefits of moving from a LAN-based company to a document-based intranet is easier access to information. It is important to distinguish between the two types of networked environments.

Local Area Networks (LANs) are file-based. This means that, to view information, you must log into the network, launch a software application, search for and retrieve the file that holds the information, open the file, and view the data.

But what if the information is stored in a file format you cannot read, because you did not have the accompanying software application? It would be inconvenient to view a document created in WordPerfect unless you had WordPerfect loaded, or unless you converted the document using your word processor's filtering utilities. Even then, the document might have imbedded formatting that could not be converted because the filtering utility unsuccessfully read the source document, and could not correctly transfer formatting information during the conversion process. Additionally, moving from one version of a software product to another—for example, moving from Microsoft Word 6.0 to MS Word for Win 95—might create problems.

Publishing on the Web has eliminated that problem by making the document itself a universal standard. The Web browser is now the productivity application. This allows a corporation, government agency, or other enterprise to make information and data available by converting existing documents to Web pages using the Internet standard HTML (HyperText Mark Up Language).

But Index Server does not just index documents created in HTML format, nor does it simply index documents in ASCII text format. Index Server also indexes documents created in Microsoft Office applications such as Excel, Word, and PowerPoint. It can also, through the use of an optional filter (called IFilter and available through Microsoft), index documents created in other word processor, spreadsheet, and presentation formats.

And it can index documents created in seven popular languages, or multilingual documents created using several languages in the same document.

Searching Over the Internet

Veteran Web surfers know and understand how to use such tools as WebCrawler, Lycos, Yahoo!, and Digital's AltaVista. You type a search keyword or phrase, and the Web search engine goes out over the Internet, locates words or phrases that correspond to the request, ranks them according to a formula, and returns the search results to the browser.

Index Server takes this concept further, by indexing not only the contents of documents, but the actual document objects themselves. Therefore, you can search not just by a document's content, but by such document object particulars as author, date, and time the document was created, and the size of the document.

With the proliferation of raw data, as well as information, Index Server can reduce the time needed for Internet or intranet queries dramatically, which translates into faster searches; happier customers; and far greater use of an organization's Internet or intranet site by all parties. And that's always good news.

Any organization that makes it easier for its people to acquire and use information will be at a greater competitive advantage. And making this technology available to its customers or consumers will help that company retain, or find, a competitive advantage.

Part
IV

Ch
11

Joining the Query "Revolution" with Index Server

Psychologists and sociologists have jump-started careers by talking about information overload. Executives, as well as decision makers, frequently are inundated with information from a variety of sources, including electronic information. Additionally, it is getting more difficult to find what you really need, information-wise, on the Internet. A method of cutting through the clutter is sorely needed.

Data versus Information

Data does not become information until the data is brought together in a format that makes it useful and relevant to the individual or organization. Numbers on a spreadsheet or data in a database do not become relevant until a method is devised to sort and analyze the data, thereby turning it into information. The query power of Index Server helps turn that data into useful information.

Information at Your Fingertips

Microsoft's phrase for turning data into information is called "Information at your fingertips," the realization of founder Bill Gates' vision to be able to retrieve entire storehouses of data and turn that data into information for your use quickly, easily, and accurately.

With Index Server and the various Microsoft Commercial Internet System applications, organizations can make their entire knowledge base available for accessing. Governments can put policies and procedures on the Web without converting existing word processor formats. Law firms will access information much more efficiently and completely than before. Companies can index entire product manuals, catalogs, and notices, again without changing their basic formats. Internet Service Providers (ISPs) will be more attractive to subscribers, because they will know their site(s) will be indexed for a more thorough search by customers and clients.

Learning the Secret of Index Server

The secret to Index Server's capabilities rests in Microsoft's decision not to tax system resources through a constant reindexing of all documents. Rather, Microsoft's process heavily relies upon NTFS, or Windows NT File System. This is why it is important that the indexing be performed on a server whose drives are formatted using NTFS.

As opposed to other methods of storing files on a computer, such as DOS' File Allocation Table or OS/2's High Performance File System, Windows NT's NTFS includes a registry that can be tied into by Commercial Internet Server applications, as well as other third-party products.

Index Server registers each document with NTFS and requests that, when a document is modified, NTFS notifies Index Server. As it monitors system resources and performance, Index Server may elect not to reindex the document immediately, opting instead for performing the index at a time of inactivity. This use of the operating system, rather than the software, to perform the task of document notification, is what allows Index Server to run on comparatively modest hardware.

Understanding Index Server's Role in Microsoft Commercial Internet System

Microsoft Index Server does not ship with Windows NT Server 4.0, and it is not part of Microsoft Commercial Internet System. Officially, Index Server is an add-in product for NT Server 4.0, and is considered part of NT's Internet Information Server (IIS).

ON THE WEB

www.microsoft.com/ntserver   Since Index Server does not ship with NT Server 4.0, you'll need to download the product from Microsoft's NT Server area on its World Wide Web site. You can download Index Server free of charge. At press time, the latest version of Index Server is 1.1.

You'll need to install some other products before you can successfully install Index Server: Internet Information Server 3.0 and Internet Explorer 3.0, for Windows NT. Each product is available for download, free of charge, from Microsoft's Web site. The products you'll want to download are Index Server 1.1 and Active Server Pages beta 2.

> **CAUTION**
>
> While Netscape Navigator and other Web browsers are satisfactory for everyday querying of indexed documents, the Web browser used for administration must be able to support client-side scripting, such as JScript or VBScript. Therefore, it is strongly recommended that Microsoft's Internet Explorer be used for all Web-based administration.

Index Server interfaces with Internet Information Server in a way similar to the way SQL Server or any other ODBC-compliant database program does. Rather than using the ODBC (Open Database Connectivity) model, IS uses its own connector model. The database returns the results, and the connector converts those results into a Web page accessible via a Web browser.

Index Server uses several file types to move information from directories holding documents to the Web browser: It uses IDQ files, which have a format and structure similar to IDC files used in Microsoft's SQL Server. Also, Index Server uses advanced HTX files that specify how the query is to be formatted and returned to the user's browser.

The following steps show how a query travels through the system:

1. The user creates a query in Web browser.
2. A query travels through Internet Information Server.
3. The query travels through IIS to Index Server.
4. Index Server locates information stored in Indexes.
5. Results are transmitted to Index Server.
6. Index Server transmits to IIS.
7. IIS returns results as an M document to Browser.

Part
IV

Ch
11

Verifying the Minimum Hardware and Software Necessary for Running Index Server

The minimum hardware requirements for operating Index Server are basically the same as the other components of Windows NT Server and the MCIS. Though Microsoft's minimum hardware configuration for NT Server is a computer running an Intel 486DX/33 processor with 12 megabytes of RAM, there are other MCIS applications that require a 486DX2/66 processor as a minimum. Therefore, it is recommended that the minimum practical configuration include a 486DX2/66 processor and 32 megabytes of RAM.

Table 11.1 describes Microsoft's minimums for Index Server.

Table 11.1   Minimum Recommended System Requirements for Index Server

System Requirement	Specifications
Hardware	32-bit x 86-compatible microprocessor (such as Intel 80486/25 or higher), Intel Pentium, or supported RISC-based microprocessor such as the MIPS R4x00, Digital Alpha, or PowerPC. You also need a VGA, or higher resolution, monitor (800×600 resolution at 256 colors is not required, but is highly recommended). To store the actual indices, Index Server needs free disk space equaling 40% of the total size of the documents to be indexed.
Software	Windows NT Server 4.0 and NT Server 4.0 Service Pack 1 for Microsoft Windows NT Internet Information Server 2.0. IIS 3.0 and Internet Explorer 3.01 for Windows NT recommended.
Memory	12M RAM minimum for x 86 systems, 16MB recommended. 16M RAM minimum for RISC-based systems. 32M RAM or greater strongly advised.
Peripherals	One or more network adapter cards if you want to use Windows NT Server with a network.

CAUTION

Some "x 86" processors not manufactured by Intel (Cyrix, AMD, and others) that support 16-bit MS-DOS and Microsoft Windows may not be compatible with Windows NT. The problem centers around non-Intel x 86 processors that feature "write-thru" cache. If you have a non-Intel x 86 processor that meets this description, check with the processor manufacturer before proceeding with any attempt at installing or configuring this software.

Practical Configuration of Index Server Hardware

The functional capabilities of Index Server are governed by:

- The number of documents in the corpus, or site where the documents are stored (also known as the virtual root)
- The size of the corpus, in megabytes
- The number of queries arriving at the server
- The kind of queries (simple versus complex)

Simple queries run fastest; more complex queries will run best on a server with a faster processor. In small operations, Index Server can perform well on a 486/66 with 16 megabytes of RAM. In larger corporate and government situations, however, much more powerful hardware is suggested. Table 11.2 gives some recommendations for installed memory.

Table 11.2   Document Indexing Speed Relative to Installed Random Access Memory

Number of Documents	Minimum Memory	Recommended Memory
Fewer than 10,000	16M for workstations	Same as minimum
10,000–100,000	32M	32M
100,000–250,000	32M	64M to 128M
250,000–500,000	64M	128M to 256M
500,000 or more	128M	256M or more

Additionally, you need to factor the size of the corpus, or volume of documents, to be indexed. Microsoft has devised a formula whereby you need an additional 40 percent of hard disk space, over and above the size of the volume. This is to facilitate the indexing process itself.

Always plan for growth in your analysis of hard disk space. Look seriously at the volume of documents to be indexed now, and try to plan for an explosive growth in the volume of these documents. One law of technology is that, once an enterprise understands the benefits of technology, its use will increase exponentially. Apply this law when assessing how much disk space is needed for indexing and storage purposes.

Part IV

Ch 11

TIP The faster the processor, the faster the queries will perform and the faster the indices will update. And the more memory you install, the better off you will be. If you have unusually large documents, a lack of memory will seriously hamper performance, or in some cases, prevent performance completely. If performance is slow, add more memory. Unlike 16-bit Windows, where adding additional memory did not always provide performance dividends, Windows 95 and Windows NT will benefit greatly from the addition of memory. Buy as much memory as your budget allows.

Workstation Requirements

Any PC or Macintosh running a Web browser and connected to the company intranet or Internet can function as a workstation. Ideally, the computer should be running Microsoft Internet Explorer 3.0 or higher Web browser to take advantage of Microsoft ActiveX technology.

NOTE Other Web browsers can be used with Index Server on the organizational intranet or Internet site to search for information, but may not support ActiveX. This will not limit basic access to indexed documents.

Downloading Index Server

Download and install the latest versions of Active Server Pages and Internet Explorer for Windows NT before attempting to install Index Server. This way, you'll ensure the latest versions of the products and minimize the possibility of these components not performing well together.

ON THE WEB

http://lisa.microsoft.com/activex/default.asp   You need to download Index Server 1.1, Active Server Pages, and Internet Explorer 3.01 (or higher) for Windows NT directly from Microsoft's Web site. Using your Web browser, connect to this site on the Internet, and proceed to the download area.

www.microsoft.com/ntserver/default.asp   You also may wish to go to Microsoft's Windows NT Server site, and read information about Microsoft's NT Server package before you proceed with the download.

www.microsoft.com/NTServerSupport/   Download NT Server 4.0 Service Pack 1 and install it before installing any other upgrades or betas.

Installing Index Server

Follow these steps to install Index Server on your system:

1. Using Windows NT Explorer, copy the downloaded Index Server file, is11enu.exe, to an empty directory on NT Server's hard disk.

2. Double-click the is11enu.exe icon to launch the installation utility.

3. You will see a dialog box similar to the one in Figure 11.1. It will ask you if you wish to install Index Server 1.1. Click Yes to proceed; otherwise, click No.

FIG. 11.1

Launching is11enu.exe brings up this confirmation screen. Click Yes to proceed.

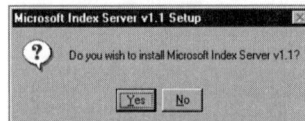

4. You must accept or reject Microsoft's License Agreement (see Figure 11.2). Read the agreement carefully. Choose Yes.

5. Next, Setup begins extracting files from their compressed state, as shown in Figure 11.3.

6. Setup is now ready to begin the actual installation of Index Server. Again, you will be asked to confirm your decision to install Index Server (see Figure 11.4). Choose Continue and proceed.

FIG. 11.2

The Microsoft License Agreement. It is a good idea to read this document carefully before proceeding. Click Yes when finished.

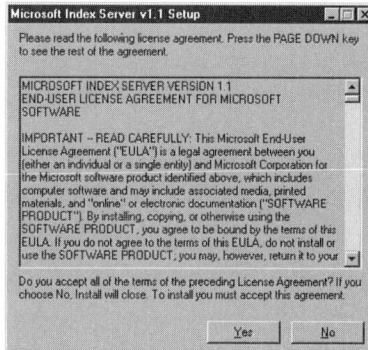

FIG. 11.3

You will see the status bar update the overall progress of the setup process as files are expanded. Note the filenames and extensions as they appear on-screen.

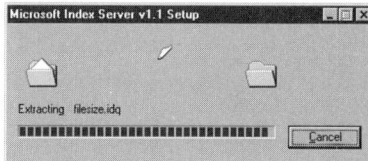

FIG. 11.4

The main Setup screen. Click Continue to proceed.

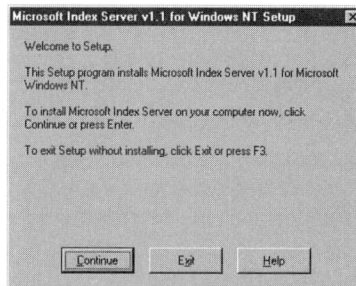

Part

IV

Ch

11

7. You will be asked to verify the destination Internet Information Server folder for the sample scripts that will be used with Index Server. You should accept the default directory, c:\InetPub\scripts, as shown in Figure 11.5, unless you installed IIS in another directory. Accept the default if you are unsure. Click Continue.

FIG. 11.5

Accept Microsoft's defaults here, unless you are certain you want the files in a separate directory.

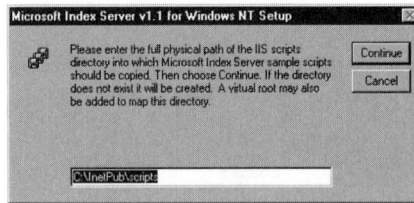

N O T E A virtual root will be created to map this directory correctly. A *virtual root* maps a directory, or folder, to a corresponding Internet volume. ▧

8. Next, Setup will ask you to identify the IIS Virtual Root into which it will install Index Server sample HTML pages. Identify the virtual root if different from Figure 11.6; otherwise, accept the defaults. Click Continue.

FIG. 11.6

The virtual root is the directory accessible to Internet/intranet users via a Web browser, after it has been mapped to a directory. Index Server will map this virtual root automatically.

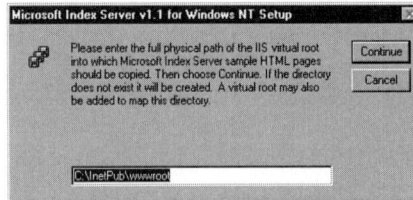

9. As shown in Figure 11.7, Setup will ask for the full path into which the Index Server Index should be stored. Accept the default if unsure. Click Continue.

FIG. 11.7

By default, the index will be positioned just off the root.

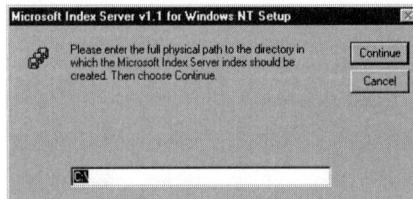

10. Setup completes the installation of Index Server by creating directories on the destination drive (see Figure 11.8), and begins copying IS files to their appropriate locations (see Figure 11.9).

T I P You may also consider putting Index Server scripts into a separate directory, index, to keep it off the root.

FIG. 11.8

Setup now creates the aforementioned directories on the hard drive.

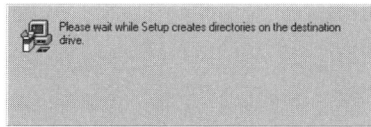

> Please wait while Setup creates directories on the destination drive.

FIG. 11.9

Setup copies Index Server files to their appropriate directories on the server.

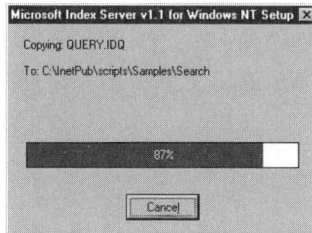

> **Microsoft Index Server v1.1 for Windows NT Setup** ☒
>
> Copying: QUERY.IDQ
>
> To: C:\InetPub\scripts\Samples\Search
>
> 87%
>
> Cancel

11. When finished, Setup notifies you with a dialog box similar to Figure 11.10. Press Exit to Windows to complete the installation.

FIG. 11.10

Copy down the URL, or location, of the sample files. You'll want to access that site (your site, actually) by using a Web browser.

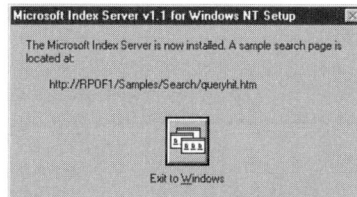

> **Microsoft Index Server v1.1 for Windows NT Setup** ☒
>
> The Microsoft Index Server is now installed. A sample search page is located at:
>
> http://RPOF1/Samples/Search/queryhit.htm
>
> Exit to Windows

Part
IV

Ch
11

NOTE The URL given in this dialog box, **http://RPOF1/Samples/Search/queryhit.htm**, is the sample search page you will use to understand how to query using Index Server. Write down this URL for use later. ▓

To confirm the successful installation of Index Server, choose Microsoft Index Server (Common) from Programs on the Start Menu to display the cascading menu selection shown in Figure 11.11. If successfully installed, there will be four separate Index Server entries on the final menu: Administration, Online Documentation, Release Notes, and Sample Query Form.

A sample query form is found by clicking on Sample Query Form (see Figure 11.12). This is the form you will use for the examples in this chapter, although you can create customized query forms by using HTML.

FIG. 11.11

Notice how Index Server has created four directories—Index Server Administration, Online Documentation, Release Notes, and Sample Query Form—off the Microsoft Index Server menu option.

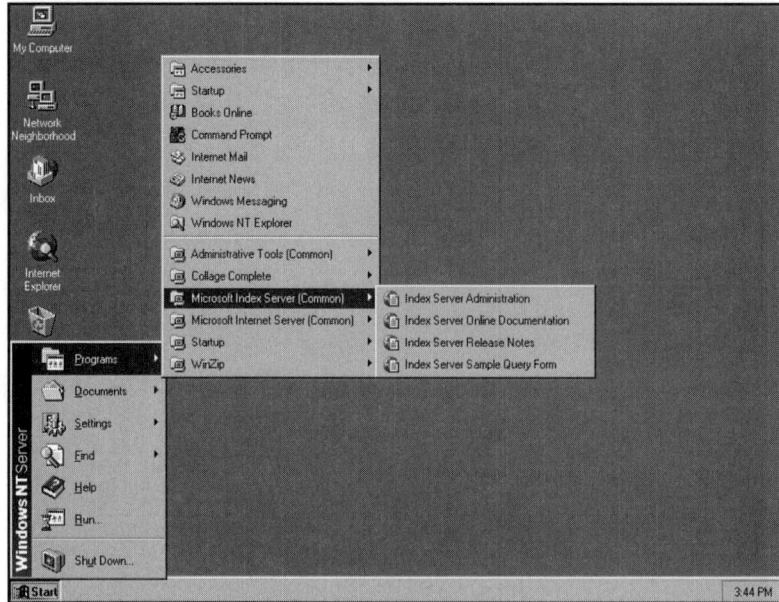

FIG. 11.12

The sample query form. Text is typed into the text box which contains the word "microsoft" in this screen.

You are now ready to proceed to the next phase.

Starting Index Server

Index Server cannot run unless Internet Information Server is started. But that process does not start Index Server. Index Server does not "start" until a search query is performed on the corpus. At that time, Index Server starts the indexing process for that particular data set. Index Server is stopped when IIS is stopped. It restarts when the next query is made.

The administration module is launched from the Start menu or, as shown in Figure 11.13, by accessing the Web Administration page from a remote workstation.

FIG. 11.13
Index Server Administration is run from a browser and features the five categories shown here.

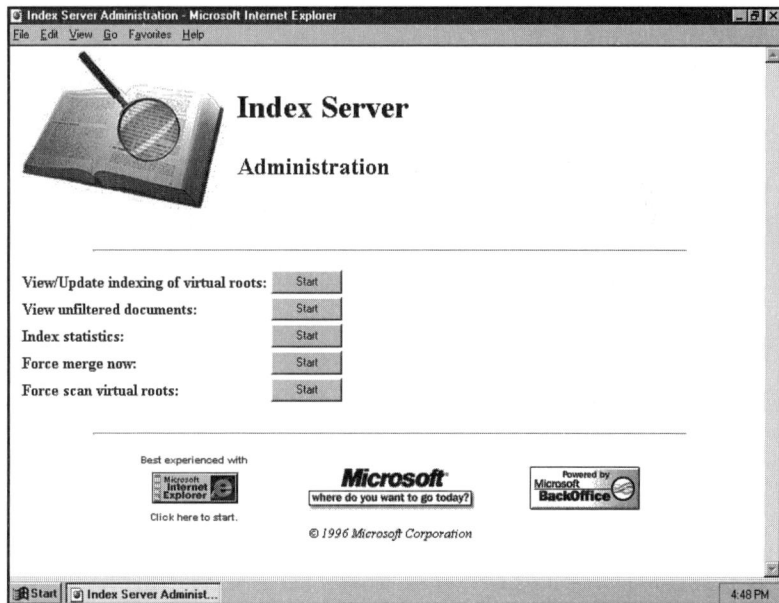

Part
IV

Ch
11

Indexing Documents

To perform a query, you must first index the document directories that are to be queried. Microsoft Index server employs several unique ways to index a document. They include:

- Indexing full text in Web pages. This allows the content of a Web document to be indexed.

- Indexing HTML properties in a document. This allows Index Server to make use of the HTML document structure as well.

- Indexing full text in Microsoft Word, Excel, and PowerPoint documents without reformatting those documents. This means Microsoft Office documents can be accessed on a Web site without converting the document to HTML—a time saver whose significance cannot be underestimated.

- Indexing other document formats. Using the optional Ifilter interface, developers can create indexes to document formats not supported natively within Index Server.

- Incremental refreshing of document indexes. Working in conjunction with the NTFS file management system under Windows NT, Index Server is notified when a document is changed or added. Indexing occurs in the background, thereby conserving precious system resources.

- Controlling indexing based on user preferences. On a server whose volume is indexed, users can determine what, if any, of their information is made available to be indexed. It also allows users to block the indexing of directories containing proprietary data.

- Indexing file and property values that enable users to query based on file size, date and time of creation, and author.

- Indexing in seven languages, including English, Spanish, French, German, Swedish, Italian, and Dutch. And the software can switch from English to another language (for example, Spanish) and back again.

- Automatically updating indexes. Index Server automatically updates its indexes in the background, eliminating the need to update those indexes manually. Also, it indexes as the documents themselves are being modified, allowing the index—along with the document—to stay current.

- Allowing administrators to know exactly who, when, where, and how many queries are being performed.

- Maintaining itself through automatic corruption detection and recovery, as well as offering 7×24 (seven days a week, 24-hour a day) maintenance, meaning the server never has to be shut down for routine Index Server administrative tasks. The server can stay up, and users can stay logged in, even during a forced index process.

- Performing these tasks while conserving system resources, thereby allowing Index Server to run on a relatively modest range of platforms.

ON THE WEB

www.microsoft.com/ntserver/search   The Ifilter Software Development Kit (SDK) is available to download without charge via Microsoft's Web site. Go there and follow the directions to locate and download the SDK.

How Indexing Works

Indexing is performed on a virtual root and its child directories. Indexing can be performed on one, all, or several virtual roots of the administrator's preference. It can be performed on some, none, or all of the child directories.

The process of indexing virtual roots Microsoft employs is known as the CiDaemon process. Index Server gives the CiDaemon process a list of documents. The process identifies the correct filter DLL and Word Breaker DLL associated with the documents to be filtered.

Filtering is performed in the background in an effort to conserve system resources and optimize overall Index Server performance.

When the Windows NT NTFS notifies Index Server that a document has changed, Index Server decides if the document will be indexed now or during a lull in activity, depending on the level of utilization of the processor and other server resources at that time. By so doing, Index Server respects and conserves system resources until such time as the server can more efficiently process the index update.

This is in contrast to other, more resource-intensive indexing solutions, where the documents are constantly polled against an existing table of authorities. Continuous polling, found in competing indexing products, robs system resources and limits the ability of the computer to do its work.

Filtering, Word Breaking, and Normalization

Filtering, also known as content filtering, allows Index Server to decode private files that would normally require the host application to perform the work. For example, many indexing applications cannot understand Word or Excel files, and consequently cannot index them. Index Server uses open standard content filters to index these files.

The system begins by determining the file type and uses the appropriate content filter. A filter DLL starts the Ifilter ActiveX interface. The CiDaemon process then begins breaking the document into "text chunks," which are passed on to Index Server.

The filter DLL can be found in the registry.

The process can also understand language changes. If a document is written in both English and Spanish, it will tag the second language text chunk as Spanish. It will then load the appropriate word breaker and normalizer (described later in this section).

These filters can also handle embedded objects. If you have an Excel spreadsheet embedded in a Word document, the filter recognizes the imbedded object and activates the appropriate filter for that object.

Word breaking is the process of converting character streams into words, all the while being mindful of inflections, breaks, and punctuation unique to different languages. Index Server has the capability of indexing words in seven languages:

- English
- Spanish
- French
- German
- Italian
- Dutch
- Swedish

Part
IV

Ch
11

Because both the Content Filter and Word Breaker are modular, they can be modified using the open standard and plugged into Index Server. This allows third-party software developers to make content filters and word breakers in languages not currently supported by Microsoft.

Normalizing cleans up the words received from Word Breaker and standardizes case, punctuation, and the removal of common words and conjunctions, referred to as "noise" words. This makes the words uniform and easier to index and access.

"Noise words" in English might include "a," "the," "of," "at," "and," and "you." There are literally hundreds more. Each language's noise file is stored in Index Server.

The advantage of filtering out these "noise words" can be found in the performance of Index Server. Filtering out these words can reduce the size of a document by up to 50 percent in the English language alone.

The software can index an English paragraph, switch to a French paragraph, then switch back to English, all through the process of Unicoding. All index information is stored as Unicode characters and all queries are converted to Unicode before processing.

T I P   You can customize a word list to include slang, local dialect, and application-specific words. You can add these words to the appropriate noise word file. You can find the English noise.enu file that contains these "noise words" at C:\WINNT\system32\noise.enu and can be viewed or edited using a text editor such as Notepad.

CAUTION

Removing words from a noise file, or removing all words from a noise file, will significantly increase the size of indexes and will take longer to index a document. Proceed with great care before altering noise.enu in any way. Make a backup copy of the file before you proceed.

Index server can also search based on proximity data; that is, the location of one word in relation to another. Many popular indexing programs do not do this, usually in an effort to conserve space. But that philosophy reduces, or eliminates, the ability of the user to search for such phrases as "Windows NT Server Performance Benchmarks." The closer the searched-for words are together, the greater the ranking given to the returned document. If the words match completely, the overall rank is elevated higher still.

Indexing Binary Files

Index Server can also index binary files, making it easy to locate image, sound, video, and executable files stored on a server.

Index Server indexes the following binary formats:

.aif.avi	.cgm	.com	.dct
.dic	.dll	.exe	.eyb
.fnt	.ghi	.gif	.hqx
.ico	.inv	.jbf	.jpg
.m14	.mov	.movie	.mv
.pdf	.pic	.pma	.pmc
.pml	.pmr	.psd	.sc2
.tar	.tif	.tiff	.ttf.wav
.wll	.wlt	.wmf	.z
.z96	.zip		

Generating Abstracts

Index Server can generate a summary, usually referred to as an *abstract*, of a document. The process is also known as characterization. By default, the characterization process is active. Changing the Registry key `GenerateCharacterization` to 0 turns off the automatic generation of abstracts. Controlling the maximum number of characters in an abstract is accomplished with the registry key `MaxCharacterization`. Changing this number can reduce or expand the actual size of the abstract generated and sent to a Web page.

Administering Index Server

Maintaining an Index Server site is easy because many of the routine tasks—and a few of the more demanding ones—are automatically performed by the software.

For example, Index Server maintains itself through automatic corruption detection and recovery. It also has complete 7×24 (seven days a week, 24-hour a day) maintenance. This is significant because it means Index Server never has to be shut down (downed) for routine tasks to be performed. System administrators can add indexes whenever they want, and users are never left without access.

The reporting and logging features of Index Server allow administrators to know exactly who, when, where, and how many queries are being performed.

All this occurs while Index Server is attempting to conserve system resources. It is this capability of the software, more than any other single element, which allows Index Server to run on a modest platform such as an Intel 486 processor.

Part
IV
Ch
11

Lost File Notifications

If the rate of file modification is unusually high, it is possible for Index Server to experience buffer overflows. Index Server automatically schedules an incremental scan of all virtual roots to correct this problem. Of course, incremental scans will take place in the background, when activity on the system is low. No manual intervention is needed.

Dropped Network Connections

If a virtual root is pointing to a remote directory or share (shared folder under Windows NT, Windows 95, or Windows 3.1), and the network connection is lost to that share, Index Server assumes it is a disconnected path and makes periodic attempts to detect the remote share to see if it is again active. Again, no manual intervention is necessary.

Corrupted Files or Faulty Filter DLLs

If corrupted files are detected, the Filter DLL will be unable to properly interpret the contents of the file. The files themselves will be marked as unfiltered and an event will be written to the Event Log. Files protected by passwords are not filtered.

You can request a list of unfiltered files by doing the following:

1. Go to Index Server Administration by choosing Start, Programs, Microsoft Index Server (Common), then choose Index Server Administration.

2. Click the Start button next to View Unfiltered Documents (see Figure 11.14).

FIG. 11.14
Click the View unfiltered documents: Start button to process the request.

3. Copy or print the list of documents that are unfiltered.

4. Click OK.

5. Using a text editor or word processor, check the document contents to make sure they are not damaged, corrupted, or otherwise unreadable.

6. If the documents are damaged, repair, restore, or otherwise replace the documents. Make sure the repaired documents rest in the same virtual roots as before.

   ▶ **See** "Mapping Document Directories to a Virtual Root," **p. 300**, for information on how repaired documents are indexed.

Faulty Filter DLLs can also cause documents to go unfiltered. To track down a problem with a Filter DLL that is suspect, an administrator needs to know where to find the Filter DLL for a particular document type.

Document DLLs and their associated Filter DLL entries can be found in the Registry under the \HKEY_LOCAL_MACHINE\SOFTWARE\CLASSES tree.

CAUTION

Editing the Registry incorrectly can be as catastrophic as a hard disk failure, sometimes with the same remedies. Corruption of the Registry can make necessary a complete reinstallation of NT Server or Index Server. If you make a mistake, the computer's configuration could be damaged. The only time you should edit the registry is if you cannot make adjustments through the user interface. Information in the IFilter SDK can give you a better understanding of when, and how, to edit within the Registry.

Part
IV

Ch
11

Query Logging

All activity under Index Server is recorded and logged by Internet Information Server. To view or print log files, or to change logging procedures, do the following:

1. Choose Programs from the Start menu, then choose Microsoft Internet Server, then Internet Service Manager or Internet Service Manager (HTML), as shown in Figure 11.15.

2. Double-click WWW (see Figure 11.16), or single-click WWW if you're performing Administration under the HTML page.

FIG. 11.15

Cascading menus off the Start button. Note the two Internet Service Manager entries.

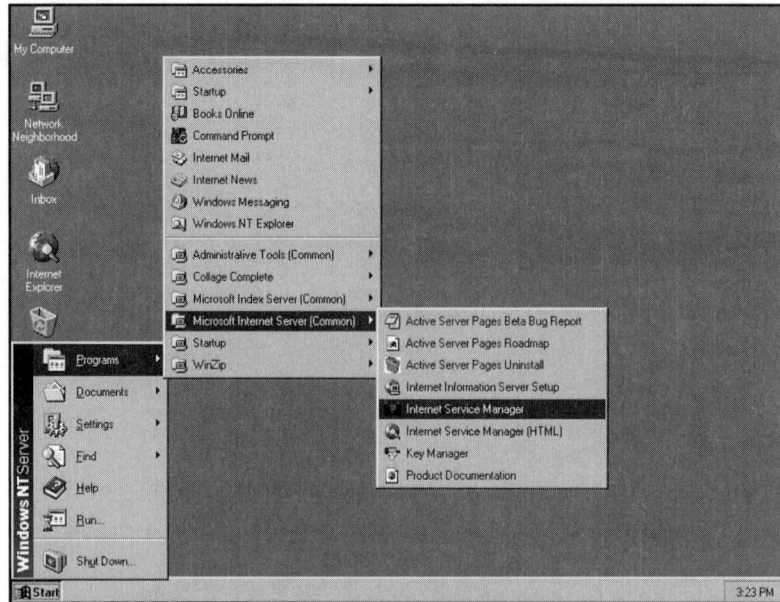

FIG. 11.16

There are three options listed here: the World Wide Web server, the Gopher server, and the File Transfer Protocol, or FTP, server. All three are running.

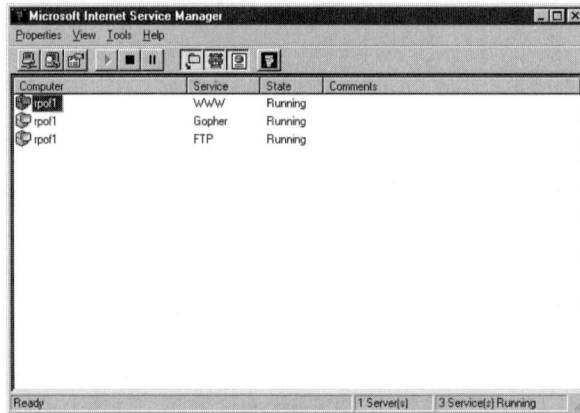

3. Choose the Logging tab in the WWW Service Properties dialog box (see Figure 11.17).

4. Copy down the name of the log file. The log file's name is INyymmdd.log, where yy represents the year, mm the month, and dd the day.

5. Launch Notepad or other text editor.

6. Go to the directory and file as listed in Logging.

7. Double-click the file name. The file will appear on-screen.

N O T E   By default, Internet Information Server keeps a daily log of activity. You can adjust the default for weekly or monthly logging, or when the log file reaches a certain size. ■

FIG. 11.17
WWW properties after
choosing the Logging
tab. Note the name and
location of the log file.
By default, Index Server
creates a new file each
day.

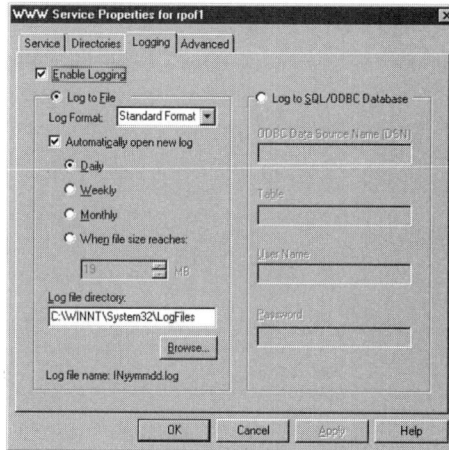

Automatic Reindexing

Index Server automatically updates its indexes in the background, eliminating the need to update those indexes manually. Also, through interaction with NTFS, Index Server can index as the documents themselves are being modified, allowing the index—along with the document—to stay current.

Indexing (Scanning) Documents

Scanning is not quite the same as indexing. *Scanning* is the procedure by which documents are identified for indexing. Before any querying can begin, you must have documents ready to be indexed. The indexing process itself takes time, so a plan of action is important. And the querying process is heavily RAM- and processor-dependent.

Occasionally, the indexing system will, of its own initiative, optimize its indexes, as well as other data structures. These tasks are designed to optimize performance, free up disk space, and open up some system RAM.

Table 11.3 gives you some guidelines regarding indexing of large volumes of information.

Table 11.3   Indexing Time Relative to Processor Speed

Processor	RAM	Estimated Index Time
Intel 486DX2/66	32M	10M per hour
Intel 486DX4/100	16M	40M per hour
Intel Pentium 100	16M	125M per hour
Dual-processor MIPS	64M	1G per hour

Filter DLLs Pre-Installed with Index Server

Index Server comes with filter DLLs pre-installed. Index Server can index the following document formats:

- HTML 3.0 or lower
- Microsoft Word
- Microsoft Excel
- Microsoft PowerPoint
- Plain (ASCII) text
- Binary files

CAUTION

Though Index Server can index files in .SAM (Ami Pro) and .WPD (WordPerfect) format, the printer formatting codes will appear in the document, as well as in the abstract. Therefore, it is recommended that the Ifilter SDK be downloaded from Microsoft's Web site and used to develop DLLs for any non-Microsoft, non-ASCII file format.

The Help Screen is a weekly question-and-answer computer column written by Scott McPherson and carried via the Knight-Ridder/Tribune News Wire to more than 300 newspapers, coast-to-coast. One of the biggest dilemmas faced by a computer columnist is that every time the column gets picked up by another newspaper, the writer gets asked the same questions, over and over again, by new readers. Creating a Web site and placing the entire inventory of old columns there would be the perfect solution for those new readers to get information specific to their needs. By using Index Server, readers will be able to query based on specific hardware and software requests. The ability to index columns and put them on a Web site for the benefit of interested readers was not posssible until now.

The Help Screen is one of several commercial sites. So, for purposes of illustrating the benefits of Index Server, the following steps will actually index the entire catalog of Help Screens from 1994 to the present.

ON THE WEB

www.integritydata.com/helpscreen/search.htm   You can access these columns by pointing your Web browser to the Integrity Data site.

Mapping Document Directories to a Virtual Root

Before you can index a directory of documents, you must first map the directory to a virtual root. It is this virtual root that will become visible to Web users.

Follow these steps to map a directory to a virtual root:

1. First, if you have not already done so, create a directory that will contain the documents to be indexed. The directory does not have to be a shared volume.

2. Copy or move the documents into the directory.

3. From the Start Button, go to Programs, Microsoft Internet Server (Common), then choose Internet Service Manager *or* Internet Service Manager (HTML).

N O T E Choosing either Internet Service Manager or Internet Service Manager (HTML) takes you to a screen where you can perform routine maintenance. Choosing ISM allows you to perform the function in an application screen; choosing ISM (HTML) takes you to a Web page to do the same housekeeping. Both applications are identical in terms of what you can do and how you do it. But, from a remote workstation, you can perform the maintenance if you use the HTML screen. ■

4. For these purposes, we will work with the HTML version of Internet Service Manager. You will see a screen similar to the one in Figure 11.18.

FIG. 11.18
Internet Service Manager as viewed from the Web. Note the tools are the same; only their location and access point are different. Any administrative procedure can be performed from either the Web page or the Windows NT screen.

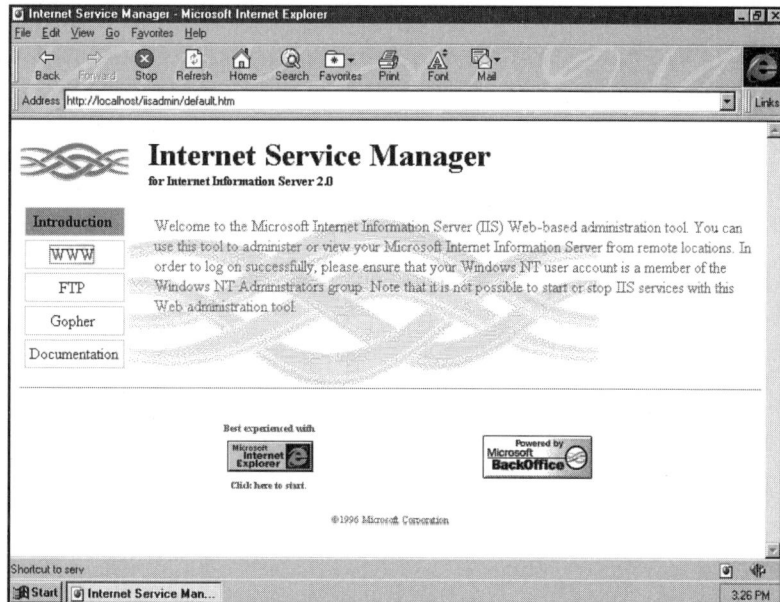

5. You have five categories: Introduction, WWW (World Wide Web), FTP (File Transfer Protocol), Gopher, and Documentation. Choose WWW.

6. From the new page (see Figure 11.19), choose Directories.

FIG. 11.19
Clicking the Logging button is the same as clicking the Logging tab metaphor, shown earlier.

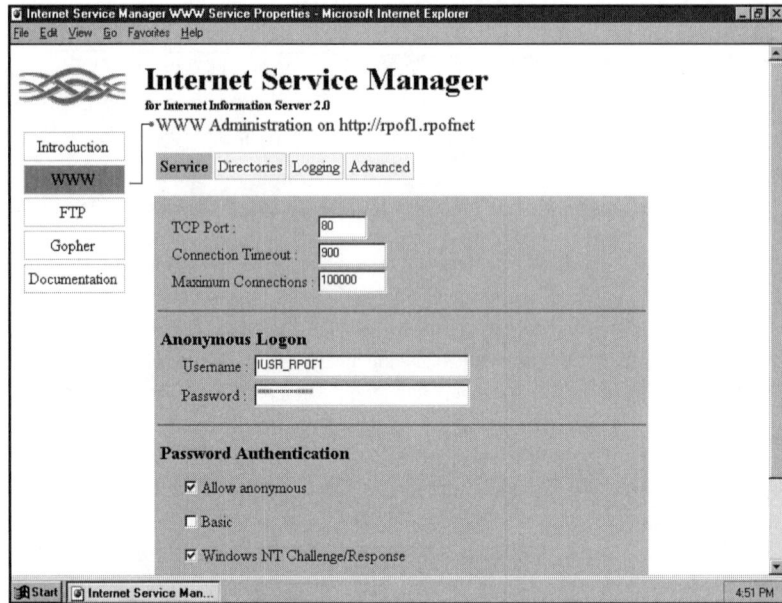

7. In Figure 11.20. you see a list of all the current Virtual Roots available on the server, along with their drive and directory (folder) mappings. At the bottom of the table, you see an empty box under the last directory entry. Click the Add button visible at the lower right corner of the screen.

FIG. 11.20
Click in the empty box immediately under C:\InetPub\wwwroot\ srchadm and then click Add.

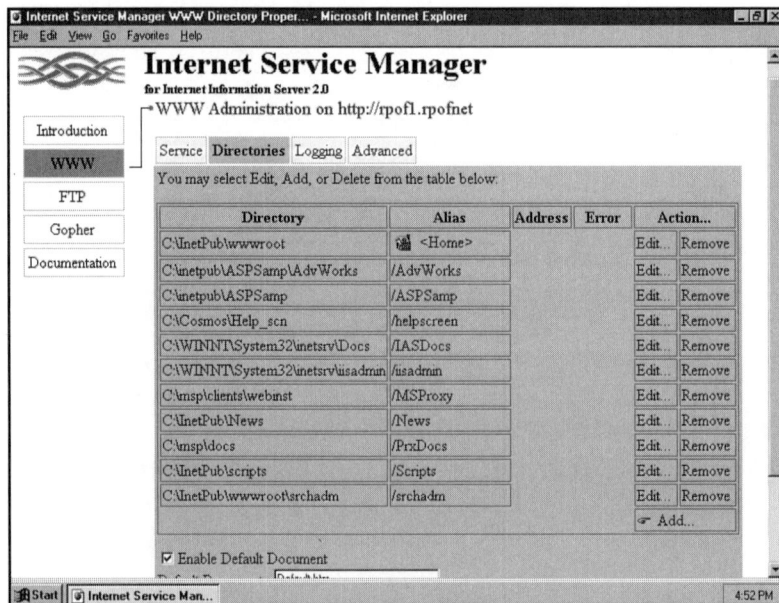

8. In the dialog box shown in Figure 11.21, click Browse.

FIG. 11.21

Click the Browse button to bring up the directory tree.

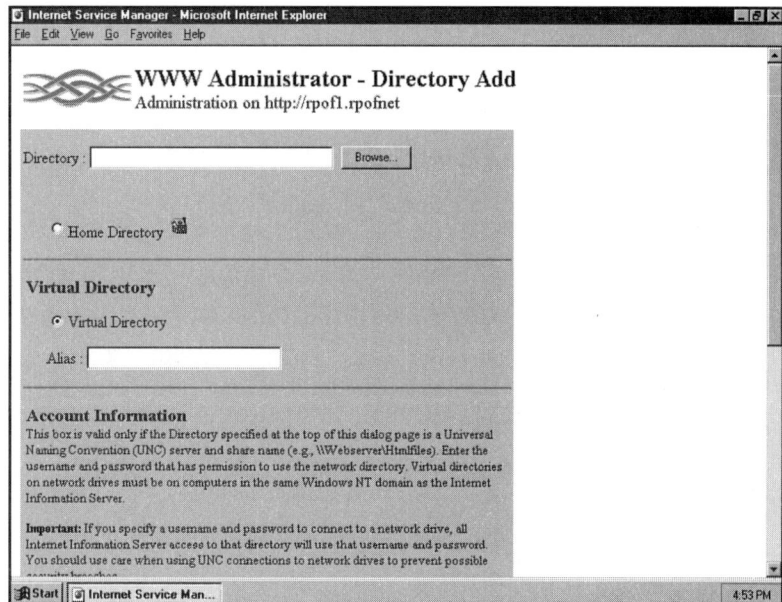

9. From the directory tree shown in Figure 11.22, choose the directory that holds your documents. In this illustration, the correct directory is C:\Cosmos\Help_scn.

FIG. 11.22

Click the directory you want to map to a virtual root. Once selected, the directory will display next to Selected Directory, located under the Select Directory page header.

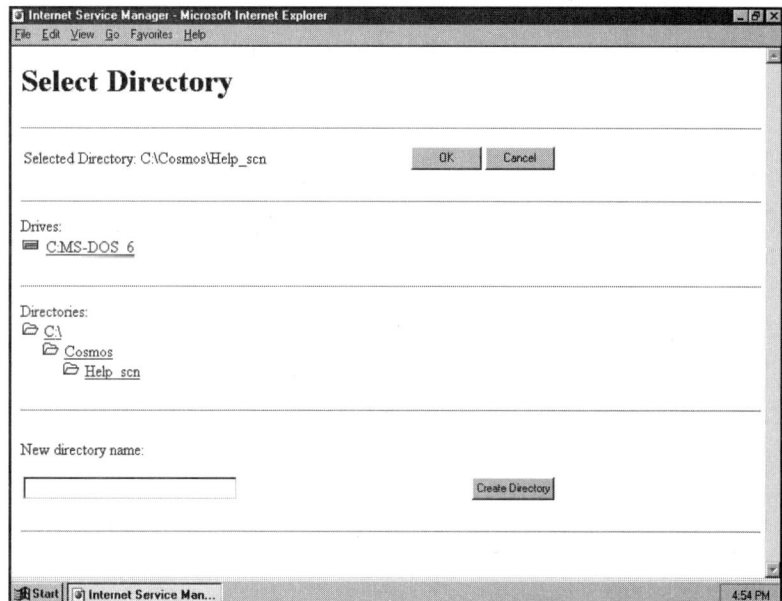

10. The value is returned to the Directory box in the Directory Add page (see Figure 11.23). Type in the alias that you want as a virtual root (in this example, the words Help Screen are typed as one string of text).

FIG. 11.23

The selected directory value is returned to the text box.

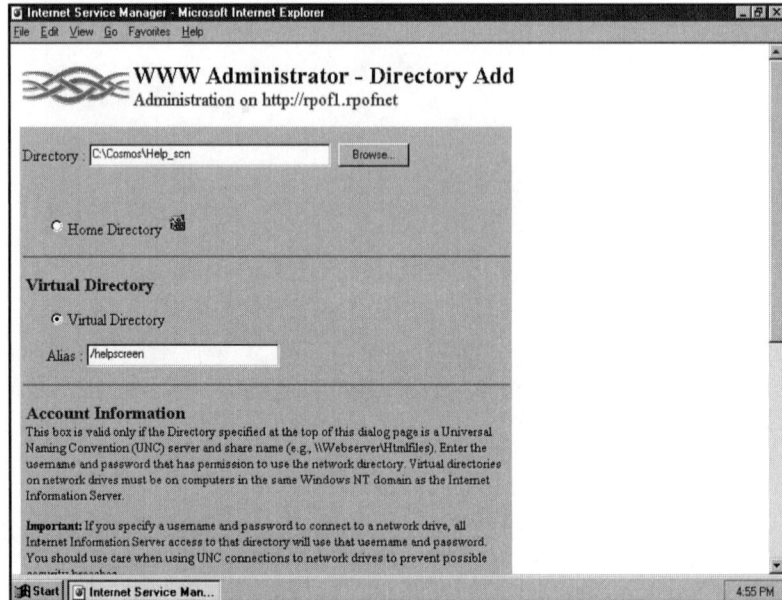

11. Scroll to the bottom of the Directory Add page and click OK. You are returned to the Internet Service Manager screen where the directory C:\Cosmos\Help_scn is now mapped to the alias /helpscreen (see Figure 11.24).

12. The directory is now ready for indexing. From the Start button, go to Programs, Microsoft Index Server (Common), and choose Server Administration.

13. Click the Start button next to Force scan virtual roots:

14. On the extreme right side of the Web page (see Figure 11.25), choose the Full Scan selection for the virtual roots you want to index. Choose all of them.

FIG. 11.24

Note the directory
C:\Cosmos\Help_scn
as well as the virtual
root /helpscreen to
which it is mapped is
included in the table.

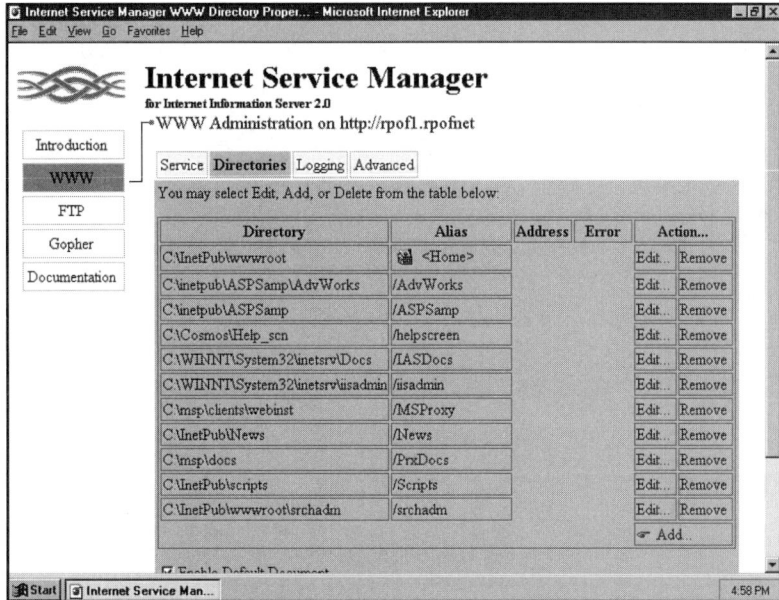

FIG. 11.25

Each virtual root is
listed with its mapped
directories. Note the
radio buttons next to
each scanning option.
This allows you to tailor
the scan (or no scan)
to each virtual root.

15. Click Submit Changes. The indexing process begins. Scroll down to the bottom of the Web page, and you will see the section marked titled Index Statistics (see Figure 11.26). The statistics can be updated by clicking the Refresh Page button under the statistics.

FIG. 11.26

The Index Statistics function in progress. Note the Refresh Page button in the lower-left corner.

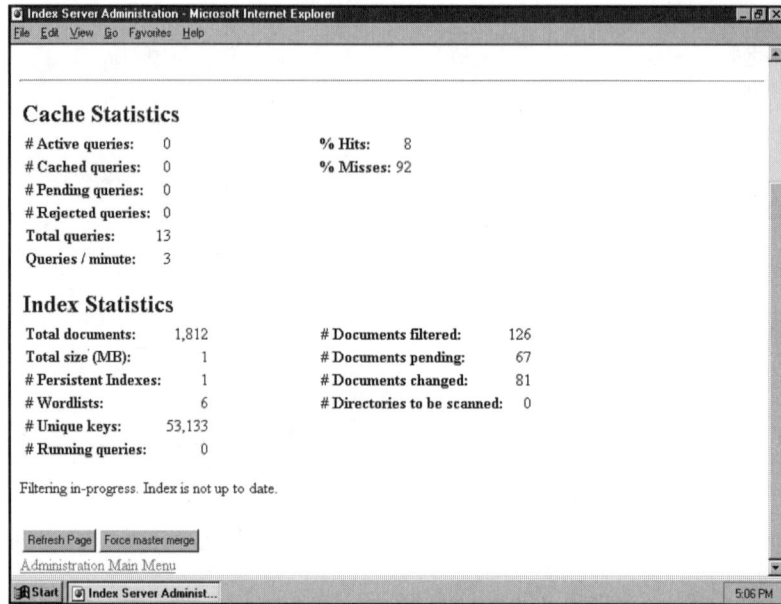

16. When the index is finished, the final statistics will appear on-screen, along with an indication that the filtering is complete and the index is up-to-date (see Figure 11.27).

T I P After indexing your virtual roots, you will want to click Force Master Merge. This forces all indexes into one huge master index. This procedure, while the preferred way to index queries, is CPU-intensive and may take some time, but it will be worth it in terms of the speed and accuracy of querying across directories.

N O T E You do not have to force a scan of a virtual root after repairing or replacing damaged or corrupted documents. Index Server will automatically sense the changed or updated files through its relationship with NTFS. Updating the index will be automatically performed. ■

FIG. 11.27
Once filtering is complete, the `All filtering is complete` statement replaces the `Filtering in progress` message.

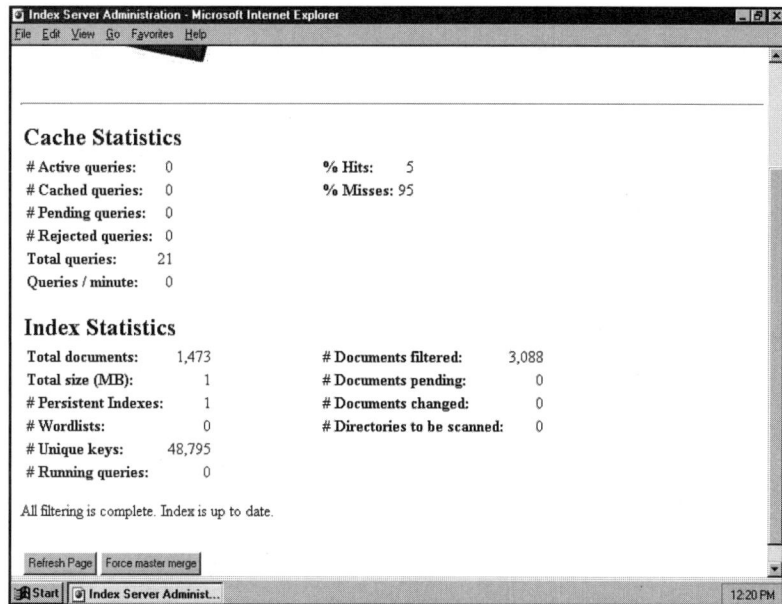

```
┌──────────────────────────────────────────────────────────────────┐
│ ◎ Index Server Administration - Microsoft Internet Explorer  _ ❐ ✕│
│ File  Edit  View  Go  Favorites  Help                          ▲  │
│                                                                   │
│  ───────────────────────────────────────────────────────────     │
│                                                                   │
│   Cache Statistics                                                │
│   # Active queries:     0        % Hits:    5                     │
│   # Cached queries:     0        % Misses: 95                     │
│   # Pending queries:    0                                         │
│   # Rejected queries:   0                                         │
│   Total queries:       21                                         │
│   Queries / minute:     0                                         │
│                                                                   │
│   Index Statistics                                                │
│   Total documents:    1,473      # Documents filtered:   3,088    │
│   Total size (MB):        1      # Documents pending:        0    │
│   # Persistent Indexes:   1      # Documents changed:        0    │
│   # Wordlists:            0      # Directories to be scanned: 0   │
│   # Unique keys:     48,795                                       │
│   # Running queries:      0                                       │
│                                                                   │
│   All filtering is complete. Index is up to date.                │
│                                                                   │
│   ┌─────────────┐ ┌───────────────────┐                      ▼   │
│   │ Refresh Page│ │ Force master merge │                          │
│   └─────────────┘ └───────────────────┘                          │
│ 🏁 Start │ ◎ Index Server Administ...           12:20 PM          │
└──────────────────────────────────────────────────────────────────┘
```

Confirming the Scan

To confirm that the Index Server has performed its tasks, follow these steps:

1. Click Start, Programs, Microsoft Index Server (Common), Index Server Sample Query Form.

2. In the query text box, type **McPherson AND Windows NT Server** (see Figure 11.28). This query separates the library of NT Server documents Microsoft inserts into the corpus from columns I have written about the product.

3. Click <u>E</u>xecute Query. If you make a mistake, click Clear and retype the query. Do this on your own indexed documents.

N O T E   In this context, the word AND represents the Boolean operator, not a noise word. ▦

In Figure 11.29, the results of that query are returned to the browser. As you can see, the indexing was successful, and a list of three columns with specific mentions of Windows NT Server has been generated.

FIG. 11.28
Typing the query into the text box. The word AND is capitalized for emphasis only; capitalization is not required.

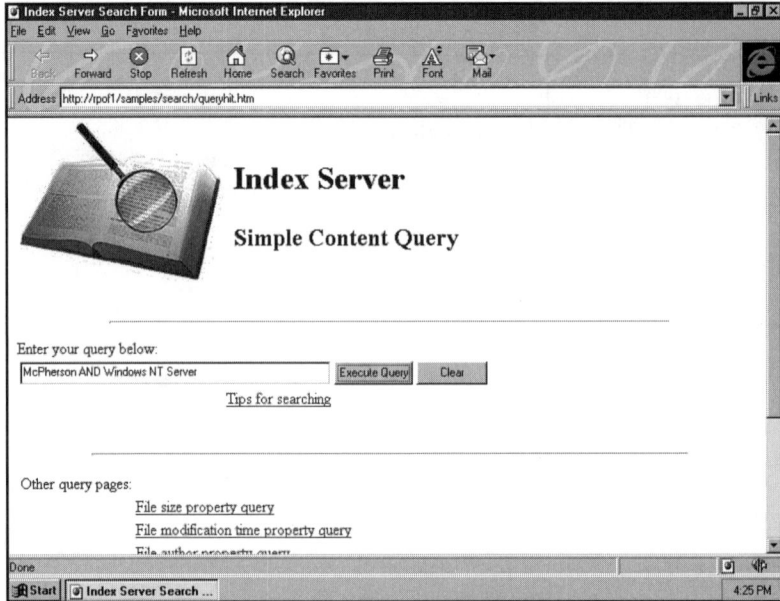

FIG. 11.29
The search results displayed as an HTML page. Note the document links, highlighted in a contrasting shade of text.

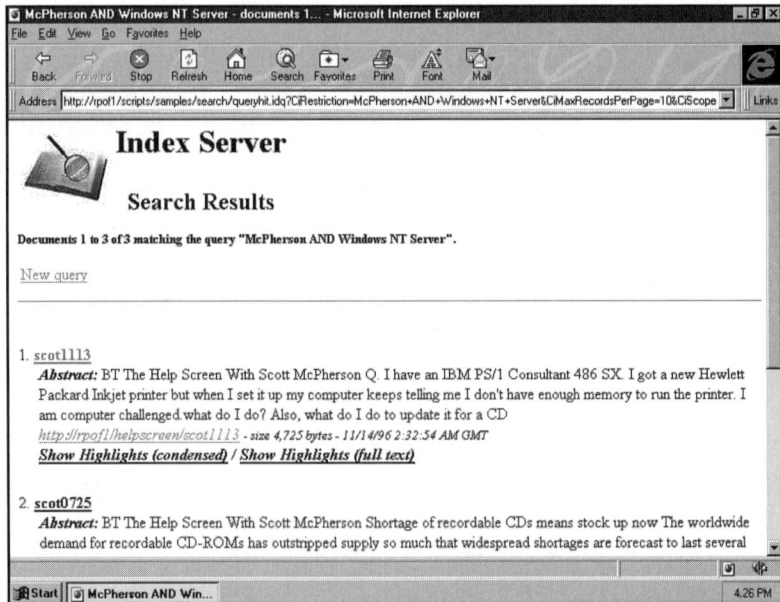

The results of the query are displayed on-screen. These results show the name of the file, the abstact of the file, the URL where the document is located, the size of the file in bytes, and the date and Greenwich Mean Time when the document was created.

There are two other options. The Show Highlights (condensed) option, when selected, shows only those portions of the document with relevance to the query. The relevant words are highlighted in a contrasting color and italicized (see Figure 11.30).

FIG. 11.30
Selecting Show Highlights (condensed) brings up only those passages with direct bearing on the search keywords.

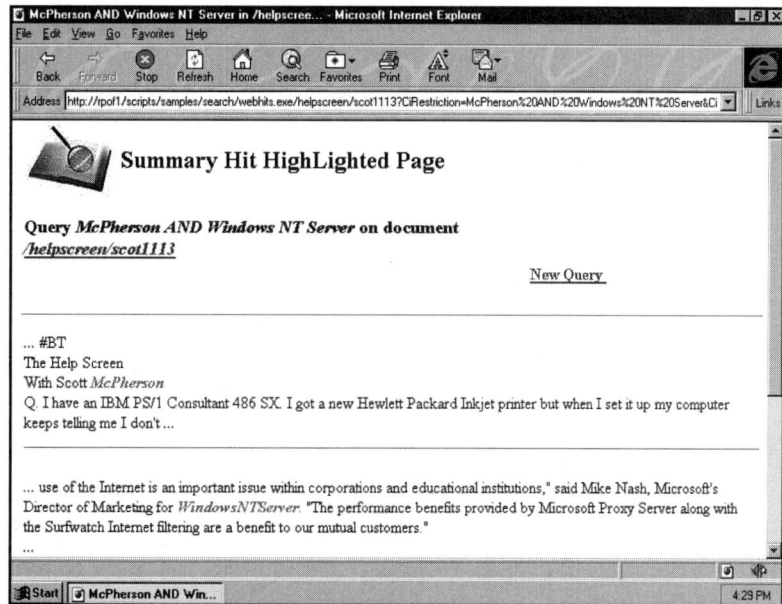

The Show Highlights (full text) option will bring up the entire document, with all relevant words and phrases highlighted and italicized (see Figure 11.31).

T I P

Use the Highlights options when possible. Choosing the file by name brings up the file as is—formatted or unformatted—while either of the Highlights options brings up the document in full format, regardless of whether it is a formatted document or just ASCII text.

CAUTION

If search results are displayed without boldface or italics, then a CGI application that comes with the Index Server did not load properly at install.

FIG. 11.31

The entire document is available under the Show Highlights (full text) option. Note the formatting of the document in this scenario, as opposed to the unformatted ASCII text output if simply selecting the document by its name.

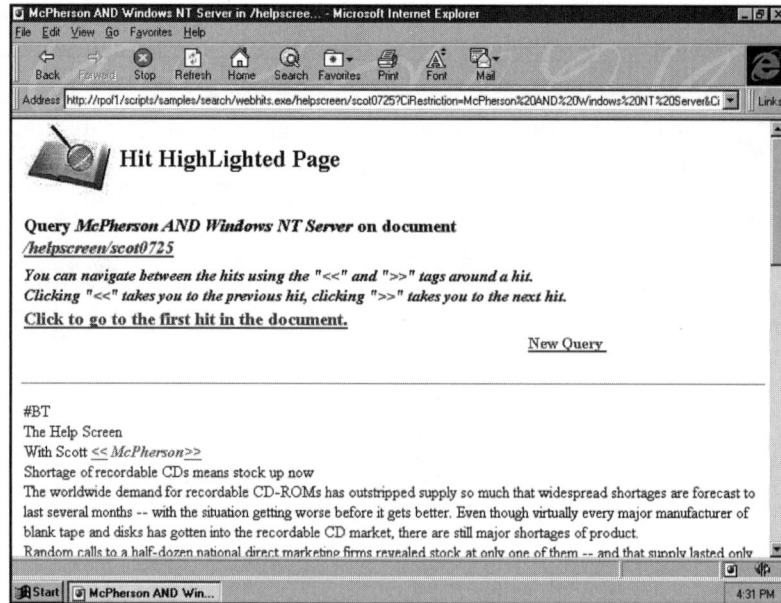

Performing Scans on NetWare and UNIX Volumes

Any volume that can be mapped as a virtual root can be indexed by using Microsoft Index Server. Unfortunately, because NetWare and UNIX do not employ NTFS, their indexes cannot be automatically updated by the system unless their physical contents were copied over to the NT volume. Also, the security measures inherent in NTFS, passed on automatically to Index Server, will not be available.

N O T E It is important to make sure there are sufficient security restrictions on these directories to protect unauthorized access. You should consult your network operating system's security options for more information on how to prevent unauthorized access to directories. ▪

Since copying entire document directories is not a practical consideration in many organizations, it is necessary to map the physical drive to a virtual root. This process is known as Setting Up a Remote Virtual Root.

Mapping NetWare or UNIX Volumes to a Virtual Root

The computer to be mapped must be present and recognized on the same *domain* as the Index Server. The machine with the volume must have the relevant directories mapped to the server running Index Server, and must be registered with Index Server. The volume(s) to be scanned must be visible to IIS.

Here are the steps you'll take to map a NetWare or UNIX volume to a virtual root:

1. From the Start Button, choose Programs, Microsoft Internet Server (Common), and then choose Internet Service Manager (HTML).
2. Choose WWW from the Categories menu.
3. Click the Directories button.
4. Click the Add button in the lower-right corner of the table.
5. In the dialog box that appears, click Browse.
6. From the directory tree, choose the NetWare or UNIX volume that contains the documents to be indexed. The value is returned to the Directory box in the Directory Add page.
7. Type the alias that you want as a virtual root.
8. Scroll to the bottom of the Directory Add page and click OK.
9. You will see that the directories are now mapped to the alias you created.
10. From the Start button, go to Programs, Microsoft Index Server (Common), and click Server Administration (see Figure 11.32).

FIG. 11.32
Choosing Index Server Administration will bring up the Web page.

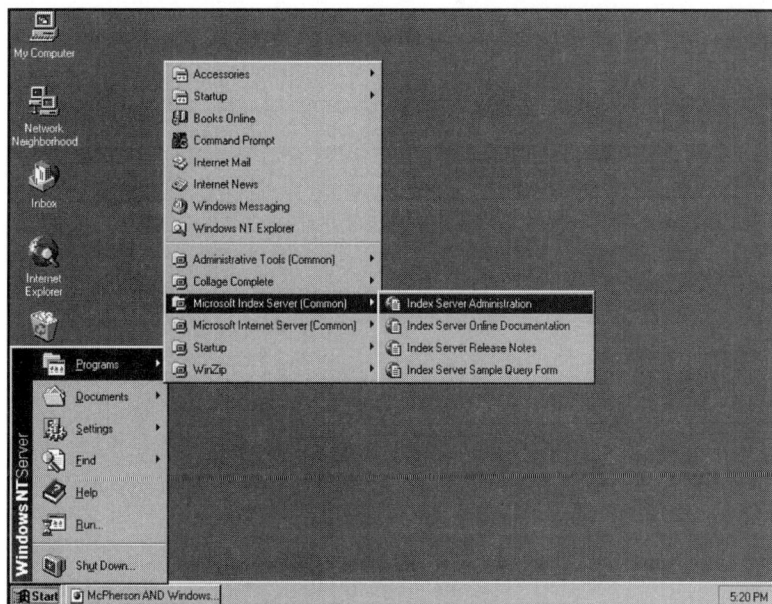

11. Click the Start button for Force Scan Virtual Roots and indexing commences (see Figure 11.33).

FIG. 11.33

Click the Start button next to Force scan virtual roots to reindex.

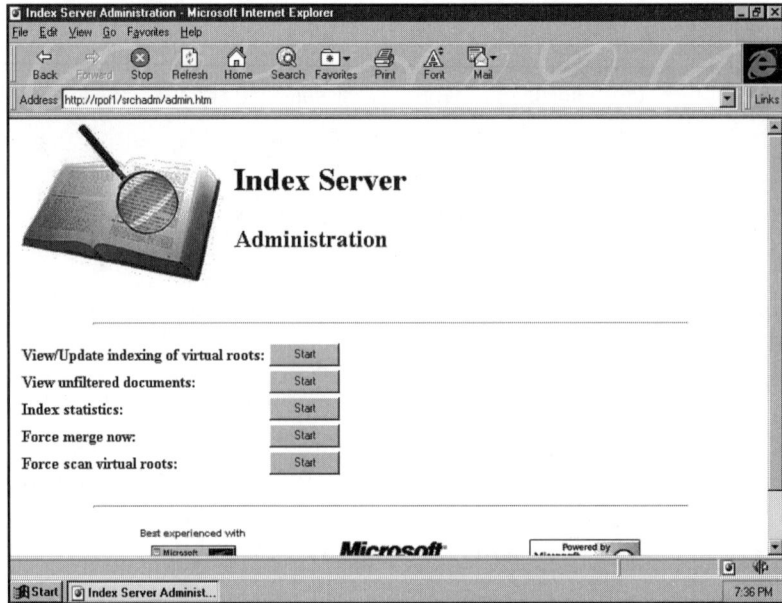

12. When indexing is finished, click View Unfiltered Documents to ensure the scan was successful (see Figure 11.34).

FIG. 11.34

Note the status of the filtering process is displayed directly under the book image.

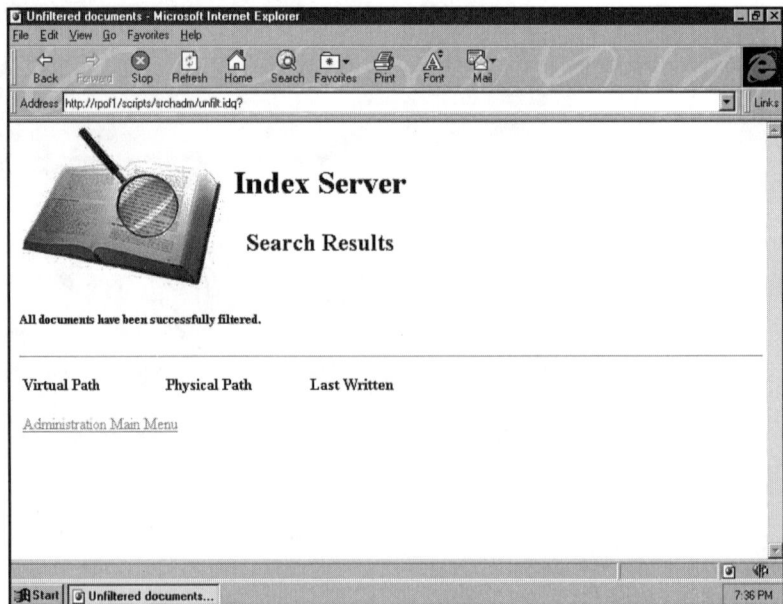

Creating Queries

To use Index Server to its fullest extent, it is important for users to know the different ways documents can be retrieved using queries.

There are three parts to a query:

- The scope of the query
- The restriction
- The result set

The *scope* tells the query engine where to look for a document. The query's *restriction* checks to see if a document should be returned. The restriction is determined by the operators submitted (Boolean operators, <, >, and so on). The *result set* returns the information and completes the query.

Here are some of the ways a query can be structured:

- You can limit the query to specific scopes.
- You can search for words, or entire phrases, within documents.
- You can search for words or phrases NEAR another set of words or phrases.
- You can search for words or phrases within textual properties.
- You can search for properties with <, <= ,=>, > against a constant such as a date, size of a file, or time.
- You can search with wild cards such as *, ?, and other expressions.
- You can search using free-text queries.

Types of Queries

The most common types of queries performed by Index Server are:

- Boolean and Proximity operator queries
- Wildcard queries
- Free-text queries
- Property value queries
- Vector Space Queries

Performing Queries

Here are some rules to follow to structure a query to return the information you need.

- Queries are not case-sensitive. You may type them in uppercase or lowercase.
- You can use Boolean operators (AND, OR, and NOT) and the proximity operator (NEAR) to modify and further narrow your query search.

■ If you search on a specific phrase, the phrase words must appear in the exact same order in the query as you wish them to appear in the document.

■ You can search for any word except for "noise words" (a, an, and, as, and so forth).

■ Punctuation marks (commas, semicolons, periods, and the like) are ignored during a search.

■ Noise words are treated as placeholders in phrase and proximity queries. For example, if you searched for "Smith for President", the results could give you "Smith for President" and "Smith and President", because "for" is a noise word.

■ To use characters such as &, |, ^, #, @, $, (,), in a query, enclose your query in quotation marks (").

■ To search for a word or phrase containing quotation marks, enclose the entire phrase in quotation marks and then double the quotation marks around the word or words you want to surround with quotes. For example, "World Wide Web or ""Web""" searches for World Wide Web or "Web".

■ The wildcard character (*) can match words with a given prefix. The query esc* matches the terms "ESC" as well as "escape."

■ Free-text queries can be specified without regard to query syntax.

■ Vector space queries can be specified.

■ ActiveX (OLE) and file attribute property value queries can be issued.

Boolean and Proximity Operators

Boolean and Proximity Operators are used to create precise queries based on the familiar operators AND, OR, NOT, or NEAR.

A search can be as easy as typing one word into the query form. But, unless that word is very unique, the result will be more documents than you cared to see. So the use of additional operators, or discriminators, is strongly suggested.

For example, if you wanted to search for the words "McPherson" AND "Macintosh", you would type the following string into the text box, as shown in Figure 11.35.

If you wanted articles written by McPherson OR articles concerning Macintosh, you would type in the query screen the words McPherson OR Macintosh.

Let's say you wanted articles about two particular Macintosh models; say, a Power Macintosh 5200 or 7200, regardless of who the author was. Type the following string into the text box as represented in Figure 11.35:

Power Macintosh 5200 OR Macintosh 7200

The word OR does not have to be capitalized, as Index Server recognizes the Boolean operator instead of the noise word. The search would result in the HTML page shown in Figure 11.36.

FIG. 11.35

Type the query in the text box provided. If you make a mistake, click the Clear button.

FIG. 11.36

The query results returned when searching for Power Macintosh 5200 or Macintosh 7200.

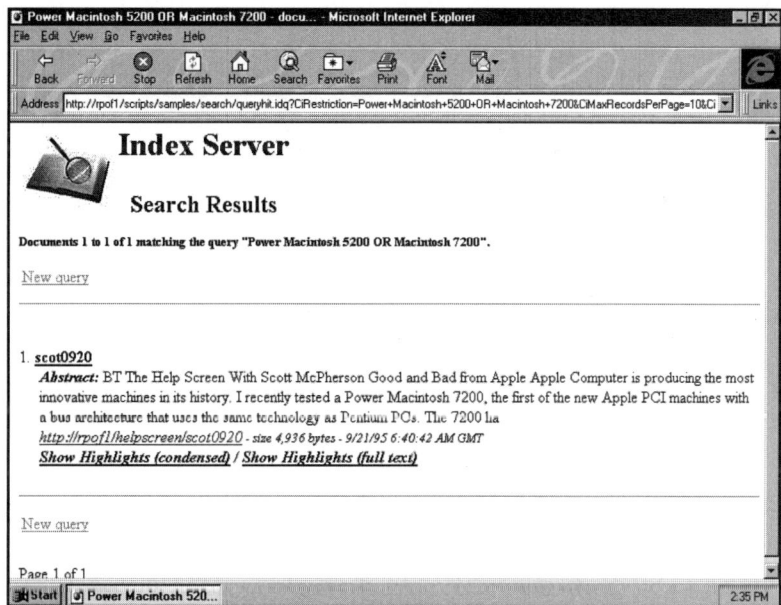

You can also search by words that lie NEAR other words. If you wanted to see all the articles written about IBM PS/1 computers with RAM information, you would type the following string into the text box:

IBM NEAR memory

Be sure to use words in a NEAR query that are not noise words. If you had typed "PS/1", the query would have yielded nothing, as P, S, and 1 would be considered noise words.

The query would return the results as shown in Figure 11.37.

FIG. 11.37
Articles on IBM PS/1 computers. Note that the abstract for the first article never mentions PS/1 computers, but clicking either of the highlighted links shows multiple notations of PS/1 computers.

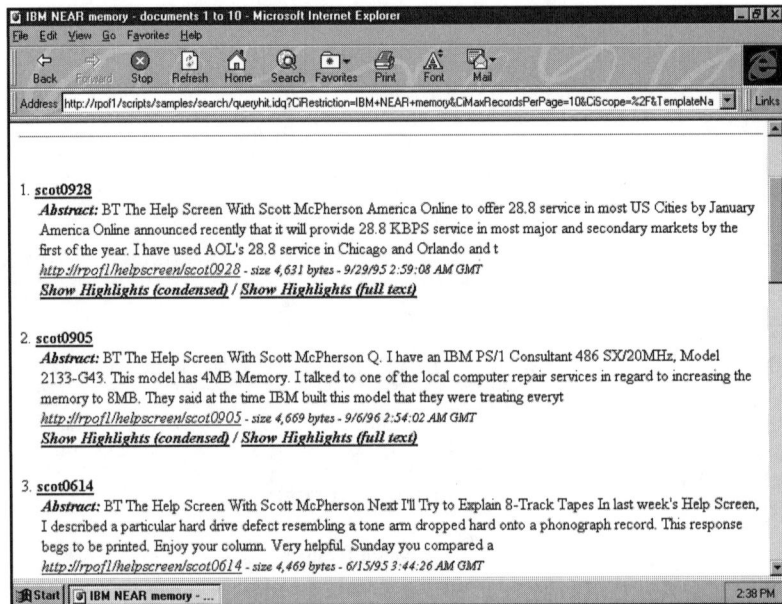

Notice how Index Server has ranked the articles. The closer the word "memory" is to the expression "IBM," the higher the rank.

Here are some rules to follow when using Boolean operators:

- The AND operator has a higher priority than OR.
- The NEAR operator will return a match if the words searched for are in the same document. However, NEAR differs from other operators because it calculates the proximity of the first expression to the second. Put another way, the rank of a page with the searched-for words closer together is greater than or equal to the rank of a page where the words are farther apart. If the searched-for words are more than 50 words apart, they are not considered near enough, and the page is assigned a rank of zero.
- NOT is used only after AND in content queries, it can only be used to exclude pages that match a previous restriction.
- For property value queries, the NOT operator can be used apart from the AND operator.

TIP Add parentheses to nest expressions within a query. The expressions in parentheses are evaluated before the rest of the query.

Use double quotes (") to indicate that a word normally used as a Boolean operator (AND, OR, and so on) should be ignored in your query. For example, "Search and destroy" will match pages with the phrase, not pages that match the Boolean expression search AND destroy. In addition to being an operator, the word AND is a noise word in English.

Likewise, a specific name can also be accessed by using quotes.

Boolean values are (t) or (true) for TRUE and (f) or (false) for FALSE.

Table 11.4 shows you some Boolean operators in other languages. The words are also considered noise words in their respective languages:

Table 11.4   Foreign Language Boolean and Proximity Operators

Language	Operators
German	UND, ODER, NICHT, NAH
French	ET, OU, SANS, PRES
Spanish	Y, O, NO, CERCA
Dutch	EN, OF, NIET, NABIJ
Swedish	OCH, ELLER, INTE, NÄRA
Italian	E, O, NO, VICINO

TIP The symbols (&, |, !, ~) and the English keywords AND, OR, NOT, and NEAR work the same way in all languages supported by Index Server.

Wildcards

Wildcards help you find pages containing words that are similar to a given word. For example, typing **cong*** would yield words including Cong., Congress, or Congressional.

You can also search for words with the same stem word. If you wanted to look up pages with the word stem "win," you would type **win**** to yield the words "win," "won," or "winning."

Free-Text Queries

Free-text queries are accomplished by attempting to find the meaning, not the exact wording, of the query. Boolean, proximity, and wildcard operators are all ignored within a free-text query by using the prefix *$contents* (italics for emphasis).

Part

IV

Ch

11

For example, if you wanted to search for a document that tells you how to perform a free-text query in Index Server, you would type:

$contents how do I perform a free-text query?

The query will yield several responses. You will find that some of these responses will be relevant, and many will not. Check the abstract of each returned document to find the one(s) that meet your criteria. It can definitely make searching for a needle in a haystack a little easier!

Vector Space Queries

Vector space queries separate their components through the use of commas. You also can assign a weight to a component by using brackets ([ ]). Also, results returned by vector queries do not have to match every item in the query. Finally, vector queries work best when the results are sorted by rank.

If you want to look up all articles I have written about Intel's Pentium OverDrive processor, knowing you would need to distinguish it from other Intel products, you might structure your query on McPherson in all documents, with processor given a weight of 5, Intel a weight of 25, and OverDrive a weight of 100, as shown in Figure 11.38.

FIG. 11.38

Structuring a Vector Space query. Note the use of an asterisk (for all documents), and the use of brackets to assign the weight given to a particular entry.

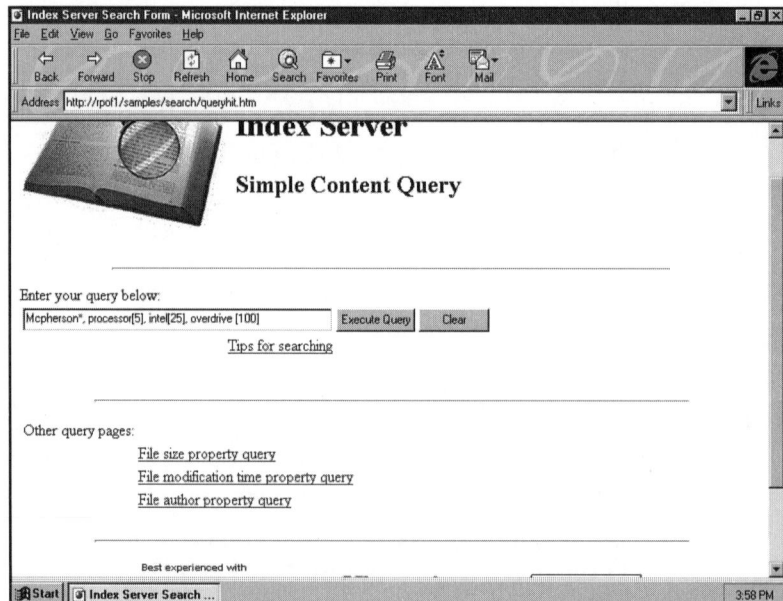

Figure 11.39 displays the results of this query.

FIG. 11.39

The abstracts of documents 2 and 3 do not show references to OverDrives because the abstracts only show the first few sentences of a document.

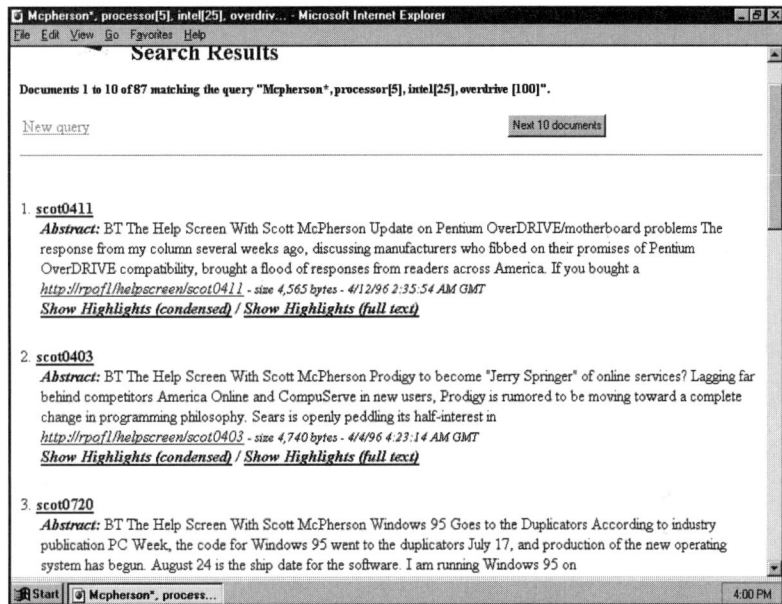

Property Value Queries

Property value queries can be used to find files that have property values that match a given criteria. The property values which you can query include file information such as size, file name, and ActiveX (OLE) properties including the document summary stored in files created by ActiveX-aware applications.

There are two different types of property queries:

- Regular expression property queries
- Relational property queries

Relational property queries contain an "at" character (@), a property name, a relational operator, and a property value. For example, to find all of the files larger than one million bytes, issue the following query:

    @size > 1000000

Regular expression property queries consist of a number sign (#), a property name, and a regular expression for the property value. For example, to find all of the Windows sound files on a server (extension .wav), issue the following query:

    #filename *.wav

Property Names   Property names are preceded by either the "at" (@) or number sign (#) character. Use @ for relational queries, and # for regular expression queries.

If no property name is specified, @contents is assumed.

Table 11.5 shows you the Properties available for all files.

Table 11.5   Property Names and their Characteristics

Property Name	Description
All	Matches any property
Contents	Words and phrases in the file and textual properties
Filename	Name of the file
Size	File size
Write	Last time the file was modified

Table 11.6 is a list of ActiveX property values for use in queries of ActiveX-aware documents (those created by ActiveX-aware applications).

Table 11.6   ActiveX Property Values

Property Name	Description
DocTitle	The document's title
DocSubject	The document's subject
DocAuthor	The document's author
DocKeywords	The document's keywords
DocComments	Author comments regarding the document

Relational Operators   Relational operators are used in relational property queries.

Use the pound (#) character before the property name if creating a regular expression in a property value, and an "at" (@) character when creating a relational expression. The equal (=) relational operator is assumed for regular-expression queries.

#filename is the only property that supports regular expressions with wildcards to the left of the text.

Date and time values use the form 1996/12/25 23:25:11:00, where 12 represents the month, 25 the day, and the time in hh:mm:ss. The first two characters of the year and the entire time can be omitted. Dates and times are in Greenwich Mean Time (GMT).

Currency values are of the form x.y, where x is the whole value amount and y is the fractional amount. There is no assumption about units.

Single-value expressions that are compared against vectors are expressed as relational operators, then a (^a) for all of or a (^s) for some of.

Numeric values can be in decimal or hexadecimal (preceded by 0x).

The contents property does not support relational operators. If a relational operator is specified, no results will be found. For example, @contents Microsoft will find documents containing Microsoft, but @contents=Microsoft will find none.

Regular Expressions   Regular expressions in property queries are defined as follows:

Any character except asterisk (*), period (.), question mark (?), and vertical bar (|) defaults to matching just itself.

Regular expressions can be enclosed in matching quotes ("), and must be enclosed in quotes if they contain a space ( ) or closing parenthesis ( )).

The characters *, ., and ? behave as they behave in Windows; they match any number of characters, match (.) or end of string, and match any one character, respectively.

The character | is an escape character. After |, the following characters have special meaning, as shown in Table 11.7.

Table 11.7   Characters and their Properties

Symbol	Function	Comments
(	Opens a group	Must be followed by a matching)
)	Closes a group	Must be preceded by a matching (
[	Opens a character class	Must be followed by a matching (un-escaped)]
{	Opens a counted match	Must be followed by a matching }
}	Closes a counted match	Must be preceded by a matching {
,	Separates OR clauses	
*	Matches zero or more occurrences of the preceding expression	
?	Matches zero or one occurrence of the preceding expression	

continues

Table 11.7   Continued

Symbol	Function	Comments
+	Matches one or more occurrences of the preceding expression	
	Anything else, including |, matches itself	

Between square brackets ([]) the following characters have special meaning:

Symbol	Function	Comments
^	Matches everything but following classes	Must be the first character
]	Matches]	May only be preceded by ^, otherwise it closes the class
-	Range operator	Preceded and followed by normal characters
	Anything else matches itself (or begins or ends a range as itself)	

Between curly braces ({}) the following syntax applies:

Symbol	Function	Comments
|{m|}	Matches exactly m occurrences of the preceding expression	$(0 < m < 256)$
|{m,|}	Matches at least m occurrences of the preceding expression	$(1 < m < 256)$
|{m,n|}	Matches between m and n occurrences of the preceding expression, inclusive	$(0 < m < 256, 0 < n < 256)$
		To match *, ., and ?, enclose them in brackets (for example, |[*]sample will match "*sample")

Query Examples

The queries you can construct are limited only by your imagination and the rules we have just reviewed. The more queries you conduct, the better you will understand the effects of the way you construct a query. Here are a few examples you can try:

Example	Results
@size > 3000000	Pages larger than three million bytes
@write > 96/10/14	Pages modified after the date
Blue Oyster Cult	Pages with the phrase "Blue Oyster Cult"
"blue oyster cult"	Same as above
@contents blue oyster cult	Same as above
McPherson and @size > 100000	Pages with the word "McPherson" that are larger than one hundred thousand bytes
"mcpherson and @size > 100000"	Pages with the phrase specified (not the same as above)
#filename *.bmp	Bitmap files (the # prefix is used because the query contains a regular expression)
@attrib ^s 32	Pages with the archive attribute bit on
@docauthor=Scott McPherson	Pages with the given author
$contents how do I log on?	Pages that match the query
@size < 100000 & #filename *.avi	Windows movie files less than 100,000 bytes in size

Part

IV

Ch

11

Custom Query Forms

With a query form, you can conveniently search for a word or phrase anywhere in a set of documents. Just fill out the form, and execute the query. After filling out the form, the user clicks the Execute Query button to start the query. The results are then displayed on the user's screen.

With Microsoft Index Server, the administrator of a Web server can create customized forms to help employees and other clients find specific information from a set of documents. For example, a form can be tailored to search for a word or phrase or for other properties such as the author or subject. You create a query form in standard HTML format, just as you would create any Web page. If you know how to write pages in HTML format, you can quickly put together a simple query form.

From Here...

In this chapter, you learned about the differences between a file-based LAN and a document-based intranet, and the role of Index Server in establishing a useful site.

You also learned how to make an indexed directory available to your audience by mapping that directory to a virtual root and considered relevant strategies and security options. Indexing documents in several languages was also discussed.

Finally, you learned how to make queries using Index Server and reviewed some common and unique query statements. For further study, be sure to read these related sections:

- To find out how to deliver highly personalized information to your users, read Chapter 9, "Understanding Commercial Internet Personalization System."

- Turn to the next chapter, "Replicating Internet Content With the Content Replication System," where you learn how to seamlessly update the information on your site.

Replicating Internet Content with the Content Replication System

As Web sites grow and user sessions increase, an organization eventually finds itself asking very specific questions about how it delivers information to the public. In particular, they'll be looking for answers to the following two questions: As more and more people get interested in the company Web site, how can you continue to deliver information as quickly as possible? Also, how can we better manage our content developers, especially when it comes to moving data from development to production?

Microsoft's Content Replication System is designed specifically for sites that reach the level of maturity where they are asking these questions. It's also a good application for young Internet sites that want to start off on the right foot because the Content Replication System will provide solutions for both of these problems.

Let's face the facts—most new sites that launch an Internet site are simply looking for fast and efficient ways to get their information onto the Web. Normally, there's very little thought put into how to build an infrastructure that will sustain the organization's growth. When a Web site blossoms, growing from 10,000 accesses a day to 2 million hits a day, site managers need to find answers to the previously mentioned questions. With the Content Replication System there is an instant and easy solution.

With problem number one—managing to deliver information quickly when your user load is rising—the obvious answer is to increase bandwidth, which is a very expensive proposition. A more practical answer is to find new ways to deliver the information. Specifically, the load can be distributed by creating mirror sites. The Content Replication System makes it very easy to create a mirror site, allowing the network to spread the load to several servers, as opposed to the one server that you started with on this Internet initiative. Sharing the load does wonders for headroom, and your computer processors need room to breathe.

With problem number two—managing content from development to production—the Content Replication System also has a solution. In the development-to-production phase of a Web site, there are plenty of opportunities for data to get lost during upload. Additionally, your Web clientele may encounter broken links if they access a page that is in the middle of being rewritten at the very moment they visit your site. (Yeah, how does ESPN update the Florida State-Florida Sugar Bowl score and add plays I just saw happen?) To make the shift to a new Web delivery infrastructure, Microsoft takes what could be a very difficult concept and makes it quite easy to deploy. In fact, you can manage the Content Replication System through Internet Explorer. It will save time and improve your organization. ■

Overviewing the Content Replication Server

When Microsoft introduced the first versions of Content Replication Server in October 1996, they painted a picture of an Internet Web site that was growing quickly and a company that needed a new way of delivering information. Not only were there bandwidth problems, but the site had a bigger issue: a growing team of Web developers who had become unmanageable.

For the record, the company was not Microsoft, and they never revealed the name of the organization to which they referred. But, of course, the solution was provided by Microsoft. Here's the solution they offered.

Issue #1—Getting Control of the Content

Understanding that Web page development is a two-pronged issue is the first step. The first half of the challenge is developing the Web page, the second half is publishing the content to the production server. Development is rarely the problem. The Internet is infectious, and more and more employees throughout the organization are motivated to develop Web pages at a fast pace.

It's the second phase that causes problems. Certainly, moving files to a production server is a simple process. But there are side effects to the file transfer process. Specifically, when users (the people surfing your Web pages) try to access pages that are in the process of being transferred to the server, the user receives a broken link—a dead end. That's unacceptable, but there is a solution. Instead of granting all developers access to the production server, create a middle ground with a pre-production server. This is a separate server, where development of new technologies can take place without putting the Web server at risk. Also, when it's time to move information from the development/pre-production server, using Microsoft's Content Replication System, there are several options for updating and posting to the development server. The administrator can choose from the following:

- *Transaction-based replication*   In this scenario, the server replicates the entire set of changes into a temporary directory and then exchanges the entire updated file at once using a renaming method.

- *Incremental Replication*   Replicates only the files that have changed since the last replication. This tool updates Web sites as fast as possible, and is great for delivering information that is changing very quickly, like poll results or a sports event.

- *Automatic File Replication*   Provides the ability to replicate based on directory change notifications.

All of these features are automated and can be configured to work within a variety of parameters. The bottom line is that with this tool you can encourage the development environment without putting the main Web server at risk.

Issue #2—Sharing the Load in a Multi-Server Environment

Suppose the company Web server can't take much more activity. The processors are already maxed out, and only one out of every three visitors can get access to the site. The company has offices around the world and is drawing interested consumers from the oddest sites. A multi-server arrangement is called for to solve this problem. With two more Windows NT Servers, the load can be shared equally when one server is overburdened with user activity. In times like these, the Content Replication System offers the following:

- *Mirroring*   Through a distributed environment, the burden associated with servers that are buckling under a large number of hits can be shared with other servers without a loss of service.

- *Geographic distribution*   This mirroring strategy involves replicating data from the main site to servers thousands of miles away. Again, a proper distribution of the load is needed to maintain customer satisfaction.

The Content Replication System boasts high-level security, easy-to-use automation, administrative features to monitor performance, and scaleability. Also, the Content Replication System is designed to keep backup copies of everything it replaces during replication, so it's easy to revert to earlier versions if you need to backtrack.

The best way to get an idea of how this tool can be used in your environment is to install the package and test the features. This is a reliable and secure program and it's worth investigating now, because it's a pretty good bet you'll need it later.

Setting up the Content Replication Server

In this chapter you learn how to set up the Microsoft Content Replication System and test its functionality. You'll be briefed on minimum system requirements, the installation steps, and then there will be several tests that introduce you to the functionality of the system and ensure that the setup process was successful.

Preparing the System

To use the Content Replication System you will need at least two servers connected to a network. However, the two-server approach will allow you to test only the push replication and the pull replication methods. To get the most out of the Content Replication System you'll need at least three NT servers. Although there will be more than one NT server involved, the setup process should be relatively easy because the setup process will be the same for each machine.

Server Requirements   The primary component of the Content Replication System is the start-point server. This is the server that holds the information to be replicated. The other pieces in the puzzle are the site staging servers, which receive the replicated information from the start-point server. That data is then forwarded to other Content Replication Servers and finally to end point servers, which handle user requests for Web pages.

> **N O T E**   There's no way to run a Content Replication Test on one NT server. Be forewarned, if you want to try to move files from one directory on your server to another directory on your server, it won't work. Presently, replication only works from server to server. ▪

Below is a list of the three servers in the system and a breakdown of the hardware requirements for each:

- *Start-point server*   Basically the company development server.
- *Staging server*   An intermediate server between the start point and end point servers.
- *End Point Server*   This is the Web server that the public accesses.

Minimum Requirements for the Start-Point Server   To deploy the Content Replication System, you need to have a minimum of two servers with at least the following configuration:

- Digital Equipment Corporation Alpha, PowerPC processor, or Intel 386+
- Windows NT Server version 4.0 or Workstation 4.0 with Internet Information Server 2.0 or later
- 16 megabytes of RAM
- Hard drive space that is at least twice the size of the content that will be replicated
- Windows NT file system (running NTFS) if the Web Administration tool will be utilized
- Microsoft Internet Explorer 3.0 or higher

Minimum Requirements for the Stager and the End Point Server

- Digital Equipment Corporation Alpha, PowerPC processor, or Intel 386+
- Windows NT Server version 4.0 or Workstation 4.0 with Internet Information Server 2.0
- 16 megabytes of RAM
- Hard drive space that is at least twice the size of the content which will be replicated
- Windows NT file system (running NTFS) if the Web Administration tool will be utilized
- Microsoft Internet Explorer 3.0 or higher

Minimum Requirements for the End Point Server (Optional)

- Digital Equipment Corporation Alpha, PowerPC processor, or Intel 386+
- Windows NT Server version 3.51 or later
- 16 megabytes of RAM
- Hard drive space that is at least twice the size of the content which will be replicated
- Windows NT file system (running NTFS) if the Web Administration tool will be utilized
- Microsoft Internet Explorer 3.0 or higher

N O T E In order for replication to take place, all three computers must share TCP/IP network connectivity. Therefore, the Content Replication Servers may also be distributed in remote locations. Of course, you must be able to ensure that the servers can locate one another over the Internet by the usual Domain Name Server, IP address, and local host. If there is a firewall in the scheme, you need to open a single port from inside and outside the firewall for port 507, which is the port for administering and running the Content Replication Service. ■

Remote Administration Requirements   Remote administration through a Web browser is built into the Content Replication Server. However, you must use Microsoft Internet Explorer 3.0 or higher.

N O T E Internet Explorer 3.0 was the first browser released that can access a Windows NT Server through the NTFS security logon procedures. The user attempting to log on to restricted access material must have a system account on the server and Log on Locally privileges. Once authenticated, the user has rights to view documents that he or she is listed as a permissive user on. For more information, consult *Special Edition Using Windows NT Server*. ■

You Have Contact   Right now is a good time to make sure that all of your servers are reachable over the TCP/IP network. Proceeding any further without that confirmation could prove to be a very frustrating experience. Checking network connectivity is conducted by Pinging the other servers that will be participating in the Content Replication Server architecture.

If you are unfamiliar with how to conduct a Ping, simply click the Start button, choose Run, and then type in the open text box **Ping** *Sitename.com* where *Sitename.com* represents the domain name of your site. The system will send a series of bits (also known as *echo signals*) through the TCP/IP protocol to that computer and report back the number of bytes that were

Part

IV

Ch

12

sent and the amount of time it took for the other computer to reply. The report appears in a command prompt window as shown in Figure 12.1. which closes automatically when the Ping is completed.

If Ping finished uneventfully, your connectivity is good. If you get a reply similar to that shown in Figure 12.1, analyze the network and correct the network connectivity before proceeding any further.

FIG. 12.1

An example of a bad Ping response.

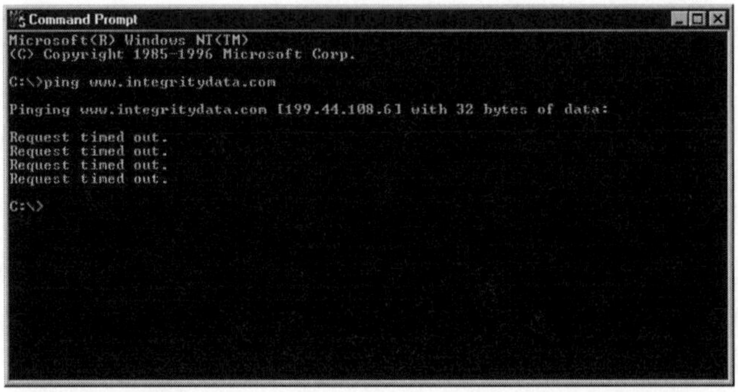

You also need to check your connectivity from a common workstation to the NT server to ensure that you have access for remote administration. Send a Ping from the client computer, in the same fashion you used to send to the servers, to test connectivity. Also, you could use Internet Explorer on the client to access the server's home page by typing in the domain name of each Content Replication Server.

Running Setup

To install the Microsoft Content Replication System, you want to do the following:

1. Make sure you are logged on to the server as an administrator and exit all running Windows programs.

2. Launch the Microsoft Content Replication System executable program (setup.exe) to begin the setup process.

3. At the Installation Welcome Screen, choose Next to set up the program, then at the License Agreement screen select the Yes button to accept the terms of the agreement and proceed with installation.

4. In the Running Services dialog box, click Yes to stop any Internet Information Server components that may remain open.

5. Type your Name and Company information, then click the Next button.

6. In the Type of Install dialog box, you have the option to choose Typical or Custom. If you choose Typical, Setup will conduct the routine install of the Content Replication System, which includes the program files, documentation files, and Web Administration files. You may choose to go the Custom route, which allows you to select the components to install. But for the first installation, a Typical install is recommended.

7. Now choose the destination directory for the Microsoft Commercial Internet System components to be installed. The default directory, c:\Program Files\MCIS should be sufficient. Click the Next button.

8. In choosing a destination directory for the Content Replication System, you will determine where the Content Replication System components will be installed. The default directory of c:\Progam Files\MCIS\CRS is fine. Click the Next button.

9. In the Content Replication Service Account dialog box, enter the user information. In this text entry box you want to type your entry so it displays the < machine_name > <account_name > for the local Content Replication Service account with administrative rights. Click the Tab button to proceed to the Password fields.

10. Type a Password and then verify the Password by retyping it. Click the Next button.

11. In the SMTP Server dialog, type the SMTP (Mail) server name and click Next.

12. In the Content Replication System TCP/IP Port dialog box, accept the default value of 507 by clicking Next.

13. For the Folder Selection select Microsoft Internet Server and click Next.

14. Confirm the Setup Information and click Next.

15. The Setup procedure begins. When the setup is complete, choose the "I would like to start the administration" tool option and click Finish to complete setup.

The Content Replication Server administrative Web page is launched. The location of the page is **http://*servername*/mcisadmin/crs/crhm.pgi**. Naturally, the name of your server will be listed in place of *servername*.

When Setup is complete the browser will launch the Web page with the administration tools.

Checking the Setup

Obviously, you want to make sure the installation was successful. If it was, the Content Replication Service, the Web administration tool, and command line interface should be installed and accessible. To verify that the Content Replication Services are installed, try the following on each of the servers where the program was installed.

Open the Services dialog box from the Control Panel to see a listing of all services that are running on the server, as shown in Figure 12.2. Review the list to ensure that Content Replication Service is listed. The service should be listed as Started and in Automatic Startup mode so the service will be launched automatically when the server is rebooted.

Part
IV

Ch
12

FIG. 12.2
The Windows NT
services list provides
details on the services
installed and their
present status.

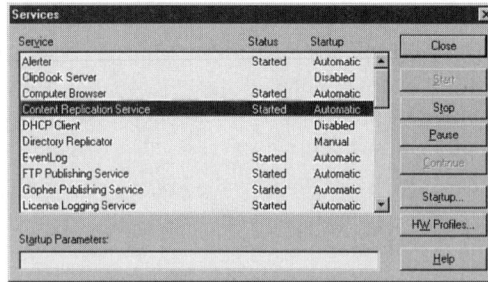

To confirm that the Web administration tool is set up properly, the procedure requires that you first launch Internet Explorer. When Internet Explorer is running, open the following location: **http://*servername*/mcisadmin/crs/crhi.pgi**. Substitute the name of your server in the *servername* portion of the Web address. If your installation was complete, you'll see the Content Replication Server Web administration page displayed, as seen in Figure 12.3.

FIG. 12.3
The Microsoft Content
Replication System
allows administration
from a Web page.

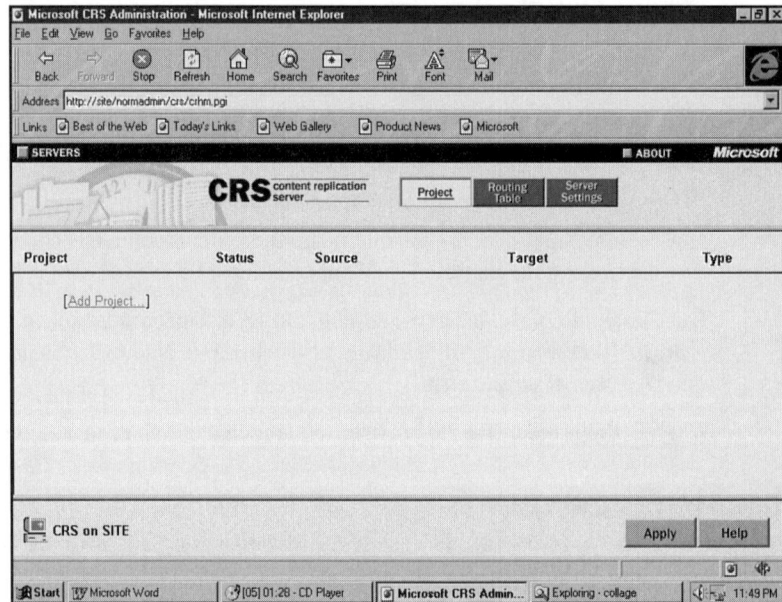

Administrators versus Users

During the setup procedure, the Content Replication System added two user groups to the Windows NT User Manager. The two new groups are Content Replication Service Users and Content Replication Service Administrators. The Users group has limited management abilities, while the Administrators have unlimited privileges, such as creating new projects, deleting projects, scheduling projects, and other administrative features, which will be outlined later in this chapter.

To use the Windows NT User Manager to add users and administrators on each server, follow this basic overview:

1. From the Start menu, choose Programs, Administrative Tools (Common), then choose User Manager for Domains, which launches the Windows NT User Manager.

2. The User Manager for Domains tool is used to manage security for domains, member servers, and workstations. Here you can add, edit, or delete user and administrator privileges. For this example, let's add a user. Select the menu option for User and then choose New User.

3. Type a Username, the user's Full Name, a Description of the user (such as technical support, project manager, and so on) who will be granted and a password. Click the Groups button.

4. Select the groups that the user should be a member of. In this case you'll choose CRS Users and click the Add button. Click OK to return to the New User information.

5. Click the Add button and you will return to the User Manager where the Username, Full Name, and Description of the new user will be displayed in the permissions list.

For more information on configuring the User Manager, please see Que's *Special Edition Using Windows NT 4.0*.

Testing the Installation

To ensure that the installation of the Content Replication Server is complete, there is a series of tests that you should run to check the functionality of the system. The following tests will be conducted:

- *Push* A replication process that happens between two servers. In this procedure, the content will be pushed from the Start Point server to a target (or staging server).

- *Parallel Replication* Similar to a Push, except in this procedure the replications will be sent to multiple target servers. Both sends will happen simultaneously.

- *Chain Replication* In this procedure, the replication will move from one server to another. However, the information will pass through an intermediate server which connects the two networks together.

- *Pull* This is a replication that is conducted between two servers. In this procedure, content is pulled from an Internet Web server and sent to a Content Replication Server.

- *Route Replication* This procedure initiates a replication through the use of routing tables.

The procedures for each of these tests are set out below. Remember that the Web browser required in each test must be Internet Explorer 3.0 or higher.

Push Replication Test For this test, you need two servers, which we refer to as "server1" and "server2". With this test, you gain an understanding of how a push project replicates files by pushing the files from the Start Point server to a Target server.

1. On Server1, launch Internet Explorer and access the administration page by going to the following location: **http://server1/mcisadmin/crs/crhm.pgi**.

2. On the Content Replication Server home page, click the Add Project button.

3. On the Add Project page, in the name box, type **pushtest**, as seen in Figure 12.4; and then select the P̲ush Replication option. Click OK.

FIG. 12.4

Using the Web interface, adding a project is a pretty easy routine.

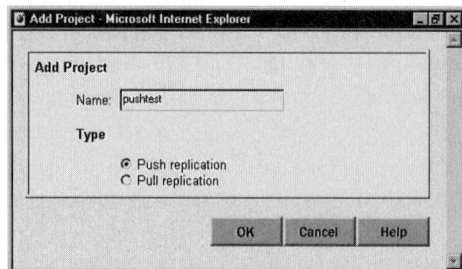

4. In the Project Directory box type **c:\project1**, which identifies the directory on the current server that contains the source files you want to replicate. Click the Add Target link.

T I P Should you choose, you can also select the Exclude This Directory option. Simply enter the name of a directory below, or within, the source directory containing the files you do not want to replicate. When the replication is conducted, no information in the directory you excluded will be replicated. You may want to use this feature when you have a directory that you don't want to transfer to the main Web server but is necessary to keep on the development server.

5. On the Add Target page, as seen in Figure 12.5, select the M̲achine radio button, type **server2** in the text box, and click OK.

FIG. 12.5

Adding a target through the Content Replication System Web utility allows ease of Administration.

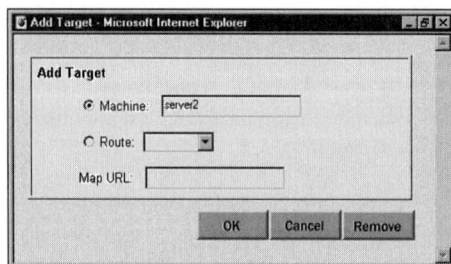

6. When you return to the main Content Replication Web Page, the project will be listed, along with the source directory that you intend to replicate, and the target computer that server1 will be interacting with. Review the results and click OK to accept the configuration.

N O T E Make sure there are files located in your source directory c:\project1. If the directory is empty, you'll have nothing to replicate to the target server. ▪

Follow these steps to configure server2:

1. On Server2, launch Internet Explorer and access the administration page by going to the following location: **http://server2/mcisadmin/crs/crhm.pgi**.
2. On the Content Replication Server home page, click the Add Project button.
3. On the Add Project page, in the Name field, type **pushtest** and then select the Push Replication option. Click OK.
4. In the Project Directory box type **c:\push1**. This identifies the directory on the current server that will receive the replication. Click OK. (No target is necessary.)

CAUTION

You can use the directory name of your choice, but be forewarned. If you replicate to the root directory, or any other directory with valuable information in it, the information contained in those files will be erased during the replication process. The Content Replication System replaces all content of a directory with the replication content.

To run the replication with the Web administration tool, follow these steps:

1. On server1, launch Internet Explorer and access the administration: **http://server1/mcisadmin/crs/crhm.pgi**.
2. On the Content Replication Server project page, click the green arrow next to the project name "pushtest," as seen in Figure 12.6.
3. Click OK when asked for confirmation. The Content Replication Service project will begin running and the content will be replicated on server2 in the c:\test1 directory.

Parallel Replication Test   To perform a parallel replication test, three servers are required. We'll refer to them as "server1," "server2," and "server3." You will need USER privileges on server2 and server3. On server1, you will need administrator privileges. After you complete this example, you should have an understanding of how a parallel replication is conducted from one server (server1) to multiple target servers. And it all happens simultaneously.

1. On Server1, launch Internet Explorer and access the administration page by going to the following location: **http://server1/mcisadmin/crs/crhm.pgi**.
2. On the Content Replication Server home page, click the Add Project button.
3. On the Add Project page, in the name box, type **paralleltest** and then select the Push Replication option. Click OK.
4. In the Project Directory box type **c:\parallel2**, which identifies the directory on the current server that contains the source files you want to replicate. Click the Add Target link.
5. On the Add Target page, highlight the Machine radio button and type into the text box **server2**. Click OK.

6. When you return to the main Content Replication Web Page, the project should be listed with the source directory that will be replicated, and the target.

7. Click the Add Target link to add a second target.

8. On the Add Target page, highlight the Machine radio button and type into the text box **server3**. Click OK.

9. When you return to the main Content Replication Web Page, both targets should be listed along with the source directory that will be replicated, as seen in Figure 12.7. Review the results and click OK to accept the configuration.

FIG. 12.6

Launching the project is as simple as clicking the green arrow.

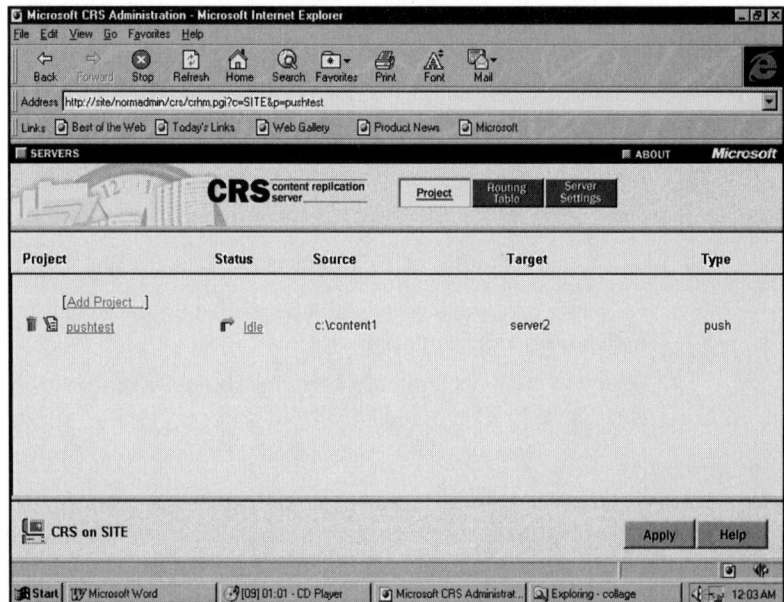

Follow these steps to configure server2:

1. On Server2, launch Internet Explorer and access the administration page at the following location: **http://server2/mcisadmin/crs/crhm.pgi**.

2. On the Content Replication Server home page, click the Add Project button.

3. On the Add Project page, in the name box, type **paralleltest** and then select the Push Replication option. Click OK.

4. In the Project Directory box type **c:\rep2**. This identifies the directory on the current server that will receive the replication. Click OK.

FIG. 12.7
It's easy to keep tabs on projects through the Web browser interface.

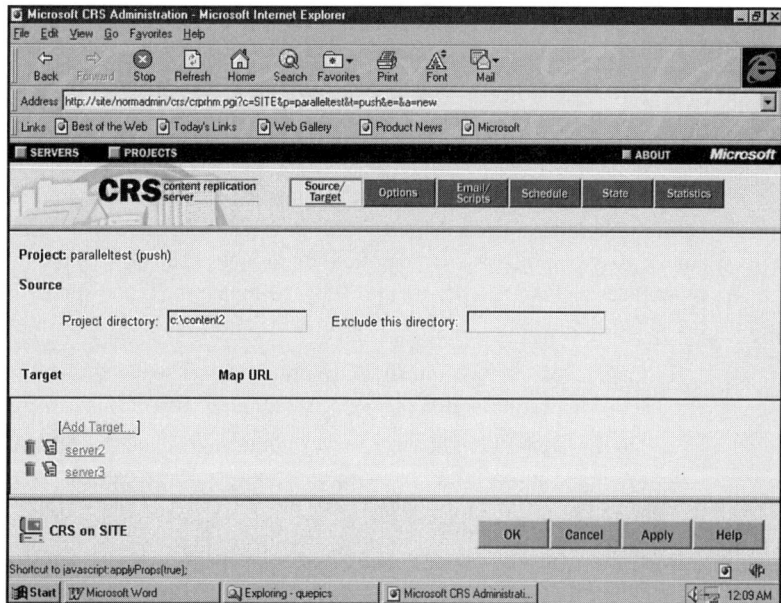

Follow these steps to configure server3:

1. On Server3, launch Internet Explorer and access the administration page by going to the following location: **http://server3/mcisadmin/crs/crhm.pgi**.

2. On the Content Replication Server home page, click the Add Project button.

3. On the Add Project page, in the name box, type **paralleltest**, then select the Push Replication option. Click OK.

4. In the Project Directory box type **c:\rep2**. This identifies the directory on the current server that will receive the replication. Click OK.

To run the replication with the Web administration tool, follow these steps:

1. On Server1, launch Internet Explorer and access the administration page by going to the following location: **http://server1/mcisadmin/crs/crhm.pgi**.

2. On the Content Replication Server project page, click the green arrow to the right of the project name "1."

3. Click OK when asked for confirmation, as seen in Figure 12.8. The Content Replication Server project should begin running and the content will appear on server2 and server3 in the c:\rep2 directory.

Part
IV

Ch
12

FIG. 12.8

It's important to make sure your project information is correct before proceeding.

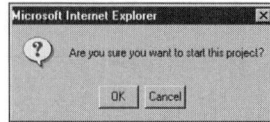

Replication Chaining Test   For the Replication Chaining test, you will need three NT servers. Again, we'll refer to them as "server1," "server2," and "server3." When you complete this example, you should have an understanding of how replication chaining is conducted from one server (server1) to another (server3), by using a transitional server (server2) to bridge the two networks.

1. On Server1, launch Internet Explorer and access the administration page by going to the following location: **http://server1/mcisadmin/crs/crhm.pgi**.

2. On the Content Replication Server home page, click the Add Project button.

3. On the Add Project page, in the name box, type **chainingtest**, then select the Push Replication option. Click OK.

4. In the Project Directory box type **c:\chain3**, which identifies the directory on the current server that contains the source files you want to replicate. Click the Add Target link.

5. On the Add Target page, select the Machine radio button and type into the text box **server2**. Click OK.

6. When you return to the main Content Replication Web Page, the target should be listed, with the source directory that will be replicated. Review the results and click OK to accept the configuration.

Next, follow these steps to configure server2:

1. On Server2, launch Internet Explorer and access the administration page by going to the following location: **http://server2/mcisadmin/crs/crhm.pgi**.

2. On the Content Replication Server home page, click the Add Project button.

3. On the Add Project page, in the name box, type **chainingtest** and then select the Push Replication option. Click OK.

4. In the Project Directory box type **c:\intermediate3** and click Add Target.

5. On the Add Target page, highlight the Machine radio button and type into the text box **server3**. Click OK.

When Server2 is set up, follow these steps to configure server3:

1. On Server3, launch Internet Explorer and access the administration page at the following location: **http://server3/mcisadmin/crs/crhm.pgi**.

2. On the Content Replication Server home page, click the Add Project button.

3. On the Add Project page, in the name box, type **chainingtest** and then select the Push Replication option. Click OK.

4. In the Project Directory box type **c:\rep3**. No target is necessary on server3 for this test. Click OK.

To run the chained replication with the Web administration tool, follow these steps:

1. On Server1, launch Internet Explorer and access the administration page by going to the following location: **http://server1/mcisadmin/crs/crhm.pgi**.

2. On the Content Replication Server project page, click the green arrow to the right of the project name, `chainingtest`.

3. Click OK when asked for confirmation. Watch the results on server2 and server3. When complete, server1 will have been replicated to the c:\rep3 directory on server3.

Pull Replication   The object of this example is to create a replication between two servers, where the content is "pulled" from an Internet Web server and placed on a Content Replication Server. The first step in configuring for a pull replication involves creating a content directory on a Web server that can be accessed by a Web address. To accomplish this, you'll need to create a Web content directory and then make it a virtual root through your Web publisher, the Internet Information Server.

To create an URL-accessible content directory on your Web server, follow this procedure:

1. On Server2, create a subdirectory named pullcontent off of the wwwroot subdirectory. Then attach it to the Internet Service Manager.

2. In the Internet Service Manager, connect to server2 and access the WWW Service entry for server2.

3. This will launch the WWW Services Properties dialog box. Now click the Directories tab and then the Add button.

4. In the Directory properties dialog box, in the directory box, type **c:\Inetpub\wwwroot\pullcontent**.

N O T E   The default location of the pullcontent subdirectory will be different for Windows NT 3.51 and 4.0. With Windows NT 3.51, the default location is c:\inetsrv\wwwroot\content4. When using Windows NT 4.0, the default location is c:\inetpub\wwwroot\content4. ■

5. In the Alias box, type **pulltest** as the virtual root alias name for the content directory.

6. Under Access, make sure Read is checked.

7. The pullcontent subdirectory will now be located in \\CRSServer2\pulltest\. Now Configure the pull replication project with the Web administration tool.

8. On Server1, launch Internet Explorer and access the administration page by going to the following location: **http://server1/mcisadmin/crs/crhm.pgi**.

9. On the Content Replication Server home page, click the Add Project button.

10. On the Add Project page, in the name box, type **pullexample** and then select the Pull Replication option. Click OK.

11. On the Source/Target page in the URL text entry box type **http://server2/pulltest**.

12. In the Levels Deep option, select All. This will cause the Content Replication Server to pull all of the content from the listed URL.

13. In the Target directory, type **c:\pulltest**. Click OK.

14. Review the main project screen to see the project that was just entered.

To run a Pull Replication test with the Web administration tool, follow these steps:

1. On Server1, launch Internet Explorer and access the administration page by going to the following location: **http://server1/mcisadmin/crs/crhm.pgi**.

2. On the Content Replication Server project page, click the green arrow to the right of the project name, pullexample.

3. Click OK when asked for confirmation. The replication project will run and the directory content on server2 should appear on server1.

Route Replication Test   For this example, three servers will be used. To stay consistent we'll refer to them as "server1," "server2," and "server3." After completing this example, you'll have an overview on using routing tables for replication.

1. On Server1, launch Internet Explorer and access the administration page by going to the following location: **http://server1/mcisadmin/crs/crhm.pgi**.

2. On the Content Replication Server Web page select the button for the Routing Table.

3. Select the Add Route option.

4. In the Add Route dialog box, type **route5** into the Name text entry field and click OK.

5. On the Routing Table Information page, leave the Local Directory box empty and click Add Server.

6. In the Add Server dialog box, enter **server2** into the Name text entry field and click OK. You'll be returned to the Routing Table Information page.

7. Choose add server on the Routing Table Information page and then type **server3** into the text entry field; click OK.

8. Click OK when returned to the Routing Table Information page.

Next, set up server2, as follows:

1. On Server2, launch Internet Explorer and access the administration page by going to the following location: **http://server2/mcisadmin/crs/crhm.pgi**.

2. On the Content Replication Server Web page select the button for the Routing Table.

3. Select the Add Route option.

4. In the Add Route dialog box type **route5** into the Name text entry field and click OK.

5. On the Routing Table Information page, type **c:\route5** for the Local Directory and click OK.

Last, set up server3:

1. On Server3, launch Internet Explorer and access the administration page by going to the following location: **http://server2/mcisadmin/crs/crhm.pgi**.
2. On the Content Replication Server Web page select the button for the Routing Table.
3. Select the Add Route option.
4. In the Add Route dialog box, in the Name box, type **route5** and click OK.
5. On the Routing Table Information page, type **c:\route5** for the Local Directory and click OK.

Here is the procedure for setting up the Replication Project:

1. On Server1, launch Internet Explorer and access the administration page by going to the following location: **http://server1/mcisadmin/crs/crhm.pgi**.
2. On the Content Replication Server home page, click the Add Project button.
3. On the Add Project page, type **routetest** in the Name text entry field and then select the Push Replication option. Click OK.
4. In the Project Directory box type c:\content5, which identifies the directory on the current server that contains the source files you want to replicate. Click the Add Target link.
5. On the Add Target page, highlight the Machine radio button and type **route5** into the text box. Click OK.
6. When you return to the main Content Replication Web Page, both targets should be listed, with the source directory that will be replicated. Review the results and click OK to accept the configuration.

With the necessary server set up, we can move on to configuring the route replication project with the Web administration tool, using these steps:

1. On Server1, launch Internet Explorer and access the administration page by going to the following location: **http://server1/mcisadmin/crs/crhm.pgi**.
2. On the Content Replication Server project page, click the green arrow to the right of the project name, routetest.
3. Click OK when asked for confirmation. The replication project will run and the content on server1 should be replicated to server2 and server3 into the c:\route5\routetest directory.

Part
IV

Ch

12

Starting Up

The launching of all projects is handled through a Web page interface. When you launch the Content Replication Service Web page, all projects will be listed on the first page, which is the Project page. From this page you can delete a project by clicking the Garbage can, or you can edit the document by clicking the edit icon. When you are ready to begin the replication procedure, simply click the green arrow and you will be prompted with a dialog box that verifies that you are ready to start the project. Click the OK button and the replication process begins.

Using the Content Replication Server

In order to effectively deploy the Content Replication server, it's important to have a basic understanding of how to monitor the performance of the Content Replication Server and how to work around potential problems. In the following section you get an overview of how to use the Windows NT Event Viewer and Performance Monitor, as well as some tools built into the Content Replication System, to monitor the progress of replication projects. There will also be some information to help you solve common problems that may occur in the use of the Content Replication Server.

Monitoring the Content Replication Server

Like any of the Microsoft Commercial Internet Servers, there are system tools designed to monitor the health of the server. Through the analysis of the following three options, you should be able to ascertain the stabilty and performance of the server:

- Event Log Viewer
- Performance Monitor
- Content Replication Administration Tools

Let's take a closer look at how to use each tool.

The Event Log The Windows NT Event Log Viewer is an excellent tool for monitoring any of the service events that are conducted by the server. Through the Event Log, administrators can monitor performance and gather useful information on errors and configuration problems that may be occurring with the Content Replication System.

The Event Viewer is in the Administrative Tools (Common) group on the Start menu. The main window for the Event Viewer provides detailed information on system events. Displayed from left to right are the date, time, source (the process that logged the event), category (relates mostly to Security issues), event (a numeric identifier), user (the user account where the event occurred), and the computer.

> **N O T E** When monitoring the Event Log, watch the symbols to the left of the date to help you understand the status of your server:
>
> - Informational events are symbolized with a letter "i" in a blue circle.
> - Warning events are symbolized with an exclamation point in a yellow circle.
> - Critical events are symbolized with a stop sign.
>
> The Error Log also will display a key icon when it has completed a successful audit, or a padlock icon if an audit fails. ▨

To obtain more information about an event, double-click the event. The Event Detail dialog box that is launched provides a description of the event. Review the event description and correct the problem accordingly.

Performance Monitor Counters   The Windows NT Performance Monitor will allow you to take a look at the performance status of the Internet Content Replication Server. The Performance Monitor is designed to allow you to review real time information on the status and health of your server by letting you view a variety of performance counters.

To access the Performance Monitor and evaluate the status of the Content Replication Service, follow these steps:

1. Click the Start button, selecting Programs, Administrative Tools, and then choose the Performance Monitor.

2. Select View, and verify that you will be viewing by Chart.

3. Choose to add to the chart by selecting Edit, then Add to Chart. You can also activate this feature by clicking the + button on the tool bar.

4. The Performance Monitor launches the Add to Chart dialog box. Some of the main features needed in the Performance Monitor are:

    - *Computer*   Select the computer you want to the monitor. Your server appears as the default. If the Content Replication Service resides on another server, click the ellipses button (…) and a select computer dialog box is launched.

    - *Object*   Used to select an object to monitor from those residing on the computer you selected.

    - *Counters*   Used to select the counter you want to monitor.

5. Leave the Computer as the default.

6. Change the Object feature to Content Replication Service.

7. Select the counter of interest. To review what the counters are designed to do, highlight the option and click the Explain button. For this test, select Bytes Total, which will record the total number of bytes sent and received by the Content Replication Service.

8. Now click the Add button and the counters will be launched.

9. Click the Done button and the Performance Monitor begins charting the graph. If you presently are not replicating any data, the chart will be flatlined at zero. To initiate a response, launch a replication project from the the Web administration page. The Performance Monitor will immediately record the status of the project.

10. Review the outcome.

You can also use the Performance Monitor's alert mode feature to automatically notify you when levels do not reach your expectations.

Here's how to set up the alert feature for Performance Monitor.

1. From the Start menu, select Programs, Administrative Tools, and then choose the Performance Monitor.

2. The Performance Monitor is launched. Select the View the Alerts button on the button bar, or choose View, Alert.

Part
IV

Ch
12

3. Choose the Add Counter button (+), or choose Edit, Add to Alert.

4. Select the Object as Processor, and the Counter at %Processor Time.

5. In the Alert if field, as an example, select the Over option and type the number 50 in the text entry field. This will cause the server to notify you whenever the server's processors reach more than 50 percent usage.

6. Click the Add button.

7. Choose Options, Alert to launch the Alert Options dialog box.

8. If an alert is necessary, Performance Monitor can be configured to Switch to an Alert View, or to Send a Network E-mail Message to the administrator. For now, let's select Switch to an Alert View.

9. The Performance Monitor will track anything that crosses the alert threshold and will log the activity on the Performance Monitor page.

10. Monitor the server resources and adjust as needed.

With this test, you can analyze the performance of the Content Replication Service against the other offerings on the server and determine whether the server is being taxed excessively.

▶ **See** "Content Replication Server," **p. 601**, for more information.

Content Replication Administration Tools   Monitoring opportunities are available from the Content Replication Service home page located at **http://*servername*/mcisadmin/crs/** (substitute the domain name of your server in place of *servername*). Whenever projects are pending, or in progress, the Web page offers a Statistics button. If you click the statistics button, you can access the following performance information:

- The Project Name
- Files sent
- Bytes sent
- Files received
- Bytes Received
- Time in seconds
- Average bytes sent per second
- Average files sent per second
- Average bytes received per second
- Average files received per second

Monitoring performance through this tool provides a quick and easy method for acquiring information about your replication projects.

Troubleshooting the Content Replication Server

Whenever you add an additional application to your server, there are opportunities for errors. It's unfortunate, but expected. Some errors are human errors, others are related to software errors. The following section provides an overview on resolving the problems that may occur during your deployment of the Content Replication System.

Startup   When the Content Replication Service fails to start, the failure may be a result of the missing program files, service account rights, or perhaps a configuration problem with the Windows NT Access Control List; in layman terms, directory permissions. We'll start by checking to see if there are missing files. Try the following procedure:

1. From the Start button, select Programs, and then the Command Prompt option.
2. At the command prompt, change to the c:\MCIS\CRS directory and type the following command: **crssrv.exe debug**, as seen in Figure 12.9.

FIG. 12.9

Review configuration problems from the command prompt with the debug tool.

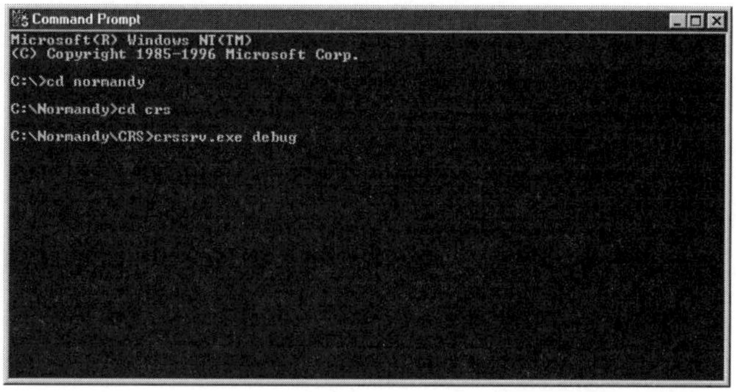

```
Command Prompt                                                    _ □ ×
Microsoft(R) Windows NT(TM)
(C) Copyright 1985-1996 Microsoft Corp.

C:\>cd normandy

C:\Normandy>cd crs

C:\Normandy\CRS>crssrv.exe debug
```

A debug routine is initiated. To review the log, type the following command:

`crs getlog`

Review the log for valid information that was detected during the debug process. You can also access the log files in the c:\MCIS\CRS\log files directory and view the text file in Notepad, as seen in Figure 12.10. Missing files will be reported. The result may indicate that a reinstall of the Content Replication Service is required.

To determine if the problem is a result of a conflict in the Windows NT Access Control List, use the Windows NT Explorer. The Content Replication Server needs access to its own program directory and also to the crstemp directory.

To review permissions, follow these steps:

1. Right-click the Start button, and choose Explore.
2. In the Windows NT Explorer, scroll to the MCIS directory and access a subdirectory called CRS. Simply highlight the directory folder, right-click the folder, and choose Properties.
3. Review the attributes for the folder and ensure that the directory Permissions and Ownership are allowing access to the Administrator of the server. Make any necessary changes.
4. Conduct the same review of the crstemp directory. Make necessary changes.

Part

IV

Ch

12

FIG. 12.10

The logfile, generated with the debug command, reveals information about the status of the Content Replication Service.

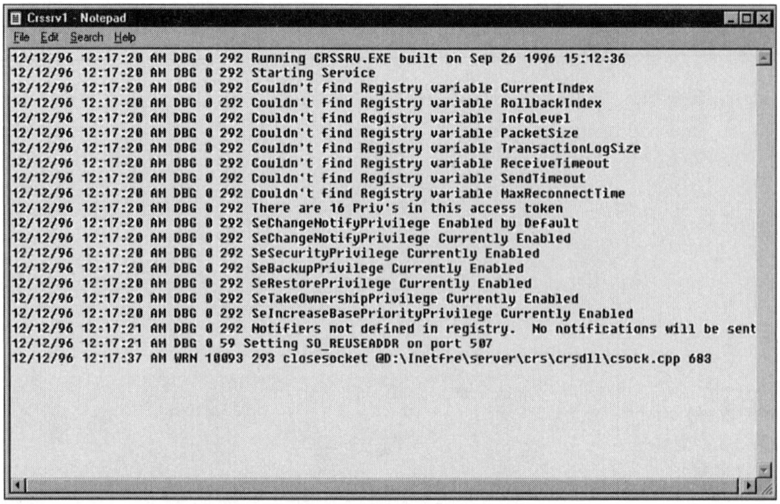

```
Crssrv1 - Notepad
File  Edit  Search  Help
12/12/96 12:17:20 AM DBG 0 292 Running CRSSRV.EXE built on Sep 26 1996 15:12:36
12/12/96 12:17:20 AM DBG 0 292 Starting Service
12/12/96 12:17:20 AM DBG 0 292 Couldn't find Registry variable CurrentIndex
12/12/96 12:17:20 AM DBG 0 292 Couldn't find Registry variable RollbackIndex
12/12/96 12:17:20 AM DBG 0 292 Couldn't find Registry variable InfoLevel
12/12/96 12:17:20 AM DBG 0 292 Couldn't find Registry variable PacketSize
12/12/96 12:17:20 AM DBG 0 292 Couldn't find Registry variable TransactionLogSize
12/12/96 12:17:20 AM DBG 0 292 Couldn't find Registry variable ReceiveTimeout
12/12/96 12:17:20 AM DBG 0 292 Couldn't find Registry variable SendTimeout
12/12/96 12:17:20 AM DBG 0 292 Couldn't find Registry variable MaxReconnectTime
12/12/96 12:17:20 AM DBG 0 292 There are 16 Priv's in this access token
12/12/96 12:17:20 AM DBG 0 292 SeChangeNotifyPrivilege Enabled by Default
12/12/96 12:17:20 AM DBG 0 292 SeChangeNotifyPrivilege Currently Enabled
12/12/96 12:17:20 AM DBG 0 292 SeSecurityPrivilege Currently Enabled
12/12/96 12:17:20 AM DBG 0 292 SeBackupPrivilege Currently Enabled
12/12/96 12:17:20 AM DBG 0 292 SeRestorePrivilege Currently Enabled
12/12/96 12:17:20 AM DBG 0 292 SeTakeOwnershipPrivilege Currently Enabled
12/12/96 12:17:20 AM DBG 0 292 SeIncreaseBasePriorityPrivilege Currently Enabled
12/12/96 12:17:21 AM DBG 0 292 Notifiers not defined in registry.  No notifications will be sent
12/12/96 12:17:21 AM DBG 0 59 Setting SO_REUSEADDR on port 507
12/12/96 12:17:37 AM WRN 10093 293 closesocket @D:\Inetfre\server\crs\crsdll\csock.cpp 683
```

To review the Service Account Rights, do the following:

1. Click the Start button, choose Programs, Administrative Tools (Common), and then select User Manager.

2. In the Groups list, double-click the CRS Administrators group.

3. Review the Members list. If the Administrator is not listed as a member, reset the account to allow the Administrator the appropriate rights.

Security   Often, when the Content Replication Server is misbehaving, it is a result of Security or Access problems. When working with multiple machines, the problem can often be solved by simply updating each server's ID, password, and rights in the User Manager. Other times, the problem can be related to the use of improper accounts, or other access or configuration problems.

If you cannot access projects through the Web administration tool, it may be because the account you are using does not have rights. In this case, you have two options:

■ Access the Windows NT User Manager, change the account rights to allow you administrative rights, and try again.

■ Restart the server and log on as the Administrator. If you still don't have rights, check to make sure the Administrator is granted privileges in the User Manager.

If you are trying to manage another server through the Web administration tool in the multi-server Content Replication Server network, do the following:

1. Click the Start button, choose Programs, Microsoft Internet Server (Common), and select the Internet Service Manager.

2. Access the service properties for the WWW service by double-clicking the computer's service name.

3. In the service properties, if the Password Authentication is configured only to Allow Anonymous, then add the Windows NT Challenge/Response option.

4. Apply the changes and return to the Content Replication Service's Web administration tool to test access.

Processing   With the Content Replication System there can be a number of processing areas to review when your service doesn't perform up to standards. When your replications slow down to a crawl, check for the following problems:

- No project on the destination server. The project names must be exactly the same on each server. Remember, if you set up a push from server1 to server2, you not only have to configure server1 to conduct the push, you also need to add a project on server2 to receive the push.

  ▶ **See** "Setting up the Content Replication Server," **p. 328**

- The remote system may be down. Try pinging the system to make sure it's active.

- The content tree is too large. If you're moving large chunks of information, it may take a long time for the replication and the transaction to be completed. A workaround for this problem is to break the content into smaller segments by sending the replications one directory at a time.

- Network seems busy. To solve this one, change the time of day for the replication.

- The replication hangs. The Content Replication Server will only attempt to recover from network failures for 30 minutes. The service will either recover or time out.

Data   With any sort of file transfer, there are opportunities for your files to be corrupted, incomplete, or wrong. When the result of your replication is fouled up, review the following:

- Corrupted Data. The first thing to check is a system error. If the system fails and is restarted during the replication process, the files will be corrupted. Attempt a resend and if the files are still corrupted, check the system for hardware problems.

- Wrong Data Replicated. This is usually the result of human error. When this occurs, analyze each server's project list to ensure that the project routes are appropriate for each stage of the replication.

- Incomplete Replication. The culprit is typically a server crash somewhere in the replication process. Check the Event Logs on each of the machines for error messages.

Part
IV

Ch
12

Replicating a Web Site Structure

With the Content Replication System, organizations can mix and match features to accomplish their replication tasks. For this service, it's all about projects. For a project to be successfully fulfilled, each server must play its role in the replication process. In this section, we'll show a test replication of the Web site managed by Integrity Data.

Integrity Data needs to move development activity off of its production server. They plan to launch a development server for their employees, and then use the Content

Replication System to update the production server. They have decided that the strategy for this project calls for a pull replication.

Here's the plan. Presently, the Web documents are kept in the root directory. The first level pages for Integrity Data are contained in this directory. There are three subdirectories, one called /products, another called /history and a third entitled /misc. Therefore, the objective is to set up a replication project from the development server to the production server that contains all the files in the root directory, along with all the files in the subdirectories, and place it in a directory on idpro called c:\html. For the purposes of this test, they have copied the file structure and placed it in directory called /test, which can be found on the server at **c:\inetpub\wwwroot\test**.

The Company has purchased an additional server and has installed Windows NT 4.0, with IIS and the Content Replication Service. They have successfully pinged the server from other machines on the network, and are ready to create a project for replication.

In order for a pull replication to work, the iddev server needs to have the content directory that contains the HTML files configured as a virtual root. It is recommended that you refer to Que's *Special Edition Using Internet Information Server 3.0* for more information on configuring the Windows NT Web server interface. Here's the step-by-step process they used for replicating the HTML files from the development server to the production server (the development NT server will be identified as "iddev" and the production NT server will be referred to as "idpro"):

1. Click the Start button, choose Programs, Microsoft Internet Server (Common), and then choose Internet Service Manager.
2. Open the WWW properties by double-clicking the WWW Service entry, and then click the directories tab and click the add button.
3. In the Directory properties dialog box, type **c:\Inetpub\wwwroot\test**.
4. In the Alias field for the Virtual Directory, type **test1** as the virtual root alias for the content directory.
5. Under Access, make sure the Read option is selected.
6. The /test directory now has the URL of **http://iddev/test1** and is ready for replication.

Next the idpro server must be set up to handle the Pull Replication. To do so, follow these steps:

1. On the idpro server, launch Internet Explorer and access the administration page at **http://idpro/mcisadmin/crs/**.
2. Click the Add Project button.
3. On the Add Project page, in the name box, type `pullid`, and then select the Pull Replication option. Click OK.
4. In the Source URL text entry box type **http://iddev/test1**, which identifies the URL on the iddev server that contains the HTML files that will be replicated.

5. Proceed to the Levels Deep option and set the configuration to 2 Levels Deep, because there are no directories that run deeper than the second level.

6. For the Target directory, type **c:\html**. This signifies where the replicated files will be placed on the idpro server.

7. Click the Schedule button, choose <u>A</u>dd schedule and set the schedule options to replicate seven days a week at 1 p.m. every day. Choose OK.

8. When you return to the main Content Replication Web Page, the schedule will be listed. Now click the E-mail/Scripts button.

9. Enter an e-mail address for notification, should a replication fail.

10. Review the results and click OK to accept the configuration.

To run the replication with the Web administration tool from idpro, use this procedure:

1. On idpro, launch a Web browser (Internet Explorer 3.0 or higher) and access the administration page by going to the following location: **http://idpro/mcisadmin/crs/ crhm.pgi**.

2. On the Content Replication Server project page, click the green arrow next to the project name "pullid".

3. Click OK when asked for confirmation. The Content Replication Service project will begin running and the content will appear on idpro in the c:\html directory.

The mission, err replication, should be accomplished. Integrity Data has successfully demonstrated a Pull Replication and the content is replicated accurately and on schedule.

Propagating Content

Reproducing any sort of content through the Content Replication System is quite easy. You can also generate replications for any type of data. In the replication process, there are a number of things happening between the servers to accomplish a routine push operation.

Setup Phase

During the setup phase, the following takes place:

- The two servers set up a TCP session over Port 507.
- A Windows NT LAN Manager authentication exchange occurs. This is the Windows NT security protocol.
- The two servers exchange version information.
- The two servers create a session context, which allows for a session to be resumed should there be an outage.
- The source server sends to the destination server a MSG_START_REPLICATION command message, which allows the machines to initialize with each other for the replication.

Part
IV

Ch
12

Replication Phase

During the replication phase, these events take place:

- The source server sends to the destination server a MSG_START_DIRECTORY command message for each directory that will be replicated.

- The source server sends to the destination server a MSG_I_HAVE_LIST command message, which contains specific information such as the creation date of the file and the last time the file was modified. The destination server responds to the message by indicating whether or not a file should be sent.

- The source and destination establish an exchange stream.

- The replicated data is transmitted.

- When the replication of each directory is complete, the source server sends a MSG_END_DIRECTORY command message, allowing the destination server to determine if any files in the directory or subdirectory have been deleted and remove that directory's content information.

- The communication between the source and destination servers continues, repeating each of the above steps for every directory, until the source system sends to the destination server a MSG_FINISH_REPLICATION command message, indicating that the replication process is complete.

- The session between the source server and the destination server is ended when the replication is finished.

What's Happening in the Back of the House

Whenever a replication is taking place, the destination server is not placing the files that are transferred into the target directory. In fact, the files are placed in the c:\crstemp directory. The files remain in the temporary directory until the replication is complete. Once the transfer is complete, the Content Replication system renames the files and places them into the target directory. As the new files are placed into the target directory, each of the files that are being replaced are renamed and sent to the c:\crstemp file. The purpose of this feature is to allow for a replication roll back should you need to revert to the earlier version of the file structure.

High End Handling of HTML Files through the Pull Replication

Whenever servers are configured for a pull replication from a Web server, the Content Replication System attempts to review all of the links on every page to determine if any new links have been added. That means if a new tag, such as IMG, HREF, or SRC, has been added, the Content Replication System resolves the absolute path to the URL and places it in the processing queue. If the page has relative paths listed, the Content Replication System resolves the link to an absolute path. If the link goes to another site, the Content Replication Server ignores it. The process continues from first level URLs through any additional tiers in the Web tree. Microsoft has created a process where all paths resolve from the base URL, as opposed to the root URL. This procedure is designed to allow the Content Replication System to maintain an accurate Web tree.

NOTE It's important for developers to understand the difference between an Absolute path and a Relative path. Absolute path names are generally used to link to remote files; for instance **"http://www.integritydata.com/index.htm/"** would be an Absolute path. Relative path names are used to link to a local file, such as "staff.html". Relative paths are relative to the file or directory you are currently in. ■

Examples of the Content Replication Server

In conversations with Microsoft consulting, the development team explained how the Microsoft Network used the Content Replication System to update its Superbowl site continuously with pictures and statistics while the game was being played. They also used the Content Replication system to broadcast up-to-date information on the Oscars as each award was given out. According to Microsoft, here's how they did it:

After setting up the replication project, they configured the options to Replicate Automatically, which means that every time a new file or image is uploaded to the source directory a replication of that update would be launched and sent to the public server, allowing the consumer the ability to acquire the most up-to-date information.

That's a useful tool and can be used for some practical everyday problems. For instance, in Tallahassee, the local government Web site could benefit from the use of the Content Replication System. Here's why: Whenever there is an election related to City government, the City's Web master manually moves an updated voting tally for each precinct every 20 to 30 minutes. This is work-intensive, because after the update is dropped into a directory on the Web master's hard drive, he launches a file transfer session and moves the file up to the City's Web site. With Content Replication, the Web master would only need to concern himself with updating information; the file transfer would be handled by the server as soon as the updates were complete.

Part
IV

Ch
12

From Here...

In this section, you gained an overview of the Microsoft Content Replication System. The Chapter outlined how to set up and use the service. There were also examples of how to replicate a site with some ideas on practical usage of the application.

- For more information on the Windows NT User Manager and Event Log, please review Que's *Special Edition Using Windows NT 4.0*.

- For additional information on hardware, see Appendix A, "Hardware Requirements."

- For a more detailed explanation on how to use the Performance Monitor, see Appendix B, "Performance Monitors Counters."

The Merchant System

Microsoft Merchant Server—Enabling Commerce on the Web

The Microsoft Merchant Server provides a comprehensive software solution for delivering a Web-based Electronic Commerce environment. Microsoft Merchant Server facilitates the rapid development of a complete shopping environment on the Web, including management of the shopper's experience, a structured order process, extensive merchandising features, and a complete Web-based administration capability. The Merchant Server provides a scalable and robust order processing engine which provides for an open architecture that third-party software developers have already embraced.

While the Merchant server provides extraordinary features and flexibility, it is also a very specific software tool catered to a very specific function. Merchant server's primary focus is the managing of the purchasing process for goods and services. Merchant server provides plenty of search features and easy access to a database over the Web, but if your primary task is not the selling of goods or services you need to take additional time to review other products contained in this book to ensure that you are applying the most appropriate software tool to your intended purpose. ■

Implementing Merchant server, the core requirements

Implementing the array of hardware and software services requires a broad range of skills, from programming to network administration.

Developing Merchant server source code

While setting up and administering a Merchant site requires network and database support, leveraging the power and flexibility of the Merchant server involves developing HTML-based template files marked up with Merchant Directives, Actions, and Value References.

Controlling transactional order processing

One of the values that Merchant provides in the site development process stems from order processing architecture which any developer must thoroughly understand to enable a Merchant site.

Administering the Merchant Server

Merchant provides both a site-wide administration environment, and the ability to custom develop a Web-based store level administration environment; both play a key role in delivering a complete commerce solution.

Understanding the Microsoft Merchant Server

The Microsoft Merchant Server runs as a single service on a Windows NT Server computer. The Merchant Store Service integrates with Microsoft's Internet Information Server's Web server and an ODBC-compliant database program to provide a complete Merchant solution. The process starts from the Web server, which is the gatekeeper of all Web-based communication. Web-based communication between the shopper's Web browser and the merchant's Web server provide the Internet-based point of entry for a shopper to the Merchant site. The Web server invokes the Merchant Store Service to request that a page be generated any time a Web browser request is received that follows the specific URL syntax required by Merchant. When this URL request is received by the Merchant Store Service, it generates the page and returns it to the Web server. The Merchant Store Service at startup opens a connection to its database through ODBC and maintains that connection for the processing of any page requests that require database lookups (which is almost every page request).

▶ **See** "Invoking a Page, the PGEN, or Action URL Syntax," **p. 369**, for additional details on the custom URL required.

This three-product architecture is complemented by additional third-party products that may be included. For example, if online credit card authorizations were enabled through Verifone's vPOS product, an additional service would be installed on the Windows NT Server. This vPOS service would be invoked by the Merchant Store Service in the event the an authorization was required during the order processing payment stage.

ON THE WEB

http://www.verifone.com   For more information about Verifone, see their site.

▶ **See** "Controlling Transactional Order Processing," **p. 370** for more information about the Order Processing Stages.

Implementing Merchant Server, the Core Requirements

Delivering an Electronic Commerce Web site based on Merchant server involves a series of technologies and software products all seamlessly working together. Implementing these technologies and software products requires a range of skill sets, computer hardware, and software tools that must be understood before you attempt to build a Merchant site. This section will thoroughly explore the requirements to building a Merchant site including:

- Skill sets necessary on your development team
- Network infrastructure which must be in place
- Software products which must be properly installed and configured
- Computer hardware configuration that must be used

Building the Development Team

Setting up a Merchant server involves several very different jobs or responsibilities. While it's possible to have a single individual who possesses all the necessary skills to completely implement a Merchant site, the more likely scenario involves two to five individuals with specific knowledge in a particular aspect of the sight development and/or implementation. The training or areas of expertise required for Merchant site creation include:

- Graphic designer familiar with multimedia for the Web
- HTML programmer
- Mark-up programmer mastering the Merchant syntax
- Database administrator with expertise in whatever database platform is selected
- Database programmer with SQL programming experience in selected platform
- Windows NT certified professional
- Network administrator familiar with your network and Internet protocols
- Web server administrator knowledgeable in Microsoft's Internet Information Server

The preceding list documents eight areas of competence that should be available as part of the development team responsible for Merchant implementation; however, many of these skills can be delivered by a group of two to three professionals. A common development team for Merchant Server includes three professionals who have the networking, database, and HTML/mark-up development skills.

The HTML/mark-up role involves the development or adaptation of graphic images for use on the Web, as well as the coding of HTML pages for use as templates as Merchant dynamically generates Web pages for the shopper at the site. The Merchant mark-up syntax will require Merchant specific training but fits closely with the skills of an existing HTML developer.

▶ **See** "Marking-up Templates, the Source Code of Merchant," **p. 363**, for more information about the tasks involved in the development of HTML/mark-up pages.

The networking professional's role involves the Windows NT Server knowledge, Web server administration experience, and Networking/Internet skills. In some cases, this individual may also become responsible for administering the database server used in your Merchant site.

▶ **See** "Administering the Merchant Server Implementation," **p. 373** for more information about the responsibilities of a Merchant administrator.

Finally the database programmer must thoroughly understand the Structured Query Language (SQL) as it relates to the specific database server you have selected for your Merchant site. The Merchant server heavily relies on a database server for operation. Many of the administrative, order processing, and shopping features are driven by SQL statements which must be adapted from sample stores. In the development process, the database programmer may also become involved in some of the HTML/mark-up development since the HTML/mark-up development becomes such a focus of the Merchant site development effort.

▶ **See** "Marking-up Templates, the Source Code of Merchant," **p. 363**, for more information about the relationship between the database and the HTML/mark-up templates.

Part
V

Ch
13

Networking Infrastructure Required

The networking infrastructure required by Merchant includes a TCP/IP based network. While the communication among the Web server, database, and Merchant can be conducted over other protocols such as IPX with Microsoft's Named Pipes, the Web server must communicate with a Web browser over TCP/IP. In addition, if the Merchant site must be accessed by shoppers over the Internet, a connection to the Internet is also required.

TIP If you already have an operational Web server functioning properly, then you have the necessary infrastructure already in place and you can skip this Networking requirement issue.

▶ **See** "Installing the Required Software Services," **p. 386**, for more information about the relationship among the Web server, Merchant server, and database server.

Identifying the Software Products Necessary

The Merchant Server product installs one service called the Merchant Store Service, but a functioning Merchant site requires, at a minimum, two additional software components. In addition to the two required components, Merchant's open architecture supports the ability to provide an almost unlimited number of additional components which can either be custom developed or provided by third-party software vendors. The two required components include:

■ Microsoft Internet Information Server's World Wide Web Service (IIS)

■ An ODBC-compliant database product

IIS must be version 1.0c or higher in order to operate with Microsoft Merchant Server version 1.0. IIS runs as a service under Windows NT and provides the communication link between the Web browser and the Merchant Store Service. All requests from a shopper's Web browser first go the Web server or IIS which then routes the request to the Merchant Store Service.

The ODBC-compliant database product represents a wide range of possible database products from vendors including Oracle, Informix, Microsoft, and many more too numerous to mention. Due to Merchant's reliance on continuous database interaction, a product such as Microsoft Access or FoxPro may present performance problems even with a low traffic sight; as a result, you should consider carefully what product you select. The remainder of this chapter and Chapter 14, "Building a Merchant System," focus on Microsoft's SQL server product when discussing Merchant site database-related issues.

ON THE WEB

http://www.microsoft.com/odbc/   For more information about ODBC compliant databases, see Microsoft's Web Site, or contact your database vendor.

N O T E The current version of Internet Information Server at the time of this book's release is 3.0. ■

Third-party products that should be considered primarily include components that act as plug-ins to the Merchant server order processing steps. The key component steps that currently have products include:

- Shipping and Handling
- Tax
- Payment

Additional order processing component steps have products under development from commercial vendors and are also areas where custom components could be developed such as the Inventory component where you might want to query a separate system carrying current Inventory information. In the shipping and handling area, consider TanData's Progistics.Merchant product. For tax calculations TAXWARE International, Inc. offers products to support complex tax requirements. And, for payment consider the first and most well known vendors including Verifone and CyberCash Systems.

ON THE WEB

http://www.microsoft.com/merchant/partners/partner5.htm For additional information on vendors, visit Microsoft's Web listing.

▶ **See** "Utilizing Third-Party Components for Extending the Process," **p. 371**

Configuring the Right Hardware Environment

The range of hardware configurations that you can implement to support a complete Merchant site range dramatically, based on your expected traffic volume. Microsoft's published minimum requirements for operating Merchant server follow the guidelines illustrated in Table 13.1. The simplest configuration you can implement involves placing your Merchant server, Database server, and Web server products all on the same single computer (assuming your database server runs on Microsoft Windows NT Server).

Table 13.1 Microsoft's Published Merchant Server Minimum System Requirements

Category	Requirement
Processor	Intel 486, Intel Pentium, or DEC Alpha
Operating system	Microsoft Windows NT Server version 3.51 or later
Web server	Microsoft Internet Information Server version 1.0c or later
Database	ODBC compliant
RAM	64M
Hard drive space	55M of available space

Part
V

Ch
13

The minimum installation we tested was a Pentium 133 computer with 64M of RAM, and the maximum configuration we tested was two multi-processor Pentium computers with 256M of RAM each. In the maximum configuration, one server was running the Web server and Merchant Router and the other machine was running Microsoft SQL Server and the Merchant

Store Service. In both environments the performance during light loads was similar. Based on feedback from Microsoft System Engineers working on Merchant server Benchmarking, we have established some general rules of thumb for assessing the required hardware configuration.

In understanding the requirements, you must take the Web server, database server, and Merchant server into consideration. Overall, the Web server tends to be RAM and not CPU intensive due to its page caching features for optimization. The database server also tends to require more RAM resources due to caching as well. The Merchant server, in contrast, relies heavily on the CPU. Overall, the Merchant server will most likely become your first bottleneck as your traffic volume grows. A high performance database like Microsoft SQL Server only represents around 7 percent of the work done in a typical page request with the Web server following similar if not lower percentages (3–4%). The Merchant server, in contrast, provides all of the dynamic page generation and order processing computing and will make up the majority of work done to generate a page for the Web browser. As a result, you should begin with a fast CPU and consider carefully your expected traffic volumes.

In addition to the distribution of work between Web, database, and Merchant servers, the type of page request also affects performance. If the order processing components are invoked by either displaying a shopping basket or conducting the checkout and payment process, additional computing is required. In general, any time that prices are displayed, it is a good bet that you have invoked a more resource intensive process. With all this in mind, a general rule of thumb for concurrent transactions on the minimum configuration that we tested would complete 10 transactions before you begin to experience a slowdown. Remember, the service will not stop—just equally slow down for all users. Also remember that a concurrent transaction could represent 10 current shoppers since shoppers are not generating page requests at the same time.

Managing the Shopper's Experience

The Merchant server provides a comprehensive environment for tracking shoppers or users as they enter and move through the pages of a site. The process begins with the initial logon and continues through the browsing of product pages and eventual check out process. Within this shopping experience, the Merchant system will manage shopper information including their tracking ID, order basket information, payment information, and any additional information the site developers chose to gather.

Controlling the Shopper as They Enter the Site

The Merchant server can manage shoppers with several methods, but all require the shopper to be issued a Shopper ID as they begin using the site. The Merchant server generates this Shopper ID during a login process which can involve a shopper simply clicking a link or form button, or the login process can entail a shopper providing some additional information such as a password. The two distinguishing categories of shopper login management can be thought of as either a membership-based community or a guest community.

In the guest community, every time a shopper visits the site a new Shopper ID is generated. This removes the need for any form of validation or login process for the shopper but results in no ability for the site to track a repeat shopper from one visit to the next. While this is the simplest site setup, losing any ability to track shopper activity over time profoundly limits the ability to customize the environment for the shopper or to accumulate any effective demographic or tracking data on shopper activity.

In contrast to the guest community, a membership community allows the shopper to re-enter the site by using the same Shopper ID generated the first time they visited the Merchant site. This enables the Merchant site to customize the environment based on information previously provided by the shopper, as well as allowing the site to accumulate information on the activity of shoppers over multiple visits. The Merchant server provides two methods of managing the login to membership based. The first method involves a customized login process based on any information stored in the shopper's database record, while the second method is simply an enhanced version of the login process that supports the use of cookies. With the use of cookies, the Merchant server automatically writes a cookie to the shopper's browser both the first time a shopper logs in and upon any subsequent visit. When the shopper first requests a page from the site, the Merchant server automatically checks for the cookie and if it exists and matches a Shopper ID in the database, the shopper will be logged in and proceed directly to the logged in shopping area. If the cookie does not exist or the cookie does not match a record in the database, the user will be required to log in by creating a new Shopper ID. Alternatively, the shopper can provide additional information that will allow the Merchant server to match the additional information with a record in the shopper table. The login process is fundamental to the Merchant server since every Hyperlink or form processed contains a special URL which includes the Shopper ID.

▶ **See** "Invoking a Page, the PGEN or Action URL Syntax," **p. 369**, for more information about Merchant server's custom URL.

Developing the Shopping Environment

While Merchant server provides a series of sample stores that include comprehensive HTML/mark-up template files (pages) for managing a shopping environment, the shopping environment can be completely controlled. In contrast to the login process that is required by Merchant server, once the shopper has been issued a Shopper ID the site can have a virtually unlimited set of pages for the shopper to explore. In general, a shopping experience will have certain key features or pages beyond the login process, but this set of features simply provides an example of the types of features that are commonly implemented and in no way reflects any limitation of the Merchant server. General pages found in the most sample stores and most Merchant server sights following the login include:

- Home page displaying featured products, promotions, and information related to the site
- Search features ranging from drill-down browsing to keyword-based lookups focused around the theme of helping a shopper to find products
- Product lists and detail pages for providing information on products

Part
V

Ch
13

■ Shopping basket to display items that the shopper has selected during their visit at the site

■ Check out pages usually including a series of two to four linear pages for completing a sale, including collecting billing, shipping, and payment information

■ Other common pages include surveys/questionnaires, and private shopper areas providing personalized information such as order history

▶ **See** "Marking-Up Templates, the Source Code of Merchant," **p. 363**, for more a detailed look at what creating a custom Page entails.

Enabling and Extending Merchandising Features

With a general overview of the login and shopping environment, your focus should turn to the core of what Merchant server provides which is a stable transactional model for processing an order. Processing an order, however, does not just take place when a shopper checks out and provides payment. Every time a shopper views a price on a product or reviews their shopping basket, Merchant server calculates all applicable discounts and promotions. This type of order processing calculation makes possible cross-sells, up-sells, and price promotions that were cost prohibitive to custom implement for most merchants in the past. The built-in merchandising calculation engine offers merchants a mechanism to ensure that any time a shopper sees pricing information, the item will be in stock with the correct sale and price promotions calculated.

The standard features available in the Adventure Works and other sample stores shipped with Merchant include the ability to provide three primary features:

■ Cross-merchandising, or the relating of one product with another so that the other items can be spotlighted on the product page of the first and at other places in the site.

■ Up-sells providing technically the same feature as a cross-sell.

■ Price Promotions offer a rule-based approach to adding pricing discounts for shoppers based on a series of rules.

Price promotions offer the most powerful of the merchandising features which come pre-built in the Merchant server product; however, additional features can be quickly added to extend the flexibility of the promotions such as a free or discounted shipping or handling option.

Managing the Shopper's Order Basket

In the process of building the shopping environment, after the searching features and the ability to display product pages have been created, the site will require the ability to allow shoppers to select a product or service they want to purchase. Most shopping sites will want to allow that shopper to continue shopping after that point by saving the item in a shopping basket for future display or eventual checkout. Merchant provides a flexible and easy-to-use series of features for managing a shopper's basket of items.

Prior to Merchant server, the process of managing a shopper's selected items prior to checkout has meant adding a record to the database for every item or creatively storing the selections in hidden fields on the form pages or as cookies on the shopper's browser. All of these creative approaches had severe limitations. Merchant server utilizes a blob data field to track shopper information about pending orders, including product SKUs and related discount, billing, and shipping information. The Merchant server controls this blob data field in the shopper's record and refers to it as the "Blackboard." The Merchant server provides the developer with a series of Actions to easily manage this system stored information, as illustrated in Table 13.2.

Table 13.2   Actions for Managing Order Items

Action Name	Description
order.additem	Adds an item to the order by passing the action either a SKU or a query which returns a single SKU.
order.delitem	Deletes an item for the order.
order.edititem	Edits an existing item in the order basket.
order.editquantities	Edits the quantities selected in an order basket.
order.clearitems	Clears all items from the order basket.

Finalizing the Order and Accepting Payment

At some point after the shopper has used the shopping environment to review products or services and add items to their shopping basket, the shopper will want to check out and purchase the products they have selected. To finalize an order, the Merchant server must successfully move through all 14 steps of the order processing pipeline. The steps can include checks ranging from shipping, handling, and tax calculations to inventory lookups and the online authorization of a credit card. Regardless of which components are set up for use and which ones are ignored the shopper must successfully pass through all 14 steps completing the Accept stage of order processing.

▶ **See** "Controlling Transactional Order Processing," **p. 370**, for more information about order processing.

Part
V

Ch

13

Marking-Up Templates, the Source Code of Merchant

During the implementation of Merchant server, the initial process will be focused on the set up of the Windows NT Server and the configuring of your database server, but quickly the emphasis will turn to enhancement of sample store templates and the development of new templates.

An HTML/mark-up template (Template) is an HTML page with Merchant-specific tags included for the dynamic generation of HTML files. The process the Merchant Store Service undertakes when a user requests a page is similar to how many dynamic page generating programs work today.

When a shopper requests a page from the Merchant site, the Web server traps the request and relays it to the Merchant Store Service. If the shopper request is a PGEN (Page Generation) request, the Merchant Store Service reads the template file and strips out all the Merchant-specific tags. These Merchant-specific tags include Directives, Actions, and Value References. The Merchant Store Service then executes all the tags and inserts the resulting information into the template. If the request is an Action (XT) request, the merchant executes the action and then goes to the template specified in the Goto or Redirect parameter processing the Redirect or Goto as a PGEN request. In addition to the PGEN and XT Web browser requests, a special MAP request is used to allow Merchant to correctly process an image map and route to the appropriate Template for PGEN processing. Assuming no errors take place, the Merchant Store Service than sends the resulting HTML file to the Web server for delivery to the requesting Web browser.

These Templates define the functional operation of the site. Through invoking Directives, Actions, and Value References, the Templates embody the business logic of the Merchant site. Templates provide the executable source code, allowing the Merchant site to interact with the database and the shopper. To set up a Merchant site, a programmer must adapt and extend the sample store templates upon which the site bases itself. Only through customizing Templates can the custom Merchant store be created.

Directives, Actions, and Value References make up the complete mark-up language of the Merchant server. In understanding how to use this mark-up language, a basic working knowledge of HTML is assumed. The mark-up language builds upon and cooperates with HTML programming. In general, whenever a tag in a Template begins with a square bracket, it is either an Action, Directive, or Value Reference, or some combination of an Action, Directive, or Value Reference. The remainder of this section provides an overview of each of these categories and illustrates briefly how these features can be used in a Template.

CAUTION

The information contained in this section is not meant to be an all-inclusive discussion of each of these features. You should refer to the Merchant Server Documentation if you are implementing Merchant Server and want a more through discussion of a particular Directive, Action, or Value Reference, or to see a complete list of the Directives, Actions, and Value References.

CAUTION

Because Merchant server evolved from Eshop's UNIX-based product, many areas of the product are case-sensitive; be careful with the use of case in programming templates.

Using Directives to Generate HTML

Directives provide commands to the Page Generator which range from running a query on the database to simply telling the Page Generator to insert a value at a particular place in the Template. The key directives include:

- Outputting of formatted values
- Running and outputting queries
- Generating hyperlinks and forms
- Conditional processing

The Merchant server provides extensive features for outputting values in particular formats from dates to money. While Value References further enhance the ability to format and manage values being output in cooperation with Directives, the Directive is responsible for actually outputting the information on a page. A list of specific commonly used Directives for outputting information is illustrated in Table 13.3.

Table 13.3   Commonly Used Directives for Outputting Information

Directive	Sample Code	Description
Value	`[value "value to output"]`	A simple value.
Time	`[time "9:30 PM"]`	A time-formatted value.
Date	`[date "11/11/97"]`	A date-formatted value.
Money	`[money "100089"]`	A money-formatted value.
Include	`[include "filetoinclude.htm"]`	Includes a Template/file, similar to IIS' Server Side Include feature.

Probably the most important Directives for managing the Merchant shopping experience revolve around accessing the database. Since the ODBC datasource is registered with the Merchant Store Service and a connection to the database is established when the Merchant Store Service starts, the process of initiating a query to the database becomes very straightforward. The one important distinction between Merchant and many other database-oriented Web products is that in the Templates you never directly reference a stored procedure or SQL statement. All queries that run against the database are stored in a database table. The table simply stores a unique name for the query which gets referenced by the Directive and then a second field for the SQL statement or stored procedure. A list of commonly used Directives for running queries is illustrated in Table 13.4.

Part

V

Ch

13

Table 13.4 Commonly Used Directives for Accessing the Database

Directive	Sample Code	Description
SQL	`[sql queryname parameter1` `...parameterN]`	Executes queries but does not return any values.
Fetchrows	`[fetchrows nameforuse` `queryname parameter1` `...paramterN]`	Executes query and returns `value` which can be referenced by the `nameforuse` value with the `eachrow` Directive.
FetchProduct	`[fetchproduct` `nameforuse skuvalue]`	Returns a specific product and invokes the query specified in the registry for products since this query gets automatically invoked in the order process.

The generating of Hyperlinks and Forms becomes a Directive that appears in almost every Template. Merchant server must create all Hyperlinks and Form tags so it can include the custom information such as Shopper ID. A detailed example of the generated URL created in Hyperlinks and Form tags will be covered later in this chapter in "Invoking a Page, the PGEN or Action URL Syntax." Specific examples of the commonly used Directives for generating Hyperlinks and Form tags are illustrated in Table 17.5.

Table 13.5 Commonly Used Directives for Generating Hyperlinks and Form Tags

Directive	Sample Code	Description
Link	`[link pagename.htm` `valuename1=value1` `...valuenameN=valueN]`	Display Value Hyperlink [/link] creator
Form	`[form pagename.htm` `valuename1=value1` `...valuenameN=valueN]` `Form Display Values [/form]`	Form tag creator

Conditional processing probably provides the Directives that a programmer will most actively be using to manage the display of the Templates being created. While Merchant server provides some of the most basic conditional processing syntax, developers familiar with more mature languages such as C++ or Visual Basic may be disappointed with the lack of certain features including `For/Next` Looping and `Select Case` statements. However, in spite of the limited language, the syntax provides most of the conditional processing you would expect in a Web-based environment. Before you make your determination about the flexibility of the language, be sure to review the features offered by combining Directives and Value References discussed following this discussion of Directives. Some commonly used conditional processing Directives are illustrated in Table 13.6.

Table 13.6   Commonly Used Conditional Processing Directives

Directive	Sample Code	Description
If Else If	`[if value operator value2] do something [else] do something else [/if]`	Standard `if` `then` processing.
Let	`[let variablename value]`	Assign a value to a variable for use within the scope of current page.

Managing Output of Information with Value References

Value References work in conjunction with Directives to manage information—both output on a page and also as input to Directives and Actions that invoke the database. Value References provide a variety of functions with a special emphasis on managing numbers or money. The list of Value References is illustrated in Table 13.7.

Table 13.7   Commonly Used Value References

Value Reference	Sample Code	Description
concat()	`[value concat(value1, value2, valueN)]`	Concatenates values provided returning a single string.
len()	`[value len("supercalifragilistic expealidocious")]`	Returns the length of the string value provided.
random()	`[value random(100)]`	Returns a number between 1 and the value passed in.
var.name	`[value var.name]`	Resolves a variable value previously set with the Let Directive.
add()	`[value add(value1, valueN)]`	Adds values returning a single value.
mul()	`[value mul(value1, valueN)]`	Multiplies values returning a single value.

Part

V

Ch

13

Inserting, Deleting, and Modifying Database Information with Actions

Actions get invoked by a Hyperlink or Form tag processing an operation similar to named function calls. All Actions focus on inserting, deleting, or modifying information in the database. In addition to the Actions provided with Merchant, you can set up your own custom named Actions as necessary to extend this type of processing. Actions operate in several key areas where the Merchant system provides Actions to ensure the integrity of the database steps that are to be performed. The categories of Actions available include:

- Shopper login and maintenance activities
- Order processing related activities
- Store administration activities
- Custom named Actions created for the site

The key shopper-related Actions include the creation of new Shopper ID or shopper record, the lookup of an existing shopper, or the maintenance of shopper information. In a guest-based community, the primary Action will only be the `shopper.guest` Action since generally no information is maintained and no return shoppers are retrieved. In this case the `shopper.guest` Action is used strictly to continually generate Shopper IDs for shoppers as they enter the site. In contrast, in a membership based community the `shopper.lookup` Action is commonly invoked to retrieve a shoppers information and ID for them to begin shopping. In addition, membership communities will often track additional information through surveys and membership sign ups which will invoke the `shopper.updateshopper` Action.

▶ **See** "Controlling the Shopper as They Enter the Site," **p. 360**

The code used to invoke the shopper Actions will exist as part of a Hyperlink of From tag Directive and take this form:

```
To begin shopping, click [xlink shopper.guest] Enter the Store [/xlink]
```

When the Template generates the page with the code previously displayed, a Hyperlink will be created with a properly formatted URL invoking the `shopper.guest` Action.

Order processing activities also heavily rely on Actions for managing both the order basket of a shopper and the information collection associated with the checkout process. The Actions associated the order process include: `order.additem`, `order.clearform`, `order.clearitems`, `order.delitem`, `order.deleteorder`, `order.edititem`, `order.editquantities`, `order.editorder`, `order.plan`, and `order.purchase`. These actions provide the stable mechanism for managing items in the shopper's basket. The `order.plan` and `order.purchase` steps go beyond the managing of a shopper's order basket and take the shopper through additional steps in the order process. The `order.plan` moves through all the order process steps prior to payment and accept while the `order.purchase` attempts to finalize the order.

▶ **See** "Finalizing the Order and Accepting Payment," **p.363**

▶ **See** "Controlling the Shopper as They Enter the Site," **p. 360**, for order process detail.

Store administration begins a discussion of an area of Merchant server functionality we have not discussed at this point. Similar to all the features that have been discussed in the management of shoppers and the shopping environment, the Merchant server provides an administrative environment where all the Directives, Actions, and Value References can be used to create an administrative environment for managing a store, including all the database information related to shoppers, purchases, and other data stored in the database. In order to further ensure security in these environments that can enable the editing of shopper information and product prices, administrative Actions have been provided which validate security as part of their process of updating the database. The administrative Actions include `admin.delete`, `admin.insert`, `admin.sql`, and `admin.update`. As the descriptions imply, these Actions provide record, delete, insert, update, and general SQL execution. These Actions have unrestricted access to the database and must be invoked by a user logged in to the administrative area.

▶ **See** "Administering a Single Merchant Store Environment," **p. 377**, for additional information on the administrative area.

Custom named Actions can be created in the Registry and allow the invoking of update, delete, and insert activities from within shopper pages. These Actions are similar to the administrative actions except that they have certain security restrictions in which parts of the database they can delete, insert, or update records.

Invoking a Page, the PGEN or Action URL Syntax

When a Directive creates a Hyperlink or Form tag, a specific set of information is included in the URL to provide information to both the Web server and the Merchant Store Service. The specific components are described in Table 13.8. The URL is illustrated in Figure 13.1.

Table 13.8   Components of a Merchant URL

Componet	Example	Description
Server Name	http://www.server.com/	General Web site address.
Environment	prd	Tag used to invoke the Router or ISAPI filter on the Web server.
Type of Store	i	Insecure or Process secure process defining whether to invoke SSL key.
Type of URL	pgen	Defining Page Generator (pgen) in contrast to Action (xt) or Map Manager (map).
Store Name	clockped	Name of store being referenced.
Shopper ID	JFN...NX	Unique shopper ID 0L for initial guest shopper and 1L for administrative user.
Template Name	dept.html	Actual Template file invoked.
Arguments	;dept_id=1	Optional arguments to pass into the dept.html page.

FIG. 13.1

Specific components of a Merchant URL, created by a Directive.

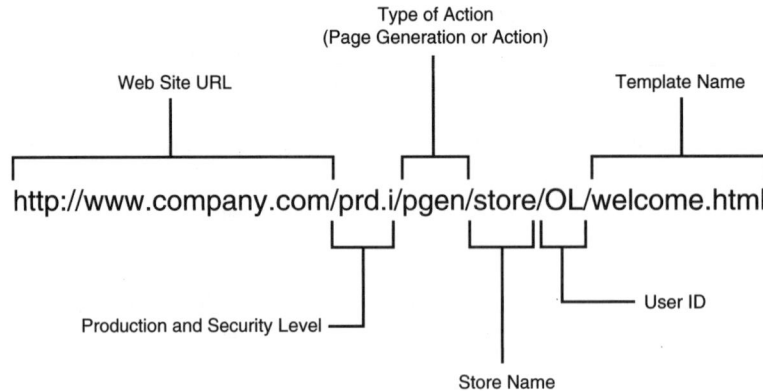

Controlling Transactional Order Processing

Order related Actions and Directives invoke the transactional order processing pipeline. The pipeline involves a series of 14 processing steps, as illustrated in Figure 13.2. At each step the components or API calls set up in the registry for that step will be invoked. The component invoked could range from an update query to decrement inventory levels in the accept step or the processing of a credit card authorization over the Internet through your merchant bank's Internet gateway in the payment step. Regardless of what activity gets performed, all steps must successfully completed prior to an order being approved.

Methods for using the 14-step pipeline fall into three major categories including: Merchant Server built-in functions, Commercially sold Merchant plug-in products, and any custom components you may create for use during the component step.

Understanding the Built-In Order Processing Functions

Merchant server built-in functions or optional functions for use during the order processing pipeline include a range of features from the copying of data to the providing simple tax calculations. While certain required validations also occur during the pipeline processing, the built-in functions illustrated in Table 13.9 are all optional components which the site developer specifies in the registry.

Table 13.9   Built-In Functions for the Purchasing Components

Name	Pipeline Step	Description
CopyData	Order Initialization	Copies information onto the blackboard for use in the order processing.
SetData	Order Initialization	Sets variables or name/value pairs to a value in the blackboard.
OrderValidate	Order Check	Checks a validation string defined in the registry against the order.

Name	Pipeline Step	Description
OrderItemValidate	Order Check	Checks a validation string defined in the registry against each item.
SaleAdjust	Item Price Adjust	Updates item price information in an order when a sale has been set up based on checking the two sale-related date values and the sale price.
ItemPromo	Item Price Adjust	Implements an item price adjustment based on registry setting.
DBOrderPromo	Order Price Adjust	Implements price promotions based on database values.
FixedShipping	Shipping	Calculates a fixed amount for shipping charges.
LinearShipping	Shipping	Calculates shipping based on multiplying a factor to a field-like quantity.
TableShipping	Shipping	Calculates shipping based on a query lookup in the database.
SimpleUSTax	Tax	Calculates tax obligation based on a registry-based list of states and their associated tax rate.
FlagInventory	Inventory	Just checks inventory to ensure non-zero value field.
LocalInventory	Inventory	Checks inventory prior to the use of the ReduceLocalInventory function.
ReduceLocalInventory	Accept	Decrements inventory by quantity of a SKU purchased.
SaveOrderToDb	Accept	Saves information about the order to the database for tracking.

Utilizing Third-Party Components for Extending the Process

Commercial software vendors released a series of products that install themselves directly into the Merchant server order process and enable extended functionality for controlling the order process. As this market of products continues to expand, the capabilities of the Merchant server will expand as well. We tested the Beta release of CyberCash's payment product and the commercial release of Verifone's product for authorizing credit cards and found both products to be relatively easy to install and operate. Both products contain Web-based administrative features for conducting authorizations, credits, and reporting. The plug-ins provide a cost effective way of rapidly extending the power of the Merchant product. Table 13.10 illustrates the commercial products either released or slated for release.

FIG. 13.2

The following illustrates the sequential order of the 14-step order processing pipeline.

14 Step
Order Processing
Pipeline

| Product Information |
| Merchant Information |
| Shopper Information |
| Order Initialization |
| Order Check |
| Item From Adjust |
| Order Price Adjust |
| Shipping |
| Handling |
| Tax |
| Order Total |
| Inventory |
| Payment |
| Accept |

Table 13.10   Merchant Third-Party Vendors

Company	Web Site	Category
CyberCash	http://www.cybercash.com/cybercash/merchants/	Payment
CyberCharge	http://www.cybercharge.com	Payment
Events Software	http://www.eventssoftware.com	Customer Service
Intactix International	http://www.intactix.com/eleccomm.html	Consumer Service
SAP's R/3	http://www.sap.com	Accounting Hook
Sterling Commerce	http://www.sterling.gentran.com/product.2/servernt.htm	Messaging/EDI

Company	Web Site	Category
T4G	**http://www.t4g.com/ productsframeset.htm**	Point of Service Application for integrating Retail system
TanData	**http://www.tandata.com/ products/index.html**	Shipping and Handling
TAXWARE Int.	**http://www.taxware.com**	Tax
Tellan Software	**http://www.tellan.com/ msmerchant.html**	Payment
Trintech	**http://ireland.iol.ie/~trintech**	Payment
Verifone	**http://www.verifone.com**	Payment
Vertex	**http://www.vertexinc.com**	Tax

Building Your Own Custom Components

In addition to the built-in Merchant functions and the third-party Merchant plug-ins available, developers can quickly build DLLs in the C programming language to enhance the functionality of the Merchant server order processing pipeline. To support this development, Merchant server has a series of API calls that allow the custom program to interact with the Merchant Store Service to read in information and write back information to the blackboard. The nine API calls provide a range of features from requesting the total number of items in the order to setting the Merchant server error condition of the order. For a detailed discussion of building custom components as well as a sample program see the Microsoft Merchant documentation installed with Merchant installed by default into the directory c:/msmerchant/docs/html/odpr24.htm.

Administering the Merchant Server Implementation

Administration of the Merchant server implementation involves a combination of using the Merchant server's graphical administration utility and registry settings in the Merchant server registry key. As the Merchant server administration utility continues to evolve, the site administrator will have to turn to the registry less and less. But currently, many of the basic settings required to configure a Merchant server store still require the site administrator to directly modify the registry; as a result, we will briefly review both the registry settings and the current capabilities of the Merchant administration utility. In addition to the administration utility and registry, the Merchant server allows the creation of a Web-based administration environment focused on modifying database related settings and information for a particular store. The directory structure displayed provides the storage area for images and template files.

Part

V

Ch

13

Working with the Merchant Server Administration Utility

The Merchant server administration utility (utility) is illustrated in Figure 13.3; it allows a series of features including but not limited to the restarting of the Merchant Store Service, the setting of debugging and caching parameters, and adding of a new store automatically.

Figure 13.3 illustrates the default tab utility providing the ability to synchronize the registry settings of a site which might span multiple computers, as well as the ability to restart both the Router or Web server and the Merchant Store Service automatically. This capability will be important during the testing stage of the site development but will hopefully not need to be used during the normal operation of the Merchant site. Two additional areas of the utility that we will explore include the Environment tab and the Add Store tab.

FIG. 13.3

Administration utility provides a range of features for managing the Merchant site.

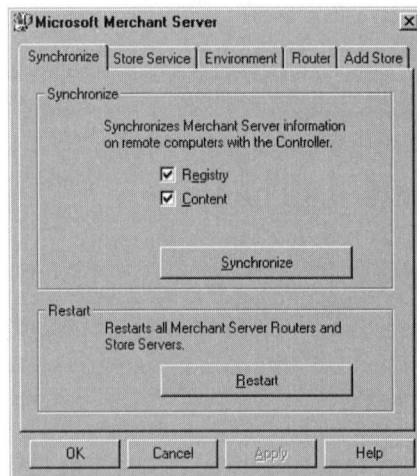

Automatically adding a new store involves the creation of a custom registry key, a series of database tables, and a custom directory tree with source code and images. The automatic adding of a new store feature, illustrated in Figure 13.4, provides a mechanism for creating all of these areas based on an existing sample store or any store that you have previously created. As displayed in Figure 13.4, you create a name for the store, a store to base your new store upon, and the selected areas to create including the registry settings, database tables, and templates/directories. This process will rename all registry settings, database tables, and files based on your new store name automatically.

The features provided with the Environment tab include the ability to set primarily the caching and debugging features of the site as illustrated in Figure 13.5. These features are interrelated and through effective utilization can significantly improve site performance both during the development phase as well as the production phase of the site. The specific check box settings include:

- Debug All Stores
- Cache Pages on Disk
- Cache Pages in Memory
- Verify Pages Are Up-to-Date

FIG. 13.4

The Add Store feature of the Merchant server utility allows the creation of a store based on any other installed store.

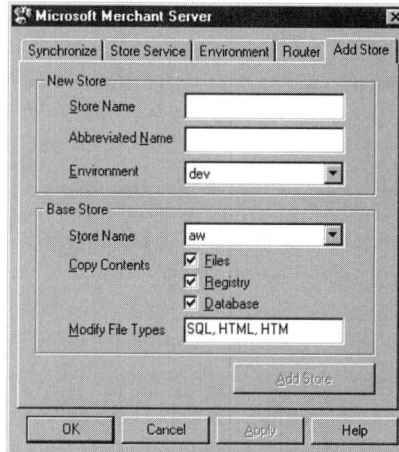

FIG. 13.5

The Environment tab of the Merchant server utility allows the setting of caching and debugging features for the Merchant site.

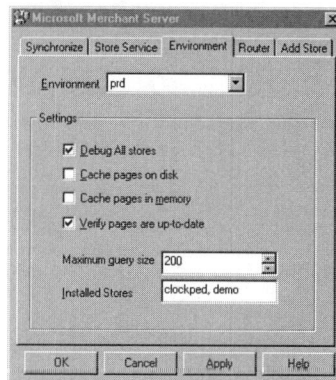

The Debug and Verify Pages options provide a key support during the development phase and should usually both be turned off during the production phase. The Caching options play a key role in the production phase but should probably both be turned off during development. The Debug feature provides comprehensive logging of Merchant Store Service activity especially related to the order process in a file designated in the root of the MSMerchant registry key under the key for log file. The Verify Pages feature forces the Merchant Store Service to evaluate the date of a file before relying on any cached information.

Part
V

Ch
13

N O T E The registry key for Merchant settings is contained under the Local Machine/Software/ Microsoft/MSMerchant. ▓

The Caching features will allow the Merchant Store Service to retain frequently request pages in their resulting HTML state either in RAM or on the hard drive. Caching files on disk will actually prompt the Merchant to write files with modified names for use on frequently requested pages.

T I P When caching files to disk, be aware that Merchant doesn't always clean up after itself and you may want to periodically review the directory when the Merchant is down to clean up the specially numbered files.

Controlling the Server through Registry Settings

The registry settings control every aspect of the Merchant Store Service and in general the Merchant site. Information stored in the registry ranges from the user name and password for connecting to the database to the file locations of all templates used. While many of these settings are configured during the installation process and subsequently maintained by the administrative utility, creating a Merchant site requires a minimum of work in the registry. The overall registry keys are illustrated in Figure 13.6.

FIG. 13.6

The registry enables the management of all settings related to the Merchant site.

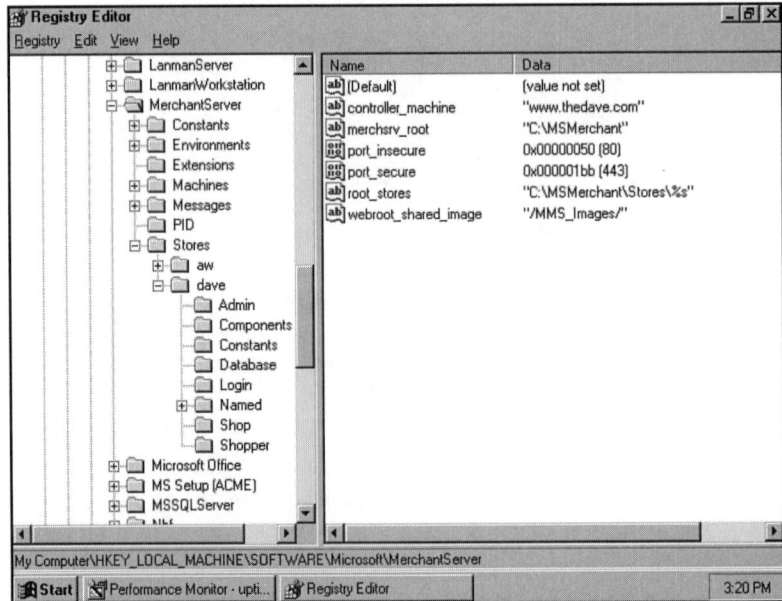

Understanding the Merchant Server Directory Structures

The Merchant server creates a series of directories for managing the images and templates in use with the Merchant server. These directories separate shared templates and images as well as separating the directories used during logon, shopping, and administrative sessions. The general directory breakout illustrated in Figure 13.7 shows the `images` directory for storing site graphics as well as the `login`, `shop`, and `admin` directories for storing templates related to those areas of functionality.

FIG. 13.7
The directory structure displayed provides the storage area for images and template files.

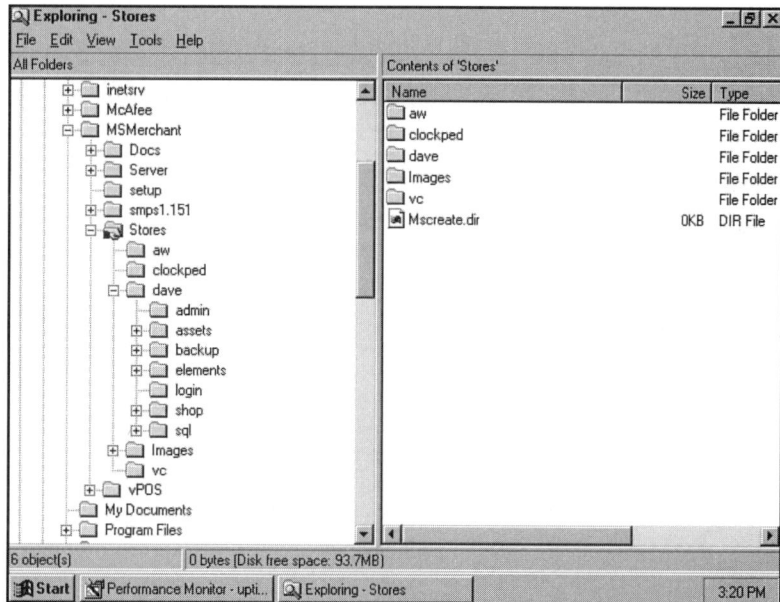

Administering a Single Merchant Store Environment

Part V
Ch 13

One aspect of administrating a Merchant store that differs from the methods discussed in the previous section, "Administering a Single Merchant Store Environment," is the Web-based administrative capabilities that can be adapted from the sample stores and enhanced. This form of administration focuses on managing information in the database. At first glance, only being able to manage the database appears as a limited area, but actually the database stores the heart of all information related to Merchant server. The key types of information maintained in the database that sample stores administer includes:

- Product SKU information
- SQL statements
- Shopper information (primarily in membership communities)
- Order information
- Traffic information

With access to all the above tables of information, an administrator has access to a full-featured environment for managing a store. Shopper information allows the resetting of passwords or general reporting. Product information provides the ability to maintain inventory and pricing information. SQL statements are at the heart of the entire site and in combination with an FTP account to alter Templates, this information can allow a developer to modify the core functionality of the site. Order and traffic information provide a vehicle for reporting and order fulfillment processing. One example of a use for the Shopper and Order information would be to build a complete Web-based customer service system for users of the site.

Benefitting from Selecting Merchant Server

Merchant server provides a series of benefits to the developer attempting to implement an Internet-based Electronic Commerce solution. In exploring the key value Merchant adds to the process we have highlighted a short list of key benefits including:

- Providing the right cost/benefit equation: MMS = extensive features + low cost
- Delivering a scaleable solution
- Driving a flexible upgrade path
- Implementing a robust order processing engine
- Opening a third party software market to rapidly extend store capabilities

When evaluating the cost/benefit proposition of options in building Web-based Electronic Commerce environment you can select from a series of development platforms for creating a custom site or you can choose from a growing set of vendors providing a partially developed solution for you to enhance and customize. Microsoft Merchant Server provides an expanding and flexible set of features with an open architecture for creating new features, but at the same time, the implementation costs are well below either a custom effort or the costs of any vendor solution with even close to the same feature set. In short, Microsoft's Merchant Server represents the beginning of what will become a maturing market for Electronic Commerce software tools.

Microsoft Merchant Server provides a scalable and flexible expansion path for sites with large expected volumes or just unpredictable volume levels. Merchant server allows the site manager to distribute the Merchant Store Services across multiple computers or have the Merchant Store Service manage the site as multiple stores, each with their own pipe to the database server. This easy centrally managed distribution of services provides a scalable environment for any site manager. In addition, the commercial products and Microsoft's commitment to the platform ensures a continued upgrade path for sites developed in this platform.

One of the key aspects to any Electronic Commerce platform is the stability of the transaction processing approach. Microsoft Merchant Server's 14-step order processing pipeline provides a robust order processing mechanism that gives the site developer granular control of the error handling and steps of the order processing engine. The stability and flexibility of the order processing pipeline is further enhanced by the ability to plug-in commercially available third party products. These products provide robust and flexible components from the calculation of shipping and tax to the processing of an online credit card authorization.

From Here...

From this overview of Microsoft Merchant Server and its capabilities, you now turn to the specifics of building a Microsoft Merchant based store in Chapter 14, "Building a Merchant System." You focus on implementing the concepts discussed in this chapter in a more hands-on fashion. Chapter 14 explores source code and specific registry configurations associated with the setup of a Merchant store and provide a more working illustration of how to apply Merchant server to your situation.

For additional discussions of some of the topics covered in this chapter, try:

- Chapter 3, "Building The Foundation," which provides a more detailed discussion about Windows NT and the Internet Information Server.
- Chapter 14, "Building a Merchant System," which provides a review of the entire setup process.
- Chapter 19, "Interpreting Logfiles and Monitoring Server Performance," which provides a discussion of monitoring issues for NT services.
- Appendix A, "Hardware Requirements," a further discussion of the hardware configuration issues brought up in this chapter.

Building a Merchant System

The process of bringing a Merchant server up—like with any complex application—will vary largely based on the features defined and the resulting complexity. A store can be a straightforward knock-off of one of the sample stores, requiring only a small amount of customization to replace graphics and text messages, or it can be a large scale development effort requiring a team of ten developers. The implementation discussed in the following example will be a straightforward knock-off of the Clock Peddler sample store. This chapter highlights areas where additional features might commonly be added but overall this will represent the simplest of implementations. ∎

Designing your store environment

The design process in Merchant Server is as important as in any application development effort and perhaps more important due to the diversity of interrelated services that must properly operate together.

Installing all the necessary software

Properly installing the software can save a large amount of time in the early debugging stages; this process generally moves so smoothly it seems trivial, or it becomes a nightmare.

Creating your customized store environment

After designing your store, properly installing all of the software, and exploring the sample stores, the task of building your own store should be a straightforward development process.

Testing and debugging your store

The final hurdle in bringing your store into production is undertaking a sufficiently thorough testing phase. This process can avoid a lot of firefighting repair efforts during the first weeks of production.

Designing Your Store

The design process, a Web-based Electronic Commerce environment, centers around the features that must be enabled in the site. The process should start from understanding the database structure and shoppers' environment (user interface). These two areas provide the central development areas for the implementation of a site. Following these areas, the order processing issues from payment to order fulfillment must be defined.

With the Merchant server product, these steps have been organized into the following process including:

1. Selecting the shopper logon model, or the aspect of the user interface relating to how a shopper enters the site, has implications for the amount of tracking and custom features you can provide. The tracking and customization capabilities available primarily depend on whether you invoke a guest- or membership-based model.

2. Designing the database record layouts involves adapting and setting up the information needed about your product or service, as well as the information tracked on the shopper and order.

3. Identifying merchandising, tracking, and reporting requirements relates also to the database layout but primarily focuses on the shopping environment and order process. Clearly understanding these requirements will determine how you handle order processing and the user interface.

4. Defining order processing components stems from understanding your product and merchandising requirements but goes beyond this in establishing payment mechanisms, tax policies, shipping calculations, handling charges, and inventory management.

5. The final design step prior to development is selecting the sample store that most closely fits the requirements you have established during the design phases. It is not possible to overemphasize the importance of correctly fitting your requirements to a sample store; this step will dramatically have an impact on the amount of development time involved in completing your site.

Defining Hardware Configuration Based on Expected Traffic

This area has been covered thoroughly up to this point but requires a brief reference due to the importance of this initial step. While the Merchant can be effectively scaled over time, you should evaluate the required resources up front based on your best guess of volume requirements. For additional information on this area visit Chapter 3, "Building the Foundation."

▶ **See** "Configuring the Right Hardware Environment," **p. 359**

This implementation relies on a Pentium 133 with 64M RAM and a 1G hard drive. The software is Microsoft Windows NT Server version 4.0, Internet Information Server version 3.0, Merchant Server version 1.0, and SQL Server version 6.5.

Selecting Shopper Logon Model

The primary shopper logon model selections include guest- and membership-based communities, with membership-based communities providing additional choices. If you select a membership community you can utilize the cookie features in Merchant and also determine an additional logon model requiring any unique logon value from an e-mail address to password.

This implementation uses a guest community, meaning that every shopper using the site is new and unique. It sacrifices tracking the shopper over time for the convenience value of not requiring the shopper to undergo any type of logon process.

N O T E   With cookies, in a membership-based community, if the shopper allows the cookie and maintains the same Web browser, the site can also bypass the logon process through Merchant server's ability to automatically log in cookied browsers. ■

Designing Database Record Layouts

The database layout design issues focus around what values must be added to the existing values found in the data structure of your selected sample store. Since Merchant server is database schema independent, the range of tables and features that can be involved in this stage can vary widely.

For this implementation, based on The Clock Peddler sample store, we will review their database schema, which includes five tables. This is the simplest of layouts and should serve as a starting point in the development of a Merchant site. The five core tables and their role is illustrated in Table 14.1. For this implementation, you do not need to change anything in the table structure provided by The Clock Peddler store.

Table 14.1   Five Tables Drive the Implementation of Merchant Discussed Here

Table Name	Description
basket	Manages order baskets
shopper	Manages shopper information, primarily IDs
product	Contains all product-related information
dept	Contains departments or categories of products
sql	Stores all named queries used by the site

Part
V

Ch
14

The simple record layout for The Clock Peddler store is illustrated by Figure 14.1. Importantly, much more complex database record layouts can be developed but are not necessary to implement a Merchant site.

FIG. 14.1

These are all the tables of a basic Merchant store.

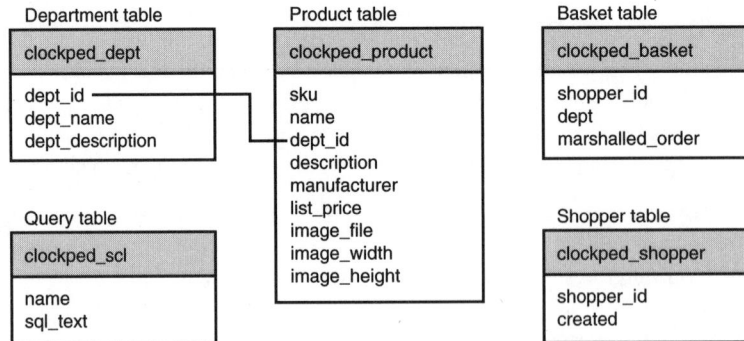

Department table
clockped_dept
dept_id
dept_name
dept_description

Product table
clockped_product
sku
name
dept_id
description
manufacturer
list_price
image_file
image_width
image_height

Basket table
clockped_basket
shopper_id
dept
marshalled_order

Query table
clockped_scl
name
sql_text

Shopper table
clockped_shopper
shopper_id
created

Identifying Merchandising, Tracking, and Reporting Requirements

Several of the sample stores come with extensive merchandising, tracking, and reporting features integrating into them. The Clock Peddler does not provide any merchandising, tracking, or reporting features. Each of these areas offers important features for the development of a comprehensive site and some of the features in other sample stores merit a brief review.

N O T E Internet Information Server provides comprehensive logging features and may also have reporting tools developed for your site. The tracking and reporting discussed here is Merchant-specific. ▪

The key merchandising features available for review in the Adventure Works sample store include: sales pricing, new product introduction, cross-sell, and price promotions. For any promotion, three steps are undertaken:

1. Information to track the promotion or merchandising features is incorporated into the database.
2. Code is added into Template files to enable the display of the particular promotion.
3. An order process component is modified if the promotion impacts the price charge on an item or order.

To enable the sale or new product introduction, four fields are added to the product table. For the sale, a price field, date begin, and date end field are stored; these fields are used to decide whether to invoke the sale price based on system date. For the new product promotion, a simple date is added to show the introduction date; the logic for what is new is set in the Template that determines whether to display the information.

Cross-sells required an entirely new table which simply relates one product to another product. This table is then queried on a product page or other place in the shopping environment to determine how and in what way to promote the cross-sell. This feature does not impact pricing and as a result does not affect the order processing component.

The final merchandising feature is the price promotion which provides a new table to track the rule-based promotions and then implements an order price adjust stage function to calculate the price promotion impact. The rule-based administrative screen which manages this table is illustrated from the Adventure Works store in Figure 14.2. The information captured included an active flag, ranking, and date range to determine if the promotion is active, followed by specific criteria evaluated with each shopper's order. The criteria include what shoppers are included, what the shopper has to purchase, what products the discount applies to, and what they get if they qualify.

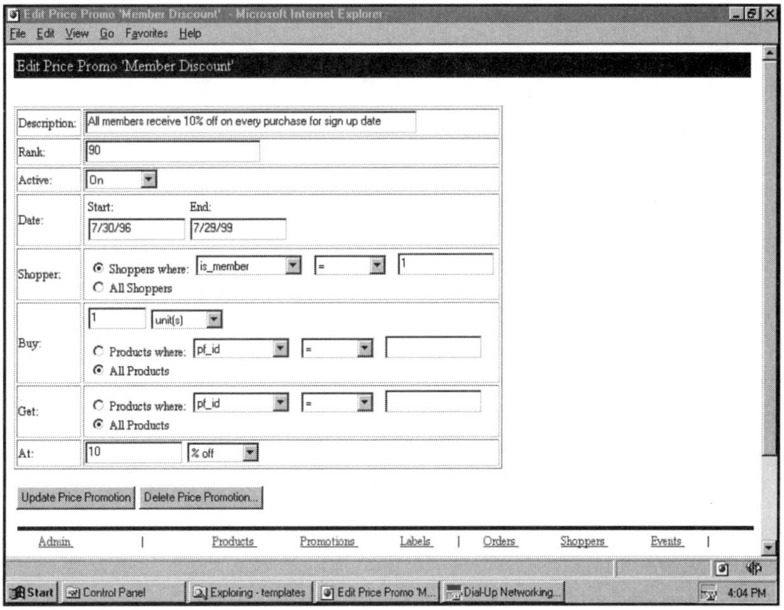

FIG. 14.2

The Web-based form allows the setup and maintenance of price promotions in the Adventure Works store.

Defining Order-Processing Components

The primary task in defining the order-processing requirements involves determining whether any third-party or custom components are required and then setting the required options and Merchant functions for completing an order. For this implementation, you invoke functions only on four stages of the order-processing pipeline. As illustrated in Registry settings in Figure 14.3, only the order initialization, shipping, and tax have function calls invoked.

In the order initialization stage, you copy billing and shipping information collected from the shopper's form into the blackboard for use in calculating tax later in the process. In the shipping stage, you calculate a fixed shipping amount followed by a simple tax calculation with the built-in simple tax function. The tax calculation applies a percentage based on shipping state information provided by the shopper. For bringing the store online, you would also want to save completed orders in the accept stage by adding a built-in function call.

Part
V

Ch
14

FIG. 14.3

The Registry illustrates the settings for the order-processing stages.

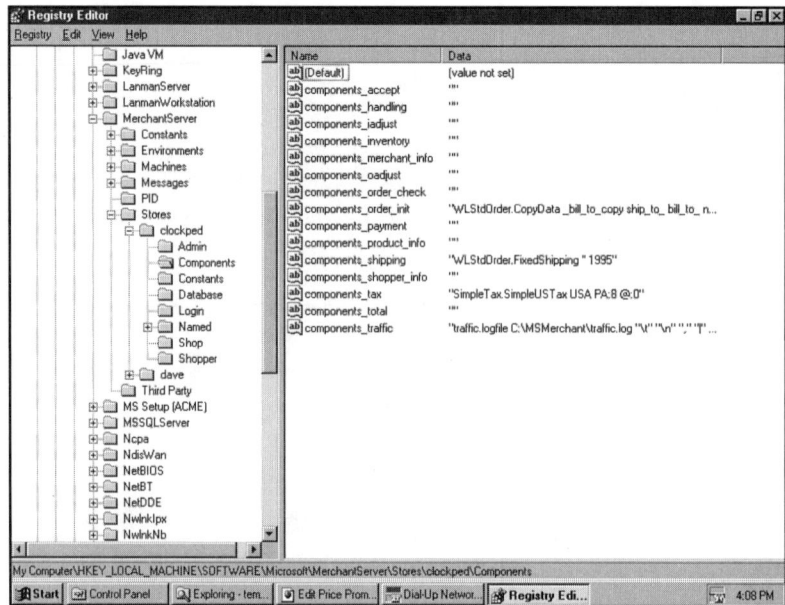

Selecting a Sample Store Template

This implementation selects The Clock Peddler store, but we have briefly reviewed the promotion features of the Adventure Works store which also has a membership-based community model for login. For your implementation, a thorough review of all sample stores should be undertaken prior to completing the design phase and beginning development.

Installing the Required Software Services

Installing the software to bring your Merchant site up requires a thorough understanding of Microsoft Windows NT Server, your database server, and Microsoft Internet Information Server. Understanding of these products is taken for granted at this stage. The following is a brief overview of how these products relate to each other for the purpose of setting up Microsoft Merchant Server software.

Running Windows NT Server and Internet Information Server

Prior to installing Merchant, Microsoft Windows NT Server with IIS should be properly installed and up and running. This step must precede the installation of the Merchant software. Test this by using a Web browser to visit your machine name and ensure that it is in fact serving up Web pages. If your Web server is up and running, you should be ready for configuring your database server and then installing Microsoft Merchant Server.

Implementing the ODBC-Compliant Database (Microsoft SQL Server)

For this implementation, Microsoft SQL Server 6.5 must be installed and properly running. In addition, ensure that a database device and database have been created with sufficient space to store the sample store tables loaded during the installation of Microsoft Merchant Server. The space necessary depends on your intended use of the SQL server; remember that with traffic-logging features, this database can grow quite quickly. For simple testing, allocate 100M to be safe.

> **N O T E** If you don't have a database up and running, you can still install the Merchant software and skip database installation. The SQL scripts for generating the sample store schema and populating the database will be stored in the directory placed by default in **c:\msmerchant\stores\%storename%\sql**. ▨

> **T I P** By default, Microsoft SQL allocates a very small amount of space for the TempDB stored in the Master database. Increase the size of this database table to 8 or 16M if you have any troubles during the installation process. You need at least 6M to run Merchant Server.

Be sure to provide sufficient SQL server security permissions to the user ID you will use for installing Merchant. You should set up an ID that you intend to allow the store to use moving forward since it will default this user name and password from the installation into your registry settings for logon. Insufficient security permissions is a common cause for failure during the database portion of the Merchant setup.

Installing Microsoft Merchant Server

The actual installation of Microsoft Merchant Server should be very clean, assuming the database and Web server are properly configured and ready. During the installation process the Merchant server will conduct the following steps:

1. Create a directory (**c:\msmerchant**) with the source code for all the sample stores.
2. Create all the registry settings (**localmachine/software/microsoft/msmerchant/**) to operate the sample stores.
3. Load its documentation in the directory and create a logical path on your Web server to reach the documentation (**/mms_docs/**).
4. Install the ISAPI filter DLL and register it in the IIS registry.
5. Install ODBC if necessary and install the Merchant administrative utility.
6. Create the sample store database tables in the database and populate the tables with data.

Part
V

Ch
14

Testing and Debugging the Default Installation

Once all of the software has been installed without error, you should be able to access the Merchant server directly by one of the structure URLs used. As a first step, open the Merchant administrative utility by selecting the Start button, Programs, Microsoft Merchant Server, Merchant Server Administrator. On the Store Service tab and the Router tab you should see the status as Running. If both these are running, then try a sample store's URL, which you can find buried in the documentation. An example URL which should work would follow the form:

```
http://computername/prd.i/pgen/storename/0L/welcome.html
```

The most common problem faced in bringing up a store is that the Store Service won't stay running when you start it, nothing works, and it eventually stops. Nine times out of ten this stems from a database connectivity problem. Open the Event Viewer found under Start, Programs, Administrative Tools, Event Viewer. If you see *unable to logon* messages anywhere, immediately turn to the permissions for the user ID being used to log on. You can check the user being invoked by reviewing the registry, as illustrated in Figure 14.4. In the key title "db_connect" the ODBC name, Username, and Password the Merchant Store Service is using to connect to the database is illustrated (**localmachine/software/microsoft/msmerchant/stores/clockped/database/**). Check with your database administrator to understand whether the user illustrated has sufficient permissions. If the user is not the problem, turn to the tables and whether they were correctly created and populated.

FIG. 14.4
Registry settings showing the ODBC datasource, user name, and password for a store.

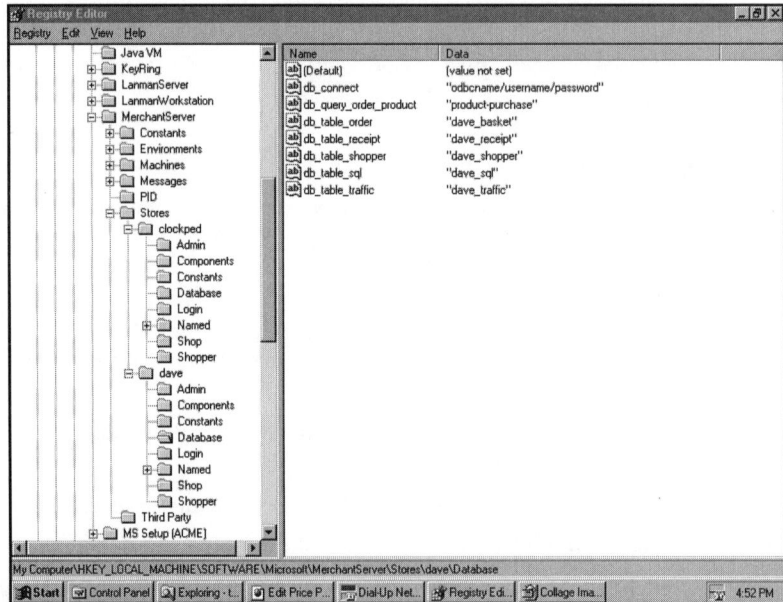

Beginning to Create Your Custom Store

The starting point for creating a new store involves selecting the sample store to use and then copying it with the Add Store tab on the Merchant administrative utility. Once the new store has been created, test it. If it works, you are ready to start the customization process. In the beginning, you should add your custom artwork to the images directory and modify the database with your design and data.

Adding a New Store Based on Sample Store Template

The Add Store process creates the database tables, registry settings, and hard drive directories customized to your new store name. If you have selected a store that fits your needs well, the implementation process will move very quickly. If none of the sample stores fit your requirements, you should still select the closest fit and then begin a process that will simply require more development effort.

Providing All Necessary Store Images

Depending on the sample store you select, your images will be stored in one or more locations. In addition, you can always reference images anywhere your Web server can reach. Images primarily include the toolbar and navigation buttons you select as well as the product art. In addition, promotional art includes sale and new product icons. Be conscious of file-naming conventions so that you may be able to dynamically build references to your file names during the page-generation process. For example, if you name your artwork associated with a product by the SKU number, you will be able to reference that file from a product page since the SKU information will be available from the database.

Customizing and Populating the Database

In customizing the database, avoid the urge to rename all the fields in use by the sample store. The sample store data fields are widely referenced in the Templates of the site and the less name changing you do, the quicker you can adapt the well-tested code provided in the sample store Templates. Adding fields to tables will by and large have no negative effect on the operation of the sample store Templates, so definitely add all the fields of information you need.

If you have not worked extensively with SQL server, you may find using a product like Microsoft Access easier for your table and SQL development. The Microsoft Access Upsizing Tool can be downloaded for free from Microsoft's Web site. This tool allows you to move tables into SQL Server, converting automatically key and trigger information.

ON THE WEB

HTTP://www.microsoft.com/   Download the Access Upsizing Tool here.

Part
V

Ch

14

For this implementation, we will leave all existing tables untouched and only add two tables for tracking orders placed. These tables, named receipt_item and receipt, will save the header and item level detail information about a completed order. An entry will be made in the Accept stage component in the registry to map order information to the table. The table fields added include the values displayed in Figure 14.5.

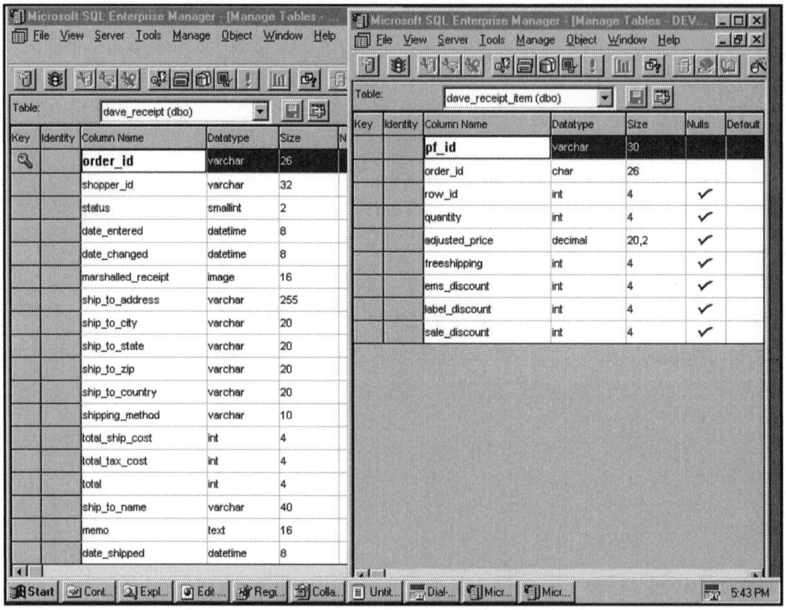

FIG. 14.5
The table layouts illustrate the tables added to track completed orders.

Checking and Modifying the Store Registry Settings

By using the Add Store feature, you set up a complete registry key for your store with the store name already customized for you. A review of the registry setting can save a lot of debugging time. The following categories represent all of the store key components you should review. The general registry settings for stores are illustrated in Figure 14.6. For this implementation, you only need to modify the Accept stage to write information to a receipt_item and receipt table you created.

General store settings, found at the root key of your store, are illustrated on the right side of Figure 14.6 and generally should not need modification with the exception of the hostname_insecure/secure. This by default may be set to your computer's NetBIOS name; this is fine when you're working locally but won't work over the Internet. If the name takes the form "www.computersite.com," you are in good shape; otherwise, you should edit this setting. This name will be inserted when the user logs on regardless of the address they use to first reach your site. The debug_order_logfile provides a useful way of tracking order activity while in test mode and can be invoked with a combination of properly pathing a file name and then turning on the Debug All Stores check box in the Merchant administrative utility. This is also where you would turn on the cookies feature if your site required it.

FIG. 14.6

Managing a store involves understanding the registry values for the section.

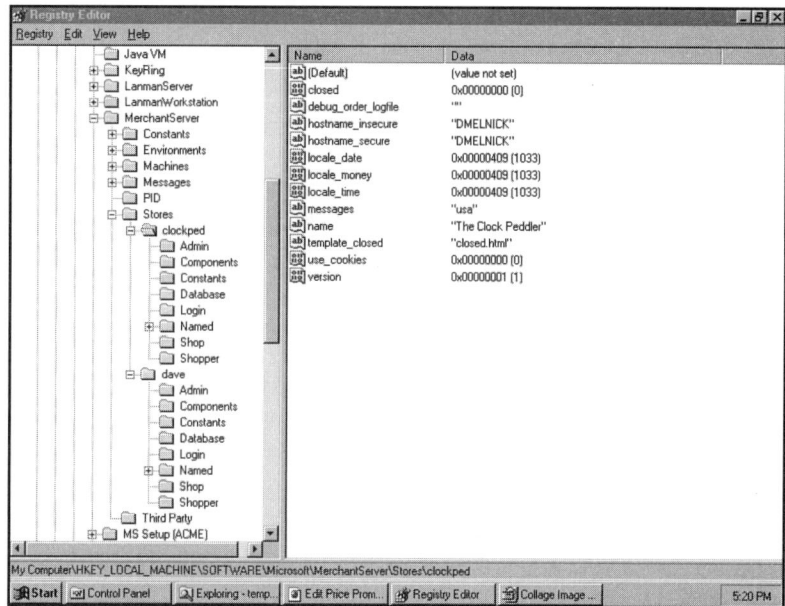

The Admin, Login, and Shop keys only refer to directory pathing to the files that the system uses. The pathing information should be correct but if you want to alter the location of files, you would do that in these keys. In contrast to the pathing keys, the Database key generally merits careful review. While the Add Store feature should have changed the table names reference, the logon information under the db_connect may or may not be the user you intend to use as you develop the site. If the Database key is in error, the Merchant Store Service will not start.

Creating constants or named actions can be done in the Constants and Named keys. Generally, these can be completely ignored; however, as you expand and develop your site you may begin to have use for these values. By default, the only entries that will be made by sample stores include setting color names as constants to refer to the numeric value of colors. In addition, Adventure Works creates Named actions for managing a part of the shopper login process.

The final area of the store registry that should be carefully reviewed is the Components key. This key maintains an entry for each stage in the order-processing pipeline and any optional functions called, third-party components invoked, or custom components added will need to be referenced in these settings. By default, this key will probably not meet your needs, and incorrect setup of a value in the Components key may prevent the Merchant Store Service from running. For this implementation, the only change that had to be added was in the Accept

Part

V

Ch

14

value of the Components key and invoked the SaveItemsToDb function twice. The key entry is partially illustrated as follows, including only the function call to save the receipt detail information:

```
WLStdOrder.SaveItemsToDb receipt_item {'_rowidx':'row_id',
➥'_product_pf_id':'pf_id',
'_oadjust_adjustedprice':'adjusted_price'}",
```

The illustrated function call entered into the Accept value invokes the SaveItemsToDb function, which writes information to database based on the parameters provided. The parameters include the table name and value pairs. The value pairs start by naming a value in the blackboard or in the current blob data field stored in the order basket table, and then by referencing a valid field in the specified table. In this case, three fields, including row ID, product ID, and the item's adjusted price, are saved.

Editing the Template Files (Source Code)

Understanding and working with Template files represents the primary programming of the Merchant site. Through adding special Merchant server tags, including Directives, Actions, and Value References, to an existing HTML page, you create the Templates used by Merchant server to dynamically generate HTML pages based on shopper requests. These Templates interact with the database to provide product and order processing pages throughout the shopper's visit to the Merchant site. In understanding the uses of Merchant's Templates in delivering a store, this section will review samples from Templates originally based on the Merchant's Clock Peddler sample store but then altered to deliver a custom store. For the most part, a simple store can be created with relatively minor adaptation of The Clock Peddler store. For this implementation, we used The Clock Peddler store to execute the Add Store feature and then adapted the Templates as illustrated in the following sections of the store. The core areas of the store Templates to modify include:

- Login process
- General shopping environment
- Order processing area of the shopping environment
- Administrative area of the site

Adapting a Login Process

The logon step occurs when the shopper enters the store through a Hyperlink referring to the standard guest shopper ID of "0L", fully illustrated as:

```
http://computername/prd.i/pgen/clockped/0L/welcome.html
```

By entering the store with a guest shopper ID, the shopper requests a page from the login stored by default in the directory **c:\msmerchant\stores\storename\login**. The specific page requested depends on the URL or Hyperlink used to enter the store; in the preceding example, the "welcome.html" page would be requested.

N O T E In a cookie-enabled store, if the auto logon feature successfully logged on the shopper, the system would automatically look for a "welcome.html" page in the shop directory, replacing the OL ID with the actual shopper ID found during the auto logon. ■

At this point, while in the guest mode, the shopper can be presented additional Hyperlinks to move to other pages, but they all must reside in the login directory. Until the shopper has logged on, they cannot access pages in the shop directory.

When adapting a login process based on a store using the guest community model, all that is required to enter the shop directory area with a generated shopper ID is the creation of a Hyperlink or Form tag that invokes the `shopper.guest` Action. The source code to invoke that page would include only:

```
To enter the store click [xlink shopper.guest]ENTER[/xlink]
```

This simple line of code will generate the complete URL for invoking the Action to create a new shopper ID for shopping in the shop directory area. This template file will reside in the login directory, which exists by default at **c:\msmerchant\stores\storename\login**. This initial file will contain whatever other HTML type code is required to display multimedia and text information.

In contrast, with a community-based model code invoking a `shopper.new` or `shopper.lookup` would be required. Unless the cookie feature is used which can automatically log in a user and move to the shop directory, this community will still start in the login area just like the guest community process. Whether by cookied automatic login or by successfully invoking a shopper Action, the shopper will move from this area to the primary directory for the site stored in the shop directory by default in **c:\msmerchant\stores\storename\shop**.

The `shopper.new` Action attempts to insert a new shopper record, generating a unique shopper ID similar to the `shopper.guest` Action, but, in this case, inserting additional fields of information based on the setup of your store. At this stage, your process can range from requiring the creation of a password to the entering of varying amounts of demographic information to be captured in the customer record. The key idea here is that a shopper record is being created which can be used in subsequent visits; therefore, information to enable a subsequent `shopper.lookup` must be stored.

The `shopper.lookup` Action is equivalent to a shopper logging on to the store. In its simplest manifestation, it is the shopper providing whatever information will allow the system to identify a unique record in the shopper table. The lookup, like the new Actions, can be customized to fit the requirements of your store. In addition to the registry and table setup required to support the login model, you can include a validation string in your HTML page to ensure that adequate information to perform the lookup has been included. A sample of a validation string would take the form of:

```
ADD VALIDATION STRING
```

> **N O T E** A validation string is also a part of the registry key associated with performing a
> shopper.lookup or shopper.new Action. ■

Regardless of the method used for logging a shopper into your store, the result is always the movement of the shopper from the login directory to the shop directory with the adding of a unique shopper ID into their URL string.

Developing Shopping Environment Pages

The Development of a shopping environment can range from an extremely simple set of features to an almost infinitely complicated range of choices and pages. For this implementation, we will focus on a relatively limited set of features based on The Clock Peddler store model. The model involves a starting page which looks up and displays the different departments available; by selecting a department the shopper is presented with a list of products which then allow the shopper to drill into details for a particular product. Once the product details are displayed, the shopper may add an item to their basket. After adding an item to their basket, an order summary is displayed which allows the shopper to either continue shopping or complete their current order. When completing an order, the shopper will move through a series of linear steps allowing the store to accumulate shipping, billing and other necessary information to finalize the order. This overall flow is illustrated by the flowchart in Figure 14.7.

FIG. 14.7
Illustration of the shopping experience flow in demo implementation site.

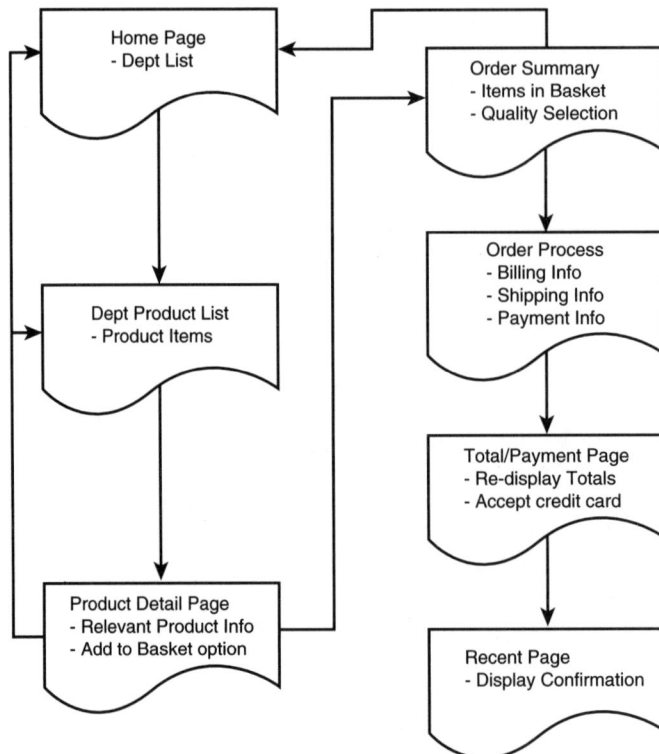

Enabling a Simple *Home Page* The Home Page of the store represents the first page a shopper visits after successfully entering the shop area. This is not the first page a shopper sees but rather the first page the shopper sees once they have passed the login stage. This page can be enhanced by any range of queries to the database, but for this implementation the Home Page focuses on only looking up information in the department table to display a list of departments enabled by Hyperlinks so that a shopper may drill into or select whatever department or category they are interested in reviewing.

TIP Providing a featured product on this page as well as options to fill out a survey or become a member are typical enhancements for the Home Page.

Since this implementation is based on a guest community, no personal information about the shopper is available for customizing the look of the page. In a membership community, customized greetings, including a shopper's name as well as shopping history information, could be displayed.

In addition to Merchant tags for displaying departments with Hyperlinks, the Home Page will include whatever graphical and textual information you determine to display, including a navigation toolbar to move throughout other pages in the site. The Merchant tags will include Directives for looking up the departments in the department table and Directives and Value References for displaying that information on the page. No Actions will be utilized on this page. The Home Page for this implementation is illustrated in Listing 14.1. The following template illustrates the tags and HTML to create the first page for the logged in shopper. The specific features include the Fetchrows Directive for executing the named search of the department database, and the Eachrow Directive for looping through the output of the records returned. In addition, Link Directives provide the creation of Hyperlinks for drilling into the Department Page, and finally Value References support the display of the information records returned from the Fetchrows lookup.

N O T E All of the listings in this chapter can be downloaded from Que's Web site— **http://www.quecorp.com/mcis**.

Listing 14.1 The Following Template Illustrates the Tags and HTML to Create the First Page for the Logged-In Shopper

```
<!--
[# #######################################]
[#                                       #]
[# HOMEPAGE.HTML                         #]
[# QUE Book Demo Program      v1.00      #]
[#                                       #]
[# (c) 1997 QUE. All rights reserved     #]
[#                                       #]
[# #######################################]
-->
<HTML><HEAD>
```

continues

Listing 14.1 Continued

```
<TITLE>The Demo Store Home Page</TITLE>
</HEAD>
[include "header.html"]

<H1>The QUE Demo Store</H1>

Welcome to our Demo Store. We have a broad
range of products you can choose from.
<BR>
Select a department below:

<UL>
[fetchrows depts "dept-list"]

[eachrow depts]
<LI>[link "dept.html" dept_id=depts.dept_id][value depts.dept_name][/link]
[/eachrow]

</UL>
[include "footer.html"]
</HTML>
```

The Fetchrows directive is used widely throughout all sites as the primary means for invoking a search on the database. The search, which is based on executing a SQL statement stored in the SQL table, can be as complex or simple as required. In the Home Page, the search provides a wildcard search of all records in the department table invoking the SQL statement illustrated as:

```
select * from demo_dept
```

The specific syntax for invoking the search follows the form:

```
[fetchrows depts "dept-list"]
```

> **N O T E** The Tfetchrows Directive could also have been used to query the records. In this case, no named query is required, only the actual table name to be queried. ▪

The Fetchrows query is invoked when the shopper requests the Home Page or logs into the store. Displaying and formatting the results of the query involves utilizing the Eachrow and Link directive with the Value Value Reference.

The Eachrow Directive always accompanies a Fetchrows Directive when the results of a search must be output on the page. The Eachrow Directive provides the mechanism to loop through the results set from the query and follows the form:

```
[eachrow depts]
[#Comment - Stuff to display]
[/eachrow]
```

The Link Directive generates a properly formatted Hyperlink inserting the required shopper ID and other values to allow a shopper to move to another page. In this case, the Link Directive allows the shopper to invoke the Department Page, drilling into and displaying the products available within a given department. The Link Directive displayed below provides the page to link to and any values to pass in as variables, in this case, the department ID:

```
[link "dept.html" dept_id=depts.dept_id]
[#Comment - Hyperlinked stuff to display]
[/link]
```

The Value References utilized for supporting the output of information retrieved with the Fetchrows Directive includes, in this case, only Value. The Value Reference precedes the variable or information to be displayed which, in this case, is the name of the department as illustrated by:

```
[value depts.dept_name]
```

CAUTION

While the Directives and Value References mentioned in the text are capitalized to recognize them as names, be careful to always make them lowercase in the code. Many areas of Merchant are case-sensitive.

Displaying Different Categories with the *Department Page*   The Department Page, similar to the Home Page, completes a relatively simple search of the product table, filtering for Active products and products which are assigned to the specific department selected. The selected department information is passed to the Fetchrows Directive from the Home Page as a variable in the URL or Hyperlink, allowing the value to be used in the SQL statement called. Once the Fetchrows Directive executes, the product records are displayed in much the same way the department information is displayed in the Home Page. In addition, the department information is also received to customize the display of the Department Page, as illustrated in Listing 14.2. The Department Page represents the second of three search pages for finding a product and provides a display of all products for a department.

Listing 14.2   The *Department Page* Represents the Second of Three Search Pages for Finding a Product and Provides a Display of All Products for a Department

```
<!--
[# #######################################]
[#                                        #]
[# DEPARTMENT.HTML                         #]
[# QUE Book Demo Program     v1.00         #]
[#                                        #]
[# (c) 1997 QUE. All rõ©xtsË eserved       #]
[#                                        #]
[# #######################################]
-->
```

continues

Listing 14.2 Continued

```
<HTML><HEAD>
     <TITLE>Department Page </TITLE>
</HEAD>
[include "header.html"]

[fetchrows deptinfo "department" args.dept_id]

<H1>[value deptinfo.dept_name]</H1>
[value deptinfo.dept_description]

<BR>
Select a product from the list below.

[fetchrows deptproducts "products-by-dept" args.dept_id]

<UL>
[eachrow deptproducts]
<LI>
[link "product.html" sku=deptproducts.sku]
[value deptproducts.name]
[/link]
by [value deptproducts.manufacturer]
[/eachrow]
</UL>

[include "footer.html"]
</HTML>
```

The two Fetchrows Directive searches used in this page include a search to find the unique department information to be displayed as header type information, as well as a general search of products from this department. The department search is like the Home Page search discussed in the previous section but with the addition of criteria identifying the unique key for the department. The product search identifies all records in the product table meeting two criteria. First, the product record must have its Active field set to true and second, it must have a department ID which matches the requested department as passed in from the Home Page. The specific SQL statement syntax for running the product search includes:

```
select * from demo_product where dept_id = convert(numeric,:1)
```

The specific syntax for invoking the search on the Department Page includes a custom name for referencing the results in the subsequent Directives and Value References as well as a named reference to the SQL statement stored in the SQL table. The third and final value illustrated below is a parameter identifying the department to filter for as illustrated:

```
[fetchrows deptproducts "products-by-dept" args.dept_id]
```

The Fetchrows query gets invoked when the shopper selects a department from the list of Hyperlinks on the Home Page. Displaying and formatting the results of the query, similar to the Home Page, involves utilizing the Eachrow and Link directive with the Value Value Reference.

Generating a Detailed *Product Page* When the shopper reaches the point of detailing a specific product, the process changes slightly. While the general Directives and Value References used are similar to the Department Page and Home Page, on the Product Page only a single record is being displayed. In addition, the Product Page must provide the ability to add a product to the shopper's basket which involves performing the Add Item action. The product page for this demonstration implementation is illustrated in Listing 14.3. The Product Page displays the product details and allows the adding of an item to the shopper's basket.

Listing 14.3   The *Product Page* Displays the Product Details and Allows the Adding of an Item to the Shopper's Basket

```
<!--
[# ######################################]
[#                                       #]
[# PRODUCT.HTML                          #]
[# QUE Book Demo Program      v1.00      #]
[#                                       #]
[# (c) 1997 QUE. All rights reserved     #]
[#                                       #]
[# ######################################]
-->
<HTML><HEAD>
      <TITLE>Product '[value args.sku]'</TITLE>
</HEAD>
[include "header.html"]

[fetchrows product "product" args.sku]

[if product.count > 0]
<H1>[value product.name] by [value product.manufacturer]</H1>

<TABLE CELLPADDING=5><TR><TD>

[if product.image_file != ""]
    <IMG SRC="[img]prodimg/[value product.image_file]">
[else]
    Image not available
[/if]

</TD><TD VALIGN=TOP WIDTH=400>

Our Price:[money product.list_price]

[xlink order.additem sku=product.sku]
<IMG SRC="[simg]addbskt.gif" ALT="Basket">
[/xlink]

<P>
[html product.description]
```

continues

Part
V

Ch
14

Listing 14.3 Continued

```
</TD></TR></TD></TR></TABLE>

[else]
    Product not available
[/if]
<P>

[include "footer.html"]
</HTML>
```

Similar to the other shopping pages, the Fetchrows and Eachrow Directive provide the mechanism to look up and display the product information. The Fetchrows Directive provides a search looking up a unique product record in the product table. Identifying a product record involves running a SQL statement which filters the product table for a unique product ID, which is passed in from the Department Page based on the Hyperlink that the shopper selects. The specific SQL statement syntax for running this search includes:

```
select * from demo_product where sku=:1
```

The specific syntax for invoking the search on the Product Page follows the form:

```
[fetchrows product "product" args.sku]
```

The Fetchrows query gets invoked when the shopper selects a product from the list of Hyperlinks on the Department Page. Displaying and formatting the results of the query, similar to the Department Page and Home Page, involves utilizing the Eachrow and Link directive with the Value and Money Value Reference. In addition to this display of product information, conditional processing and the use of the sites first Action get processed in the Product Page.

The use of Actions and conditional processing introduces the first point at which features beyond simple database lookups are required to enable the Merchant site. The Actions and conditional processing, like the login steps, differentiate the Merchant and other products from the simple database access tools being used to custom build shopping environments. As we continue to move into the order processing, additional features will be illustrated that further differentiate the Merchant from other commerce products. The primary conditional processing Directives used are shown in Listing 14.3. The Product Page displays the product details and allows the adding of an item to the shopper's basket to include the If/Else Directives. They are used twice with one example being a check of whether the Fetchrows search returned any product records. The following example uses the Count property of the recordset returned by the Fetchrows to determine if more than 0 records were returned:

```
[if product.count > 0]
```

The Action set up in the Product Page focuses on adding an item to the shopper's basket. This use of the Order.AddItem Action is set up as a Hyperlink using the Xlink Directive, as displayed as:

```
[xlink order.additem sku=product.sku]
```

N O T E   One limitation of the `Order.AddItem` Action is the inability to add more than one item at a time. Hopefully, a remedy is on the way, but at this time that is a limitation that requires creative workarounds if you need to add multiple items at once. ▪

"Implementing Order-Processing Pages" details the order-processing pages illustrated in Figure 14.7; the process of enabling a shopping experience up to the point of adding an item into the basket is the critical success factor in closing a sale. The shopping environment must be easy to navigate, providing shoppers with the ability to quickly identify products they wish to purchase. In addition, the site should provide cross-sell and up-sell features to help shoppers find products they hadn't realized they wanted to purchase.

As illustrated in Figure 14.7, the shopping environment can be enabled in as little as three templates. Since the templates dynamically generate pages based on database queries, three pages provide sufficient templates to enable the shopper to review all the products in the store quickly and easily. The three pages include the `Home Page` listing departments, `Department Page` listing products, and `Product Page` listing details of a product. Additional pages that could quickly be added range from enhanced keyword or other search features to survey and membership signup areas. During the review of these pages, you should focus on the types of enhancements you might add, and while some ideas will be presented, you should view this as a starting point for developing a shopping environment. The limitations are only defined by your imagination.

Implementing Order-Processing Pages

Implementing Order-Processing, like the implementation of a general shopper environment, can range widely in the level of complexity. Generally, increasing the features of the Order-Processing area involves extending the Order-Processing components in the Registry as opposed to adding complexity to the template files. However, the template developer must ensure that the pages provide the information required for processing the order components. This implementation focuses on providing the most basic functionality and can be complemented by a wide range of extended features for shipping, handling, payment, inventory, and other processes.

Four pages represent the heart of order-processing for this example, including the `Order Summary Page`, `Order Process Page`, `Total/Payment Page`, and `Receipt Page`. These pages continue to rely on Directives and Value References but include the use of Actions for processing the order components to complete the transactional order process.

Implementing the *Order Summary Page*   The `Order Summary Page` displays the shopper's current order basket illustrating all products selected and allowing the shoppers to specify quantities to order as well as providing the ability to remove items from the order basket. The `Order Summary Page` acts as both a confirmation when an order is added to the shopper's basket from the `Product Page`, and as the first of four steps in the process of completing an order.

Part
V

Ch
14

The Order Summary Page invokes the order-processing component by displaying the shopper's basket. This, unlike a lookup in the shopping environment pages, involves requesting order basket information from the Merchant with the Order.AddItem Directive. The order basket data is stored on the Merchant "blackboard" represented by a blob or binary field of data in the basket table. No direct query can access this information, and as a result specific Directives are used to add, modify, and delete basket information. The code is illustrated in Listing 14.4. The Order Summary Page illustrates the code required to display items in a shopper's basket with the Actions necessary to purchase or update the order. Both display the items in the shopper's basket and provide the Actions to update, clear, or purchase.

Listing 14.4 The *Order Summary Page* Illustrates the Code Required to Display Items in a Shopper's Basket with the Actions Necessary to Purchase or Update the Order

```
<!--
[# #######################################]
[#                                        #]
[# ORDER-SUMMARY.HTML                     #]
[# QUE Book Demo Program      v1.00       #]
[#                                        #]
[# (c) 1997 QUE. All rights reserved      #]
[#                                        #]
[# #######################################]
-->
<HTML><HEAD>
<TITLE>DEMO Order Summary Page</TITLE>
[nocache]
</HEAD>

[include "header.html"]

<H1>Shopping Basket</H1>

[fetchitems orderitem order.items]

[if orderitem.count > 0]
    You have [value orderitem.count] item
[if orderitem.count > 1]s[/if] in your shopping basket:
    [xform order.editquantities]
        <TABLE BORDER=0>
            <TR>
                <TH ALIGN=LEFT>Label</TH>
                <TH ALIGN=LEFT>Qty</TH>
                <TH ALIGN=LEFT>Description</TH>
                <TH ALIGN=CENTER>Unit Price</TH>
                <TH ALIGN=CENTER>Total Price</TH>
                <TH></TH>
            </TR>
            [eachrow orderitem]
                <TR>
```

```
                        <TD>
                        [value orderitem.sku]
                        </TD>
                        <TD>
                          <INPUT TYPE="Text"
                          NAME="[value orderitem.rowidx]"
                          SIZE=3,1
                          VALUE="[value orderitem.quantity]">
                        </TD>
                        <TD>
                          [value orderitem._product_name]
                        </TD>
                        <TD ALIGN=RIGHT>
                          [money orderitem._product_list_price]
                        </TD>
                        <TD ALIGN=RIGHT>
                          [money orderitem._oadjust_adjustedprice]
                        </TD>
                        <TD>
                          [xlink order.delitem index=orderitem.rowidx]
<IMG SRC="[simg]buttons/btnremove1.gif" BORDER=0 ALT="Delete item">[/xlink]
                        </TD>
                        </TR>
                        [/eachrow]

[# show subtotal: ]
                        <TR>
                        <TD COLSPAN=4 ALIGN=RIGHT> <STRONG>Subtotal: </STRONG></TD>
                        <TD ALIGN=RIGHT> [money order._oadjust_subtotal] </TD>
                        </TR>
                </TABLE>

                <P>
                To change an item's quantity,
                edit the number and press "Update Basket".
                <P>

<TABLE><TR><TD>
                <INPUT TYPE="Image"
                        VALUE="Update Order"
                        SRC="[simg]btnupdatebskt.gif"
                        ALT="Update Basket">
        [/xform]
        </TD>

        <TD>
        [xform order.clearitems]
            <INPUT TYPE="Image"
                    VALUE="Clear Order"
                    SRC="[simg]btnempty.gif"
                    ALT="Clear Basket">
        [/xform]
        </TD>
```

continues

Listing 14.4 Continued

```
    <TD>
    [form "orderform.html"]
        <INPUT TYPE="Image"
                VALUE="Purchase"
                SRC="[simg]btnpurchase.gif"
                ALT="Purchase">
    [/form]
    </TD></TR></TABLE>
[/if]

[if orderitem.count == 0]
    <BLOCKQUOTE>
        <STRONG>Your basket is empty.</STRONG>
    </BLOCKQUOTE>
[/if]

<P>
[include "footer.html"]
</HTML>
```

The key features included in the preceding code include the use of several Actions including the `Order.DelItems`, `Order.ClearItems`, and `Order.EditQuantities`. In addition, the Order Summary Page introduces the `Fetchitems` and `Xform` Directives for retrieving the information in the order basket. Outside of the use of these Actions and the new `Fetchitems` Directive, the code involves primarily plain HTML, conditional processing Directives, and Directives for formatting and outputting information.

The new Actions illustrated provide straightforward and somewhat automated handling of the order basket. With both the deleting of items and the clearing of items in the basket, no special parameters or code are required to implement these features. The editing of quantities does require a quantities field but basically operates automatically.

> **N O T E** Unlike the `Order.AddItem` Action, `Order.EditQuantities` will update multiple records at a time. ▨

> **N O T E** By invoking the `Fetchitems` Directive, the order process is invoked even without an Action being run. Be careful in development if you are having failures displaying a basket page because it could be due to a failure in the Order-Processing Components. ▨

Collecting Information for the *Order Processing Page* The Order Processing Page is primarily a data entry form with the exception that at the end of entering the data, the form processed by this page invokes the `Order.Plan` Action. `Order.Plan` completes all processing steps in the order except payment and acceptance. This is a final check prior to finalizing the order. In order to pass this step, shipping, tax and any other components invoked must successfully complete. The data entry form excepts billing, shipping, and contact information prior to moving into the Total/Payment Page. The reason for separating the Total/Payment Page from the Order Processing Page is to allow shipping and tax information like ship to state to be entered for final price calculation. If no shipping or tax charges apply, these steps could be combined.

Confirming the Order with the *Total/Payment Page*   The Total/Payment Page allows the confirmation of a complete price including the all shipping and tax information completed on the previous page and stored in the "blackboard." The code for capturing the data entry and displaying the total order is illustrated in Listing 14.5. The Total/Payment Page illustrates the data entry and order summary code for showing the "blackboard" fields stored about the order.

Listing 14.5   The *Total/Payment Page* Illustrates the Data Entry and Order Summary Code for Showing the "Blackboard" Fields Stored About the Order

```
<!--
[# ######################################]
[#                                     #]
[# TOTAL-PAYMENT.HTML                   #]
[# QUE Book Demo Program    v1.00       #]
[#                                     #]
[# (c) 1997 QUE. All rights reserved    #]
[#                                     #]
[# ######################################]
-->
<HTML><HEAD>
     <TITLE>DEMO site Totals and Payment Page</TITLE>
[nocache]
</HEAD>

[include "header.html"]

<TABLE WIDTH=500>
<TR><TD>
Purchase Price is [money order._total_total].  Enter
credit card and press the "Purchase" button below.
</TD></TR>
</TABLE>
<P>

<TABLE BORDER=0>
    <TR><TD ALIGN=RIGHT WIDTH=100>
<B>Subtotal:</B>
    </TD><TD ALIGN=RIGHT>
[money order._oadjust_subtotal]
    </TD></TR><TR><TD ALIGN=RIGHT>
<B>Tax:</B>
    </TD><TD ALIGN=RIGHT>
```

continues

Listing 14.5   Continued

```
[money order._tax_total]
    </TD></TR><TR><TD Align=RIGHT>
<B>Shipping:</B>
    </TD><TD ALIGN=RIGHT>
[money order._shipping_total]
    </TD></TR><TR><TD ALIGN=RIGHT>
<B>TOTAL:</B>
    </TD><TD ALIGN=RIGHT>
[money order._total_total]
    </TD></TR></TABLE><P>

[sxform order.purchase]
[verifywith "_total_total" "ship_to_zip" "_tax_total"]

    <TABLE><TR><TD></TD><TD ALIGN=CENTER COLSPAN=4>
<STRONG>Credit Card Information</STRONG>
    </TD></TR><TR><TD ALIGN=RIGHT>
<B>Name on card:</B>
    </TD><TD COLSPAN=4>
<INPUT TYPE="text" NAME="cc_name" SIZE=70,1>
    </TD></TR><TR><TD ALIGN=RIGHT>
<B>Card Number:</B>
    </TD><TD COLSPAN=4>
<INPUT TYPE="text" NAME="_cc_number" SIZE=70,1>
  </TD></TR><TR><TD ALIGN=RIGHT>
<B>Type:</B>
  </TD><TD>
<SELECT NAME="cc_type">
  <OPTION VALUE="Visa"> VISA
  <OPTION VALUE="Mastercard"> MasterCard
</SELECT>
  </TD>

  <TD ALIGN=RIGHT>
<B>Expiration Date:</B>
  </TD><TD>
<SELECT NAME="_cc_expmonth">
  <OPTION VALUE=1> Jan
  <OPTION VALUE=2> Feb
  <OPTION VALUE=3> Mar
  <OPTION VALUE=4> Apr
  <OPTION VALUE=5> May
  <OPTION VALUE=6> Jun
  <OPTION VALUE=7> Jul
  <OPTION VALUE=8> Aug
  <OPTION VALUE=9> Sep
  <OPTION VALUE=10> Oct
  <OPTION VALUE=11> Nov
  <OPTION VALUE=12> Dec
</SELECT>
  </TD><TD>
<SELECT NAME="_cc_expyear">
  <OPTION VALUE=1996> 1996
```

```
            <OPTION VALUE=1997> 1997
            <OPTION VALUE=1998> 1998
            <OPTION VALUE=1999> 1999
            <OPTION VALUE=2000> 2000
            <OPTION VALUE=2001> 2001
        </SELECT>
          </TD></TR><TR><TD></TD><TD COLSPAN=4>
        <INPUT TYPE="Image" VALUE="Purchase" SRC="[simg]btnpurchase.gif">
          </TD></TR></TABLE>
        [/sxform]

        [include "footer.html"]
        </HTML>
```

The key point in this section is the use of order fields in the display of a totaled order. The fields displaying the totals, such as order._oadjust_subtotal, order._total_total, and order._shipping_total are logically constructed based on the field names and order processing components invoked. Review the log file for a display of the field names for reference on the purchasing pages.

NOTE The Log File gets set as a registry setting at the root of the Merchant registry key. If logging is turned on, the initializing of all of these variables will be documented in the log file created. This log file represents a quick way of validating field names. In general, the referencing of the sample store templates will be very applicable to your custom store. ▪

Finalizing the Order with the *Receipt Page* The receipt page is generated by the invoking of the Order.Purchase Action which finalizes the order by successfully completing all steps in the order-processing pipeline. This page provides the shopper with any receipt type information the store determines should be displayed, as well as shipping tracking numbers and additional instructions if available or necessary. For this implementation, only a simple order ID is displayed as illustrated by the code from the Receipt Page in Listing 14.6. The receipt simply acknowledges that the Order.Purchase Action completed successfully, letting the shopper know that their order was completed. The order ID displayed for tracking to the shopper is a good example of an obscure string that should probably be translated into a readable number. However, this just illustrates that opportunity to begin improving upon this basic store illustrated in this chapter.

**Listing 14.6 The Receipt Simply Acknowledges that the *Order.Purchase*
Action Completed Successfully**

```
<!--
[# ######################################]
[#                                      #]
[# RECEIPT.HTML                         #]
```

Part
V

Ch

14

continues

Listing 14.6   Continued

```
[# QUE Book Demo Program      v1.00        #]
[#                                         #]
[# (c) 1997 QUE. All rights reserved       #]
[#                                         #]
[# #######################################]
-->
<HTML>
<HEAD>
<TITLE>QUE Demo Store Purchase Receipt</TITLE>
</HEAD>

[include "header.html"]

<H1>Purchase Confirmed</H1>

Your order number is <STRONG>[value args.order_id]</STRONG>.
Please record it for referencing your order.
<P>
If you want to continue shopping, simply return to the
[link "main.html"]lobby[/link].

[include "footer.html"]

</HTML>
```

Modifying a Sample Store's Administration

Enabling a Web-based administration environment provides a flexible method for rapidly modifying a store without modifying code. Due to Merchant's dependence on the database for storing configuration information such as SQL statements, a Web browser using the same types of templates enabled in the shopping and login areas can effectively modify many aspects of a store site. While not attempting to define all the possible applications of the administrative environment, the following provides a brief overview of some of the features built into the sample stores, as well as some uses beyond that of the sample stores.

The basic features enabled in many of the sample stores include:

- Editing products
- Modifying departments/categories
- Managing shopper information
- Creating and editing price promotions
- Enabling traffic and order reporting
- Modifying SQL statements

Additional features you may consider implementing include providing the ability to modify database-stored headers and footers.

The standard sample store features enabled basically focus on editing fields stored in the database tables of the site. As a result, whenever you add a new table to your store you should consider the administrative implications of that new information being stored. The most useful and common implementation is the ability to modify product, department, and shopper information. This ranges from descriptions to prices and only involves executing saved SQL statements with the same types of Directives used in the shopping environment. If your site makes use of price promotions and traffic tracking, these become excellent areas to build administrative pages for as well.

Carefully review the administrative sample store templates. The code is well organized and effectively provides a modular set of templates that can be easily adapted as you add new tables to the site. Investing some time during the initial development of the site to understand the organization of this code can quickly provide you with a powerful administrative component for your store.

Moving beyond the templates that are provided with the sample store administrative areas, the first and biggest value comes from storing headers and footers for different areas of your store in a database table. By storing text fields that can contain HTML code for display at the top and bottom of your pages, you can almost completely control the look of your site from font size and color to backgrounds and toolbars. While these features are not found in any of the sample stores, they can be easily implemented and can prevent the need to edit source code when changes to the overall look and feel of the site are required.

Testing and Debugging Your Store

While a wide range of testing and debugging steps should be investigated for any site implementation, the following highlights some basic steps. As with any application, a change control process and specification should be part of the development process; however, some quick areas for review during the development and testing phase include:

- Setting the store options for debugging
- Monitoring the Event Viewer

Setting the store for debugging and specifying a log output file in the registry for capturing information will provide the only method for understanding what is happening during the order-processing components. While turning on debugging allows details of page errors to be displayed when an error occurs moving from one page to another, the order-processing components are harder to identify. Since the order process invokes several API calls and processing steps during one-page execution, understanding the failure requires more information than Merchant provides on the result page when an error occurs. The log file tracks both errors and non-errors that take place during the order-processing steps and can help you identify variable naming problems among others.

A second area that can sometimes be overlooked is the Windows NT Event viewer. The Merchant Server does a good job of tracking errors in the event viewer relating to the Store Service. The Event Viewer will be most useful when the Store Service is failing to start, or

Part
V

Ch

14

stopping for some unknown reason. While many developers may immediately turn to their database server setup or Web server setup, this can quickly become hours of wasted time. The Event Viewer will quickly alert the developer to what is most likely a database permissions or other database problem.

Putting Your Store into Production

Once the store goes into production, the developer and administrator's attention quickly turns to how to enhance or upgrade the site without destabilizing the production environment. While Merchant teases the developer with options for Production, Staging, and Development in the Environment tab of the Merchant Server Administrative utility, these features are currently not yet operational. The most commonly used approach is to create a mirrored version of the site for Staging and Development. As a rule, the Web-server component of the site is fairly robust since it only relies on the ISAPI filter, and as a result there is little risk in sharing a Web server with both Production and Development sites. The Store Service, on the other hand, is much more sensitive to a problem in a site, and while bad code in templates is not a problem, if the database or registry settings of a development store have problems, it will bring the whole Store Service to a stop. Therefore, share Web servers, share Store Services once the database and registry are stable, and isolate stores that do not yet have stable databases and registry settings (such as order-processing components).

Once a store is in production, the primary role becomes monitoring performance. Watch for CPU bottlenecks or slowdowns by logging your performance monitoring. The Performance Monitor can track the performance of the Store Service and the CPU providing the critical site performance information you need in determining when to upgrade or scale your site's hardware configuration.

From Here...

At this point, you have covered all the areas of developing a complete commerce site. Monitor the Microsoft Web site at **HTTP://www.microsoft.com/merchant/** and the many vendors such as payment vendors at **HTTP://www.cybercash.com** and **HTTP://www.verifone.com** for additional news and information. From here, you may consider some additional areas of this book for more in-depth coverage of topics introduced in this chapter. For additional information, try the following chapters:

- Chapter 3, "Building The Foundation," provides a more detailed discussion about Windows NT and the Internet Information Server.

- Chapter 13, "Microsoft Merchant Server—Enabling Commerce on the Web," provides a more high level review of the Merchant Server product.

- Chapter 19, "Interpreting Logfiles and Monitoring Server Performance," provides a discussion of monitoring issues for NT services.

- Appendix A, "Hardware Requirements" is a further discussion of the hardware configuration issues brought up in this chapter.

The Active Server

Introduction to Internet Information Server 3.0

The Web has been undergoing an explosive growth in recent months, but what a lot of people don't realize is that for every Web site, there also has to be a Web server. With the growing complexity of the average Web user's wants, the server software has to grow with it. Microsoft's Internet Information Server is one of the programs cresting the wave of this trend. ■

All about Internet Information Server 3.0

Get the goods on Microsoft's latest extension to its Internet Information Server.

Two primary distinctions of a Web site

The debate rages: static versus dynamic. But just what are they?

The development of active content over the ages

A treatise tracing the history of content's ability to change to suit the situation.

Getting Active Server Pages online

A quick breakdown of installing Internet Information Server 3.0 on your NT 4.0 system.

Overview of Internet Information Server 3.0

Web servers have come a long way. Historically, it's been ancient steam-driven software, understood by a select few in the bowels of the IS department, that parceled out precious content. Then came the PC revolution, bringing server power in bite-sized chunks to desktop units everywhere. Microsoft jumped on the bandwagon with Internet Information Server 2.0 (IIS 2.0). Following that comes version 3.0.

IIS 3.0 isn't a total rework of IIS 2.0; rather, it's an extension to IIS 2.0's functionality. While a major upgrade in and of itself, the majority of "base" functionality is still the same. Instead of revamping the entire package, Microsoft has added new modules, or extensions, to the existing server. This makes upgrading and installing incredibly simple. There are many new improvements, such as an up to 30 percent speed increase. The reliability has been extended as well, supposedly allowing thousands of hits per second. Most importantly, Microsoft has included scripting language support. This means that you can insert programming functionality into your Web documents by using VBScript or JavaScript. The rest of the software industry has not been sitting on its laurels, as there will soon be script interpreters for Perl and Rexx available through third-party publishers.

With this sort of power available to both site administrators and designers, our concept of what a Web site should be is rapidly changing. The traditional brochure "display" site, or the turbocharged, ever-changing "active" site becomes the new choice faced by potential Web site owners.

Static versus Dynamic Web Sites

If a site's information does not change, or does not *need* to change over a long period of time, it's known as a *static* site. A large percentage of the existing sites on the Web at this point are static in nature.

Let's take the example of our good friend Marcel. Marcel is the vice-president of Quality Control for the BigCo Corporation (his Dad is chairman of the board). Marcel has led a happy life, almost totally responsibility-free. Suddenly he is faced with a dramatic assignment that could change the nature of his existence: define the company's Web presence.

Immediately he is plunged into the maelstrom of jargon that surrounds any computer-related industry. Marcel knows only that he has lots of money to spend on this project, and that his father would be displeased if the staid, rich BigCo Corporation was in any way misrepresented. Marcel contracts the New Age Design firm in New York for a quick, traditional, brochure page (see Figure 15.1).

BigCo's site doesn't change. It's a large, boring investment brokerage that is perfectly happy with the Web site it has. This is known as a *static* Web site. The information's nature is such that it can remain the same for quite some time. In the case of BigCo, it could include a mission statement, a vague assurance of quality and safety, and perhaps a listing of when the annual general stockholder's meeting occurs. None of this information would have to be altered except in the case of a radical change (new ownership, change in mission statement, or hostile takeover). Marcel has fulfilled his duty admirably. While there is nothing wrong with a static site, it's rapidly becoming the lowest common denominator on the Web.

FIG. 15.1
BigCo serves a typical example of a static site. The content on it would change perhaps once a year.

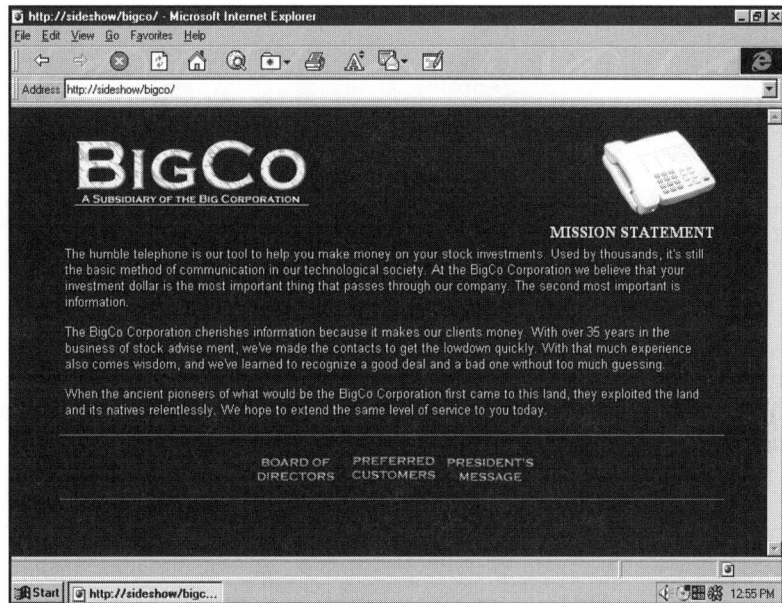

When a site's content needs to change, and does so without human intervention, it's known as a *dynamic* site. The dynamic site is slowly gaining more prominence as the tools to create them become easier to use.

Jose works for the big restaurant chain Herb's Mostly Identifiable Greasy Chicken Parts as Public Relations Manager. It is he who has to deal with the many food poisoning cases Herb's is famous for. One day while being cross-examined in court he has the idea of trying to improve Herb's image by having a self-congratulatory Web site done.

The harried executives love the idea, and reward Jose by immediately putting him in charge of the new Web project. Jose has been doing some research, and is rapidly discovering that a Web site can do a whole lot more than claim, "Now Salmonella Free!" He quickly jots down his ideas for a possible Web site and sends them off to Site Corporati, based out of San Francisco. Site Corporati responds warmly, and soon enough Jose has a Web site that reflects most of his desires.

The information on Herb's site changes often, based on real-time events occurring at the various restaurants. This is known as *dynamic* behavior. A visitor to Herb's site could be informed of how many seats are left in a particular restaurant at that time, what the dinner entrée special is, and whether it's currently happy hour in the Herb's nearest you. They can also access static information such as the menu, how long the restaurant is open, and Herb's Food Preparation Disclaimer. A Web site requires at least some static content to maintain continuity and cohesion.

FIG. 15.2

Herb's site offers online examples of using Active Server Pages and ActiveX components to create dynamic content.

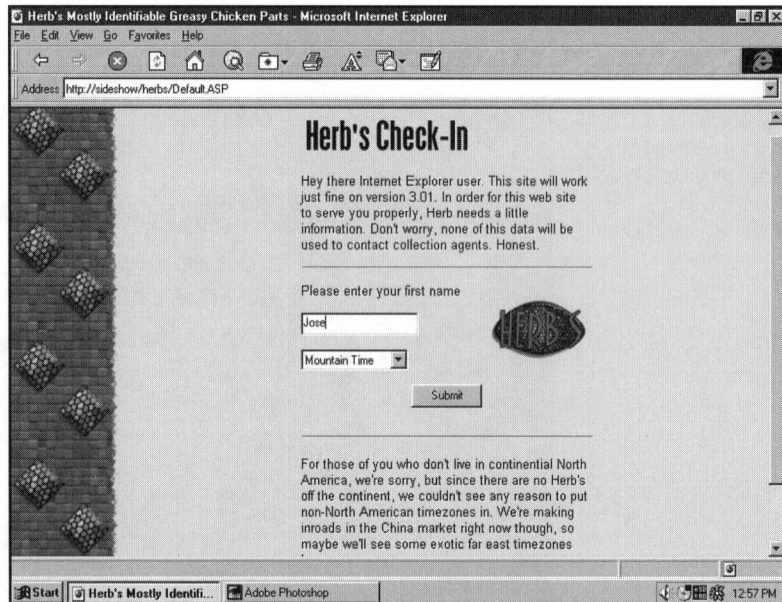

Jose's idea is an unqualified success. Many vegetarian groups support Herb's openly when they read that no animals are killed for the production of Herb's cuisine. Just as many food poisoning cases are reported, but potential plaintiffs are scared off by the daunting Food Preparation Disclaimer. Jose is promoted to fast-track management and is responsible for creating robust franchises in China. However, because of the advanced features of Herb's Web site, a higher-end server is required, as well as special Web server software. Luckily, Herb's Information Services section has the Web site hosted by someone with Microsoft's Internet Information Server 3.0, which handles both the traffic and complex interactivity generated by Jose's Web site.

Being static can still have its benefits. Many people don't want or even need the ability to have a constantly updated site. They know what they want to say, and only want to say it once. However, more and more people are finding out that they require a dynamic site to fulfill their needs. A dynamic site means complication, in both hardware and software. Special software is required to manipulate the server input and output, which in the past has proven to be both expensive and arcane. Fortunately, the means to do so have been getting easier and easier as time goes on.

Viewing Dynamic Sites

Unfortunately, current browser technology doesn't totally facilitate viewing of a dynamic site. Because Web transfers are a single-state process (they're either on or off), changes could occur to a Web page that you're not aware of until you "refresh" them. A simple way around this is to set your browser to refresh files on every visit to a site as opposed to the default "refresh every time you start your browser."

Another option as a Web designer is to include the tag <META=PRAGMA-NOCACHE>, which prevents the page itself from being included in a browser's cache, effectively forcing the browser to refresh each time. As a short-term solution, simply click Refresh in your browser when you suspect a change has occurred.

The Evolution of Dynamic Content

Dynamic content provision has appropriately undergone a constant process of refinement to get to where it is today. While the desire to present "active" content has been around for as long as Web sites have existed, it is only recently that technology has evolved sufficiently to fulfill it. However, the philosophies behind which method to use to serve active content vary wildly.

Common Gateway Interface (CGI)/Internet Service API (ISAPI)   CGI, or Common Gateway Interface, was one of the first solutions to the conundrum faced by those wanting to serve dynamic content. Common Gateway Interface is an alternate data stream handler. Instead of flowing data to the screen, it's redirected to a Web page, through a "gateway." Oddly enough, ISAPI, or Internet Service Application Programming Interface, follows the same philosophy. The idea behind both is this: The data is in here; the user is out there. CGI and ISAPI act as a filter between the two, allowing manipulation of the data before it sees the user.

This sounds perfect, right? Well, unfortunately, it isn't. Common Gateway Interface is described as *out of process*. This means it handles one thing at a time, returns its results, and *stops*. The CGI is single-process based, and is not very flexible with multiple processes that occur simultaneously. CGIs are resource intensive because once they're called, they have to do their job, return the data, and terminate. This process is duplicated *every time* the CGI is accessed, for every user accessing it. This quickly adds up to a large system load.

The Internet Service Application Programming Interface tries to address some of these problems. At heart, they're both the same—a filter between the data and the user. ISAPI differs in one important aspect, however; it is what's known as *in process*. This is more flexible than "out of process" because it allows the application to exist in several states. An ISAPI application can be called, return data to the user, do something else, read in from the database, return more data to the user, and then pause. An ISAPI process never properly terminates, because it runs under the purview of the Web server itself. ISAPI's advantage over CGI is its integration with the Web server. CGI's clumsiness resulted from the fact that it had no real communication with the server except at the very beginning and end of its activation. An ISAPI application maintains contact with the server constantly, and is therefore able to insert outgoing data, and read incoming data, all while running on the same copy of itself. A CGI that could service 1,000 users would have to run 1,000 times. An ISAPI application would have to run but once.

Let's continue to use the Herb's Mostly Identifiable Greasy Chicken Parts example, as there's enough interactivity there to generate examples for *three* books. Case in point: The reservation system. In order for this to work, a restaurant has to have a database that's up to date with its seating plan. Staff at Herb's mark tables as taken, and users approaching from the Web then see what is available and what is not when they "update" the page. The functionality required is this: The site has to be able to access a database, take information from it, and then format the data to present to the Web audience. Either a CGI or ISAPI application is capable of this, although it would take some work to program it.

Just about every server in the known universe can support CGI applications. Several, but not all, server programs support ISAPI commands. There are a few other third-party solutions out there, which include Netscape Server Application Programming Interface (NSAPI), which is comparable to ISAPI.

The problem with both CGI and ISAPI is that they're essentially programming tools. The average designer or administrator isn't going to know how or want to know how to make a complex application using either. Fortunately, there's a much less complex (and less powerful) alternative in Server Side Includes.

Server Side Include (SSI)   The Server Side Include (SSI) philosophy is a little different. Instead of providing flexible (and arcane) tools to manipulate an HTML document, SSI grants the ability to use several predefined constants. These can vary from simple things like the time or date, to the name of the current user's computer, or network address. An SSI could be used for fancying up a site, but for the most part its functionality is mere window dressing.

In the example of Herb's Web site, the only possible use a Server Side Include could have is if a user were looking at the hours of operation/happy hour figures. A Server Side Include of the current time could be displayed next to both figures, and it would be up to the user to figure out if the restaurant was closed or open at that time. A CGI or ISAPI application could tell the user directly if the place was open for business.

While valuable, the Server Side Include is by no means a complete solution. It totally cuts out any notion of interactivity, nor does it allow a server to "remember" variables that aren't predefined. Finally, a Server Side Include doesn't have any means for interacting with a database.

Internet Database Connector (IDC)/(HTX)   When you think data, you think database. There are entire hordes of ugly, unorganized data out there that people never see because it doesn't get put into a database, and is therefore unmanageable. Enabling a Web site to access a database increases its potential power considerably, and has long been the Holy Grail of both Web designers and administrators alike. The Internet Database Connector is certainly considered a step in the right direction.

IDC is a standardized format to join the Internet and a database together. In the case of Herb's, say there was a different special entrée every week, and this information was stored in a database at Herb's Mostly Identifiable Greasy Chicken Parts Central. When the week passes, a stored procedure changes the database entry for "Special of the Week." The Web site requests the special because a user has just "hit" it. The database is called and returns the info to be presented to the user ("Country Fried Ham"). However, in order for the data to be formatted properly, it has to be in an .HTX file. An extension of the .HTM file, the .HTX is a normal Web page in all respects save one: By using special scripting tags, the author can format data inserted from a database. The IDC/HTX combination works in a one-two punch. The data is collated using the IDC filter, and then is inserted in the proper place using the HTX scripting format.

While IDC allows for input and retrieval of data to a database, it has no real front-end capabilities. The actual interface control is limited, and the syntax is arcane. However, the obtuse nature of IDC/HTX is slowly being overcome. As of Microsoft Office 95, there was an add-on utility to generate IDC/HTX files from an Access database. As of Access 97 this functionality is included in the package itself. While this is a step in the right direction, it still limits output formatting somewhat. What's needed as a total solution is some combination of the precise control of ISAPI, the ease of an SSI, added to the database functionality and formatting of IDC/HTX.

Active Server Pages (ASP)   At the pinnacle of the Darwinian active content evolution lies the crafty, tool-using Active Server Page. IDC/HTX was a format introduced in Internet Information Server 1.0, and many Web designers applauded the sudden database powers granted to them. But it wasn't enough, and with the introduction of IIS 3.0 comes the ASP or Active Server Page.

N O T E   Even though ASP supports several varieties of scripting language, for simplicity's sake VBScript will be the example language of choice in this chapter. ▪

Active Server is a leagues-wide step on the road to true dynamic content. Instead of memorizing a whole new command syntax, the functionality behind Active Server Pages is already existing scripting languages. VBScript, JavaScript, and Perl are just some of the possible choices you have when making an Active Server Page. CGI and ISAPI are very powerful, but their final form is still a program. The Active Server Page is comparable to the "Visual" programming movement, except instead of using basic Windows parameters to define the interface, you're using Web-compliant HTML.

ASPs allow us to fulfill that long-lost dream, having real variables on a Web page. If you want a visitor to Herb's to have the accurate time, you can ask them what time zone they're from, and store it in a variable. You can then use a comparison method and do some simple arithmetic to display a person's time, in their time zone, as in the following VBScript example, Listing 15.1.

N O T E   This Listing is available on one of Que's Web pages. Find it at **http://www.quecorp.com/mcis**. ▪

Listing 15.1   Example Code Determining the Effects of Timezones on the Date and Time

```
<% Select Case Session("Timezone")
Case "Pacific"
```

continues

Listing 15.1 Continued

```
CurrentHour = CurrentHour - 1
If CurrentHour = -1 then
CurrentDayInt = CurrentDayInt - 1
If CurrentDayInt <=0 then
CurrentDayInt = 7
End If
End If

Case "Mountain"
CurrentHour = CurrentHour

Case "Central"
CurrentHour = CurrentHour + 1
If CurrentHour = 24 then
CurrentDayInt = CurrentDayInt + 1
If CurrentDayInt> 7 then
CurrentDayInt = 1
End If
End If

Case "Eastern"
CurrentHour = CurrentHour + 2
If CurrentHour> 23 then
CurrentDayInt = CurrentDayInt + 1
If CurrentDayInt> 7 then
CurrentDayInt = 1
End If
End If
Case "Atlantic"
CurrentHour = CurrentHour + 3
If CurrentHour> 23 then
CurrentDayInt = CurrentDayInt + 1
If CurrentDayInt> 7 then
CurrentDayInt = 1
End If
End If
Case "Newfoundland"
CurrentMin = CurrentMin + 30
If CurrentMin>= 60 And CurrentHour = 23 then
CurrentDayInt = CurrentDayInt + 1
If CurrentDayInt> 7 then
CurrentDayInt = 1
End If
End If
Case Else
CurrentHour = CurrentHour
End Select %>
```

As the preceding code illustrates, VBScript is still a powerful programming language that enables you to assign and use variables, and do logic comparisons and arithmetic. Procedures that were normally the purview of programmers and administrators are now firmly thrust into the designer's hands. The tools have become simplified enough that only a modicum of programming knowledge is required, instead of the "Two Years of C Programming" program.

Unfortunately, VBScript is not Visual Basic 4.0. Because the IIS 3.0 implementation had to support a very general base, hardware-specific functions such as file I/O and database functionality are not supported directly. However, there are now server-side components that allow access to these functions. While the implementation is not as smooth as VB 4.0, it is still oceans ahead of any other method out there.

Server Side Includes are effectively integrated into the ASP functionality. Their role has changed to a more administrative level, however, as SSIs are used more to complement ASP script. When it comes to covering CGI/ISAPI's turf, Active Scripting does the job pretty well, too. There is more interactivity, less complex coding, and the added bonus of being interpreted. Interpreted code can be changed on-the-fly, instead of having to be recompiled like traditional programs. If you wanted to add the obscure Newfoundland time zone in Canada, you could simply edit the Active Server Page like any other HTML document. There's no compiling and no replacing executables.

For example, take Herb's Mostly Identifiable Greasy Chicken Parts Web site. Every item on Jose's wish list would be possible using Active Server and the Server Components. Because you're using a programming language to do the instruction work, you can do all sorts of IF/THEN clauses, FOR/NEXT loops, or even a CASE statement—all of the logic chopping data manipulation tools you need to do the job. Add that to the Active Database Object and File System component, and all the features of the Herb's site go from unattainable to easily conquered.

Installing and Configuring Internet Information Server 3.0

Referring to Internet Information Server 3.0 only as a Web server is misleading. IIS 3.0 is actually a package of solutions that extend the IIS 2.0 framework for the World Wide Web, Gopher, and FTP. The predominant piece of IIS 3.0 is the Active Server Pages (ASP) application, formerly known as "Denali." ASP is the Web server extension that introduces server side processing and the component extensions. In addition to ASP, IIS 3.0 includes: Index Server (1.1), NetShow and NetShow Live, Crystal Reports for IIS, FrontPage, and a few other smaller pieces.

You can obtain the different pieces of IIS from the Microsoft Web site at **http://www.microsoft.com/iis**. The crucial component for you to retrieve and install is ASP, as that is what is explored in the next chapter. The other components extend functionality depending on your needs. These components are:

- *Index Server*   The Microsoft Index Server provides you with a method of creating an indexed and searchable database of documents. This is a search engine facility which lets you provide the ability to search HTML pages, or even Microsoft Word Documents within your site. Index Server provides several neat tricks, such as context highlighting.

- *NetShow and NetShow Live*   In the quest for real-time multimedia over the net, Microsoft has introduced NetShow. NetShow is the Microsoft framework for transmitting streaming audio or video to clients over the Internet or an intranet. NetShow is intended for pre-recorded material, while NetShow Live is intended for real-time broadcasts. NetShow is Microsoft's answer to on-demand broadcasting.

- *Crystal Reports for IIS* Crystal Reports from Seagate Software is an industry standard report generation system. CR for IIS provides comprehensive and powerful tools for analyzing database sources and creating Web-ready reports. In addition to this, CR for IIS provides a flexible method of reporting statistics for your own Web server using the IIS log files or database logs.

- *FrontPage* The Microsoft FrontPage product is a WYSIWYG (What You See Is What You Get) Web authoring and management tool. FrontPage operates through a visual editor for authoring, a site administration tool, and optional server extensions which allow the tools to directly communicate and update the Web server in real-time. These tools allow the user to interact with a FrontPage-enhanced server, but is not the actual FrontPage editing utility. Both novice and advanced Web developers may be interested in taking advantage of what FrontPage has to offer.

To install and run IIS 3.0 you must be running Microsoft Windows NT Server 4.0. You can install some of the components to operate in a more limited capacity on Windows NT Workstation 4.0. Active Server Pages also functions as an extension to the Microsoft Windows 95 Personal Web Server for local development. Each component has specific requirements for storage and memory, depending on your needs. Consult the information provided with each component for specific requirements and installation instructions.

Installing Active Server Pages is a simple task on any machine. Once you have the ASP self-installing archive, you may begin the installation. Make sure that you have all other programs closed at the time to ensure a proper installation. To begin your installation, double-click the installer's icon and follow these steps:

1. Once the installer has extracted the required files, the setup program begins by displaying an End User License Agreement for you to review. Once you have read and agreed to it, click the I Agree button to continue.

2. Click the Next button to proceed to the installation process.

3. If your current World Wide Web, FTP, or Gopher services are running you will receive a warning dialog box asking you if Setup can stop the services before continuing, as shown in Figure 15.3. Click the Yes button to proceed.

FIG. 15.3

If current Internet Information Server services are running, you are asked to stop them before proceeding with the installation.

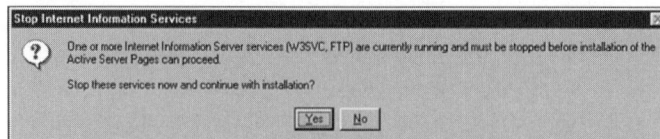

4. A dialog box appears, allowing you to select the options for installation. By default, all three options are selected for installation (see Figure 15.4). Select the options you want to install and click the Next button.

FIG. 15.4
By default, the ASP
setup has you install
not only the Active
Server, but also ODBC
3.0 and the tutorial
files.

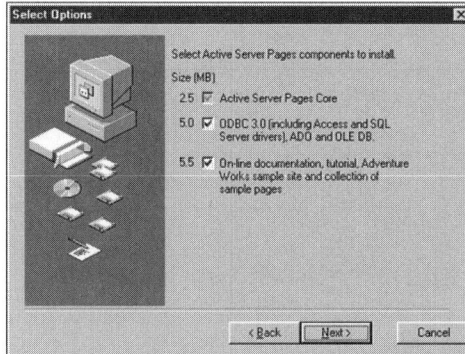

5. The next dialog box enables you to specify a destination path for the ASP Samples and tutorial files if you chose to install them (see Figure 15.5). Set the directory to the path you desire and click the Next button to begin the installation process.

FIG. 15.5
You have the option of
specifying a destination
path for tutorial and
sample files, if you
choose to install them.

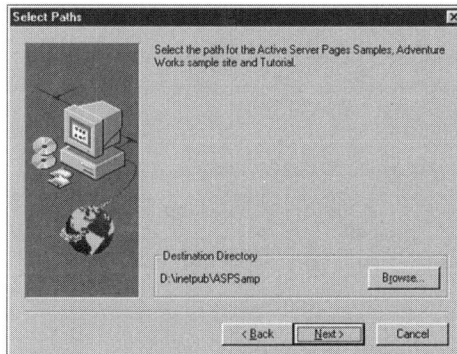

6. Once installation is complete, a summary dialog box appears to inform you what has been installed. Click OK to continue.

7. For your reference, an icon called Active Server Pages Roadmap is added to your Start Menu. This is a crucial reference for ASP authoring. A dialog box appears to inform you of the change. Click OK to continue.

8. ASP requires a few updates to the NT operating system. As you are installing ASP onto a Windows NT based system, you are prompted to install NT Service Pack 1a (see Figure 15.6). If you have already installed this service pack or a later one, click No. If you have not yet done so, click Yes to install the service pack.

9. Finally, Setup prompts you whether you want to restart the IIS services (World Wide Web, FTP, or Gopher), as shown in Figure 15.6. If you want to do so, click Yes; otherwise, click No.

FIG. 15.6

NT administrators should be familiar with NT Service Packs. ASP requires Service Pack 1a or later. If you do not have it installed, you must do so for ASP to function properly.

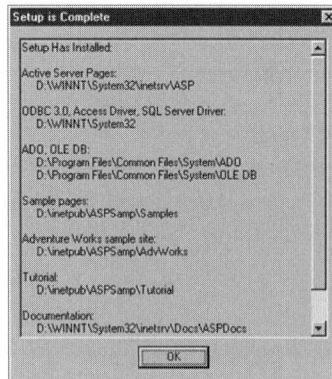

After the installation is complete, you may need to restart your server. To begin authoring sites that take advantage of ASP functionality, be sure to refer to the ASP Roadmap. This sizeable reference includes comprehensive information on ASP components and scripting, as well as several tutorials and samples.

From Here...

Time's winged chariot catches up with us all, and Internet Information Server 3.0 is just another example of that. The audience for active content is becoming more and more demanding. Older implementations of dynamic sites such as CGI, SSI, and IDC/HTX can't cut it any more. That's where Active Server Pages come in. Simpler to write than CGI/ISAPI applications, more powerful than SSI, and an easier incorporation of IDC functionality makes ASP a powerful contender of the dynamic content wars.

More importantly though, is the fact that Active Server has reduced the knowledge level for creating complex projects considerably. Just as there was a desktop publishing revolution, there will also be a Web publishing revolution, and Internet Information Server will be spearheading it. Here are some chapters that will hopefully help you further your goal of learning Internet Information Server 3.0:

- Chapter 16, "Serving Active Content on the Internet," deals with the specifics of Server components and their labor-saving efficiency.
- Chapter 20, "Developing an Intranet with MCIS Servers," gives you a helping hand in plunging into the chancy world of intranet development.

Serving Active Content on the Internet

Not satisfied with dry and static sites? Then active content is the thing for you. This chapter explores in closer detail exactly what active content is, and how Internet Information Server 3.0 will do almost everything you need. ■

Scripting your content

By using IIS 3.0's flexibility and power, you can deliver your content to any browser regardless of what browser the visitor is using.

Using the included components

Internet Information Server 3.0 includes several useful components for delivering dynamic content within your Web site. These seemingly simple tools will allow you to turn your Web sites into Web applications.

All this and examples too

Once again we will be using the Herb's restaurant Web site as the primary example of Active Scripting functionality.

Activating with Scripts

In the quest for providing a rich and changing experience for visitors, Web site designers and content providers used to rely on server-side engines to send information to a traditionally "dumb" client—the Web browser. With the advent of client-side interactivity through newer technologies like Java, JavaScript, and Visual Basic Script, designers have been able to offload a great deal of the work onto the client. Designers chose to do this because, in the past, if a designer could implement what they wanted, it would have either taken up too many resources or would have proven too difficult to do on the server. Microsoft Internet Information Server 3.0 (including the Active Server Pages component previously known as "Denali") has created an exciting platform that allows designers to implement functionality on the server side. This functionality can operate with lower overhead than CGI or ISAPI programs, and provides the ease of use that new scripting languages have provided.

Active Server Pages (ASP) is one of the essential components that comprises IIS 3.0. Active Server Pages is a server-side scripting environment that functions as an extension to Microsoft Internet Information Server 2.0, Microsoft Peer Web Services, and the Microsoft Personal Web Server for Windows 95. By using ASP, you can create dynamic and interactive Web applications which use the high-performance advantages of the server.

Platform Independence

Unlike client-side scripting that requires a client browser capable of processing the scripting language, Active Server Pages empowers your Web server to process the scripts on the Web server side, generating pure Hypertext Markup Language (HTML), which is delivered to the client browser. Because none of the scripting code is observable on the client side, a Web developer can create extended functionality that relies on user interactivity and can deliver the appropriate content to the visitor. The processing of the script is entirely transparent to the visitor—they are never aware of back-end services.

This allows a visitor using *any* World Wide Web browser, whether it be Netscape Navigator, Microsoft Internet Explorer, or the "Wonder Browser of the Week," to view the page as it was intended. The only limitations on how the visitor will view your site is with what file types you are using for your content (for example, if your page references a .PNG format image, most older Web browsers will not be able to view it). In addition to this flexibility, a great deal of extensibility is achieved without requiring extensions to the client side. This translates into an effortless visit on the part of the user, which allows them to concentrate on the content that you are dispensing to them. With authoring growing increasingly more complex and intricate in supporting multiple browser platforms, the ability to create your site in a manner that is viewable by nearly everyone on the Internet is appealing.

Scripting Language Independence

ASP provides the two industry standard scripting languages built-in: Visual Basic Script (VB-Script) and JavaScript (actually Microsoft JScript, a JavaScript-compatible language). These two languages should be familiar to you if you have worked with client-side scripting in the past. VBScript is a subset of Microsoft's popular Visual Basic language, which is relatively simple and robust. JavaScript (related only to Sun Microsystems' Java by name, not by architecture) is a more complex and advanced scripting environment created by Netscape. Both languages have a loyal following and allow a great deal of intricate interactivity.

Not to be limited to the two basic languages, ASP supports add-in languages through extensions to the architecture. Popular scripting languages in the UNIX world are Perl and Python, both of which are used in creating server-side CGI programs. These two languages are available through third-party language components. If a need arises for the addition of a new scripting language, any developer can create a new extension to fulfill the need.

Server Components

Developers are growing increasingly aware of client-side "ActiveX" components that allow them to extend the client browser. These components, similar in concept to Netscape Plug-Ins, function as OLE (a core Windows subsystem) objects that can carry out basically any task a developer sets out for them. To bring this flexibility to the server side, IIS 3.0 supports server-side components that allow developers to extend the capabilities of the server beyond its basic features. This attribute translates into a healthy boon for site developers who feel they need to create more advanced and powerful sites.

Several components are included in IIS 3.0 that carry out different tasks that can enhance the Web developer's work. As with language extensions, if a developer recognizes a need for an enhancement to IIS, it does not require rewriting the server itself but can be achieved through server-side components. This allows developers to offer third-party tools and products to strengthen the IIS platform without relying on Microsoft to implement it in the next release of the Web server.

File Syntax

Active Server Pages deliver information through Hypertext Markup Language (HTML) files. The key difference between static content and "active content" pages is how the HTML file is formatted and what it contains inside. Scripting for the client side takes place in the average HTML file by using the `<SCRIPT>` `</SCRIPT>` anchors, with the code lying in between the two anchors. If a developer wants to script for the server side, the scripting code must lie between the `<%` and `%>` anchors. This signifies server-side scripting, and will be processed before the client views it. The client browser will never see the code between the two anchors, only what code is generated as a result of its processing.

Scripting for the server side is identical in syntax to scripting for the client side. The differences appear in what you are doing with the information and what objects you are manipulating. For example, you would not control user interface objects on the server side as they do not have a UI. The server-side components offer a different set of features and capabilities and are handled accordingly. That aside, the underlying concepts for the scripting remain the same throughout.

To ensure proper delivery of information, IIS 3.0 uses smart handling of HTML files to tell it how to handle the delivery. For static content delivery, the HTML file can have the extension of .HTM or .HTML. For server-side processing of scripts and components, the HTML file must have the extension .ASP. This signals IIS 3.0 to process the information within the file before delivering it to the client browser. If you contain server-side scripting in a file with an .HTM extension, the scripting will not be processed.

Compile-Free Updates

Unlike ISAPI and most CGI programs, creating ASP pages requires no *compilation* on the part of the developer. For most development languages, the developer must turn his or her instructions (code) into a machine-understandable form through compilation. ASP pages are internally compiled by IIS 3.0 and Active Server Pages without any intervention from the developer. When you modify your ASP page, IIS detects that a change has been made to the file since it was last compiled and quickly recompiles it for delivery. Because this is entirely transparent to the user and the developer, this results in a very quick turnover in development time. If you need to make a change, you can do so quickly and see the results immediately. However, because every ASP page has to be compiled through the server, they also create overhead. If you create a file that incorporates scripting code of any kind, its extension must be .ASP in order for the server to process it properly. If your file has no Active Server Pages functionality within it, then you should use whatever extension is appropriate for that file, be it .HTM, .HTX, and so forth.

ON THE WEB

http://www.microsoft.com/iis   For more information you should go to Microsoft's Internet Information Server Web site.

Server-side components, like client-side components, still require traditional compilation, as they are not created in a scripting environment. Instead, they are developed in a traditional development environment using the standardized API (Application Programming Interface) for IIS. This work is usually done in an environment like Microsoft Visual C++, Microsoft Visual Basic, or Borland Delphi. The important thing to keep in mind is that server-side components are not part of IIS but an extension to the server; thus, they are created and compiled like traditional programs and referenced within ASP pages through scripting.

Included Active Server Components

ASP includes a set of components available for use by site developers. These components are an excellent example of how server-side components can empower developers to create more advanced and effective Web sites. Microsoft created several components that fulfilled an existing need to highlight the possibilities of server-side components. These components replace what used to be carried out either by a CGI or manually by the developer. The included components are: Ad Rotator, Browser Capabilities, Database Access, Content Linking, and File System.

Part

VI

Ch

16

Each component is aimed to fulfill a specific niche or need. All components use a variety of properties and methods for scripts to manipulate and use. We will explore each of the components and how they function. From the previous chapter, we will use the delectable "Herb's Mostly Identifiable Greasy Chicken Parts" as our sample site. Only brief code excerpts and screen shots will be shown within this chapter. To view the full sample site, you will find it on Que's Web site—**http://www.quecorp.com/mcis**. The sample site goes into more depth about the activation process for each component, including sample code. Before viewing the example, please follow the instructions provided in the "Readme.HTM". This file details the few simple steps you will need to follow to set up the "Herb's" site on your own machine to view it properly.

If you need more comprehensive information on the components discussed within this chapter, or Active Server Pages in general, you should refer to the Microsoft Active Server Pages Roadmap included with IIS 3.0 ASP. The Roadmap completely details each component with scripting information and several examples. You will find a link to the Roadmap in your Start Menu after installing Active Server Pages.

Ad Rotator

The signature horizontal banner for advertising has become a mainstay for most commercial Web sites. The actual size and shape of the advertisement makes no real difference; it is the task of displaying and controlling these "nagbars" that has become an increasingly bigger chore for administrators. In addition to the administrative headaches, they present a looming problem for designers and developers in how to integrate them into a site while maintaining uniformity and backward compatibility. Most sites use a series of CGI programs for controlling how frequently a banner appears, and where it should be linked. In addition to the presentation, these CGIs usually map statistics for "click-throughs," or how many times a user clicked a banner to continue, where they were visiting, and so on. The monitoring of click-throughs is usually the task of the "hit counters" that appear on many Web pages.

The Ad Rotator component is a clever extension to IIS that addresses these key concerns in a simple fashion (see Figure 16.1). The component automates the rotation of the banner for each time a page is reloaded by using a Rotator Schedule file. The schedule file is a simple text file formatted to specify the dimensions of the advertisement and the URLs for the individual banners, in addition to alternate text and a redirectional URL. You can also assign "impressions" to a particular banner to set the relative weight or frequency of the advertisement. This translates into how often a visitor will see a particular banner over another.

FIG. 16.1

For a more thorough description of the code behind the ad rotator, check out your copy of Herb's site on this book's CD.

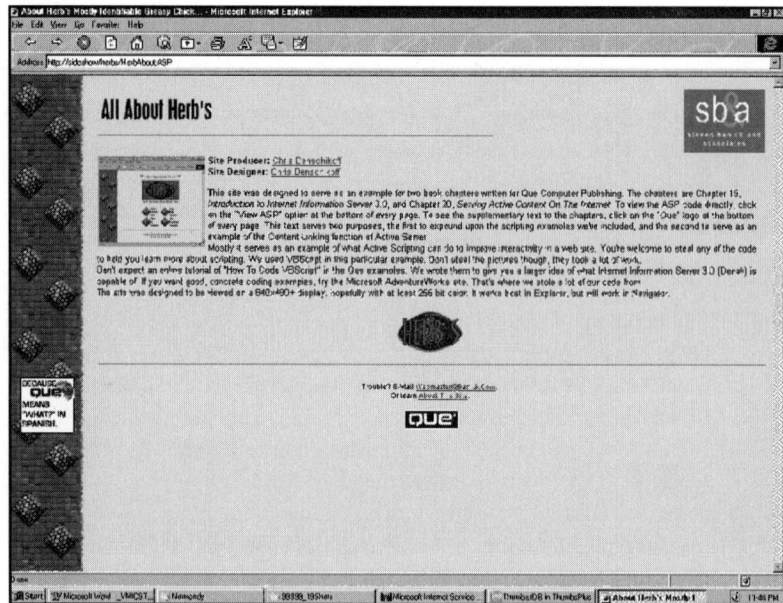

In addition to the Rotator Schedule, you may optionally use a Redirection File that allows finer control over user redirection. The Redirection File also allows you to include scripting to count the number of "click-throughs" for a particular banner and save the information, or to perform calculations based on the number of visitors. This information is invaluable for advertisers and site operators alike and once required specialized CGI programs to track.

Our Sample Site: Herb's

As you may remember from the last chapter, Jose was given the responsibility of creating and maintaining the Web site for "Herb's Mostly Identifiable Greasy Chicken Parts." Recognizing the benefit of online advertising, Jose decided to include a series of alternating box advertisements within the Herb's Web site. Jose saw it as an excellent way to pad out the cost of maintaining the site and sucking up to suppliers for a better deal. The site developers, Site Corporati, integrated the Microsoft "Ad Rotator" component for the site, beginning with five ads.

Jose began by deciding on five separate advertisements, where they would link to, and the frequency that they would appear on-screen. The Site Corporati team went to work by first creating a Rotator Schedule file that lists the five advertisements, as shown in Listing 16.1.

N O T E   All of these listings can be found on Que's Web Site—**http://www.quecorp.com/mcis**.

Listing 16.1   The AdRot.TXT File Is the Rotator Schedule File that Contains Information on the Separate Advertisements, Their Associated URLs, and the Frequency that They Will Appear

```
WIDTH 80
HEIGHT 80
BORDER 0
*
LilHerbAd1.GIF
-
Eat At Herb's - For the Children's sake
20
MicroAd.GIF
http://www.microsoft.com
Microsoft - Because we like sucking up to them
20
QueAd.GIF
http://www.que.com/mcp
Read Que Books - Because they pay us in American $$$
20
SBAAd.GIF
http://www.banick.com
Steven Banick & Associates - Get Savvy, Get Cool
20
Mst3KAd.GIF
-
Enjoy the comic stylings of this guy and two robots
20
```

N O T E

Once the Rotator Schedule file was in place, Site Corporati simply inserted two lines of HTML code into the site, consistent with the appearance design they had decided on. These two lines instruct ASP to insert the appropriate advertisement when the page is processed before delivery to the visitor's browser. Once this was inserted, the advertisements and the Ad Rotator were off and running.

Listing 16.2   Taken from the Front Page of Herb's Site, but Present Throughout, These Two Lines of Code Instruct Active Server Pages to Insert the Next Ad

```
<% Set ad = Server.CreateObject("MSWC.AdRotator") %>
<%= ad.GetAdvertisement("adrot.txt") %>
```

Browser Capabilities

An increasingly frustrating and unrewarding task for site developers is to create fantastic sites that function in any browser, yet still use all of the "Whiz bang" features that visitors and advertisers expect. This usually involves maintaining several different "versions" of the Web site that perform properly for specific browsers, or stripping a site down to baseline compatibility and sacrificing some of the potential present in newer browsers. Neither of these options is appealing and cause significant stress on the part of developers.

The Browser Capabilities component empowers your scripts with the ability to recognize what the client's browser is capable of handling. This in turn gives your active site the ability to alter itself, determines what content is appropriate to deliver, and what doesn't work. This is due to the mechanics of how Web browsers connect to Web servers. Browsers automatically send a "User Agent" header in an HTTP request that identifies the browser and its appropriate version number. By comparing the browser and its version to an internal list of browsers and capabilities, the Browser Capabilities component can accurately determine what the visitor's browser is capable of doing and what it isn't.

This component uses a resource file called "browscap.ini" that contains information on different browsers and their capabilities. If a new browser is released, or you discover that an existing browser can (or can't) do something, it is a simple task to edit the resource file. The browscap.ini is a simple formatted text file which lists the browser, its version, and a list of capabilities.

For sections within your site that require browser-capabilities detection, you create a server-side script that calls the component. Depending on the results returned from the component, your script could decide how to present the information as is required (see Figure 16.2).

FIG. 16.2

The Browser Capabilities component can tell you quite a lot about a user's browser type and preferences. You could use this information for marketing or just to smooth navigation of your site.

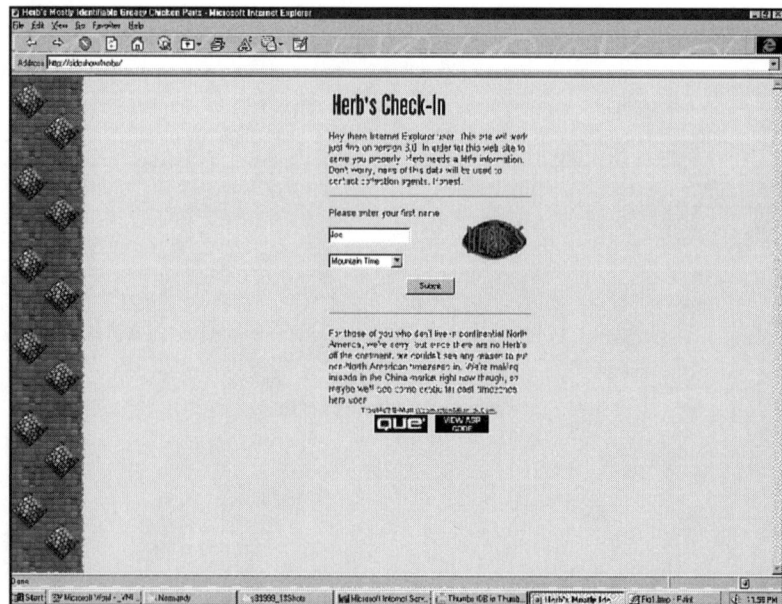

Database Access

Dynamic Web sites usually require a database to store information for retrieval when needed. Previously, reading (and writing) database information for a Web site needed either CGI/ISAPI programs or an existing database connector (like IDC/HTX or a third-party product). The Database Access component allows you to use ActiveX Data Objects (ADO) to send and retrieve information stored in a database. This is all achieved directly within your ASP page, as opposed to an external program or file.

Part VI

Ch 16

Database access lets a developer store dynamic information within a database for easier manipulation or change. Rather than manually editing each HTML file that contains information that should change, the developer only needs to update the information in one central location: the database. The ASP pages then retrieve the most up-to-date information available from the database for presentation. This can also be done in reverse. Information retrieved from a visitor on the Web site, likely through a form, can be stored within the database. This is ideal for tracking users, access, and client information, for example.

The component works by using the ActiveX Data Objects, which uses standard ODBC (Open Database Connector) data sources and OLE DB providers. By using the Windows standard for database communication, the component can communicate with any type of database that has a driver installed on the system. This means that you are not limited to just using Microsoft Access or SQL Server databases—you may also use dBASE resources, Oracle, and many others. ODBC provides a standardized framework for communicating with databases, which leaves you to be concerned only with what data you need to manage back and forth; not the trivial bottom-line mechanics of getting it in and out of the database. Additionally, Microsoft Access 97 lets you directly export database information as an .ASP file for convenience (see Figure 16.3). This is ideal if you are not familiar with the SQL syntax.

FIG. 16.3

Adding database functions to Web sites is an incredible leap that could be used for maintaining news articles to diary entries. Or, in this case, the specials in a greasy chicken place.

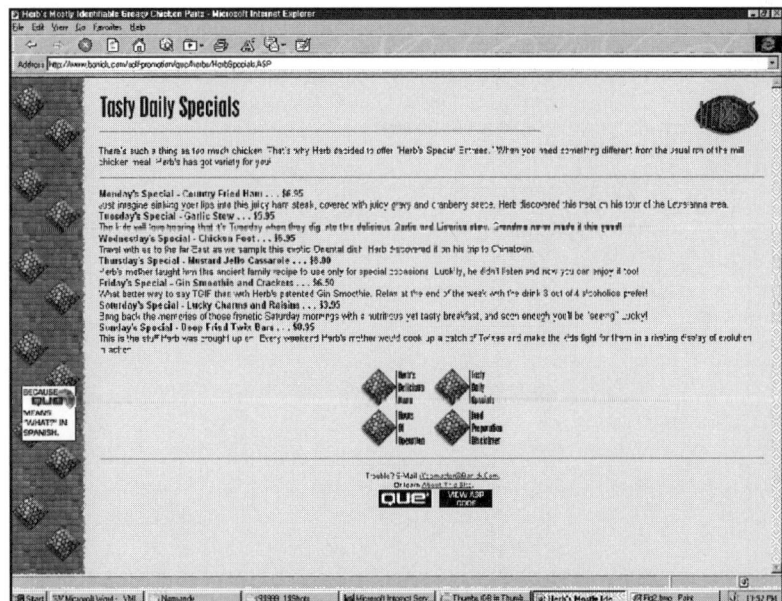

Our Sample Site: Herb's

Jose created a headache for himself. When he sat down with the Web designers, he had decided to implement a "Specials" section to Herb's Web site that would highlight the particular special of the day. The problems began when the management staff decided that the Wednesday special, "Twinkies Au Gratin," just wasn't performing as well as they would have liked and decided to replace it. This translated into Jose having to hire someone (in this case, the original designers at Site Corporati) to update the pages where this was referenced. "What a pain!" Jose thought to himself. "It would be a lot easier if it could just tie into our Point of Sales..." Bingo, he thought.

Jose decided that a short-term cost now would be better than an ongoing expense later, so he contracted the designers to have the daily specials information retrieved from the corporate database. This meant that any time the menu was changed at the head office, it would automatically change in the Web site. No tedious editing...hooray!

In the Herb's site, the Database Access component was integrated to retrieve information from a simple Microsoft Access database through ODBC, the standard for database communications in Windows. This required a "Data Source Name" (DSN) to be specified on the Web server for the code to reference. Once the DSN was set up and pointing to the Access database, the ASP page could have industry-standard SQL (Structured Query Language) database statements inserted directly into the page, as opposed to relying on external CGI or ISAPI programs.

When it was all said and done, Jose managed to turn an entire page into a few simple lines of ASP code (see Listing 16.3), which were inserted into the specials page. From then on, whenever someone visits the page, the most recent information is retrieved.

Listing 16.3 The Specials.ASP Page Illustrates How Simple It Is to Add Live Database Connectivity. Note the SQL Statements that Appear Directly in the Code

```
<%
Query = "SELECT * FROM Specials WHERE ID=" & CurrentDayInt
Set Conn = Server.CreateObject("ADODB.Connection")
Conn.Open Session("ConnectionString")
Set RS = Conn.Execute(Query)
= RS("Specials")
RS.Close
Conn.Close
Set RS = Nothing
%>
```

Content Linking

If you are dealing with a large, multi-page site that has a great amount of content, then the Content Linking component will be a lifesaver. In the past, a developer had to manually keep track of consecutive pages and the links in between. It was only possible to create crude interfaces for switching pages directly by number, or by next and previous pages in consecutive numbers. The Content Linking component allows you to manage a list of pages or URLs so that they may be manipulated like the pages in a book. This allows you to create an interface that makes true use of a "Next Page" or "Back" without any trickery—the component knows exactly where a visitor has been in the list, and where to go next.

In addition to easier page management, the component also is capable of generating automatic content lists and navigational links. Imagine if you had to create a site containing hundreds of pages of reference material. The laborious task of manually creating sections and contents, as well as linking all of the pages as needed would surely drive you mad (or at least cramp your hands). With the Component Linking component, you would create a simple formatted text file containing the URLs and a description for each individual page. Once that's completed, you create one standardized page for displaying the contents, including navigational controls, with a script to read in the appropriate page of content (see Figure 16.4). As a visitor advanced to the next page, the component would fetch the next page and insert it into the standardized page. No mess!

FIG. 16.4

Content Linking lets you create quick and easy tables of contents or paging systems.

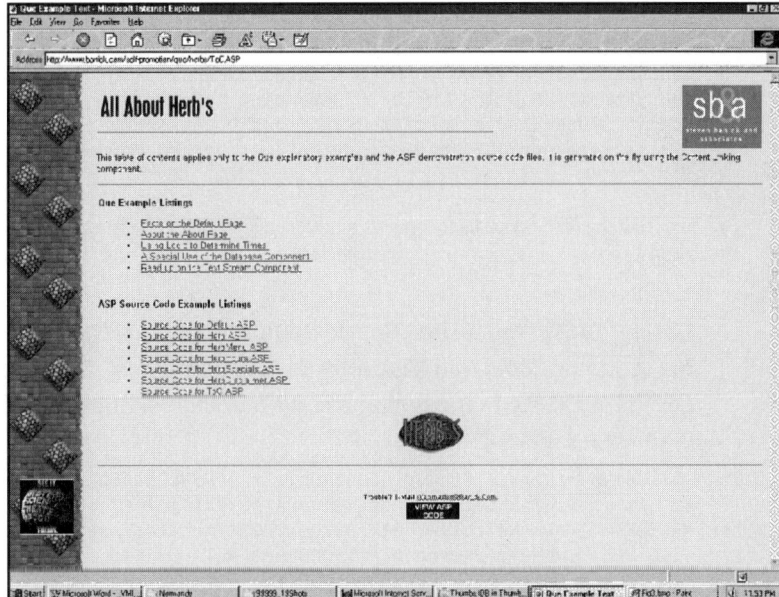

Our Sample Site: Herb's

Jose was immensely pleased with himself. Herb's site was growing in popularity and he was receiving (in his eyes) a well-deserved pat on the back from upper management. At the request of his superior, Big Lou, Jose was given the task of documenting the entire Herb's site so that the efforts could be duplicated in the new corporate concept restaurant, "Smilin' Ed's Kentucky Roasted Potato Barn." Hoping for that lucrative promotion to the new company, Jose again contracted the now fat and bloated Sites Corporati to fully document their efforts on the site's activation.

To Sites Corporati, this presented a simple problem. This would result in a large number of pages explaining each active aspect of the site. Navigation and maintenance of the pages could grow to be a headache. Knowing better than to doubt the all-knowing Microsoft, the designers implemented the Content Linking component to handle the multiple pages of documentation. This allowed the designers to add new pages by simply adding them to the list of URLs (see Listing 16.4) and letting the component handle the building of a table of contents. Site Corporati had to make sure that each line in the NewLink.TXT file was separated with a carriage return and line feed. From there, the designers only had to design one page with the code to insert the navigational tools.

Listing 16.4   The NewLink.TXT File Contains a List of Pages in the Form of URLs. These Pages Comprise the "Document" that Is Readable. By Adding a Description of the Page, a Table of Contents Can Be Automatically Generated as Needed

```
DefaultAbout.ASP Facts on the Default Page
QueAbout.ASP About the About Page
MenuAbout.ASP Lowdown on Herb's Menu
HoursAbout.ASP Using Logic to Determine Times
SpecialsAbout.ASP A Special Use of the Database Component
DisclaimerAbout.ASP Read up on the Text Stream Component
```

The inserting of the document contents and the navigational buttons was a simple task, as shown in Listing 16.5.

Listing 16.5   The Actual Script Code to Insert the Document Contents and Navigational Tools Is a Matter of Only a Few Lines. This Allows You to Have a Lot of Flexibility in Designing the Appearance Without Worrying About Flowing in the Material

```
<%  Set NextLink = Server.CreateObject ("MSWC.NextLink") %>
<%  If (NextLink.GetListIndex ("newlink.txt") > 1) Then %>
<A HREF="  <%= NextLink.GetPreviousURL ("newlink.txt")  %>  ">
<IMG SRC="Image/Backward.GIF" BORDER=0 ALT="Previous"></A>
<%  End If  %>
<FONT FACE="Arial" SIZE=-2>
<A HREF="ToC.ASP">Table of Contents</A>
<A HREF="  <%= NextLink.GetNextURL ("newlink.txt")  %>  ">
<IMG SRC="Image/Forward.GIF" BORDER=0 ALT="Next"></A>
```

File System

The File Access Component is a deceptively simple yet powerful component for developers. The component uses two objects—the FileSystem and the TextStream objects. Both of these objects provide you direct access to the server's file system within your page. By using these two objects, you may control and directly modify files, as well as retrieve directory structures. This allows you to create complex, file-based Web applications.

The FileSystem object works through two methods—one to create a text file and the second to open a text file. From that point, your ASP page may modify the contents of the file as required, as shown in Figure 16.5. The TextStream object allows you sequential access to a file, usually text. This allows you to read and write to a file in steps.

Part

VI

Ch

16

FIG. 16.5

Putting long, boring legal documents that change all the time into a Web site is just one of the applications of the File System Object.

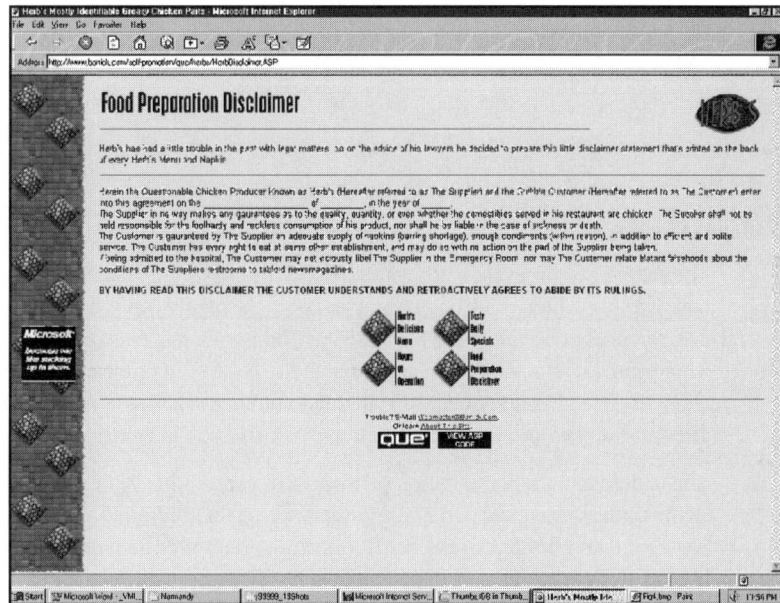

Our Sample Site: Herb's

Thanks to a nasty case of under-prepared food (a hallmark of Herb's), the corporate lawyers quickly and politely informed Jose that he would need to add a disclaimer to the Web site that had also been put into action at all of the stores on the back of the napkins. Because Jose hates legalese (thanks to that "bump and run" in '86), he took the disclaimer file straight from the corporate drone lawyers and passed it off to Sites Corporati to include into the site. Looking for a way to pad out their resume without having to manually retype the entire disclaimer, the designers implemented the FileSystem component to directly read in the file as-is from the legal department. Everyone kept their sanity this way, and the lawyers didn't look cross-eyed at anyone who made a typo.

continues

continued

Because the contents of the disclaimer were already stored in a standard text file, all the designers needed to do was to insert the scripting code to read it in. The few lines required are shown in Listing 16.6. The plan in the future is to have a rotating series of disclaimers and random first lines for the contents, but that has yet to be approved by the lawyers.

Listing 16.6   The Disclaimer Is a Good Example of Reading in the Contents of an Outside File. You Can Keep Existing Formatting of a Page While Taking the Material from Other Sources

```
<%
Set FileObject = Server.CreateObject("Scripting.FileSystemObject")
Set Instream = FileObject.OpenTextFile (Server.MapPath ("/Herbs") &
    "\Disclaimer.txt", 1, FALSE, FALSE)
DisclaimerText = Instream.ReadAll
= DisclaimerText
%>
```

From Here...

The Active Server system allows you to do things you normally could not. Even more important, it allows you to do things that you could do before, only *much easier*. The most important design concept behind all of the ActiveX Components is centralization. The Ad Rotator takes what is normally a messy job and puts all the control in one central file. If you want to make changes, you change one text file instead of many sub files. Both the Database Object and the Text Stream component allow you to put information in central points to include in Web sites.

The design and implementation of advanced, content-heavy sites is becoming easier and easier as the tools to effectively manage and present data are honed. Microsoft's Internet Information Server 3.0 and the Active Server Pages component are the next link in a chain leading inexorably to a newer and better interface between Web and user. Many of the Microsoft Commercial Internet System services include active server components that you can manipulate from within ASP.

Now that you have expanded your knowledge base for Serving Active Content, you should look into these chapters:

- Chapter 18, "Server Administration Via the Web," covers the ins and outs of administering a server remotely, and the tools built into IIS 3.0 to do so.
- Chapter 20, "Developing an Intranet with MCIS Servers," tells you why IIS 3.0 is one of the best choices for a start in the growing intranet market.

Administration, Data Access, and Extended Capabilities

Using the Microsoft Proxy Server

Meet the Proxy Server

Learn what a Proxy Server does and how it can make your Internet site faster and more secure.

Manage the Proxy Server

See how to install and configure the Proxy Server. Learn what's required in the day to day administration.

Use the Proxy Server cache

Learn how caching can reduce the bandwidth your site uses and improve client service.

Secure your site

See how the Proxy Server can help protect your site against hacker attacks and unwanted visitors.

Is the Internet a safe place to go? That's the multi-million dollar question.

Is it safe to surf the Web? Of course it is, but is it safe to put your company on the Web? That is a more difficult question. In a recent survey by Warroom Research, Inc. of Baltimore, MD, 58 percent of 236 companies polled reported hacker attacks within the previous 12 months. Fifty-seven of those companies were hit at least 11 times during that period. One-third of the attacks cost the companies at least one million dollars to repair the damage.

Obviously the Internet can be a dangerous place to put valuable company information. However, you would not want to walk down a city street with a roll of cash visible in your hand. You would want to hide the money in your pocket. Likewise, if you leave your Internet site or network visible for all to see, you ask for trouble. The Microsoft Proxy Server gives you the ability to "hide" your network and help protect your data.

This chapter takes a look at the Microsoft Proxy Server and how to use it. You learn how to set up clients and how to help speed up the network using the caching capabilities of the Proxy Server. You will also see how a well configured cache can greatly reduce your network bandwidth usage. ■

Introducing the Proxy Server

A *proxy server* is a server configured to act on behalf of assigned clients.

When a client application makes a request for data from the Internet, a proxy server responds by translating the request and passing it to the Internet. When a computer on the Internet responds, the proxy server passes that response back to the computer that made the request. The proxy server is a gateway between the client computers and the Internet.

A gateway is special software, or a computer running special software, that enables two different networks to communicate. A proxy server provides a gateway between your network and the Internet. You configure a proxy server to enable your workstations to communicate with remote services on the Internet. You select the appropriate hardware for a gateway computer, adequate bandwidth for the Internet connection, and choose the level of security for protecting your network. The gateway acts as a barrier that allows you to make requests to the Internet and receive information, but does not allow access to your network by unauthorized users.

Microsoft Proxy Server listens to the computers on your network, translating requests and passing them to the Internet, then passes responses back to the client. Thus the Microsoft Proxy Server handles all direct interaction with the Internet for the computers on your network. This provides one layer of protection between you and the outside world. If the client requests a cached document then the Proxy server fills the requests directly from the cache, further protecting and speeding up the network.

Exploring the Proxy Server

The Microsoft Proxy Server supports all Internet protocols, including WWW (HTTP), FTP, RealAudio, VDOLive, IRC, and mail and news protocols. Support for Novell's IPX/SPX transport eliminates the need for installing TCP/IP on the network. Internet sites can be accessed by Web browsers running on any operating system, and by all 16- and 32-bit Windows Sockets applications.

With Microsoft Proxy Server you can:

- Extend Internet applications to every desktop on your internal network by configuring the client applications to utilize the Proxy Server.

- Improve performance and access for Internet-based services on your network by utilizing the caching capabilities of the Proxy Server. Cached copies of popular Web pages can be maintained locally and updated automatically.

- Provide secure access between your private network and the Internet by configuring the Microsoft Proxy Server to grant or deny outbound Internet access by user, service, port, or IP domain. Access to specific domain sites can be blocked easily.

- Integrate proxy services closely within your current network operating system. Microsoft Proxy Server provides tight integration with Microsoft Windows NT Server and Microsoft Internet Information Server, resulting in a high level of performance and ease of administration.

Preparing to Install the Microsoft Proxy Server

The Microsoft Proxy Server Setup program installs the following on a server:

- The Web Proxy service
- The WinSock Proxy service
- A shared network directory containing a client Setup program
- The online documentation in HTML format
- The administrative components

Before You Begin

Before you begin the installation process, the following must already be installed on the server:

- Microsoft Windows NT Server version 4.0
- Microsoft Internet Information Server version 2.0 or later
- The Windows NT Server 4.0 Service Pack 1
- The TCP/IP network protocol

N O T E The server computer can be configured as a stand-alone server, a primary domain controller (PDC), or a backup domain controller (BDC). However, for the highest security level and best performance it is recommended that you install Microsoft Proxy Server on a computer configured as a stand-alone server. For best cache performance, it is strongly recommended that at least one disk drive on the server computer be configured as a Windows NT File System (NTFS) volume. ■

▶ **See** "Using Windows NT Server 4.0," **p. 46**, if you need help installing and configuring Windows NT or IIS.

Setting Up the Disk Drives

Microsoft Proxy Server can be installed on computers that have their hard disks configured as either file allocation table (FAT) or NTFS volumes. However, for security and performance, it is recommended that at least one of the server's hard disks be configured as an NTFS volume. This enables the Proxy Server to take advantage of Windows NT security and auditing capabilities.

> **CAUTION**
> Once a FAT volume is converted to an NTFS volume, it cannot be converted back to FAT.

The Web Proxy service of Microsoft Proxy Server stores cached Internet objects on one or more of the server's drives. You will select these drives during installation. For best cache performance, it is strongly recommended that all the drives having space allocated to the cache be configured as NTFS drives.

Depending on the number of clients using the Proxy Server, the size of the cache can grow rapidly. You should plan on allocating as much drive space for the cache as possible. The larger the cache, the less bandwidth you will use.

TIP If your current server disk volume is formatted to use FAT partitions, before or after installing Microsoft Proxy Server you can convert these partitions to NTFS using the Convert program included with Windows NT Server. Convert does not overwrite data on the disk.

Setting Up the Network Adapters

Before you install Microsoft Proxy Server, verify that the network adapter cards are installed and configured properly. To create a secure configuration, the Microsoft Proxy Server computer must have at least one network adapter connected to your network, plus one network adapter connected to the Internet.

If you need to install additional network cards, go ahead and install them now. Once they are installed you can configure them through Control Panel.

To configure additional network adapter cards, follow these steps:

1. Open Control Panel.

2. Double-click the Network application, and then click Adapters to display that property sheet.

3. Add the additional network adapter card by clicking the Add button in the Adapters property sheet.

FIG. 17.1

Select your adapter from the Network Adapter list box.

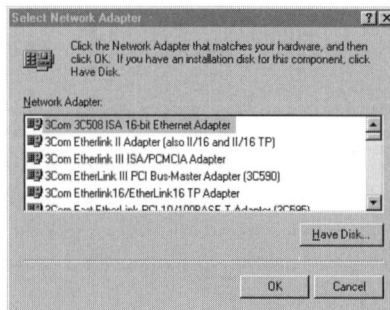

4. Select your adapter from the list shown in Figure 17.1 and click OK.

After Windows NT installs the software for your adapter you will need to restart your system. Then you will need to configure the TCP/IP settings for your adapters.

To configure TCP/IP settings for internal and external network adapter cards, follow these steps:

1. Open Control Panel and Network application again.

2. Click the Bindings Tab.

3. Select show bindings for all adapters.

4. Select the Adapter connected to the Internet.

5. Set the binding to TCP/IP, as shown in Figure 17.2, so that it can communicate over the Internet. When binding this network card to TCP/IP, you are prompted for the card's Internet Protocol address. This address is usually supplied by your Internet Service Provider (ISP).

FIG. 17.2

Bind the external network adapter to the TCP/IP protocol.

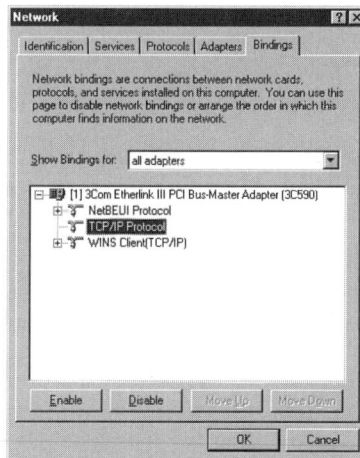

Part

VII

Ch

17

> **CAUTION**
>
> If the external network adapter card will be used to connect to the Internet, it must be bound only to the TCP/IP protocol. In particular, do not bind IPX/SPX or NetBEUI to the externally connected cards. If you bind protocols other than TCP/IP to the card you open your network to attacks utilizing those protocols.

6. Select the Adapter connected to the internal network

7. Set the protocol bindings for the internal network adapter card.

   If the server will be running the Web Proxy service, the network adapter card connected to the private network must be bound to TCP/IP in addition to your internal protocols. If the server will be running the WinSock Proxy service, the network adapter card connected to the internal network can be bound to TCP/IP, IPX/SPX, or both.

8. Click OK and restart the system.

N O T E A Microsoft Proxy Server computer should have only one IP default gateway. The IP address of the default gateway should be configured on the external network adapter card only. ▪

You can choose to implement Microsoft Proxy Server on a server that has only one network adapter card. This configuration can be used to provide some limited Proxy functions such as:

- A Caching service for internal Web Proxy clients
- An IP application-level gateway to support internal IPX clients that use the WinSock Proxy service
- An IP default gateway

The Local Address Table

During Microsoft Proxy Server installation you are asked to complete the Local Address Table Configuration dialog box. The information you provide is used to create a Local Address Table (LAT). This section describes the LAT, tells you what the LAT does, and shows you how the LAT is defined.

During Microsoft Proxy Server installation, the Setup program helps you create a list of the IP addresses that make up your internal network. The information you provide is used to create the Local Address Table (LAT).

The Setup program installs the LAT on the server. The file containing the LAT is named Msplat.txt and on the server its default location is C:\Msp\Clients. The Microsoft Proxy Server Setup program also installs a client Setup program into this directory.

The LAT is defined during Microsoft Proxy Server installation when you complete the Local Address Table Configuration dialog box. The LAT consists of a series of IP address pairs. Each address pair defines either a range of IP addresses (from the first, lower address to the second, higher address), or a single IP address (if both addresses of the pair are identical).

Each IP address pair identifies either a range of addresses, or a single IP address. Do not mistake the second entry for a subnet mask. It looks like a routing table, but it is very different.

Changing Service Ports

The Web Proxy service uses the port set for the WWW service as its listen-on port. The default is port 80. If you want to use a different port, use the Internet Service Manager to change the WWW service port number. You must do this before installing the Proxy Server.

To change the port, use this procedure:

1. Open the Internet Service Manager from the Start menu.
2. Double-click the computer name next to the WWW Service.
3. In the Service tab of the WWW Service Properties window, type the port number in the TCP Port box, as shown in Figure 17.3, and then click OK.
4. From Internet Service Manager, stop and restart the WWW service.

During Microsoft Proxy Server setup, the Setup program reads this port number from the Windows NT registry and adds it to the WebProxyPort field of the Mspclnt.ini client configuration file that Setup adds to the server's Mspclnt client installation share. When a client computer installs the client software from that share the client's browser is configured to use this port on the proxy.

FIG. 17.3

Set the Port Number in the <u>T</u>CP Port text box.

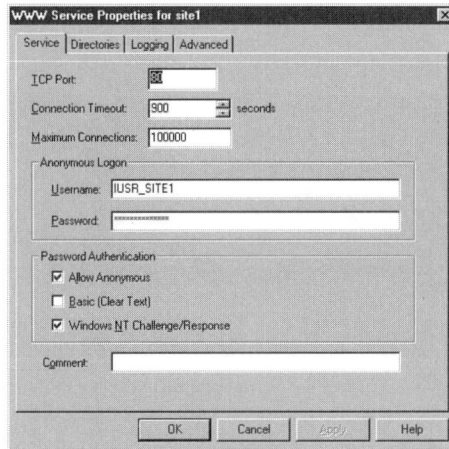

If you change the WWW service port number after installing Microsoft Proxy Server, you must edit the WebProxyPort value in the Mspclnt.ini file in the server's Mspclnt share. If browser clients of that server are not already configured to use that port, also use each browser's configuration interface to configure the browser to use the new port number.

Installing the Proxy Server

To install Microsoft Proxy Server first verify that the server has Windows NT Server version 4.0 and Microsoft Internet Information Server (IIS) version 2.0 installed. Then restart the system and log on using an account that has administrative privileges on the server. Follow these steps to install Proxy Server:

1. Open the folder for the Microsoft Proxy Server and run Setup.

2. Choose the Installation Options button (see Figure 17.4) to display the Installation Options dialog box. To decide which Microsoft Proxy Server components to install, select or clear the check box for each option.

FIG. 17.4

Click the Installation Options button to proceed.

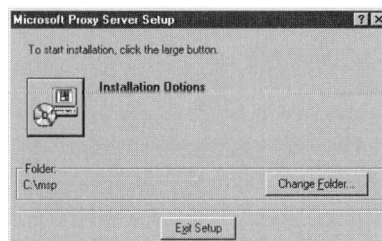

The Installation Options dialog box allows you to install the following items, as shown in Figure 17.5:

- Proxy Server
- The Administration Tool
- Install Documentation
- By default, all components are selected

FIG. 17.5

Choose the components to install here.

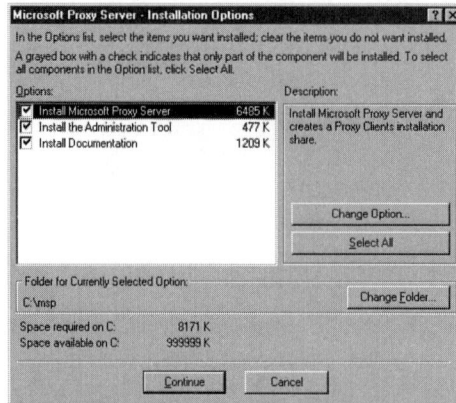

3. When the installation options are set appropriately, click Continue. The Microsoft Proxy Server Cache Drives dialog box appears. The server's local drives are listed.

4. To assign a disk to store the cached data, select the drive from the list.

5. When configuring the cache drives you must, at a minimum, allocate at least one drive and 5M for caching. Microsoft recommends that you allocate at least 100M plus 0.5M for each Web Proxy service client. For example, if a server will be servicing 85 Web Proxy clients, it is recommended that you allocate 145M or more to the cache. For each server the optimal cache allocation varies depending on load and configuration, but in general, increasing the disk space allocation benefits the cache.

   Allocate space from a drive to the cache in increments of 5M. If you assign a number to the cache that cannot be evenly divided by 5, the allocation is rounded down to the next lowest 5M increment. For example, if you assign 144M to the C drive, 140M is actually allocated from that drive to the cache.

   Type the number of megs you determine in the Maximum Size (M) box, and then click Set.

NOTE You should only use NTFS drives for the cache. This allows them to take advantage of the NT file compression and block size features. This will maximize the efficiency of the drive use process.

6. Repeat Steps 4 and 5 as often as necessary to assign additional drives to store cached data.

7. When all drives have been assigned, click OK. The Local Address Table Configuration dialog box appears, as shown in Figure 17.6. This dialog box is used to define all the internal IP addresses of your network, and to exclude all external IP addresses.

FIG. 17.6

Use the Local Address Table Configuration box to define your internal network.

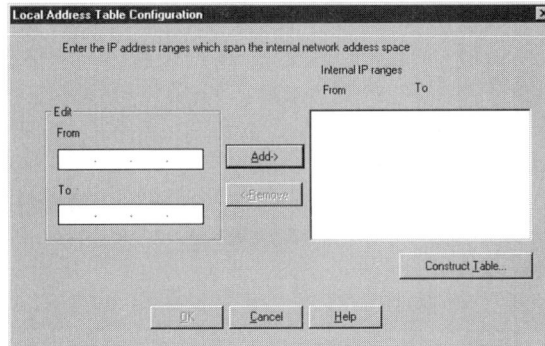

8. Click the Construct Table button. The Construct Local Address Table dialog box appears (see Figure 17.7).

FIG. 17.7

This is where you will build the Local Access Table.

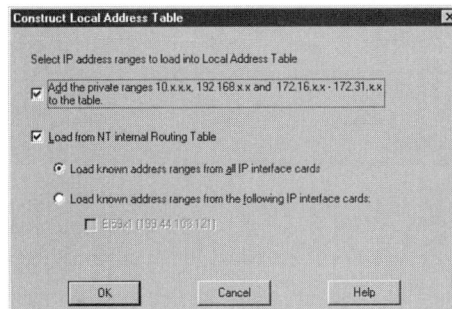

9. Select Load from NT Internal Routing Table.

If you do not know which of the server's network adapter cards are connected to the internal network, select Load known address ranges from all IP interface cards.

If you know which of the server's network adapter cards are connected to the internal network and which are connected to the Internet:

Select Load known address ranges from the following IP interface cards to load only those IP addresses associated with the server's internally connected cards.

Then, in the list of network adapter cards, select the check box for each of the internally connected cards, and clear the check box for each of the externally connected cards.

10. When you have completed the Construct Local Address Table dialog box, click OK. The Local Address Table Configuration dialog box returns. A list of IP address pairs is displayed in the Internal IP Ranges box.

Part

VII

Ch

17

11. Verify that the entries in the Internal IP Ranges box correctly identify your internal network. Add any needed IP address pairs until all addresses of your internal network are defined. Remove any IP address pairs that define external (Internet) addresses.

To add a range of IP addresses to the list, under Edit type a pair of addresses in the From and To boxes, and then click the Add button.

12. When the LAT configuration is properly set, click OK.

After the setup of the LAT is finished, the Client Installation/Configuration dialog box appears. Figure 17.8 shows the dialog box where you enter information that is used by the client Setup program.

FIG. 17.8

The options available in the Client Installation/ Configuration dialog box control how the client Setup program configures clients and security options.

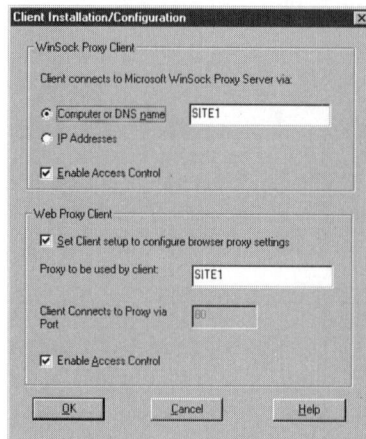

The choices in the WinSock Proxy Client section of the dialog box allow you to specify how the client Setup program will configure WinSock Proxy clients that will be installed from this server. Select either Machine or DNS Name or IP Addresses. If you select Machine or DNS Name, verify that the name is correct.

When the Enable Access Control check box is selected, WinSock Proxy service security is enabled, and only those clients that have been assigned permissions are able to use the WinSock Proxy service on this server. If you clear this check box, all internal clients will be able to use the WinSock Proxy service on this server. By default, this check box is selected.

The options in the Web Proxy Client section allow you to specify how the client Setup program configures Web Proxy clients that install from this server. If the clients are using Microsoft's Internet Explorer or Netscape's Navigator you can select the Set Client Setup to Configure Browser Proxy Settings to have the client Setup program configure the browsers as a Web Proxy client.

If you select this option, verify that the name shown in the Proxy to be Used by Client box is correct. Also verify that the Client Connects to Proxy Via Port value displays the port number that Web Proxy clients will be configured to use. The value in this box cannot be changed here.

It is the TCP port number that is set for Internet Information Server, and is changed using the Internet Service Manager to administer the WWW service.

When the Enable Access Control check box is selected, Web Proxy service security is enabled. When this check box is cleared, the Web Proxy service will not attempt to validate connections from clients. By default, this check box is selected.

When the Client Installation/Configuration dialog box is complete, the setup program proceeds with the installation of the Microsoft Proxy Server. When it is finished you will not be prompted to restart the computer. Go ahead and restart the system and then we will look at how you administer and configure the Proxy Server.

Administering the Proxy Server

The Proxy Server is administered using the Internet Service Manager. However, you can (and probably should) set up an administrative workstation. This allows you to configure and administrate the Proxy Server from a remote location. Since the Proxy Server utilizes the Internet Service Manager, it has the same easy to use features as many of the other MCIS Servers.

Setting up an Administrative Workstation

You can install the administration tool for the Web Proxy and WinSock Proxy services without installing Microsoft Proxy Server. The administration tool can be installed on computers running either Windows NT Server or Windows NT Workstation. In either case you must also install the appropriate Internet Information Server.

To install the Administrative tools, use this procedure:

1. From the root directory of the Microsoft Proxy Server compact disc or from a shared network folder, run Setup.
2. Select the Install Administration Tool check box and clear the Install Proxy Server check box.
3. Click OK. The setup program will proceed to install the Administrative Tools.

To open and use the administration tool, follow these steps:

1. From the desktop, click Start, select Programs, and then select Microsoft Proxy Server.
2. Click Internet Service Manager.
3. The Microsoft Internet Service Manager window is displayed. It lists the Internet services available on the local computer. Because Microsoft Proxy Server is not installed on this computer, the Web Proxy and WinSock Proxy services are not included in the list.
4. Choose Properties, Connect to Server. The Connect to Server dialog box appears.
5. Type a server name in the Server Name box, and then click OK, as shown in Figure 17.9.

FIG. 17.9

Enter the name of the
Proxy Server here.

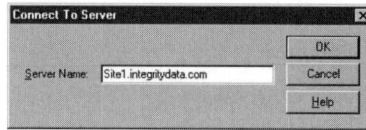

The Internet services available on that server will now be listed in Internet Service Manager. If that server has already had Microsoft Proxy Server installed, the Web Proxy and WinSock Proxy services appear in the list.

You may now administer the Web Proxy and WinSock Proxy services on that server.

Configuring the Proxy Server

For configuring access to Web Proxy and WinSock Proxy services, it is recommended that you add users to groups, and then assign permissions to those groups. By using group assignments, you can simplify the administrative tasks needed to grant or revoke user permissions for Microsoft Proxy Server. These groups can be set up using the Windows NT Administrative Tools. For help in using these tool please refer to Chapter 3, "Building the Foundation," or Que's *SE Using Windows NT 4.0*. You can also refer to the Windows NT Books online documentation found under the accessories menu.

A number of considerations can affect how you choose to configure or install Microsoft Proxy Server on your network. Configuring server network adapter cards and TCP/IP ports correctly is an important consideration. Also, for networks that use other TCP/IP services such as DNS, WINS, DHCP, or multiple gateways, further considerations apply when using Microsoft Proxy Server on your network. We will address these issues in this section.

To configure Microsoft Proxy Server services with the Internet Service Manager, follow these steps:

1. Click Start, select Programs, select Microsoft Proxy Server, and click Internet Service Manager.
2. The Microsoft Internet Service Manager window is displayed. All installed Internet services for the current server are listed.
3. If you will be managing a remote server, connect to that server.
4. To connect to a specific server, choose Properties, Connect to Server and complete the Connect to Server dialog box that appears. To connect to all Microsoft Proxy Servers on your network, choose Properties, Find All Servers.

N O T E The WinSock Proxy service on other server computers is not detected when it is used. To connect to WinSock Proxy service for different computers, use Connect to Server and specify the server name for connection. ▨

5. To administer a server's Internet service, double-click the computer name next to the service name.

To administer a server's Web Proxy service, double-click the computer name next to that service.

To administer a server's WinSock Proxy service, double-click the computer name next to that service.

The Service Properties window for the selected service appears, as shown in Figure 17.10.

FIG. 17.10

The Proxy Service Properties window is where you configure the service.

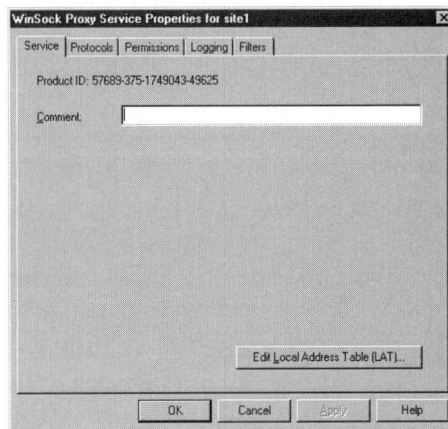

The Service Tab is where you will edit the LAT. Follow these steps:

1. Click the Service Tab.
2. Click the Edit Local Address Table (LAT), Configuration button.
3. Add or Remove IP addresses as necessary.
4. Click OK to save your changes.

Configuring TCP/IP Ports

Ports are used in TCP/IP to name the ends of logical connections that carry long-term conversations. A port allows transport protocols such as the User Datagram Protocol (UDP) and Transmission Control Protocol (TCP) the capability of handling communications between multiple hosts. It also allows a communication to be uniquely identified. The WinSock Proxy service uses ports extensively to provide a way of redirecting applications.

For the purpose of providing services to unknown callers, a service contact port is defined. Each WinSock Proxy-enabled application specifies a port to be used as the contact port on the server for TCP or UDP. To some extent, these same port assignments are used with UDP. In order to use UDP, the application must supply the IP address and port number of the destination application.

Ports are identified by a positive integer. The range for assigned ports allows 4-digit port numbers up to 9999. The assigned ports use a small portion of the range of possible port numbers, allowing other unassigned port numbers to be designated as alternatives if the initial port is not available.

Ports can be designated to use either TCP or UDP as the transport-level protocol specifying how ports send and receive data. In addition, port assignments are enabled separately for inbound ports and outbound ports on Microsoft Proxy Server. Inbound ports are used to listen for client requests from Internet clients, and outbound ports are used to listen for requests from clients on the internal network.

The Microsoft Proxy Server uses application service ports for the WinSock Proxy service. In order for each Windows Sockets-based application to work through a network connection, ports are used in combination with IP addressing to form a "socketed" connection.

When ports are defined for the WinSock Proxy service, port permissions can be assigned to users for each application defined on the Microsoft Proxy Server. If you want to enable access to inbound and outbound service ports separately for users on your network, you can create additional protocol definitions in WinSock Proxy service properties for that purpose.

To configure ports for individual services, use this procedure:

1. Start the Internet Services Manager.
2. Click the WinSock Proxy Services Property for the desired Server.
3. Click the Protocols Tab.
4. Select the Service you want to edit, and then choose Edit.
5. Modify the Service definition as you want, as shown in Figure 17.11.
6. Click OK.

FIG. 17.11
Edit port configurations here.

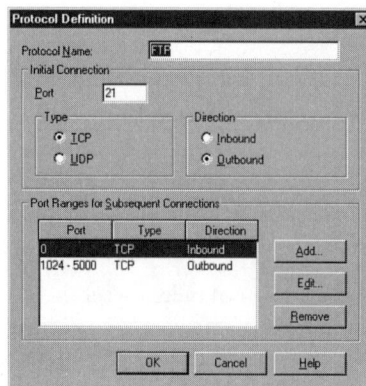

You also grant or remove permissions to groups or users through the Permissions tab by using this procedure:

1. Click the Permissions tab.

2. Choose the Protocol from the drop-down menu.

3. Figure 17.12 shows where you can Add or Remove the groups or users you choose.

4. Click OK.

FIG. 17.12

Grant permissions to groups or users in the Permission Properties sheet.

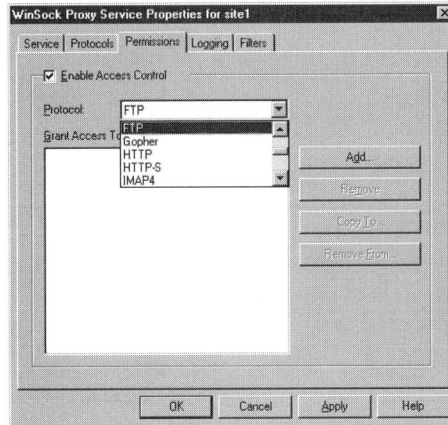

The Logging tab allows you to configure the Proxy Server Log functions for your specific site needs:

1. Click the Logging Tab.

2. Configure Logging as described in section "Logging WebProxy Activities." Figure 17.13 shows the options available in the Logging Properties sheet.

3. Click Apply to initiate your changes.

FIG. 17.13

Indicate whether to send your logs to files or a database.

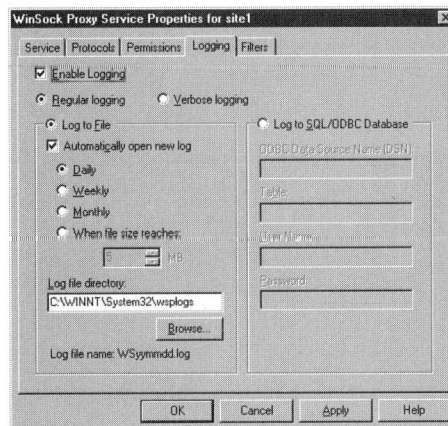

The Filters Tab allows you to enable or disable IP Filtering. If you choose to enable IP Filtering use the following procedure:

1. Click the Filters tab.

2. Check the Enable Filtering box to enable IP Filtering.

3. Choose whether to grant or deny access by default.

4. Add IP addresses as necessary to configure your network, as shown by Figure 17.14.

5. Click Apply to initiate your changes.

FIG. 17.14

Set IP Filtering rules in the Filters Properties sheet.

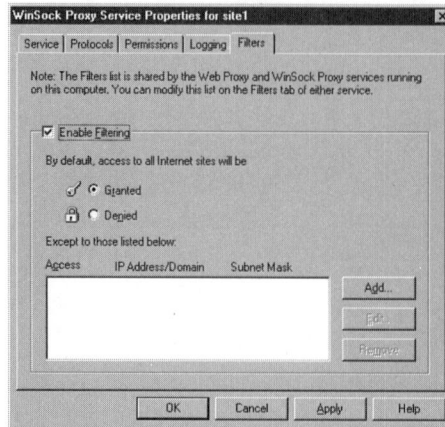

Configuring the Local Access Table (LAT)

During Microsoft Proxy Server installation the Setup program helps you create a list of the IP addresses that constitute your internal network. The information you provide is used to create a table, called the Local Address Table (LAT), that defines your network. IP addresses that are external to your network are specifically excluded from this table. The server maintains the master copy of the LAT, and a copy is downloaded to client computers.

The Setup program creates the original copy of the LAT. After installation, the server's copy of the LAT can be modified by using Internet Service Manager.

Modifying the LAT   You can modify the existing LAT, adding to or removing from IP address pairs provided by the Windows NT Server internal routing tables. To modify the LAT, use this procedure:

1. Open the Internet Service Manager and double-click the WinSock Proxy service.

   The Service Properties window appears.

2. Select the Service tab.

3. Click the Edit Local Address Table (LAT) button.

   The Local Address Table Configuration dialog box appears.

Verify that the entries in the Internal IP Ranges box, shown in Figure 17.15, correctly identify your internal network. Add any needed IP address pairs until all addresses of your internal network are defined. Remove any IP address pairs that define external (Internet) addresses.

- To add a range of IP addresses to the list, under Edit type a pair of addresses in the From and To boxes, and then click the Add button.

- To add a single IP address to the list, under Edit type the same address in both the From and To boxes, and then click the Add button.

- To remove an IP address or address pair from the list, select it from the Internal IP Ranges box, and then click the Remove button.

FIG. 17.15
Add or Remove
IP Pairs.

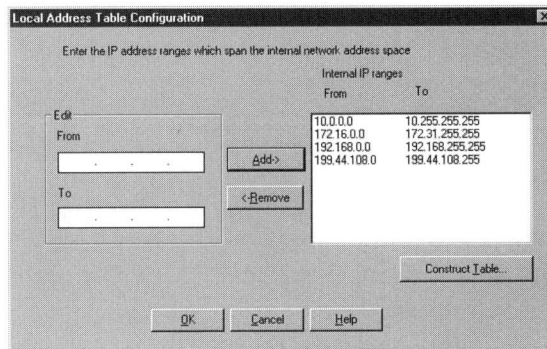

Part
VII

Ch
17

Be sure to exclude from the LAT any IP addresses associated with Internet-connected network adapter cards on servers running Microsoft Proxy Server. These are external IP addresses and should not be included in the LAT.

When the configuration is properly set, click OK until you return to the WinSock Proxy service and the Service Properties window. Stop and start the WinSock Proxy and Web Proxy services. The LAT changes will not take effect on the server until the services are restarted.

Rebuilding the LAT   You can also completely replace the LAT, generating a new list of IP address pairs from internal routing tables used by Windows NT Server.

To replace the LAT and generate a new list of addresses, follow these steps:

1. Double-click the computer name next to the Web Proxy or WinSock Proxy service. The Service Properties window appears.

2. Select the Service tab.

3. Click the Edit Local Address Table (LAT) button. The Local Address Table Configuration dialog box appears.

4. Click the Construct Table button. The Construct Local Address Table dialog box appears.

5. If you wish to add private address ranges select the Add the private ranges check box.

6. Choose the network adapter cards on the server whose IP addresses will be included in the LAT.

7. Select Load from NT Internal Routing Table.

   If you do not know which of the server's network adapter cards are connected to the private network, select Load known address ranges from all IP interface cards.

   If you know which of the server's network adapter cards are connected to the internal network and which are connected to the Internet:

8. Select Load known address ranges from the following IP interface cards to load only those IP addresses associated with the server's internally connected cards.

9. Then, in the list of network adapter cards, select the check box for each of the internally connected cards.

10. Clear the check box for each of the externally connected cards.

11. When you have completed the Construct Local Address Table dialog box, click OK. The Local Address Table Configuration dialog box returns. A list of IP address pairs is displayed in the Internal IP Ranges box.

12. Verify that the entries in the Internal IP Ranges box correctly identify your internal network. Add any needed IP address pairs until all addresses of your internal network are defined. Remove any IP address pairs that define external (Internet) addresses.

13. When the LAT configuration is properly set, click OK.

14. Stop and start the WinSock Proxy and Web Proxy services.

Configuring the Web Proxy Service

In order to configure the Web Proxy Services you must:

■ Set up permissions to determine which Windows NT groups or users are granted the ability to use each of the Internet protocols supported by the Web Proxy service.

■ Set up filtering to determine the specific Internet sites that all users of the Web Proxy service are allowed to access.

■ Set up caching to determine the way that the Web Proxy service caches Internet objects returned by client requests.

■ Set up logging to determine how Web Proxy service activity is saved in the Web Proxy service log.

Selecting the Client Authentication Method   There are three types of client authentication methods that can be used by the Web Proxy service:

■ Anonymous

■ Basic

■ Windows NT Challenge/Response

The client authentication method used by the Web Proxy service is actually set in the WWW service of Microsoft Internet Information Server (IIS), as shown in Figure 17.16. To set the WWW service authentication method and the Web Proxy authentication method, follow these steps:

1. Open the Internet Service Manager

2. Double-click the Server name next to the WWW Service. The WWW Service Properties dialog box appears.

3. Select the Service tab.

4. Under Password Authentication, select one or more authentication methods:

   • Allow Anonymous

   • Basic (clear text)

   • Windows NT Challenge/Response

5. Click OK.

FIG. 17.16
Set the Client
Authentication method
here.

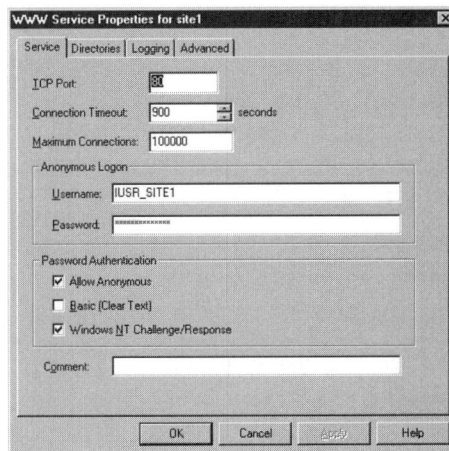

This procedure sets the authentication method for one server. If your network has more than one server running the Web Proxy service, repeat the procedure for each server.

Granting Permissions to Proxy Users When Microsoft Proxy Server is first installed, by default there are no Proxy permissions granted. You must grant Proxy permissions to users or groups in order for them to use the services.

If you enabled Anonymous authentication in the WWW service, all users on the internal network will have access and you do not need to grant Proxy permissions.

If you disabled Anonymous authentication in the WWW service and have enabled Basic or Windows NT Challenge/Response authentication, you must grant Proxy permissions before users can access the Internet using the Web Proxy service.

Part

VII

Ch

17

> **N O T E**   Users will not be able to gain access to the Msp\Clients share folder before Proxy
> permissions are granted. ▨

Proxy Permissions determine which users or groups of users can access the Internet by using
a specific protocol through the Web Proxy Server. Permissions are granted separately for each
protocol. The available Web Proxy service protocols are:

- ■ *FTP Read*   File Transfer Protocol. This allows you to download files through your
  browser.
- ■ *Gopher*   Allows you to access links and files on Gopher Servers via your browser.
- ■ *WWW*   HTTP and HTTPS (secure HTTP) protocols for the World Wide Web. Allows
  browser access to the Web.
- ■ *Secure*   Allows various Secure Socket Layer (SSL) connections. By default this includes
  SNEWS, but other protocols can be configured using the Windows NT registry.

T I P   It is a good idea to use the User Manager for Domains to create user groups for those users who need
access to a particular protocol or sets of protocols. Then you can apply permissions to groups, rather
than to individual users.

To grant permission to use Proxy protocols, use this procedure:

1. Open the Internet Service Manager.
2. Double-click the server name next to the Web Proxy service.
3. Click the Permissions tab.
4. Select the Enable Access Control check box.
5. Review the current permissions.

Select a protocol from the Protocol box, shown in Figure 17.17, and review the users and
groups granted the right to use that protocol.

FIG. 17.17
Review the access lists
for the various
protocols.

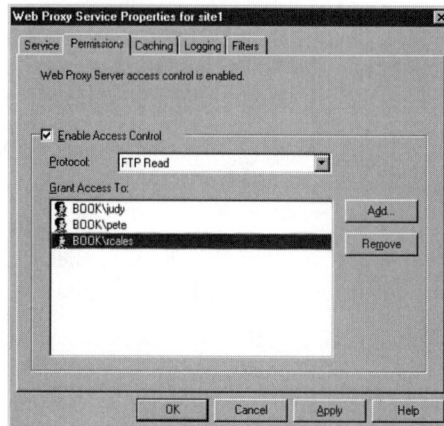

N O T E When you select a protocol from the `Protocol` list, the `Grant Access To` box displays the users and groups that are already granted permissions for that protocol. ▪

To grant a user or group the right to use a protocol on this server, follow these steps:

1. Select the protocol from the list in the Protocol box.
2. Choose Add.
3. Complete the Add Users and Groups dialog box, shown in Figure 17.18.

FIG. 17.18

Add users as needed in the Add Users and Groups dialog box.

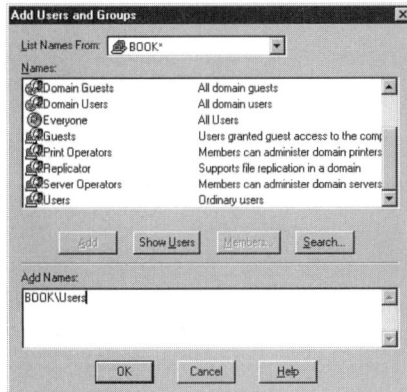

To remove a user or group follow the same steps, but choose Remove instead of Add. When permissions are set appropriately for the selected protocol:

1. Select another protocol from the list, and grant or remove permissions as necessary.
2. When all protocols have their permissions set appropriately, click OK.

This procedure sets permissions for one server. If your network has more than one server running the Web Proxy service, repeat the procedure for each server.

Controlling Web Proxy User Access to Internet Sites In today's business and political climate, corporate liability is a major concern. There are many types of information available from your Internet Site. If you are concerned over the material that may be downloaded or accessed from your site, filtering gives you an option.

You can allow or prevent client access to specific Internet sites. This is called filtering, and it is accomplished on a per-server basis. It applies to all users who access the Internet from your site, using either Web Proxy or WinSock Proxy services.

Filtering allows you to prevent access to a single computer, a group of computers, or an Internet domain. You can control access by IP address, subnet mask, and domain name.

To configure filtering for Internet Sites, follow these steps:

1. Open the Internet Service Manager.

Part

VII

Ch

17

2. Open the Web Proxy Service Properties window for the server to be administered.

3. Click the Filters tab.

4. Select the Enable Filtering option.

5. Select the filtering mode. Set an overall policy first, then specify exceptions to that policy.

You can also deny users access to specific Internet sites by using this procedure:

1. Select Granted.

2. Add sites to the Except to those listed below list. Users will be allowed access to all other Internet sites.

Access can be allowed to specific Internet sites only. You can select Denied, and then add sites to the Except to those listed below list. Users will be denied access to all other Internet sites.

To create a new filter, follow these steps:

1. Click Add and complete the dialog box that appears.

2. Select Single Computer to filter a single computer. If you select this option, you must also enter that computer's IP address in the IP Address box.

3. Select Group of Computers to filter a group of computers. If you select this option you must enter an IP address in the IP Address box, and a subnet mask in the Subnet Mask box.

4. Select Domain to filter a domain, as shown in Figure 17.19. If you select this option, enter a domain name in the Domain box.

FIG. 17.19

Filter out unwanted addresses for single computers, computer groups, or an entire domain.

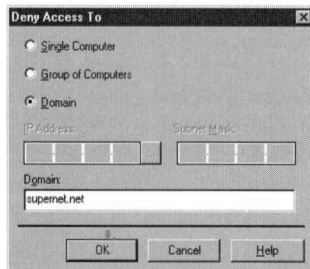

5. When you have completed the dialog box, click OK. The Filters property sheet returns, with the new filter added to the Except to those listed below list.

6. Repeat Step 5 until all needed filters are defined for this server.

7. To alter a listed filter, select it from the list, click Edit, and modify the settings in the dialog box that appears.

8. To remove a filter from the list, select the item and click Remove.

9. Click OK to save your filters.

NOTE Only the selected mode, Granted or Denied, is in effect. When you switch between modes, filters created for the deselected mode are retained, but are not in effect. ■

This procedure sets up filtering for one server. If your network has more than one server running Microsoft Proxy Server, repeat the procedure for each server.

Configuring the Cache

In addition to controlling access to and from your internal network the Microsoft Proxy Server can also improve your overall Internet or intranet access time. It accomplishes this by caching documents on its hard drive. This can prevent several clients from having to download the same documents time and again. It also results in lower bandwidth usage and faster response time.

Basic Cache Configuration

In order to take effect of the caching abilities of the Proxy Server we need to tell it what to cache and how long to keep the data before refreshing.

To configure the cache, follow these steps:

1. Open the Internet Service Manager.
2. Open the Web Proxy Service Properties window for the server to be administered.
3. Select the Caching tab, shown in Figure 17.20.
4. Check the Enable Caching box.
5. In the Cache Expiration Policy window move the slider toward Always Request Updates to maintain the freshest cache data. Move the slider toward Fewest Internet Requests to allow objects in the cache to be used for the maximum Time-To-Live (TTL).

FIG. 17.20
This is where you configure the cache settings.

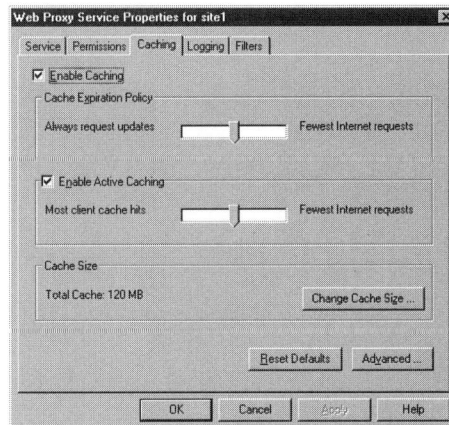

Part VII
Ch
17

> **TIP** The longer the TTL the quicker the server response time will be. However, if you set it for to long, the cached data may not be current.

6. Set the E_nable Active Caching option. Active caching uses the cache to ensure the freshness and availability of certain HTTP data. The cache manager creates its own request for an object, without client prompting, when the TTL has expired or is near expiration.

7. Use the Active Caching slider to specify how frequently objects in the cache are updated. Set the slider toward Most client cache hits to update the cache frequently. Set the slider toward Fewest Internet Requests to minimize the number of times Microsoft Proxy Server makes requests to update objects in the cache.

8. Review the cache space allocation shown in Total Cache. To change the drives and the amount of disk space allocated to the cache, click the Change Cache Si_ze button and complete the Microsoft Proxy Server Cache Drives dialog box.

9. When the cache is configured appropriately for this server, click OK.

Advanced Cache Configuration

You can use the advanced options to specify a maximum size allowed for:

- Cached objects
- Filter cache objects
- Returning expired objects from the cache when the requested Internet site is unavailable and the cache does not contain an unexpired copy of the requested object

Follow these steps to set the advanced cache options:

1. Open the Internet Service Manager.

2. Open the Web Proxy Service Properties window for the server to be administered.

3. Click the Caching tab. The Microsoft Proxy Server Cache Drives property sheet appears.

4. Click the Ad_vanced button. The Advanced Cache Policy dialog box appears, as shown in Figure 17.21.

5. To limit the size of cached objects, select the _Limit Size of Cached Objects to check box and type the size in kilobytes in the adjacent box. Objects larger than the specified size will not be cached.

6. To specify that cached objects will be sent to the client when the object is in the cache and the Internet server is unavailable, select the _Return expired objects when site is unavailable check box. Objects in the cache will be used even if they are expired. By default, this option is selected.

FIG. 17.21
Advanced Cache
configuration can be
done here.

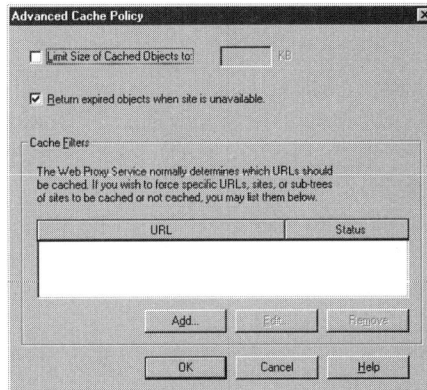

7. Review and if necessary modify the Cache Filters list, which contains the currently configured cache filters. The URL column displays the URL that will be filtered, and the Status column shows whether that URL will always be cached or will never be cached.

8. When the advanced options are set appropriately, click OK in the Advanced Cache Policy dialog box.

9. When the Caching property sheet reappears, click OK again.

Microsoft Proxy Server determines which Internet objects will be cached. Optionally, you can create cache filters, which specify URLs that will always be cached or will never be cached.

When a URL is configured to never be cached, its objects will not be stored in the cache. When a URL is configured to always be cached, objects from that URL will be cached. This can be useful if, for example, you want to specify a wildcard filter to deny caching from a specific site, and then create another filter to re-enable caching from a sub-tree of that site.

To administer cache filters, follow these steps:

1. Open the Advanced Cache Properties dialog box.

2. Click Add and in the URL box shown in Figure 17.22, type the URL to be filtered.

FIG. 17.22
Build URL filter rules
here.

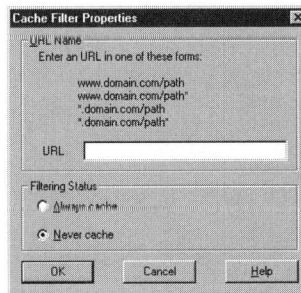

3. Select Always cache or Never cache. Select Never cache to prevent caching from the URL entered in the URL box. This is the default selection.

   Select Always cache to always cache Internet objects returned from the URL listed in the URL box. Use this option when you have already specified a wildcard filter to deny caching of all Internet objects from a site, and want to re-enable caching of objects from a particular sub-tree of the site.

4. When the filter is configured appropriately, click OK. The Advanced Cache Policy dialog box returns.

Reallocating the Cache

Always locate the cache on one or more hard drives installed on the computer running Microsoft Proxy Server. You cannot use network drives to store cached data. You should choose a hard disk of sufficient size to make the cache as large as possible. Using multiple drives is a good idea, because breaking a very large cache into several smaller caches can provide faster access to data. It is also a good idea to store the logs and the cache on different volumes. This will help prevent the log files from using up space needed for the cache.

As discussed previously, you should allocate a minimum of 100M plus .5M per client. You should also allocate the cache in 5M increments, as this is the factor the Proxy Server utilizes.

What happens if you need to add space to the cache or want to reconfigure the way you laid the cache out? You need to look at reallocating the cache drives.

To change the drives and the amount of disk space allocated to the cache:

1. Open the Internet Service Manager.

2. Open the Web Proxy Service Properties window for the server to be administered.

3. Click the Caching tab.

4. Click the Change Cache Size button and the Microsoft Proxy Server Cache Drives dialog box appears, as shown in Figure 17.23.

5. Review the existing drive and cache size configurations.

FIG. 17.23
You can reconfigure cache drives here.

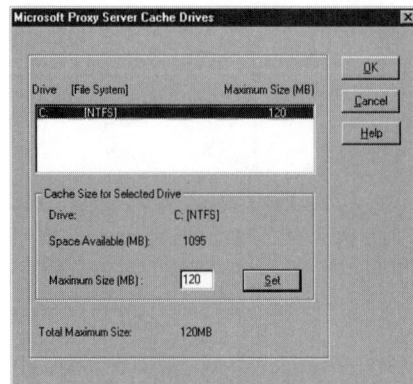

The list under Drive displays all the local drives installed on the server, identified by drive letter and file system type. If a drive is configured to cache, the amount of allocated space is shown in the Maximum Size (M) column. If a drive is not configured to cache, this column is empty.

The total disk space, in megabytes, allocated to the cache is shown at the bottom of the dialog box, in Total Maximum Size (M). This value is the sum of all entries in the Maximum Size (M) column.

To set up a drive to store cached data, use this procedure:

1. Select the drive from the list.
2. Type a number in the Maximum Size (MB) box.
3. Click Set.

The number you type will become the maximum amount of space, in megabytes, that the cache can use on that drive. The number you type must be less than the value shown next to Space Available (M).

To stop storing cached data on a drive:

1. Select the drive from the list.
2. Type **0** in the Maximum Size (M) box.
3. Click Set.

> **CAUTION**
>
> If you stop storing cached data on a drive all cached data on that drive will be lost.

To reallocate the amount of cache on a specific drive:

1. Select the drive from the list.
2. Type a new value in the Maximum Size (M) box.
3. Click Set.

> **CAUTION**
>
> If you modify an existing cache drive and reduce the `Maximum Size (MB)` value, some cached data on that drive might be lost.

   If you increase the Cache Size (MB) value, the new setting takes effect immediately. There is no effect on the data already cached on that drive.

4. When the drives and space allocations are set appropriately, click OK.
5. When the Caching property sheet reappears, click OK again.

Part
VII

Ch
17

Stopping the Cache

If for some reason you should need to halt the cache while leaving the Proxy Server running, you will need to:

1. Open the Internet Service Manager.
2. Open the Web Proxy Service Properties window for the server to be administered.
3. Click the Caching tab.
4. Clear the Enable Caching check box.
5. Click OK.

Logging Web Proxy Service Activity

The Microsoft Proxy Server can log information about all Internet requests made by Web Proxy service clients. It can log to a text file or to a table in an ODBC-compliant database.

The information is logged to a text file, by default. After installing Microsoft Proxy Server, you can set the configuration parameters for text file logging, or you can set up logging to an ODBC-compliant database.

To log Web Proxy information to a text file and set the logging parameters:

1. Open the Internet Service Manager.
2. Open the Web Proxy Service Properties window for the server to be administered.
3. Click the Logging tab. Make sure the Enable Logging option is selected.
4. Select either Regular Logging or Verbose Logging.

   Regular Logging records only a subset of all available information for each Internet access. This option reduces the disk space needed for a log file. Verbose Logging records all available information for each Internet access.

5. Make sure the Log to File option is selected.
6. Select or clear the Automatically open new log option.

   Select this option to periodically create a new Web Proxy service log file. When a new log file is started, the old log file is closed. Clear this option to use the same Proxy log file continuously.

   If you select the Automatically open new log option, specify the interval used to open a new log file. Select Daily, Weekly, Monthly, or When File Size Reaches, as shown in Figure 17.24. If you select When File Size Reaches, also enter a value in the MB box.

7. Review and if appropriate change the log file directory. To change this location, type a new path in the Log File Directory box, or click Browse and complete the dialog box that appears. It is possible to log to a remote drive, but you really should store your Proxy log file on a local disk.

8. Click OK.

FIG. 17.24

Choose Daily, Weekly, or
Monthly logging.

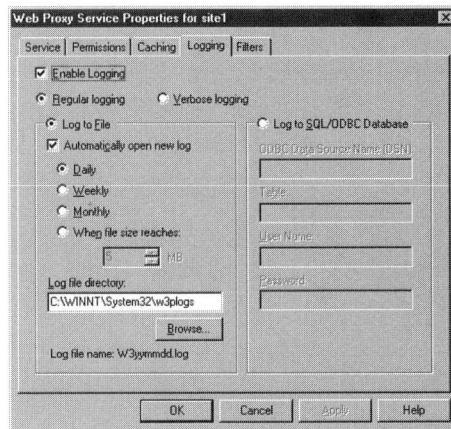

If you decide you want to send the log data to a database, you will need to configure the logging
for an ODBC-compliant database.

> **CAUTION**
>
> Be very careful when setting up logging. Large sites can generate several megs of log files per day, which can
> quickly fill the available hard drive space.

To log Web Proxy service information to an ODBC-compliant database:

1. Install the database.
2. The database can be installed on the local computer or a remote computer.
3. Create a table in the database, with the fields necessary to support the service data.
4. Install the ODBC driver for the database you are using.
5. Create a System Data Source Name (system DSN) for the database that will receive the logging.
6. Open the Internet Service Manager and choose the Logging tab for the Web Proxy Service Properties window.
7. Select the Enable Logging option, then select Log to SQL/ODBC Database, as shown in Figure 17.25.
8. Configure the logging options.

TIP Turn off Internet Information Server (IIS) logging when Web Proxy service logging is enabled. The IIS log
is a subset of the information stored in the Web Proxy service log. Since the information is duplicated,
you can improve performance by turning off IIS logging.

Part
VII

Ch
17

FIG. 17.25

You can also send your logs to a database.

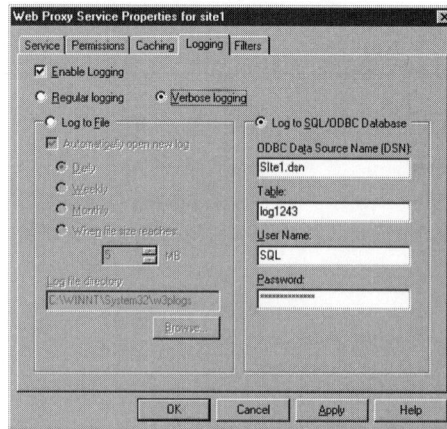

Configuring Proxy Server Clients

During Microsoft Proxy Server setup, you were asked to complete the Client Configuration dialog box. The options in this dialog box are used to create a Mspclnt.ini file, which is installed on the server, along with a client Setup program. Later, when a client connects to the server and runs the client Setup program, the Mspclnt.ini file is copied to the client, and configures the client.

To edit the server's Mspclnt.ini file, which is installed into the Msp\Clients folder on the server, you must either use a text editor or run the Microsoft Proxy Server Setup and reinstall the server.

If you need to change a client's copy of the Mspclnt.ini file after a client has been installed, you can:

■ Refresh the client's copy of the file by downloading the current version from the server, or

■ Use a text editor to modify the client's copy of the Mspclnt.ini file.

Running Client Setup

You can set up a client computer by using either the Setup program or a Web browser.

To set up a client computer using the Setup program, use this procedure:

1. Connect to the server's Mspclnt share folder.
2. From the Mspclnt share, run Setup.
3. Click Install Client, shown in Figure 17.26.
4. Click OK.

FIG. 17.26

Install the client software.

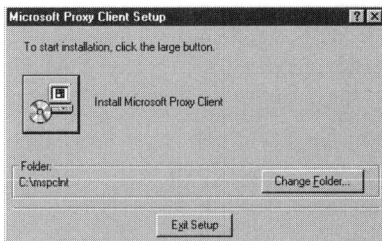

The client components will be installed, and the client computer will be configured according to the settings of the Mspclnt.ini file.

To set up a client computer using the client's Web browser, connect to the server's installation page by typing the URL **http://*Servername*/MSPROXY** for the URL for the present location of the client installation Web page. Once the client installation Web page is loaded, follow the on-screen instructions to run Setup and install client components.

If the browser proxy settings configured by client Setup are not appropriate for a particular client, or if a client's Web browser is not Microsoft Internet Explorer or Netscape Navigator, then you must use the Web browser's own configuration interface to specify the name of the computer running Microsoft Proxy Server and the protocol port number.

Part

VII

Ch

17

Web Proxy Clients

The term Web Proxy client refers to a client computer whose Web browser is configured to use the Web Proxy service on a Microsoft Proxy Server. Usually, this is accomplished by running the client Setup program.

If the browser proxy settings configured by client Setup are not appropriate for a particular client, you can reconfigure that client's Web browser after installing the client software. Each browser is configured through its own user interface. Typically, an application's settings are found in menu items called Options, Preferences, or Settings.

When you run client Setup, it will configure Microsoft Internet Explorer as a client of Microsoft Proxy Server. However, you can also use the Internet application in Control Panel to specify the name of the Microsoft Proxy Server and the protocol port number. Internet Explorer uses the settings from the Internet application, but other client applications may have their own locations for their proxy service settings.

To configure the Internet application with a Microsoft Proxy Server name and protocol port number:

1. Open Control Panel and click the Internet icon.
2. Select the Connection tab, and then select the Use Proxy Server check box.
3. Click the Settings button and choose the service(s) you want to use the Proxy Server, as shown in Figure 17.27.

FIG. 17.27

You can also configure the client here in Microsoft's Internet Explorer.

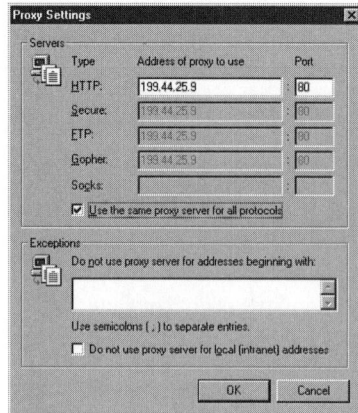

4. Enter the address of the Proxy Server in the address field.

5. Enter the Port Number in the Port field.

6. If you are using the same Proxy server for all services, check the Use the Same server for all Protocols box.

7. Enter any addresses you do not want to use the Proxy Server for in the Exceptions Box.

8. Check the Do Not Use Proxy for Local Intranets box, unless you want to use a Proxy within your intranet.

Configuring the Server's Browser

If you use a browser running on the Microsoft Proxy Server, and that browser is configured as a client, you must configure it to use the IP address of the server's network adapter that is connected to the internal network. If you configure the server's browser to use the computer or DNS name, this name can be resolved to the IP address of a network adapter card connected to the Internet. When this occurs, requests from that browser will be filtered and an `Access is denied` error will be returned.

WinSock Proxy Security

The WinSock Proxy service provides secure communication between your network and remote Internet computers that support Windows Sockets applications. It uses Challenge/Response authentication to authenticate all users.

Also, you can use WinSock Proxy as an IP gateway for IPX networks. This allows IPX/SPX clients on an internal network to access TCP/IP resources on an external network. An application level proxy uses two separate service connections: An IPX connection on the internal network between the WinSock Proxy server and client, and an IP connection between the WinSock Proxy server and a remote server on the Internet. Because separate connections and different routing protocols are used on the internal and external networks, the risk of outside intrusion is reduced. Only the computer running Microsoft Proxy Server is visible to other Internet servers.

You can use the WinSock Proxy access control to select whether to administer permissions individually by user, or allow all users to use the WinSock Proxy service.

When access control is enabled, authentication is done on each WinSock Proxy request to determine if each user has appropriate permissions for the service being requested. You can control which application ports can be used and who can use them.

When access control is disabled, the WinSock Proxy service does not verify users. Access to all WinSock Proxy server ports and protocols is possible for valid users on the server computer.

The Permissions property sheet of the WinSock Proxy Service Properties window in the Internet Service Manager is used to set permissions for WinSock Proxy users.

WinSock Proxy Clients

The term *WinSock Proxy client* refers to a client computer that is configured to use the Web Proxy service on a Microsoft Proxy Server. The WinSock Proxy client components are installed when you run the client Setup program. The client Setup program does not configure individual Windows Sockets applications. Instead, the client computer is configured to use the WinSock Proxy service on a server. All Windows Sockets applications on that computer access the Internet through the WinSock Proxy service on the Microsoft Proxy Server.

The WinSock Proxy service supports Windows Sockets version 1.1. Before a Windows Sockets application can access the Internet through Microsoft Proxy Server, the server must be configured to permit access for the required protocol on the required outbound and inbound ports.

The WSP Client Application Use the WSP Client application in Control Panel to enable or disable the client, change the server from which client configuration files are downloaded, and download updated copies of the configuration files.

After a computer has the WinSock Proxy client software installed, it is able to use Windows Sockets applications to access Internet sites through the Microsoft Proxy Server. However, unless the WinSock Proxy client is turned off, the computer will be unable to access any Internet sites through a dial-up connection. You can turn the WinSock Proxy client on and off by using the WSP Client application in the Control Panel.

To turn the WinSock Proxy client on or off, use this procedure:

1. From the client computer, open Control Panel and double-click the WSP Client icon. The Microsoft WinSock Proxy Client dialog box appears.
2. Select or clear the Enable WinSock Proxy Client check box, shown in Figure 17.28.

   To turn on the WinSock Proxy client software select the Enable WinSock Proxy Client check box.

   To turn off the WinSock Proxy client software clear the Enable WinSock Proxy Client check box.
3. Click OK, and then reboot the computer.

FIG. 17.28

Turn Proxy services on or off.

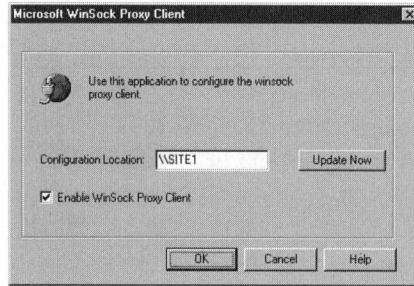

Manually Editing the Mspclnt.ini File   In some cases it may be necessary to manually edit the Proxy client files. The Mspclnt.ini file contains the client configuration. The master copy of the Mspclnt.ini file is created by the Microsoft Proxy Server Setup program and is stored in the Clients folder on the server. A copy of the Mspclnt.ini file is stored in the Mspclnt folder on the client. The Mspclnt.ini file can be modified by using a text editor.

The following is a sample Mspclnt.ini file.

```
[Master Config]
Path1=\\SITE2\Mspclnt\
[Servers Ip Addresses]
Name=SITE
[Servers Ipx Addresses]
Addr1=00004970-0240e768477g
[Common]
Port=1745
Configuration Refresh Time (Hours)=6
Set Browsers to use Proxy=1
WWW-Proxy=SITE2
WebProxyPort=80
```

Table 17.1 describes the entries in the Mspclnt.ini file.

Table 17.1   Proxy Client Configuration References

Section	Entry	Description
[Master Config]	Path1	A UNC path to the shared network directory on the server, containing the master copy of the client configuration files.
[Servers IP addresses]	Name	The computer or DNS name for the WinSock Proxy server used by the client. (This entry will not appear if an IP address is used.)
[Servers IP addresses]	Addr1	The IP address of the WinSock Proxy server used by the client. (This entry will not appear if a computer or DNS name is used.) Additional entries are shown as Addr2, Addr3, and so on.

Section	Entry	Description
[Servers Ipx Addresses]	Addr1	The IPX address of the WinSock Proxy server. Additional entries are shown as Addr2, Addr3, and so on.
[Common]	Port	The port Microsoft Proxy Server uses for the control channel. This value will rarely be changed. It should be changed by the administrator on the server's master copy of the Mspclnt.ini file only if there is a conflict with another service on the server. This value should never be edited in the client's copy of the Mspclnt.ini file.
[Common]	Configuration in Refresh Time	At this interval, specified in hours, the client will ask (Hours) the server to download a fresh copy of the Local Address Table (Msplat.txt).
[Common]	Set Browsers to use Proxy	In the server's file, set this value to 1 to have the client Setup program configure the client computer's browser to use the proxy server defined in the WWW Proxy field. Set the value to 0 to prevent the client Setup program from configuring clients to use a proxy server. This field has no effect on the client's version of the file.
[Common]	LocalDomains	A list of suffixes for names that will be resolved locally, separated by commas (,). Domain names that end in the listed strings are resolved at the client.
[Common]	WWW-Proxy	In the server's file, if Set Browsers to Use Proxy is set to 1, the client Setup program will configure client browsers to use the proxy server named here. This field has no effect on the client's version of the file.
[Common]	WebProxyPort	The listen-on port used by the Web Proxy service. In the server's file, if Set Browsers to Use Proxy is set to 1, the client Setup program will configure client browsers to use the port named in that box. This should be the same port number that is set for the WWW service of Internet Information Server.

Part
VII

Ch
17

You can manually edit each of the entries as necessary. As on any situation where you edit a configuration file, be certain you have a valid backup.

Configuring Windows Sockets Applications   Most applications do not require Advanced configuration to work with the WinSock Proxy service. In most cases, the default WinSock Proxy configuration will work with no need for further modification. However, in some situations the advanced options discussed in this section may be necessary.

Configuration information can be set for all WinSock Proxy applications in two ways:

- *Global configuration* These settings are configured by adding a new section in the Mspclnt.ini file. Settings made in this way will be used for all applications.

- *Application-specific configuration* These settings are set for each specific Windows Sockets application. They are stored by creating an additional file named Wspcfg.ini for each application that needs custom configuration. This file should be located in the same file directory where the application is installed.

The WinSock Proxy service will first look for an Wspcfg.ini file in a client application directory. If one is not found, WinSock Proxy service will use the settings found in the Mspclnt.ini file.

The following is a sample client section in an Mspclnt.ini file:

```
[Wsp client]
Disable=0
NameResolution=R
LocalBindTcpPorts=7777
LocalBindUdpPorts=7000-7022, 7100-7170
RemoteBindTcpPorts=30
RemoteBindUdpPorts=3000-3050
MultipleAccessTcpPorts=100-300
MultipleAccessUdpPorts=500-900, 1000-2000
ProxyBindIp=80:10.52.144.103, 82:10.51.0.0
```

Table 17.2, WinSock Proxy Service Configuration Options, describes the possible entries that can be used in a configuration file.

Table 17.2 WinSock Proxy Service Configuration Options

Entry	Description
Disable	Disables WinSock Proxy service functionality; all functions are directly forwarded to the system. Note if the Disable value is set to 0, all following file entries are ignored.
NameResolution	By default, resolution for all dot-convention names is redirected. Forces name resolution to local (L) or redirected (R), as specified.
LocalBindTcpPorts	Specifies a TCP port, list, or range that will be bound locally.
LocalBindUdpPorts	Specifies a UDP port, list, or range that will be bound locally.
RemoteBindTcpPorts	Specifies a TCP port, list, or range that will be bound remotely.
RemoteBindUdpPorts	Specifies a UDP port, list, or range that will be bound remotely. By default, this is set to 6970-7170 to support client computers running RealAudio player version 2.1 or newer. If this entry does not appear in the Mspclnt.ini file, when RealAudio player version 2.1 or newer is used with Microsoft

Entry	Description
	Proxy Server it will display "Buffering 18" in the status bar, and will not play sound. To resolve this condition, click the Stop button, and then click the Play button.
MultipleAccessTcpPorts	Specifies a TCP port, list, or range used by a server application, so an accept operation on these ports is intended to serve clients both locally and on the Internet. By default, the socket is considered of client process with one connection, so the listening socket is reused. Requires that the port will be available both on the client and Microsoft Proxy Server.
MultipleAccessUdpPorts	Specifies a UDP port, list, or range used by a server application, so an accept operation on these ports is intended to serve clients both locally and on the Internet. By default, the socket is considered of client process with one connection, so the listening socket is reused. Requires that the port will be available both on the client and Microsoft Proxy Server.
ProxyBindIp	Specifies an IP address or list that will be used when binding with a corresponding port. Used by multiple servers that use the same port and need to bind to different ports on Microsoft Proxy Server.

Part VII

Ch 17

Changes to a Mspclnt.ini should only be made when absolutely necessary and only when a backup of the original file has been made. Use a text editor only, as any formatting codes will render the file useless.

Securing the Microsoft Proxy Server

The Microsoft Proxy Server provides a secure gateway between your internal network and the Internet. As a network administrator, you can use the default configuration to set up Microsoft Proxy Server quickly. Once the server is installed, you can closely administer Microsoft Proxy Server services to grant or deny access to users, services, ports, or domains that you specify.

How Secure Is Proxy Server?

Microsoft Corporation suggests that Proxy Server actually offers 99 percent of the security provided by a hardware-based firewall. Those readers for whom security is a critical issue will want to explore the issue of site security further than the discussions provided in this chapter and the Proxy Server documentation. You might want to start with Que's *Running a Perfect Web Site, 2nd Edition,* which addresses security and firewall issues, and *Windows NT Server Security Handbook* (slated for publication in May, 1997).

By default, Internet users are prevented from connecting to your internal network by these default settings:

- Disabling IP forwarding on the server. IP forwarding (IP routing) normally allows packets to be forwarded on the internal network. By disabling this feature for the server, all connections must be placed remotely by using the Microsoft Proxy Server.

- Denying listening on inbound service ports. This prevents Internet users from initiating connections on any service ports you do not specifically enable inbound access to.

Web Proxy Security

The Web Proxy service uses the same password authentication options for client requests as Internet Information Server (IIS).

A client logon request occurs whenever a client request is forwarded to a Server using IIS or Microsoft Proxy Server. The logon process is used to determine if the client is allowed or denied access to a resource on the server. An authentication is the way the server validates users when processing logon requests. An authentication can be as simple as assigning and encoding a password for the user, or it can involve several secure and encrypted process communications between the client and server.

In addition to the options for authenticating users, Web Proxy offers the option to enable or disable access control. For simplified management of the Web Proxy service, you can disable access control. This is useful if anonymous user access is all that is needed for users on your network. For management of individual users on your network, access control can be enabled so that you can fully administer individual security for each user on your network.

When access control is enabled, Web Proxy clients on your network are verified by using a combination of Web Proxy service permissions and the password authentication settings applied for IIS services. The password authentication options for IIS users include the following:

- *Anonymous Logon*   This is a standard way to provide a single guest user account that is assigned reading and browsing privileges only. This account allows shared access for all users who request documents on an Internet server.

- *Basic Authentication*   This is a standard way to validate HTTP users by using encoded clear-text passwords and user names. This type of authentication is specified in HTTP standards established by the World Wide Web Consortium and the Conseil Europeen pour la Recherche Nucleair (CERN).

- *Challenge/Response Authentication*   This is a secure standard for validating clients that Microsoft has developed. This type of authentication is very secure and uses encryption to transmit security information. You can only use this with clients that support the standard.

Authentication is set within the Service property sheet of the WWW service of IIS. The option to enable or disable access control for Web Proxy is set within the Permissions property sheet of the Web Proxy service. Both of these services are configured by using Internet Service Manager.

Configuring Access Control for the Web Proxy Service

When access control is enabled, verification is performed on each Web Proxy request to determine if the user has appropriate permissions assigned for the type of service being requested. When access control is disabled, the Web Proxy service ignores user permission settings, and all requests are accepted.

Anonymous Logon   Anonymous logon is a method that uses a standard logon account to provide guest access to resources on the Internet. To establish anonymous logon, a user account is first created and assigned limited privileges on a server. In standard TCP/IP, the user name for this account is "anonymous." "Anonymous" is entered at a server logon prompt. The server will then prompt for an e-mail name be entered as a logon password. Once the user has completed the "anonymous" logon, rights granted are typically read-only access to a limited set of data.

When a server is first installed with Internet Information Server, IIS creates a default anonymous user account named IUSR_*computername*, where *computername* is the NetBIOS name for the server. This account is allowed permissions by default to the Web Proxy service. This user does not need to be assigned further user permissions in the Web Proxy service properties to enable anonymous logon for proxy users.

The IIS WWW service provides three authentication check boxes:

- Allow Anonymous
- Basic (Clear-Text)
- Challenge/Response

If you select Allow Anonymous without also selecting one of the other types of authentication, the Web Proxy service services all user requests and all included items on the Permissions property sheet are disabled.

Part

VII

Ch

17

> **CAUTION**
>
> If anonymous logon is allowed, all client applications use it. To force proxy users to log on with an account and password, disable anonymous logon. You can still grant unrestricted access to the Web Proxy service by disabling access control in the Permissions property sheet.

Use this procedure to enable anonymous logon to Microsoft Proxy Server:

1. From Internet Service Manager, double-click the computer name next to the WWW service. The WWW Service Properties window is displayed.

2. Click the Allow Anonymous check box in the Password Authentication section to select it.

3. Click Apply, and then click OK.

Clear-Text Logon   Basic authentication is a standard HTTP mechanism that sends and receives user information as clear text. Passwords and user names are encoded but not encrypted in this type of authentication.

Basic authentication is used by Web Proxy service whenever any one of the following occurs:

- The Basic (Clear Text) check box is selected on the Service property sheet in WWW service properties.
- The server and client are both enabled to use Challenge/Response authentication.
- The client request could not be processed by using anonymous logon account.
- The Enable Access Control check box on the Permissions property sheet for the Web Proxy service properties is selected.

In basic authentication, the client is responsible for prompting the user for user name and password credentials. The credentials are then encoded and sent to the server. The user name must be an account on the computer running IIS or in a trusted domain of that computer. When using a trusted domain account, the user name must contain the domain name in the following format: username=domain\account.

> **CAUTION**
>
> User credentials can be decoded easily by using utilities such as UUdecode. For some client types, such as UNIX-based Web clients, basic authentication is the only available means of establishing password-required access to Web published files. If you allow access from the Internet to Microsoft Proxy Server or another Windows NT-based server on your internal network, HTTP basic authentication offers poor security.

If you need to support other client types that are not Windows-based, you should consider a supplementary encryption method. If your network supports only Windows-based clients, you should use a more secure authentication mechanism that supports link encryption, such as Challenge/Response authentication.

To enable basic authentication, create a local group and grant it permission to use a Web Proxy protocol. Users are then granted access by assigning each user membership in this local group. To create and modify groups and user accounts, use User Manager for Domains. For more information, see Chapter 3, "Building the Foundation."

There are two ways to enable basic authentication. The easy way uses this procedure:

1. Open the Internet Service Manager and then double-click the computer name next to the WWW service.
2. Select the Basic (Clear Text) check box in the Password authentication section of the dialog box shown in Figure 17.29.
3. Clear the Windows NT Challenge/Response check box.
4. Clear the Allow Anonymous check box.
5. Click Apply, and then click OK.

FIG. 17.29

Set the authentication method here.

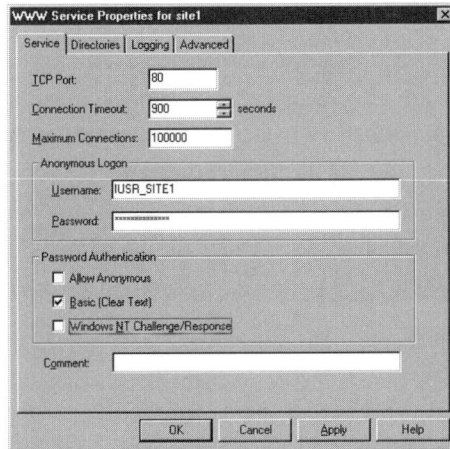

6. Double-click the computer name next to the Web Proxy service.

7. Click the Permissions tab (see Figure 17.30).

8. To allow all users rights to all Web Proxy services clear the Enable Access Control check box.

9. To set limited user access to Web Proxy services, select the Enable Access Control check box. If you enable access control, you will need to assign user permissions for access rights to each service.

10. Click Apply, and then click OK.

FIG. 17.30

Set user permission in the Permissions Properties sheet.

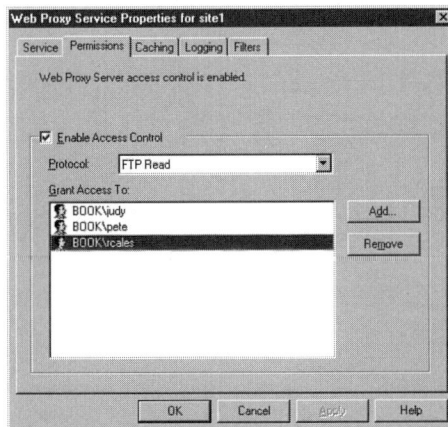

Part
VII

Ch
17

The more complex procedure requires following this procedure:

1. Open the Internet Service Manager, and then double-click the computer name next to the WWW service.

2. Select the <u>B</u>asic (Clear Text) check box in the Password Authentication section.

3. Clear the Windows <u>N</u>T Challenge/Response check box.

4. Clear the A<u>l</u>low Anonymous check box.

5. Click <u>A</u>pply, and then click OK.

6. Double-click the computer name next to the Web Proxy service.

7. Click the Permissions tab.

8. Enable Access Control.

9. Add users permissions for Web Proxy services.

10. Add the IUSR_*computername* user to permissions lists for Web Proxy services (see Figure 17.31).

11. Click <u>A</u>pply, and then click OK.

FIG. 17.31

Be sure to add the IUSR_*computername* user to the permissions list.

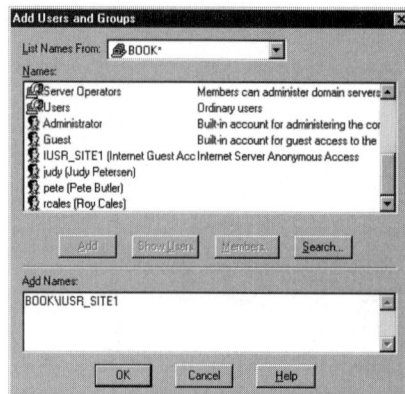

This more complex method allows you to grant access to specified users only and not the entire internal network.

Challenge/Response Authentication   Challenge/Response authentication is a security mechanism. Unlike basic authentication, which forwards user names and passwords as cleartext from client to server, Challenge/Response authentication follows a more complex process that requires multiple communications between the client and server.

In a challenge-and-response sequence, the client computer uses its established user logon information to identify itself to the server. The user is not prompted to enter these user credentials. Instead, the information is available after the user first logs on to a Windows NT-based computer.

Challenge/Response authentication only works where the client and server computers are located in the same or trusted domains.

There are two ways to enable Challenge/Response authentication. To allow all users within the Domain to access the resources, follow these steps:

1. Open the Internet Service Manager, and then double-click the computer name next to the WWW service.
2. Select the Windows NT Challenge/Response check box.
3. Select the Allow Anonymous check box.
4. Clear the Basic (Clear Text) check box.
5. Click Apply, and then click OK.
6. Double-click the computer name next to the Web Proxy service.
7. Click the Permissions tab.
8. To allow all users access to Web Proxy services clear the Enable Access Control check box.
9. To set limited user access to Web Proxy services, select the Enable Access Control check box. If you enable access control, you need to assign user permissions for access rights to each service.
10. Click Apply, and then click OK.

The second method is more complex but will allow you to control access on a user-by-user basis:

1. Open the Internet Service Manager, and then double-click the computer name next to the WWW service.
2. Select the Windows NT Challenge/Response check box in the password Authentication section.
3. Clear the Basic (Clear Text) check box.
4. Clear the Allow Anonymous check box.
5. Click Apply, and then click OK.
6. Double-click the computer name next to the Web Proxy service.
7. Click the Permissions tab.
8. Enable Access Control.
9. Add users to permissions lists for Web Proxy services (FTP Read, Gopher, WWW, Secure).
10. Add the IUSR_*computername* user name to permissions lists for Web Proxy services that will allow anonymous use.
11. Click Apply, and then click OK.

Part
VII

Ch
17

For Challenge/Response authentication to be used, the Web browser for each client must support it. Currently, Microsoft Internet Explorer 3.0 is the only browser that supports this option with Microsoft Proxy Server.

From Here...

This chapter covered a lot of tough material. This is one of the most difficult and also one of the most important parts of being an Internet administrator. If you are going to invest a lot of time and money into building an Internet site, you really should protect it. If you decide to go with a more powerful firewall solution, then the Proxy Server can be even more helpful in speeding up data transfer.

You have learned how to set up and configure the Proxy Server. You also learned how to install and configure the client software and make changes as necessary. Hopefully you also have a better understanding of how Windows NT security features can make your site safer and more easily managed.

- For more background on Windows NT 4.0, turn to Chapter 3, "Building the Foundation."
- Move on to Chapter 18, "Server Administration Via the Web," where you learn how to administer the Microsoft Commercial Internet servers from the Web.

Server Administration Via the Web

This chapter covers server administration under the Microsoft Commercial Internet System. By the end of this chapter, you'll have a good understanding of all issues regarding site administration, troubleshooting, and security. You will know how to monitor multiple servers, stop, start, and optimize services, and perform remote administration by using a Web browser. ■

Configuring the Internet Service Manager

The Internet Service Manager is the cornerstone of Windows NT's Web management. From this application, you'll manage Internet services and servers.

Configuring WWW, FTP, and Gopher services

Setting up Windows NT's Internet Information Server's main components—Web, FTP, and Gopher services—along with ways to configure different types of access for different classes of user.

Creating a secure Internet site

The main types of Internet security options are discussed in depth, including Windows NT's Challenge/Response and Basic Authentication.

Server administration

There are several ways to manage user accounts and other server functions using NT Server 4.0's tools. One of these tools features remote server management over the Web.

Understanding the Relationship Between MCIS, Windows NT, and Internet Server Management

A major benefit of using Microsoft Commercial Internet System is its tight integration with Windows NT Server and Internet Information Server for administrative and configuration duties. NT Server's administration and built-in security tools, coupled with Microsoft Internet Information Server and the Web, give system administrators great flexibility in optimizing and configuring MCIS whether in the office or at a remote location.

In addition to routine maintenance and support, ISM gives you total control over all facets of Internet security, from mapping directories to virtual roots, to setting privileges across the domain.

Managing Web Services with the Internet Service Manager

The task of managing the actual content and operation of Web services under Windows NT falls to the Internet Service Manager. This tool allows for the management of three basic categories under Internet Information Server:

- Servers
- Services
- Property Sheets

Using ISM, an administrator can manage virtually any situation effectively, including:

- Granting access to sensitive files and directories to individual users over the Web, provided they use Microsoft Internet Explorer or the Web's Secure Sockets Layer (SSL)
- Revoking or limiting access to files and directories to individual users
- Revoking or limiting access to entire groups or domains
- Monitoring all requests, especially ones turned down repeatedly for a lack of authentication
- Starting, pausing, or stopping Internet services for maintenance or changing of permissions
- Mapping directories to aliases, or virtual roots, on Web, FTP, and Gopher servers
- Other administrative tasks

Administering MCIS Under NT and IIS

There are three ways to administer the Microsoft Commercial Internet System under Windows NT Server and IIS:

- Using the Internet Service Manager application that comes with IIS
- Using Internet Service Manager as an interactive Web application
- Using Windows NT's administrative and management tools, including command-line operation

There are two versions of Internet Service Manager—a full-featured version that runs as a Windows NT Server application, and an HTML version for use on the Web under Internet Explorer or any other browser that supports Windows NT Challenge/Response Authentication. We will cover NT Challenge/Response and Web browsers later, under the section titled "Web Browsers and Security."

N O T E Currently, only Microsoft Internet Explorer 2.x and higher Web browsers support Windows NT Server Challenge/Response Authentication. The latest version of Internet Explorer for Windows 95, Macintosh, and Windows NT is 3.

Remote Administration Via the Web

The reason the various IIS components can be managed remotely under a Web browser is because of Microsoft's use of what is known as Remote Procedure Calls, or RPCs, in the development of IIS.

By allowing Internet administration through the use of these RPCs, coupled with Windows NT's automatic knowledge of user rights and privileges and the security options built in to Internet Explorer 3, an individual with administrative privileges can log on and make changes to the domain containing the Commercial Internet System through Internet Information Server, even though that person may be half a world away. All Internet servers in the domain can be managed using ISM. Likewise, access to directories, properties, and services can be controlled.

Though the prospect of using the Web to remotely administer WWW services is appealing, there are limitations to its everyday use. These limitations are:

- Although any Web browser can be used, only MSIE (Microsoft Internet Explorer) supports Challenge/Response. Other Web browsers will have to use either Basic Authentication or SSL.
- When using the Web to configure the Internet server, do not turn off Basic authentication while using a non-IE browser. You'll cut yourself off.
- If you stop a service, you'll be unable to restart it by using the Web browser.

Advantages of Using the ISM Windows NT Application

Though there are two versions of Internet Service Manager—the NT application and the HTML version for use on the Web under Internet Explorer—there are many advantages to using the NT application as opposed to the Web version. You'll have a greater range of options, including:

Part VII
Ch
18

- The capability of using User Manager for Domains, Performance Monitor, Event Manager, and other server- and workstation-based NT Server management tools

- The capability of generating keys and certificates using Key Manager (something you can't do under the Web browser version)

- The capability of starting, stopping, and pausing various WWW services, including WWW, Gopher, and FTP (you cannot stop and start services under the Web browser)

- A faster response using the NT application as opposed to the Web browser

- Administrative access to all other NT-based controls, in case you need to configure additional NT Server security options

N O T E   Microsoft has built functionality into its Internet Explorer 3.x Internet browser software that simply does not exist under Netscape, Mosaic, or other browsers. This includes support for ActiveX applications over the Web. In this chapter, we are specifically referring to support for Windows NT's Challenge and Response system. Internet Explorer 3 supports Challenge and Response, making it at this time a more secure Web browser when used in conjunction with Internet Information Server and Microsoft's Commercial Internet System. This is by design. ■

Installing Internet Service Manager

Internet Service Manager is an installation option available during installation of Internet Information Server. By default, ISM is installed and configured. But the HTML version of ISM is *not* installed by default. You must choose it.

This fact will necessitate checking to verify the installation of, or lack of, ISM's HTML format. The following instructions will guide you through that process.

When you install IIS, you have the option of installing both the NT application and the HTML page onto the server. Though the default is to install only the NT application, we recommend you install both versions of ISM. You can add the HTML version at a later time, if you want to.

To install HTML support for ISM, perform the following steps:

1. From the Start menu choose Programs, Microsoft Internet Server, then choose Internet Information Server Setup.

2. Click OK to select the default directory for ISM.

3. Click OK to start the Internet Information Server setup program (see Figure 18.1).

4. Click Add/Remove to see what components are installed (see Figure 18.2).

N O T E   This is where you install the other Internet components—FTP, Gopher, and, if you want connectivity to a SQL server now or later, the ODBC Drivers and Administration. ■

FIG. 18.1

Choose OK to enter the Setup program.

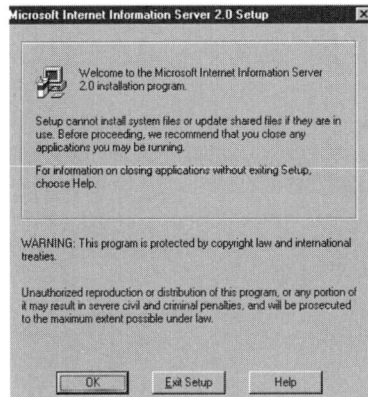

FIG. 18.2

IIS at installation. Make sure the HTML version of Internet Service Manager is selected if you want to perform Web-based administration.

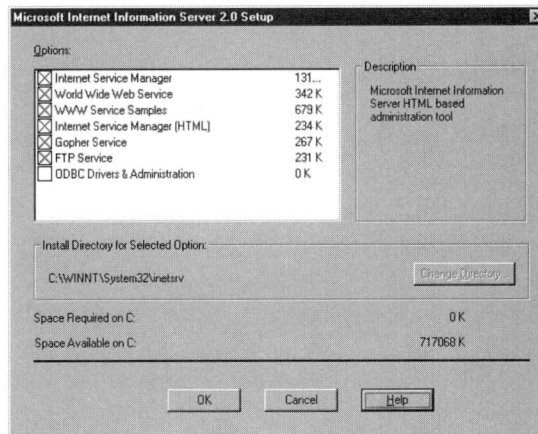

Part

VII

Ch

18

5. In the Options list box, seen in Figure 18.2, make sure the option Internet Service Manager (HTML) is selected. If selected, HTML support is installed. Exit the Setup program by clicking Cancel until you have completely exited Setup and are back at the Windows NT Desktop.

   If the HTML support box is unchecked, you'll have to install it in order to have Web administration capability.

6. Make sure any other option you want to install now is selected. When all options are set, click OK.

T I P Turn off any option that is already installed; you don't want to install it again.

7. When prompted, make sure the Windows NT Server CD-ROM is in the correct drive, or that the installation points to the drive and directory where the download of Internet Information Server is stored.

8. When ISM installation is complete, exit the Setup program and restart Windows NT and launch the Internet Service Manager (HTML). You will see a screen similar to the one in Figure 18.3, indicating the HTML administrative module is successfully installed.

FIG. 18.3

The Internet Service Manager HTML console.

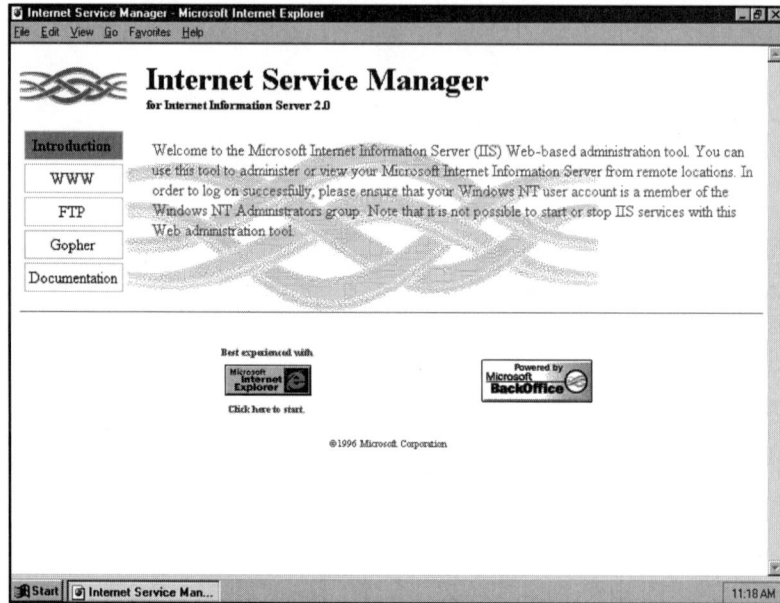

N O T E   In order to log on, the Windows NT user account must have Administrator privileges. Also, you will be unable to start or stop IIS services from the Web console. ■

Activating Internet Service Manager

The two Internet Service Manager options are found in the Microsoft Internet Server folder on the Programs menu. To launch Internet Service Manager from the Start menu, choose Programs, Microsoft Internet Server, then choose Internet Service Manager or Internet Service Manager (HTML). Or, from Microsoft Internet Explorer, go to the URL that contains ISM.

In Figure 18.4 you see the heart of Internet Service Manager—the main Report screen. Although there are three main views, Reports is the default under ISM. The other two views, Servers and Services, will be described shortly.

FIG. 18.4

The Microsoft Internet Service Manager Reports view.

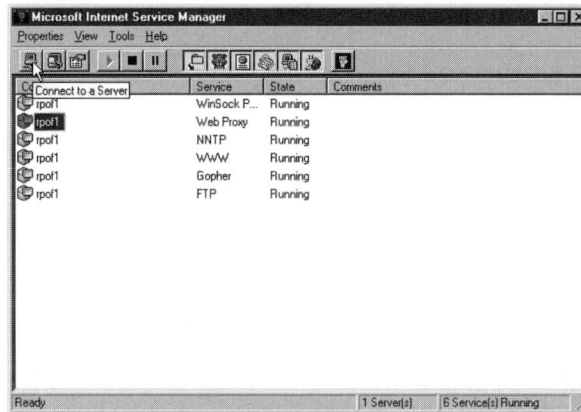

Let's learn about the different buttons on the button bar, located just below the Title and Menu bars.

Icon	Button Name	Description
	Server Connect	Connects you to a specific Internet server in your domain
	Find Internet Servers	Locates all MCIS or NT-based Internet servers in the domain
	Properties	Brings up the Property Sheets for a particular server or service
	Start Service	Restarts or resumes a service that has been paused or stopped
	Stop Service	Halts a particular service
	Pause/Continue Service	Toggles between pausing and resuming a service
	View FTP Servers	Finds all FTP servers in the domain
	View Gopher Servers	Finds all Gopher servers running within the domain
	View WWW Servers	Finds all WWW servers within the domain

The remaining buttons relate to optional servers that may or may not be loaded under MCIS. For our purposes, we have loaded MCIS News Server and Microsoft Proxy Server for

Part
VII

Ch
18

Windows NT Server. Proxy Server actually loads two Virtual Servers: Web Proxy Server and WinSock Proxy Server. Here are these buttons:

Icon	Name	Description
	View NNTP Servers	Shows you all MCIS News Servers within the domain
	View Web Proxy Servers	Displays all Proxy servers within the domain
	View WinSock Proxy Servers	Displays all proxies with responsibility for handling dial-up connections to Web servers in the domain
	Key Manager	Displays information on creating, importing, exporting, and restoring keys and certificates for SSL, or Secure Sockets Layer

N O T E To see the use of the HTML Internet Service Manager, go to the section covering the configuration and management of Gopher services, titled "Implementing Gopher."
The entire section uses the HTML version of ISM to illustrate Gopher management. ■

Configuring the Servers

Using ISM, system administrators can track, monitor, and configure each server within a domain. This task is best performed using the NT application of ISM. Options for working with each server are available from within several views: Report, Server, and Services view.

To find all servers in the domain, click Find All Servers from the ISM Properties menu. The Microsoft Internet Service Manager dialog box, shown in Figure 18.5, appears, indicating that the search is being conducted.

FIG. 18.5
ISM is searching for all servers on the network. Click STOP if the request takes too long, or was performed in error.

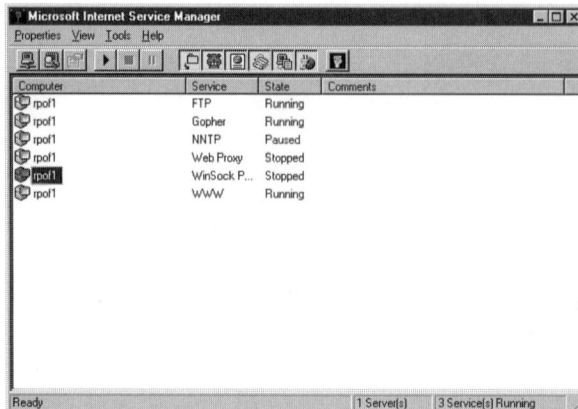

Report View

When the servers on the network are located, all servers will be listed in the ISM Report page which is the default view for ISM (see Figure 18.6). Note the services that are indicated as *running* on the server.

FIG. 18.6

ISM reports all the services found and the operational status of all services found. The report has been sorted.

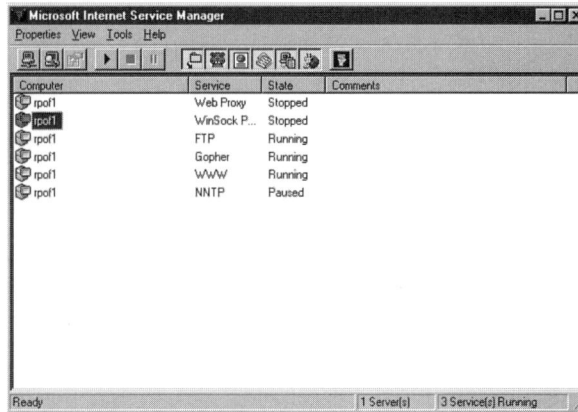

Choose View, Sort to sort the report first by server, then by service, then by status as ordered in Figure 18.6.

Server View

Choose View, Servers to change to Server view where the standard Explorer window features are used (see Figure 18.7). A computer icon represents each server in the domain. Choose the plus (+) or minus (-) icon next to a server to expand or collapse the display of services found on each server.

FIG. 18.7

Only one server resides in the domain depicted in this expanded Server View. Note the of status—Running, Stopped, or Paused—of each service, which is echoed in the traffic signal icon adjacent to each service.

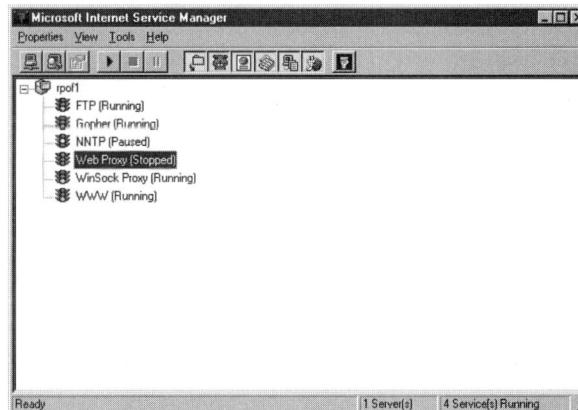

Part

VII

Ch

18

In the screen, you will see the expanded tree view of all services running on the server. Microsoft uses a traffic light metaphor to determine the status of each service. By using the buttons on the toolbar, a service can be started, stopped, paused, or continued. The change in status is then indicated adjacent to the service.

Services View

The final viewing option is the Services View. Choose View, Services to see the view where services are prioritized (see Figure 18.8).

FIG. 18.8

Note in Services view services are shown, but not servers.

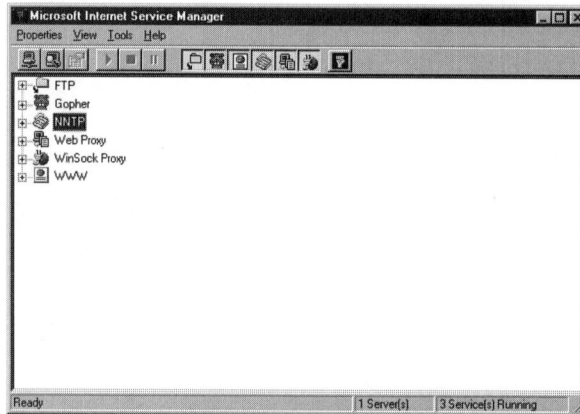

Any of the services shown in Figure 18.8 can be expanded to see the servers corresponding to each service, along with their status both as text and as the traffic light metaphor (see Figure 18.9), by choosing the service or the adjacent plus (+) icon.

FIG. 18.9

Each service now displays its corresponding server and status.

Configuring World Wide Web (WWW) Services

You are about to contribute to the spectacular growth of the World Wide Web. The ease with which you can configure and commission a Web site using Windows NT, IIS, and MCIS should show why the Web has become such a hot property.

Configuring a Web site involves several steps. These steps will, in large part, be mirrored for the other two Internet services: FTP and Gopher.

The Service Property Sheet

From ISM, choose WWW in either the Reports View or the Services View. You will see a dialog box with four tabs (or buttons), shown in Figure 18.10.

The tabs correspond to the WWW Services you will need to administer: Services, Directories, Logging, and Advanced. These four categories are described in greater detail later in the chapter.

First, let's look at the Service tab. This tab covers technical specifications for the WWW site, including the physical TCP port used, the number of users, and basic login information.

FIG. 18.10

The Service property sheet for the WWW service. Note the User ID IUSR_RPOF1 has been entered and the Basic (Clear Text) option is not selected. This permits only Anonymous and NT Challenge/Response logins to the WWW server.

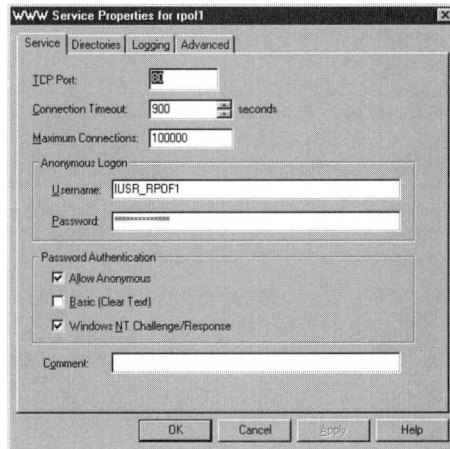

Part

VII

Ch

18

- The TCP Port is set for the default value of 80. If you plan to publish your WWW site, leave the default. If you plan to hide your WWW site, change the value.

T I P If you plan on changing the TCP Port number for *any service*, not just WWW, change the port number to a figure higher than 1023. Port numbers 0 through 1023 are governed by the Internet Assigned Numbers Authority (IANA) and are called "Well Known Port Numbers." Therefore, you would risk a conflict with another port number if you changed the number below 1023.

- *Connection Timeout* The default is 900 seconds (15 minutes) before automatic logout. If you want to reduce this time to conserve concurrent logins, or save money on connection charges, reduce this value.

■ *Maximum Connections*   The default is 100,000 concurrent users. Please note that this figure is hardware- and bandwidth-dependent. Due to bandwidth limitations, it is hard to imagine connecting 100,000 users to your server through anything other than a T-3, 45-megabit network connection directly hard-wired into the greater Internet.

■ *Anonymous Logon*   This is set to the default Username of IUSR_*computername* (all anonymous users), where *computername* is the default anonymous account created when you installed Internet Information Server. The Password was randomly generated when the account was created. The random generation of a password for an anonymous login is normal here.

N O T E   You can view the specific rights and permissions for the default anonymous account, IUSR_*computername*, by using User Manager for Domains, located under Programs, Administrative Tools, on the Start button. ■

There are three options under Password Authentication:

■ *Allow Anonymous*   Permits anonymous logins to your Web site. This is normal; most Internet sites permit anonymous access because Web administrators could never handle the huge number of hits, or accesses, that each major Web site receives each day. Permitting anonymous logins, and then regulating their access to only public areas, solves most Web-based administrative problems.

■ *Basic (Clear Text)*   Enables Basic Authentication. Basic Authentication does not encrypt user names or passwords, however, so this form of security is vulnerable to intrusion.

■ *Windows NT Challenge/Response*   This is the most secure form of standard, non-SSL security. Using Internet Explorer, versions 2.x and higher, you can require a user ID and password before a user can access sensitive material such as pages, files, and folders on the Web server.

By checking the Windows NT Challenge/Response and Allow Anonymous boxes, and leaving Basic Authentication unchecked, only public pages and those files and directories protected by NT Challenge/Response and IIS security are accessible to Web users.

N O T E   In order for NT Challenge/Response to be activated via the Web, the user logging in to the server must have a User ID and password that is registered within the domain. Therefore, make sure each Web user that will use Challenge/Response is registered by using User Manager for Domains. ■

Mapping WWW Directories

You can map directories to a virtual root, or to virtual roots, by using the Directories Property Sheet. To verify directory mappings, or to map a new directory to a WWW alias, do the following:

▶ **See** "Mapping Document Directoriesto a Virtual Root," **p. 300**, for additional understanding of virtual roots, directories, and mapping.

1. Choose Directories in the WWW Service Properties Sheet to display the Directories page (see Figure 18.11).

FIG. 18.11

The Directories property screen shows the available directories and their aliases. Note the unchecked box marked Directory Browsing Allowed.

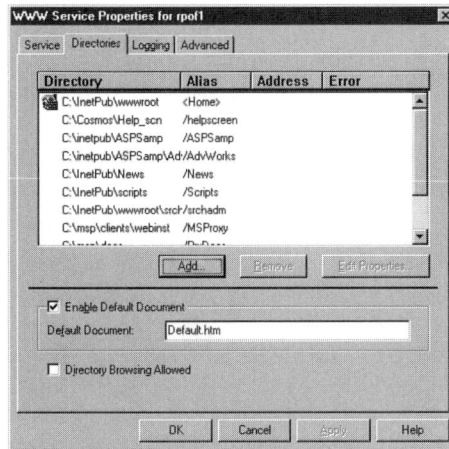

2. Choose A<u>d</u>d, then click the <u>B</u>rowse button.

3. Locate the directory you want to map to an alias. Choose the directory; the directory name will be returned to the Directory text box (see Figure 18.12).

4. Indicate whether you want the directory's real name (the Home Directory) used, or if you want to map this directory to an alias as a Virtual Directory.

5. Type in the name of the alias to which you want to map the directory.

6. Indicate whether the access is Read, Execute, or both, and then choose OK.

FIG. 18.12

The Directory box, with the returned directory listed inside of it. Note the Alias typed in the text box.

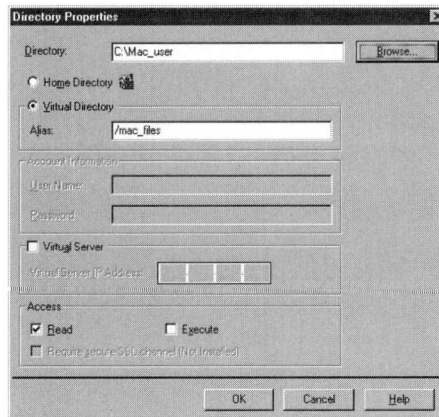

N O T E Unless you want to be able to change the material in your Virtual Directory, only select the <u>R</u>ead option.

N O T E In some cases, you may want to assign an alias to this directory, or group of directories, and create a Virtual Server for administrative purposes. You can then assign this Virtual Server an IP address by typing the IP address in the space provided. ▪

In the example presented, we have selected a Macintosh directory on NT Server to be mapped. This allows the mapping of documents prepared by Mac users to appear on the same Web site as Windows and Windows NT files and directories.

Additionally, Mac users can also access the WWW services, as long as their account name and password are present in the User Manager for Domains. If they are using a recent version of Internet Explorer, they can also use the Challenge/Response security model.

In Figure 18.13, the results of choosing the Directory Browsing Allowed box in the WWW Directories property sheet are shown. Note how clicking that option brought up a tree display of all files on the directory and the file attributes. Each file name is hyperlinked to the file itself; clicking the file once takes you to the document's page. Though this is not a preferred activity, activating Directory Browsing Allowed can have positive effects in intranet situations for quick document sharing.

N O T E The argument against implementing directory browsing is that, once selected, you may expose directory contents to unauthorized users. If you do not specify a default page, the Web page automatically returns a listing of files in the target directory, similar to that shown in Figure 18.13. It is therefore good policy to have both a default page in the directory to be browsed, as well as a limitation (or ban) on browsing directories, unless it is in your organization's interests to allow this. ▪

FIG. 18.13

The results of choosing the Directory Browsing Allowed box in the directory property sheet. Note each file's hyperlink and attributes.

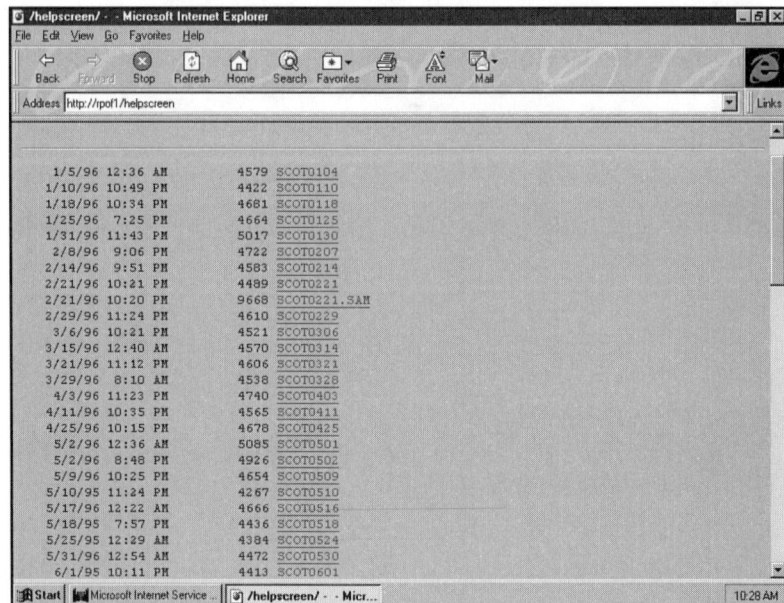

Logging Activities

You can view and print the contents of a log file record of all activities on the WWW server. This log can be configured to create a new file as often as you want.

In Figure 18.14, you can see the contents of the Logging page.

FIG. 18.14

The options for changing log settings under the Logging page. Note the shaded SQL/ODBC option boxes.

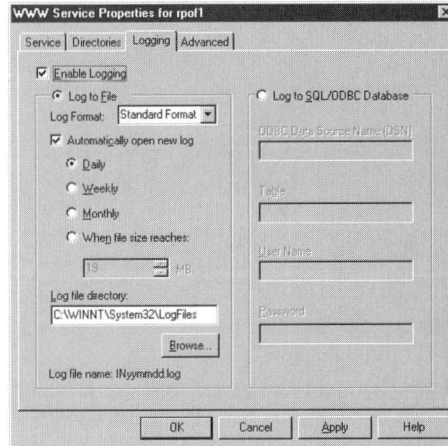

The Enable Logging option is selected by default, allowing the automatic creation of logfiles. You can have a standard log format, or NCSA format, logfile. An advantage to using NCSA format is the ability to import the log into Access to keep a record of activity.

The Automatically open new logfile is also selected by default. This creates a new logfile at the interval you choose: Daily, Weekly, Monthly, or When the file becomes too large. You determine the maximum size of the file, in megabytes.

Finally, if SQL Server is active in the domain, you can choose to Log to SQL/ODBC Database. This option is shown as unavailable in Figure 18.14.

Advanced Property

In Advanced Properties, you can configure IIS to grant or deny access to individuals or groups of people. Let's assume you have a malcontent intranet user who is abusing Web privileges.

▶ **See** "Configuring Security for Your Site," **p. 512**, for a detailed discussion of how this property sheet is used as part of an overall security strategy.

You can follow these simple steps to block the unwanted abuser:

1. Click Add in Advanced Properties (see Figure 18.15).

FIG. 18.15

Note the default of either Granted Access or Denied Access. This makes it easier to satisfy individual cases by including or excluding the greater number of people.

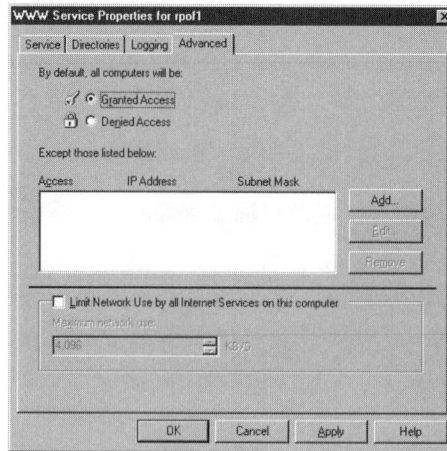

2. Type the IP address of the unwanted user. Use the actual physical IP address; DHcP will not work well.

3. The IP address appears in the box below, along with a lock icon. This signifies that Web services have been denied for this user.

Limiting Network Usage

Because of hardware limitations, there may be a need to share Internet resources on a computer. This is especially true if a server must handle Web, FTP, and Mail services simultaneously.

It is too easy for Web users, by their innocent actions, to monopolize all available bandwidth on a Web server. Therefore, it is advisable to experiment with limiting bandwidth on a WWW server.

If you experience problems with speed, access to other Internet resources, or other performance issues, you may want to limit the size, in kilobytes, of all Web traffic.

To activate this feature, check the box labeled Limit Network Use by All Internet Services on this computer. Accept the default of 4096K for Web services; you can adjust this value later if necessary.

Configuring FTP Services

FTP, or File Transfer Protocol, is one of the original ways to move files across the Internet. With the growth of Hypertext Transport Protocol, or HTTP, it would be logical to think FTP's usefulness as an Internet tool was waning. Nothing could be further from the truth.

FTP is the only way to copy files across the Internet. Because it is reliable, large files can be moved across long distances with minimal errors. Also, because logging on to an FTP server is relatively easy, FTP remains a favorite of Internet users. It is also essential for any Internet site that has files to distribute on an everyday basis, such as software and hardware companies. It also is important for cross-platform movement of files, say, from Macintosh to UNIX to Windows platforms.

Most Web browsers now support FTP, but many people prefer to use FTP software to move files from Point A to Point B.

N O T E Microsoft Internet Explorer, Netscape Navigator, and other browsers automatically log the user in to FTP sites that permit anonymous logins.

Logging In to an FTP Site

The preferred method of logging in to an FTP site is *anonymously*. Because FTP sites are commonly used to distribute files, patches, and drivers, it would be a nightmare for network administrators to attempt to issue a user ID and password to every user. So, the concept of using "anonymous" as the user ID and the user's e-mail address as the password came into vogue.

The IIS FTP site accepts anonymous as the standard login. But, there are precautions you should take to ensure anonymous is the *only* login you can have in to FTP.

Once logged in, FTP users navigate around the directories within the site. Users can then copy files, possibly upload files, and log out.

Why Use Only Anonymous Logins?

FTP sites support only two types of user logins: anonymous and Basic Authentication. Additionally, Microsoft's FTP Server allows, if left unmodified, FTP logins using the NT username and password.

As an example, if a user on RPOF1 was named Harold, and FTP allowed Harold to log in, he would type the following in the URL box in a Web browser:

ftp://harold@rpof1

and FTP would grant him access using the permissions granted under NT. Under this scenario, if Basic Authentication is employed on an FTP site, and an unauthorized user stole an administrator's password, that person could navigate into the FTP site and conduct mass mischief. Therefore, it is advisable to completely eliminate any possibility of an unauthorized login via FTP.

The anonymous login used by most Web browsers activates the account IUSR_*computername*, where *computername* is the name given to your server. By default, this account, as well as a random password, was created at the time IIS was installed on the primary domain controller or stand-alone server. If you are using a primary domain controller or secondary controller, the default account is copied to all the other servers in the domain automatically, so you do not have to deal with individual anonymous user issues on individual servers.

By viewing the account in User Manager, under Server Administration, you can see how the user is configured.

Configuring an FTP Site

Configuring an FTP site is extremely straightforward. Using ISM, either from the NT application or the Web page, choose FTP, then select FTP. You will note five tabs (buttons, if on the Web), marked Service, Messages, Directories, Logging, and Advanced. We'll take these tabs in the order they appear.

Service   Choose Service to see a box similar to the one in Figure 18.16. Note the boxes marked TCP Port, Connection Timeout, Maximum Connections, and three other options at the bottom of the box.

FIG. 18.16

The FTP Service Property Sheet. Pay close attention to the two Anonymous options at the bottom of the window.

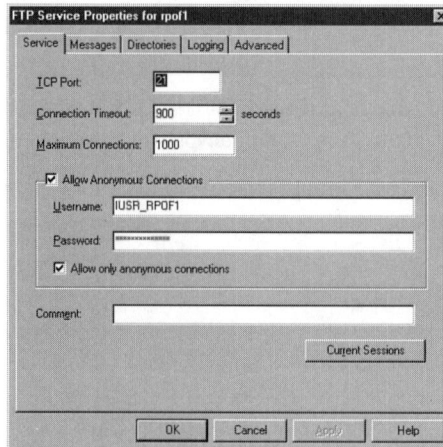

Let's take a look at the individual components of the Service tab:

■ *TCP Port*   The TCP Port value represents the default for all FTP sites: 21. There is no reason to change this value unless you wish to "hide" your FTP site, similar to the hiding of the WWW site illustrated in the previous section (see the following Caution).

CAUTION

Changing this value will render your FTP site invisible to normal users. Do not change this value if you intend to use your FTP site for public access. Also note that the same numbering restrictions discussed in the WWW Service Properties section must be followed for FTP and Gopher sites, in order to avoid clashes with other Well Known Port Numbers.

- *Connection Timeout*   Connection Timeout is the time, in seconds, before the FTP server returns an error message regarding the amount of time the connection was idle (without activity). The default is 900 seconds, or 15 minutes. You may want to reduce this figure to save time and minimize the possibility of errant activity.

- *Maximum Connections*   The Maximum Connections option determines the maximum number of connections that can occur on one server at one time. The default is 1,000 simultaneous connections. While an average FTP site may require more simultaneous connections, it is hard to imagine an FTP site requiring more, unless the site is extremely popular and contains very eagerly sought-after files.

  The two remaining boxes govern the security issues surrounding FTP and, as such, command great attention:

- *Anonymous Connections*   Also available in the Service dialog box are the options Allow Anonymous Connections, and Allow Only Anonymous Connections, as shown in Figure 18.16.

TIP   For security reasons, you want to check both the Allow Anonymous Connections as well as the Allow Only Anonymous Connections. By default, the Allow Only Anonymous Connections box is unchecked.

Part
VII

Ch

18

Checking the box marked Allow Only Anonymous Logins disables any other permission granted under Windows NT, and means no one can enter an FTP site and create havoc by masquerading as an administrator or other authorized user.

Messages   The Messages tab allows you to prepare custom messages when someone logs into your FTP site. To create messages, do the following:

1. Choose the Welcome Message text box and type your greeting (see Figure 18.17). We've kept it short and sweet!

2. Click the Exit Message text box. Now your typed message will appear when users exit the FTP server.

3. Click the Maximum connections message text box. Now your typed message will appear any time 1,000 users are active and FTP user 1,001 tries to access the service while it is at maximum capacity.

4. Click Apply, and then OK.

N O T E   Your Welcome, Goodbye, and Maximum messages will not appear when accessing FTP sites while using Web browsers such as Netscape or Microsoft Internet Explorer.

Directories   By configuring this property screen, you can point FTP users straight to a virtual or real directory or directories on your server where you will store files for copying, or downloading. This directory can be an actual directory on the server, or it can an *alias*—that is, a name different from the actual name of the directory.

FIG. 18.17

The Messages page, showing the creation of Welcome, Goodbye, and Maximum messages.

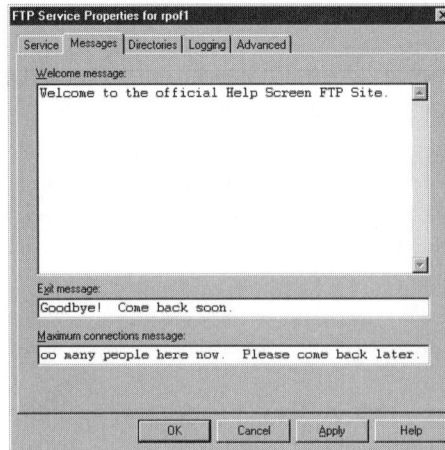

When an alias for a directory is provided, the alias can then be mapped to a virtual directory, which is made up of other files and directories whose contents are fused into one non-physical directory for the sake of FTP access. For example, you could take several directories and subdirectories and create a virtual directory. You would then map that virtual directory to the FTP server.

In Figure 18.18, we have mapped the helpscreen directory on my site to a virtual directory and given it the alias /helpscreen for instant recognition for my readers. To add directories for games, drivers, patches, demonstration software, and other files or programs later, those directories are simply mapped to the virtual directory /helpscreen. Readers would then be able to download, or copy, those files and programs for use on their own computers.

To map a directory to your FTP server, follow these steps:

1. Select Properties from the Services window.

2. Click the Browse button and navigate through the directory tree structure to find the directory, or directories, to map. Click the directory to highlight it and choose OK.

3. Choose Select Home Directory to have the directory name appear on the FTP site, or

4. Choose the Virtual Directory radio button if you want the directory to be mapped to a virtual directory.

5. Click in the Alias text box and type the name of the alias you are giving to the virtual directory.

6. Click OK.

FIG. 18.18

The directory
c:\cosmos\help_scn
has been mapped to
the virtual directory
alias /helpscreen for
FTP access.

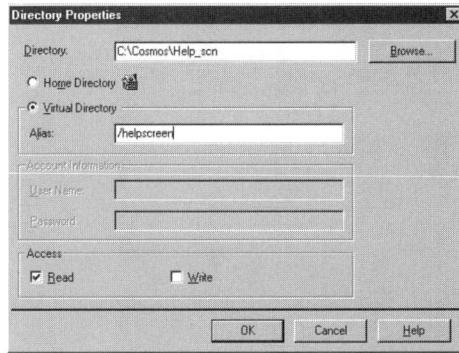

There are two additional areas in Properties: the Underline{U}ser Name and Underline{P}assword text boxes. These options are unavailable unless you activate the Underline{W}rite option. You can then assign a default login and password for individuals who can upload files via FTP to the server's directory.

For example, you may have specific needs—such as allowing anonymous users access to certain directories on your FTP site, but allowing for special, limited access to secure, confidential directories for special needs. In that case, you may map certain user IDs and passwords to certain directories, keeping the mainstream user limited to the default directory structure only.

Part
VII

Ch

18

CAUTION

Enabling the Write option can open the door to unauthorized access to an FTP site. For occasional uploads, consider instead having a file e-mailed as an attachment. If the file is too large, or you expect everyday uploads, activate this feature, but consider changing User IDs and passwords on a frequent, perhaps daily, basis.

After the directory (or directories) is selected and an alias has been assigned, FTP Service Properties for rpof1 properties sheet, shown in Figure 18.19, appears where you can confirm the directory and its alias as well as deciding which Directory Listing Style you prefer, either UNIX or MS-DOS.

N O T E The UNIX style of directory listing uses the forward-slash key, today simply called the slash key (/). The MS-DOS style is more familiar to everyday users, and uses the backslash (\) key. ▧

FIG. 18.19

Click Apply after you have completed your preferences. You can add more directories by clicking the Add button before you leave this screen.

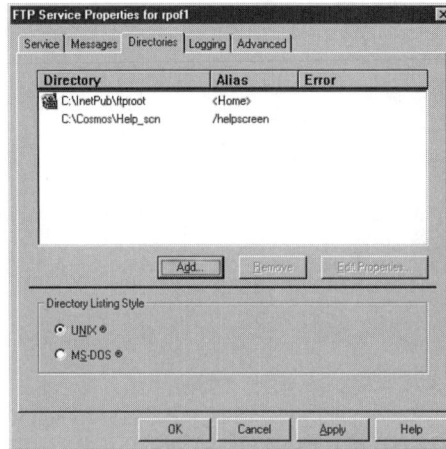

Your directories will now appear in a hypertext box on your Web browser, or will appear as text in a text-based FTP software product. The directories, and their contents, will appear in the familiar "tree" structure, with directories and subdirectories branching off the root.

Implementing Gopher

Gopher combines the tree structure and the publishing ease of the FTP protocol with the hyperlinked custom menus and document links that typify the Web. Before the Web became popular, Gopher was the preferred way Internet users surfed the Information Highway. In the early 1990s, before the Internet moved from an educational to a commercial medium, Gopher was developed by the University of Minnesota (also known as the Golden Gophers). Like FTP, it is considered a *legacy system*, meaning it is an older way of doing things. Legacy also implies that, even though it's old, you'll want to maintain some backward compatibility. Unlike FTP, however, Gopher doesn't appear headed for a renaissance any time soon. Determine your needs carefully.

To set up a Gopher site, just copy your files to the gopher home directory. Users can then browse Gopher as they do FTP and WWW. The logon in Gopher is anonymous only, so no secure logins are possible. It is clear, then, that it is not wise to use Gopher for sensitive files, as there is no secure way to retrieve them without making them available to all Gopher users.

To configure Gopher for use with MCIS, follow these steps. In the interest of displaying the Web capabilities of the ISM module, and since Gopher has no real security features, the Gopher illustrations will feature HTML format.

To configure Gopher services from the Internet System Manager (HTML), choose Gopher, and then choose Service to see the page shown in Figure 18.20.

FIG. 18.20

The HTML version of ISM, with the Gopher Administration page active. Note the pointer leading from the Gopher button directly to the URL of the server.

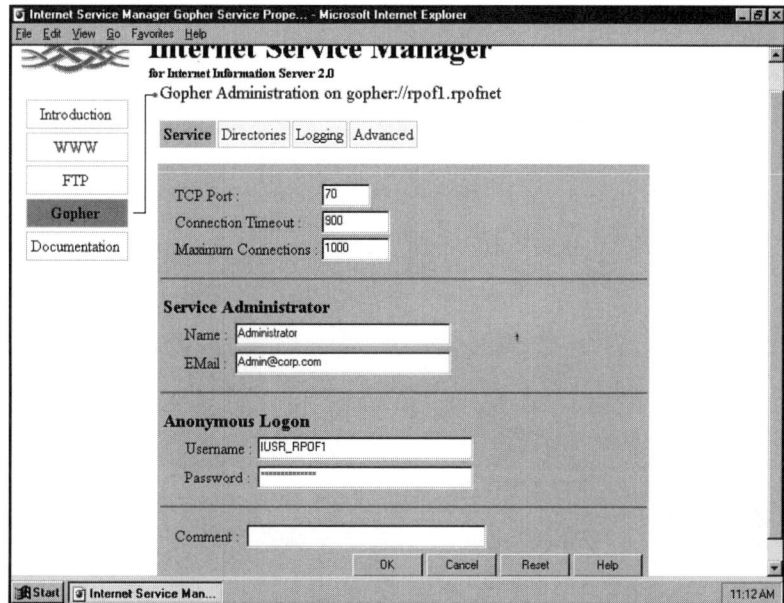

The TCP Port is set to 70, the default for Gopher. You can "hide" your Gopher server by changing its TCP Port, but there in no purpose in doing so. Note the Connection Timeout and Maximum Connections values are dramatically reduced from other services. This is partially because few people use Gopher anymore, and therefore Gopher takes fewer resources relative to overall system access points such as WWW.

Service Administrator is the system administrator, with the e-mail box and address listed. Under Anonymous Logon, note the by-now-familiar IUSR_computername user ID and randomly generated password.

N O T E You do not see any boxes allowing for specific logon access. Again, that is because Gopher does not support dedicated user IDs or passwords. ▦

Gopher Directory Mapping

You have the ability to map Gopher directories to an alias on the server, as you did FTP and Web services.

To map a directory to an alias, do the following:

1. Select Directories from the ISM HTML page. Note the root directory for Gopher services, and the empty box below it.

2. Click the Add button. You will be presented with a directory tree from which you can make your directory selections.

Part

VII

Ch

18

3. Click the directory to highlight it and choose OK.

4. Choose Select Home Directory if you want this directory's name to appear on the Gopher site as it is on the actual server, or

   Choose Virtual Directory to have the directory mapped to a virtual directory and enter the name of the alias for the virtual directory.

5. Click OK.

The directory name is now returned to the box as shown on the Directories page (see Figure 18.21).

FIG. 18.21

The directories page, listing the alias for each directory mapped. Note how closely the Web options correspond to those in the NT version of ISM.

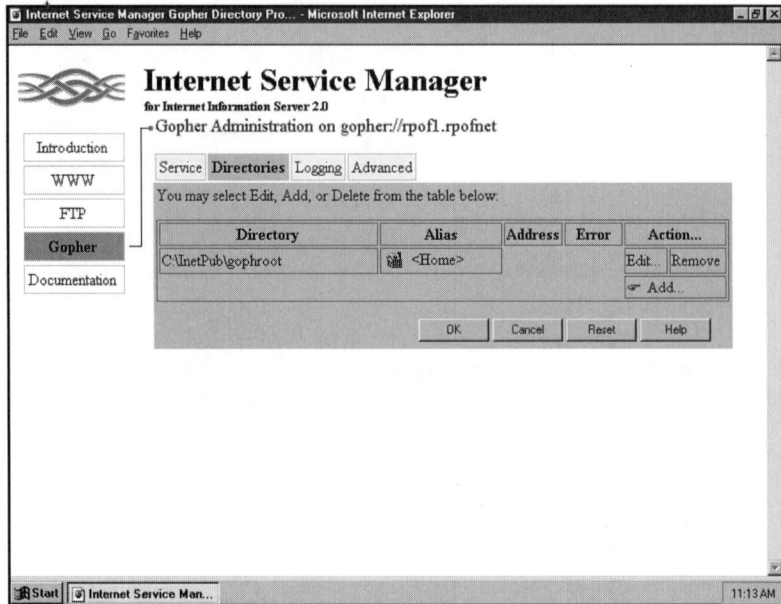

Logging System Events in Gopher

As in the other services, you can generate logs of Gopher events for analysis by performing the following steps:

1. From the ISM Gopher page, choose Logging to display the Logging dialog box, shown in Figure 18.22.

2. By default, Log to File is selected as the installation option. Select Log to File if it is not active.

3. Verify that Automatically Open New Log is active. This is also the default setting.

4. If you want to change the frequency for making a new log file, do so now. If not, it is recommended that the default of Daily be selected.

5. Note the log file directory for future reference.

FIG. 18.22
The Logging page, with the default options selected.

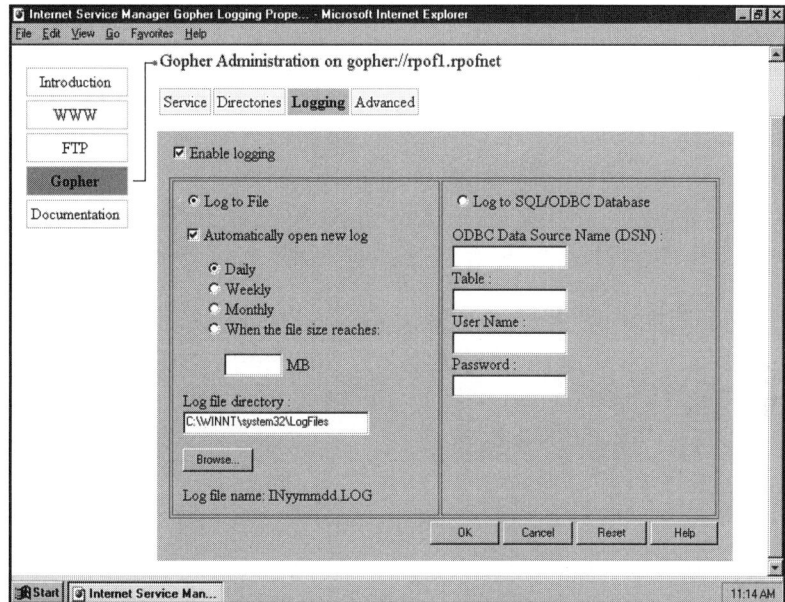

N O T E As in the other Internet services, you can enable SQL/ODBC connectivity here as well, but you will not be able to provide the recommended layer of security here that you can provide in other protocols. ▓

Advanced Options Under Gopher

Unlike standard Gopher, you can limit or prohibit access to Gopher services through IIS. This option gives administrators the ability to deny Gopher services to all users except the administrator.

In the following example, you can easily configure Gopher to deny access by default, and allow selected users to access the Gopher site.

1. From the Gopher ISM page, choose Advanced to see the screen in Figure 18.23.

2. Single-click Click Here to Set the Default to *Deny Access*. You will be taken to a page similar to that shown in Figure 18.24.

3. Click Set default to deny and add your address to the grant list. This action only allows the administrator's User ID to the Grant list.

FIG. 18.23

In the Advanced screen under Gopher in ISM. Note the pointer hand signifying that particular area of screen is actively linked to another page.

Pointer hand ──

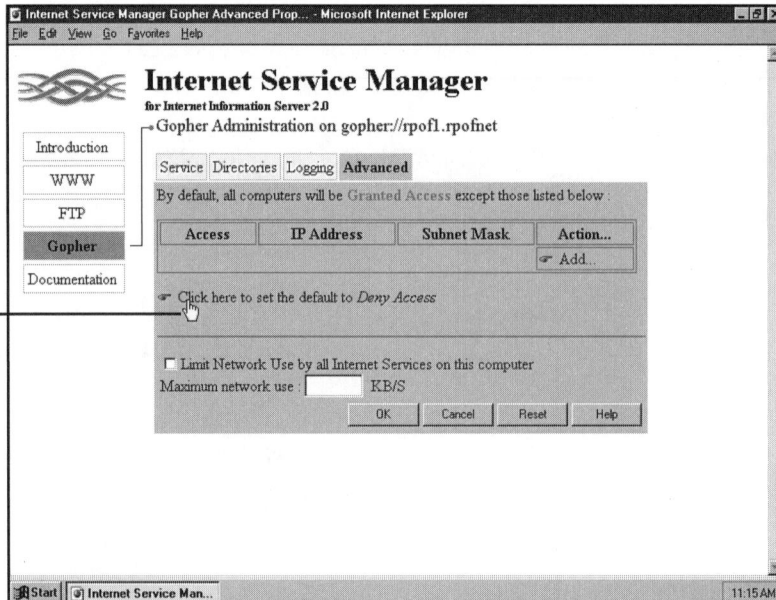

FIG. 18.24

The Set Default to Deny screen. Note its heading at the top of the HTML page.

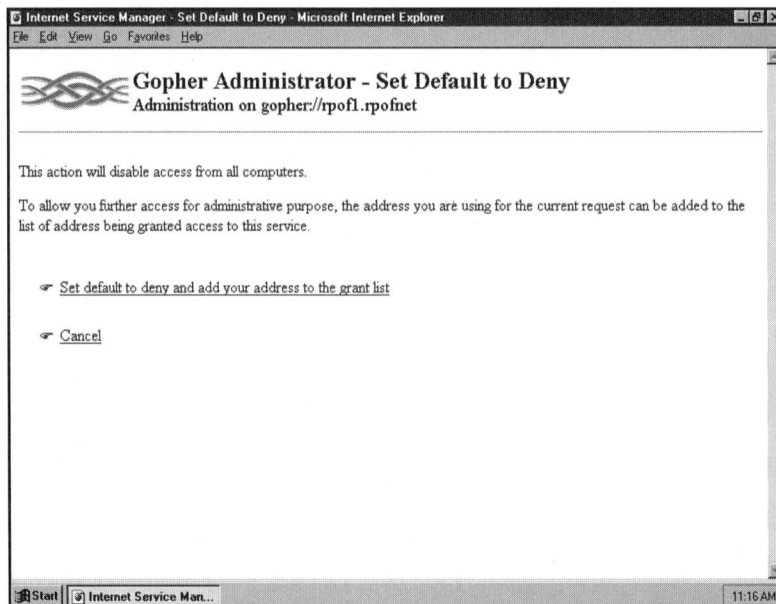

4. Note the changes as represented by Figure 18.25, and then click OK to complete the task. All Gopher services are now off limits.

FIG. 18.25

The access Granted is visible, along with a key, instead of a lock, for the administrator. To set the default back to Grant Access, just click the Grant Access area.

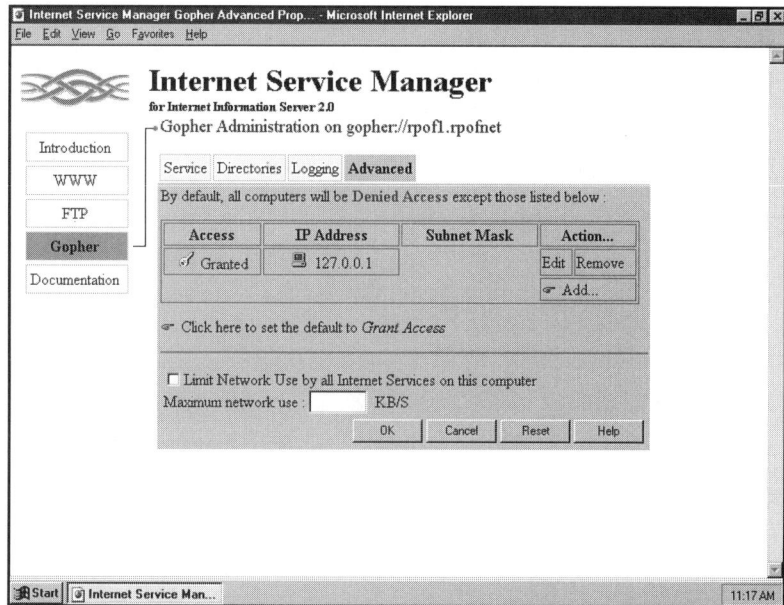

> **N O T E** It can be argued that this is the only area in the HTML version of Internet Service Manager that actually allows you to functionally stop an Internet service remotely using the Web page. ▓

WAIS Searching and Tags

By default, *Wide Area Information Search*, or *WAIS*, is not activated by Internet Information Server. This is probably due to the fact that Gopher is not the hot item it used to be years ago, and this was overlooked.

It can, however, be activated using the Registry.

In the following example, the Registry is edited to activate WAIS.

1. Launch REGEDIT.EXE.
2. Find the entry:

```
HKEY_LOCAL_MACHINE_SYSTEM
        \CurrentControlSet
                \Services
                        \GopherSVC
                                \CheckForWAISDB
```

You should see a window similar to the one in Figure 18.26.

FIG. 18.26

Using the Registry Editor, you can locate the entry for WAISDB. By changing the value to (1), you enable and activate WAIS for Gopher.

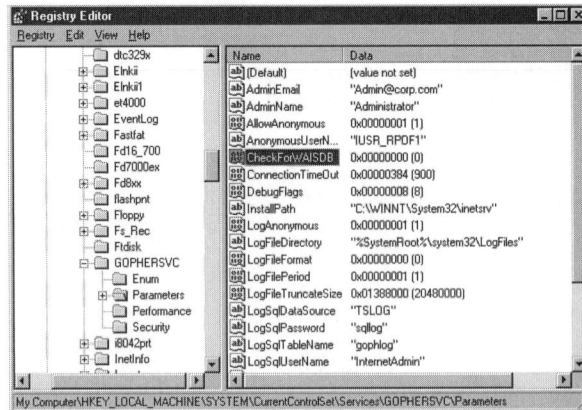

3. Using great care, change the value (0) next to WAIS to (1).

4. Close REGEDIT.EXE.

CAUTION

Mistakes made when editing the Registry can cause serious problems. Avoid this by backing up the Registry regularly by exporting it to a file. Then the Registry can easily be restored when needed.

Note the value for WAIS in the Registry is (0). You'll need to set it to (1) to activate WAIS. Tag files are used to annotate files with other attributes for the benefit of Gopher users. For more information on Gopher tags, refer to your Microsoft documentation.

Configuring Security for Your Site

The biggest wonder of the Internet surely must be its ability to link users across the planet in one huge "cloud," giving a user in Turkey the ability to access your MCIS site, wherever it is located. But with this opportunity comes risk. Usually, this Internet risk takes the form of tampering, hacking, and malicious mischief.

The overwhelming majority of Internet users are good, curious people exercising their Internet privileges with nothing but goodwill on their minds. But there are evil, maladjusted people who enjoy nothing more than committing mischief (and worse) on undefended, or underdefended, networks. Don't let your network fall prey to these malcontents.

Security issues must be recognized and dealt with holistically, if your MCIS site is to be safe from intruders. A security plan should incorporate all of the following elements, each of which will be discussed in the following sections:

■ Erecting Firewalls

■ Authenticating Users

■ Protecting Files and Folders

■ Limiting Access

Erecting Firewalls

As discussed elsewhere in this book, there are many ways to connect to the Internet. Most organizations will find their needs best met by using dedicated lines into, and out of, their network. Their connections will probably be either 56K or T-1 and T-3 lines, although smaller organizations will move to ISDN service when it is available in their area. A very small percentage of organizations will want to publish Web and FTP services using dial-up connections.

The most common method of "hard wiring" into the Net is through the use of a router. Routers connect networks to other networks, or, in this case, from a network to the Internet. The following best describes the concept of routing:

NETWORK ➡ WEB SERVER ➡ ROUTER ➡ CLOUD (INTERNET)

These hardware routers can be configured to accept or reject one- or two-way Internet traffic. This means if a company wants to surf or crawl the Web without allowing incoming packets to infiltrate their intranet, they may configure the router appropriately.

Routers can also be configured to stop certain IP addresses, or groups of addresses, from reaching your site. This concept is known as *packet filtering*. The router monitors incoming packets and filters out, or prevents, certain IP addresses from hitting your Internet server. This is usually referred to as *building a firewall*.

Microsoft has taken the concept of building firewalls to the software level through the use of two other products: Microsoft Proxy Server, which offers other firewalls to the administrator, and built-in firewalls in the Windows NT/Internet Information Server software. Proxy Server is discussed in Chapter 17, "Using the Microsoft Proxy Server." We will give examples of limiting access by certain IP addresses in this chapter.

Part

VII

Ch

18

Authenticating Users

The second popular concept to limiting Internet access is through the use of user identification names, or User IDs, and passwords. The method of using names and passwords is called *authentication*.

The need for authentication depends upon such considerations as whether or not you will use the Internet site for commerce, specifically transacting business using credit card numbers; or using the Web and FTP to move sensitive files or corporate secrets across the Internet; or whether you are simply publishing public information that is not a trade or other forms of secrets.

Web Browsers and Security   There are four methods of Web authentication. They are:

■ NT Challenge/Response

■ Basic Authentication

■ Anonymous Logons

■ The Secure Sockets Layer, or SSL

Each method of Web security has its own configuration options, and each has its limitations. For these reasons, unless you are running a closely administered intranet with one standard Web browser and a need to limit access of authenticated users on a regular basis, it is difficult to imagine using one security method on your system. Instead, a policy of using multiple security layers is recommended.

Figure 18.27 illustrates the security procedures used when a user requests data in a Microsoft Internet Information Server environment.

FIG. 18.27

The security features makes certain checks; the process is similar to a flow chart.

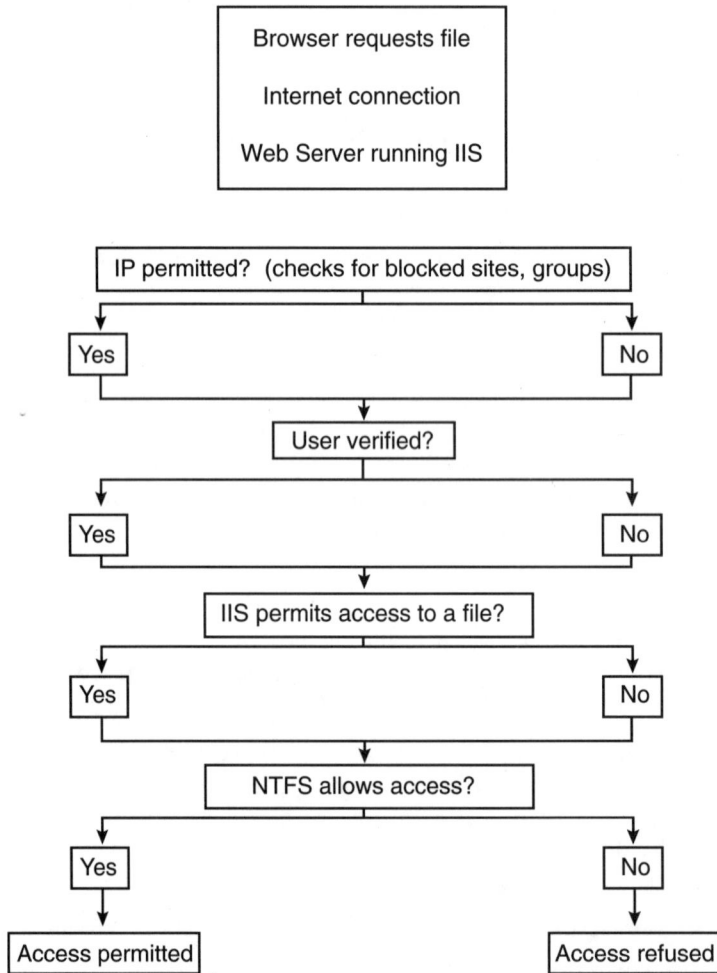

Browser requests file

Internet connection

Web Server running IIS

IP permitted? (checks for blocked sites, groups)

Yes   No

User verified?

Yes   No

IIS permits access to a file?

Yes   No

NTFS allows access?

Yes   No

Access permitted   Access refused

NT Server Challenge/Response and Internet Explorer 2.x and Higher Web Browsers   Using Microsoft Internet Explorer 2.x and higher Web browser software, Internet users can actually be exposed to the Challenge/Response security model. This is because Microsoft has taken NT Server Challenge/Response authentication and elevated it from mere network status to true Internet-tested security through the use of its Web browser, Internet Explorer.

NT Challenge/Response and other authentication methods can coexist because IIS broadcasts both methods of authentication every time a resource is accessed that requires authentication of the user, and the Internet Explorer browser senses, and responds to, this authentication request. Other browsers may or may not recognize NT Server Challenge/Response.

In Challenge/Response Authentication, the User ID and password are encrypted; that is, they are scrambled and left indecipherable by all but the most powerful decryption devices. The challenge/response model is broadcast first by IIS, followed by Basic Authentication. MSIE, being challenge/response-aware, reacts and interacts with IIS. The next level of security, namely the user restrictions and permissions through NTFS, then kicks in to regulate access to organizational resources.

N O T E   Because of its capability to be used within Microsoft Internet Explorer Web browsers, it is highly recommended that NT Challenge/Response authentication be used on organizational intranets or in Internet situations where sensitive information must pass between client and server. ▪

Part VII

Ch 18

Limitations of Challenge/Response   Other Web browsers, however, do not recognize Challenge/Response, and do recognize the second IIS security protocol, commonly referred to as Basic Authentication. The big problem with Basic Authentication, however, is that the User ID and password are broadcast unscrambled; this leaves the site exposed if a scheme is being employed that is deliberately trying to access a site unethically.

Basic Authentication   All popular Web browsers support Basic Authentication, which is the standard user ID and password combination. The problem with using Basic Authentication over the Internet is that Basic Authentication transmits an unscrambled user ID and password over the Internet. This lack of encryption, or scrambling of information, is a security risk that administrators need to address when designing a site and determining what information is to be made available to these users. It is generally considered a bad idea to use simple Basic Authentication when publishing, or making available-sensitive information and files on the Internet.

Anonymous Logon   This procedure is the most common on the Internet. Again, virtually all Web browsers support anonymous logons. It is by far the most popular way to access Web sites; indeed, when accessing a Web site, it is usually accomplished automatically, as an anonymous user. Rights and privileges have already been set by the system administrator or Webmaster. Users are not aware of any other rights, because You Don't Know What You Don't Know, as they say in the business. Ignorance is bliss; users may feel the whole world in their hands (or on-screen), but the reality is, access is only being allowed to what the anonymous configuration and directory settings say can be accessed.

The Secure Sockets Layer (SSL)   The Secure Sockets Layer was developed to allow standard Web browsers to use a process called *cryptography* to secure the integrity of data transmissions over the Internet.

The Secure Sockets Layer is a *protocol*, or standard way of doing things, that was submitted to the standards authority W3C, the World Wide Web Consortium. W3C is a task force charged with the responsibility of finding safer ways to perform tasks over the Internet, including financial transactions. The Secure Sockets Layer protocol, when added to Basic Authentication, creates a situation that is, perhaps, the most secure in the entire Internet. Using SSL, all data transmissions between server and client are completely secure; so secure, in fact, that SSL is used for financial transactions over the Internet, including credit card transactions.

What happens when SSL is invoked is that the server and the client agree on what level of security is to be used (commonly referred to as a "handshake"). Once SSL is invoked, all data—coming both upstream and downstream—is encrypted, including all user IDs, passwords, and even the URL that is being accessed!

This encryption also includes credit card numbers and any other sensitive information.

Once SSL is activated on a server, any Web browser capable of supporting SSL can access SSL-protected files and folders. But once SSL is activated, ONLY SSL-aware users can access the material in these specially coded folders. This is because SSL will actually encode the files and folders with additional information designed to protect the contents of those folders from intrusion. This requires the use of the instruction "https://" instead of the familiar "http://" instruction when locating a Web page.

To activate SSL, you must generate a security code called a Key Pair, and then secure what is called an SSL Certificate. Certificates can be ordered from companies called Certificate Authorities. An example of a Certificate Authority is VeriSign.

ON THE WEB

http://www.verisign.com/microsoft/   VeriSign can be contacted via the Web by accessing VeriSign. Full instructions on obtaining Key and Certificate Pairs can be downloaded there.

There is a button at the end of the button bar in the Internet Service Manager screen, or an option that is accessed off the View menu, called the Key Manager. From the Key Manager, you can create key and certificate requests and perform other maintenance as required to support SSL.

Follow this procedure to create a new key:

1. From the Menu Bar, choose Key, Create New Key. The Create New Key and Certificate Request dialog box shown in Figure 18.28 appears.

2. In Key Name, enter a name for the key. Enter a Password. Remember, alphanumeric and mixed case works best.

FIG. 18.28

Set up key preference in the Create New Key and Certificate Request dialog box.

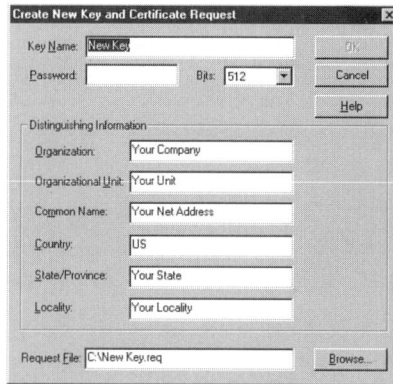

3. For Bits, the American default is 1024 bits long. The International version is 512 bits long. The greater the number of bits in the key, the greater the security.

4. Enter the name of your Organization and the Organizational Unit.

5. Under Common Name, type the domain name of the server, such as **www.rpofnet.com**.

6. Provide the Country 2-letter designation, such as US, UK, and so forth.

7. Enter the State/Province and the City such as Miami, Tallahassee, or Atlanta.

8. Finally, enter the name of the Request File that will be generated. Here, the filename is c:\New Key.req.

9. When all text boxes are complete, click OK. A screen that requires retyping the password appears. Retype the password.

The key is generated. When the key generation is finished, a screen appears, telling you to request a certificate, similar to Figure 18.29.

After closing the dialog box, a screen appears that confirms that there is not a valid key until the Certificate is received and installed, as shown in Figure 18.30.

FIG. 18.29

The New Key Information dialog box. Choose OK to forward your key to a Certificate Authority to complete the process.

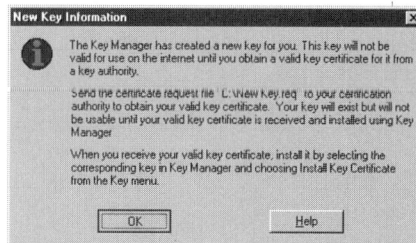

Part

VII

Ch

18

FIG. 18.30

The Key Manager screen once a key is generated. Note the text just under the dialog box, indicating the status of the key and the fact the key is not yet valid.

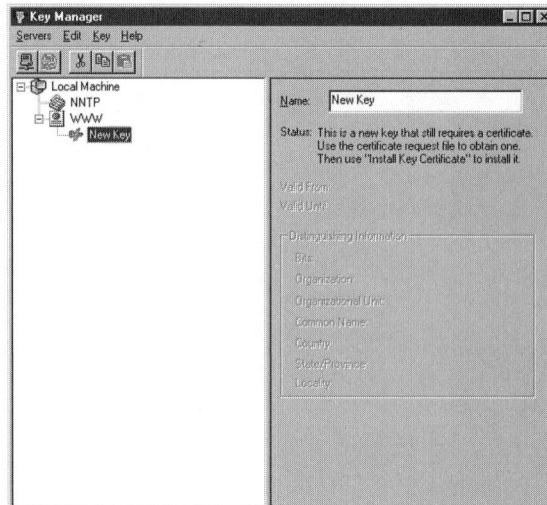

Installing Certificates   You will receive a signed Certificate from the Authority you used. You now must load the certificate in order to complete the task. Follow these instructions:

1. Launch ISM and click Key Manager.
2. Select the key pair that matches the one you requested and that matches your signed certificate.
3. Choose Key, Install Key Certificate.
4. Choose the certificate file from the available list and click Open.
5. Type in the password used to generate the key pair. This combines both the key pair and the password.
6. Choose Servers, Commit Changes Now.
7. Click OK to complete your key pair and certificate.

Backing Up a Key Pair   Once you have a key file, you should immediately move to make a backup, or archive, copy of the file. The copy can be made to floppy disk or removable media, such as tape or removable optical drives.

Backing up a key file involves using Key Manager. Here's how:

1. From Key Manager, choose Key, Select Export Key.
2. Select Backup File, read the documentation, and then click OK.
3. Click once in the File Name Box and type in the name of the key file.

Key Manager automatically names the key and adds the extension .REQ. The file is copied to the hard drive. It can now be backed up, either as a stand-alone archive, or as part of an ongoing backup scheme.

Restoring or Loading a Backed-Up Key The concept of backing up means preparing for disaster. Unfortunately, disasters sometimes happen. This section helps you to restore and recover a key from a catastrophic disaster.

To restore a backed up key, follow these steps:

1. Launch Key Manager.
2. Choose Key, Import Key.
3. Select Backup File (see Figure 18.31).
4. Find the name of the key and select Open.

FIG. 18.31
Key Manager during a key restoration project. The safest bet is to copy the key to a floppy disk or tape for safekeeping. By selecting Backup File, you are preparing to load the archived key back onto the server.

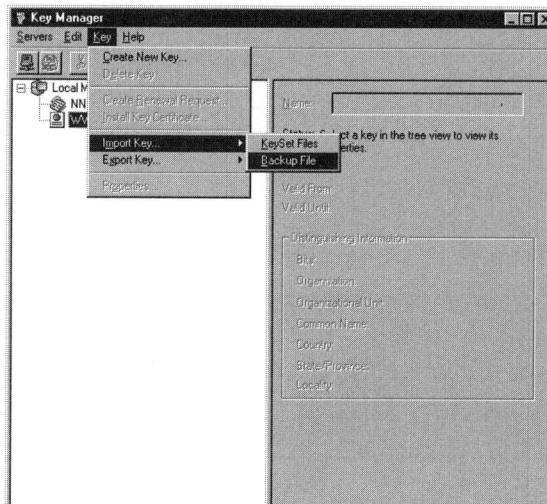

Changing Directory Settings to Require the Secure Sockets Layer (SSL) After the key and certificate are installed on the server, you can now configure directories to require Basic Authentication with SSL for maximum privacy and security. Remember that once a directory is configured to require SSL, it can only be accessed using SSL.

The following steps will allow you to configure SSL:

1. Launch Internet Service Manager (NT Version).
2. Open the WWW Service and choose the Directories tab.
3. Select the Advanced folder then choose Edit, Properties.
4. Select the Require Secure SSL Channel. Click OK.
5. Check the protocols that will be used according to the key and certificate. Choose OK.

Protecting Files and Folders

Windows NT Server has a thorough and comprehensive series of features designed to protect files and folders. These methods include NTFS, ACLs, and other permissions. By using these options, you can safeguard the files and folders from intrusion, just as you can safeguard access to your site.

Some of these options have been discussed earlier in this chapter. We will show you some additional ways to protect files and folders.

First Line of Defense—The Windows NT Server Operating System

NT Server was designed from the ground up with security in mind. As a next-generation operating system, NT designers were able to learn from the security breaches which have victimized other Network Operating Systems as well as anticipate some new ways that hackers might be able to penetrate. With this pursuit of security a major priority of NT, Microsoft made a security system that was not just redundant; it was scalable, too.

Windows NT security is based on a system of user accounts and passwords. You assign a user to an account, and assign that user a password.

TIP Ideally, that password should contain upper- and lowercase letters, as well as numbers to make detection difficult. By making the password case-sensitive, you can make it much more difficult to detect. For example, the password "NutZ2U" is made up of upper- and lowercase letters and a number.

This system of using User IDs and passwords is commonly referred to as NT Challenge/ Response Authentication. It is the first line of defense against unauthorized access.

When you assign a user account, whether in User Manager or one of the Administrator Wizards, you assign rights and permissions to the user's account. If your server is a Primary or Secondary Domain Controller, that user information is automatically transferred to the other servers within the domain.

N O T E If your machine is not a primary or secondary domain controller, you'll have to shoulder the responsibility of copying user information from server to server yourself. For this reason, it is sometimes helpful to create a master Anonymous account that was not generated by IIS, and copy that new master anonymous user to each WWW server in your domain. ■

The Windows NT File System (NTFS) registers those permissions and restrictions on folders and files throughout the domain. You can, therefore, deny or limit access to certain files and folders; you also can block copying, writing, or executing those resources entirely.

Additional IIS File and Folder Safeguards

Building on the NT security model, IIS implements its own level of user security. Using the Internet Service Manager, administrators can set Read- or Execute-only permissions on virtual directories within a domain.

The methods for changing those permissions on directories was described earlier in this chapter.

Licensing Issues Under Windows NT and Internet Information Server

One of the most attractive features regarding Internet Information Server is its licensing flexibility. For example, Internet Information Server includes an unlimited client license as part of its software, making it an extremely cost-effective way of publishing across the Web, even if that data is confidential.

Let's look at an example of how IIS can save a company thousands of dollars in licensing fees. An organization sets up NT Server and installs Internet Information Server. This organization has 100 remote field representatives, each with their own method of accessing the Web.

From within NT Server, either from User Manager or by using the Administrative Wizard, you create a separate User ID and password for each field representative. Then, using IIS, you map the sensitive directories to virtual roots that can only be accessed by NT Challenge/Response.

Now, you can allow authorized users, whether they are remote users or office-bound employees who access the company intranet using a Web browser, to log on by using Internet Explorer Web browser, and access Web pages that require NT Challenge/Response without requiring a corresponding client license. This means organizations can actually use a 5-user NT Server to create an Internet gateway that will serve hundreds!

The rule of thumb here is simple. If NT Server is used as an Internet server, you will not need individual licenses for each user, even if that user is authenticated using NT Challenge/Response. If NT Server is used for file and print services, however, in situations such as the Internet, or if connections are made using NT Server Remote Access Services (RAS), then a valid license is required.

Part
VII

Ch
18

Limiting Access

There may be times when it is necessary to limit access to your Internet site to IP addresses that do not follow rules, log in excessively, or are suspected of causing problems. Additionally, there are situations, such as corporate intranets wired to the greater Internet, that might call for filtering out or blocking *all* incoming IP addresses. The system administrator starts by excluding everyone first, then adding outside access to authorized users a group at a time.

Limiting Access Under IIS

As discussed earlier, by building on the NT security model, IIS implements its own level of user security. By using the Internet Service Manager, administrators can set Read- or Execute-only permissions on virtual directories within a domain. Additionally, access can be granted—or denied—to individual users, or groups of users through restrictions on the IP addresses of those users.

As you see in Figure 18.32, you can configure the ISM WWW Service property sheet to block or grant access to individual users, groups of users, or all users.

FIG. 18.32

Note the two options:
Granted Access and
Denied Access. By
clicking the Add button,
you can include or
exclude anything from
individual IP addresses
to entire domains from
WWW access.

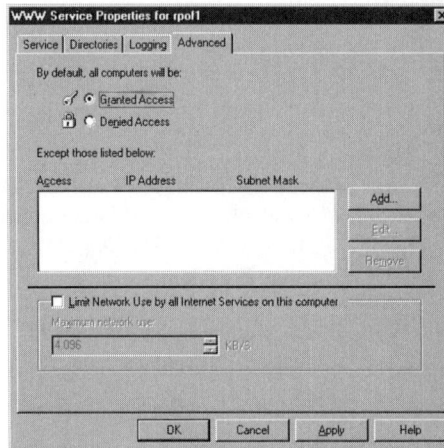

To limit access to a site, you should first determine whether you want the default to be unfettered access or tightly restricted access. This is another area where NT security is strong.

Limiting Access to Your FTP Site

There may be circumstances where you need to "hide" your FTP site from everyday users or snoops. The dilemma in this scenario is, you still need to provide FTP service to remote users.

One answer is to disable the "allow only anonymous connections" from the Services Property Sheet under ISM and then make User IDs and passwords the only way to get into your FTP site. The problem with this solution is that, by doing so, it opens your FTP site to a possible breach of security from unauthorized users.

The reason for this is that, once you have created individual IDs and passwords within FTP, you cannot limit access to specific areas of the site By keeping only anonymous logins, you, by default, limit the scope of access, and can secure your FTP site from intruders.

The other solution is to change the TCP Port variable. Normally, the TCP Port variable is set to the default of 21. If you wish to hide your FTP site from everyday users, set the TCP Port variable to a number higher than 1023. This "hides" your site.

N O T E   Changing these values affects both the FTP Server and the FTP client. If you wish to "hide" only the Server value, you'll need to change the entry in the Registry. ▦

Here's how to change the Registry to hide the server value from within the Registry:

1. Start REGEDIT.EXE. This launches the Registry Editor.
2. Click the HKEY_LOCAL_MACHINE window.
3. Find this key:

```
\System
        \CurrentControlSet
\Control
        \ ServiceProvider
\ServiceTypes
        \MSFTPSVC
```

CAUTION

Again, changing Registry entries can be hazardous if a mistake is made. Registry entries govern virtually all operations of the computer. Exercise extreme caution when editing the Registry. Back up the Registry just in case.

4. Choose MSFTPSVC and then select the TepPort value.
5. You will see the DWORD Editor dialog box. Click Decimal.
6. Enter 1024 as the new port value in the Data box.
7. Click OK.
8. Close the Registry Editor.

N O T E   You will now be typing command line instructions to keep the Service file from overriding the work you have just entered in the Registry. ▦

9. Go to the NT Command Prompt (accessible from the Programs menu off the Start button).
10. Type the following lines:

    cd %systemroot% \system32\drivers\etc
    ren services services.ok

11. Exit the command prompt window.
12. Go to Internet Service Manager and select FTP.
13. Click the Stop button to stop the service.
14. Click the Start button in ISM to restart FTP.

FTP has now been restarted with the new settings.

Part
VII

Ch
18

Server Administration Using NT Server Tools

NT Server gives the system administrator some potent configuration and monitoring tools, even without the Internet Service Manager. Each of these tools can mean a world of difference to the network professional.

User Manager for Domains

One of the most powerful and important tools in the NT arsenal is User Manager for Domains, also known simply as User Manager. This is where all user rights are initially assigned, along with some other important configuration issues.

In order to access User Manager, perform the following steps:

1. Open the User Manager from the Start menu.

2. User Manager opens to a view of all authorized users who have been installed in the domain. But our quarry is the elusive IUSR_RPOF1, the anonymous file. We'll take a look at how the file is configured.

3. Choose the IUSR_RPOF1 file to display its properties (see Figure 18.33). Note the buttons at the bottom of the box:

FIG. 18.33

The properties for the anonymous user file IUSR_RPOF1.

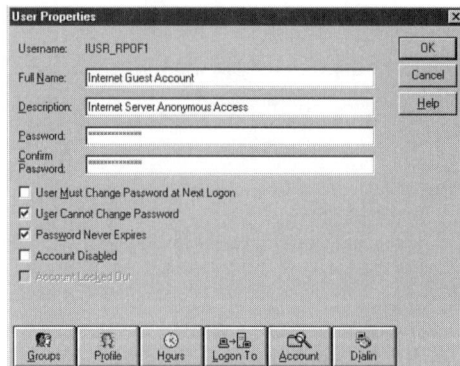

Clicking the "Groups" button reveals a list of groups the user account is assigned to:

- *Groups* denotes what groups the user is a member of (see Figure 18.34).

FIG. 18.34

Group Membership shows both Member of and Not member of.

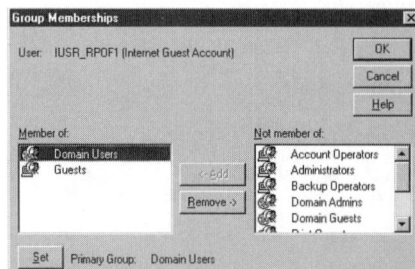

■ *Profile* shows the user profile (see Figure 18.35).

FIG. 18.35

There are no profiles for the anonymous logon.

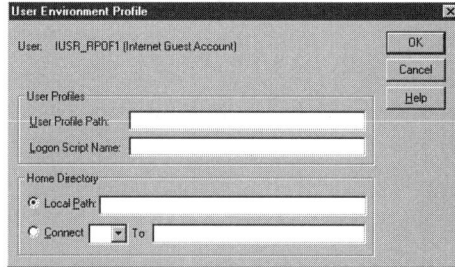

■ *Hours* indicates the hours the user is entitled to access the system (see Figure 18.36).

FIG. 18.36

By default, **IUSR_computername** has a full 24 hours of access every day.

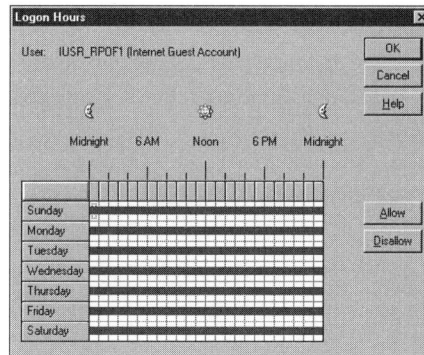

■ *Logon To* indicates what servers, and services, the user can access.

■ *Account* gives information about the expiration, duration, and whether the user is a global, or a local, client (see Figure 18.37).

FIG. 18.37

By default, the account never expires, and is a global account.

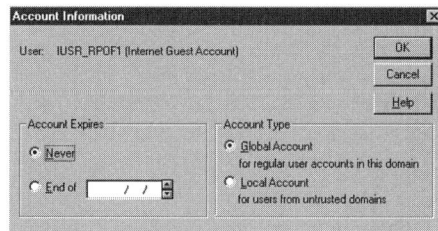

■ *Dialin* indicates whether the user can call into the system, and whether the system is programmed to call back the user for security reasons (see Figure 18.38).

FIG. 18.38

The Dialin Information dialog box. If this were a regular user, there might be a configuration that allowed for a callback once contact was made with the server. The concept of callbacks increases security, for it allows only calls made from known locations.

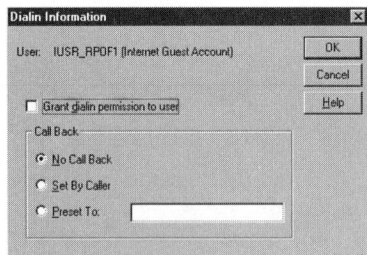

User Manager also allows the administrator to assign and change some other basic user permissions by using the Policies menu.

Follow these steps to assign additional permissions by using the Policies menu:

1. Choose Policies, Account. The Account Policy dialog box opens (see Figure 18.39). By default, the account cannot be locked out, and a blank password is permitted. Change settings as necessary, and then choose OK.

FIG. 18.39

The defaults for passwords for the anonymous logon. The user is configured for maximum flexibility and no user can lock out the anonymous user.

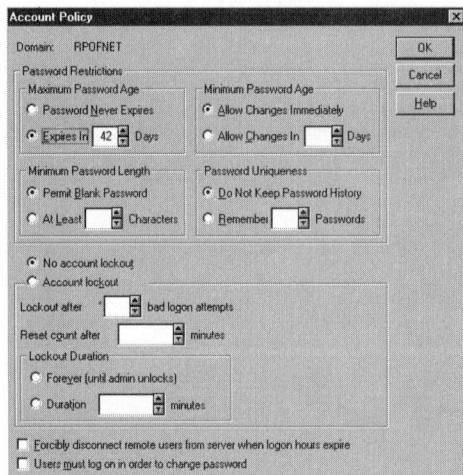

2. Choose Policies, User Rights to see the User Rights Policy dialog box, seen in Figure 18.40. You can Add or Remove rights from this dialog box.

3. Pull down the Right menu to view the different rights options.

The Audit Policy dialog box enables you to configure different audit options for each user. By default, the boxes are unchecked because Audit is turned off.

FIG. 18.40

The User Rights Policy dialog box is selected through the use of pull-down menus.

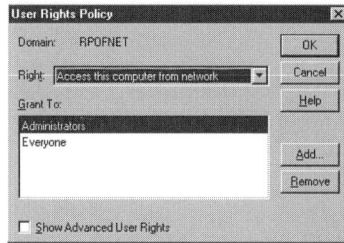

N O T E Make sure Audit is turned on in Server Administration before trying to assign Audit Policies to any users. It won't work. ▪

In Figure 18.41, an administrator is preparing to add events to a user profile.

FIG. 18.41

Audit policies are selected by clicking the appropriate individual check boxes.

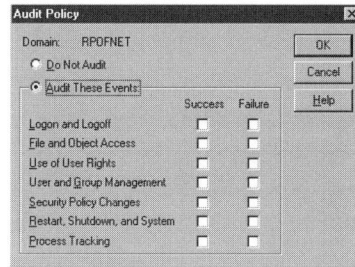

Monitoring Events with the Event Viewer

Event Viewer, another NT Server Administrative Tool, is very helpful for determining what events were successful, what activities were not, and who is trying to access what resources when.

In Figure 18.42, you can see the different kinds of events that are reported. There are browser logins, AppleTalk logins, Print requests, and other activities.

In Figure 18.43, an AppleTalk event that was shaded with a warning light has been opened with a double-click. The description of the incident is in the Event Detail dialog box. An administrator can now look for similar instances of the problem and correct it.

Double-clicking an Information Box reveals the circumstances behind the event; in this case, the stoppage of the MCIS News Server. Restarting the server is recorded under a separate event.

Part
VII

Ch
18

FIG. 18.42

The Event Viewer gives you a concise look at all activities of NT Server, including Internet and intranet activities.

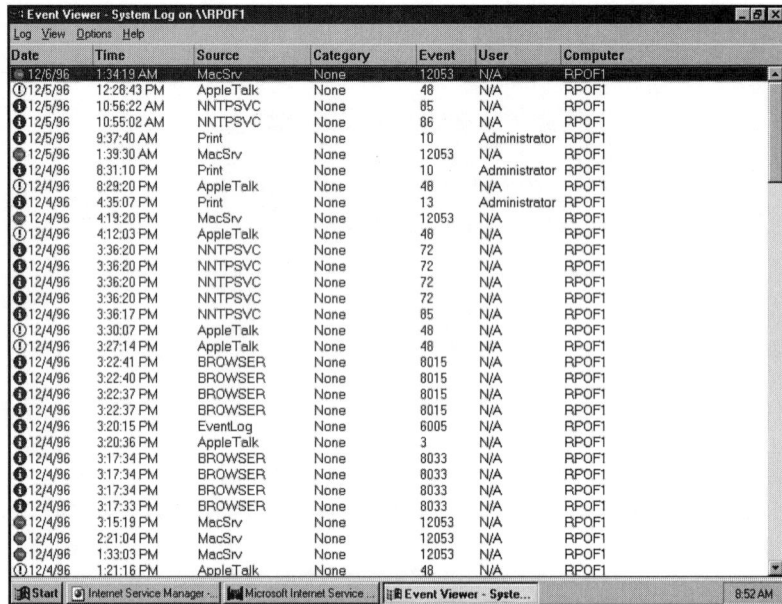

FIG. 18.43

Double-clicking an Event brings up the Event Detail dialog box. The information box displays a message explaining the reason for the warning.

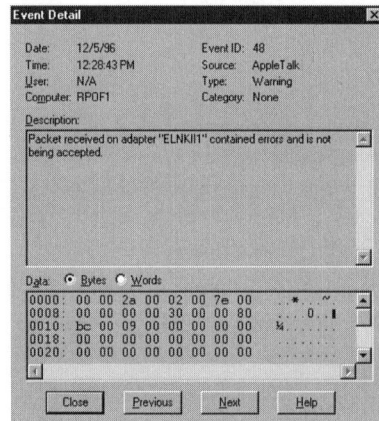

In Figure 18.44, an entry in the log has been selected, regarding the status of the NNTP Service.

FIG. 18.44

The information box displays that the News Server has been stopped.

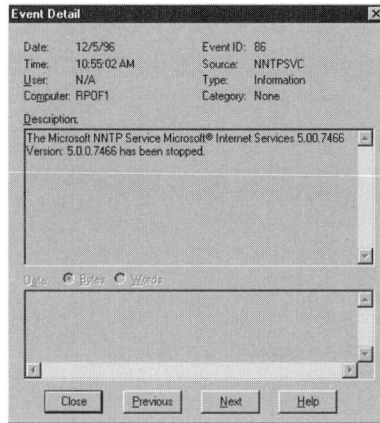

Checking System Performance with Performance Monitor

Performance Monitor is yet another NT Server Administrative Tool with great value for the IIS administrator. Performance Monitor tracks all processor, cache, and interrupt utilization issues and reports them as graphs in real-time.

The administrator can configure Performance Monitor to check different hardware and operating system functions; Figure 18.45 shows Performance Monitor is recording DPC time, Interrupt time, Processor time, Privilege time, and User time.

Part
VII

Ch
18

FIG. 18.45

Performance Monitor displays results as real-time information in a full-color graph.

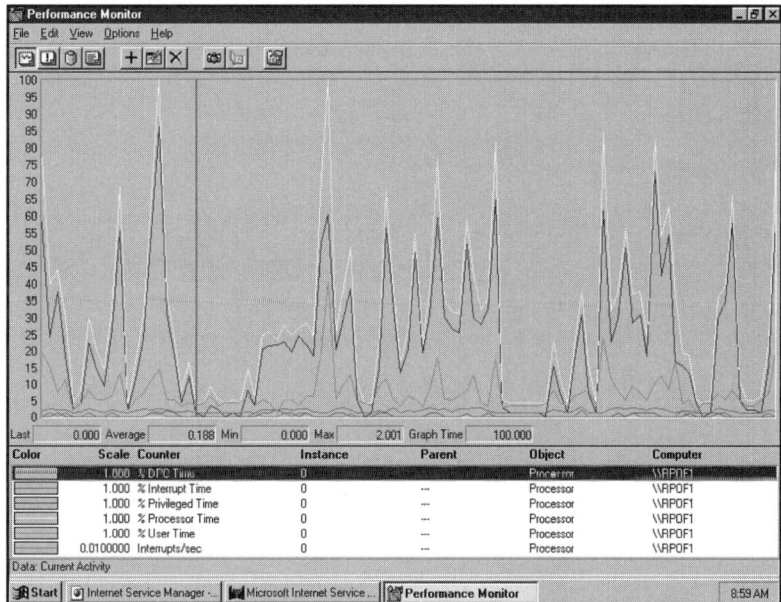

Configuring Directories Using NT's Access Control List

One of the built-in management tools under Windows NT, the Access Control List (ACL) is a solid performer. By using ACL you can assign permissions to the actual directories themselves.

In Windows NT Explorer, right-click the directory whose properties you want to configure. Choose Properties to see the Properties dialog box, shown in Figure 18.46. Of the three tabs in the Properties dialog box, General and Sharing are not significant to this chapter; we are concerned with Security.

Click the Permissions button.

FIG. 18.46

Click the Permissions button to pull up information on the selected directory.

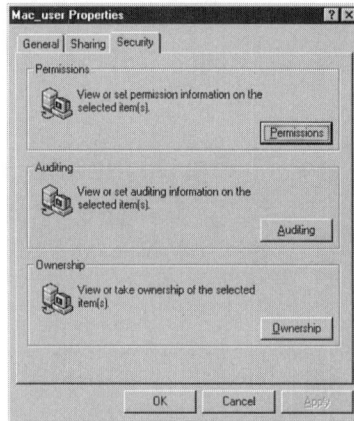

The Directory Permissions box (see Figure 18.47) displays what groups get to do what activities within the directory. Choose Add to enable additional user categories to the directory list.

FIG. 18.47

The Directory Permissions box. Choosing Add will bring up the other users allowed on the server for inclusion to the Permissions list.

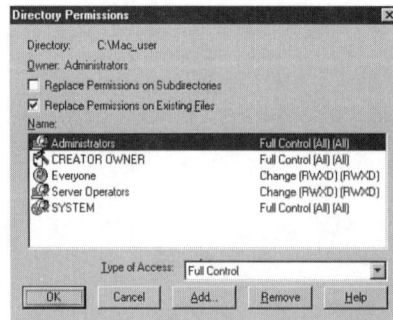

Figure 18.48 shows three groups ready to add to the Add Name list: Domain Users, Domain Administrators, and Domain Guests. Note the type of access NT has designated to these users (located at the bottom of the window): Read only.

FIG. 18.48

You can display a drop-down menu to change Type of Access.

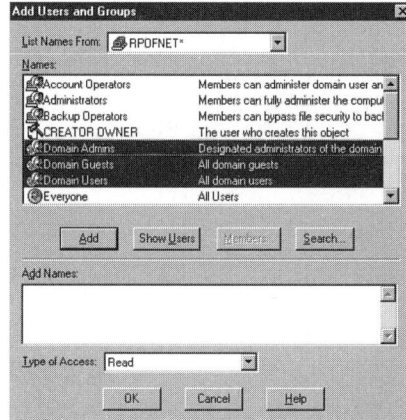

When the desired groups are selected, select the Add button so that the names appear in the Add Name list box, and then choose OK. The groups are added to the list in Directory Permissions (see Figure 18.49).

FIG. 18.49

The added user groups, with permissions next to their names.

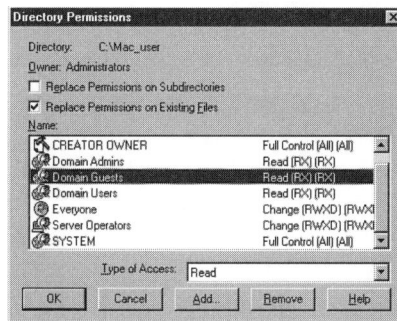

Auditing

Choosing the Auditing option allows administrators to monitor who is accessing what directory and when accesses occur. No audit events are automatically selected. When directories have been set for auditing, events can be activated by choosing to audit Success or Failure (see Figure 18.50), and then choosing Add.

FIG. 18.50

The Directory Auditing dialog box with two user groups—Domain Guests and Domain Users—now engaged. The audit list has been modified to ask for failed access attempts only. This will help determine any problems with file access, as well as trying to find any unauthorized attempts to penetrate the server.

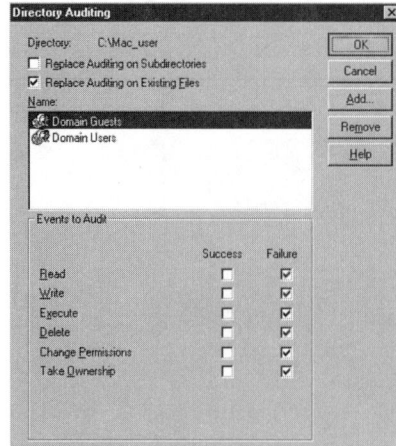

Server Administration Via the Web

Microsoft has recently issued a tool that allows system administrators to administer Windows NT Server 4.0 from any remote location using a Web browser. The application, Web Administration for Microsoft Windows NT Server, is available for download from Microsoft's World Wide Web site.

ON THE WEB

www.microsoft.com/windows/common/aa246.htm   Visit this site to download Web Administration from Microsoft.

TIP   The tool is also available on the companion CD-ROM to the Microsoft Windows NT Server Resource Kit, available in bookstores and computer retailers.

Any Web browser that supports Basic Authentication is capable of running Web Administration. Microsoft heavily recommends its Internet Explorer 3.x Web browser software, as Web Administration also supports Windows NT's Challenge/Response system. Also, you need to run Internet Information Server 2.0 or higher with Web services enabled.

Versions of Web Administration are available for the major platforms that Windows NT Server ships on: Intel, Digital Alpha, Power PC (PPC), and UNIX.

Installing Web Administration

Web Administration for Microsoft Windows NT Server installs on the server itself. A simple setup program installs and configures the software for use.

Server Administration Using a Web Browser

The administrative tasks you can perform using Web Administration include:

- Creating and deleting user accounts
- Rebooting the server
- Listing print queues and jobs within each queue
- Changing user passwords
- Sending messages to all users logged into the server
- View shares for all services
- Creating and configuring user groups and domains

Figure 18.51 shows the main page of the utility.

FIG. 18.51
The main page of the Web Administration utility as seen through Microsoft Internet Explorer 3.1 for Windows NT. Web Administration features most of the administration tools as found in the User Manager for Domains.

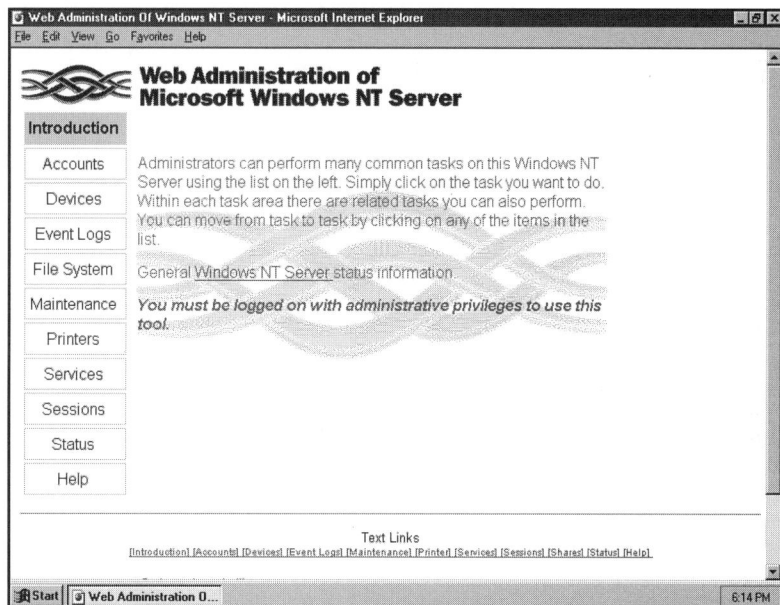

From Here...

You now have the basic concepts of server administration. In the next chapter, you take those concepts and expand on them, especially learning how to read and understand logfiles. You will also learn other valuable tips on how to monitor server performance.

For further study, be sure to read these related sections:

- Chapter 3, "Building the Foundation," gives you the concepts with which you'll build a better understanding behind the interrelationship of these programs.
- Appendix A, "Hardware Requirements," will give you more information and technical specifications on setting up and optimizing IIS.

Interpreting Logfiles and Monitoring Server Performance

How to benefit from the system logfiles

Learn how to take a look under the hood of your Web server to get a grasp on what the users are really interested in at your site.

How to use an SQL server to interpret logfiles

Gain an understanding of how to use your database program to dissect the usage information gathered by the IIS server.

How to use other tools for logfile analysis

Get an overview on other logfile analysis products provided by other companies.

A lot of time and effort goes into developing a company Internet/intranet strategy. Businesses are spending time and money to reach their public and enhance their means of communication. The Microsoft Commercial Internet System offers you a News Server, Chat Server, an Indexing system, a Merchant Server, Membership controls, and a Mail Server as solutions.

You can deliver all sorts of features. And when you develop a strategy that incorporates all of these applications, you have a winning site, right?

Wrong! You can develop application upon application and unveil the latest whizbang tricks. But that's not the answer.

Developing a winner is about connecting with people. After all, these are the people who you're paid to reach. To make contact, you need to know what they want. Interestingly, if your Web site has been operational and accessible to the public for any length of time, the information you're searching for is already located on your server's hard drive, buried in cryptic documents called the logfile.

The logfiles generated by the Internet Information Server capture specific information about the users who are accessing your site. For instance, in the logfiles you'll find the IP address of the incoming request, what the request was for, and whether the information requested was received successfully. With that information alone, you'll be able to determine who the users are, what they are most interested in, and whether you delivered their request to them without error. That sort of information will let you know whether you're making any headway with your clients.

This chapter is designed to provide you with information on how to monitor your success through analysis of the logfiles. There will be an explanation on what's contained in the system logfiles, how to interpret the data into readable charts, and different techniques for monitoring performance. ■

Understanding System Logfiles

Inside the logfiles is the information that will help you determine your success. If you're communicating with the masses, you need a tool to determine your effectiveness. My friend Andrew says that logfiles are to the Internet what Nielsen ratings are to television. He's right; this is where the demographic information on the makeup of your audience is located.

There are a few basic pieces of information you'll want to know to understand the effectiveness of your present interactions on the Web:

- Who are your users?
- What are they interested in?
- When are they visiting the site?
- Where are they coming from?
- Why are they visiting the site?

If you know the answers to these questions, you can make real progress in the communications game.

The quickest way to separate novices from seasoned professionals in the Web analysis world is knowing the difference between a hit and a user session. In other words, be wary of the server administrator who says his site had 2.5 million hits last month, as if it were over 2 million users. In reality, he's lucky if that equates to over 200,000 user sessions. Granted, 200,000 user sessions is nothing to sneeze at, but it's a far cry from 2.5 million visitors. Here's the reality—a *hit* is a single request for a page or a file; a user session includes all the hits and requests that a unique user generated. A user session is considered terminated when there is no activity for an extended period of time. In one user session, the user can generate hundreds of hits, but it still only counts as one user session.

What Information Does the Logfile Capture?

The Microsoft Internet Information Server captures the following data in the logfiles:

- Client's IP address
- Client's username (if a login was required)
- Date

- Time
- Service (any services listed in the IIS, such as the Index Server, News, WWW, FTP, and so on)
- Computer Name (this is the server name the client is accessing)
- IP address of the server
- Processing time
- Bytes received
- Bytes sent
- Service status code
- Windows NT status code
- Name of the operation
- Target of the operation

Of course, when that information is placed in a logfile, as seen in Figure 19.1, it's hard to tell what's what.

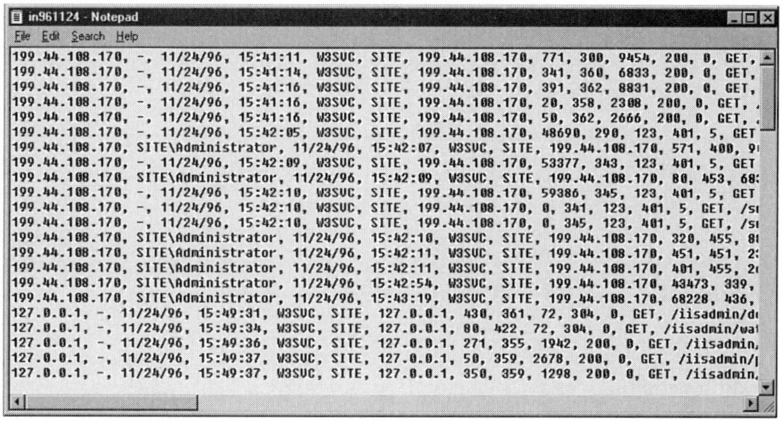

FIG. 19.1

As you can see, there's a lot of cryptic information to sift through in the logfile.

Below is an example of what a single record in an Windows NT logfile would look like:

```
199.44.108.170, -, 11/24/96, 5:00:16, W3SVC, SITE, 199.44.108.170, 391,
362, 8831, 200, 0, GET, /images/icon.gif, -,
```

Let's diagnose the transaction. The first entry in the table says that an anonymous client with the IP address of 199.44.108.170 downloaded (issued a GET command for) the file icon.gif a little after 5 AM on November 24, 1996, from a server named SITE with the IP address 199.44.108.170. Th,e 362-byte Web server request was processed in 391 milliseconds, was error free, and returned 8,831 bytes of data to the anonymous client.

Part
VII

Ch
19

N O T E   All fields are terminated with a comma (,). The hyphen acts as a placeholder if there is no valid value for a certain field. ▩

Now imagine a 500M logfile gathered during a month, with thousands of lines of transactions. Certainly, you wouldn't conduct a manual, line-by-line analysis. Instead, you can design a custom database, or purchase a third-party program that will do the work for you. Figure 19.2 gives an example of a report generated by a log analysis program called Webtrends.

FIG. 19.2

Logfiles start making sense when you can lift out the data that's most important to you and your organization.

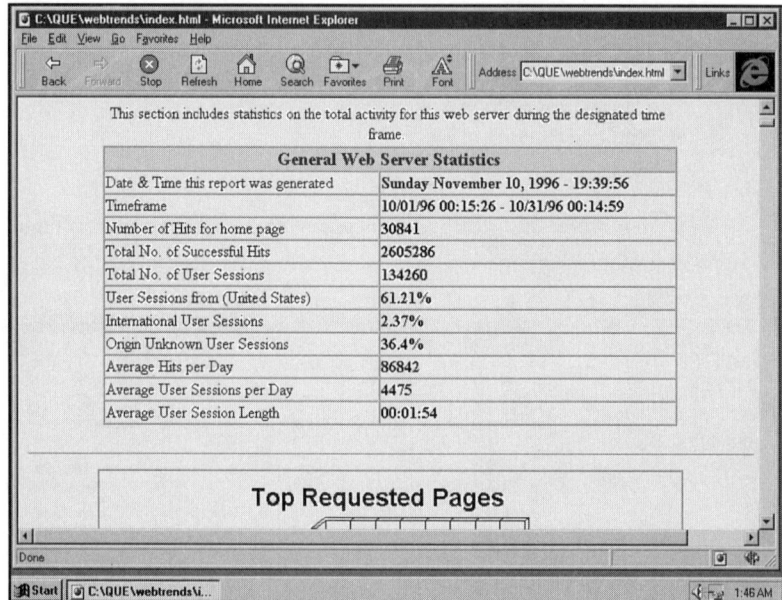

The General Web Server Statistics table shown in the figure:

General Web Server Statistics	
Date & Time this report was generated	Sunday November 10, 1996 - 19:39:56
Timeframe	10/01/96 00:15:26 - 10/31/96 00:14:59
Number of Hits for home page	30841
Total No. of Successful Hits	2605286
Total No. of User Sessions	134260
User Sessions from (United States)	61.21%
International User Sessions	2.37%
Origin Unknown User Sessions	36.4%
Average Hits per Day	86842
Average User Sessions per Day	4475
Average User Session Length	00:01:54

Later in this chapter, we explore log interpretations through a Microsoft SQL Server 6.5 database in the section "Using SQL Server to Interpret Logfiles," and offer leads to some excellent log analysis programs that are available in "Third Party Reporting Tools."

The bottom line is, it's not too difficult to make sense out of these logs. And, when you start to analyze that data, you can begin to get a handle on who is visiting your site, and what they want. For instance, with the right tools, you can determine:

- The continent, country, region, state, city, and ZIP code of users. Through reverse domain name lookup, the IP address can be translated into a domain name. When the domain name is compared with a database containing domain registration information, the specifics on the domain are returned.
- The top resources being accessed by your users.
- The least accessed resources.
- The peak hours, as seen in the WebTrends report in Figure 19.3.
- If errors are occurring.

FIG. 19.3
Your logs can help you
determine when your
server is under the
most strain.

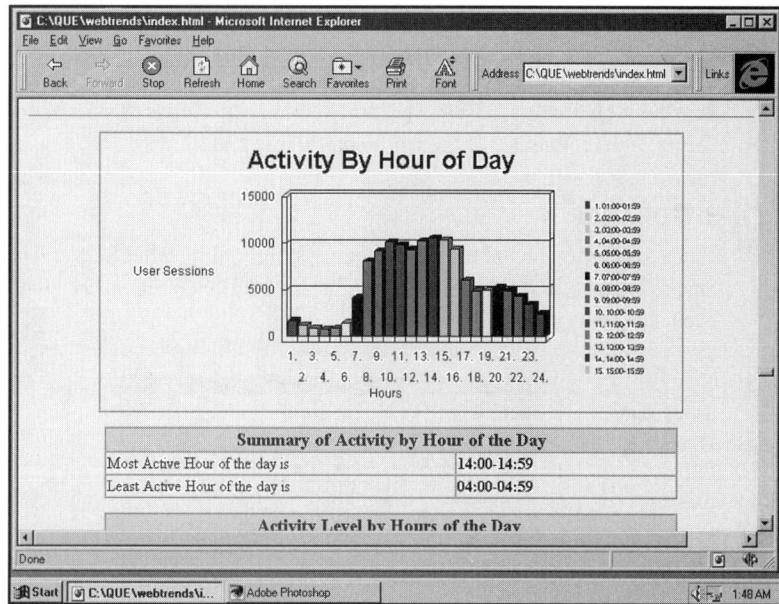

This information will provide a good foundation for making informed decisions on future development and should help in gauging the future direction of your company's Internet strategy.

For instance, let's say there is a lot of effort going into the development of the company's news server. According to your analysis, it's rating poorly on the activity meter. The numbers can be the result of several factors. Perhaps it's the obvious—your news feed doesn't contain the information your users need. However, what if users aren't accessing the news server because it hasn't been marketed properly? It may be time to add a link on your home page to the news feed. Then again, maybe there has been a problem with user errors when attempting to access the news server. If that's the problem, with a little maintenance, your users will be able to access an error-free news server.

You can learn a lot from the system logfiles.

However, the information you find in logfiles is not always bulletproof. Remember, the digital revolution is still young, and the rules are being written as technologies are designed. Tools for Internet activity analysis have been a virtual afterthought. With the Microsoft Commercial Internet Servers, there hasn't been a huge amount of progress in the analysis features. However, the logfile that can be generated by the Windows NT Internet Information Server is every bit as good as any logfile, and the logfile is the closest thing we have to a true record for analysis. View it with a grain of salt, though, because what you interpret from logfiles will hardly ever be the complete truth.

Doug Linder, Synetics Webmaster at the National Archives and Records Administration, said it best in his article "Interpreting WWW Statistics." "As you look at the statistics, I cannot stress strongly enough that they should only be used as very general trends and not as gospel truth.

These numbers could easily be off (on the low side) by significant percentages. They are not, by any means, "Hard numbers," he continues, "is that a fault with the software? The hardware? The operation of the system? No. The inaccuracy of the numbers is simply a byproduct of the way the Web functions. Even the most technically advanced sites have only a general idea of the amount and nature of the traffic on their servers."

Logfile Options

When you set up any of the Microsoft Commercial Internet Servers, you have the option to enable logging, and generate a file for analysis. The configuration options are the same with each server, as seen in Figure 19.4.

FIG. 19.4

Logging options include logging to a text file or to an SQL/ODBC database.

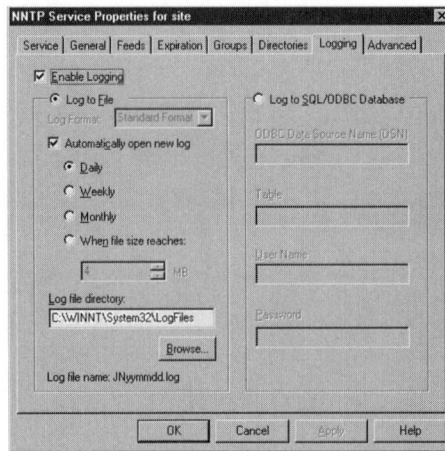

This section describes setting up the Log to File option. You can also log to SQL/ODBC which is covered later in the chapter in "Using SQL Server to Interpret Logfiles." Follow these steps to enabling logging of any installed servers:

1. Click the Start button, choose Programs, Microsoft Internet Server, and then choose the Internet Service Manager.

2. Select the service of your choice from the list of services and access the configuration files by choosing Properties, Service Properties.

3. From the Service Properties page, select the Logging tab.

4. Select the Enable Logging option by clicking the checkbox.

5. Select the Log Format type:
   - *Standard format*   The Windows NT log format
   - *National Center for Supercomputing Applications (NCSA) Format*   Traditional UNIX style logfile
6. Select the Automatically Open New Log option by clicking the checkbox.
7. Choose the appropriate logging option, either:
   - <u>D</u>aily
   - <u>W</u>eekly
   - <u>M</u>onthly
   - W<u>h</u>en file size reaches a particular size

TIP   For most administrators, it's a good idea to generate a daily log, because the logfiles are inaccessible for review when the logfile is being generated. If there is a problem or a need for quick analysis, you don't want to have to shut your server down to peruse the logfile. If you run a daily log, you have access to information that's no more than 24 hours old. If a daily log seems like overkill, you may want to at least create a weekly log.

---

8. Identify the Logfile directory.
9. Click the <u>A</u>pply button and the logfiles will begin generating.

Logfile Types

The standard Microsoft Internet Information Server Logfile format contains good information, but there are a few more key elements that can be gathered to enhance the logfile output. Some third-party vendors have created plug-ins to generate a Microsoft IIS extended logfile format. Along with the usual logfile output, the extended logfile format includes the user agent log and the referrer log.

Here's what those features offer:

- *Referrer log*   The Referrer log captures the Web page the user came from before accessing a Web page on your site. This log will help you to determine the sites that are funneling users to your site, as displayed in the WebTrends table in Figure 19.5.
- *Agent log*   Agent logs record the browser or client software used to access your Web pages. Information such as the table shown in Figure 19.6 can help you determine whether your user base can handle the latest Web browser features. Different Web browsers offer different features. You want to offer features that your public can access.

Part
VII

Ch
19

FIG. 19.5

It's nice to know which sites are pointing users in your direction.

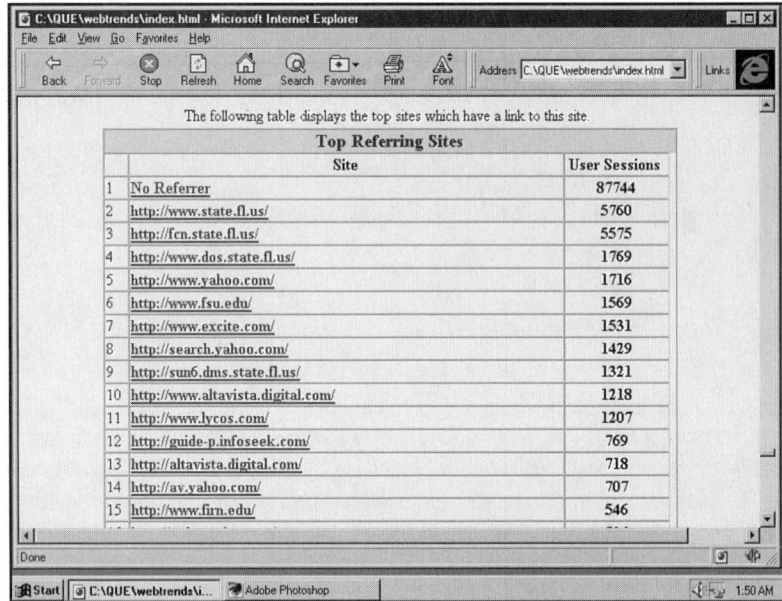

The following table displays the top sites which have a link to this site.

	Top Referring Sites	
	Site	User Sessions
1	No Referrer	87744
2	http://www.state.fl.us/	5760
3	http://fcn.state.fl.us/	5575
4	http://www.dos.state.fl.us/	1769
5	http://www.yahoo.com/	1716
6	http://www.fsu.edu/	1569
7	http://www.excite.com/	1531
8	http://search.yahoo.com/	1429
9	http://sun6.dms.state.fl.us/	1321
10	http://www.altavista.digital.com/	1218
11	http://www.lycos.com/	1207
12	http://guide-p.infoseek.com/	769
13	http://altavista.digital.com/	718
14	http://av.yahoo.com/	707
15	http://www.firn.edu/	546

FIG. 19.6

The Agent Log provides excellent information on which browsers your users have installed.

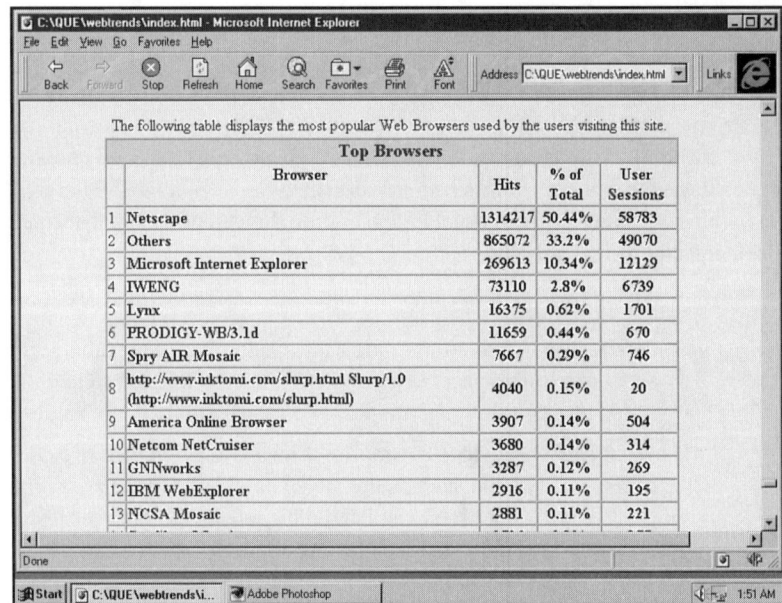

The following table displays the most popular Web Browsers used by the users visiting this site.

	Top Browsers			
	Browser	Hits	% of Total	User Sessions
1	Netscape	1314217	50.44%	58783
2	Others	865072	33.2%	49070
3	Microsoft Internet Explorer	269613	10.34%	12129
4	IWENG	73110	2.8%	6739
5	Lynx	16375	0.62%	1701
6	PRODIGY-WB/3.1d	11659	0.44%	670
7	Spry AIR Mosaic	7667	0.29%	746
8	http://www.inktomi.com/slurp.html Slurp/1.0 (http://www.inktomi.com/slurp.html)	4040	0.15%	20
9	America Online Browser	3907	0.14%	504
10	Netcom NetCruiser	3680	0.14%	314
11	GNNworks	3287	0.12%	269
12	IBM WebExplorer	2916	0.11%	195
13	NCSA Mosaic	2881	0.11%	221

Converting Logfile Formats

If you have created Microsoft Internet Information Server logfiles and have a third-party analysis program available before you analyze the logfile, you may be required to convert the files from Windows NT 4.0 IIS logs into Common Log Format. Typically, the most common universal log formats are the NCSA Common Log Format, developed by the National Center for Supercomputing Applications (NCSA) Common Logfile format and the EMWAC log format, developed by the European Microsoft Windows NT Academic Centre (EMWAC). If you need to make such a conversion, the Microsoft Internet Information Server provides the Microsoft Internet Log Converter (Convlog.exe).

The program's sole objective is to convert files in the IIS log format to the NCSA or EMWAC format. Unfortunately, this feature is not available in a graphic user interface. All conversions take place at the command prompt.

Follow these steps to conduct a conversion:

1. Click the Start button, select Programs, and then choose Command Prompt.
2. At the command prompt, type **convlog** without parameters to see syntax and examples.
3. To convert logs to other formats, begin by adding convlog.exe (in the \Inetsrv folder, by default) to your path.
4. In a command-prompt window, type the convlog command. See the following syntax and examples. Add the appropriate syntax and parameters for the conversion.

Syntax   With the following options, administrators can dictate the output directory, temporary file directory, and the cache size.

```
convlog -s[f¦g¦w] -t [emwac ¦ ncsa[:GMTOffset] ¦ none]
-o [output directory] -f [temp file directory] -h LogFilename
-d<m:[cachesize]>
```

Parameters   Here are all of the switches that can be used at the command line to conduct the file conversion:

```
-s[f¦g¦w]
```

The following switches specify the service which converts log entries:

```
f = Process FTP log entries
g = Process gopher log entries
w = Process WWW log entries
```

The default for the -s switch is to convert logs for all services.

```
-t [emwac ¦ ncsa[:GMTOffset] ¦ none]
```

specifies the destination conversion format. The default is to create output files in EMWAC format.

Part

VII

Ch

19

`-o [output directory]`

specifies the directory for the converted files. The default is the current directory.

`-f [temp file directory]`

specifies a temporary directory to hold temporary files created by convlog. The default is C:\Temp or the directory specified by the "tmp" environment variable.

`-n[m:[cachesize]¦i]`

specifies whether to convert IP addresses to computer or domain names. The default is to not convert IP addresses.

`m[cachesize]`

specifies to convert IP addresses to computer names. The default cache size is 5000 bytes.

`i`

specifies to not convert IP addresses to computer names.

`h`

displays Help.

`LogFilename`

specifies the name of the log to be converted. Convlog will display the file name for the converted file.

`-dm:[cachesize]`

converts IP addresses in NCSA log format to computer names or domain names. The default is to not convert IP addresses. The default cache size is 5000 bytes.

An example of the use of convlog with some of the parameters just described is:

```
convlog -sf -t ncsa -o c:\logs in*.log
```

which converts an ftp log into an NCSA log, with the converted file saved to the c:\logs directory)

Using SQL Server to Interpret Logfiles

Whenever you access the log properties for Internet Information Services, the default selection is always to log to a file. However, if you prefer to collect your logs in a database, you need to install Open Database Connectivity (ODBC) version 2.5 and the Microsoft SQL Server version 6.5 database. This section will provide an overview of the steps to creating the database. If you are unfamiliar with Microsoft SQL Server 6.5, it is recommended that you refer to Que's *Special Edition Using SQL Server 6.5.*

CAUTION

Take notice: Logging to an Open Data Base Connectivity (ODBC)/SQL server may be a poor decision, because the process is slower than logging to a file. According to Microsoft, the process for generating an ODBC log will occupy processing power and decrease the performance of your server. The bottom line is that it requires more time, memory, and disk resources to perform the task. Suffice it to say that you'll probably want to avoid using the SQL server and simply log the file.

Creating the Database

If we haven't talked you out of it yet, please feel free to continue on. For this feature, the database requires you to follow the standard Windows NT database design model, which is the Microsoft SQL Server 6.5 client/server database environment. If you're experienced with SQL Server, this outline should help. However, if you have never worked with SQL Server before, skip this section until you get a handle on Microsoft SQL Server 6.5. Please refer to Que Publishing's *Special Edition Using Microsoft SQL Server 6.5* for specific help.

1. Create a table that conforms to the sizes of the fields for your Microsoft SQL Server database program.

   The logtemp.sql file, located in the c:\winnt\system32\inetsrv\ directory, includes the following text that outlines the sizes of the fields for a table:

   create table inetlog (ClientHost varchar(255), username varchar(255), LogTime datetime, service varchar(255), machine varchar(255), serverip varchar(50), processingtime int, bytesrecvd int, bytessent int, servicestatus int, win32status int, operation varchar(255), target varchar(255), parameters varchar(255))

2. Using this information, set up a database on your server and create a system Data Source Name.

N O T E You can decrease your time investment on this database by simply running the logtemp.sql file from within SQL Server 6.5 by using the query tool. ▨

Part

VII

Ch

19

To Log to a Database

Follow these steps to have the Internet Information Server log its activity to the database you just created:

1. Click the Start button, select Programs, then Microsoft Internet Server, and then the Internet Service Manager.

2. Double-click the service you want to log to a database.

3. Click the Logging tab.

4. Select the Enable Logging check box.

5. Select Log to SQL/ODBC database, as seen in Figure 19.7.

FIG. 19.7

Setting up the server to log to a SQL database.

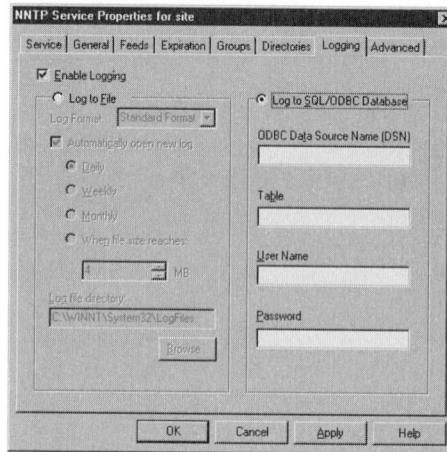

6. In the ODBC Data Source Name (DSN) box, type the system DSN that you added in Step 2 of the previous procedure.

7. In the Table field, type the name of the table (not the file name of the table).

8. In the User Name and Password fields, type a user name and password that is valid for the computer on which the database resides.

9. Click Apply and then click OK.

Your SQL database should now be receiving the logfile information.

Using Third-Party Reporting Tools

There are a number of tools out there that do a superb job of analyzing logfiles. All aim to offer detailed statistics, a look at developing trends, and impressive graphics to help make sense of the numbers. This section looks at two different third-party options: WebTrends and Interse's Market Focus. With tools like these, it really doesn't make much sense to design your own database to display statistics. These packages are easy to work with and deliver excellent reports.

Web Trends

WebTrends is a 32-bit application that provides well-organized statistical information with lots of colorful graphs that show trends, usage, and market share. Reports can be generated as HTML files for viewing with any Web browser or as Microsoft Word documents. This program, which can be downloaded from the company's Web page as seen in Figure 19.8, is designed to post-process the logfiles.

ON THE WEB

http://www.webtrends.com   Check out this site for the newest release of WebTrends.

FIG. 19.8

Download the latest version of the software and access the most up-to-date information about the product.

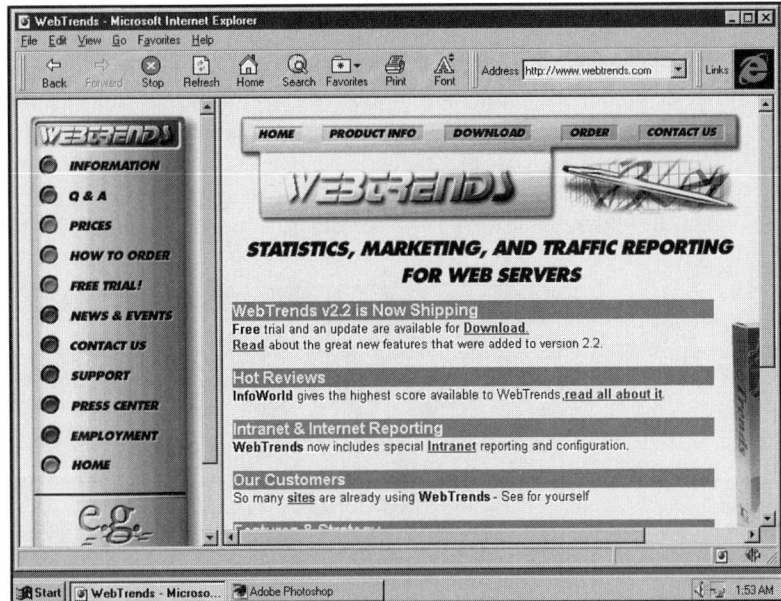

When you're ready to run a report, you launch WebTrends, point the program to the logfile you want to analyze, and the process begins.

The latest version, WebTrends 2.2, includes a custom Microsoft IIS ISAPI plug-in for logging the previously mentioned Extended logfiles.

Along with generating standard log information, WebTrends also provides:

- Reverse DNS Lookup
- Agent/Browser information
- Referring Site/URL information
- Cookies for accurate User Session Logging
- Compatible with IIS 2.0 and 3.0

TIP WebTrends has been my analysis software of choice since November, 1995. It's easy to work with and fairly intuitive. The only downside is that it does not create a database to plug in your most recent statistics. A database would provide an excellent way to analyze statistics over a long period of time. WebTrends' suggested fix for getting those results is to manually paste the logfiles of several months' statistics together, then run the program over the reconstructed log to generate a report of several months of statistics. When I started analyzing the logs for my organization in late 1995, the monthly reports were only 40M in size. Now the files are over 600M per month. Pasting these files together is simply not an option. Other than that, this software is fabulous.

For your convenience, a trial version of WebTrends is available on the Que Web site at **http://www.quecorp.com.mcis**.

Other Databases

The recommended third-party database of choice is Intersé Market Focus. By the way, according to the company's Web page, the product is pronounced In-ter-say. Intersé Corporation was acquired by Microsoft Corporation on March 3, 1997. The product will be integrated into the BackOffice product group. This program builds a database that allows you to reconstruct the actual visits, users, and organizations that interact with your Internet site. The information is delivered in a very logical fashion, as seen in Figure 19.9.

FIG. 19.9

Intersé offers easy-to-read tables.

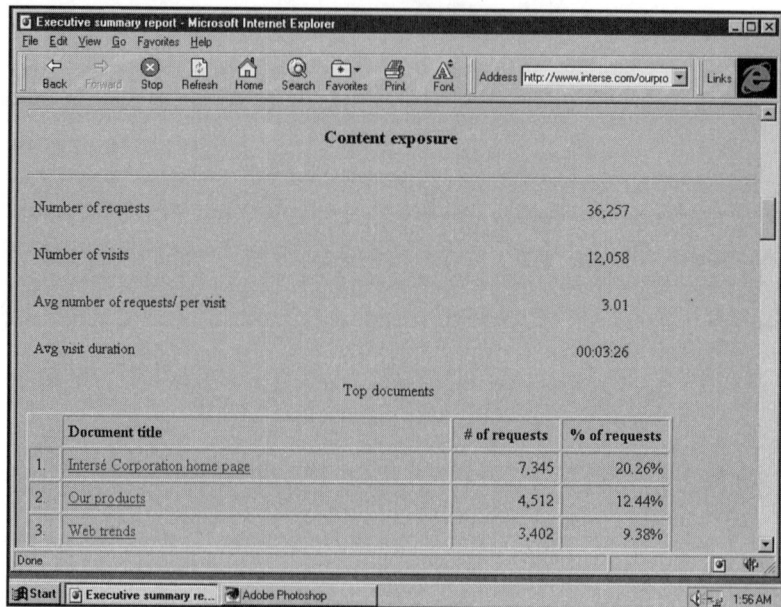

Like WebTrends, Intersé creates 3-D graphics and tables for a professional quality, custom report. Also, the developer's version of this product supports SQL Server databases, providing you with client/server capabilities. Intersé, like WebTrends, also processes the logfiles. However, every logfile that is analyzed is stored in a database, which allows you to compare the old logs with the new in a database environment.

Intersé also has a plug-in to generate an extended logfile and allows users to both create Microsoft Word and Microsoft Excel reports.

Along with Intersé, there are many other great log analysis tools on the market. Many users choose to stick with Crystal Reports, from Seagate Software, which is currently distributed with IIS 3.0. This excellent tool is also very easy to implement with MCIS.

Monitoring Performance

Although logfiles are an excellent source for server usage history, they don't provide you with live data for measuring your server's performance. The best tool for analyzing the live performance is the Performance Monitor. Certainly, the logfiles can give you an idea of how your server is performing, but administrators need to proactively monitor server performance to identify potential problems. The Performance Monitor is the avenue for a live account of server activity.

The Windows NT Performance Monitor

The Windows NT Performance Monitor offers a wide array of tools for measuirng the services offered by the Internet Information Server. This means that for every component offered with the Microsoft Commercial Internet Server package, there are specialized tools for monitoring the effectiveness of your server and building a profile of your site.

To obtain real benefits, incorporate regular analysis of the Performance Monitor into your network management responsibilities. The Performance Monitor offers the following functionality:

- *Charting*   A real-time graph of the item you selected, displayed through a live monitor. You can view the data as a line graph or a bar chart.

- *Alerts*   Alerts allow you to monitor a variety of logs without actually having to be on standby watching the output. You simply set some threshhold levels for the items you are interested in monitoring, and configure the server to either write an entry in the Event Log, or send a network message with the specifics of the alert.

- *Logfiles*   Based on the performance statistics you are charting, the Performance Monitor will place the information in a logfile that can be exported and viewed in programs like Microsoft Excel or Microsoft Access.

This is the tool that will help you determine how your server is holding up. With features that are automated to alert you when there are problems, this is something you can't live without. Of course, the features don't come without a price. The Performance Monitor uses additional system memory, so use it with care.

Gathering Real Time Statistics

The Windows NT Performance Monitor will enable you to take a look at the performance status of any of the Internet Information Services. Whether you need specifics on the Chat Server, Web Server, the Mail Server, or the News Server, the Performance Monitor will allow

Part

VII

Ch

19

you to review the status and health of your server. You have the ability to view over 80 different performance counters, designed to give you the most informed information about your server's health.

▶ **See** "Personalization Server," **p. 604**

To access the Performance Monitor and evaluate the status of any of your services, follow these steps:

1. Click the Start button, choose Programs, Administrative Tools, and then choose the Performance Monitor. The Performance Monitor is launched.

2. Choose View, Chart.

3. Add to the chart by choosing Edit, Add to Chart. You can also activate this feature by clicking the + button on the toolbar.

4. The Performance Monitor launches the Add to Chart dialog box. Some of the main features needed in the Performance Monitor are:

    - *Computer*   Select the computer you want to monitor. Your server appears as the default. If you want to monitor a server that resides in another location on the network, click the ellipses button (. . .) and a Select Computer dialog box is launched.

    - *Object*   Used to select an object to monitor from those residing on the computer you selected.

    - *Counters*   Used to select the counter you want to monitor.

5. Leave the Computer as the default.

6. Change the Object feature to the server of your choice.

7. Select the counter of interest. To review what the counters are designed to do, highlight the option and click the Explain button.

8. Now click the Add button and the counters will be launched.

9. Click the Done button. The Performance Monitor begins charting the graph.

You can also exploit the Performance Monitors alert mode feature to automatically notify you when levels do not reach your expectations.

Here's how you set up the alert feature for Performance Monitor:

1. Click the Start button, select Programs, Administrative Tools, and then choose the Performance Monitor.

    The Performance Monitor is launched.

2. Select the View the Alerts button on the button bar, or choose View, Alert.

3. Click the Add Counter button (+), or choose Edit, Add to Alert.

4. Select the Object as one of the installed Microsoft Commercial Internet Servers, and pick one of the Counters to view.

5. In the Alert if field, select Under and enter the threshold so that when the server crosses that threshold, you'll be notified.

6. Click the <u>A</u>dd button.

7. Choose <u>O</u>ptions, <u>A</u>lert to launch the Alert Options dialog box.

8. If an alert is necessary, performance Monitor can be configured to Switch to an Alert View, or <u>S</u>end network a message to the administrator. For now, select Switch to an Alert <u>V</u>iew.

The Performance Monitor will track anything that crosses the alert threshold and will log the activity on the Performance Monitor page. Monitor the server resources and adjust them as needed.

From Here. . .

At the conclusion of this chapter, you should have a general understanding of how logfiles are generated, with an idea of how to analyze these logs for the purpose of reviewing the effectiveness of your Web site.

■ For further information on the Internet Information Server, please refer to Que's *Special Edition Using Internet Information Server 2*.

■ For further information on SQL Server 6.5, please refer to Que's *Special Edition Using SQL Server 6.5*.

Developing an Intranet with MCIS Servers

Over the last three years Internet hype has grown to the point of hysteria. Startup companies make millions on IPOs and every blue-chip company in America is looking for a way to leverage the "new market." Yet, the computer industry pundits are saying that the Internet is not the killer app. If a technology that has created billions of dollars in stock offerings and more than a 50 percent growth rate is not "the gold mine" then what is?

The intranet. It is estimated that there are more than four times as many "invisible hosts" on the Internet as there are public hosts. Millions of companies around the world have internal LANs. Most of these have no intention of connecting them to the Internet and the ones that do fear for the security of their data. Yet the majority of these organizations are coming to see the tremendous benefits inherent in the Internet model. The ability to share information in a near-seamless environment is a long-sought goal. The Microsoft Commercial Internet System helps make that goal a reality.

This chapter looks at intranets and how they differ from the Internet. It also explores how the various components of the Commercial Internet System can be used in an intranet. You look at how planning an intranet requires a different strategy from a normal Web site. Finally, you examine some examples of the Commercial Internet System in corporate intranets. ■

Explore the private net

Learn the differences between the Internet and intranets. See how intranets can boost the bottom line and increase employee satisfaction.

Plan your intranet

Determine who needs to be involved in planning an intranet. What information should be distributed and how? Discover what you need to know to build a successful intranet.

MCIS and the intranet

See how the different MCIS components can be used to construct a dynamic effective intranet.

Living, breathing, and growing intranets

Take a look at some actual intranets and see what works.

Understanding Intranet Concepts

There are several fundamental differences between an intranet and the Internet. While some are obvious and relatively trivial, others are more subtle but extremely critical. This section looks at these differences and explores the benefits of using an intranet.

An *intranet* is a private network that uses Internet software and standards, such as TCP/IP. Yet it is also much more. An intranet allows companies to more effectively:

- *Gather and distribute information*   Companies can use an intranet to distribute important information across departments and locations. By utilizing HTML pages and Web servers, employees can have access to corporate policies and documents. Forms can be used to gain employee input and ideas.

- *Communicate with its employees*   E-mail can allow nearly instant communication. By using attachments, companies can transfer documents directly to recipients without using faxes or couriers.

- *Automate the training process*   Multimedia training solutions can be implemented to deliver on-demand training solutions.

- *Promote company news and events*   Current events and company news can be sent directly to employee desktops. Human Resource departments can distribute information easily to all employees regardless of location.

- *Hold meetings and conferences*   Teleconferences can be conducted instead of employees having to travel to meetings.

- *Share documents and files*   Files and documents can be shared and exchanged across a company without waiting for couriers and deliveries.

- *Collaborate on projects*   Whiteboard applications can allow staff spread across locations to jointly edit documents in real time.

- *Improve workflow by enabling groupware applications*   Calendars, schedules, and projects can be accessed across the company.

- *Improve access to corporate databases*   SQL links and forms can be used to improve access to legacy databases.

- *Increase productivity by enabling a common application interface*   Browsers can be used to provide a uniform interface across disparate platforms.

An intranet differs from the Internet in several ways:

- *Intranets are not normally open to the public*   They are designed for internal needs, rather than external interactions. A well-designed intranet helps a company conduct business in a more efficient manner.

- *Intranets are concerned more with performance than appearance*   The typical Web designer spends hours designing the perfect graphics and effects. Intranet designers like to make things look good, but they are more interested in how well it works.

■ *Intranets carry confidential corporate information whereas Internet site information is intended for all to see*   Intranet information is often critical to a business and therefore highly confidential.

■ *Intranet information content is more important than presentation*   Along with how well an intranet communicates information, is what it actually says. The bottom line for an intranet is usefulness. Sure, it needs to communicate, but make the information pertinent and concise.

■ *Intranets can more easily contribute to the "bottom line."*   Intranet content is company-specific, rather than of general interest. Content is directed at improving performance and efficiency.

Planning an Intranet

Developing an intranet plan is similar to designing an Internet site. However, there are some significant differences in goals and implementation. In this section we will look at some of the more important design considerations.

Audience

An intranet is designed to reach the management and employees of an organization. Therefore, all design decisions are structured around reaching this audience. The very nature of an intranet creates a kind of captive audience. The designers can worry less about drawing visitors to their site and more about fulfilling the needs of the existing users.

An intranet may also be made available to suppliers or vendors. This allows an organization to build stronger relationships with key suppliers, by giving them direct access to selected information. They can more easily share product development and sales data. It can also foster tighter integration of business processes. This can have a dramatic impact on the bottom line.

In some cases the intranet may be later connected to the Internet. If this is the case then greater care must be given to how information is presented. The designers need to differentiate between public and private areas of the network. Security of the internal LAN must also be considered.

All of these audiences raise different concerns. However, if you are going to develop an effective intranet you must identify who will be using your site.

Type of Information

Now that you know who will be using your site, what do they need? The next step is deciding what your users need from an intranet.

An intranet can do many things. It can be used for information distribution. Intranets can allow a company to centrally locate important documents and information such as:

■ Corporate Policies

■ Employee Benefits

- Internal Job Openings
- Sales Information
- Newsletters
- Event Schedules
- Press Releases

All of this information and more can be disbursed electronically. This allows employees and staff to be kept current on company events and policy changes.

An intranet can also be used as a complete "front-end" for the corporate desktop. Microsoft and Netscape are both developing the next generation of browsers. These new releases will replace the desktop used by the operating system. Using the browser as a desktop will allow intranet designers to display links to static information pages next to actual applications. Users will have a seamless interface between applications and the intranet.

This will simplify the process of developing an interactive intranet. Today there are few organizations that make use of the full power of an intranet. These companies have reduced personnel costs by using their intranet for things such as:

- *Online Training*   Utilizing custom multimedia applications, full training programs have been developed. These can be as simple as new employee orientation or as complex as having a new employee fill out all of their required paperwork online. Other organizations have developed continuing education courses for employees scattered around the world. The employees can receive the training they need without the expense of travel.

- *Database Integration*   Many corporations have developed extensive databases. These databases may reside in different locations scattered around the world. Many times the databases have evolved over time on several different platforms. Normally if an employee is assigned to research a particular topic, she might have to spend days contacting the various departments to gain the required information. Utilizing Internet Search Engine technology and legacy interfaces searches now can be done in a fraction of the time. An intranet designer can develop search forms that interface with all of an organizations databases, regardless of platform or location.

An intranet can be used for these tasks and more. The designers must know exactly what kind of information will be distributed and gathered via the intranet. They must also understand the way that transfer of data will take place. Will it just be static pages or will there need to be links to databases and search engines?

Locations

The next thing that must be considered is location. Does your organization have multiple sites or is there just the one? A company with only one location has a much easier time designing an intranet than one with several. The single site allows the designers to jump more quickly into the actual content and development. Companies with more than one site must decide if all of them are going to be linked together or if some will be left out. If it is an international company the designers must also look at language and time differences. Representatives from each site as well as each department must be included in the design process. If the intranet is to be successfully implemented it must work as well in the Middle East as it does in Chicago.

Connectivity

Even if you are only designing for a single site you still have to consider connectivity. What is the status of your LAN? Are all of your users connected? What network protocol are you using? Are all of your workstations using the same operating system? If not, what common interface will you use?

If you are designing an intranet which must service multiple sites you still need to answer those questions. In addition you need to examine these questions:

- Do you already have a wide area network (WAN)?
- If a WAN is already in place, does it have sufficient bandwidth to carry additional traffic?
- Do you need to purchase additional network hardware?
- Will new servers be required at the remote sites or can it all be centrally located?
- If the intranet is going to be "the company interface," do you have sufficient redundancy?

Security

Before an organization implements an intranet it must rethink the nature of employee-to-corporation and employee-to-employee relationships. When every employee has the ability to instantly communicate work, thoughts, gripes, experiences, and solutions to every other employee a new set of responsibilities for all members of the corporate community will be created.

Not discussing and planning for the increases in individual power and responsibilities is potentially dangerous. While most security measures are focused on better firewalls, systems administrators know that the real security problem is with the malicious insider or disaffected employee. There needs to be a discussion between management and staff about what constitutes productive use of the intranet and Internet on company time. Employees need to think about just what is offensive to others in the way of personal or work communications. Everyone must realize that not everyone is interested in their opinion on every subject matter at hand.

These issues are not new. What is new is that intranets bring more people in contact than ever before within the company. Corporate systems, cultures, and procedures must adapt themselves to this shift in relationships.

A malicious employee could potentially remove vital corporate information from the intranet. Therefore, a security plan is a vital part of any intranet design. Who will have access to what information or which resources is a critical decision.

In addition to an inside attack intranet developers must also examine the threat of outside attack. Is there a connection to the Internet? Does the organization have an effective firewall? Are there modems connected to critical systems? A standard security review should be conducted on the existing infrastructure and appropriate steps should be taken before an intranet is implemented.

ON THE WEB

www.cert.org Additional information on intranet and Internet security can be found at this site.

Who Runs the Show?

An Internet site has a fairly basic management structure. The IS department actually makes the site happen. Marketing and Sales will contribute information and Corporate Management will set the tone. An intranet is a more complicated animal. Since an intranet's goal is to serve an entire organization, it must naturally address a wide cross-section of needs. Each department will have a different agenda of things to be accomplished. At the very least these departments should be involved in the planning process.

- IT/IS Department will be responsible for infrastructure planning and development and applications development.

- Human Resources will supply employee related information and applications policies on employee groups, and internal communications. They will also develop training programs to be used on the intranet.

- Legal will need to develop communications and network usage policies.

- Major user communities will develop the demand and prioritization of content and applications.

- All must, of course, be justified to Accounting, the department that will get you the funding support needed to implement the plan.

Using MCIS to Build an Intranet

The Microsoft Commercial Internet System provides an excellent basis for building a corporate intranet. Windows NT Server 4.0 and the Internet Information Server form a stable robust foundation for the system. The system's ease of use and common interface make it ideal for small organizations who are new to intranets. Larger corporations will be able to make use of the native NT stability and security in the Commercial Internet System.

The Mail Server

The foremost internal need of any organization is communication. The Mail Server is the fundamental basis of communication within the Commercial Internet System. By using the Mail Server, companies can enable communication between any of their staff in any location. They can also build stronger relationships with vendors and related organizations. Automated e-mail responses can free Human Resource departments from answering the same questions over and over again. Instead of sending expensive faxes to remote offices, e-mail important documents as attachments (see Figure 20.1). This not only reduces long-distance bills, it also routes the documents to the exact person who needs to have it. Faxes often are made to public areas and are not secure. If you interface the Mail Server with the Microsoft Exchange server you have a complete communication solution. The Exchange server provides you with a group messaging and collaboration system, while the Mail Server provides the e-mail and SMTP platform.

▶ **See** "Administering the Internet Mail Server," **p. 150**, for information on how to use the Internet Mail Server.

FIG. 20.1
E-mail can be the foundation of an intranet

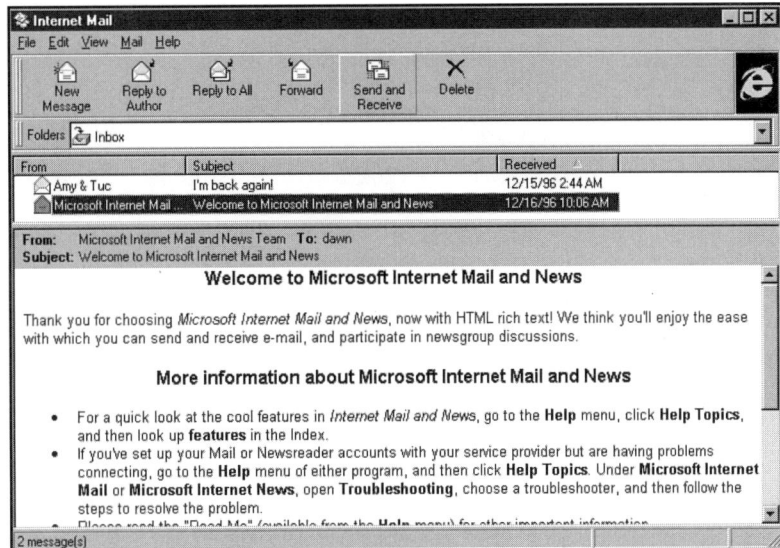

The Internet News Server

Discussion groups can help a company focus on a particular idea or problem. The difficulty with forming these types of groups has always been scheduling time for them to meet and budgeting the travel required. The Internet News Server removes both obstacles. Now an organization can create discussion groups on any topic they desire. Participants can join in as their schedules permit. Individuals do not have to worry about missing something and the discussion is open 24 hours a day. If you choose, the discussion can be open to everyone. What before would have been impossible is now a no-brainer. If you have 10,000 employees they can all participate. If you have a need for a private discourse, that's no problem either.

The Internet News Server can be a valuable part of an intranet strategy. Implementing it is the same as for an Internet. The only difference would be if you chose not to receive any news from outside your organization. Then you would only have local groups and not have any type of a News Feed.

The News Server gives companies the ability to not only host discussion groups. It can also be used to download news from UseNet news groups. There are groups that deal with almost every topic conceivable. These can be a valuable source of information. Answers to specific problems as well as general market information can be had through UseNet.

Part
VII

Ch
20

Corporations can also improve their name recognition and public image by allowing employees to participate in the online support and business forums in UseNet (see Figure 20.2). When others come to see your staff as a valuable online resource, it can result in additional sales and opportunities for the business.

FIG 20.2

UseNet groups can hold the answers to many problems.

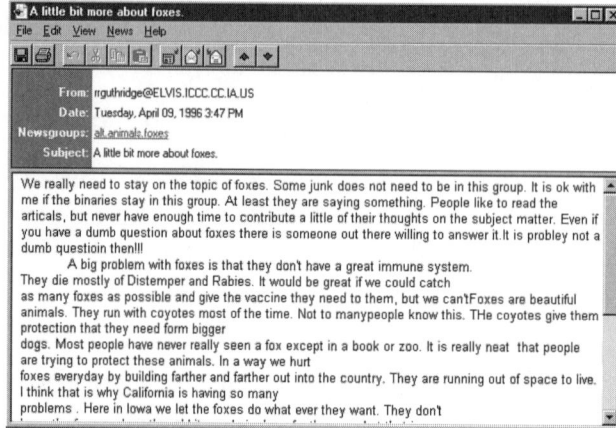

The Personalization System

The Personalization Server allows an intranet staff to meet more of the individual employee needs with less staff. In a static intranet setting, users would be given one or two choices from the information shown on any given interface. The appearance would be governed by others and they would have little, if any, choice about the content presented. Now, with the Personalization Server, users can have a choice. They can now adjust the appearance to meet their preferences. They can also have a choice in what information is displayed on their desktop, as shown in Figure 20.3. If they want to know when new training is available they can be notified. If they want to keep an eye on promotion opportunities they can see job listings. Users can have the capability to modify their desktop within the limits set by the intranet designers. This capability to make each desktop unique would have been almost impossible before; now, it's part of the package.

▶ **See** "Taking Advantage of a Personalized Site," **p. 224** for more information on the Personalization Server.

FIG. 20.3
Employees can choose
what information they
want on their desktop.

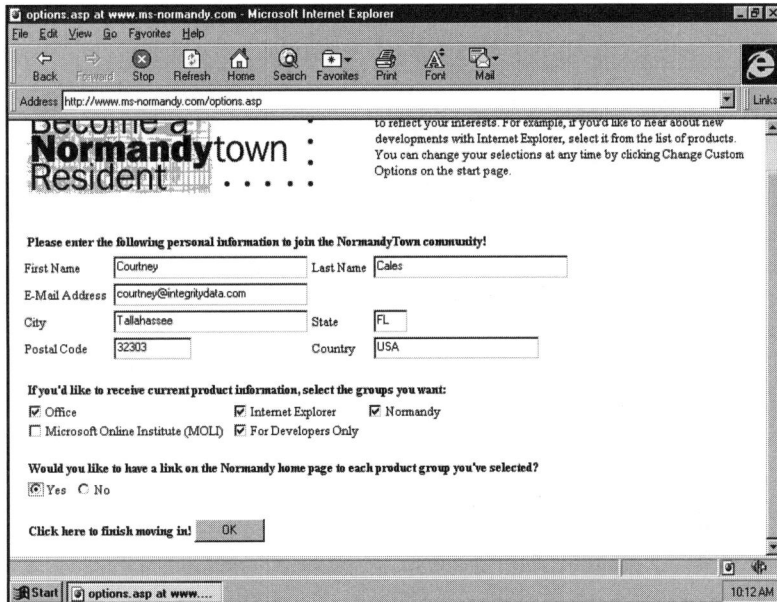

The Internet Locator Service

How many people today have the time to travel to meetings? In today's world we are all far too busy for most of the meetings we have to attend. On top of that, when we have a problem with our computer or an application, we can lose hours waiting for a technician. The Internet Conference System can resolve some of these problems. By integrating Microsoft's NetMeeting and Conference Servers intranet designers can eliminate some costly travel time. Employees spread across multiple locations can have an online conference via NetMeeting. They can share and mark up documents and communicate via audio and video links in the NetMeeting program. This capability alone can save corporations hundreds of thousands of dollars per year in travel expenses and lost time.

The Internet Chat Server

The chat server application allows users to have real-time communications through a browser. There's no need to launch another application, such as NetMeeting. This works conveniently through the browser. There are many other potential uses for the chat server; for instance, sales and technical support can be offered from anywhere in the world. Many businesses are not ready to spend thousands of dollars on video-conferencing systems, yet they can still benefit from long distance meetings with the Conference servers.

▶ **See** "Introducing Microsoft Commercial Internet Chat Server," **p. 192**, for more information on the Internet Conference System.

Part
VII

Ch
20

Over all, the Membership System will be very helpful in knowing who is using the intranet and what they are using it for. This information is necessary for planning future development of an intranet site.

The Proxy Server

An intranet can have access to the Internet or it can be isolated. Either way, the Microsoft Proxy Server should be a part of the intranet strategy.

If your intranet is connected to the outside world then security is a concern. While the Proxy Server is only part of a security platform, it is a useful part. By using the Proxy Server, administrators can help you control and monitor access to specified sites. With Proxy Server, you can limit what services a user has access to. If you want to limit certain users to e-mail only the Proxy Server can do this. It can also allow you to log which users are using which services. The Proxy Server can also act as an IPX to TCP/IP gateway. This enables you to access TCP/IP services without enabling the protocol on individual workstations. This makes it more difficult for outsiders to mount an attack against your network. The Proxy Server also enables caching on the Internet Site. This can improve performance by keeping a local copy of high access files.

If you have a standalone intranet, the Proxy Server can still contribute to the efficiency of your site. By using it to cache documents, you can reduce the load on other servers. Administrators can choose to limit services to users within the intranet via the WinSock filters. If you are communicating via a WAN, the Proxy Server can be used to secure individual sites from unauthorized access.

Each of these Commercial Internet System components can help to create a dynamic, effective intranet. The next section takes a look at some sample intranets and how they are using the Commercial Internet System.

Examples of Intranets

Intranets are considered by many to be the wave of the future. Many corporations have intranet plans in the works. The Commercial Internet System has generated much interest within the corporate community. It holds great promise for reducing the level of difficulty in rolling out an intranet.

Microsoft developed the system mostly for its own internal needs. For example, the Content Replication Server was used to update the Superbowl 95 site. The Mail Server was an answer to their need for an in-house SMTP mail solution. NetMeeting and the Conference Servers were developed as part of the Microsoft Network. This helps to contribute to the suitability of the Commercial Internet System for intranet use.

Integrity Data

Integrity Data had been looking at developing its own intranet for some time. We hoped to use the intranet to solve some recurring problems. Since we are a technology solutions provider, we have access to all of the newest software. One of our major concerns was finding the proper Groupware package. We also conduct a lot of business on and around the Internet. This meant that whatever package we chose needed to integrate as seamlessly as possible with the Internet and the World Wide Web. Many of Integrity Data's customers have needs that could potentially be solved by an intranet. One of these was an improved help desk system. Another client was looking for a common interface for several different systems.

The Microsoft Commercial Internet System was chosen as the development platform for the Integrity Data intranet (see Figure 20.4).

FIG. 20.4
Integrity Data built their intranet on the Commercial Internet System.

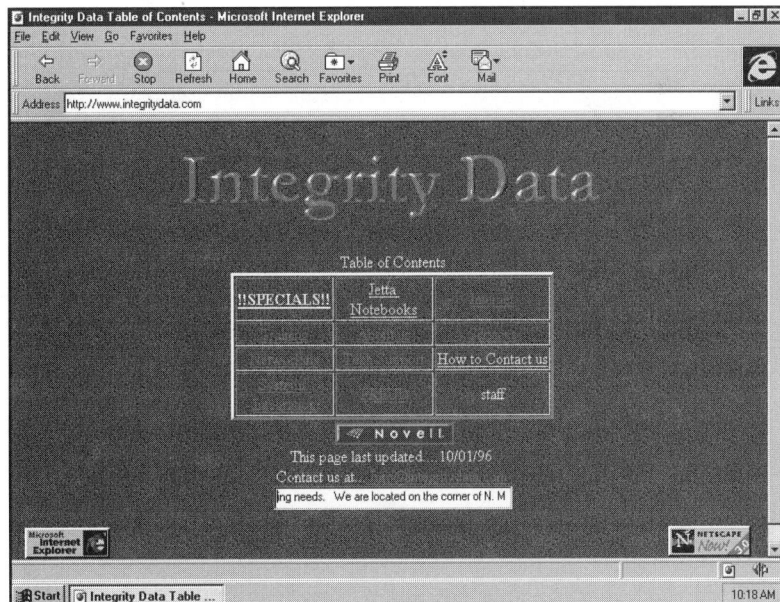

Four of the main components have been used in the development of the intranet:

- *The Mail Server*   This is the backbone of our in-house communication. One of the first steps was integrating the Mail Server with the Microsoft Exchange Server. This allows the staff to have seamless access to Internet mail, intranet mail, and faxes. Service technicians and salespeople can call into the intranet using Windows NT remote access services and check their e-mail and calendars. Microsoft's Schedule+ is shared via the Exchange Server so that technicians and salespeople can update their schedules as needed. Internet Mail is used to communicate with clients as well as vendors.

- *The News Server*   Integrity Data follows a large number of industry-specific UseNet news groups. We use these to get answers to specific questions as well as to answer problems as they are able. The News Server allows us to access the groups we need without having to sort through the thousands of unwanted groups. Integrity Data also has started several local groups of interest to our customers. This allows us to respond to non-critical problems and questions in a group format. One of the side benefits of this is that many times one customer will respond to a different customer's problem without an Integrity technician's involvement. So not only are we able to respond to a customer's needs, sometimes they solve the problem without even knowing it.

- *The Conference Servers* Everyone at Integrity Data complains of being overworked and underpaid, especially the technicians and help desk personnel. Customer problems come first so it could be several hours or days before an internal problem is addressed. This seemed to mirror the problems that several of our customers were having. In order to address this Integrity Data decided to utilize the conference servers to develop a virtual help desk. We were able to construct a series of help desk HTML pages. These pages ran on the Internet Information Server and were only accessible through the intranet. Then NetMeeting was installed on every desktop and laptop. Now when a user had an application problem they could bring up the proper Chat page and communicate directly with the application specialist. If necessary the specialist could use NetMeeting to immediately correct the problem. No more waiting for the user and the application specialist did not have to leave their office. This has enabled the help desk to increase the number of client problems addressed and to improve the number of problems successfully resolved.

- *The Proxy Server* Integrity Data has a complete firewall system in place. This means that we use the Proxy Server primarily as a caching server. This enables us to cache frequently accessed pages locally. This helps reduce the required access times to those pages. We also are experimenting with the IP filtering options on the Proxy Server. In today's world prudent businesses take a proactive approach to legal issues. Since there is the possibility for abuse of Internet access, Integrity Data is testing the feasibility of blocking access to specific sites.

State Agency

An agency of the State of Florida has long been on the forefront of Internet development. One of the most impressive elements of their intranet is its training component. Interactive multimedia training modules have been developed for most positions. The trainee can sit at a desktop computer and receive the needed training. This enables the agency to provide training on demand and not have to tie up valuable instructors with a single student. The agency plans to integrate this training with the Conference Servers. This way an instructor could interact with multiple students via chat clients and NetMeeting. These students could be scattered across the state and still have real-time answers to their individual questions. A single instructor will be able to cover the whole state without all of the travel expense.

From Here...

This chapter looked at how some of the components of the Commercial Internet System are used to develop an intranet. Also check out these chapters for related information:

- Chapter 2, "Getting Started with Microsoft Commercial Internet System," provides detailed descriptions of each of the MCIS servers as well information about how to plan an Internet site.

- If you need help with setting up or configuring Windows NT or the Internet Information Server you can find it in Chapter 3, "Building the Foundation."

Part
VII

Ch
20

Appendixes

Hardware Requirements

All of the Microsoft Commercial Internet Servers have the
same minimum requirements as Windows NT Server
version 4.0 and the Internet Information Server version
3.0 as described in the following table:

Category	Requirement
Server Hardware	32-bit x 86-compatible microprocessor (such as Intel 80486/ 25 or higher), Intel Pentium, or supported RISC-based micro-processor, such as the Digital Alpha or PowerPC
Software	Windows NT Server version 4.0 and Internet Information Server version 3.0
Memory	Minimum 12 megabytes (M) of RAM for x 86 systems (16M recommended) Minimum 16M of RAM for RISC-based systems

However, this is only a minimum requirement for running a single component of the Commercial Internet System. These requirements will for the most part allow only a minimum number of clients. The following sections list Microsoft's recommended configurations for scaling the various components. ■

Internet News Server

According to Microsoft, a dual-processor P166 with 256M of RAM can scale up to 3,000 concurrent users of the Internet News Server. Larger sites that intend to serve thousands, or tens of thousands of users, need only configure additional servers. Multiple server configurations require a Master/Slave configuration. This will allow managers to dedicate a Master server to downloading news. The slave servers will have direct access to the Master to process client requests.

The amount of storage space required depends on how many discussion groups you want to carry and how long you want to store them. There are over 20,000 newsgroups on the Internet. In order to make all of these groups available to your users, you will need to download over 1G of articles per day. A significant amount of this space is eaten up by binary images. You can reduce the amount of storage space required by reducing the expiration times on those groups. Realistically though, you will need at least 9G of storage space if you intend to carry a full news feed.

If your installation is running out of storage space, you may want to increase the physical disk space or eliminate some groups from your feed. Remember to plan for peak loads. Also, you can spread articles over multiple machines by putting different newsgroups on different virtual roots.

If your newsfeed averages 250 megabytes per day, you may want to plan for 300 megabytes to cover busy periods. If the news articles will be retained for one week, the total requirement would be 2100 megabytes, or 2.1G. Additional space is also required for file overhead. This overhead includes 540 bytes per article plus one byte per 128 articles. The average size of an article is approximately 2K. By dividing the number of megabytes in your daily newsfeed by 2K, file overhead can be approximated.

Index Server

On a Microsoft Windows NT Server, the minimum hardware required for the Index Server is the same as that for IIS. However, on a Windows NT Workstation, you need a minimum of 16 megabytes of RAM.

Index Server program files require anywhere from 3 to 12 megabytes of disk space, depending upon the number of languages installed. The disk space needed for storing Index Server data depends upon the size of the corpus and the type of documents. You need to have at least 40 percent of the size of the corpus in free disk space to Index. However, indexing can require much more space than 40 percent of the original. Some real world applications have needed almost 100 percent of the original corpus.

The optimum configuration depends upon the size of the corpus, the number of documents, and the search load on the server.

The minimum configuration requirements for the Index Server are basically the same as for Microsoft Windows NT Server but the configuration for optimum performance depends upon the number of documents, size of the data corpus, and the rate of queries. A 486/DX4-100 computer with 32M of memory running Windows NT Server 4.0 services queries well if the number of simultaneous queries is not too high. For a small organization, this may be sufficient; but for a larger group serving more users, better hardware is recommended.

The following table shows recommended memory configuration based on the number of documents. The size of the corpus affects the disk space needed for storing Index Server data. The disk space needed for Index Server data in all the cases is approximately 40 percent of the size of the corpus. While the average usage is less than 30 percent of the corpus, the peak usage of disk space can be 40 percent.

Number of Documents	Minimum Memory (in Megabytes)	Recommended Memory (in Megabytes)
Fewer than 10,000	16 for Workstation 32 for Server	Same as minimum
Fewer than 100,000	32	32
100,000–250,000	32	64–128
250,000–500,000	64	128–256
500,000 or more	28	256 or more

A faster CPU and more memory improves the performance of indexing as well as the speed of queries. If the number of documents is very large, not having enough memory will seriously affect performance. If you see that performance is slow when Index Server is running, add more memory to improve the situation.

Internet Mail Server

Internet e-mail is the core function of most Internet sites. This is not the area to skimp on hardware. A reliable e-mail system can make up for many other site deficiencies. Table A.1 shows you the elements of the Mail Server systems, which have the following minimum requirements on top of the standard Windows NT 4.0 requirements:

Table A.1   Mail Server System's Minimum Requirements

Processor	RAM (in Megabytes)	Hard Drive Storage
Routing Table Database Server		
Intel 486+, Digital Equipment Corporation (DEC) Alpha, or PowerPC	16 minimum	1 gigabyte (G) hard drive for SQL Server and basic database setup, plus 0.5G per million users
Mailbox File Server		
Intel 486+, DEC Alpha, or Power PC	16	1G minimum, or the number of anticipated mailbox accounts multiplied by the maximum size allowed for mailboxes, plus 30% for system overhead
SMTP and POP3 Servers		
Intel 486+, DEC Alpha, or Power PC	16	1G hard drive

Depending upon the size of your organization, you may choose to run all of the Mail Server components on a single server or you may decide to run them separately. Large organizations will need to bring multiple servers online.

The processing of Mail is not very intensive; storage is the major concern. Use Microsoft's formula to determine the required Mailbox Fileserver storage space. Let's look at a corporation with 10,000 employees needing e-mail. If they set a mailbox limit of 1M, they would require 13G of hard drive space. In addition, they would need to develop SMTP and POP servers to handle the client requests.

Microsoft is also releasing a version of the Mail Server that does not require SQL. This version will be ideal for smaller sites and many businesses that are not servicing thousands of mailboxes. The non-SQL version was not available to us, so there are no hardware requirements for this system. According to Microsoft, the non-SQL version would be able to run everything on a single server.

Internet Chat Server

The Chat Server requirements are dependent upon the number of concurrent users you expect to serve. Following are the configurations Microsoft recommends:

Requirement	Up to 1,000 Concurrent Users (Minimal)	5,000–10,000 Concurrent Users (Recommended)	30,000-50,000 Users in 16,000 Channels (Optimal)
Hardware	1 computer 64 megabytes (MB) RAM 1 gigabyte (GB) hard disk space	3 computers 2 CPUs each 128M RAM 2G hard disk space	10 computers 4 CPUs each 256-512M RAM 2-4G hard disk space
Example Platforms	Single Intel 586+ 133 MHz or single Alpha	Dual Pentium 133 MHz or 200 MHz Alpha	Quad Pentium 133 MHz

It is important to understand that the Chat Server is scaleable. Therefore, if your particular Chat Service expands beyond your present design, you can add additional capabilities as described in Chapter 8, "Adding a Chat Server."

Internet Locator Server

Running the Locator Server on one computer is suitable for small to medium installations. Increased load or performance requirements may be met by running multiple Locator Server computers. The more queries per second the more NT servers will be required.

ILS requires the same minimum configuration as Windows NT Server version 4.0 and Microsoft Internet Information Server, as described next.

Category	Requirement
Server hardware	32-bit x 86-compatible microprocessor (such as Intel 80486/25 or higher), Intel Pentium, or supported RISC-based microprocessor, such as the Digital Alpha or PowerPC
Software	Windows NT Server version 4.0 and Internet Information Server version 3.0
Memory	Minimum 12 megabytes (M) of RAM for x 86 systems (16M recommended) Minimum 16M RAM for RISC-based systems

Microsoft conducted quantitative performance evaluation tests on the search portion of the Beta 2 version of the Internet Locator Server. Most of the system test and evaluation used the following configurations:

- A computer with one Alpha processor and 32M memory
- A computer with one x 86 processor and 32M memory

For administration and testing purposes, your site should include a client computer with the following software:

- Microsoft Windows 95 or Windows NT Workstation version 4.0
- Microsoft Internet Explorer version 3.0a or later
- The client portion of the Microsoft Internet Mail and Microsoft Internet News components
- Microsoft NetMeeting

Content Replication Server

The following table lists the requirements for the start-point, site staging, and end-point servers.

Requirement	Start-Point Server	Site Saging Server	End-Point Server
Software	Windows NT Server 4.0, Windows NT Workstation 4.0 Internet Information Server (IIS) 3.0 (required for using the Web Administration tool), or Administration Windows NT 4.0 Service Pack 1	Windows NT Server 4.0 Internet Information Server (IIS) 3.0 (required for using the Web Server 3.51 tool), or Windows NT 4.0 Service Pack 1	Windows NT Server 4.0 Internet Information Server (IIS) 3.0 (required for using the Web Administration tool), on Windows NT Intel-based systems only (does not support the Web Administration tool), or Windows NT

Start-Point Requirement	Site Saging Server	Server	End-Point Server
			4.0 Service Pack 1
Web browser	Internet Explorer 3.01 or Netscape Navigator 3.0	Internet Explorer 3.01 or Netscape Navigator 3.0	Internet Explorer 3.01 or Netscape Navigator 3.0
Hardware	486 processor, 16M of RAM, and hard disk space equal to at least twice the volume to be replicated	486 processor, 16M of RAM, and hard disk space equal to at least twice the volume to be replicated	486 processor, 16M of RAM, and hard disk space equal to at least twice the volume to be replicated
RISC system	Runs on RISC systems supported by Windows NT Server 4.0; 16M of RAM	Runs on RISC systems supported by Windows NT Server 4.0; 16M of RAM	Runs on RISC systems supported by Windows NT Server 4.0; 16M of RAM
Connectivity	Shared TCP/IP CRS servers in remote locations must be able to locate one another by DNS server, IP address, local hosts or Imhosts, or Windows Internet Name Service (WINS) server.	Shared TCP/IP CRS servers in remote locations must be able to locate one another by DNS server, IP address, local hosts or Imhosts, or WINS server.	Shared TCP/IP CRS servers in remote locations must be able to locate one another by DNS server, IP address, local hosts or Imhosts or WINS server.

Personalization Server

The requirements for setting up Microsoft Personalization Server depend on the administrator's decisions on a number of issues.

Storage Capacity

The required storage capacity for the User Property Database is a combination of the anticipated number of users of your Web site, the amount of information you plan to store for each user, and how much your site will use the Voting component. The following table charts required storage space for a typical site; your storage needs may vary.

The following assumptions were made: 100 properties stored for each user, 20 bytes per property, two votes stored at any given time.

Number of Users	User Property Database Storage	Vote Database Storage
1 thousand	2M	32K
10 thousand	20M	320K
100 thousand	200M	3.2M
1 million	2G	30M
10 million	20G	300M

How Many Servers?

The number of Web servers your site needs is largely determined by:

- Number of HTTP requests received by your site per second at peak load as determined by examining log files or by using Performance Monitor
- Percentage of those requests that are for personalized Web content built
- Complexity of those personalized pages

Estimating the exact number of servers needed depends on a large number of variables that affect a Web server's exact performance, such as:

- RAM
- CPU speed and power
- CPU type
- Server architecture
- Network bandwidth
- Script complexity

The delivery of a personalized Web page requires a lot more processing power than a static page containing two images and some text. The more complex the site, the more processing power you will need. According to Microsoft, a 120 MHz quad processor with 128M of RAM can efficiently handle the following:

Page Request/sec	Requests/day	Web Servers Needed	File Servers Needed
1	86,400	1	0 (same server)
10	860,000	2	1
50	4,300,000	10	1
100	8,600,000	20	2

Sendmail Traffic

The number of SMTP servers needed by the Sendmail component is directly related to the estimated maximum number of e-mail messages sent per second. Sendmail is typically used to thank users for submitting information or to deliver the submitted information to an e-mail box. In those cases, the number of messages needed per second is usually low. The following table suggests the number of SMTP servers that you will need based on the estimated use of Sendmail.

The numbers were calculated for an SMTP server running on a single-processor Pentium 133 with 32M of RAM.

E-Mail Messages/sec	E-Mail Messages/day	Number of SMTP Servers Needed
1	86,400	1
5	432,000	2

Membership Server

The Membership Server is a high-impact, high-overhead system. While it adds considerable capabilities and value to an Internet site, it comes at a high price. This component of the Commercial Internet System can easily be the most resource-intensive part. However, it can easily make up for this in increased revenues.

Backend Server Requirements

The Membership System is designed for optimum performance when the Backend services each run on a separate machine. This means one or more separate NT servers for each of the following:

- Security Database
- Membership Agent
- Member Services
- System Administration
- Event Collector (if installed)

Table A.2 gives you the minimum requirements for each of the Membership Server components:

Table A.2   Membership Server Requirements

Processor	OS	RAM (M)	Hard Drive Storage	Software
Security Database Servers				
i486/33+, Digital Equipment Corporation (DEC) Alpha, or PowerPC	Microsoft Windows NT Server version 4.0 with Service Pack 2	64	1G minimum for SQL Server and the basic database setup, plus 0.5G per 1 million users	Microsoft SQL Server version 6.5
Membership Agents				
i486/33+, DEC Alpha, or PowerPC	Microsoft Windows NT Server version 4.0 with Service Pack 2	32	1G minimum (the amount of space you need depends on the anticipated volume of billing events and the capacity of the Billing Event Collector)	NTFS file system in which the events will be stored Microsoft Content Replication System (if you're using the Billing feature)
Web Applications: Member Registration, Member Change Template, Member Administration				
I486/33+, DEC Alpha, or Power PC	Microsoft Windows NT Server version 4.0 with Service Pack 2 Information Server	32	1G minimum	Microsoft Internet Explorer version 2.0 or later with Active Server Pages feature and World Wide Web (WWW) services enabled
Event Collector Server				
i486/33+, DEC Alpha, or PowerPC	Microsoft Windows NT Server version 4.0 with Service Pack 2	32	1G minimum (the amount of space needed will depend on the anticipated volume of billing events)	Microsoft Content Replication System

Connectivity Requirements

In any Membership Backend deployment, the basic network connectivity will require considerable planning and work to ensure not only proper communication between components but also the security of the system. Your connectivity hardware and software should meet the following requirements:

Internet

- 56K (or greater) leased line for the link from the Application Server to the Membership Agent. This will typically be the Internet link.
- The Membership Agent requires TCP/IP connectivity on port 568 to the Internet.
- CRS requires TCP/IP connectivity on port 507 between the Membership Agent and the Event Collector.
- The Membership Agent DNS (Domain Name System) hostname and IP address must be correctly configured on a DNS server that is visible to the MBS Broker servers.
- All Backend components must be able to freely communicate with other Backend components, with no port/protocol limitations.

LAN

- All Backend components must be located on a high-speed secured LAN for performance, reliability, and security.
- Although all MBS Backend components are located on this secured LAN, only the Web Application servers and Membership Agents are also accessible from the Internet.
- Network planning, configuration, and topology *must* ensure that the LAN environment remains secure even if a server is compromised or fails, while also allowing the component servers to communicate with one another freely.

Address Book Server

The Address Book Server will run on the minimum Windows NT Server 4.0 set-up. However, in larger environments additional capacity is required.

This section describes a sample hardware and software configuration for a five-million-member ABS database being accessed by a large community.

SQL Database Server

The following hardware and software are required for the SQL database server:

- Four i386+, DEC Alpha, or Power PC processors
- 512M RAM
- Hard disk with 1G of free space for SQL Server and basic database setup, plus 2G per million users

- Microsoft Windows NT Server version 4.0
- Microsoft SQL Server version 6.5

ABS Server

The following hardware and software are required for the ABS server:

- Dual i386+, DEC Alpha, Power PC processor
- 128M RAM
- 5M of free disk space
- Microsoft Windows NT Server version 4.0
- Microsoft Internet Information Server version 3.0
- The World Wide Web (WWW) service

Performance Monitor Counters

Windows NT Server 4.0 includes a Performance Monitor tool which is used for monitoring computer performance. When you monitor a system, you actually monitor its parts. A set of counters exists for the processor, memory, cache, hard disk, processes, and other parts that produce statistical information. Certain counters are standard; others are added with the installation of new software.

You can choose to chart performance when you want to, or you can set system alerts for any specific counters. By setting alerts, you can choose to have any of the following responses occur when a counter reaches a predefined limit:

- The active monitoring view for Performance Monitor changes to the Alert view and the Alert window displays information about the reason for the alert.
- The event that caused the alert status is logged in the Application log of the Event Viewer.
- An alert message is broadcast over the network by the server.

You do not need special privileges to open Performance Monitor. However, you do need to be logged on as a member of the Administrators group to use the diskperf command. ■

Monitoring Disk Performance

The diskperf command turns the counters for disk activity on and off. Diskperf works for a local or a remote computer. After restarting the computer, you can use Performance Monitor to view disk performance data.

To activate the physical and logical disk counters:

1. Log on as a member of the Administrators group.
2. At the command prompt, type diskperf to view Help information on how to turn diskperf on and off and how to specify a remote computer's name.
3. Follow the instructions to turn diskperf on or off.
4. To activate the disk performance counters, reboot the server.

N O T E Activating object counters for performance monitoring will increase disk access time. When you are finished with diskperf you should turn it off. ■

Launching Performance Monitor

To start Performance Monitor, use this procedure:

1. From the Start Menu, choose Programs.
2. Choose the Administrative Tools program group, then select Performance Monitor.

To view counters, follow these steps:

1. Choose File, New Chart.
2. Choose Edit, Add to Chart. The Add to Chart dialog box appears.
3. Select an object from the Object list. For example, you might select WinSock Proxy Server. The counters for that object appear in the Counter list.
4. Select a counter from the Counter list, and then choose Add.
5. Repeat Steps 2, 3, and 4 to add additional counters.
6. When all counters have been added, choose Done.

The display returns to the Performance Monitor and information about the selected counters is displayed.

Each component will have its own list of performance counters. Following are lists of the counters broken down by server. Each counter is accompanied by a brief description of its function.

Index Server Counters

Table B.1 lists all the .htx variables available for statistics. The Content Index performance object variables begin with CiAdminIndex while Http Content Index object variables begin with CiAdminCache.

Table B.1   The .HTX Variables

.htx Variable Performance	Monitor Field	Description
CiAdminCacheActive	Active queries	The number of queries being executed currently
CiAdminCacheCount	Cache items	The number of cached queries
CiAdminCacheHits%	Cache hits	Percent of HTTP requests that used an existing cached query
CiAdminCacheMisses%	Cache misses	Percent of HTTP requests that executed a new query
CiAdminCachePending	Current requests queued	The number of queries awaiting execution
CiAdminCacheRejected	Total requests rejected	Total queries rejected because the query engine was busy
CiAdminCacheTotal	Total queries	Total queries executed since starting Web server
CiAdminIndexCountDeltas	(not applicable)	Total documents indexed or deleted since the last master merge
CiAdminIndexCountFiltered#	Documents filtered	Total documents filtered since starting Index Server
CiAdminIndexCountPersIndex	Persistent indexes	Total shadow indexes and master indexes in catalog

continues

Table B.1   Continued

.htx Variable Performance	Monitor Field	Description
CiAdminIndexCountQueries	Running queries	Count of queries with open cursors against the catalog. Note that this may differ from the total cached queries because queries may be enumerated (nonindexed), and some quiescent cached queries may still hold cursors open.
CiAdminIndexCountToFilter	Files to be filtered	Total documents added or modified since they were last filtered
CiAdminIndexCountTotal	Total # documents	Total documents in the catalog
CiAdminIndexCountUnique	Unique keys	Total unique words in the catalog. This counter is updated only after a master merge.
CiAdminIndexCountWordlists	Word list	Total word lists in catalog
CiAdminIndexMergeProgress	Merge progress	The percent of current merge that is completed. Equals 100% when no merge is in progress.
CiAdminIndexSize	Index size (in megabytes)	Size of index, including in-memory word lists, on-disk shadow indexes and master indexes, but not the property cache, in megabytes
CiAdminIndexStateAnnealingMerge	n/a	True if an annealing merge is in progress
CiAdminIndexStateMasterMerge	n/a	True if a master merge is in progress
CiAdminIndexStateScanRequired	n/a	True if the catalog needs to be rebuilt, which happens automatically when appropriate
CiAdminIndexStateShadowMerge	n/a	True if a shadow merge is in progress

News Server Counters

The two objects for which the NNTP server maintains counters are NNTP Server Svc and NNTP Server Client Requests. The list of counters, with descriptions for these objects, are listed in the Tables B.2 and B.3.

Table B.2 NNTP Server SVC Counters

Symbol	Name	Description
NNTP_ARTICLE_MAP_ENTRIES_COUNTER	Article Map Entries	Total entries inserted into the NNTP server's article-mapping table
NNTP_ARTICLE_MAP_ENTRIES_PERSEC_COUNTER	Article Map Entries/sec	The number of entries inserted per second into the server's article-mapping table
NNTP_ARTICLES_EXPIRED_COUNTER	Articles Expired	Total articles that have expired on the server since it was last started
NNTP_ARTICLES_EXPIRED_PERSEC_COUNTER	Articles Expired/sec	The number of articles expired per second on the server since it was started
NNTP_ARTICLES_POSTED_COUNTER	Articles Posted	Total articles posted to the server
NNTP_ARTICLES_POSTED_PERSEC_COUNTER	Articles Posted/sec	The number per second of articles posted to the server
NNTP_ARTICLES_RECEIVED_COUNTER	Articles Received	Total files received by the server
NNTP_ARTICLES_RECEIVED_PERSEC_COUNTER	Articles Received/sec	The number per second of files received by the server
NNTP_ARTICLES_SENT_COUNTER	Articles Sent	Total files sent by the server
NNTP_ARTICLES_SENT_PERSEC_COUNTER	Articles Sent/sec	The number per second of files sent by the server

continues

Table B.2   Continued

Symbol	Name	Description
NNTP_ARTICLES_TOTAL_COUNTER	Articles Total	Total files transferred by the server (Articles Sent plus Articles Received)
NNTP_BYTES_RECEIVED_COUNTER	Bytes Received/sec	The number of data bytes received per second by the server
NNTP_BYTES_SENT_COUNTER	Bytes Sent/sec	The number of data bytes sent per second by the server
NNTP_BYTES_TOTAL_COUNTER	Bytes Total/sec	The number of bytes that are transferred per second by the server
NNTP_CONTROL_MSGS_FAILED_COUNTER	Control Messages Failed	Total control messages that have failed or have not been applied by the server
NNTP_CONTROL_MSGS_IN_COUNTER	Control Messages Received	Total control messages received by the server
NNTP_CURRENT_ANONYMOUS_COUNTER	Current Anonymous Users	Total anonymous users connected to the server currently
NNTP_CURRENT_CONNECTIONS_COUNTER	Current Connections	The current number of connections to the server
NNTP_CURRENT_NONANONYMOUS_COUNTER	Current Users NonAnonymous	Total nonanonymous users connected to the server currently
NNTP_CURRENT_OUTBOUND_CONNECTS_COUNTER	Current Outbound Connections	Total current outbound connections being made by the server
NNTP_HISTORY_MAP_ENTRIES_COUNTER	History Map Entries	Total entries inserted into the server's history-mapping table
NNTP_HISTORY_MAP_ENTRIES_PERSEC_COUNTER	History Map Entries/sec	Total entries inserted per second into the server's history-mapping table
NNTP_MAX_ANONYMOUS_COUNTER	Maximum Anonymous Users	The maximum number of anonymous users connected to the server simultaneously

Symbol	Name	Description
NNTP_MAX_ CONNECTIONS_COUNTER	Maximum Connections	The maximum simultaneous connections to the server
NNTP_MAX_ NONANONYMOUS_COUNTER	Maximum NonAnonymous Users	The maximum nonanonymous users connected to the server simultaneously
NNTP_MODERATED_ POSTINGS_FAILED_COUNTER	Moderated Postings Failed	Total moderated postings the server has failed to send to an SMTP server
NNTP_MODERATED_ POSTINGS_SENT_COUNTER	Moderated Postings Sent	Total moderated postings the server has attempted to send to an SMTP server
NNTP_OUTBOUND_ CONNECTS_FAILED_COUNTER	Total Outbound Connections Failed	Total outbound connections that the server has failed to make
NNTP_OUTBOUND_ LOGON_FAILED_COUNTER	Failed Outbound Logons	Total outbound logons that the server has failed to complete
NNTP_SESS_FLOW_ CONTROL_COUNTER	Sessions Flow Controlled	Total client sessions currently in a flow-controlled state in the server
NNTP_TOTAL_ ANONYMOUS_COUNTER	Total Anonymous Users	Cumulative total of anonymous users who have connected to the server
NNTP_TOTAL_ NONANONYMOUS_COUNTER	Total NonAnonymous Users	Cumulative total of nonanonymous users who have connected to the server
NNTP_TOTAL_OUTBOUND_ CONNECTS_COUNTER	Total Outbound Connections	Total outbound connections that have been made by the server
NNTP_TOTAL_PASSIVE_ FEEDS_COUNTER	Total Passive Feeds	Total passive feeds accepted by the server
NNTP_TOTAL_PULL_ FEEDS_COUNTER	Total Push Feeds	Total push feeds made by the server
NNTP_TOTAL_PUSH_ FEEDS_COUNTER	Total Pull Feeds	Total pull feeds made by the server
NNTP_TOTAL_SSL_ CONNECTIONS_COUNTER	Total SSL Connections	Total SSL connections that have been made to the server

continues

Part VIII

App B

Table B.2 Continued

Symbol	Name	Description
NNTP_XOVER_ENTRIES_COUNTER	Xover Entries	Total of xover entries in the xover table of the server
NNTP_XOVER_ENTRIES_PERSEC_COUNTER	Xover Entries/sec	The number of entries per second inserted into the xover table of the server

Table B.3 NNTP Server Client Requests

Symbol	Name	Description
NNTP_CMDS_ARTICLE_COUNTER	Article Commands	Total ARTICLE commands received by the NNTP server since it was last started
NNTP_CMDS_GROUP_COUNTER	Group Commands	Total GROUP commands received by the NNTP server since it was last started
NNTP_CMDS_HELP_COUNTER	Help Commands	Total HELP commands received by the NNTP server since it was last started
NNTP_CMDS_IHAVE_COUNTER	Ihave Commands	Total IHAVE commands received by the NNTP server since it was last started
NNTP_CMDS_LAST_COUNTER	Last Commands	Total LAST commands received by the NNTP server since it was last started
NNTP_CMDS_LIST_COUNTER	List Commands	Total LIST commands received by the NNTP server since it was last started
NNTP_CMDS_NEWGROUPS_COUNTER	Newgroups Commands	Total NEWGROUPS commands received by the NNTP server since it was last started
NNTP_CMDS_NEWNEWS_COUNTER	Newnews Commands	Total NEWNEWS commands received by the NNTP server since it was last started
NNTP_CMDS_NEXT_COUNTER	Next Commands	Total NEXT commands received by the NNTP server since it was last started

Symbol	Name	Description
NNTP_CMDS_PERSEC_ ARTICLE_COUNTER	Article Commands/sec	Total ARTICLE commands per second received by the NNTP server since it was last started
NNTP_CMDS_PERSEC_ GROUP_COUNTER	Group Commands/sec	Total GROUP commands received per second by the NNTP server since it was last started
NNTP_CMDS_PERSEC_ HELP_COUNTER	Help Commands/sec	Number of HELP commands received per second by the NNTP server since it was last started
NNTP_CMDS_PERSEC_ IHAVE_COUNTER	Ihave Commands/sec	Number of IHAVE commands received per second by the NNTP server since it was last started
NNTP_CMDS_PERSEC_ LAST_COUNTER	Last Commands/sec	Number of LAST commands received per second by the NNTP server since it was last started
NNTP_CMDS_PERSEC_ LIST_COUNTER	List Commands/sec	Number of LIST commands received per second by the NNTP server since it was last started
NNTP_CMDS_PERSEC_ COUNTER	Newgroups Commands/sec	Number of NEWGROUPS commands received per second by the NNTP server since it was last started
NNTP_CMDS_PERSEC_ NEWNEWS_COUNTER	Newnews Commands/sec	Number of NEWNEWS commands received per second by the NNTP server since it was last started
NNTP_CMDS_PERSEC_ NEXT_COUNTER	Next Commands/sec	Number of NEXT commands received per second by the NNTP server since it was last started
NNTP_CMDS_PERSEC_ POST_COUNTER	Post Commands/sec	Number of POST commands received per second by the NNTP server since it was last started

Part
VIII

App
B

continues

Table B.3   Continued

Symbol	Name	Description
NNTP_CMDS_PERSEC_ QUIT_COUNTER	Quit Commands/sec	Number of QUIT commands received per second by the NNTP server since it was last started
NNTP_CMDS_PERSEC_ STAT_COUNTER	Stat Commands/sec	Number of STAT commands received per second by the NNTP server since it was last started
NNTP_CMDS_ POST_COUNTER	Post Commands	Total POST commands received by the NNTP server since it was last started
NNTP_CMDS_ QUIT_COUNTER	Quit Commands	Total QUIT commands received by the NNTP server since it was last started
NNTP_CMDS_ STAT_COUNTER	Stat Commands	Number of STAT commands received by the NNTP server since it was last started
NNTP_LOGON_ ATTEMPTS_COUNTER	Logon Attempts	Total logon attempts that have been made to the NNTP server
NNTP_LOGON_ATTEMPTS_ PERSEC_COUNTER	Logon Attempts/sec	Number of logon attempts per second that have been made to the NNTP server
NNTP_LOGON_ FAILURES_COUNTER	Logon Failures	Total logons that have failed
NNTP_LOGON_FAILURES_ PERSEC_COUNTER	Logon Failures/sec	Number of logons per second that have failed
NNTP_REVERSE_ ATTEMPTS_COUNTER	Reverse Authentication Attempts	Total reverse AUTHINFOs made by the NNTP server
NNTP_REVERSE_ATTEMPTS_ PERSEC_COUNTER	Reverse Authentication Attempts/sec	Number of reverse AUTHINFOs made per second by the NNTP server
NNTP_REVERSE_ FAILURES_COUNTER	Reverse Authentication Failures	Total failed reverse AUTHINFOs made by the NNTP server

Symbol	Name	Description
NNTP_REVERSE_FAILURES_ PERSEC_COUNTER	Reverse Authentication Failures/sec	Number of failed reverse AUTHINFOs made per second by the NNTP server

Mail Server

Mail Server contains two categories of Performance Monitor counters, the Component SMTP and Component POP3 Performance Monitor counters, which are detailed in Tables B.4 and B.5.

Table B.4 Component SMTP Performance Monitor Counters

Name	Description
Bytes Sent Total	The total number of bytes that have been sent
Bytes Sent/sec	The rate per second that bytes are sent
Bytes Received Total	The total number of bytes that have been received
Bytes Received/sec	The rate per second that bytes are received
Bytes Total	The total number of bytes that have been sent and received
Bytes Total/sec	The rate that bytes are sent and received
Message Bytes Sent Total	The total number of bytes that have been sent in messages
Message Bytes Sent/sec	The rate per second that bytes are sent in messages
Message Bytes Received Total	The total number of bytes that have been received in messages
Message Bytes Received/sec	The rate per second that bytes are received in messages
Message Bytes Total	The total number of bytes that have been sent and received in messages
Message Bytes Total/sec	The rate per second that bytes are sent and received in messages
Messages Received Total	The total number of messages that have been accepted

continues

Table B.4 Continued

Name	Description
Message Received/sec	The rate per second that messages are being received
Avg Recipients/msg Received	The average number of recipients per inbound message
% Recipients Local	The percent of messages that will be successfully delivered to local recipients
% Recipients Remote	The percent of messages that will be successfully delivered to remote recipients
Messages Refused for Size	Total messages that were rejected because they were too big
Messages Refused for Address Objects	Total messages that were refused because of no address objects
Messages Refused for Mail Objects	Total messages that were refused because of no mail objects
Messages Delivered Total	Total messages delivered to local mailboxes
Messages Delivered/sec	The rate per second that messages are delivered to local mailboxes
Message Delivery Retries	Total local deliveries that were retried
Avg Retries/msg Delivered	The average number of retries per local delivery
NDR's Generated	Total non-delivery reports that have been generated
Local Queue Length	Total messages in the local queue
Retry Queue Length	Total messages in the retry queue
Number of MailFiles Open	The ratio of handles to open mail files
Number of QueueFiles Open	The ratio of handles to open queue files
Messages Sent Total	The number of outbound messages sent
Messages Sent/sec	The number of outbound messages sent per second
Message Send Retries	Total outbound message sends that were retried
Avg Retries/msg Sent	Average retries per outbound message sent
Avg Recipients/msg Sent	The average recipients per outbound messages
Remote Queue Length	Total messages in the remote queue

Name	Description
DNS Queries Total	Total of DNS lookups
DNS Queries/sec	The number of DNS lookups per second
Inbound Connections Total	The total inbound connections received
Inbound Connections Current	The total number of client sessions currently connected
Outbound Connections Total	The total outbound connections attempted
Outbound Connections Current	The connections outbound currently
Outbound Connections Refused	Total outbound connection attempts that were refused by remote sites
Total Connection Errors	The total number of connection errors
Connection Errors/sec	The connection errors per second

Table B.5 Performance Monitor Counters

Name	Description
Authentication Attempts	Total authentication requests issued using the AUTH command
Authentication Attempts/sec	The number of incoming authentication requests per second
Bytes Received Total	The number of bytes received
Bytes Received/sec	The number of bytes received per second
Bytes Sent Total	The number of bytes sent
Bytes Sent/sec	The rate that bytes are sent per second
Bytes Total	The number of bytes sent and received
Bytes Total/sec	The number of bytes sent and received per second
Challenge/Response Auth Attempts	Total attempts to open a session using the AUTH authentication method
Challenge/Response Auth Attempts/sec	The attempts per second to open a session with the AUTH method
Challenge/Response Auth Failures	The number of failures to open a session with the AUTH method

continues

Part

VIII

App

B

Table B.5 Continued

Name	Description
Clear-text Auth Attempts	Total attempts to open a session with the USER/PASS authentication method
Clear-text Auth Attempts/sec	The attempts per second to open a session with the USER/PASS method
Clear-text Auth Failures	Total failures to open a session with the USER/PASS method
Current Async IO Buffers	The number of asynchronous I/O buffers currently in use
Current Connections	The number of connections currently in use
Current Mail Bags	The number of mail bags in use currently by connected clients
Delete Message Requests	Total DELE command requests to delete messages
Delete Message Requests/sec	Total incoming message-delete requests per second
Deleted Messages	Total messages deleted with the DELE command
Deleted Messages/sec	The number of messages deleted per second
Digest Attempts	Total digest-based authentication requests issued, using the APOP command
Digest Attempts/sec	The number of incoming digest-based authentication requests per second
Download Message Requests	Total RETR command requests to retrieve message
Download Message Requests/sec	The number of incoming retrieve message requests per second
Downloaded Messages	Total messages retrieved with the RETR command
Downloaded Messages/sec	The number of messages retrieved per second
Headers Downloaded	Total headers downloaded with the HEAD command

Name	Description
Headers Downloaded/sec	The number of headers downloaded per second
Inbound Connections	The number of inbound connections received
Inbound Connections Current	The number of connections that are currently inbound
Inbox Open Attempts	Total attempts to open an inbox
Inbox Open Attempts/sec	The number of attempts per second to open an inbox
Inbox Open Failures	Total failures to open an inbox
Invalid Command Requests	Total invalid or unsupported requests
Invalid Command Requests/sec	The number of incoming invalid or unsupported requests per second
Maximum Async I/O Buffers	The maximum number of asynchronous I/O buffers used
Maximum Connections	The maximum number of connections
Maximum Mail Bags	The maximum number of times all connected clients have collected mail messages
Message Bytes Sent Total	Total bytes sent in messages
Message Bytes Sent/sec	The number of bytes sent in messages per second
Message List Requests	Total LIST command requests for message information
Message List Requests/sec	The number of incoming message list requests per second
Message Stats Requests	Total STAT command requests for messages stats
Message Stats Requests/sec	The number of incoming message stats requests per second
No Operation Requests	Total of no-operation (NOOP) command requests
No Operation Requests/sec	The number of incoming NOOP requests per second

continues

Part

VIII

App

B

Table B.5 Continued

Name	Description
Open Message Files	Total files opened by POP3 Server
Password Attempts	Total pass commands issued with the PASS command
Password Attempts/sec	The number of incoming password attempts per second
Protocol Errors	Total protocol errors received
Protocol Errors/sec	The number of protocol errors that are received per second
Quit Attempts	Total quit commands issued with the QUIT command
Quit Attempts/sec	The number of incoming quit requests per second
Reset Requests	Total requests with the RSET command to reset the deleted messages
Reset Requests/sec	The number of incoming reset requests per second
Unique ID Listing Requests	Total UIDL command requests to list unique message IDs
Unique ID Listing Requests/sec	The number of incoming message unique ID requests per second
User Requests	Total user commands issued with the USER command
User Requests/sec	The number of incoming user commands per second

Chat Server

The Microsoft Internet Chat Server includes counters for monitoring the flow of information; that tally local and remote client and server connections and disconnections; the rate of collisions and errors; available memory and other performance issues. The counters are described in Table B.6.

Table B.6 Internet Chat Server Performance Monitor Counters

Name	Description
Channel Creates/sec	The number of new channels created per second
Channel Deletes/sec	The number of channels deleted per second
Channel Joins/sec	The number of clients joining channels per second
Channel Parts/sec	The number of clients leaving channels per second
Client Bytes Received/sec	The number of bytes received from client connections per second
Client Bytes Sent/sec	The number of bytes sent to client connections per second
Client Connections/sec	The number of client connects per second
Client Disconnects/sec	The number of client disconnects per second
Client Messages Received/sec	The number of messages received from client connections per second
Client Messages Sent/sec	The number of messages sent to client connections per second
Current Anonymous Clients	The total of currently connected anonymous clients
Current Authenticated Users	The total currently connected authenticated users
Current Channels Available	The total channels available currently
Current Direct Servers	The total servers currently connected directly to this chat server
Current Invisible Clients	The total invisible clients connected currently
Current Local Clients	The total local clients connected to this chat server currently
Current Members Available	The total members available on the chat server currently
Current Remote Clients	The total clients connected currently as remote proxies from another chat server
Current Remote Servers	The total servers connected currently as remote proxies from another chat server

Part

VIII

App

B

continues

Table B.6   Continued

Name	Description
Current Servers	Total local and remote servers connected to the chat network currently
Current Unknown Clients	Total clients in the process of logging on but not yet identified by protocol type
Input-Saturation Client Disconnects	Total clients that have been disconnected due to input flooding
Memory Allocated	The bytes of memory currently allocated by the chat server
Operator-Killed Client Disconnects	The total clients disconnected due to an operator-kill action
Output Buffers	The total output buffers that are in the queue for transmission by the chat server
Output-Saturation Client Disconnects	The total clients disconnected because of output saturation
Server Bytes Received/sec	The number of bytes per second that have been received from server connections
Server Bytes Sent/sec	The number of bytes per second that have been sent to server connections
Server Input Pegged	Total times the server input buffer was filled on read
Server Messages Received/sec	The number of messages per second that have been received from server connections
Server Messages Sent/sec	The number of messages per second that have been sent to server connections
Socket Failures	The total of socket failures
Socket-Error Client Disconnects	Total clients disconnected due to a socket error
Socket-Error Server Disconnects	Total servers disconnected due to a socket error
Timeout Server Disconnects	Total servers disconnected due to a timeout
Timeout-Related Client Disconnects	Total clients disconnected due to a timeout
Total Authentication Failures	Total of authentication failures
Total Channel Collisions	Total channel collisions that have occurred on the chat server

Name	Description
Total Channel Creates	Total channels that have been created
Total Channel Deletes	Total channels that have been deleted
Total Channel Joins	Total clients that have joined channels
Total Channel Parts	Total clients that have parted channels
Total Client Bytes Received	Total bytes that have been received from client connections
Total Client Bytes Sent	Total bytes that have been sent to client connections
Total Client Connects	Total clients that have been connected
Total Client Disconnects	Total clients that have been disconnected
Total Client Messages Received	Total messages that have been received from client connections
Total Client Messages Sent	Total messages that have been sent to client connections
Total Connection Attempts	Total connections that have been attempted
Total Members Created	The cumulative total of members that have been created
Total Nick (Alias) Collisions	The total nick, or alias, collisions that have occurred
Total Operator Kills	The total operator kills that have been issued
Total Remote Servers	The cumulative total of servers connections that have ever been made as a remote proxy from another chat server
Total Server Bytes Received	The number of bytes that have been received from server connections
Total Server Bytes Sent	The number of bytes that have been sent to server connections
Total Server Disconnects	The number of servers that have been disconnected due to timeouts and errors
Total Server Messages Received	The number of messages that have been received from server connections
Total Server Messages Sent	The number of messages that have been sent to server connections

Locator Server

Internet Locator Server Performance Monitor counters are utilized through the "LDAP Server" perfmon object. The counters are described in Table B.7 that follows.

Table B.7   Internet Locator Server Performance Monitor Counters

Symbol	Name	Description
LDAP_ILS_APPS	ILS Applications	Total of ILS application structures allocated
LDAP_ILS_APPS_PROPS	ILS Apps Properties Requests	Total of ILS applications that have set properties
LDAP_ILS_APPS_PROPS_PER_SEC	ILS Apps Properties Requests/sec	The number of ILS applications per second that are setting properties
LDAP_ILS_ASSOCS	ILS Associations	Total of ILS association structures allocated
LDAP_ILS_DIRECTORIES	ILS Directory Requests	Total times an ILS directory has been called
LDAP_ILS_DIRECTORIES_PER_SEC	ILS Directory Requests/sec	The number of times per second that an ILS directory is being called
LDAP_ILS_REFRESH_USERS	Refresh ILS User Information	Total times the ILS user information has been refreshed
LDAP_ILS_REFRESH_USERS_PER_SEC	Refresh ILS User Information/sec	The frequency with which ILS user information is being refreshed
LDAP_ILS_REGISTER_APPS	ILS Apps Registrations	Total ILS applications registered in the database currently
LDAP_ILS_REGISTER_APPS_PER_SEC	ILS Apps Registrations/sec	The number of ILS applications being registered in the database per second
LDAP_ILS_REGISTER_USERS	ILS User Registrations	Total ILS users registered in the database currently

Symbol	Name	Description
LDAP_ILS_REGISTER_ USERS_PER_SEC	ILS User Registrations/sec	The number of ILS users being registered in the database per second
LDAP_ILS_RESOLVES	ILS Resolve Requests	Total requests for ILS name resolution
LDAP_ILS_RESOLVES_ PER_SEC	ILS Resolve Requests/sec	The number of requests per second for ILS name resolution
LDAP_ILS_ UNREGISTER_APPS	ILS Apps Unregistration Requests	Total requests to remove ILS applications from the database
LDAP_ILS_UNREGISTER_ APPS_PER_SEC	ILS Apps Unregistration Requests/sec	The number of requests per second to remove ILS applications from the database
LDAP_ILS_ UNREGISTER_USERS	ILS User Unregistration Requests	Total requests to remove ILS users from the database
LDAP_ILS_UNREGISTER_ USERS_PER_SEC ILS	ILS User Unregistration Requests/sec	The number of requests per second to remove users from the database
LDAP_ILS_USER_PROPS	ILS User Properties Requests	Total of ILS users that have set properties
LDAP_ILS_USER_ PROPS_PER_SEC	ILS User Properties Requests/sec	The number of ILS users setting properties per second
LDAP_ILS_USERS	ILS Users	Total ILS user structures allocated
LDAP_ILS_USERS_ TIMED_OUT	ILS Users Timed Out	Total ILS users who were timed out
LDAP_ILS_USERS_ TIMED_OUT_PER_SEC	ILS Users Timed Out/sec	The number of ILS users being timed out per second

Part
VIII

App
B

Content Replication Server

The Content Replication Server uses the following Performance Monitor counters for its components and operations, as shown in Table B.8.

Table B.8   The Content Replication Server Performance Monitor Counters

Symbol	Name	Explanation
CRS_API_CALLS_PER_SEC	API Calls/sec	The number of API calls per second
CRS_API_CALLS_TOTAL	API Calls Total	Total API calls since the service started
CRS_AUTH_ATTEMPTS_COUNTER	Replication AUTH Attempts	Total attempts to start a replication
CRS_AUTH_FAILURE_COUNTER	Replication AUTH Failures	The number of failures to start a replication
CRS_AUTH_PER_SEC_COUNTER	Replication AUTH Attempts/sec	The number of attempts per second to start a replication
CRS_BYTES_RCVD_PER_SEC_COUNTER	Bytes Received/sec	The number of bytes received per second
CRS_BYTES_RCVD_TOTAL_COUNTER	Bytes Received Total	The total of bytes received
CRS_BYTES_SENT_PER_SEC_COUNTER	Bytes Sent/sec	The number of bytes sent per second
CRS_BYTES_SENT_TOTAL_COUNTER	Bytes Sent Total	The total of bytes sent
CRS_BYTES_TOTAL_COUNTER	Bytes Total	The total of bytes sent and received
CRS_BYTES_TOTAL_PER_SEC_COUNTER	Bytes Total/sec	The number of bytes sent and received per second
CRS_CONN_LOST	Number of Lost Connections	Total lost connections recorded by CRS
CRS_CONN_LOST_PER_SEC	Number of Lost Connections/sec	The number per second of lost connections recorded by CRS
CRS_DIR_CHG_NOTIFY	Directory Change Notifications	Total directory change notifications received since the service was started
CRS_DIR_CHG_NOTIFY_PER_SEC	Directory Change Notifications/sec	The number of directory change notifications received per second

Symbol	Name	Explanation
CRS_ERR_PER_SEC_COUNTER	Errors/sec	The number of protocol errors received per second
CRS_ERR_TOTAL_COUNTER	Errors Total	Total protocol errors received
CRS_FILES_DEL_COUNTER	Files Deleted Total	Total of files deleted
CRS_FILES_DEL_PER_SEC_COUNTER	Files Deleted/sec	The number of files deleted per second
CRS_FILES_RECV_COUNTER	Files Received Total	Total of files received
CRS_FILES_RECV_PER_SEC_COUNTER	Files Received/sec	The number of files received per second
CRS_FILES_SENT_COUNTER	Files Sent Total	Total of files sent
CRS_FILES_SENT_PER_SEC_COUNTER	Files Sent/sec	The number of files sent per second
CRS_HEART_BEAT_COUNTER	Service Alive	Indicates whether the service is still processing requests
CRS_HEART_BEAT_SEC	Service Alive/sec	Indicates every second whether the service is alive
CRS_PRI_API_CALLS_PER_SEC	Privileged API Calls/sec	Total privileged API calls per second
CRS_PRI_API_CALLS_TOTAL	Privileged API Calls Total	Total privileged API calls made since the service was started
CRS_REPL_CONCURR_COUNTER	Maximum Concurrent Replications	The maximum number of concurrently running replications
CRS_REPL_CURR_COUNTER	Connections Current	The number of current connections
CRS_REPL_RETRANS	Retransmits	The retransmits that have occurred since the service was started
CRS_REPL_TIME	Replication Time	The duration, in seconds, of the last replication

Part

VIII

App

B

continues

Table B.8   Continued

Symbol	Name	Explanation
CRS_REPL_TOTAL_COUNTER	Connections Total	Total connections received
OBJECT_CRS	Content Replication Service	Represents the global counters for content replication

Personalization Server

The Personalization Server makes use of Performance Monitor counters for the User Property Database and the Vote and Sendmail components which are provided here.

User Property Database

Table B.9 shows you the User Property Database counters.

Table B.9   Performance Monitor Counters for the User Property Database

Counter Name	Description
Total Reads Attempted	Total attempted User Property Database reads that have been performed
Total Reads	Total User Property Database reads that have been performed
Attempted reads/sec	The number per second of attempted User Property Database reads
Reads/sec	The number per second of User Property Database reads
Total Writes Attempted	Total attempts to write to the User Property Database
Total Writes	Total User Property Database writes that have been performed
Attempted writes/sec	Number of attempts per second to write to the User Property Database
Writes/sec	The number of User Property Database writes per second
Total GUID Creates	Total Globally Unique IDs (GUIDs) that have been created for the first time
GUID creates/sec	The number of new users added per second

Counter Name	Description
Total File Creates	Total new user files that have been created
File creates/sec	The number of new user files created per second
Last User File Size	Average size of the User Property file written to disk during the last operation
Max. User File Size	The largest User Property file that has been written to disk
Last Property Count	Total user properties stored in a user file during the last operation
Max. Property Count	The largest number of user properties that have been stored in a user file
Last Properties Read	Total user properties accessed in the last operation
Max. Properties Read	The largest number of user properties read per transaction
Last Properties Changed	The number of user properties changed during the last operation
Max. Properties Changed	The largest number of user properties changed in a transaction
Current Connections	Total Property database reads or writes being processed currently
Max Connections	The largest number of User Property Database reads or writes that have been simultaneously processed
Last Read Time	The amount of time that it took to read the user properties into memory in the last operation
Max Read Time	The longest that it has ever taken to read the user properties into memory
Last Write Time	The length of time that it took to write the user properties to disk in the last operation
Max Write Time	The longest time it has taken to write the user properties to disk
Total Error Count	Total errors that have occurred

Vote and Sendmail Components

Table B.10 details the Voting and Sendmail Performance Monitor counters.

Table B.10   The Voting and Sendmail Performance Monitor Counters

Counter Name	Description
Avg Latency	The average number of milliseconds that this method takes to execute
Max Latency	The longest that this method has taken to execute
GeNames/sec	The average number of times per second that a script has referred to this method
Total GetNames	The total number of times that a script has referred to this method
Invokes/sec	The average number of times per second that a script has called this method
Total Invokes	The total number of times that a script has called this method

Membership System

The role of the Membership System is to provide support services for MSIC components such as the Microsoft Commercial Internet System News Server, Internet Address Book Server, and Microsoft Commercial Internet System Mail Server. Therefore, many of the necessary performance monitor counters are provided by these applications rather than Membership System. Membership System includes performance counters for the Membership Agent on the Membership Backend, for Membership Broker, and for the Membership Simulator.

Membership Agent Counters

The Membership Agent maintains counters under the Membership Agent Object, which utilizes the following Performance Counters (see Table B.11).

Table B.11   Membership Agent Object Performance Monitor Counters

Symbol	Name	Notes
COUNTER_SICILY_ALTERED_PACKETS	Altered Packets Received	Number of packets with modified contents
COUNTER_SICILY_BILL_REQS_FAILED	Billing Request Failures	Number of billing events rejected by the Membership Agent

Symbol	Name	Notes
COUNTER_SICILY_BILL_REQS_PER_SECOND	Billing Requests Received/sec	Number of billing requests received per second. Microsoft suggests that if this rate remains at more than 10-20, service is overloading the billing system submission system.
COUNTER_SICILY_BILL_REQS_RECEIVED	Billing Requests Received	Total number of billing request events received
COUNTER_SICILY_BILL_REQS_SUCCEEDED	Billing Request Successes	Total successful billing events received
COUNTER_SICILY_CONNS_TIMED_OUT	Connection Time-outs	Number of Brokers failing to authenticate within 30 seconds of connection
COUNTER_SICILY_CURRENT_ICP_CONNECTIONS	Brokers Connected	Number of Brokers currently connected
COUNTER_SICILY_FAILED_AUTHENTICATION_COUNT	Logon Operation Failures	Number of failed Broker logons
COUNTER_SICILY_GET_RIGHTS_COUNT	Retrieve-Rights Requests Received	Total retrieving-account-rights requests being received
COUNTER_SICILY_GET_RIGHTS_FAILURES_COUNT	Retrieve-Rights Request Failures	Total failed retrieving-account-rights requests
COUNTER_SICILY_GET_RIGHTS_FAILURES_PER_SECOND	Retrieve-Rights Request Failures/sec	The number of retrieving-account-rights request failures per second
COUNTER_SICILY_GET_RIGHTS_PASSTHRU_COUNT	Retrieve-Rights bypass Cache	Total retrieving account-rights requests that pass directly to the database, bypassing the cache
COUNTER_SICILY_GET_RIGHTS_PASSTHRU_PER_SECOND	Retrieve-Rights bypass Cache/sec	The number per second of retrieving-account-rights requests that pass directly to the database, bypassing the cache

continues

Table B.11   Continued

Symbol	Name	Notes
COUNTER_SICILY_GET_RIGHTS_PER_SECOND	Retrieve-Rights Requests Received/sec	The number of retrieving-account-rights requests being received per second
COUNTER_SICILY_ICPAUTHS_FAILED	Broker Authorization Failures	Total number of failed authentications
COUNTER_SICILY_ICPAUTHS_FAILED_PER_SECOND	Broker Authorization Failures/sec	The number of failed authentications per second. Sustained positive values could be an indication of attempts to invade the system.
COUNTER_SICILY_ICPCONNECTIONS_DROPPED	Broker Connections Dropped	Total number of Broker connections that have been closed by the Membership Agent
COUNTER_SICILY_ICPCONNECTIONS_DROPPED_PER_SECOND	Broker Connections Dropped/sec	Number per second of Broker connections closed by the Membership Agent.
COUNTER_SICILY_ICPPERMANENT_ATTEMPTS	Logon Attempts from Permanently Blacklisted Brokers	The Membership Agent shuts down the connection whenever such an attempt is detected
COUNTER_SICILY_ICPTEMPORARY_ATTEMPTS	Logon Attempts from Temporarily Blacklisted Brokers	The Membership Agent shuts down the connection whenever such an attempt is detected
COUNTER_SICILY_MSEC_PER_FAILURE	<Not assigned>	Reserved for Future Counters
COUNTER_SICILY_MSEC_PER_REQUEST	<Not assigned>	Reserved for Future Counters
COUNTER_SICILY_MSEC_PER_SUCCESS	<Not assigned>	Reserved for Future Counters
COUNTER_SICILY_NUMBER_OF_FAILED_LOGINS	Logon Operation Failures/sec	The number per second of user authorizations that fail

Symbol	Name	Notes
COUNTER_SICILY_ NUMBER_OF_REQUESTS	Requests Processed/sec	Number of requests processed per second. Microsoft suggests that a sustained rate in excess of 90 is a heavy load of requests.
COUNTER_SICILY_NUMBER_ OF_SUCCESSFUL_LOGINS	Logon Operation Successes/sec	Number of successful logons completed per second
COUNTER_SICILY_ NUMBER_OF_THREADS	Active Threads	Number of processing threads running currently
COUNTER_SICILY_ OUTSTANDING_BUFFERS	Outstanding Buffers	Total Broker writes waiting to complete
COUNTER_SICILY_ OUTSTANDING_CONTEXTS	Outstanding Contexts	Total Broker contexts waiting to complete
COUNTER_SICILY_ REUSED_ADDRS	Existing Connections Dropped	Number of times a Broker tried to connect to the server while already connected
COUNTER_SICILY_SUCCESS_ AUTHENTICATION_COUNT	Logon Operation Successes	Total number of successful logons
COUNTER_SICILY_TOTAL_ CURRUPT_PACKETS_RECEIVED	Corrupt Packets Received	Cumulative total of corrupt packets received from Brokers
COUNTER_SICILY_TOTAL_ ICP_CONNECTIONS	Total Brokers Connected	Cumulative total of unique Brokers that have connected
COUNTER_SICILY_TOTAL_ INVALID_PASSWORDS	Invalid Passwords Received	Cumulative total of invalid passwords received
COUNTER_SICILY_TOTAL_ INVALID_USERNAMES	Invalid User Names Received	Cumulative total of invalid user names received

continues

Part
VIII

App
B

Table B.11 Continued

Symbol	Name	Notes
COUNTER_SICILY_TOTAL_REQUESTS_RECEIVED	Buffers Received	Total number of requests received
COUNTER_SICILY_TOTAL_RESPONSES_RECEIVED	Responses Sent	Cumulative total of Broker responses sent

Member Services/System Admin

The Member Service applications incorporate Performance counters under the Registration Object. Table B.12 is a list of available counters.

Table B.12 The Member Service Registration Object Performance Monitor Counters

Symbol	Name	Notes
SSO_LATENCY_INVOKES_AVG	Avg Latency	Average time taken by the execution of this method
SSO_LATENCY_INVOKES_MAX	Max Latency	Maximum time taken by the execution of this method
SSO_NUM_GETNAMES	GetNames/sec	Number of IDispatch::GetNamesOfIDs calls per method per second
SSO_NUM_GETNAMES_TOTAL	Total GetNames	Total of IDispatch::GetNamesOfIDs calls per method
SSO_NUM_INVOKES	Invokes/sec	The number of IDispatch::Invoke() calls per method per second
SSO_NUM_INVOKES_TOTAL	Total Invokes	Total of IDispatch::Invoke() calls per method
SSO_PERF_OBJECT	SignUp	SignUp Component Statistics

Membership System Admin

System Administration maintains counters under several SysAdmin Objects which are listed and described in the following sections.

AccessPlan Object   Table B.13 shows you the performance counters that are contained in the AccessPlan Object.

Table B.13   AccessPlan Object Performance Monitor Counters

Symbol	Name	Notes
SSO_LATENCY_INVOKES_AVG	Avg Latency	Average time taken by the execution of this method
SSO_LATENCY_INVOKES_MAX	Max Latency	Maximum time taken by the execution of this method
SSO_NUM_GETNAMES	GetNames/sec	Number of IDispatch::GetNamesOfIDs calls, per method, per second
SSO_NUM_GETNAMES_TOTAL	Total GetNames	Total of IDispatch::GetNamesOfIDs calls per method
SSO_NUM_INVOKES	Invokes/sec	Number of IDispatch::Invoke() calls per method per second
SSO_NUM_INVOKES_TOTAL	Total Invokes	Total of IDispatch::Invoke() calls per method
SSO_PERF_OBJECT	SignUp	Access Plan Component Statistics

SecToken Object   Table B.14 presents the performance counters that are contained in the SecToken Object.

Table B.14   SecToken Object Performance Monitor Counters

Symbol	Name	Notes
SSO_LATENCY_INVOKES_AVG	Avg Latency	Average time taken by the execution of this method
SSO_LATENCY_INVOKES_MAX	Max Latency	Maximum time taken by the execution of this method
SSO_NUM_GETNAMES	GetNames/sec	Number of IDispatch::GetNamesOfIDs calls, per method, per second

continues

Table B.14   Continued

Symbol	Name	Notes
SSO_NUM_GETNAMES_TOTAL	Total GetNames	Total number of IDispatch::GetNamesOfIDs calls per method
SSO_NUM_INVOKES	Invokes/sec	The number of IDispatch::Invoke() calls per method per second
SSO_NUM_INVOKES_TOTAL	Total Invokes	Total of IDispatch::Invoke() calls per method
SSO_PERF_OBJECT	SignUp	Security Token Component Statistics

UserAccount Object   The following performance counters are included in the UserAccount Object (see Table B.15):

Table B.15   UserAccount Object Performance Monitor Counters

Symbol	Name	Notes
SSO_LATENCY_INVOKES_AVG	Avg Latency	Average length of time taken by the execution of this method
SSO_LATENCY_INVOKES_MAX	Max Latency	Maximum length of time taken by the execution of this method
SSO_NUM_GETNAMES	GetNames/sec	Number of IDispatch::GetNamesOfIDs calls per method per second
SSO_NUM_GETNAMES_TOTAL	Total GetNames	Total of IDispatch::GetNamesOfIDs calls per method
SSO_NUM_INVOKES	Invokes/sec	Number of IDispatch::Invoke() calls per method per second
SSO_NUM_INVOKES_TOTAL	Total Invokes	Total of IDispatch::Invoke() calls per method
SSO_PERF_OBJECT	SignUp	User Account Component Statistics

UserGroup Object   The UserGroup Object contains the following performance counters, as shown in Table B.16.

Table B.16   UserGroup Object Performance Monitor Counters

Symbol	Name	Notes
SSO_LATENCY_INVOKES_AVG	Avg Latency	Average time taken by the execution of this method
SSO_LATENCY_INVOKES_MAX	Max Latency	Maximum time taken by the execution of this method
SSO_NUM_GETNAMES	GetNames/sec	Number of IDispatch::GetNamesOfIDs calls per method per second
SSO_NUM_GETNAMES_TOTAL	Total GetNames	Total of IDispatch::GetNamesOfIDs calls per method
SSO_NUM_INVOKES	Invokes/sec	Number of IDispatch::Invoke() calls per method per second
SSO_NUM_INVOKES_TOTAL	Total Invokes	Total number of IDispatch::Invoke() calls per method
SSO_PERF_OBJECT	SignUp	User Group Component Statistics

Address Book Server

The Address Book Server uses these Performance Monitor counters (see Table B.17).

Table B.17   Address Book Server Performance Monitor Counters

Symbol	Name	Description
LDAP_BYTES_RCVD_PER_SEC	Bytes Received/sec	The number of bytes received per second
LDAP_BYTES_RCVD_TTL	Bytes Received	The number of bytes received
LDAP_BYTES_SENT_PER_SEC	Bytes Sent/sec	The number of bytes sent per second

continues

Table B.17   Continued

Symbol	Name	Description
LDAP_BYTES_SENT_TTL	Bytes Sent	The number of bytes sent
LDAP_CONNECTIONS_CURRENT	Current Connections	The number of connections currently active to the LDAP server
LDAP_CONNECTIONS_TOTAL	Connections	The total number of Received LDAP server connections that have been received
LDAP_CREATES	Creates Processed	The total number of ABS database create operations processed
LDAP_CREATES_PER_SEC	Creates Processed/sec	The average number of ABS database create operations processed per second
LDAP_DELETES	Deletes Processed	The total number of ABS database delete operations processed
LDAP_DELETES_PER_SEC	Deletes Processed/sec	The average number of ABS database delete operations processed per second
LDAP_ILS_APPS	ILS Applications	The number of ILS application structures allocated
LDAP_ILS_APPS_PROPS	ILS Apps Properties Requests	The number of ILS applications that have set properties
LDAP_ILS_APPS_ PROPS_PER_SEC	ILS Apps Properties Requests/sec	The rate that ILS applications are setting properties

Symbol	Name	Description
LDAP_ILS_ASSOCS	ILS Associations	The number of ILS association structures allocated
LDAP_ILS_DIRECTORIES	ILS Directory Requests	The number of times an ILS directory has been called
LDAP_ILS_DIRECTORIES_PER_SEC	ILS Directory Requests/sec	The rate that an ILS directory is being called
LDAP_ILS_REFRESH_USERS	Refresh ILS User Information	The number of times the ILS user information has been refreshed
LDAP_ILS_REFRESH_USERS_PER_SEC	Refresh ILS User Information/sec	The rate that ILS user information is being refreshed
LDAP_ILS_REGISTER_APPS	ILS Apps Registrations	The number of ILS applications currently registered in the database
LDAP_ILS_REGISTER_APPS_PER_SEC	ILS Apps Registrations/sec	The rate that ILS applications are being registered in the database
LDAP_ILS_REGISTER_USERS	ILS User Registrations	The number of ILS users currently registered in the database
LDAP_ILS_REGISTER_USERS_PER_SEC	ILS User Registrations/sec	The rate that ILS users are being registered in the database
LDAP_ILS_RESOLVES	ILS Resolve Requests	The number of requests for ILS name resolution

Part
VIII

App
B

continues

Table B.17 Continued

Symbol	Name	Description
LDAP_ILS_RESOLVES_PER_SEC	ILS Resolve Requests/sec	The rate of requests for ILS name resolution
LDAP_ILS_UNREGISTER_APPS	ILS Apps Unregistration Requests	The number of requests to remove ILS applications from the database
LDAP_ILS_UNREGISTER_APPS_PER_SEC	ILS Apps Unregistration Requests/sec	The rate of requests to remove ILS applications from the database
LDAP_ILS_UNREGISTER_USERS	ILS User Unregistration Requests	The number of requests to remove ILS users from the database
LDAP_ILS_UNREGISTER_USERS_PER_SEC	ILS User Unregistration Requests/sec	The rate of requests to remove ILS users from the database
LDAP_ILS_USER_PROPS	ILS User Properties Requests	The number of ILS users that have set properties
LDAP_ILS_USER_PROPS_PER_SEC	ILS User Properties Requests/sec	The rate that ILS users are setting properties
LDAP_ILS_USERS	ILS Users	The number of ILS user structures allocated
LDAP_ILS_USERS_TIMED_OUT	ILS Users Timed Out	The number of ILS users who were timed out
LDAP_ILS_USERS_TIMED_OUT_PER_SEC	ILS Users Timed Out/sec	The rate ILS users are being timed out
LDAP_MODIFIES	Modifies Processed	The total number of ABS database modify operations processed

Symbol	Name	Description
LDAP_MODIFIES_PER_SEC	Modifies Processed/sec	The average number of ABS database modify operations processed per second
LDAP_QUERY_NOT_ALLOWED	Query Form Not Allowed	Number of queries not serviced because the query was not in a valid form
LDAP_QUERY_NOT_FOUND	Query Not Found	Number of queries that resulted in the search item not being found
LDAP_QUERY_TOO_BROAD	Query Too-Broad	Number of queries not serviced because the result set would be too large
LDAP_QUERY_TOTAL	Queries Received	The total number of ABS database queries performed by the server
LDAP_QUERY_TOTAL_PER_SEC	Total Queries/sec	The rate that the server is processing ABS database queries
LDAP_REQUEST_QUEUE_LENGTH	Queue Length	The number of requests currently waiting in the queue
LDAP_WP_AUTHORIZATION_FAILURES	WP Authorization Failures	The total number of White Pages authorization failures

Part VIII

App B

Proxy Server

When Microsoft Proxy Server is installed on a new installation of Windows NT Server, three additional Performance Monitor objects are created:

■ *Web Proxy Server Cache* This object type includes counters specific to URL caching performed by the Web Proxy service.

- *Web Proxy Server Service*   This object type includes counters specific to the Web Proxy Server service.
- *WinSock Proxy Server*   This object type includes counters specific to the WinSock Proxy Server service.

These three Performance Monitor objects contain all of the additional performance counters that are added for monitoring Microsoft Proxy Server.

The counters in the Web Proxy Server Cache object include counters specific to URL caching performed by the Web Proxy service. Table B.18 describes those counters.

Table B.18   Web Proxy Server Cache Performance Monitor Counters

Name	Description
Active Refresh Bytes Rate	The number of bytes per second retrieved from the Internet to refresh in advance the popular URLs in the URL cache on disk
Active URL Refresh Rate	The number per second of popular URLs in the cache that are preemptively refreshed from remote URL sources on the Internet
Bytes Committed Rate	The number of bytes per second committed to storage in the URL cache
Bytes in Cache	Total bytes in the URL cache currently
Bytes Retrieved Rate	The number of bytes per second retrieved from disk storage in the URL cache
Max Bytes Cached	The maximum bytes that have been stored in the cache
Max URLs Cached	The maximum URLs that have been stored in the cache
Total Actively Refreshed URLs	The cumulative total of popular URLs in the cache that have been preemptively refreshed from the Internet
Total Bytes Actively Refreshed	The cumulative total of bytes retrieved from the Internet to preemptively refresh popular URLs in the cache
Total Bytes Cached	The cumulative total of bytes stored in the URL cache
Total Bytes Retrieved	The cumulative total of bytes retrieved from the URL cache

Name	Description
Total URLs Cached	The cumulative total of URLs that have been stored in the cache
Total URLs Retrieved	The cumulative total of URLs that have been retrieved from the cache
URL Commit Rate	The number of URLs per second being stored to the cache
URL Retrieve Rate	The number of URLs per second being retrieved from the cache
URLs in Cache	The number of URLs in the cache currently

The counters in the Web Proxy Server Service object include counters specific to the Web Proxy service. Table B.19 describes those counters.

Table B.19   Web Proxy Server Service Performance Monitor Counters

Name	Description
Cache Hit Ratio (%)	The percent of all requests to Web Proxy Server that were served using cached data
Client Bytes Received/sec	The number of data bytes per second being received by Web Proxy Server from Web Proxy clients
Client Bytes Sent/sec	The number of data bytes per second being sent by Web Proxy Server to the Web Proxy clients
Client Bytes Total/sec	The sum of Client Bytes Sent/sec and Client Bytes Received/sec. This is the total rate of all bytes transferred between Web Proxy Server and Web Proxy clients.
Current Users	The number of users currently connected to Web Proxy Server
DNS Cache Entries	The current number of DNS domain name entries cached by Web Proxy Server
DNS Cache Flushes	The total number of times that the DNS domain name cache has been flushed or cleared by Web Proxy Server
DNS Cache Hits	The total number of times a DNS domain name was found within the DNS cache

continues

Table B.19 Continued

Name	Description
DNS Cache Hits (%)	The percentage of DNS domain names served by the Web Proxy Server cache, out of the total of all DNS entries that have been retrieved by Web Proxy Server
DNS Cache Retrievals	The total number of DNS domain names that have been retrieved by Web Proxy Server
FTP Requests	The number of FTP requests that have been made to Web Proxy Server
Gopher Requests	The number of Gopher requests that have been made to Web Proxy Server
HTTP Requests	The number of HTTP requests that have been made to Web Proxy Server
HTTPS sessions	The total number of secure HTTP sessions serviced by the Secure Sockets Layer (SSL) tunnel
Inet Bytes Received/sec	The rate at which data bytes are received by Web Proxy Server from remote servers on the Internet
Inet Bytes Sent/sec	The rate at which data bytes are sent by Web Proxy Server to remote servers on the Internet
Inet Bytes Total/sec	The sum of Inet Bytes Sent/sec and Inet Bytes Received/sec. This is the total rate for all bytes transferred between Web Proxy Server and servers on the Internet.
Maximum Users	The maximum number of users that have connected to Web Proxy Server simultaneously
Sites Denied	The total number of Internet sites to which Web Proxy Server has denied access
Sites Granted	The total number of Internet sites to which Web Proxy Server has granted access
SNEWS Sessions	The total number of SNEWS sessions serviced by the Secure Sockets Layer (SSL) tunnel
SSL Client Bytes Received/sec	The rate at which Secure Sockets Layer (SSL) data bytes are received by Web Proxy Server from secured Web Proxy clients
SSL Client Bytes Sent/sec	The rate at which Secure Sockets Layer (SSL) data bytes are sent by Proxy Server to secured Web Proxy clients

Name	Description
SSL Client Bytes Total/sec	The sum of SSL Client Bytes Sent/sec and SSL Client Bytes Received/sec. This is the total rate for all bytes transferred between Web Proxy Server and secured Web Proxy clients.
SSL Sessions Scavenged	The number of Secure Sockets Layer (SSL) sessions closed because of idle timeout and excessive SSL demand
Thread Pool Active Sessions	The number of sessions being actively serviced by thread pool threads
Thread Pool Failures	The number of requests rejected because the thread pool was overcommitted
Thread Pool Size	The number of threads in the thread pool
Total Cache Fetches	The total number of requests that have been served by using cached data from Web Proxy Server cache
Total Failing Requests	The total number of Internet service requests that have failed to be processed by Web Proxy Server due to errors. Errors can be the result of Web Proxy Server failing to locate a requested server URL on the Internet, or because of the client being denied access to the requested URL.
Total Internet Fetches	The total number of requests that have been served by using data retrieved from servers on the Internet
Total Requests	The total number of Internet requests that have ever been made to Web Proxy Server
Total SSL Sessions	The total number of Secure Sockets Layer (SSL) sessions serviced by the SSL tunnel
Total Successful Requests	The total number of Internet requests that have been successfully processed by Web Proxy Server
Total Users	The total number of users that have ever connected to Web Proxy Server
Unknown SSL Sessions	The total number of unknown Secure Sockets Layer (SSL) sessions serviced by the SSL tunnel

The counters in the WinSock Proxy Server object provide statistics about the WinSock Proxy service, as shown in Table B.20.

Table B.20   WinSock Proxy Server Performance Monitor Counters

Column 1	Column 2
Accepting TCP Connections	The number of connection objects that wait for TCP connection from the client after a successful remote connection
Active Sessions	The number of active sessions
Active TCP Connections	The number of active TCP connections
Active UDP Connections	Total number of active UDP connections
Available Control Worker Threads	The number of control channel worker threads that are available or waiting in the completion port queue
Available Data Worker Threads	The number of data-pump worker threads that are available or waiting in the completion port queue
Back-Connecting TCP Connections	Total number of connections that are waiting for an inbound connect( ) call to finish. These are connections from the WinSock Proxy service to a client after the WinSock Proxy service accepted a connection from the Internet on a listening socket.
Bytes Read/sec	Number of bytes read by the data-pump per second
Bytes Written/sec	Number of bytes written by the data-pump per second
Connecting TCP Connections	Total number of connections that are waiting for a remote connect( ) call to finish
Control Worker Threads	The number of control channel worker threads that are alive
Data Worker Threads	The number of data-pump worker threads that are alive
Failed GetXByY	Number of calls to gethostname/gethostbyaddr that have failed
Listening TCP Connections	Number of connection objects that wait for TCP connections from the Internet (after a successful listen)

Column 1	Column 2
Nonconnected UDP mappings	The number of mappings for UDP connections
Pending GetXByY	Number of calls to gethostname/gethostbyaddr that have not yet returned
Successful GetXByY	Number of calls to gethostname/gethostbyaddr that have returned successfully

Part
VIII

App
B

Glossary

Alias   A name different from the actual name of something, such as a file, a device, or a directory. Aliases are used extensively in the BackOffice and Microsoft Commercial Internet Services applications. For example, in Internet News Server, an alias is a list of newsgroup specifications. When configuring SMTP for the Mail Server, an alias is the account which will receive all mail for a user. When an alias for a directory is provided while configuring World Wide Web services, the alias will be mapped to a virtual directory made up of files and directories available for FTP access.

anonymous   Because of the huge number of hits, or accesses, that many Internet sites receive, particularly FTP sites that are commonly used to distribute files, patches, and drivers, issuing a user ID and password for each visitor would be an administrative nightmare. As a result, the concept of using "anonymous" as the user ID and the user's e-mail address as the password came into vogue. Permitting anonymous access, and then limiting anonymous access to only public areas, solves most Web-based administrative problems.

Athena   The code name for the Microsoft Internet Explorer version 3.0 Mail and News client.

bandwidth   A measurement of frequency stating the capacity of a communications channel, or the amount of information and the rate of speed it travels through the network. Typically, bandwidth is stated as bits per second (bps) or cycles per second (Hertz, or Hz).

Basic Authentication A user authentication that does not encrypt user names or passwords, which can leave systems vulnerable to intrusion. FTP sites support only two types of user logins: anonymous and Basic Authentication. Basic Authentication is listed as Basic (Clear Text) in some dialog boxes.

Challenge/Response An authentication method that requires a user ID and password before a user can access sensitive material such as pages, files, and folders on the Web server. With Challenge/Response, the User ID and password are encrypted, indecipherable by all but the most powerful decryption devices, making this the most secure form of standard, non-SSL security. Windows NT Challenge/Response uses Windows NT system accounts to authenticate users.

Common Gateway Interface (CGI) A standard for running external applications, known as "gateways" because they provide an interface between external information sources and the server, World Wide Web HTTP servers. By using CGI scripts, a user can fill in the blanks in a Web page to join a site or search for information. The external program, such as a search engine or mailer program, processes the information, and a new Web page is generated containing information for the user, such as a search result or confirmation.

cookie A handle or transaction ID that stores small bits of information about a user and their preferences, which a Web server stores onto and reads from the user's computer. A cookie might store a user's personalized view of a Web site, the items a user adds to a merchant "shopping cart," or authentication information for a registered user of a Web site so that signing in is not required every time the user accesses that site. Cookies are used to maintain state between otherwise stateless HTTP transactions.

daemon The UNIX term for a background program that runs all the time. See **inetd**.

Denali The code name for the Internet Information Server, version 3.0.

File Transfer Protocol (FTP) A set of rules (protocol) for exchanging files on the Internet. An FTP client program is used by hosts to contact another host and transfer files with it. Web browsers can serve as FTP clients for anonymous FTP downloading of files.

file transfer protocol (ftp) A standard for the error-free transmission of files over telephone lines.

firewall Hardware or software that restricts or blocks outside access to a private network. This is usually accomplished by the use of a router to filter packet traffic. Proxy servers can be used as a mediator, processing and responding to outside information requests and messages without allowing direct access to the systems behind the firewall. Although very effective, security problems often are caused by a malicious insider or disaffected employee against whom the firewall offers no protection.

gateway A device (software or a computer) that enables two networks to communicate. A gateway might connect two PC networks, a LAN, and a WAN or EtherNet to AppleTalk, or may connect a PC-based network to a mainframe. Unlike a bridge, which is a sophisticated buffer, a gateway processes information and may perform protocol and bandwidth conversion.

Gateways can also act as barriers, allowing, for example, requests to be made to the Internet and receive information, but not allow access to a network by outsiders.

HTML editor Software used to mark up document text by inserting the tags that Web browsers interpret. HoTMetaL and HotDog are two of the early HTML editors, but the increased use of the Internet has resulted in HTML editors built into some word processors, such as WordPerfect 7, and HTML editor "assistant" add-ins available for download at the Microsoft Web site for Microsoft's desktop applications. Microsoft's Front Page HTML editor, included with Windows NT 4.0, represents the next level of editors, adding additional features such as Active Server Pages support.

Hypertext Markup Language (HTML) The conventions for marking portions of a document so that when the document is viewed with a parser (a Web browser), the marked text appears in a format such as bold, or the text becomes a hyperlink (a link to another HTML document). Using HTML, tags consisting of a <, instructions, or parameters and another >, like <HEAD>, are embedded in the text to define fonts, graphics, hypertext links, and other details. An HTML document can be created using a HTML editor or a standard word processor, but must be converted to and saved in HTML format before the document can be displayed as a Web page. The Web browser determines how to handle the marked text in HTML documents.

Hypertext Transport Protocol (HTTP) A client-server TCP/IP protocol that supports document delivery to a Web browser from a Web server. HTTP defines URLs and how URLs are used to retrieve files on the Internet, making it possible to embed hyperlinks in Web pages that can be clicked to begin data transfer. The user only needs to provide a location to store the retrieved data.

Hypertext Transport Protocol, Secure (HTTPS) An HTTP variation used by Netscape for processing secure transactions using Secure Socket Layers (SSL). In Netscape Navigator, use `https://` followed by the URL for connecting to HTTP servers using SSL when this security is needed.

inetd A UNIX daemon that runs continuously, listening to all ports for requests for Internet service. When a request is received, inetd starts the daemon responsible for providing the requested service. Inetd acts as a "super daemon," making it unnecessary to run other daemons constantly.

Internet Relay Chat (IRC) A real-time Internet service. When combined with an IRC client program that displays a list of the current IRC channels (chat sessions), the user can watch what other users are typing on-screen and respond as desired.

InterNIC A consortium of AT&T, providing Internet directory and database services, Network Solutions, Inc., which provides Internet registration of new domain names and IP addresses, and the National Science Foundation. When establishing a domain, it is necessary to register it with the InterNIC, which can be done by completing the registration form at the InterNIC Web site, **rs.internic.net**.

kernel The essential part of an operating system, responsible for low-level hardware interfaces, security, resource allocation, and the like.

Part

VIII

App

C

key pair   A public key/private key pair. See **public key encryption**.

Lightweight Directory Access Protocol (LDAP)   A protocol for accessing online directory services. LDAP is a relatively simple protocol for updating and searching directories running over TCP/IP. The LDAP interface provides an Internet-standard-based protocol which allows third-party Internet client applications to access the Internet Locator Service for dynamic directory information, such as a user's current IP address. A service provider can also use an HTTP interface or a User Location Protocol (ULP) to access directory information. An LDAP directory entry is a collection of attributes with a name, called a distinguished name (DN). LDAP directory entries are arranged hierarchically with countries appearing at the top of the tree, states or national organizations below them, with entries representing people, organizational units, printers, documents, and so on following.

Malta   The code name for Microsoft's Backend.

Memphis   The code name for Microsoft Windows 97.

named pipe   A UNIX pipe, named using the "mknod" command, which allows unrelated processes to communicate with one another.

Network News Transfer Protocol (NNTP)   A protocol for the distribution, inquiry, retrieval, and posting of UseNet news articles over the Internet. It is designed to be used between a news reader client and a news server. NNTP is a simple ASCII text protocol, making it possible to connect to the news server using telnet if a news reader is not available.

Normandy   The code name for the Microsoft Commercial Internet Services.

Open Data Base Connectivity (ODBC)   A standard for accessing different database systems. ODBC was defined by the SQL Access Group and designed as a programming interface to support SQL access to the popular databases such as Paradox, dBASE, Btrieve, Excel, Access, and text.

pipe   Originally, a UNIX temporary file which receives output from one command and sends input to another command. The kernel suspends and activates the sending and receiving commands as needed. In later versions of UNIX, the pipe can be named and then implemented as a local socket pair. See **kernel** and **named pipe**.

POP3   Version 3 of the Post Office Protocol, a protocol designed to allow single user hosts to read electronic mail from a server. POP3 is an Internet mail standard that establishes how a computer connected to the Internet can be used as a mail-handling agent. Messages arrive at a user's electronic mailbox housed on a POP3 server computer. The user can access mail from any computer, such as the office workstation or home PC. A POP-compatible mail program on the user's computer establishes the connection with the POP server and detects new mail. The mail can then be retrieved by the user.

public key encryption   A method of encryption that uses a public key for encrypting messages and a private key for decryption. The key holder sends the public key to others to use to encrypt messages to be sent to the user. The key holder then uses the private key to decrypt any received messages. Public key cryptography is available to any Internet user for a nominal fee by accessing **http://www.verisign.com/microsoft/**.

Registry   Windows NT 4.0 stores configuration information for all system components and installed applications in a database called the Registry. Stored as proprietary binary format files but easily accessible by running RegEdit, the Registry is organized hierarchically and consists of topics called "keys" with values divided into logical units called "hives." The Registry files are named for each hive (except HARDWARE, which resides in memory only) without a file extension, and are saved by default, along with corresponding .LOG files, in the \winnt\system32\config\ folder.

Remote Procedure Call (RPC)   A procedure that sends executable requests from one computer to another. Microsoft's IIS and MCIS servers support Internet administration through the use of RPCs, making it possible to manage servers remotely using a Web browser.

scalability   The ability to perform adequately when the demand increases significantly. For example, a server with ten clients may perform adequately but with a thousand clients it might fail to meet response time requirements. MCIS servers are referred to as "highly scalable" because the software can handle a few, thousands, or millions of users. Accommodating heavy user demand while providing good performance may require the addition of resources such as more hard drive space, faster processors, and additional servers.

Secure HTTP (SHTTP)   See **Hypertext Transport Protocol, Secure** and **Secure Sockets Layer**.

Secure Sockets Layer   A security standard developed by Netscape Communications to allow Web browsers to use a process called cryptography to secure the integrity of data transmissions over the Internet. When SSL is invoked, the server and the client agree on the security level used (a handshake) and all data, including all user IDs, passwords, and even the URL that is being accessed, is encrypted using a public key encryption to ensure the information cannot be intercepted. SSL works with any Internet tools, unlike Secure Hypertext Transport Protocol (secure HTTP or SHTTP), which is specific to the Web and incompatible with SSL.

Sicily   The code name for the Microsoft Commercial Internet System Membership Broker.

Simple Mail Transfer Protocol (SMTP)   A TCP/IP-dedicated protocol that transfers electronic mail between machines. SMTP receives messages from a user's mail program and places them in an outgoing queue. When a connection is made with remote machines using SMTP and the status of the connected machines is verified, information about the first mail message and its sender is transmitted, the information is acknowledged by the other server, and then the message is transmitted using TCP/IP. An **SMTP server** performs mail delivery for **remote SMTP servers** and **mail clients**.

Simple Network Management Protocol (SNMP)   An Internet-standard protocol for collecting and transmitting management or status information about the operation of networks, computers, and attached devices, such as printers. A management information base (MIB) in memory is used to gather the data on network or computer performance, which is then transmitted to a central console for display.

Part

VIII

App

C

socket A pipe for incoming and outgoing data on a network.

Structured Query Language (SQL) A search question language which IBM developed for use in mainframe and minicomputer systems. SQL consists of a small number of commands (about 30) that are combined in a fashion that reads like English-language sentences to request information from a relational database.

Telnet A method used to connect two computers, providing a terminal connection to the remote machine. When a Telnet program is used to connect to a Telnet server, the user can perform any tasks the Telnet server (called a host resource) provides. Also, Telnet is the Internet standard protocol for remote login.

Tigris The code name for the Microsoft Commercial Internet News Server.

token An access control object for a service or content area. The Mail, News, and Chat services require rights to a special token to perform authentication for users. When a user is added, the user's e-mail name, security token, and IP address must be specified. Once added, this listing can be modified only by a user with the same security token as the user who created the listing.

Transmission Control Protocol/Internet Protocol (TCP/IP) A large set of protocols for reliably connecting together two computers on the Internet. Because of differences in vendor designs, a common set of openly published standards was seen as the best solution to transferring data between Internet-connected computers. These standards have come to be known collectively as TCP/IP. TCP manages the transmission of data on networks and IP actually transmits the data. With TCP/IP, the sending computer continues to send the data until notified by the receiving computer that all the data has been received, a method known as Positive Acknowledgment with Re-Transmission (PAR).

Unicode A 16-bit character code that covers all of the world's written languages, including Cyrillic, Chinese, Greek, Roman, and so on. The Index Server software can index an English paragraph, switch to a French paragraph, then switch back to English, all through the process of Unicoding. All index information is stored as Unicode characters and all queries are converted to Unicode before processing.

URL (Uniform Resource Locator) A character string that describes the location of a document on the Internet. An URL consists of several parts:

Part	Description
http://	Indicates a WWW document
www.integritydata.com/	The domain name of the computer where the document resides
training/webdoc7.html	Any directory structure on the computer and the document name

Stated as a complete URL, this would be **http://www.integritydata.com/training/webdoc7.html**.

virtual A computer representation or simulation. Virtual memory, for example, functions as RAM but uses a portion of the hard disk space to store data instead of in electronic memory. A virtual disk can be created in memory or be a directory structure mapped so it appears to the user as a separate drive.

Virtual Root A directory, or folder, including child directories, mapped to a corresponding Internet volume. Before documents can be indexed using Index Server, you must first map the directory where the documents are stored to a Virtual Root. This Virtual Root will be visible to Web users.

Wide Area Information Search (WAIS) A distributed information retrieval system. Clients use WAIS to retrieve text or multimedia documents using keywords. The search returns a list of documents, ranked according to the frequency of occurrence of the keyword(s) used in the search. WAIS uses simple natural language input, indexed searching, and a relevance feedback mechanism which uses the results of initial searches to narrow future searches. ●

Part
VIII

App
C

Index

C

X-Z

Check out Que® Books
on the World Wide Web
http://www.quecorp.com

As the biggest software release in computer history, Windows 95 continues to redefine the computer industry. Click here for the latest info on our Windows 95 books

Make computing quick and easy with these products designed exclusively for new and casual users

Examine the latest releases in word processing, spreadsheets, operating systems, and suites

The Internet, The World Wide Web, CompuServe®, America Online®, Prodigy®—it's a world of ever-changing information. Don't get left behind!

Find out about new additions to our site, new bestsellers and hot topics

Desktop Applications & Operating Systems

que® new **users**

what's new?

Que's Publishing Areas

Windows 95

Internet And New Technologies

Calendar of Events

DEVELOPER AND EXPERT USERS

ZD ZIFF-DAVIS PRESS

Que's Top 10 Titles

Macintosh & Desktop Publishing

In-depth information on high-end topics: find the best reference books for databases, programming, networking, and client/server technologies

A recent addition to Que, Ziff-Davis Press publishes the highly-successful *How It Works* and *How to Use* series of books, as well as *PC Learning Labs Teaches* and *PC Magazine* series of book/disc packages

Stay on the cutting edge of Macintosh® technologies and visual communications

Find out which titles are making headlines

With 6 separate publishing groups, Que develops products for many specific market segments and areas of computer technology. Explore our Web Site and you'll find information on best-selling titles, newly published titles, upcoming products, authors, and much more.

- Stay informed on the latest industry trends and products available

- Visit our online bookstore for the latest information and editions

- Download software from Que's library of the best shareware and freeware

que®

Complete and Return this Card
for a *FREE* Computer Book Catalog

Thank you for purchasing this book! You have purchased a superior computer book written expressly for your needs. To continue to provide the kind of up-to-date, pertinent coverage you've come to expect from us, we need to hear from you. Please take a minute to complete and return this self-addressed, postage-paid form. In return, we'll send you a free catalog of all our computer books on topics ranging from word processing to programming and the internet.

Mr. ☐   Mrs. ☐   Ms. ☐   Dr. ☐

Name (first) ☐☐☐☐☐☐☐☐☐☐☐☐ (M.I.) ☐   (last) ☐☐☐☐☐☐☐☐☐☐☐☐☐☐☐

Address ☐☐☐☐☐☐☐☐☐☐☐☐☐☐☐☐☐☐☐☐☐☐☐☐☐☐☐☐☐☐☐☐☐☐☐☐☐

City ☐☐☐☐☐☐☐☐☐☐☐   State ☐☐   Zip ☐☐☐☐☐ ☐☐☐☐

Phone ☐☐☐ ☐☐☐ ☐☐☐☐   Fax ☐☐☐ ☐☐☐ ☐☐☐☐

Company Name ☐☐☐☐☐☐☐☐☐☐☐☐☐☐☐☐☐☐☐☐☐☐☐

E-mail address ☐☐☐☐☐☐☐☐☐☐☐☐☐☐☐☐☐☐☐☐☐☐☐

1. Please check at least (3) influencing factors for purchasing this book.

Front or back cover information on book ☐
Special approach to the content ☐
Completeness of content ☐
Author's reputation ☐
Publisher's reputation ☐
Book cover design or layout ☐
Index or table of contents of book ☐
Price of book ☐
Special effects, graphics, illustrations ☐
Other (Please specify): _____ ☐

2. How did you first learn about this book?

Saw in Macmillan Computer Publishing catalog ☐
Recommended by store personnel ☐
Saw the book on bookshelf at store ☐
Recommended by a friend ☐
Received advertisement in the mail ☐
Saw an advertisement in: _____ ☐
Read book review in: _____ ☐
Other (Please specify): _____ ☐

3. How many computer books have you purchased in the last six months?

This book only ☐   3 to 5 books ☐
books ☐   More than 5 ☐

4. Where did you purchase this book?

Bookstore ☐
Computer Store ☐
Consumer Electronics Store ☐
Department Store ☐
Office Club ☐
Warehouse Club ☐
Mail Order ☐
Direct from Publisher ☐
Internet site ☐
Other (Please specify): _____ ☐

5. How long have you been using a computer?

☐ Less than 6 months   ☐ 6 months to a year
☐ 1 to 3 years   ☐ More than 3 years

6. What is your level of experience with personal computers and with the subject of this book?

	With PCs	With subject of book
New	☐	☐
Casual	☐	☐
Accomplished	☐	☐
Expert	☐	☐

Source Code ISBN: 0-7897-1016-1

7. Which of the following best describes your job title?

Administrative Assistant .... ☐
Coordinator .... ☐
Manager/Supervisor .... ☐
Director .... ☐
Vice President .... ☐
President/CEO/COO .... ☐
Lawyer/Doctor/Medical Professional .... ☐
Teacher/Educator/Trainer .... ☐
Engineer/Technician .... ☐
Consultant .... ☐
Not employed/Student/Retired .... ☐
Other (Please specify): _____ ☐

8. Which of the following best describes the area of the company your job title falls under?

Accounting .... ☐
Engineering .... ☐
Manufacturing .... ☐
Operations .... ☐
Marketing .... ☐
Sales .... ☐
Other (Please specify): _____ ☐

9. What is your age?

Under 20 .... ☐
21-29 .... ☐
30-39 .... ☐
40-49 .... ☐
50-59 .... ☐
60-over .... ☐

10. Are you:

Male .... ☐
Female .... ☐

11. Which computer publications do you read regularly? (Please list)

_____
_____
_____
_____
_____
_____
_____
_____
_____
_____

Comments: _____
_____
_____

Fold here and scotch-tape to mail

MACMILLAN COMPUTER PUBLISHING USA

A VIACOM COMPANY

Technical Support:

If you need assistance with the information in this book or with a CD/Disk accompanying the book, please access the Knowledge Base on our Web site at **http://www.superlibrary.com/general/support**. Our most Frequently Asked Questions are answered there. If you do not find the answer to your questions on our Web site, you may contact Macmillan Technical Support **(317) 581-3833** or e-mail us at **support@mcp.com**.